MOUNTAIN RESORTS

Ecology and Law in Modern Society

Series Editors:
Richard O. Brooks
Professor Emeritus, Vermont Law School, USA
and
Ross A. Virginia
Environmental Studies Program, Dartmouth College, USA

This series presents a legal and ecological perspective on important environmental issues such as declining biodiversity and the ecological significance of endangered species, the effects of pollution on natural and managed systems, the ecology of fragile ecosystems (mountains, grazed lands), and pollution and its effects on ecosystem services. The scientific basis for understanding important areas of environmental law will be presented by experts in their fields. The formulating of environmental law to influence human activities will be analyzed by leading legal scholars. The central legal cases and challenges will be explored and the resulting success of the statutes considered. It is the intent of the series to provide a balance in the treatment of legal and ecological material not traditionally found in environmental law texts.

Also in the series

Law and Ecology
The Rise of the Ecosystem Regime
Richard O. Brooks, Ross Jones and Ross A. Virginia
ISBN 978-0-7546-2038-9 (Hb) and 978-0-7546-2316-8 (Pb)

Mountain Resorts
Ecology and the Law

Edited by

JANET E. MILNE
Vermont Law School, USA

JULIA LEMENSE
Eastern Environmental Law Center, USA

ROSS A. VIRGINIA
Dartmouth College, USA

Routledge
Taylor & Francis Group
LONDON AND NEW YORK

First published 2009 by Ashgate Publishing

Published 2016 by Routledge
2 Park Square, Milton Park, Abingdon, Oxfordshire OX14 4RN
711 Third Avenue, New York, NY 10017, USA

First issued in paperback 2016

Routledge is an imprint of the Taylor & Francis Group, an informa business

British Library Cataloguing in Publication Data
Mountain resorts : ecology and the law. - (Ecology and law in modern society)
1. Natural areas - Law and legislation - United States
2. Habitat conservation - Law and legislation - United States 3. Mountain resorts - Environmental aspects - Case studies 4. Natural areas - Law and legislation - Canada
5. Habitat conservation - Law and legislation - Canada
6. Mountain resorts - Environmental aspects
I. Milne, Janet E. II. LeMense, Julia III. Virginia, Ross A.
346.7'3046784

Library of Congress Cataloging-in-Publication Data
Milne, Janet E.
Mountain resorts : ecology and the law / by Janet E. Milne, Julia LeMense, and Ross A. Virginia.
p. cm. -- (Ecology and law in modern society)
Includes bibliographical references and index.
ISBN 978-0-7546-2315-1
1. Environmental law--United States. 2. Environmental policy--United States. 3. Ecosystem management--Law and legislation--United States. 4. Biodiversity conservation--Law and legislation--United States. 5. Ecology--United States. 6. Mountain resorts--United States. I. LeMense, Julia. II. Virginia, Ross A. III. Title.

KF3775.M62 2008
346.7304'672--dc22

2008030269

ISBN 13: 978-1-138-27746-5 (pbk)
ISBN 13: 978-0-7546-2315-1 (hbk)

Contents

List of Figures ix
List of Tables xi
List of Contributors xiii
Preface xvii
Acknowledgments xix
List of Abbreviations xxi

1 The Landscape of This Book 1
Janet E. Milne

PART I THE MOUNTAIN ECOSYSTEM

2 An Ecosystem Approach to Mountain Resorts 23
Ross A. Virginia

3 Plant Communities and Vegetation Processes in the Mountain Landscape 39
G. Richard Strimbeck

4 Water Quantity and Quality in the Mountain Environment 65
James B. Shanley and Beverley Wemple

5 Effects of Mountain Resorts on Wildlife 99
Allan M. Strong, Christopher C. Rimmer, Kent P. McFarland and Kimberly Hagen

PART II LOON MOUNTAIN, NEW HAMPSHIRE
United States Federal Law and Mountain Resort Development in the National Forest
Roger Fleming

6 An Introduction to Loon Mountain and the Loon Resort 129

7 The Legal Foundation for the South Mountain Expansion Proposal: The Early Permits and the Forest Management Planning Regime 145

8 The South Mountain Expansion: Did the National Forest Planning and Environmental Impact Statement Framework Cause Decision-Makers to Take an Ecosystem-Based Approach? 159

9 Can Other Federal Laws Contribute to an Ecosystem-Based Approach to Resort Development? 191

10 Conclusions from the Loon Resort Experience 201

PART III WHITEFACE MOUNTAIN SKI CENTER, NEW YORK
Olympic Legacies and Adirondack Park Plans
John S. Banta

11 An Introduction to the Whiteface Mountain Ski Center and the Legal Framework 211

12 The Legal Regime Affecting Whiteface Mountain: Does It Take an Ecological Approach? 227

13 The Legal Regime Affecting Private Lands Around Whiteface: Does It Take an Ecological Approach? 253

14 Conclusion 265

PART IV KILLINGTON RESORT, VERMONT
Can a Mountain Ecosystem be Protected When the Law Protects its Parts? The Case of Act 250 and Killington Resort
Julia LeMense and Jonathan Isham

15 An Introduction to Killington Resort, Its Expansion Plans, and the Issues 271

16 Vermont's Act 250 and the Early Battles at Parker's Gore East 279

17 Expansion in the Wake of Parker's Gore East: The Interconnect, the Woodward Reservoir, and the Resort Village 301

18 Conclusion 323

PART V MONT TREMBLANT, QUEBEC
Canadian Law and the Ecological Footprint of a Four-Season Resort
Jane Matthews Glenn

19 An Introduction to Mont Tremblant and the Issues 331

20 Intrawest's Development of the Skiable Domain 347

21 Base Camps, Golf Courses and Land Protection at the Mountain's Base 373

22 Legal Diversity and Legal Ecosystems 411

PART VI A VISION FOR THE MOUNTAINS

23 The Challenges of Joining Ecology with the Law: A Vision for the Mountains 419
Janet E. Milne and Ross A. Virginia

Index *447*

List of Figures

1.1 Location of the Case Study Resorts 7

4.1 Typical Annual Cycle of Precipitation and Streamflow 68
4.2 Theoretical Shift in Storm Hydrograph to Earlier and Higher Peak Flows as a Result of Land Disturbance and/or Development 77
4.3 Outline of Study Watersheds on the East Slope of Mt. Mansfield, Vermont 92
4.4 Water Yield Increases Following Forest Harvest in Paired Watershed Studies in the Northeastern U.S., with Water Yield Difference in Mt. Mansfield Case Study (MM) Described Herein 93
4.5 Comparison of West Branch and Ranch Brook Streamflow Hydrographs During Snowmelt, 2001 93
4.6 Comparison of West Branch and Ranch Brook Streamflow Hydrographs During a Series of Rainstorms, July 2001 94
4.7 Stream Fluxes of Chloride and Suspended Sediment at West Branch and Ranch Brook Gages, Water Years 2001, 2002, and 2003 94
4.8 Eastern Slopes of Mt. Mansfield, Vermont, and Ski Trails of the Stowe Mountain Resort 96

5.1 Bicknell's Thrush (Stratton Mountain, Vermont) 101
5.2 Bicknell's Thrush Nest with Nestlings (Mt. Mansfield, Vermont) 101
5.3 Northern Dusky Salamander (Smuggler's Notch, Vermont) 107
5.4 Spring Salamander (Smuggler's Notch between Stowe and Cambridge, Vermont) 107
5.5 Effects of Fragmentation and Edge Effects on Forest Area and Populations of Two Hypothetical Species with Limited Gap-Crossing Abilities on Stowe Mountain Resort 111
5.6 Effects of Fragmentation and Edge Effects on Forest Area and Populations of Two Hypothetical Species with Limited Gap-Crossing Abilities on Stratton Mountain Resort 112

6.1 Loon Mountain and its Regional Setting 133
6.2 Loon Resort and the Proposed South Mountain Expansion, as proposed in 1999 140

8.1 Alternative Ponds for Snowmaking 180

11.1	Whiteface Mountain and its Regional Setting	214
11.2	Whiteface Summit Overlooking Lake Placid	217
11.3	The Mix of Public and Private Land in the Adirondack Park	222
12.1	Whiteface Mountain Ski Center's Existing Trails and Proposed Tree Island Pod, 2007	233
12.2	Master Plan's Classifications for the Forest Preserve	236
12.3	The Tree Island Pod, 2004 Proposal and 2006 Modifications	246
12.4	Whiteface Mountain Trails and the Tree Island Pod, 2008	247
12.5	Gauging Weir on the Ausable River	249
13.1	Adirondack Park Agency's Intensity Guidelines for Private Land	259
15.1	Killington Resort and its Regional Setting	272
16.1	Killington Resort and Surrounding Area, 1985	289
16.2	Killington Resort and Surrounding Area, 1997	297
19.1	The Setting of Mont Tremblant Park	335
19.2	Mont Tremblant and its Base Camps	336
20.1	The Land Exchange	352
20.2	Mont Tremblant's Ski Slopes	354
21.1	Municipality of Mont Tremblant's Existing Development	382
21.2	Golf Courses and Domaine St. Bernard	400
23.1	A Conceptual Model for Possible Application to Mountain Ecosystems	423
23.2	A Conceptual Diagram of a Mountain System to Include the Interactions Between Science and Research, the Stakeholders, and the Resultant Law that Comes to Bear on the Development and Operations of Mountain Resorts	439

List of Tables

1.1 Selected Operational Features of the Case Study Resorts 9
1.2 Selected Legal Features of the Case Study Resorts 13

2.1 Properties, Characteristics, and Sensitivities of Mountain Ecosystems 25

3.1 Community and Landscape Processes Affected by Mountain Resort Development 62

5.1 Species that May Suffer Population Declines as a Result of Habitat Fragmentation Associated with Mountain Resorts 116

15.1 The Changing Ownership of Killington Resort 276

16.1 The Ten Act 250 Criteria 283

19.1 Intrawest Resort Revenues by Segment, 1999–2002 337

List of Contributors

John S. Banta is Counsel to the New York State Adirondack Park Agency in Ray Brook, New York, USA, where he advises on the implementation of full range of environmental policy matters under the Agency's jurisdiction. He previously was the Agency's Deputy Director, Planning for more than two decades. He started his career as a land use attorney in Chicago and subsequently worked on national and international land use and environmental issues for The Conservation Foundation in Washington, D.C.

Roger Fleming is an attorney for Earthjustice, a nonprofit public interest law firm in the United States, and is an adjunct professor at the University of Maine School of Law, USA. In addition to handling a wide range of federal legal issues in prior positions with the United States Environmental Protection Agency and the Conservation Law Foundation, he currently works extensively with legal regimes that affect ocean ecosystems. He graduated with honors from Ithaca College, Cornell University, and Vermont Law School, and lives in Appleton, Maine, with his wife Amy, their son Miles, and their two overactive weimaraners, Gompers and Scout.

Jane Matthews Glenn is a Professor at McGill University, Montreal, Canada, where she has a joint appointment in the Faculty of Law and the School of Urban Planning; she is also a member of the McGill School of Environment and the Institute of Comparative Law. She has a B.A. (Hons.) and an LL.B. from Queen's University, Kingston, Ontario, Canada, and a doctorate in public law from the Université de Strasbourg, France.

Kimberly Hagen is currently Executive Director of the Vermont Energy Education Program. She spends the summers teaching high school students about amphibians, particularly salamanders, in central Vermont, USA.

Jonathan Isham, Jr., is the Luce Professor of International Environmental Economics at Middlebury College, Vermont, USA. The co-editor of IGNITION: WHAT YOU CAN DO TO FIGHT GLOBAL WARMING AND SPARK A MOVEMENT (Island Press), he has served on advisory boards for Focus the Nation, Climate Counts, and the Vermont Governor's Commission on Climate Change and is an advisor to 1Sky, the Presidential Climate Action Project, and the Climate Project. He has published articles in Nonprofit and Voluntary Sector Quarterly, Quarterly Journal of Economics, Rural Sociology, Society and Natural Resources, and Vermont Law Review, among other journals.

Julia LeMense is a staff attorney and the Executive Director of the Eastern Environmental Law Center, a nonprofit public interest environmental law firm in the US. Ms. LeMense was the founding Assistant Director of the Vermont Law School Environmental and Natural Resources Law Clinic and an assistant professor of law, and was a visiting assistant clinical professor of law at Rutgers Law School-Newark and a staff attorney in the Rutgers Environmental Law Clinic. Ms. LeMense earned her B.A. from Michigan State University, her J.D. from the University of Iowa College of Law, and her LL.M. in environmental law from Vermont Law School.

Kent P. McFarland is a conservation biologist with the Vermont Center for Ecostudies in Norwich, Vermont, USA, a recent offshoot of the Vermont Institute for Natural Science. Kent McFarland received his B.S. in Environmental Studies from Allegheny College, and his M.S. in Environmental Studies from Antioch University New England. His current research focuses on ecology and conservation of birds in the Northeast, and butterfly ecology and conservation in Vermont.

Janet E. Milne is Professor of Law at Vermont Law School in South Royalton, Vermont, USA, and the founding Director of the Environmental Tax Policy Institute at Vermont Law School. She teaches land use law and environmental taxation and has a particular interest in the question of the choice of policy instruments in environmental protection.

Christopher C. Rimmer is Director of the Vermont Center for Ecostudies in Norwich, Vermont, USA, a recent offshoot of the Vermont Institute for Natural Sciences. His research centers on ecology and conservation of mountain birds in the Northeast and Hispaniola, with special focus on Bicknell's thrush.

James B. Shanley is a research hydrologist with the U.S. Geological Survey in Montpelier, Vermont, USA. His research interests are watershed hydrology, effects of acid rain, chemical and hydrologic responses to climate change, and mercury contamination. Since 1991 he has directed the Sleepers River Research Watershed in Danville, Vermont, one of 5 sites of the USGS Water, Energy, and Biogeochemical Budgets (WEBB) program.

G. Richard Strimbeck, a plant ecologist and ecophysiologist, is an associate professor of plant physiology in the Department of Biology at the Norwegian University of Science and Technology in Trondheim, Norway. Since received a Masters of Science in Field Naturalist Studies and a Ph.D. in Natural Resources from the University of Vermont, he has studied the effects of acid precipitation and winter injury on red spruce populations in Appalachian and Adirondack mountain forests, participated in field studies in forest ecology in Costa Rica, Puerto Rico and Chile, served as a consulting ecologist in green certification assessments of private and public forest in New York and New England, and now in Norway continues his research on mechanisms for frost tolerance and injury in conifers.

Allan M. Strong is Assistant Professor in the Rubenstein School of Environment and Natural Resources at the University of Vermont, USA. His research and teaching center around avian ecology and conservation in high elevation forests, temperate grasslands, and tropical forests.

Ross A. Virginia is Myers Family Professor of Environmental Science at Dartmouth College in Hanover, New Hampshire, USA, where he is also Director of the Institute of Arctic Studies. An ecosystem ecologist, his research is focused on climate change and its effects on biogeochemical cycling and soil biodiversity, especially in polar ecosystems. He is the co-editor of the Ashgate book series on Ecology and Law in Modern Society.

Beverley Wemple is Associate Professor of Geography at the University of Vermont, USA. She has expertise in hydrologic modeling, and her research focuses on the hydrologic impacts of forest management, in particular the effects of forest roads and mountain development. She recently served on a committee of the National Academy of Sciences to study these effects.

Preface

The series, Law and Ecology in Modern Society, is based upon the premise that the scientific discipline of ecology rests (or should rest) at the heart of environmental law and the environmental problems it addresses. The introductory volume, *Law and Ecology: The Rise of an Ecosystem Regime*, traced in broad terms the history of ecology and environmental law with special attention to their development during the last half of the twentieth century. However, the introductory volume left a variety of unanswered questions for future volumes. This is one of those volumes.

The methods and conclusions of the present volume, *Mountain Resorts: Ecology and the Law*, fully realize the intention of the series. The book is the result of a carefully planned series of interdisciplinary meetings. Ecologists, planners, economists and lawyers prepared and redrafted papers on ski area development and its ecological consequences within mountain ecosystems. Some of the authors also described and assessed the environmental laws designed to mitigate these consequences. Janet Milne has carefully introduced these papers, knitted them together to highlight their interconnections and offered some thoughtful conclusions. Thus, Milne and her co-authors fashion a vivid example of how the ecological sciences, if employed correctly, can yield an understanding of the environment and guide environmental law in its efforts to protect that environment.

Richard O. Brooks
Professor Emeritus, Vermont Law School, USA

Acknowledgments

This book is the product of the efforts of many people over a number of years to whom we owe significant thanks. After being a gleam in the eye of Richard Brooks, the book was launched as the combined effort of Ashgate Publishing and the Vermont Law Review, which organized a symposium on mountain resorts in 2001 and published the resulting papers. Kara Sweeney and Jennifer Feely, the law review's symposium editors, were instrumental in organizing the conference, and the law review editorial board and its editor-in-chief, Alexander Arpad, produced the resulting volume of the Vermont Law Review (Volume 26, Number 3 (Spring 2002)). The Canadian Embassy, McGill University, and Vermont Law School contributed generously to the symposium. Funding from the Canadian Embassy facilitated subsequent meetings of the contributors, and the Environmental Studies Program at Dartmouth College also provided support for this project. Eric Miller, who participated as an editor of this book during its initial phase, was pivotal in soliciting and shaping the contributions from the ecologists. John Banta and the Whiteface Ski Center kindly made arrangements for the contributing authors to meet at Whiteface as they explored their ideas about the book. Jeff Polubinski, Robert Gruenig, Anne Drost, and Bob Sachs delivered papers at the conference and generously participated in meetings following the conference, and Richard Brooks continued to lend a helping hand along the way. Numerous students at Vermont Law School assisted with research over the years; Albert Fox, Sarah Belcher, and Melissa Lewis provided valuable review of draft chapters; Judy Hilts compiled the final electronic manuscript; and Heather Carlos created the maps essential for locating the mountain resorts and explaining their expansion.

No doubt there are others who are not named by oversight, for which we apologize, but the proverbial bottom line is perhaps apparent. This has been an extraordinary collective effort for which we owe very broad thanks. And most particularly, deep thanks go to the contributors to this volume, who have worked through the iterations with patience and perseverance, often as their night job. It is only with their commitment over the years that this book has come to fruition. We thank them not only for their efforts but also for all that we have learned from them in the process.

The Editors

List of Abbreviations

AGIR	Alliance pour un Gestion Intégrée et Responsable du basin versant de la rivière du Diable
ANR	Vermont Agency of Natural Resources
APA	Administrative Procedure Act
ASC	American Skiing Company
ATVs	all-terrain vehicles
BAPE	Bureau d'audiences publiques sur l'environnement
C.C.Q	Civil Code of Quebec
CEQ	Counsil on Environmental Quality
CLD	Centre local de développement
CRELA	Conseil régional de l'environnement des Laurentides
CWA	Clean Water Act
CWE	Cumulative Watershed Effects
DEC	Department of Environmental Conservation
DEIS	Draft Environmental Impact Statement
DES	Department of Environmental Services
EIA	Environmental Impact Assessment
EIS	Environmental Impact Statement
EMS	environmental management system
EPA	Environmental Protection Agency
EPSCoR	Experimental Program to Stimulate Competitive Research
ESA	Endangered Species Act
FEIS	Final Environmental Impact Statement
FGEIS	Final Generic Environmental Impact Statement
FMF	February Median Flow
GIS	geographical information system
LAI	leaf area index
LMP	Loon Mountain Project
LMRC	Loon Mountain Recreation Corporation
LUDP	Land Use and Development Plan

MIS	Management Indicator Species
MOA	Memorandum of Agreement
MOU	Memorandum of Understanding
MRC	Regional County Municipality
MUSYA	Multiple Use Sustainable Yield Act
NEPA	National Environmental Policy Act
NFMA	National Forest Management Act
NFS	National Forest Service
NGOs	nongovernmental organizations
NPDES	National Pollution Discharge Elimination System
NSAA	National Ski Areas Association
ORDA	Olympic Regional Development Authority
PUD	Planned Unit Development
PVA	population viability analysis
RGGI	Regional Greenhouse Gas Initiative
ROD	Record of Decision
SEIS	Supplemented Environmental Impact Statement
SEQR	State Environmental Quality Review
SUP	Special Use Permit
TMDL	Total Maximum Daily Load
UQCN	Union québécoise pour la conservation de la nature
USEPA	U.S. Environmental Protection Agency
VCE	Vermont Center for Ecostudies
VINS	Vermont Institute of Natural Science
VNRC	Vermont Natural Resources Council
VSAA	Vermont Ski Areas Association

Chapter 1
The Landscape of This Book

Janet E. Milne[1]

Over the course of hundreds of million years, the slow but extraordinary movement of tectonic plates formed the predecessors of the modern Adirondack, Laurentian, Green and White Mountain ranges in northeastern North America.[2] Thirteen thousand years ago, the glaciers of the last ice age began retreating, leaving the wear of their grinding force.[3] The mountains slowly built their coverings of soil and trees and stood relatively unaltered by human activities until the late 1800s and early 1900s when some slopes were cleared for timber, only to return to trees again with the natural forces of regeneration by forest succession. Nevertheless, human use of these mountains continued throughout the twentieth century. People started using the slopes for downhill skiing in the 1930s,[4] for the construction of second homes in the 1960s, and today for activities that span the four seasons of the year.

Just as human activities on and around the mountains have evolved and diversified, so by necessity have the laws governing human activities in these ranges. Over the years, the United States and Canadian governments acquired large portions of these mountain terrains, gaining ownership control over their fate, and they enacted environmental regulations that attempted to mitigate the impact of human activities on the mountains. As ecological and environmental sciences have become more sophisticated, they increasingly have viewed each component of the environment as part of the ecosystem and analyzed how the functions of each component influence the health of the whole. But have environmental laws mirrored science's evolution by also viewing the mountains as part of an ecosystem when they regulate human activities at mountain resorts? And can the law effectively use science to take an ecosystem perspective? These

---

1 The author dedicates her work on this book to her father, George McLean Milne, who was inspired by and tended the landscape throughout his life, and her mother, Janet Odell Milne, who was a born editor.

2 *See generally* Bradford B. Van Diver, Roadside Geology of Vermont and New Hampshire 23–34 (1987); Natural Resources Canada, Geoscape Québec, geoscape.nrcan.gc.ca/Quebec/heritage_e.php (last visited Jan. 24, 2008).

3 Chet Raymo & Maureen E. Raymo, Written in Stone: A Geological History of the Northeastern United States 139 (1989).

4 Randall H. Bennett, The White Mountains: The Alps of New England 144 (2003).

are the questions that lie at the heart of this book.[5] The following chapters explore these questions as they focus on the ecology and law of four mountain resorts in northeastern United States and southeastern Canada—resorts at Loon Mountain in New Hampshire, Whiteface Mountain in New York, Killington and Pico in Vermont, and Mont Tremblant in Quebec.

A Bird's Eye View of the Landscape of This Book

Who: A diverse cast of resort operators, recreational users, local residents, environmental organizations, ecologists, lawyers, and governments at the local, state or provincial, and federal levels.
What: Mountain resorts in their ecosystems.
Why: A chance to determine whether we take an ecosystem perspective in evaluating and regulating human impacts on mountains, moving beyond the traditional approach to environmental protection.
Where: Four mountain resorts in northeastern United States and southeastern Canada that serve as case studies.
When: Looking at the state of science and the law now and possibilities for the future.

Before delving into the details of these mountain ecosystems and their legal regimes, it is perhaps useful to set these mountain resorts in the context of the evolution of snowy mountain resorts more generally, to consider why we chose these particular resorts, and to define what we mean by an ecosystem perspective. Just as the tectonic plates joined together to form the mountain ranges, our merging of the mountain resorts and the concept of an ecosystem perspective creates the landscape of this book.

Mountain Resorts

Northern mountain resorts are inextricably linked to skiing, which began as a form of recreation in the late 1800s more in the style of what we now know as cross-country skiing. One account cites Norwegians using skis in 1868 to travel from Telemark to Oslo, Norway, for social purposes,[6] and another acknowledges the Scandinavians' role in bringing skiing to the United States, where the first ski club was formed in California in 1867 and the first ski team in Minnesota in 1886.[7] Ski clubs sprang up in Europe in the late 1800s and international competitions started

5 *See generally* Richard O. Brooks, Ross Jones & Ross A. Virginia, Law and Ecology: The Rise of the Ecosystem Regime 26–32 (2002) (describing ecosystemic regimes as social institutions or clusters of institutions designed to govern ecosystems).

6 Simon Hudson, Snow Business: A Study of the International Ski Industry 8 (2000).

7 Hal Clifford, Downhill Slide 9–10 (2002).

in the early 1900s, but alpine or downhill skiing did not appear at international competitions until after World War I.[8] Among the people credited for the transition to modern downhill skiing were Mathias Zdarsky in Austria, who invented a type of stem turn and taught people to climb mountains and ski down in the late 1800s; Hannes Schneider, who started a ski school after World War I in St. Anton am Arlberg, Austria, where he taught his Arlberg method of skiing that used a system of turns and more sophisticated skiing equipment; and Sir Arnold Lunn, who invented the slalom race.[9] In 1927, the Arlberg Ski Club sponsored the first alpine-only skiing competition (downhill and slalom),[10] and the Arlberg technique crossed the Atlantic in the late 1920s, where college and urban ski clubs, such as the Dartmouth Outing Club and the Appalachian Mountain Club in Boston, took up the sport.[11] Nordic skiing and ski jumping competitions were held at the first Winter Olympic Games in 1924 in Chamonix, France, and subsequent games, including the 1932 Olympics in Lake Placid, New York. Alpine skiing made its Olympic debut in 1936 in Garmisch-Partenkirchen, Germany.[12]

Not surprisingly, mountain resorts developed along with the interest in recreational skiing. The custom of winter mountain resorts reportedly started in 1866 when the owner of a hotel in St. Moritz invited his British summer guests to visit off-season to hike and climb,[13] and skiing became an important addition over time. Although ski resorts generally did not have ski lifts until the 1930s, the Lauterbrunnen-Murren railway line carried skiers up into the Swiss Alps in the winter of 1910–1911,[14] and following World War I ski resorts such as St. Anton, St. Moritz, and Davos flourished in Europe.[15] The ski resorts were farming communities that developed skiing and tourism as additional lines of business, the ownership of which was spread among numerous farmers and entrepreneurs.[16]

The first mechanized ski lift in the United States was a simple rope tow powered by a Model T Ford, erected in 1934 in a cow pasture in Woodstock, Vermont, just 20 miles from today's Killington resort.[17] In 1936, the Union Pacific Railroad took a more sophisticated approach in developing Sun Valley in Idaho. Then-chairman Averill Harriman strove to bring the European resort tradition to the United States, but he created a corporate-owned resort from scratch in the middle of the wilderness. It opened complete with a $1.5 million lodge, swimming pool, skating rink, Saks

---

8 Annie Gilbert Coleman, Ski Style 43–4 (2004).

9 *Id.*

10 *Id.* at 44.

11 *Id.* at 50–52.

12 David Miller, Athens to Athens: The Official History of the Olympic Games and the IOC, 1884–2004, at 461, 466, 471, 483–84 (2003).

13 Hudson, *supra* note 6, at 8.

14 *Id.* at 8–10.

15 Coleman, *supra* note 8, at 44–45.

16 *Id.* at 43; Hudson, *supra* note 6, at 32.

17 Ellen Lesser, *Commemorative Album, America's First Ski Tow: Gilbert's Hill 1934* (1983) (on file at Dartmouth College's Rauner Library).

Fifth Avenue store, beauty treatments, Austrian ski instructors, and the first chairlift in the United States.[18] Not all resorts in the United States were created with this style or flare, but it served as a harbinger for the character of American resorts of the future.

With the increase in popularity of skiing over the decades, the mountain resort industry and skiing have grown around the globe.[19] During the 1990s, 4,500 resorts with 26,000 ski lifts hosted 390 million skier visits.[20] According to 1996 statistics, Japan was home to the largest number of resorts (700), followed by Austria (550), the United States (516), Switzerland (480), France (431), Sweden (340), the former Czechoslovakia (300), Italy (260), and Canada (245). Japan also was the leader in the number of skier visits, claiming 19.2 percent of the market, followed by France (14.4 percent), the United States (13.9 percent), Austria (11 percent), Italy (9.5 percent), Switzerland (8 percent), and Canada (5.6 percent),[21] although Japan dropped to fourth rank in a 2002 study of later years.[22] The global ski industry generates direct revenues approaching $9 billion annually.[23]

The range of activities at the resorts has also expanded over time. In many areas, resorts now offer glade skiing, replicating the experience afforded on European alpine slopes, and snowboarding, which became an official Olympic event in 1998. The increase in the number of non-skiers who visit resorts in the winter and the decrease in the number of hours that skiers spend on the slopes have gone hand-in-hand with the rise of other resort-based forms of entertainment, such as indoor tennis, spas, and hot-air ballooning, in addition to shopping, dining, and the traditional après-ski activities. Moreover, resorts increasingly are seeking to attract visitors on a four-season basis by featuring hiking, biking, tennis, paragliding, rock-climbing, and other forms of entertaining during the warmer months when the slopes and facilities otherwise would lie fallow.[24] In some cases, real estate development has become a significant part of the resort owners' financial portfolio, giving the owners the opportunity to increase their return by selling fractional or whole ownerships in condominiums and second homes and by obtaining management fees for managing rentals to non-owners.[25]

According to an industry survey, ski resorts in the United States received an estimated 57 million visits during the 2004–2005 winter season (measured by

18 Coleman, *supra* note 8, at 75–76; Hudson, *supra* note 6, at 10.

19 For additional information on the history of skiing in the United States, see Clifford, *supra* note 7, Coleman, *supra* note 8, and Bob Sachs, *National Perspective on Mountain Resorts and Ecology*, 26 Vt. L. Rev. 515 (2002).

20 Hudson, *supra* note 6, at 28 (citing statistics published by Ski Area Management in 1996).

21 *Id.*

22 A. Lazard, *Ski Winter: World Flat*, 23 Ski Area Management 24, 25 (Sept. 2002).

23 Daniel Scott, *Global Environmental Change and Mountain Tourism*, in Stefan Gössling & C. Michael Hall, Tourism and Global Environmental Change 56 (2006).

24 Hudson, *supra* note 6, at 164–65.

25 *See generally* Clifford, *supra* note 7.

skier and snowboarder days), continuing the strong, stable national record that has prevailed since the start of the new millennium. Although down 0.3 percent from the 2003–2004 season and 1.2 percent from the record high 2002–2003 season, four of the best seasons on record for United States resorts have occurred since 2000.[26] During the 2005–2006 season, Canada's ski resorts reported 19 million visits, reflecting a steady increase in the number of skier visits.[27]

Although data on the Canadian mountain resort industry are limited, information about resorts in the United States provides some insight into the current financial profile of the resort industry. According to an industry survey of U.S. resorts after the 2004–2005 season, gross revenues for resort owners in the Northeast averaged $18.5 million, with a $3.7 million operating profit. The figures were higher for the Rocky Mountains, where the resorts are larger and averaged $32.6 million in revenues and $9.4 million in operating profit. Average revenue per skier visit averaged $67.14, of which $30.73 (almost 46 percent) came from lift tickets and $36.41 from non-ticket revenue. Seventy-five percent of the resorts that responded to the survey remained open during the summer months, offering activities such as dining, lodging, golf, chairlift rides, mountain biking, water parks and alpine slides, but these summer activities generated on average only 6.7 percent of annual revenues. Thus, the winter activities have remained the primary source of revenue for the resort operators despite the trend toward four-season operation, and the employment patterns follow in tandem. Resorts responding to the survey indicated that they employed on average 767 people, but 669 of those were seasonal employees only.[28] Consequently, the resorts nationwide would appear to generate a primary and secondary economy for their communities that is significant, but often seasonal, in nature.

As mountain resorts have proliferated globally, expanded in size, and diversified their range of activities, their ecological footprint potentially grows larger as well. Although we have not found a comprehensive analysis of the ecological impacts of mountain resorts in North America, a study by the United States Environmental Protection Agency in 2000 provides a sense of perspective on some of the resource demands of skiing relative to other forms of recreation in the United States. It found that ski resorts used 50 billion gallons of water annually for snowmaking—about 85 percent of the water used for activity-specific tourism and recreational activities

26 National Ski Area Association, Economic Analyses of United States Ski Areas, at ES-1 (2005).

27 Canadian Ski Council, 2005–2006 Canadian Snow Industry in Review 1 (2006). As in recent years, 84 percent of the visits were from Canadians, who traditionally support winter sports. In 2005, 4.1 million Canadians aged 12 or older participated in alpine or cross-country skiing or snowboarding, representing nearly 15 percent of Canada's total population. The share of visits from the United States has declined from 7 to 4 percent, perhaps due to a stronger Canadian dollar making the trip less attractive for Americans, but growth among overseas visitors more than compensated for the difference. *Id.* at 1–2.

28 National Ski Area Association, Economic Analyses of United States Ski Areas ES-1, 6, 11, 19–20, 22, 43 (2005) (based on survey of 105 ski resorts).

in the United States.[29] If one assumes 57 million skier visits, this means that each skier visit required, on average, almost 900 gallons of water for snowmaking. To provide the skiing opportunity, resorts also consumed 5.6 trillion British thermal units (Btus) of energy per year, compared to 18 trillion for the activity-specific tasks of the other recreational sectors combined. Adding the energy demands of lodging, restaurants, and retail shops associated with the resorts, the energy consumption rose to 9.1 trillion Btus, but that total is relatively small compared to the 210-trillion-Btu consumption level for all recreational sectors combined, taking into account the activity-specific and related demands.[30]

Our Case Study Mountain Resorts

Four mountain resorts in the northeastern United States and southeastern Canada are the focus of this book: Loon Resort in New Hampshire, located in the heart of the White Mountains; Whiteface Mountain Ski Center near Lake Placid, New York, the home of two Olympic competitions in the Adirondack Mountains; Killington Resort in the Green Mountains of Vermont, midway between the White Mountains and the Adirondacks; and Mont Tremblant to the north in the Laurentian Mountains of Quebec, Canada. (See Figure 1.1).

These mountains sit on the edges of three major metropolitan populations thirsty for sources of recreation and outdoor experiences. To the south of the mountains, the New York City metropolitan area, the largest metropolitan area in the country, is home to 19 million people,[31] and the Greater Boston metropolitan area of Massachusetts offers another 4.5 million.[32] These two metropolitan areas almost merge as growth has expanded along the corridor between the two, accentuating by

29 United States Environmental Protection Agency, A Method for Quantifying Environmental Indicators of Selected Leisure Activities in the United States, EPA-231-R-00-001, at 43 (2000). To bring water usage down to the single-resort scale, one of the snowmaking systems at Killington Resort uses 720,000 gallons of water an hour for the part of its system that covers 80 acres with 240 snow guns. Killington Resort, Snow You Can Depend On, at www.killington.com/winter/mountain/stats/snow_you_can_count_on/index.html (last visited Feb. 1, 2008). During the 2005–2006 season, Loon Resort used 230 million gallons of water in its snowmaking system. Press Release, Loon Mountain, Snowmaking Improvements and Upgrades Ensure Top-rated Terrain at Loon Mountain (Winter 2006/2007).

30 United States Environmental Protection Agency, A Method for Quantifying Environmental Indicators of Selected Leisure Activities in the United States, EPA-231-R-00-001, at 43 (2000). The study covered skiing, golf, fishing, hunting, boating, waterside activities, conventions, amusement parks, museums and historical sites, and casinos. The "activity-specific" use of water does not include water used for associated lodging, restaurant or retail activities. *Id.; see also* Sachs, *supra* note 19, at 526–29.

31 U.S. Census Bureau, Statistical Abstract of the United States 26 (2008) (Table 20).

32 *Id.* at 24.

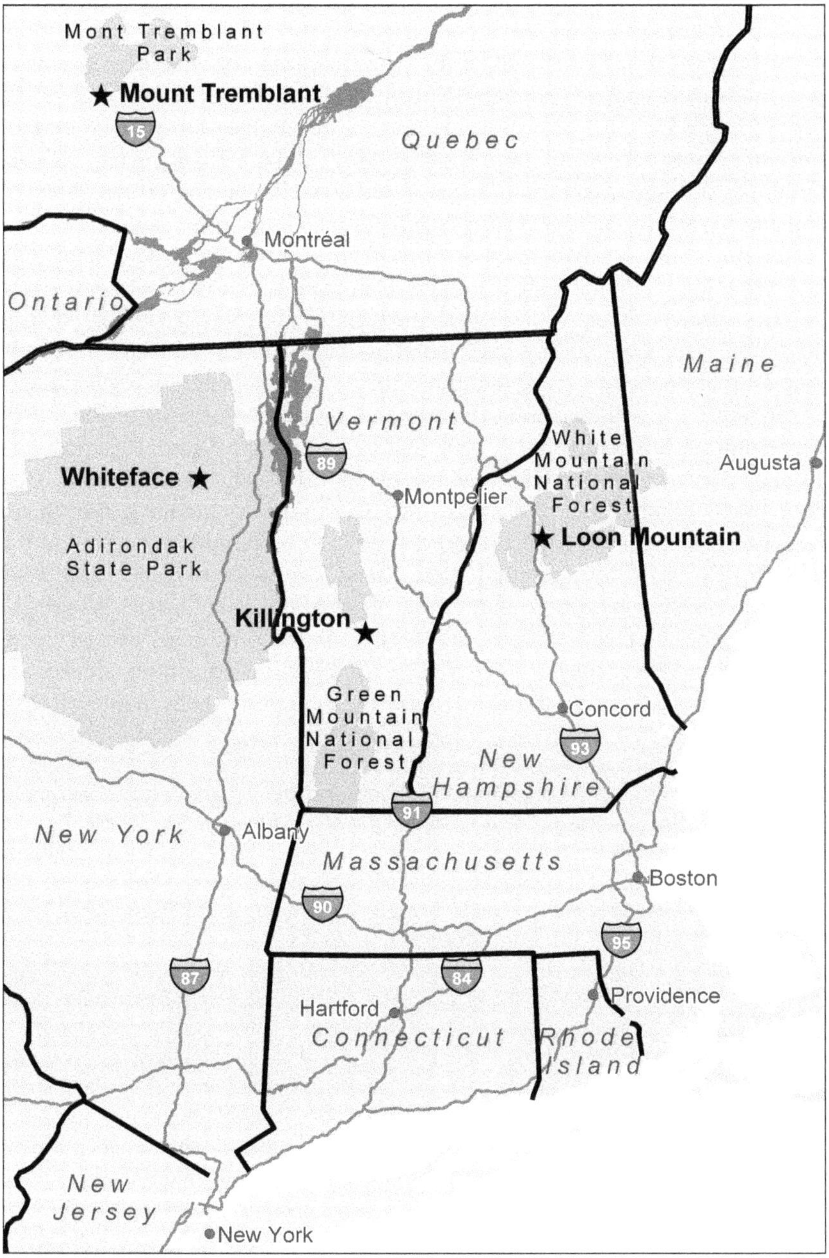

Figure 1.1 Location of the Case Study Resorts

Data Sources: DMTI Spatial, Inc.; ESRI; US Geological Survey Center for Earth Resource Observation and Science; National Aeronautics and Space Administration; National Geospatial Intelligence Agency; Tele Atlas North America, Inc.

contrast the alluring rural nature of northern New York, New Hampshire, Vermont, and Quebec. On the northern edge, the Montreal metropolitan area, the second largest in Canada, contains another 3.6 million people who can seek recreation to the south in the United States or to the north at Mont Tremblant.[33] The northeast region as a whole consists of 48 million people,[34] and others, of course, choose to travel to these destinations from farther afield as well. Although often competing for business, each of the four resorts has distinct features. (See Table 1.1).

Loon Resort at Loon Mountain, located in large part on the federal lands of the White Mountain National Forest in New Hampshire, is a family-oriented resort with four-season activities (but no golf course). It is undergoing a major expansion of its South Peak area, adding new snowmaking, two new lifts, and 50 acres of new trails that opened in 2007, and more lifts, trails and amenities scheduled for the near future.[35] Loon Mountain Recreation Corporation was the original owner and operator of the resort, but it was acquired by Booth Creek Resorts, Inc., a significant player in the United States' mountain resort industry. Until 2007, Booth Creek owned Loon, Waterville Valley, and Cranmore Mountain Resort in New Hampshire, making it the largest resort owner in New Hampshire, as well as three mountain resorts in the western United States, Northstar-at-Tahoe and Sierra-at-Tahoe in California and the Summit at Snoqualmie near Seattle, Washington. Ownership of Loon changed again in 2007, but the resort expansion discussed in the chapters on Loon focus in large part on the period when Booth Creek owned the resort.[36] Those chapters show how federal law governing the White Mountain

33 Statistics Canada, Population and Dwelling Counts, for Census Metropolitan Areas, 2006 and 2001 Censuses, www12.statcan.ca (last visited Jan. 31, 2008).

34 *See* U.S. Census Bureau, *supra* note 31, at 17 (Table 12, population of New Jersey, New York, Connecticut, Massachusetts; Maine, New Hampshire, Vermont); Statistics Canada, Population and Dwelling Counts, for Canada, Provinces and Territories, 2006 and 2001 Censuses, www.statcan.ca (last visited Feb. 1, 2008).

35 The 2007 expansion represents only 35 percent of the total planned on-mountain expansion. Press Release, Loon Mountain, Loon Mountain Invests Over $10 Million to Prepare for New South Peak Expansion Slated to Open December 15, 2007 (on file with author).

36 In 2007, Booth Creek sold the assets of Loon and the three western resorts for $172 million (including $15.5 million for Loon) to CNL Income Properties, Inc.—a real estate investment trust in Orlando, Florida, that has a portfolio of dozens of life style and recreational properties in North America, including ski resorts, golf courses, amusement parks, and marinas, but Loon Mountain Recreation Corporation, still owned by Booth Creek, continued the management functions at Loon under lease. *See* CNL Income Properties, Inc., Final Prospectus (Form 424(b)(3)), at 5 (Apr. 26, 2007); CNL Income Properties, Inc., Supplement No. Five dated March 7, 2007 to Prospectus dated April 4, 2006 (Form 424(b)(3)), at 3 (Mar. 7, 2007); CNL Income Properties, Inc., Quarterly Report (Form 10-Q), at 18 (May 11, 2007). Booth Creek itself was also sold to three of its principals, including Chairman George Gillett, owner of the Montreal Canadiens hockey team and Liverpool soccer club. Aldo Svaldi, *Soccer Gets Big-Time Backers Kroenke, Anschutz, Gillett All Betting on Sport's Growth*, Denver Post, Feb. 12, 2007, at C-01. In late 2007, Booth Creek sold Loon Mountain

Table 1.1 Selected Operational Features of the Case Study Resorts

Characteristics	Loon Mountain	Whiteface Ski Center	Killington Resort	Mont Tremblant
Location	White Mountains New Hampshire, US	Adirondack Mountains New York, US	Green Mountains Vermont, US	Laurentian Mountains Quebec, Canada
Height (feet)	3,050	4,867 (Whiteface) 3,676 (Little Whiteface)	4,241 (Killington) 3,967 (Pico)	3,176
Vertical Drop (feet)	2,100	3,430 (3,166 lift serviced)	3,050	2,116
Principal Owner of the Mountain	United States (National Forest Service) and Booth Creek (at base)	State of New York	State of Vermont and American Skiing Corporation	Province of Quebec and Intrawest Development Corporation
Principal Owner/ Operator of the On-Mountain Resort Activities	Booth Creek and its subsidiary Loon Mountain Recreation Corporation	Olympic Regional Development Authority	American Skiing Corporation	Intrawest Development Corporation
Ski Trails	23.4 miles 53 trails 324 skiable acres 6 tree skiing areas	18 miles 76 trails 225 skiable acres 28.5 acres of tree skiing	87 miles 200 trails 1,215 skiable acres 141 acres tree skiing	47 miles 94 trails 631 skiable acres
Snowmaking coverage	96%	98% (on trails) 190 guns; 33 miles of pipe	62% 1,435 guns; 88 miles of pipe	1,037 snow guns
Did the resort operator develop associated residential and commercial facilities?	Yes (limited at mountain base)	No (support facilities are located only in the nearby villages)	Yes (primarily residential on slopes and base)	Yes (new mountain villages)

Statistical Sources: www.loonmountain.com; www.whiteface.com; www.killington.com; www.tremblant.ca (last visited Jan. 22, 2008).

Note: Owners and operators are indicated as of 2006, to reflect the key players during the period covered in this book. Statistics about trails and snowmaking are accurate as of winter 2007–2008.

[*footnote continued*] Recreation Corporation to Boyne USA, Inc., which now holds the lease to operate at Loon and, through Loon Mountain Recreational Corporation, operates the resort for CNL Income Properties, Inc. *See* CNL Income Properties, Inc., Post-effective Amendment Nine to Form S-11 for Registration under the Securities Act of 1933 of Securities of Certain Real Estate Companies, at 6 (Jan. 15, 2008); Press Release, Both Creek Ski Holdings, Inc., Booth Creek Ski Holdings, Inc. Transfers Control of Loon Mountain and the Summit-at-Snoqualmie Ski Resorts to Boyne, USA, Inc. (Oct. 5, 2007) (on file with author).

National Forest sets the legal framework for evaluating permits to use federal land for the mountain resort and Booth Creek's ability to expand the resort. They also discuss how federal law addresses the residential growth now occurring on private land at the base of the mountain.

The Whiteface Ski Center on Whiteface Mountain lies in the midst of the New York State's Adirondack Park and is operated by a public authority created by the State of New York, the Olympic Regional Development Authority, making it the only resort in this book that is not operated by a for-profit corporation. Under the New York Constitution, the state-owned preserve in which Whiteface is located generally must be kept "forever wild," and the Constitution strictly limits the activities that can occur on the slopes of Whiteface. Consequently, the mountain is home to the ski slopes but, unlike the other resorts in this book, the bulk of other resort activities—hotels, shops, restaurants, golf courses, and condominiums—are conducted off-mountain by numerous private entrepreneurs in the nearby townships of Lake Placid and Wilmington. Unlike some resorts, Lake Placid attracts more people during the summer than the winter. The chapters on Whiteface examine how the unique legal regime of the Adirondack Park has influenced the character and development of this mountain resort, both on the mountain and in the surrounding communities.

Killington and Pico are neighboring mountains in central Vermont that together form Killington Resort, the largest ski resort in the eastern United States with 200 trails and 33 lifts spread over more than 1,200 skiable acres.[37] American Skiing Company acquired the resort in 1996[38] and was the owner during the period of time discussed in this book. The ski slopes of the mountain, owned in large part by the State of Vermont, are leased to the American Skiing Company, but significant development has occurred on the private land on the mountain flanks. Facilities that support the four-season use line the five-mile road to the base of the ski slopes, and condominiums and houses climb the mountain from the base. For the past decade, American Skiing Corporation had been one of the biggest players in the mountain resort industry with holdings from Maine to California, but the financial burden of its national expansion led to the sale of all but one of its properties to various buyers between late 2006 and mid-2007: Steamboat in Colorado; Attitash in New Hampshire; Sugarloaf/USA and Sunday River in Maine; and Mount Snow, and Killington Resort in Vermont.[39] The Killington Resort is now owned by a joint venture between SP Land Co., a Dallas-based company that will focus on real estate development, and Powdr Resorts, a company that owns a number of ski

37 Killington Resort Website, http://www.killington.com/about_us.html (last visited June 12, 2007).

38 Meg Lukens Noonan, *What's Doing in Killington*, N.Y. Times, Jan. 5, 1997, at 5-16.

39 Steve Syre, *Back to the Future?* Boston Globe, May 31, 2007, at D1; Steve Syre, *American Skiing Rejects Otten Bid for Sunday River, Sugarloaf*, Boston Globe, June 6, 2007, at C5.

resorts in the western United States and will manage the mountain operations.[40] But American Skiing Company's plans for the resort in its ten-year ownership created the springboard for the future. The chapters on Killington Resort explore how Vermont's unique land use permitting law, Act 250, addressed American Skiing Company's proposals to expand its snowmaking operations, to construct a trail and lift system connecting Killington and Pico, and to build a mountain village.

One of North America's oldest ski areas, Mont Tremblant lies north of Montreal in Quebec's Mont Tremblant Park. The resort is owned and operated by Intrawest ULC, the largest ski resort operator in Canada and owner of 11 mountain resorts across Canada and the United States,[41] including Whistler Blackcomb Ski Resort, the venue of the 2010 Winter Olympics near Vancouver, Canada. Since Intrawest acquired the lease to operate on provincial park land at Mont Tremblant in 1991, it has steadily upgraded and expanded the resort on park land and land it owns. Although the traditional villages of the municipality of Mont Tremblant are nearby, Intrawest built a major, full-service, European-style village at the base of the mountain, giving this resort a different profile from the other three in this book. It is now a full year-round resort that offers 38 restaurants, 43 shops, golf courses, tennis, and festivals that draw visitors from across North America and Europe,[42] and those activities will expand further as it continues its $1 billion expansion. Billed as the "largest tourism project underway in North America,"[43] the 10-year project includes new slopes, a new mountain village, and the addition of more four-season activities.[44] The chapters on Mont Tremblant investigate the intricate matrix of federal, provincial, municipal, and contract laws within which the resort has grown.

Why focus on these mountain resorts, which are lower in altitude and smaller in trail size than their counterparts in western North America? Within a relatively small region, stretching slightly over 150 miles north to south and slightly under 150 miles east to west, these four resorts provide multiple and very different lenses through which the authors and readers of this book can look to determine how the law shapes activities on the mountains. The mountains' proximity means that these resorts share many ecological features, creating a relatively similar ecological

---

40 Ben Hewitt, *As Big Company Sells Resorts, Hopes Rise for a Northeast Revival*, N.Y. Times, Mar. 23, 2007, at F8; telephone interview by Eric Goldwarg with Tom Horrocks, Killington Communications Manager (June 8, 2007).

41 Intrawest Quick Facts, http://media.intrawest.com/icr/intrawest/pdf/Intrawest_Quick_Facts2007.pdf (last visited July 19, 2007). From its origins as a residential and urban real estate development firm in 1976, Intrawest expanded into resorts in the 1980s and now owns private golf and beach resorts clubs as well, employing 22,000 people, reporting revenues of $1.6 billion (U.S. dollars), and hosting 8 million skier visits annually. *Id.* Privately held, it was acquired by Fortress Investment Group LLC in 2006 for $1.8 billion. Peter Edmonston, *Mission Acquirable? Breaking the Code*, N.Y. Times, Apr. 4, 2007, at H2.

42 Mont Tremblant Media Kit 5, http://ww1.tremblant.ca/pdfs/media/Media_kit.pdf (last visited June 13, 2007).

43 *Id.* at 15.

44 *Id.*

framework for analyzing the impact of various types of human activities and very different legal regimes. In short, they provide a workable framework for broad-ranging and comparative analysis.

These resorts also share a feature common to a number of other mountain resorts—the operation of resorts at the intersection of public and private ownership. Mountains in North America frequently are owned by the government, but the resorts themselves are often operated by the private, entrepreneurial entities. These public and private forces meet as the mountain resorts evolve over time, and the law influences the interaction. The four resorts in this book provide four different sets of circumstances for examining whether the law considers the ecosystem as a whole—public and private lands together—as the law plays a role in authorizing, denying, or influencing the evolution of the resorts.

In addition, during the time period for the case studies, the resorts at Loon, Killington, and Mont Tremblant were owned and operated by some of the most significant players in the mountain resort industry in North America, allowing one to examine the interactions of major resort operators with the law. Whiteface offers the interesting contrast of a mountain facility run by a governmental entity, rather than a for-profit corporation.

The laws at work at the array of mountain resorts provide enormous diversity across the case studies. The presence of federal land at Loon Mountain invokes significant federal environmental laws that help shape the activities on and near the mountain through the process of evaluating national forest management plans, proposed permits to use federal land, and expansion proposals. Environmental impact statements play a significant role in these evaluations. At Whiteface Mountain, the New York Constitution places limits on the state-run activities on the mountain, state law requires periodic planning for the Whiteface Ski Center, and a state-level permitting system overlays local land use regulation of privately owned land. In Vermont, a unique state law requiring state administrators to conduct an environmental review of significant development activities has played a major role in defining the terms under which the Killington Resort operates, while local land use plans also set parameters for activities at the mountain base. At Mont Tremblant, negotiations between the resort operator and provincial and municipal governments, provincial laws that require integrated local planning processes, and federal and provincial environmental impact assessment requirements have influenced the nature and extent of the resort, as have activity-specific environmental laws. Consequently, these four resorts provide a wealth of opportunities to evaluate how different types of legal regimes consider the mountain ecosystem—planning, permitting, environmental impact assessment, negotiated agreements, private land trusts, and more. (See Table 1.2).

At the same time, these mountains resorts share many characteristics with less exotic landscapes. This book, therefore, may offer some broader insights into the relationship between ecology and the law. Although the mountains stand high above the landscapes in which they sit, they are relatively low in altitude by international standards, ranging from 2,871 to 4,867 feet, and only two of the mountains have

Table 1.2 Selected Legal Features of the Case Study Resorts

Characteristics	Loon Mountain	Whiteface Ski Center	Killington Resort	Mont Tremblant
Key Expansion Activities Reviewed in This Book	Original permit Expanded trails Snowmaking Residential development	Expanded trails Snowmaking Growth in surrounding communities	Land swap Expanded trails and lifts Snowmaking New mountain village	Land swap Expanded trails Mountain villages Golf courses Land trust
Key Governing Laws	National Forest Management Act (planning process) National Environmental Policy Act (impact assessment process) Federal Clean Water Act (permit process) Endangered Species Act (species and habitat conservation)	New York Constitution (limits on uses) Adirondack Park Agency Act (state planning process for public land and permitting process for private land) Environmental Quality Review Act (state impact assessment process) Local zoning	Vermont's Act 250 (permit process) Associated state laws (permit process) Local zoning (planning process)	Quebec's Parks Act Quebec's Environment Quality Act (permit process) Canada's Environmental Assessment Act (impact assessment process) Contract law Quebec's Act Respecting Land Use Planning and Development (planning process)

alpine terrain. Many of the ecological relationships described in this book are analogous to those in other settings (especially temperate deciduous and coniferous forests); many of the laws governing these mountains are at work in other types of landscapes; and many of the challenges of taking an ecosystem perspective are common to situations well beyond the confines of these mountains.

The Ecosystem Perspective: Defining Our Challenge

The question that lies at the heart of this book is whether the law considers the effects of human activities on mountains' ecosystems when it regulates activities at mountain resorts. Does the law take an ecosystem perspective?

This inquiry must start with the question of what we mean by an "ecosystem perspective." The defining characteristic of an ecosystem perspective is that it puts the spotlight on the ecosystem as a whole, not on any one particular element or set of interactions within the greater ecosystem. As Ernest Callenback wrote, ecology is "the science that studies the marvelously complex interrelationships of life forms on the planet Earth."[45] We are looking not at specific environmental problems in isolation, such as threats to the habitat of bears or thrushes, or the quality of mountain streams. Instead, we are focusing on the interrelationships among numerous plants and animal species and the air, water and soil in which they live. These interrelationships create a complex basis for the sustainable existence of each component of the system. Collectively they form an ecosystem—"a dynamic complex of plant, animal, and microorganism communities and the nonliving environment interacting as a functional unit."[46]

A number of significant environmental laws in the United States and Canada originally were not based on an ecosystem perspective, because they focused on specific pollutants that jeopardized the quality of certain components of the environment, such as water or air. For example, in the United States, the federal Clean Air Act of 1970 established air quality standards for air pollutants, the Federal Water Pollution Control Act Amendments of 1972 regulated discharges into navigable waters, and the Resource Conservation and Recovery Act in 1976 created a regime governing hazardous waste.[47] As explored at length in the first book in this series, LAW AND ECOLOGY: THE RISE OF THE ECOSYSTEM REGIME, the science of ecology and ecosystems evolved contemporaneously with legal regimes designed to protect the environment; an understanding of ecosystems was not the conceptual predicate for designing the legal regimes in many instances in the United States and Canada.[48] As understanding of ecosystems has developed, however, some laws have embraced an ecosystem perspective from the start, and some have adapted to the broader, ecosystem perspective in the way in which they are implemented.[49] And as we start the new millennium, studies of environmental problems increasingly are calling for using management strategies that are based on the all elements of the ecosystem.[50]

The benchmark we use for evaluating whether laws today embody an ecosystem perspective is whether they are designed or implemented in a way that takes into account the multi-faceted complexities and interrelationships of the ecosystem. Similarly, when government is making decisions in its capacity as a landowner, the key characteristic of an ecosystem-based decision is whether government

45 ERNEST CALLENBACK, ECOLOGY: A POCKET GUIDE 1 (1998).

46 CONVENTION ON BIOLOGICAL DIVERSITY, art. 2, 31 I.L.M. 818 (entered into force Dec. 29, 1993).

47 *See generally* BROOKS ET AL., *supra* note 5, at 26–32 (2002); MARY GRAHAM, THE MORNING AFTER EARTH DAY 27–50 (1999); RICHARD J. LAZARUS, THE MAKING OF ENVIRONMENTAL LAW 67–97 (2004).

48 *See* DAVID R. BOYD, UNNATURAL LAW: RETHINKING CANADIAN ENVIRONMENTAL LAW AND POLICY 233–34 (2003); BROOKS ET AL., *supra* note 5, at 26–32.

49 *See* BROOKS ET AL., *supra* note 5, at 35, 368–72.

50 *See, e.g.*, U.S. COMMISSION ON OCEAN POLICY, AN OCEAN BLUEPRINT FOR THE 21ST CENTURY 61 (2004); MILLENNIUM ECOSYSTEM ASSESSMENT SYNTHESIS REPORT 17 (2005).

considers the impacts on ecological interrelationships, not just the impact on one component of the ecosystem.

For example, when a mountain resort wants to use water for snowmaking, do the laws or governmental landowners consider just the effect on the water body itself, or are they also concerned about how changes in water level may affect wildlife and plant life in and around the water body, and the ecological ripple effects of those changes in wildlife and plant life? And do they consider how using the water to improve snow cover may affect the patterns of snowmelt on the slopes, which may in turn affect wildlife and plant life? Or if a resort wants to clear land to expand the network of trails, does the law look beyond just the trees that will be cut and consider how those changes in vegetation may influence the ability of wildlife species to cross the new gaps in forest cover? And does the law consider the effect of the changes in vegetation on the rate of the flow of water down the slopes, which in turn may affect the quality or quantity of water in streams and, therefore, the habitat of aquatic species?

If the law and the governmental decision-makers, as regulators or landowners, take the broader view, then they are using an ecosystem perspective. As one commentator has stated, "[u]nder an ecosystem approach, decisions are made by measuring effects on systems rather than on their constituent parts in isolation from each other."[51]

In this book we test the ecosystem perspective at mountain resorts. Authors explain what they know about the mountain ecosystem—the interrelationships among soil, plant life, animal life, and water resources—and how human activities at mountain resorts affect those interrelationships, not just any one particular element of the ecosystem. They look at the extent to which widely ranging legal regimes consider the ecosystem as a whole, not just one particular element of the ecosystem, when they generate decisions about whether to allow certain human activities to occur on the mountains. If laws do consider the ecosystem, how do they do so? If they do not, in what ways do they fail? Are there ways either to implement or to restructure these legal regimes in order to more effectively incorporate the ecosystem perspective?

We consciously do not adopt any particular term of art for describing a benchmark for analysis other than our own term "ecosystem perspective" as described above. In the past two decades, terms such as ecosystem management and adaptive management have come into vogue to try to capture an approach to environmental protection that broadens the focus to take the ecosystem into account. Ecosystem management, however, has different meanings to different people,[52]

---

51 Bruce Pardy, *Changing Nature: The Myth of the Inevitability of Ecosystem Management*, 20 Pace Envtl. L. Rev. 675, 678 (2003).

52 *See, e.g.*, Robert Keiter, *Biodiversity Conservation and the Intermixed Ownership Problem: From Nature Reserves to Collaborative Processes*, 38 Idaho L. Rev. 301, 317 (2002); Richard Haeuber & Jerry Franklin, *Perspectives on Ecosystem Management*, 6 Ecological Applications, No. 3, at 692, 693 (1996). Compare, for example, the definition

and it embodies not just the concept of considering ecological interactions but also specific concepts about how the law or managers should achieve an ecosystem-based decision. The ultimate goal of this book is not to analyze legal regimes against any particular, pre-selected solution. Instead it is, quite simply, to explore the extent to which governmental decision-making considers the ecosystem.

Applying the Ecosystem Perspective to the Mountain Resorts

In taking an ecosystem perspective, the first issue is how one defines the ecosystem, which is not an easy threshold question. Because an ecosystem is a functional concept, not a spatial concept, we ideally would define the relevant ecosystem in functional terms, looking at all of the on-mountain and off-mountain interrelationships relevant to the functioning of mountain life. For purposes of this book, however, we have chosen a spatial definition out of necessity. We are primarily limiting the inquiry to the geographic mountain resort—the mountain and the immediate residential and commercial community that serves the mountain resort, which may be on the mountain or near its base. Thus, the authors look primarily at the ecological interrelationships within that spatial area and the human activities that occur within that geographic domain.

By limiting the exploration to the geographic area of the mountain resort, we undoubtedly are shearing off midway many chains of ecological interrelationships that arise in the mountain resort area but extend far beyond. For example, activities at the mountain resorts generate carbon emissions and nonpoint-source water pollution that flow out from the resort, affecting ecological interrelationships beyond the spatial confines of the resort. Conversely, we are not tracking back to their source interrelationships that result from actions occurring beyond the mountain resort and that have direct ecological impacts on the mountain ecosystem. Emissions from coal-fired power plants hundreds of miles away contribute to acid rain that can affect the soil and plant life on mountains;[53] airborne mercury from distant power plants enter the food supply for birds and fish;[54] national and global emissions of greenhouse gases contribute to climate change that can significantly affect the mountain environment;[55] and human activities in the winter habitats of

of ecosystem management used in *The Report of the Ecological Society of American Committee on Scientific Basis for Ecosystem Management*, 6 Ecological Applications 665 (1996), and the definition used in the 1995 report, Interagency Ecosystem Management Task Force, The Ecosystem Approach: Healthy Ecosystems and Sustainable Economies.

53 *See, e.g.*, Kate M. Joyce, *Who'll Stop the Rain?* 7 Albany L. Envtl. Outlook J. 94 (2002).

54 *See, e.g.*, Hubbard Brook Research Foundation, Mercury Matters: Linking Mercury Science and Public Policy in the Northeastern United States 16 (2007).

55 *See, e.g.*, Janine Bloomfield, Seasons of Change: Global Warming and New England's White Mountains (1997); Mylvakanam Iyngararasan et al., *The Challenges*

migratory birds that spend summers in the mountains can render the population more vulnerable. To follow all the interrelationships to their logical conclusions would yield a more accurate, but potentially overwhelming ecosystem inquiry.

Thus, out of the necessity of keeping the scope manageable, we have limited the inquiry to the ecosystem on and at the base of the mountain and the ways in which that ecosystem is affected by activities on and at the base of the mountain. But this limitation itself illustrates the first challenge of the ecosystem perspective: the need to constrain the analysis to a workable scope at the cost of forsaking the theoretically pure and potentially very important tracing of all components of the ecosystem.

We also confess from the start that the state of knowledge about our mountain ecosystems is not as comprehensive as we ideally would need to fully evaluate how the law deals with the human impacts on the ecosystem. A paper written in preparation for the Bishtek Global Mountain Summit in 2002, held as part of the International Year of the Mountains, captured the nascent state of research on mountains in general:

> With regard to science, until the 1970s mountains were considered as marginal by the leading natural and social sciences. This attitude has changed with the rapidly growing interest in environmental problems, natural resources, and mountain societies. The close relationships between natural processes and human activities in mountain areas ha[ve] created a high demand for interdisciplinary and transdisciplinary research, including traditional knowledge. … The International Year of the Mountains must be the beginning of a new research effort toward sustainability science for mountain environment and development and for the highly complex highland-lowland interactions.[56]

As readers will see in subsequent chapters, scientists are learning more about the ecosystems of the mountains that are the focus of this book, but there is more yet to learn.

The details of the ecosystem-based analyses in this book may seem inconsequential when set against the scale of geological history and the advance

of Mountain Environments: Water, Natural Resources, Hazards, Desertification, and the Implications of Climate Change, in MARTIN F. PRICE ET AL., eds., KEY ISSUES FOR MOUNTAIN AREAS 20–24 (2004); Daniel Scott, *Global Environmental Change and Mountain Tourism*, in STEFAN GÖSSLING & C. MICHAEL HALL, EDS., TOURISM AND GLOBAL ENVIRONMENTAL CHANGE 60–61 (2006); J. Kevin Healy & Jeffrey M. Tapick, *Climate Change: It's Not Just a Policy Issue for Corporate Counsel—It's a Legal Problem*, 29 COLUM. J. ENVTL. L. 89, 108 (2004). *See also* B. BAUDO, G. TARTARI ET AL., MOUNTAIN WITNESSES OF GLOBAL CHANGES (2007) (discussing the Himalaya-Karakoram Range).

56 Bruno Musserli & Edwin Bernbaum, *The Role of Culture, Education, and Science in Sustainable Mountain Development*, in MARTIN F. PRICE ET AL., EDS., KEY ISSUES FOR MOUNTAIN AREAS 211–12 (2004).

and retreat of glaciers. But living, working, sporting, and governing in the present, we can still confront and explore the ecosystem as we know it today and consider our relationship to it in its current form. Just as the shape of mountains changes over the course of time with the inherent forces of nature, so does the shape of lives and laws change with the forces of human will.

The Pages Ahead

Following this introductory chapter, the book contains six parts—the ecology of the mountains in Part I, the law of the mountains in Parts II through V, and concluding thoughts in Part VI. The first part, which contains four chapters, lays the scientific foundation by exploring what we know about the mountain ecosystem in our resort areas. Chapter 2 introduces the four featured mountains and explains basic ecological principles. It also illustrates the types of ecological interrelationships at work on the mountains and how mountain resort activities affect those interrelationships, drawing from analyses provided in the subsequent three chapters. Chapter 3 describes the vegetative aspects of the mountain ecosystem; Chapter 4 examines the hydrological patterns; and Chapter 5 focuses on wildlife in the mountain ecosystem. Readers who want to learn more about the ecology of the mountains and the ecological impacts of resort activities should read those three chapters, but those who are less scientifically oriented and more interested in the legal aspects may find that Chapter 2 provides sufficient background to proceed directly to Part II of the book.

In examining the law of the mountains, Parts II through V take a case study approach for each of the four mountain resorts—Loon Mountain (Part II, Chapters 6 through 10), Whiteface Mountain (Part III, Chapters 11 through 14), Killington Resort (Part IV, Chapters 15 through 18), and Mont Tremblant (Part V, Chapters 19 through 22). The case studies explain the key environmental laws operating at each resort and evaluate those laws from an ecosystem perspective. They focus on various types of human activities at the resort that have been subject to a governmental review process—permits required to operate on federal land (Loon), land exchanges to allow the resort expansions (Killington and Mont Tremblant), more extensive trail systems and snowmaking facilities (all four resorts), mountaintop lodges (Whiteface and Mont Tremblant), new or expanded mountain villages at the mountain base (Loon, Killington, and Mont Tremblant), growth beyond the mountain base (Whiteface), and expanded recreational activities, such as golf courses (Mont Tremblant), to give some examples.

For each of the activities subject to a governmental process or constraint, the question is whether the relevant body of law requires or allows the introduction of an ecosystem perspective into the decision-making. But as readers will find, it is not just a question of what the government requires and what the resort operator must show. It is also very much a matter of who else becomes interested in the proceedings and whether they have the legal right to be involved, such as abutting landowners, concerned citizens, environmental organizations, chambers of commerce, and others who can inject an ecological or economic perspective and influence the outcome. The plots can be thick with personalities and procedures, showing how form can shape substance. And the result is sometimes the product of the words of the law and sometimes the leverage that the law creates for negotiations.

In the course of these accounts, readers will see that the law in many instances is still grappling with the challenge of how to fully take into account the "marvelously complex interrelationships of life," so the book concludes in Part VI with some observations about the challenges and opportunities for more fully implementing ecosystem-based approaches to the law. It identifies some of the lessons that emerge from the book, both in terms of the extent of the scientific understanding of the mountain ecosystem and the law's ability to achieve an ecosystem perspective. Sifting through the collective experience at these resorts, it finds insights, which, in pragmatic ways, could yield larger ecosystem-based rewards under the law in the future, but it also reaches further, proposing ways to improve both science and the law so that they may better appreciate the complexities of the mountain ecosystem.

When the Rio Earth Summit adopted Agenda 21 in 1992, it officially elevated the global awareness of both the importance of mountain ecosystems, which cover 24 percent of the world's land surface,[57] and the risks they face:

> Mountains are an important source of water, energy and biological diversity. Furthermore, they are a source of such key resources as minerals, forest products and agricultural products and of recreation. As a major ecosystem representing the complex and interrelated ecology of our planet, mountain environments are essential to the survival of the global ecosystem.[58]

Please read on for the tales of four specific mountains, what we know about their ecological interrelationships, and the extent to which the law considers those interrelationships as resorts expand on their slopes.

---

57 Martin F. Price, *Introduction: Sustainable Mountain Development from Rio to Bishkek and Beyond*, in PRICE, *supra* note 56, at 1–9.

58 United Nations Conference on Environment and Development, Agenda 21, at 13.1, U.N. Doc A/Conf.151/26 (1992). Agenda 21 led to a decade of mountain study and the designation of 2002 as the International Year of the Mountain, which in turn generated significant study of and attention to mountains. *See* PRICE, *supra* note 56, at 1–9.

PART I
The Mountain Ecosystem

Chapter 2
An Ecosystem Approach to Mountain Resorts

Ross A. Virginia

Mountain ecosystems occupy about one-quarter of the earth's land surface and approximately 10 percent of all people live in mountainous regions.[1] To understand mountains as ecosystems that provide important resources and services to people, it is essential to understand the fundamental properties of ecosystems and their processes and how ecosystems respond to human use and disturbance. The emerging field of sustainability science provides a framework for considering the "dynamic interactions between nature and society, with equal attention to how society shapes the environment and how environmental changes shape society."[2]

This chapter explores the key components that make up the mountain ecosystem with an emphasis on processes and features sensitive to human activities, especially resort development. A general conceptual model of ecosystem and human interaction is presented in Chapter 23 as a basis for understanding how resorts may affect mountains. Chapters 3 through 5 provide more specific studies of important ecological interactions common to mountains and how mountains respond to development. A general understanding of mountains as ecosystems is necessary for evaluating how legal regimes may or may not protect the integrity of mountains while allowing sustainable levels of development and use.

The Science of Ecology and the Ecosystem Concept

Ecology is the study of the relationship of organisms and their environment (see the Glossary at the end of this chapter for definitions of common terminology used in ecology and ecosystem science). The discipline of ecology grew from the work of the great naturalists dating from Aristotle and extending to Charles Darwin. Naturalists described the diversity of the natural world and recorded the behavior

---

The author thanks Richard O. Brooks for his research, writing and concepts that contributed invaluably to this chapter.

1 Christian Korner & Masahiko Ohsawa (coordinating lead authors), *Mountain Systems, in Ecosystems and Human Well-Being: Current State and Trends*, The Millennium Ecosystem Assessment Series, Vol. 1 681–716 (R. Hassan et al. eds., 2005).

2 W.C. Clark & N. M. Dickson, *Sustainability Science: The Emerging Research Program*, 100 Proc. Nat. Acad. Sci. 8059–61 (2003).

of species and of species interactions. In the early twentieth century, natural history became quantitative and scientists began to analyze the spatial distribution and abundance of species, and groups of species, forming communities. Henry Cowles and Henry Gleason, who argued about the definition of biological communities and the environmental and biological factors controlling their diversity and changing composition through time, championed this tradition.[3]

As our knowledge of community ecology grew, new questions arose about the functioning of communities, about the larger scale processes mediated by organisms (for example, production and nutrient cycling), and on the role of biodiversity in controlling ecosystem dynamics. The early formulations of these questions led to the concept of the ecosystem as a functional unit in the natural world. The British ecologist Arthur Tansley first coined the term "ecosystem" in 1935. It is perhaps ironic that about the time of the invention and use of the rope tow—a 1930s invention that gave rise to the modern ski industry—ecosystem ecology was just beginning to be formulated.[4]

In its most general definition, an ecosystem encompasses all the organisms of a given area and their relationships with one another and the physical or abiotic environment. A focus on the ecosystem as a fundamental unit of study (and later land management) represented a shift from studying the ecology and behavior of individual organisms and communities to the study of processes and how they influence, or are influenced by, organisms and their interactions with the environment. The premise of the ecosystemic legal regime concept proposed by Brooks, Jones, and Virginia is that the ecosystem, which contains the dynamic interactions between life and the environment, should be the focal point for the joining of ecology and the law and "*that ecology is the central discipline for understanding both a viable environment and the modern threats to that environment*."[5]

The works of Eugene Odum and his seminal text, published in 1953, best date the rise of ecosystem ecology.[6] Odum gave credit to Ernst Haeckel, who in 1869 coined the term "ecology" and emphasized its holistic vision. But unlike the vague philosophical notions of holism, Odum and his fellow scientists brought to bear the concept of systems on the study of nature. By using the term "systems," Odum

---

3 *See generally* Frederic E. Clements, *An Analysis of the Development of Vegetation (1916);* H.C. Cowles, *The Ecological Relationships of the Vegetation on the Sand Dunes of Lake Michigan*, in 27 Botanical Gazette 95–391 (1899). For an overview of the development of ecology and ecosystem science as disciplines see Frank Benjamin Golley, A History of the Ecosystem Concept in Ecology: More than the Sum of the Parts (1993).

4 The history of ecology and its relationship to environmental law is set forth in Richard Brooks et al., Ecology and Law: The Rise of the Ecosystem Regime (2002).

5 *Id.* at 3.

6 Eugene Odum, Fundamentals of Ecology (1953). In addition to numerous updates of this work, in 1996 Odum published Ecology: A Bridge Between Science and Society, which he intended to be a "citizens guide" for other disciplines, including the law.

Table 2.1 Properties, Characteristics, and Sensitivities of Mountain Ecosystems

Property	Characteristics and Sensitivities
Soils	• shallow in depth and very slow to develop • low fertility • easily eroded • soil nutrients, such as nitrate and phosphate, can degrade surface and groundwater quality
Streams	• subject to wide ranges in seasonal flow from snow melt that affect stream biota and nutrient export • stream water diversions for snowmaking alter natural flow and may impact stream biodiversity
Trees	• stabilize soil and nutrients • alter microclimate • recovery following harvest or disturbance is through the slow process of ecological succession • loss of the forest canopy accelerates erosion and increases the potential for invasion by exotic species
Wildlife	• resort development increases the frequency of interactions with people • forest clearing alters habitat quality for wildlife through its influence on plant community composition and structural diversity of the forest

emphasized the study of the emergent properties of ecosystems, processes, and behaviors that come from the complex interactions among the interdependent components of the system. In our case, using a systems approach requires taking a view of snowy mountain resorts within the context of their interdependent biological (species diversity) and physical components (soils and climate), which together with their interactions characterize the mountain ecosystem. A logical extension of this systems viewpoint is the addition of human activities that impinge on mountains and the social dynamics between development and environmental regulation.

What Makes a Mountain?

In this book, we trace the impacts of resorts on mountains as tightly regulated yet fragile ecosystems, functioning in response to climate and its biological and physical properties. Resorts exert their influence on mountains through impacts on soils, snow, and water, and in turn, the interactions of these ecosystem components affect the cycling and movement of inorganic elements that influence the living communities of the mountain (see Table 2.1). This biological diversity shapes the mountain's aesthetics, soils, and hydrology. Although human action also shapes the mountain, the starting points are the mountains themselves before human development and ski resorts arrived.

Mountains are easily recognized but less easily defined.[7] A mountain is a landform that extends in elevation above the surrounding terrain within a limited area. One person's hill is another's mountain. The elevation and local relief is the product of geological history and the parent material and soil characteristics. A universal characteristic feature of mountains is their elevational-zonation driven by the cooling of air with increasing elevation (environmental lapse rate).[8] Mountains experience, and contribute to, a unique climate by increasing precipitation and by hosting distinct communities that are associated with increasing elevation and cold tolerance.

Mountains around the world are classified in various ways, including the nature of their geological origin (e.g., volcanic) and the earth processes responsible for their uplift (e.g., faulted-rock fracture and movement along fault zones, and folded-collisions of continental plates arising from plate tectonics which produce folds creating raised mountains and valley depressions), their respective sizes, and their location.[9] Appreciating the variation in ecology is also important to understanding and managing mountain ecosystems. Variation occurs across a wide range of spatial scales from individual mountains and their local variation (for example, north versus south facing slopes), mountain ranges, mountain chains, and mountainous regions, to include adjacent ecosystems influenced by processes occurring on the mountains. Another distinction often set forth in mountain studies is also important for our study: the distinction between high mountains (dominated by treeless tundra or rock), where glaciation, frost action, and mass wasting are the dominant mountain processes, and middle or low elevation mountains which are largely forested and are best understood as variants of forest ecosystems. The mountains we will describe fall into this latter category.

It is within the context and contours of these mountain characteristics that the more specific aspects of its ecosystem components and functions take place.[10] These components are the local climate; local variation in landforms and soils, slope and aspect; hydrology and stream dynamics; and the distribution of biota with elevation. Importantly to the land manager or developer, the local mountain climate will vary depending in part on the elevation and topography, which regulate the interception of precipitation, creating higher precipitation rates of rain

---

7 *See generally* KORNER & OHSAWA, *supra* note 1.

8 The environmental lapse rate is the decrease in environmental temperature observed with increasing elevation, which averages 6.49 °C/1000 m (3.56 °F or 1.98 °C/1000 ft) from sea level to 11 km (36,090 ft). Brian J. Harshburger et al., *Seasonal and Synoptic Variations in Near-Surface Air Temperature Lapse Rates in a Mountainous Basin*, 47 J. APPLIED METEOROLOGY AND CLIMATOLOGY 24961 (2008).

9 For a general description of the geology of mountains and the dynamics of the earth's surface, see JOHN MCPHEE, BASIN AND RANGE (1981).

10 For an excellent overview of mountain components and processes, see LARRY W. PRICE, MOUNTAINS AND MAN: A STUDY OF PROCESS AND ENVIRONMENT (1981). This study concentrates on, but is not limited to, the high mountains.

and snow on the mountain than in surrounding areas. The upper reaches of the mountains store water in the forms of ice and snow, releasing water when and if the temperatures change, which has important implications for stream life and for storage of water at lower elevations behind dams or as groundwater. The soils, especially on higher elevations, are likely to be shallow, coarse and rocky, acidic, unstable, infertile, and immature.[11] Once disturbed, these soils are easily eroded and become difficult or impossible to revegetate over short time scales.

Northeastern Mountains

The formation of mountains in the northeastern United States and Canada is a fascinating story beginning with colliding tectonic plates, leading to uplift, volcanic activity, and cycles of glaciation and erosion. It is this history of recent glaciation that gives northeastern mountains their more rugged terrain and young soils when compared to their unglaciated counterparts of the Appalachian Mountains to the south. Only recently did the vast human enterprise of lumbering, which left most mountain areas covered only by a young second growth of forest cover, play a role.[12]

The four resorts featured in this book—Loon Mountain in the White Mountains of New Hampshire, Killington Mountain in the Green Mountains of Vermont, Whiteface Mountain in the Adirondacks of New York, and Mont Tremblant in the Canadian Laurentians of Quebec, Canada—are located in mountain ranges that at first glance appear to be extensions of the Appalachian Mountains extending from Newfoundland, Canada south to Alabama.[13] Careful study, however, reveals that they are the product of different processes of mountain formation over a period of 130 million years, and that the Adirondacks are more properly an extension of the Laurentian Mountains. Despite these differences, all were affected by the more recent ice age, which eroded their shapes to roughly that which we observe today.

More than 11,000 years ago at the close of the Wisconsin Glaciation, the trees reappeared on the glacially cleaned mountains. Black spruce (*Picea mariana*) and paper birch (*Betula papyrifera*) spread in open forests throughout the area. At the same time, the animal communities found today became established. The forest canopy closed in, and the tundra began to disappear, leaving only small remnants of tundra above 4,500 feet. Spruce and fir came to dominate in the higher

11 In the case of the mountains, their geological formation and their subsequent glaciation and weathering contribute to their soil quality.

12 A good non-technical account of the formation of the northeastern mountains is in Betty Flanders Thomson, The Changing Face of New England (1977).

13 For one study of the Appalachian mountains, see Robert A. Brune, The Appalachian Trail: History, Humanity and Ecology (1980).

elevations. Eastern white pine (*Pinus strobus*), paper birch, and oaks (*Quercus* spp.) replaced spruce (*Picea* spp.) and fir (*Abies* spp.) on the lower elevations as the climate approached the current conditions. Later, hemlock (*Tsuga canadensis*), beech (*Fagus grandifolia*), maple (*Acer* spp.), and chestnut (*Castanea dentata*) moved in. What emerged is a mosaic of "biophysical regions" of mountains and valleys throughout Southern Quebec, New York, Vermont, and New Hampshire; the mountains we discuss are parts of those mountain regions.

Loon Mountain, New Hampshire[14]

Loon Mountain is located in the White Mountain National Forest. New Hampshire's White Mountains are another segment of the Appalachian Mountains, extending 87 miles long and up to 20 miles wide. This range contains many of the highest mountains in the Northeast, with several sub-ranges. The White Mountains include the Presidential Range, and their best known member, Mount Washington, rises 6,290 feet above sea level and is the highest peak east of the Mississippi River. The White Mountains were preceded by the Acadian Mountains and were formed when a mass of molten rock and magma welled up and solidified into a dome of resistant granite. Thus, they are unlike the folded mountains of the Adirondacks with their resulting ravines protecting some vegetation from exposure. The peaks of the White Mountains were sculpted by the glaciers, which sometimes left broad flat outwash plains known as "intervals" and also produced steep glacial cirques such as Tuckerman's Ravine, U-shaped valleys, and "notches"—rounded passes carved by the glaciers.

Loon is by no means one of the highest of the White Mountains, rising only to a height of about 3,300 feet. Soils vary in depth over the bedrock and as the slopes rise, with gradients ranging from 20 percent to 80 percent, the soils grow shallower. These soils, often with underlying bedrock or hardpan, have a medium to high permeability and have significant capability to erode. The soils are anchored by vegetation, similar to the other White Mountains. The hardwoods, spruce, fir, and hemlock dominate the lower levels, although there are some openings. There is a high canopy formed by trees 8 to 20 inches in diameter, and 40 to 80 feet tall. A mixed shrub layer can be found beneath the canopy. Ground cover of ferns, bunchberry (*Cornus canadensis*), club mosses, and mountain sorrel (*Rumex* spp.) complete the picture. The natural openings in the canopy include a variety of shrubs—mountain ash (*Sorbus americana*), sheep laurel (*Kalmia augustifolia*), and huckleberry (*Vaccinium* spp.), as well as sedges and rushes in the wet areas.

---

14 *See generally*, William Sargent, A Year in the Notch: Exploring the Natural History of the White Mountains (2001); F. Herbert Bormann and Gene Likens, Pattern and Process in a Forested Ecosystem (1981); and Betty Flanders Thomson, The Changing Face of New England (1958); *see also* U.S. Dep't of Agriculture, Forest Service, Loon Mountain Ski Resort Development and Expansion: Final Environmental Impact Statement (Feb. 2002).

The mountain waters feed the Pemigewasset River, whose tributary, the East Branch, runs alongside the mountains. The Pemigewasset's confluence with the East Branch serves a drainage area of the surrounding 25 miles. The river is subject to flooding in March and April and low flows in the summer and the depths of winter. There are numerous brooks and two well-known ponds—Little Loon Pond and Loon Pond. Loon Pond is a 19-acre pond located at 2,400 feet. There is limited inflow into Loon Pond. The ground water on the mountain is limited, but of high quality. In recent years, since the closing of the paper mills, the quality of the East Branch is good, with the exception of the high nitrate and phosphorus levels at the sewage inflow area. Loon Pond is mildly acidic.

The aquatic life in the river includes trout species, fall fish (*Semotilus corporalis*), slimy sculpin (*Cottus cognatus*), long nose sucker (*Catostomus catostomus*), and dace, as well as a variety of macro-invertebrates. There has been a recent return of brook trout (*Salvelinus fontinalis*) and an effort to restore the Atlantic salmon (*Salmo salar*). The ponds have limited fish life due to snowmelt and draw downs, but an abundance of insect life can be found around the ponds. There are 144 species of wildlife in this mountain area, some of which are game animals including white-tailed deer (*Odocoileus virginianus*), black bear (*Ursus americanus*), moose (*Alces alces*), ruffed grouse (*Bonasa umbellus*), eastern gray squirrel (*Sciurus carolinensis*), mink (*Neovison vison*), red fox (*Vulpes vulpes*), raccoon (*Procyon lotor*), fisher (*Martes pennanti*), and eastern coyote (*Canis latrans*). Other species of special note are the bog lemming (*Synaptomys borealis*) and the northern flying squirrel (*Glaucomys sabrinus*). The bald eagle (*Haliaeetus leucocephalus*), peregrine falcon (*Falco peregrinus*), and golden eagle (*Aquila chrysaetos*) migrate through the area.

The area in question, like all of the White Mountains, was lightly populated. The early settlers logged the land and consequently the forest is a second growth forest. The present nearby towns of Lincoln and Woodstock, as well as citizens of the states and the tourists, influence the mountain in various ways. The town runs a solid waste incinerator that has only recently been improved and that may have had impacts on the soils of the mountain. The sewage is treated and dumped in the river. Highways are nearby, having some, but not severe, effects on air quality. Electrical transmission lines, substations, and distribution lines are in proximity to the mountain. Any effects that the mountain resort and its planned expansion may have will supplement already existing environmental effects on the mountain.

Killington Mountain, Vermont[15]

Killington Mountain is the second highest mountain (4,241 feet above sea level) on the eastern side of the Green Mountain range, which is part of the larger Appalachian

15 This account of Vermont's Green Mountains is based on the following works: Harold A. Meeks, Time and Change in Vermont: A Human Geography (1986); John Elder, Reading the Mountains of Home (1998); U.S. Dep't of Agriculture, Forest Service, Forest

chain. The Green Mountains run along the spine of Vermont for about 250 miles. Killington is viewed as part of the Southern Green Mountains biophysical region bordering on the lowland hills areas, which is part of the Piedmont Connecticut River Valley region. As a consequence, Killington is part of each of the four great watersheds that cover Vermont.

The Green Mountains support only a small acreage of tundra on two of its mountains. Perhaps the most important aspect of the Green Mountains and Killington is its forested landscape composed of cold-climate and northern hardwood forests. On Killington, there is also krummholz, the subalpine vegetation zone in which dense thickets of spruce and fir are stunted and twisted by the forces of wind and ice. Forest communities, including those on Killington, experience disturbances, partly due to the severe weather (for example, wind and ice storms) and the forces of fire, wind, erosion, insects, disease, and mass wasting, which may be followed by processes of succession. These forces of disturbance are less severe today due to the forested nature of these mountains.

The vegetation of Killington and Vermont's mountains is generally affected by the pattern of wetlands, including peat lands (bogs and fens), marshes (sedge meadow and marshes proper), swamps (shrub and forested swamp), seasonal wetlands (vernal ponds), and open water. Since the forested areas are not unlike those of nearby Loon Mountain described above, the forest wildlife is also very similar.

Several communities unique to mountain areas include upland mountain communities and cliffs and rock falls. These provide specific kinds of habitats both for plants and animals, including swallows, hawks, turkey vultures (*Cathartes aura*), snowy owls (*Bubo scandiacus*), and blue birds (*Sialia sialis*), many of which make use of the openings in mountain forests. The cliff and rock fall communities support ravens and falcons, and the talus slopes of loose broken rock harbor snakes and lizards.

Killington, like the other mountains, saw substantial human development before the advent of the ski resort. In addition to lumbering, the mountain was a center for sheep raising, which denuded many of Vermont's mountains by the end of the 1800s. In 1879, the Summit House was built as part of the growth of non-ski mountain resorts of the period. In the early 1900s, land in the proximity of the mountain was held for the mining of marble, but the Vermont Marble Company gave up the land to establish the Long Trail in the early 1900s.

Plan Monitoring and Evaluation Report, Green Mountain National Forest (2004); Jan Albers, Hands on the Land: A History of the Vermont Landscape (2000); Christopher Klyza & Stephen C. Trombulak, The Story of Vermont: A Natural and Cultural History (1999); Peter Marchand, Life in the Cold (1991), David Dobbs & Richard Ober, The Northern Forest (1995); Charles W. Johnson, The Nature of Vermont: Introduction and Guide to a New England Environment (1980); Robert L. Hagerman, Mansfield: The Story of Vermont's Loftiest Mountain (1975); and Karen D. Lorentz, Killington: A Story of Mountains and Men (1990).

Whiteface Mountain, New York[16]

Whiteface Mountain is part of the Adirondack Mountain range in northeastern New York and extends southward from the St. Lawrence River Valley and Lake Champlain to the Mohawk River Valley. These mountains, although appearing to be part of the Appalachians, were formed as part of the same geological processes that formed the Laurentians, discussed in more detail below. The Adirondack region covers 5,000 square miles and contains up to 100 peaks ranging in height from 1,200 feet to 5,000 feet above sea level. Some of the higher peaks, like Whiteface, at 4,867 feet, reveal rock walls with vertical escarpments. More than 200 lakes of irregular shape dot the landscape. A large part of the area is still in a primitive, natural condition and Whiteface sits almost in the middle of a variety of Adirondack wilderness areas, including the High Peaks wilderness area consisting of many mountains equal or exceeding its height. Thus, unlike the undulating Green Mountains of Vermont, Whiteface reflects its unique history of mountain formation, the product of an upthrust distinct from the formation of the other northeastern mountains in the United States. Also unlike Killington, which is a brief ride from the lowlands and farmlands of the Connecticut River valley, Whiteface is in "mountain country"—a different world from the fields of the Lake Champlain valley.

Given its more rugged topography and steep slopes, there is little wonder that its soil is limited in depth and fertility and is highly erodible. Its vegetation, like the rest of the Adirondacks, progresses from hardwood forests of maple and beech on its more limited lower slopes to conifer forests of red spruce (*Picea rubens*) and balsam fir (*Abies balsamea*) upwards towards the summit. Unlike most of the other mountains we studied, this mountain has a significant krummholz area.

When one views the Adirondacks, one is struck by the large number of lakes and rivers running throughout the region. From the peak of Whiteface, 65 lakes can be seen. Its surface waters drain into the West Branch of the Ausable River and its four tributaries. There are approximately 13 acres of wetlands, either forested or scrub-shrub, many adjacent to the river.

Owing to its isolation and large elevation gain, Whiteface has a high diversity of plant species, of which at least 16 plant species have been designated as rare, threatened, or endangered (with serious implications for development). Many of these species are associated with the alpine meadow and alpine krummholz community. Whiteface also supports at least 46 mammalian species, 11 amphibian species, and five reptile species. Twenty-one bird species have been identified and another 63 are listed as probable inhabitants of the area. Large, wild trout are present in the Ausable River, but not in high numbers.

---

16 The following description is based on: Commission on the Adirondacks in the Twenty-First Century, 1 Technical Reports (1990); Philip Terrie, Contested Terrain: A New History of Nature and People in the Adirondacks (1997); and Philip Terrie, Forever Wild: Environmental Aesthetics and the Adirondack Forest Preserve (1985).

Like the other mountains, Whiteface saw substantial development before the advent of its ski area, including logging and recreation. However, the most significant development on the mountain was a controversial road to its summit, and a bobsled run in nearby North Elba was part of its gradual development as a winter center for the Olympics and then a major resort area.

Mont Tremblant, Quebec[17]

Located in the southern Laurentian highlands, not far from Montreal, Mont Tremblant is 3,176 feet high. The Laurentian region is bounded by the St. Lawrence, Ottawa, and Sanguenay Rivers and is one of the oldest mountain areas of the world. It forms a rocky erosional plane with crests of only about 3,000 feet. It is heavily forested, primarily by boreal forest. The highlands are composed of igneous rock of the Canadian Shield, a plateau 1,500 to 2,500 feet in elevation. The 1- to 1.7-billion-year-old rocks of the Canadian Shield are metamorphosed granite and gneiss. They have been faulted, uplifted and eroded to a relatively low elevation. The glaciation of a million years ago scraped the plateau surface bare in many sections and vegetation remains sparse on thin soils. The ice deepened the valleys creating a dramatic topography. The later drainage of the glaciers as they retreated resulted in a series of terraces and plains along the river valleys.

Located on the edge of the northern boreal forest, the lower vegetation includes maples and birches, but most of the area's vegetation is dominated by conifers, including spruce and balsam. There is abundant fauna, including moose, bear, fox, hare, and beaver, as well as 193 species of birds and numerous fish species.

The Laurentians were first inhabited by indigenous peoples and then settled early by marginal farmers. Farming gave way to large-scale lumbering activity. This lumbering activity, along with proximity to water, rail, and an urban center, made the Laurentians a major contributor to Canada's early economic development.

Mountains and Change

The major areas of ecosystem ecology that hold special application for analyzing the relationships between resorts and mountains are studies of the factors controlling plant (forest) productivity, nutrient cycling, and species diversity. The integrity of these processes and attributes is central to the recovery of ecosystems through

17 This overview of Mont Tremblant is taken from the following: Parcs Quebec, Parc National du Mont-Tremblant in En Coulisses (2006–2007 Tour); Quebec Societe de law Faune et Des parc du Quebec, Plan Directeur: Parc du Mont-Tremblant (2000); Francois Courchesne et al., *Recent Changes in Soil Chemistry in a Forested Ecosystem of Southern Quebec, Canada*, 69 Soil Science Am. J. 1298–1313 (2005); and Robert Schiemenauer et al., *High Elevation Fog and Precipitation Chemistry in Southern Quebec, Canada*, 29 Atmospheric Environment 2235–52 (1995).

time from either natural or human caused disturbances. Thus, productivity, nutrient cycling (especially nutrient losses), and biodiversity change are useful metrics for evaluating the response of mountain ecosystems to development pressure.

Mountains are dynamic; environmental conditions and ecological processes change widely in time and with elevation. The zonation of life on mountains reflects variation in the biodiversity of plant, animal, and soil communities, with biodiversity generally declining with elevation. Fire, drought, frost, and biological events such as the outbreak of pathogens and pests can "stress" mountain ecosystems and alter their health. Ecosystems that possess an ability to withstand stress without a loss of function are called resistant, and similarly, if they can recover rapidly from disturbance they are called resilient. Ecosystems that show large decreases in productivity and biodiversity when disturbed have low resistance and can be considered fragile.

Mountain ecosystems, in general, are considered fragile with low resistance and long recovery times, especially if the thin layer of soil is damaged following the loss of vegetation. Within this overall pattern of fragility, mountain ecosystems with greater biodiversity are hypothesized to experience less change in response to a given level of disturbance and will also exhibit more resilience, recovering to pre-disturbance levels of function at a faster rate.[18] This relationship points to the potential importance of maintaining or enhancing biodiversity to increase the stability of mountain ecosystems as they face pressures from human activities.

Primary Ecological Consequences of Resort Development

Chapters 3, 4, and 5 reveal the basic structure of northeastern mountain ecosystems, describe the ways in which they function, and most importantly address key ecosystem responses to development that should be considered by the legal community. The authors of these chapters stress the primary importance of the extent and condition of forest cover (and its subsequent influences on soil erosion), the spatial scale of development (from single tree to large clearings) and its impact on habitat suitability for wildlife, and the general significance of maintaining biodiversity (including protection from invasive species).

The analysis in this volume shows that the most consequential ecological changes resulting from resort development start with the decision to change the natural vegetative cover. This action is likely to trigger changes in the wildlife patterns, which often produces a cascade of effects on the plant community. At the same time, the changes in the vegetation can result in changes in the quantity and quality of water flows, which in turn have reciprocal effects on ecological communities.[19]

---

18 C. Folke et al., *Biological Diversity, Ecosystems, and the Human Scale*, 6 Ecological Applications 1018–24 (1996).

19 For more information about these concepts, refer to the discussion *infra*, Chapter 3 at pages 26–28.

For example, Chapter 3 discusses how ski trail clearing changes the composition and pattern of plant life on the mountain, which in turn can affect wildlife. The construction of ski trails fragments previously solid forest blocks, and skiers' demands for isolated experiences tend to maximize the degree of fragmentation. Fragmentation poses the greatest ecological challenge for wildlife species that require uninterrupted blocks of forest habitat larger than the islands of cover remaining between the trails, and for species that have difficulty crossing open gaps. It may also encourage other species that are habitat generalists to move into the area, changing the balance for existing species that are more specialized in their choice of habitat. In addition, the introduction of trails into previously unfragmented forest can affect the ability of plant life associated with older age forests to disperse and may provide opportunities for invasive species to become established.[20]

Apart from fragmentation, the creation of trails can have other direct ecological effects. The trails may cut through areas where natural patch communities exist—distinct communities of interdependent plants and animals located in natural openings in the forest such as outcrops of bedrock and headwater seeps. Blasting and leveling activities associated with trail creation may destroy key components of patch communities including seeps and vegetation, causing dependent species to lose breeding and forage habitat. Clearings may also reduce the habitat available to species that have specialized requirements.[21]

In addition, by creating open spaces with less protective vegetative cover, the forest floor becomes more vulnerable to erosion and nutrient loss from leaching. These soil and nutrient fluxes may affect the habitat for plants and associated animals, especially for aquatic species, by degrading water quality. Clearing areas for slopes and the subsequent increased human activity on those slopes can lead to soil compaction and enhanced rates of runoff, exacerbating the risk of erosion. As detailed in Chapter 4, open slopes may also alter precipitation and hydrology. More rain and snow may fall or accumulate on the cleared slopes, affecting runoff and habitats linked by water. The addition of machine-made snow will further affect the snow deposition patterns and the timing and amount of runoff, while the withdrawal of surface water for snowmaking can impact local water supplies and their aquatic communities.

The discussion provided in Chapter 5 emphasizes the profound effects of habitat fragmentation on populations. For example, trail clearing creates new forest edges, which in turn can generate a new mosaic of habitat types that alter biodiversity. The introduction of light from the forest edge leads to different patterns and types of vegetation. Shade-tolerant species that inhabit the darker interior of the forest may not tolerate the additional light and the ingression of new species, including harmful invasive species, from seeds carried to the new edge by wind or birds. These changes in vegetation can also have a significant influence on

20 *Id.*
21 *Id.*

wildlife. Chapter 5 describes how edge sensitive bird species can be impacted by tree removal because new edge habitats attract predators and nest parasites. There may be fewer insects for birds, while amphibians requiring humid conditions and leaf litter may be impacted because this habitat is less likely to exist in areas exposed to light and wind.[22] Additionally, expansion of lift capacity can result in even greater human use of the mountain during the winter, and often during other seasons for mountain biking or hiking, increasing the risk of more snow and soil compaction, erosion, and disturbance of fragile cover and breeding habitat.[23]

As readers will find in the subsequent chapters, there are many other resort-related activities that can have significant ecological effects as well. They include difficult issues such as the creation of impervious surfaces at the mountain base and storm drainage, the use of fertilizers and pesticides for landscaping, salt to de-ice roads, and the entire set of interacting issues around secondary growth generated by the resorts. Our aim in this brief introduction was to illustrate by example the type of ecological interactions occurring in the mountain ecosystem and the inherent complexity of those interactions.

Mountain Ecosystem Models

Beyond our understanding of the general ecosystem relationships among vegetation, soils, biodiversity, and ecosystem processes, we lack detailed models of mountain ecosystems to guide the formation and use of a site-specific, ecologically based law. Unlike wetlands, rivers, lakes, forests, and other ecological systems, mountains do not have any unified ecological model. On the contrary, collections of research on mountain systems reveal separate treatments of mountain origins, abiotic components, geomorphic processes, vegetation, water, and wildlife.[24] This failure to develop a unified model explicitly for mountain ecosystems is undoubtedly due to the complexity of the system and the extent to which, at least for the lower mountains, the function of mountains can be viewed as a special case of forest models.

Nevertheless, a montane model is desirable, if it can be developed. More specifically, the model would show how the unique montane characteristics affect the system and how development on mountains, whether ski or other developments, affect the system. Such a model would suggest how a legal regime might be organized to regulate development on the mountain. For scientific purposes, such a conceptual model would, over time, by attention to its components, lead to a quantitative analysis of mountain processes.[25] We conclude this volume by

---

22 *Id.*

23 *Id.*

24 For one recent overview of mountain literature, see generally PRICE, *supra* note 10.

25 It is important to emphasize that models need not be quantitative. Recently, nonquantitative models have been employed to help guide the Comprehensive Everglades

presenting a modeling framework for evaluating the impacts of resort development and operation on the functioning of mountain ecosystems.

Conclusions

This brief introduction to ecology, mountain ecology, and the individual ranges and mountains on which the mountain resorts examined in the volume are located provides the basis for looking more holistically at mountain components, structures, and processes. Mountain resorts and ecosystems provide many essential services that have economic and aesthetic value.[26] These services emerge from the collective activities of organisms and their life processes (for example, production and consumption) on the condition of the environment. Ecosystem services are many and in the case of mountains include production of wood, the cycling and purification of water, aesthetic values, and recreational opportunities such as hiking and skiing. The sustained provision of these services requires an optimal level of biodiversity to maintain the intricate relationships between producers, consumers, and decomposers that regulate the flow of energy and nutrients. Mountain development that alters forest cover and species biodiversity and/or the relationships between key species in the ecosystem can be expected to have important effects on other species and the main nutrient cycling processes that regulate the health of the forest and of the mountain. Finding a legal regime to protect these complicated ecological interrelationships is essential to achieve a sustainable future for mountain resort ecosystems.

Glossary of Ecology and Ecosystem Terminology

See Richard Brooks et al., *Ecology and Law: The Rise of the Ecosystem Regime* (2002), for a more detailed description of the use of these terms and concepts as applied to the disciplines of ecology and environmental law.

Field of Study

Ecology: the scientific study of the processes influencing the distribution and abundance of organisms, the interactions among organisms, and the interactions between organisms and the transformation and flux of energy and matter.

Ecosystem ecology: the integrated study of biotic and abiotic components of ecosystems and their interactions. This science examines how ecosystems

---

Restoration Program. John C. Ogden et al., *The Use of Conceptual Ecological Models to Guide Ecosystem Restoration in South Florida*, 25 WETLANDS 795–809 (2005).

26 *See generally*, NATURE'S SERVICES: SOCIETAL DEPENDENCE ON NATURAL ECOSYSTEMS (C. Gretchen ed., 1997).

function and relates this to their components such as chemicals, bedrock, soil, plants, and animals. A major focus of ecosystem ecology is on functional processes, ecological mechanisms that maintain the structure and services produced by ecosystems. These include primary productivity (production of biomass) and nutrient cycling.

Landscape ecology: considers the development and maintenance of spatial heterogeneity (pattern) on biotic and abiotic processes, and the management of that heterogeneity (for example to maintain biodiversity).

Levels of Ecological Organization

Ecological community: all the organisms (e.g., plants, animals, microorganisms) that live in an area and interact with each other.

Ecosystem: a natural unit consisting of all plants, animals and microorganisms in an area functioning together with all the nonliving physical factors of the environment.

Landscape: a heterogeneous land area composed of interacting ecosystems that repeat in similar form throughout.

Ecosystem Properties

Biodiversity: the variation of life-forms within a given ecosystem, biome or for the entire Earth. The amount of biodiversity is often used as a measure of the health of an ecological system (community, ecosystem).

Emergent properties: ecosystem properties that are derived from the complex interdependencies that develop within or among ecosystems that cannot be predicted from the component parts alone.

Resistance: the tendency of an ecological unit or process to show relatively little response to disturbance.

Resilience: the tendency for an ecological unit or process to return to its former state or condition (equilibrium) following disturbance.

Ecosystem Processes

Productivity: the net amount of biomass (or carbon) gained by an ecosystem per unit area per time by the process of photosynthesis.

Ecosystem functioning: the sum total of processes such as the cycling of matter, energy, and nutrients operating at the ecosystem level.

Biogeochemical cycling: the transport and transformations of chemical elements as they move through both "bio"tic (living) and "geo"logic (soil and rock) compartments of an ecosystem in a cyclical pathway. Examples are the cycling of essential elements for plant growth such as carbon, nitrogen and phosphorus.

Ecological succession: the process in which communities of plant and animal species in a particular area are replaced over time by a series of different and often more complex communities. Succession typically follows large-scale disturbances such as fire or forest harvest.

Ecosystems and People

Ecosystem services: vital services provided by natural ecosystems include the purification of air and water, detoxification and decomposition of wastes, regulation of climate, regeneration of soil fertility, and production and maintenance of biodiversity, from which key ingredients of our agricultural, pharmaceutical, and industrial enterprises are derived.

Chapter 3
Plant Communities and Vegetation Processes in the Mountain Landscape

G. Richard Strimbeck

Introduction: The View from the Top

On a clear day, the view from the summit of any of the major mountain resorts in northeastern North America can be spectacular. The horizon is defined by sinuous blue crests of ancient ranges—New York's Adirondack Mountains, New Hampshire's White Mountains, Vermont's Green Mountains or Quebec's Laurentians, depending on the vantage point. Lakes, ranging in size from mountain ponds to the great swath of Lake Champlain, punctuate a rolling sea of green. The slopes of nearby mountains are mostly cloaked in forest, while the forest on the resort's own slopes is dissected into strips, patches, and artificial glades by the ski lift and trail network. The lower ends of the ski trails merge with acres of open ground surrounding the base lodge and parking lots. In the resort towns near the mountain base, condominiums, second homes, businesses, and golf courses often fill the valley and spread out onto the town's secondary roads, with homes-with-a-view scattered among the trees on some of the lower slopes and hilltops.

The view from the top is what draws many visitors, whether they have journeyed via a ski lift, a toll road, or a hiking trail. The resulting irony is that mountain development, like the development of seacoasts, lakeshores, and other natural settings, compromises the view and many other aspects of the natural environment that people have come to enjoy. Stretching from valley golf courses, restaurants, and ski shops to the cafeteria at the top of the lift, the Northeast's larger resorts affect areas measured in square kilometers, often spanning the watersheds of several mountain streams. Those areas include a variety of different ecological communities: forests, stream banks, wetlands, and natural or manmade ponds. These communities are developed, maintained, and linked by various ecological processes such as ecological succession, the flow of surface and ground water, energy flow, nutrient cycling, and the movements of animals and plants.[1] Human activities centered on the resort may affect these key ecological processes, thereby altering the structure and function of individual communities—or even the entire network.

---

1 R.E. Ricklefs et al., *Conservation of Ecological Processes*, The Environmentalist: Commission on Ecological Papers No. 8, at 8 (1984).

An insightful and useful analysis of the ecological impact of resort development requires an assessment that matches the scale of the resort itself. This is the realm of landscape ecology, a discipline derived from community and ecosystem ecology that has emerged over the last 25 years and seeks to understand and explain phenomena occurring at a scale larger than the ecosystem. The spatial distinction between an ecosystem and a landscape is defined by the investigator, and a landscape implicitly contains a diversity of community types (while an ecosystem need not) and generally implies a larger scale. A landscape is a mosaic of different vegetation or community types, often arranged in a more or less predictable pattern resulting from the natural and human processes that affect plant establishment and growth. Landscape ecology is "the study of the causes and consequences of spatial patterns on the landscape."[2] It explores "how a heterogeneous combination of ecosystems is structured, how it functions and changes over time," and the "spatial and temporal interactions and exchanges across ecosystem boundaries."[3] (Editors' note: Chapter 2 contains definitions of a number of key terms that ecologists use when discussing ecosystems.)

This chapter draws on the principles of landscape ecology to describe the overall plant community structure of the mountain landscape of the northeastern United States and the adjacent Canadian provinces. It then discusses the dynamics of forest communities, with an emphasis on the ecological processes that control the development, maintenance, and biodiversity of forests, and some thoughts on how these may be affected by resort development. The third section discusses ecological processes and human impacts in wetland, outcrop, and other communities that occupy only a small proportion of the landscape but function as important elements in landscape diversity. Alpine plant communities are uniquely vulnerable to human impacts and are discussed in a separate section. Because resort development can create opportunities for the spread of invasive plant species, a brief final section outlines the potential for the spread of these species in and around mountain resorts.

The Mountain Vegetation Mosaic

The view from the top provides a first impression of the broad ecological structure of the mountain landscape in the northeastern United States. In summer, the lower slopes of the mountains are covered with the bright green of deciduous trees. The darker evergreen color of coniferous trees covers the higher elevations and in some areas forms isolated patches scattered among the deciduous trees. Different tree

---

2 Robert Leo Smith & Thomas M. Smith, Ecology and Field Biology 450 (6th ed. 2001). For a more comprehensive introduction to landscape ecology, see Monica G. Turner, Robert H. Gardner, and Robert V. O'Neill, Landscape Ecology in Theory and Practice (2001).

3 Smith & Smith, *supra* note 2, at 11.

species produce subtle variations in the forest canopy's color and visual texture. These differences are often most obvious in fall when birches and aspens turn bright yellow, maples turn orange and red, and beech and oak turn tan or rust brown.

In landscape ecology, this continuous expanse of forest covering most of the area is called a matrix because it provides large, continuous areas of forested habitat for other plants and animals.[4] An old adage says that in presettlement times an adventurous squirrel could easily travel for miles across the unbroken forests of the northeastern mountain landscape without touching the ground or leaving a particular forest type. Present-day forests are fragmented and no longer offer squirrels such an easy journey, but the forests have partially recovered from the logging and land clearing of the last two centuries, restoring much of the continuity, but not the full diversity, of the forest matrix.

The matrix is punctuated by openings where the tree cover is thin or absent. Some openings, such as logging clearcuts or land cleared for housing, development, or ski trails, are created by humans. Areas where trees have been felled by wind, ice, and snow, along with cliffs, ledges, landslides, and wetlands, are natural openings created by natural processes. The contributions these openings make to landscape diversity and dynamics depend on their size, distribution, and what is going on in them. These islands of unique natural habitat in the surrounding sea of forest are called disturbance patches, and are important reservoirs of biodiversity because they provide habitat for plant and animal species that do not survive in the forest. Through the process of secondary succession (a predictable sequence of plant communities following disturbance, caused in part by plants that alter soils and environmental conditions to favor the establishment of a new suite of species[5]) the forest matrix will eventually reclaim these patches over a period of tens of years to a few hundred. Other, more permanent patches occur in areas where local conditions, such as thin or wet soils or steep slopes, prevent tree growth over long periods of time. These are sometimes referred to as patch communities because they support a distinct and persistent assemblage of plants and animals that do not change through time to reach the climax community type for the area (the long-lived community type reached by the process of secondary succession).[6]

The matrix, disturbance patches, and patch communities together form a mosaic of community types that interact to support the full range of natural ecological processes and biodiversity of the region as a whole. Large-scale resort development may affect not only the ecological processes within a particular community, but also the processes that link communities and create the emergent or unique properties of the landscape.

---

4 Monica G. Turner, Robert H. Gardner & Robert V. O'Neill, Landscape Ecology in Theory and Practice 3 (2001).

5 *See* Henry H. Horn, *The Ecology of Secondary Succession*, 5 Annual Rev. of Ecology & Systematics 25–37 (1974).

6 Elizabeth H. Thompson & Eric R. Sorenson, Wetland, Woodland, Wildland: A Guide to the Natural Communities of Vermont 188, 309 (2000).

While the matrix is a continuous expanse of forest in which it can be difficult to find hard boundaries separating different types of forest, it can be useful to recognize the different assemblages of tree and associated species by subdividing it into different community types. This approach can help identify areas that harbor rare species and understand the ecological processes that maintain them. Disturbance patches and patch communities may have more recognizable boundaries and, especially in the case of the more permanent patch types, support unique and stable communities.

Ecological communities are interacting assemblages of living organisms occupying a particular area.[7] For example, in a northern hardwood forest, neighboring trees interact by competing for light. Shrubs, wildflowers, and ferns compete for space under the forest canopy. Deer, caterpillars, and other browsing and grazing species interact with the plants they eat and with the predators that hunt them. Fungi decompose fallen leaves and wood, returning nutrients to the soil for plants to reuse. All of these species are tied together in a web of interactions of different strengths. Some species and their interactions may be central to the normal function of the community while the absence of other species may not significantly affect the overall character and function of the community. The most important species include dominant species, such as the trees that occur in high abundance and biomass and so define the physical structure of the community and provide much of its energy, and so-called keystone species, often predators that keep herbivore populations in check, that have a disproportionate effect relative to their abundance or biomass.[8]

Communities are usually defined and named in terms of the dominant species that occupy most of the available space and provide the overall structure of the community. Forest communities are dominated by and named for their most important species of trees, which occur together because they have similar temperature, moisture, or other environmental requirements. In addition to the dominant species, communities include an array of other species, ranging from shrubs, wildflowers, and ferns, to mammals, birds, insects, and fungi. Some of these species are found in a broad range of community types, while others are more faithful (endemic) to a particular community or found only in specialized sites within a community.[9]

The mountain climate becomes cooler and moister with increasing elevation, resulting in different community types occurring in broadly defined elevation bands or life zones. Because community composition changes gradually with elevation and is affected by other factors such as latitude, soils, and slope steepness, the boundaries of montane forest communities can be indistinct, and there can be substantial overlap in the overall elevation range of different forest community types.[10]

---

7 Smith & Smith, *supra* note 2, at 383.

8 *See* L.S. Mills et al., *The Keystone-Species Concept*, 43 BioScience 219–224 (1993).

9 *See* Thompson & Sorenson, *supra* note 6, at 58.

10 *Id.* at 17, 107. *See also* Smith & Smith, *supra* note 2, at 546; Heinrich Walter, Vegetation of the Earth and Ecological Systems of the Geosphere (2d ed. 1979).

Forests

The Vermont community classification system developed by Thompson and Sorenson provides one classification system that can help describe the northeastern forests. Although different regions have developed different classification systems, they usually agree on the most broadly distributed community types, but differ in detail.[11] The Vermont community classification system defines "[t]he Northern Hardwood Forest Formation of Vermont [a]s part of a broad forest region where sugar maple, American beech, yellow birch and hemlock predominate."[12] Depending on local conditions and history, these species may be associated with several others, most commonly the deciduous white ash, basswood, and red oak, and the coniferous eastern white pine, and red spruce. Where these and other species are important components of the forest canopy, the Vermont classification system describes distinctive community types such as Hemlock-Northern Hardwood Forest or Mesic Red Oak-Northern Hardwood Forest. The unadorned Northern Hardwood Forest community, sometimes called beech-birch-maple forest, is the most abundant community type in the formation and is the most broadly distributed forest community type in the northeastern tier of the United States and the southern parts of the adjacent Canadian provinces. Northern hardwood forests, in the northeastern mountains, grow from the valley floors up to elevations of around 2,600 feet (800 meters) above sea level.[13]

Above 2,600 feet, climate and soil conditions favor the growth of two evergreen coniferous species, red spruce and balsam fir.[14] These are the mainstay of the Spruce-

11 All the northeastern states have natural heritage programs that have developed community classification systems to aid in biodiversity conservation. *See* Thompson & Sorenson, *supra* note 6, at 58 (describing "natural community types based upon years of study of Vermont's natural communities").

12 *Id.* at 129.

13 *Id.* at 94, 131–32.

14 *Id.* at 107. The relative advantages of evergreen growth have long been debated in ecological literature. Many point to the advantages of already having a crop of leaves at the start of a short and cool growing season. Smith & Smith, *supra* note 2. Others, however, point out that coniferous forests also grow in regions like the Pacific Northwest, where the climate is far more equitable. Additionally, most subtropical and tropical forests are also evergreen. *See, e.g.*, P.B. Reich et al., *Leaf Life-Span in Relation to Leaf, Plant, and Stand Characteristics Among Diverse Ecosystems,* 62 Ecological Monographs 365, 366 (1992) (describing Waring and Franklin's theory). This competing theory suggests that long-lived (one year or more) evergreen leaves make more efficient use of nitrogen, a critical nutrient in most terrestrial ecosystems, so that trees with long-lived leaves are found in areas where the climate or geological conditions result in the development of nitrogen-poor soils. *Id.* (citing F. Stuart Chapin, III, *The Mineral Nutrition of Wild Plants*, 11 Ann. Rev. Ecology & Systematics 233, 242–43 (1980); Brian F. Chabot & David J. Hicks, *The Ecology of Leaf Life Spans*, 13 Ann. Rev. Ecology & Systematics 229, 230–31 (1982)). In an age where industrial and automotive emissions have substantially increased the amount of nitrogen in

Fir Northern Hardwood Formation and the Montane Spruce-Fir Forest communities that cover most northeastern summits above 2,600 feet.[15] Because red spruce does not grow well at elevations over 3,500 feet (1,100 meters), balsam fir is the single dominant tree species from there to the treeline at about 4,000 feet (1,200 meters). The formation also includes the Montane Yellow Birch-Red Spruce Forest community, a transition between Northern Hardwood Forest and Montane Spruce Fir Forest that is found at elevations of around 2,000 to 3,000 feet (600 to 900 meters). Some other forest types in the formation, such as Lowland Spruce-Fir Forest, are found in lowlands in the northernmost parts of the northeastern states and similar areas in Canada, and may be part of the forest matrix surrounding resorts in these areas.[16]

While changes in local climate associated with elevation are the major cause of the shift from deciduous to coniferous forest cover, local soil conditions are a close second. Patches of coniferous forest often grow on top of ledges in a few inches of soil that developed over rock left bare by glacier ice around 10,000 years ago.[17] The surrounding hardwood forest grows in deeper soils developed from glacial till, a mix of rock fragments ranging in size from microscopic silt particles to boulders that is dropped in place by melting ice.[18] A blanket of glacial till, a few inches to several feet thick, covers most of the uplands in the northeastern region, but knobs and ledges of bedrock poke through this blanket on mountains, hilltops, and steep or convex slopes.[19] The thin soils that develop over bare rock are mostly organic matter, the partially decomposed remains of leaves and other plant parts. These organic soils are more acidic and nutrient-poor than the mineral soils that develop from till, and favor the growth of conifers with their long-lived leaves.[20]

Competition

Worldwide, forests grow wherever plant growth is not severely limited by environmental stresses such as low temperature or drought, and where injuries

---

the precipitation falling on these forests, the debate is of more than scholarly importance, for nitrogen saturation could fundamentally alter nutrient cycling and community composition of coniferous forests. John D. Aber et al., *Nitrogen Saturation in Northern Forest Ecosystems,* 39 BioScience 378, 379 (1989); Reich et al, *supra*, at 384.

15 Thompson & Sorenson, *supra* note 6, at 107.

16 *Id.* at 109, 115, 119.

17 Peter J. Marchand, North Woods 3–6, 37–39, 104 (1987). This can be observed directly during a hiking or skiing trip in the northeastern mountains. Patches of conifers are frequently observed on top of open ledges or on convex ridges, areas where glacial till is thin or absent. An excellent example is the Bamforth Ridge of Camel's Hump, which is visible south of Interstate 89 between Burlington and Montpelier, Vermont.

18 The Bamforth Ridge and similar settings also provide evidence of this phenomenon. The conifers occur primarily on convex sections of the ridge, which are often quite ledgy, while deciduous trees fill in concave pockets where there are deposits of till.

19 Thompson & Sorenson, *supra* note 6, at 62.

20 *Id.* at 106.

caused by fire, wind, or other processes are not so severe as to make life as a tree impossible.[21] Under these conditions, competition for resources, particularly light, becomes a driving force in the development and structure of plant communities. Trees invest most of their phosynthetically captured carbon to producing woody roots below ground and trunks and branches above ground. Wood is primarily dead structural tissue (cellulose and lignin) that serves to anchor the tree in the ground, support leaves high above the ground in the forest canopy, where the most light is available, and conduct water and nutrients from the roots to the leaves.[22] Put more simply, trees are tall because they compete with each other for light.

Trees provide the basis for vertical stratification of the community. A well-developed northern hardwood forest may have a canopy layer of dominant trees with leaves in full sun, an understory layer of smaller trees, a shrub layer, and an herb layer. The understory trees, shrubs, and herbaceous plants scavenge for the light that filters through the canopy, often by means of intriguing anatomical and physiological adaptations.[23] This vertical structure provides habitat diversity for the animals in the community, with many species concentrating their activities in a particular layer.

Shade tolerance, or ability to grow from seed in the shaded forest interior, is one way to rank trees. Intolerant trees, such as aspens and birches, require direct light to grow, and their seeds often germinate only in direct sunlight. At the other end of the scale, seeds from the most tolerant trees, such as American beech and eastern hemlock, will germinate in shade, and the seedlings and saplings can survive and grow slowly in the shade of taller trees for long periods of time. When neighboring trees die or fall, established saplings of more tolerant trees rapidly emerge to take their place in the canopy. As long as the forest canopy remains more or less closed, more tolerant trees replace less tolerant trees over time. The logical endpoint of this process is a forest canopy composed only of the most shade tolerant species. In northern hardwood forests, the most tolerant species is not a hardwood, but a conifer—eastern hemlock, a tree with dense foliage that produces

21 Walter Larcher, Physiological Plant Ecology 433 (Joy Wieser trans., Springer-Verlag 3d ed. 1995) (1975).

22 *Id.* at 145–46.

23 For example, the cells of the upper epidermis of leaves act as lenses that focus light into the interior of the leaf to increase the efficiency of photosynthesis. In shade leaves, which are generally quite thin, the upper epidermal cells are spherical in shady conditions which gives a shallow focal depth appropriate for the thin leaves. William K. Smith et al., *Leaf Form and Photosynthesis* 47 BioScience 785, 786 (1997). Some shade-adapted plants are so light-sensitive that they may be damaged by direct sunlight. In order to avoid an overdose of light, one common understory plant of northeastern forests, wood sorrel, rapidly folds its leaves from a horizontal to a vertical position when exposed to spots of sunlight that penetrate the forest canopy. S.B. Powles, *Leaf Movement in the Shade Species Oxalis oregana. II. Role in Protection against Injury by Intense Light,* Carnegie Institution of Washington Yearbook 63–69 (1981). *Oxalis oregana* is a western species of wood sorrel but the same phenomenon is readily observed in the northeastern *Oxalis acetosella.*

shade so deep that even many ferns and other forest floor species cannot survive under it.[24] Consequently, if competition for light were the only factor controlling forest development, our forests would be considerably less diverse.

Disturbance and Recovery

The intense competition for light is moderated by the destructive-creative processes collectively referred to as disturbance. Disturbance is anything that kills or reduces the vigor and function of living plants or plant parts en masse.[25] Fire is the dominant disturbance in dry western forests and in some uncommon forest types in the Northeast.[26] In the northeastern mountains, the most important cause of disturbance is wind. Wind can break off and uproot individual trees in patches ranging from one tree to areas tens of hectares or, more rarely, a few hundred hectares in size.[27] The 1998 ice storm[28] that, according to some interpretations, devastated[29] mountain forests throughout the Northeast, provided an intermediate form of disturbance. The storm partially opened canopies of hardwood forests by breaking off tops and branches of birches and other vulnerable trees. On steeper slopes, landslides may open up patches ranging in size from less than one to many hectares.

---

24 Thompson & Sorenson, *supra* note 6, at 69, 86–87.

25 A more precise and generally accepted definition is: "any relatively discrete event in time that disrupts ecosystem, community, or population structure and changes resources, substrate availability, or the physical environment." The Ecology of Natural Disturbance and Patch Dynamics 7 (S.T.A. Pickett & P.S. White eds., 1985).

26 *See* Thompson & Sorenson, *supra* note 6, at 68 (stating that fire is a minor player in Vermont forests because of the moist climate, but fire can spread and affect the structure in some drier areas).

27 Jeffrey R. Foster & William A. Reiners, *Vegetation Patterns in a Virgin Subalpine Forest at Crawford Notch, White Mountains, New Hampshire,* 110 Bull. of Torrey Botanical Club 141, 141 (1983); James R. Runkle, *Disturbance Regimes in Temperate Forest, in* The Ecology of Natural Disturbance and Patch Dynamics 29 (S. T. A. Pickett & P. S. White eds., 1985).

28 Margaret Miller-Weeks et al., The Northeastern Ice Storm 1998: A Forest Damage Assessment 6 (1999), *available at* http://www.fs.fed.us/na/durham/ice/public/pub_file/ice99.pdf (last visited May 31, 2005).

29 A Washington Post reporter described the ice storm in Maine as an "ice-borne apocalypse." Blaine Harden, *Maine Struggles to Unbutton Last Week's Devastating Coat of Ice*, Wash. Post, Jan. 14, 1998, at A3, *available at* A031998 1998 WL 2461871. A U.S. Forest Service official described forests as "ripped apart by bombs." Fred Bayles, *Ice Will Melt, Misery Will Remain: $1 Billion in Damage in New England,* USA Today, Feb. 18, 1998, at 3A, *available at* 03A1998 1998 WL 5715434. Major disturbances like the 1988 Yellowstone fire or the 1998 ice storm are often met with some hand-wringing in the press, in part because of the very real economic impact on harvestable timber or the maple syrup industry. Rick Hampson, *Ice Storm Taking a Toll on Millions of Trees*, USA Today, Jan. 15, 1998, at 4A, *available at* 04A1998 WL 5713137. Many ecologists, however, greet disturbances with a certain delight in seeing large-scale ecological processes at work.

Disturbance triggers secondary succession, usually resulting in the reestablishment of forest cover over the disturbed area within 50 to 100 years. As described above, one way of interpreting the general pattern of forest succession and ecosystem development is the competition for light, with intolerant species moving in rapidly after disturbance, only to be shaded out by more tolerant species over time. The details of succession often vary widely and depend on the size, intensity, and timing of the disturbance event. Various models have been proposed to explain patterns of succession in different environments,[30] but these patterns all depend to some extent on the growth and reproductive strategies of the individual species that appear on the stage at different times.

Seed dispersal, seed germination, and seedling establishment are key processes in the life histories of plants and usually involve trade-offs between dispersal distance and seed size.[31] Reproduction is a high-risk lottery for all trees. While every seed can potentially grow into a mature tree, only a few of the millions of seeds produced by a tree during its lifetime will survive their first year.[32] Most of the seeds of some species, like the acorns of oaks, are eaten by rodents, deer, turkey, or other seed predators. In addition, seeds may fail to find suitable conditions for germination, and those that do germinate may be unable to establish roots and leaves before running out of energy.[33] Herbivores, drought, or other environmental influences may kill those seeds that do germinate. The risk of dying remains high until the tree is fully established as a sapling, a process that may take years.

The risk of early mortality is highest for early-successional tree species like aspens and birches. These species broadcast small, lightweight seeds far from the parent tree relying on the wind for dispersal in order to increase the chance that they will fall in a recent disturbance patch, the only place where they stand a chance of survival.[34]

Like birds' eggs, seeds contain both an embryo and some nutritive tissue, called endosperm, that contain enough energy for the embryo to produce a root and expand its seed leaves, or cotyledons, as it germinates. Small, light seeds, like those of birch and aspen, contain little reserve energy as endosperm, and thus lack

---

30 *See, e.g.*, J.H. Connell & R.O. Slatyer, *Mechanisms of Succession in Natural Communities and Their Role in Community Stability and Organization*, 111 AMERICAN NATURALIST 1119–44 (1977).

31 Charles D. Canham & P.L. Marks, *The Response of Woody Plants to Disturbance: Patterns of Establishment and Growth, in* THE ECOLOGY OF NATURAL DISTURBANCE AND PATCH DYNAMICS 197, 200–04 (S.T.A. Pickett & P.S. White eds., 1985).

32 J.P. KIMMINS, FOREST ECOLOGY 344 (1997). Mortality in later stages in the life cycle is reflected in the age structure of tree populations. William B. Leak, *Age Distribution in Virgin Red Spruce and Northern Hardwoods*, 56 ECOLOGY 1451, 1451 (1975).

33 Canham & Marks, *supra* note 31, at 204–05.

34 Paul R. Laidly, *Bigtooth Aspen* (Populus grandidentata Michx.), *in* SILVICS OF NORTH AMERICA: VOL. 2, HARDWOODS 544, 546 (1990) [hereinafter SILVICS OF NORTH AMERICA]; G.G. Erdmann, *Yellow Birch (*Betula alleghaniensis Britton), in SILVICS OF NORTH AMERICA 133, 135.

the energy to push a root down through layers of decomposing leaves to reach the soil. Consequently, early-successional species often require exposed mineral soil as well as direct sunlight to germinate and establish effectively. These conditions are often found in disturbed patches created by landslides and under the tipped-up root masses of wind-felled trees. Larger seeds, such as acorns and beech nuts, can only travel away from the parent tree with the help of animals, with a substantial risk of consumption rather than dispersal. If this obstacle is overcome, the combination of their large size and energy reserves and shade tolerance enables them to establish roots through a thick forest floor litter layer and grow into the undisturbed soils of the forest interior.[35]

In large disturbance patches, the first arrivals are often not trees, but shrubs and herbaceous species that live for a few years in the full sun before the more competitive trees move in and shade them out. These earliest-successional species are often called fugitive species because they are always on the run from one disturbance patch to the next. While wind-dispersed species, including sedges and grasses, may be among the early arrivals, other species such as raspberries, blueberries, viburnums, and elderberries, employ the services of birds to disperse their seeds. Birds digest the pulp of berries and other kinds of fruit, but the seeds survive the quick passage through the birds' short digestive tract and are often deposited far from the parent plant, with a little "fertilizer" for an added boost.[36] Some studies in tropical forests show that the availability of perches in openings, for fruit-eating birds to roost on as they void their waste, is a key ingredient in the successful dispersal of these plant species.[37]

Not all reproductive strategies follow the size-distance rules described above. The seeds of some species will accumulate and survive in the soil for years without

---

35 Some statistics may help drive home the differences between the reproductive strategies of different tree species. A single red oak acorn weighs on the order of 5,000 times more than a bigtooth aspen seed and 1600 times more than a yellow birch seed. Most of the difference is in the endosperm of the seed. The yellow birch trees in a northern hardwood forest produce anywhere from 2.5 to 90 million seeds per hectare per year, while red oaks produce only about 50,000 seeds per hectare in good seed years. Yellow birch seeds can blow 400 meters over crusted snow and sufficient seed to ensure reproduction can be found 100 meters from the edge of a northern hardwood forest. Wind can carry aspen seeds many kilometers. *See generally* Silvics of North America, *supra* note 34. Most red oak seeds fall under the parent tree and are consumed by deer, turkeys, and squirrels, but blue jays may carry individual seeds over a distance of a kilometer or more. Susan Darley-Hill & W. Carter Johnson, *Acorn Dispersal by the Blue Jay (Cyanocitta cristata)*, 50 Oecologia 231, 232 (1981); W. Carter Johnson & Thompson Webb, III, *The Role of Blue Jays (Cyanocitta cristata L.) in the Postglacial Dispersal of Fagaceous Trees in Eastern North America*, 16 J. of Biogeography 561, 563 (1989).

36 G.W. Wendel, *Pin Cherry* (Prunus Pensylvanica), *in* Silvics of North America, *supra* note 34, at 587, 589.

37 T.R. McClanahan & R.W. Wolfe, *Accelerating Forest Succession in a Fragmented Landscape: The Role of Birds and Perches*, 7 Conservation Biology 279, 285–87 (1993).

germinating.[38] This accumulation of dormant seeds in the soil is called a seed bank. These seeds germinate only when the soil is warmed and the seeds are stimulated by direct sunlight.[39] Many species of hardwoods are able to sprout from stumps or roots, a valuable strategy following logging or other disturbance that does not uproot the tree.

While early succession in large forest openings may require long-distance seed dispersal, there is more of a scramble for the available space in small patches. There may be many species that can potentially grow in a small opening, and those that establish first can dominate the patch for decades. Some early-successional species like white pine and yellow birch can remain in the canopy for a long and productive lifetime, stretching to hundreds of years, before they are felled by wind or killed by disease.

Disturbance has the effect of "setting back the clock" on forest succession and has a rejuvenating influence on forest ecosystems unless soils are damaged by excessive erosion. The forest matrix of the northeastern mountains is a mosaic of disturbance patches of varying age, supporting forests in different stages of secondary succession. As older patches mature, disturbance opens up new patches. At a very large scale in a landscape not influenced by humans, the proportion of land under patches of a certain age may not change much over time. Therefore, the average species composition of the landscape does not change, even as local patches change dramatically due to the cycle of disturbance and recovery. This is called a shifting-mosaic steady state, and it allows early- and mid-successional species to persist in the landscape as they move from patch to patch as the older patches are taken over by late-successional species.[40] The interplay between episodic disturbance and succession helps prevent late-successional species like hemlock and beech from taking over the entire region, thereby maintaining a higher level of diversity in forest types and their inhabitants.

While all forests worldwide incorporate some level of disturbance, the kind, frequency, and intensity of disturbance varies widely between different forest types. In a landmark study, Jeffrey Foster and William Reiners measured disturbance patches in pristine northern hardwood and spruce-fir forests in Crawford Notch, located in New Hampshire's White Mountains.[41] They found that large disturbance patches 100 years or less in age, formed mostly from wind disturbance, occupied about 7 percent of the area under study. They also estimated that small canopy openings caused by the death or fall of individual trees or small groups of trees covered about 24 percent of the total area. In the higher elevation fir forests, wind disturbance is more frequent and may take the form of fir waves that occupy as much as 33 percent of the total area. Combining these influences,

---

38 Wendel, *supra* note 36, at 589.

39 *Id.* at 590.

40 F. Herbert Bormann & Gene E. Likens, Pattern and Process in a Forested Ecosystem: Disturbance, Development and the Steady State 174–76 (1979).

41 Foster & Reiners, *supra* note 27, at 141.

Foster and Reiners estimated that 39 percent of the subalpine landscape was in natural disturbance patches ranging in size from single-tree gaps to 16-hectare wind disturbance patches.[42]

Apart from the obvious disturbance associated with clearing for ski trails and base area amenities, resort development may alter the disturbance regime in more subtle ways. One is by providing exposed edges to the forest stand where there is an increased likelihood of damage due to wind, either by blowing trees down or by rocking them violently so that their roots are damaged and the trees are weakened, eventually to be finished off by insects and fungi. A study of root movement and injury in spruce-fir forest noted that all mature trees within 25 meters (82 feet) of a ski trail edge were dead. Root movements ranged up to 60 millimeters (2.5 inches), and movement and associated damage was generally more severe on wind-exposed edges. [43] The edges of forest fragments often have more light, warmer temperatures, and drier air than the forest interior. Many forest interior species cannot tolerate these conditions or may not be able to compete with edge species that take advantage of the light, so that community composition can be quite different near the forest edge. There is also evidence that edge effects and patch size may affect other ecological processes that control plant establishment and survival.[44]

Recent developments in the ski industry may be adding new disturbances to mountain landscapes. Opening and maintenance of artificial glades for skiers can dramatically alter the vegetation structure and expand the effects of development into forested areas beyond the traditional boundaries of the ski trails. Furthermore, the growth of out-of-bounds skiing has led increasing numbers of skiers into forested areas accessible from ski lifts, sometimes on undeveloped parts of the mountain far from the lifts themselves. While the direct impacts of a few skiers are undoubtedly small, sharp ski edges and falling bodies can damage shrubs and saplings, and the cumulative impacts of hundreds or thousands of skiers a

---

42 *Id.* at 150–51.

43 D.M. Rizzo, & T.C. Harrington, *Root Movement and Root Damage of Red Spruce and Balsam Fir on Subalpine Sites in the White Mountains, New Hampshire*, 18 Canadian Journal of Forest Resources 991–1001 (1988).

44 A study of Western wake-robin (*Trillium ovatum*, a forest wildflower) dynamics in old-age remnants in Oregon found almost no reproduction within sixty-five meters of clear-cut edges. Erik S. Jules, *Habitat Fragmentation and Demographic Change for a Common Plant: Trillium in Old Growth Forest*, 79 Ecology 1645, 1651 (1998). A subsequent study found that this was likely due to reduced pollination efficiency and increased seed predation by rodents, rather than a direct response of the plants to changed environmental conditions. Erik S. Jules & Beverly J. Rathcke, *Mechanisms of Reduced Trillium Recruitment Along Edges of Old-Growth Forest Fragments*, 13 Conservation Biology 784, 790–91 (1999). In small rain forest fragments in Bolivia, herbivorous leafcutter ants defoliate more tree seedlings and saplings, apparently because there are fewer ant-eating predators in the fragments. Madhu Rao et. al., *Increased Herbivory in Forest Isolates: Implications for Plant Community Structure and Composition*, 15 Conservation Biology 624, 626, 630 (2000).

year over many winters could be more considerable. These potential impacts are largely unexplored. Heavy use may also move and compact the snow, affecting the patterns of deposition and melting, potentially adding additional stress to tree roots and forest floor plants in the form of ice encasement[45] or a shortened growing season.[46]

Old-Age Forests—A Special Habitat

The Crawford Notch study suggests an estimated disturbance frequency of 200 to 300 years for an average point on a northeastern mountainside.[47] However, the large wind disturbance patches occurred mainly on exposed ridges and convex slopes. In addition, the authors found old-age stands, with some trees more than 300 years old, growing in protected locations along streams.[48] These findings are an example of how mountain topography produces both high-turnover areas, where large-scale disturbance is more frequent, and low-turnover, sheltered areas that may experience long periods of time without extensive disturbance. Single-tree gaps occur in both areas, so even old-age stands are not immune to small-scale disturbance. The large and frequent disturbances in high-turnover areas prevent the majority of the forested area from maturing to an old-age condition, but any unaltered mountain landscape will also contain pockets of old-age forests.

While the canopy trees of old-age forests may be the same mix of species as those in younger forests, these forests often contain more diversity in the understory.

---

45 Ice encasement is a well-known cause of winter stress and injury to cereal and pasture crops and golf greens, but its importance in natural communities seems to be largely unexplored. A. Bertrand & Y. Castonguay, *Plant Adaptations to Overwintering Stresses and Implications of Climate Change*, 81 CAN. J. BOT. 1145–1152 (2003).

46 T. Keller et al., *Impact of Artificial Snow and Ski-slope Grooming on Snowpack Properties and Thermal Regime in a Subalpine Ski Area,* 38 ANNALS OF GLACIOLOGY 314–318 (2004).

47 Foster & Reiners, *supra* note 27, at 142.

48 *Id.* Many competing definitions for "old-growth forest" have been proposed, and in some cases misapplied, to the point where the term lacks precision and meaning. David A. Orwig et al., *Variations in Old Growth Structure and Definitions: Forest Dynamics on Wachusett Mountain, Massachusetts*, 11 ECOLOGICAL APPLICATIONS 437, 437–38 (2001) (noting that the study of forests in the Wachusett Mountains in Massachusetts was "strikingly different" than "old-growth forests described by earlier ecologists and foresters"). The term has also become politically and socially charged by the debate over spotted owls, jobs, and other attributes of forests in the Pacific Northwest. Like many other ecologists, I substituted "old-age" here to describe stands of trees that have matured enough to incorporate key characteristics attributed to old-growth, such as uneven-aged canopy and downed logs in all stages of decay. In northeastern forests these characteristics take at least 200 years to develop. Lucy E. Tyrell & Thomas R. Crow, *Dynamics of Dead Wood in Old-Growth Hemlock-Hardwood Forests of Northern Wisconsin an Northern Michigan*, 24 CANADIAN J. OF FOREST RESEARCH 1672, 1681–1683 (1994).

The understory may include assemblages of common and uncommon plants that are rarely found together in a single area, as well as rare, threatened, or endangered species that are adapted to unique conditions found in the old-age forest interior. Gifford Woods, a seven-acre old-age[49] stand of hemlock-northern hardwood forest near Killington in Vermont, contains 13 species of trees, 14 species of shrubs, 19 species of ferns, and 65 species of grasses, sedges, and wildflowers, for a total of 111 species.[50] None of these species are rare, but it is unusual to find them all in the same small area.

While there is less biological diversity overall in high-elevation spruce-fir forests, the trained eye can spot diversity in the form of mosses and liverworts. A survey of old-age spruce-fir stands in the White Mountains found nine trees, six shrubs, 20 herbs, 16 mosses, and seven liverworts, for a total of 58 species.[51] Epiphytic lichens[52] are also easily overlooked, but may be among the most sensitive indicators of forest age, with dozens of species that are more or less faithful to old-age forests. Old-age northern hardwood and spruce-fir stands may house as many as 136 and 115 different species of epiphytic lichens, respectively.[53]

Old-age forests may also develop microsites appropriate for highly-specialized flowering plant species. For example, the cranefly orchid (*Tipularia discolor*) is most often found on or near rotting logs, and experimental studies show that the

---

49 Gifford Woods has been altered by some human activities, including management as a sugarbush, so it should not be taken as fully representative of undisturbed northern hardwood forest. Nevertheless, the relatively high species diversity within this small stand gives some idea of the potential diversity in undisturbed old-age forest. F.H. Bormann & M. F. Buell, *Old-Age Stand of Hemlock-Northern Hardwood Forest in Central Vermont*, 91 BULL. OF TORREY BOTANICAL CLUB 451, 452 (1964).

50 *Id.* at 451, 454.

51 H.J. Oosting & W.D. Billings, *A Comparison of Virgin Spruce-Fir Forest in the Northern and Southern Appalachian System,* 32 ECOLOGY 84, 90–91 (1951).

52 Epiphytes are plants that grow on the stems, branches, or leaves of other plants, and are particularly conspicuous in tropical rain forests and other moist forest types. In northeastern forests, numerous species of epiphytic lichens grow on the trunks, branches, and boughs of the trees in moist spruce-fir forests. Lichens, such as the old man's beard lichen (*Usnea* species), are a symbiotic association between a fungus and a green algae or cyanobacterium (formerly called blue-green algae). The fungus produces the overall structure of the lichen and provides a home for its photosynthetic partner, which occurs as scattered microscopic cells in a tangle of fungal threads. Lichens are often quite sensitive to the physical and chemical environment, including the textures of the surfaces they grow on. The bark on the trunks and branches of different tree species present a wide range of possible substrates. Lichens also grow slowly and reproduce and disperse primarily by fragmentation, so it can take a long time for them to find and establish appropriate substrates. IRWIN M. BRODO ET AL., LICHENS OF NORTH AMERICA 3–4, 6–7, 30, 45 (2001).

53 Steven B. Selva, *Using Lichens to Assess Ecological Continuity in Northeastern Forests, in* EASTERN OLD-GROWTH FORESTS: PROSPECTS FOR REDISCOVERY AND RECOVERY 35, 36–45 (Mary Byrd Davis ed., 1996).

seeds germinate best in soils containing decomposing wood.[54] It is no accident that orchids figure prominently on many endangered species lists. Orchids have the smallest seeds of flowering plants and most species must establish a mutualistic or, in some cases, parasitic relationship with a fungus to survive and grow.[55]

Although limited in present distribution, old-age forests act as reservoirs (refugia) of biodiversity from which various species may move out into surrounding forests as they mature or recover from disturbance and develop appropriate habitat.[56] Many forest interior species have limited dispersal capacity, hindering their ability to find appropriate habitat over long distances. For example, in hardwood forests many herbaceous wildflower species produce seeds that are dispersed by ants.[57] As ants usually have limited foraging ranges, these seeds are carried only short distances from the parent plant. The rate of movement across the landscape for these plants is slow and may be blocked by habitat inhospitable to the dispersers. Preservation of old-age forest patches is critical to maintaining biodiversity and a seed source for younger forest patches in various stages of succession. Ski trails and the more extensive open patches and corridors of the resort base and village areas are likely significant barriers to the movement of the seeds of late-successional flowering plant species and to the dispersal fragments of many lichen species.

Forest Fragmentation

Habitat fragmentation[58] is a major concern in the conservation of forest biodiversity. In landscapes where forest cover is reduced to scattered remnants, no one fragment may be of sufficient size to support viable populations of all species, and dispersal between fragments is restricted by declining biodiversity and life history strategies of the species present. Intensive logging fragmented nearly the entire forest area of the northeastern mountains before and around the turn of the twentieth century.[59] Although continuous forest cover is largely reestablished,[60] much of the forest is less than 100 years old due to more recent logging of secondary growth. The region's forests prove to be remarkably resilient with regard to the reestablishment of the

---

54 Hanne N. Rasmussen & Dennis F. Whigham, *Importance of Woody Debris in Seed Germination of Tipularia Discolor* (*Orchidaceae*), 85 Am. J. Botany 829, 830 (1998).

55 *Id.* at 833.

56 Glenn R. Matlack, *Plant Species Migration in a Mixed-History Forest Landscape in Eastern North America*, 75 Ecology 1491, 1498–1500 (1994)

57 Andrew J. Beattie & David C. Culver, *The Guild of Myrmecochores in the Herbaceous Flora of West Virginia Forests*, 62 Ecology 107, 111–12 (1981).

58 *See generally* David Lindenmayer & Joern Fischer, Habitat Fragmentation and Landscape Change: An Ecological and Conservation Synthesis (2006).

59 *See generally* Lloyd C. Irland, The Northeast's Changing Forest (1999).

60 Ralph J. Alig & Brett J. Butler, U.S.D.A. Forest Service, Area Changes for Forest Cover Types in the United States, 1952 to 1997, with Projections to 2050, General Technical Report PNW-GTR-618 (1999).

coarse-level structure of forest communities, but restoration of a broader range of biodiversity and ecological functioning in the region may take considerably longer. All of the forested areas within the case studies detailed in this volume have been logged and impacted by human activities, and thus represent the mixed age mosaic of forest community types described earlier.

In this context, fragmentation of forested watersheds by small scale or isolated ski trail development is largely a local concern, as long as forest continuity is maintained in the surrounding area. This is an increasing challenge as resorts trigger new development pressures in regions contiguous or within easy reach of the resort. The central processes of competition, disturbance, and succession can work to maintain a base level of biodiversity as long as continuity is also maintained. Large resorts, such as Killington, affect several adjacent watersheds and disturb a larger part of the forested landscape, which may present challenges for the conservation of animal species and the maintenance of forest diversity, as will be discussed later in this chapter.

Local fragmentation may affect the reestablishment of species found in old-age forest fragments. In the presettlement landscape of the northeastern mountains, before the intensive land clearing and logging of the nineteenth century, there was likely a much higher proportion of old-age forests in the landscape.[61] Reconstruction of presettlement forest composition based on land survey records shows that late-successional species are less abundant in the modern landscape, with American beech at only about 20 percent of its former abundance, and hemlock and red spruce at 70 and 90 percent, respectively.[62] In a landscape recovering from regional deforestation, with old-age forest found only in a few scattered remnants, the present-day rarity of some interior species associated with old-age forest may be due in part to their limited dispersal abilities and loss of habitat.[63] Ski trails and

---

61 The names of ski trails at some resorts reflect, perhaps poignantly, the logging history of the region. At Loon Mountain, for example, 'Bucksaw,' 'Pickaroon,' and 'Walking Boss' are the names of a few trails. Loon Mountain Resort, Winter 2001-02 Trail Map, http://www.loonmtn.com/info/winter/statmap.asp (last visited May 31, 2005).

62 C.V. Cogbill, *Vegetation of the Presettlement Forests of Northern New England*, 102 Rhodora 250, 269–70 (2000). These changes in abundance may also be caused by introduced pests and diseases and anthropogenic stresses such as the beech bark scale insect or acid rain, which is an important contributor to red spruce decline. A.H. Johnson et al., *Synthesis and Conclusions from Epidemiological and Mechanistic Studies of Red Spruce Decline, in* Ecology and Decline of Red Spruce in the Eastern United States, vol 96, at 365–411 (C. Eagar & M.B. Adams eds., 1992).

63 In a study of plant species migration rates in a hardwood forest landscape in Pennsylvania and Delaware, species richness in successional stands declined with distance from older stands, and rates of migration of forest floor species ranged from undetectable to > 2m per year, depending on the mode of dispersal. Glenn R. Matlack, *supra* note 56, at 1498–1500. A study in Belgium found similar results. Beatrijs Bossuyt et al., *Migration of Herbaceous Plant Species Across Ancient-Recent Forest Ecotones in Central Belgium*, 87 J. of Ecology 628, 635–36 (1999).

larger openings associated with resort development could further curtail the ability of these species to disperse across the landscape.

Animal predator-prey interactions are affected by human activities and also influence forest communities. Owls, weasels, and pine marten prey on the squirrels, mice, and voles that are major seed predators in northern hardwood and spruce-fir forests. The marten is extirpated over much of the region, and owls require large areas of continuously forested habitat. The absence of predators of small mammals could result in increased rates of seed predation and, therefore, alter reproductive success for many tree and understory species. Because wolves are also extinct throughout the northeastern region, deer and moose herds have reached sufficient density to affect understory plants and tree regeneration over much of the region, particularly where human hunting pressure is also reduced.[64]

Fragmentation and loss of forest biodiversity may be even more of a concern in the valleys than on the ski slopes. Base area and village development may result in more extensive clearing or fragmentation of valley bottom forests that may include forest types that are not as well-represented in the overall landscape as those on the slopes. Where valley bottoms are more continuously cleared, they may present a major barrier to the dispersal of less mobile species.

Patch Communities and Special Habitats

Out-of-bounds and backcountry skiers take particular pleasure in finding natural openings on a densely forested slope, for they combine the freedom of movement on an open groomed slope with the pleasures of first tracks in powder snow. Few pause to consider the ecological processes that produce such openings, but hidden under the snow are variations in soil conditions that can prevent or restrict the growth of trees and dense understory vegetation, producing patch communities that differ markedly in composition and structure from the surrounding forest. The most common causes of openings on forested slopes are landslides, bedrock outcrops, and headwater seeps. Natural glades may also occur in areas of deep snow accumulation on lee slopes, where persistent snow cover may inhibit tree seed germination and growth.[65] On more level terrain, including valley bottoms and natural terraces or pockets on a forested slope, vernal pool, marsh, or bog communities may develop. These patch communities support distinctive assemblages of plants and animals that add considerably to the overall biodiversity of the landscape. These may include rare, threatened, and endangered species that are found only in the localized environment of the habitat patch.[66]

---

64 R.M.A. Gill, *A Review of Damage by Mammals in North Temperate Forests: Impact on Trees and Forests*, 65 FORESTRY 363, 364–65, 370, 373 (1992).

65 W.A. Reiners & G.E. Lang, *Vegetational Patterns and Processes in the Balsam Fir Zone, White Mountains, New Hampshire*, 60 ECOLOGY 403, 413 (1979).

66 THOMPSON & SORENSON, *supra* note 6, at 241.

Outcrop communities occur where glacial ice, water, or landslide erosion leave an expanse of bedrock that is not steep enough (60 degrees or more) to be considered a cliff. Outcrops are largest and most common on mountain summits and ridge tops, but smaller examples can be found on convex slopes. In the late nineteenth and early twentieth centuries, intensive logging on some mountains resulted in slash fires, which were followed by rapid soil erosion, exposing outcrops in areas that previously supported forest growing in a thin veneer of soil.[67]

While lichens and some mosses can grow on bare rock, the grasses, sedges, wildflowers, and shrubs that dominate outcrop communities grow in crevices or small pockets of mineral soil and must be tolerant of limited rooting space and dry and sometimes nutrient-poor conditions. Different kinds of outcrop communities are recognized based on the chemistry of the bedrock and the overall climate, with boreal outcrops found at higher elevations and temperate outcrops at lower elevations. Calcareous or limey bedrock produces higher pH and nutrient availability than other rock types, such as granite or noncalcareous schist, and often supports a greater variety of plants, including numerous rare species.[68]

Many of the natural openings enjoyed by skiers are seeps—areas where ground water flows out of the soil, often at the headwaters of small mountain streams. The openings occur on concave slopes or where bedrock or impermeable soil forces groundwater to the surface. The soils are too wet and soft to support trees, so a variety of ferns, sedges, grasses, and wildflowers take their place. Seeps are also important breeding areas for salamanders and feeding areas for bear.[69]

The rivers and their surrounding lowlands also support a variety of small riparian and wetland communities.[70] In wetlands, the depth, seasonal fluctuations, and chemistry of surface water are the primary factors that determine community composition and structure.[71] The structure of riparian communities, including floodplain forests, riverside outcrops, and rivershore communities growing in mud, sand, or gravel, is controlled largely by the sediment deposition and disturbance patterns associated with flooding. Base area and village development may affect lowland communities, either by direct impacts or by altered hydrology and sedimentation associated with roads and snowmaking. Some of the larger streams may be reengineered with riprap, bridges, or culverts, all of which can directly alter riverbank communities.

Large, long-lived patch communities may support populations that are basically self-sufficient, where natural growth and reproduction are sufficient to maintain the species' presence in the patch. In smaller patches, on the other hand, some

67 *Id.* at 113, 209.

68 *Id.* at 210, 216.

69 *Id.* at 303–04.

70 William S. Keeton et al., *Mature and Old-growth Riparian Forests: Structure, Dynamics, and Effects on Adirondack Stream Habitats*, 17 Ecological Applications 852–68 (2007).

71 Thompson & Sorenson, *supra* note 6, at 239–40.

species may be at risk of local extinction, due to fluctuations in environmental conditions that cause mortality or reproductive failure. These species can only be replaced by immigration from neighboring patches. Long-distance processes of pollination, seed dispersal, or, in the case of animals, immigration and emigration of adults and juveniles, may also link populations in neighboring patches into a single metapopulation.[72]

Resort development activities that affect the distribution of patch communities in the landscape, or the metapopulation processes that link, then could affect the dynamics and viability of populations within these patches. This is a concern for some animal species, notably moths and butterflies with caterpillars that specialize in one or a few food plants. Development over and around existing patches, both on the mountain and in the valley, may effectively remove some species. For example, ski trail, lift, and road construction often involve blasting of bedrock outcrops, which destroys existing patches. In addition, other activities, such as snowmaking and road development, may indirectly affect patches, particularly seeps, wetlands, and riparian communities, by altering hydrological conditions. Large openings, such as roads and ski trails, could block dispersal between patches. Current laws and regulations control development that directly affects larger wetlands and some riparian communities, but largely ignore outcrops and small wetland patches, such as seeps.

Alpine Communities

At the highest elevations in the northeastern mountains, life as a tree becomes impossible, primarily due to low temperature stress and secondarily due to wind.[73] Low temperature stress takes two forms—the acute effects of extreme low temperature in winter, and the chronic effects of low average temperatures during the growing season.[74] While extreme low temperature can directly injure plant cells, most plants living in cold-temperate and boreal environments have anatomical and physiological adaptations that allow them to survive extreme cold. Adaptation to cold has two major requirements: a period of cold-hardening before the onset of freezing conditions, and energy to drive the biochemical reactions involved in preparing tissues and cells for survival in below-freezing temperatures. Furthermore, fully cold-hardened plants are partially or fully dormant so that

---

72 Isabelle Olivieri & Pierre-Henri Gouyon, *Evolution of Migration Rate and Other Traits: The Metapopulation Effect*, in METAPOPULATION BIOLOGY: ECOLOGY GENETICS, & EVOLUTION 293, 294 (Ilkka Hanski & Michael E. Gilpin eds., 1997).

73 *See* C.B. Vostral et al., *Water Relations of New England Conifers and Factors Influencing Their Upper Elevational Limits. I. Measurements*, 22 TREE PHYSIOLOGY 793–800 (2002); L.R. Boyce et al., *Water Relations of New England Conifers and Factors Influencing Their Upper Elevational Limits*. II. Modeling 22 TREE PHYSIOLOGY 801–06 (2002).

74 LARCHER, *supra* note 21, at 372–74.

photosynthesis is slowed or stopped altogether. In alpine environments, freezing can occur during any month of the year, so plants must maintain some level of readiness at all times. These influences affect the overall energy allocation of the plant, diverting energy away from growth and reproduction.[75]

The low average temperature of the alpine environment also places stringent limits on the total amount of energy available for survival, growth, and reproduction. All biological processes, including photosynthesis, are slowed by low temperature. In alpine areas, the growing season is two months or less, and the average temperature of the warmest month of the year is less than ten degrees Celsius. This cold, short season limits plant growth, so that the overall productivity of alpine communities is roughly one tenth that of forest communities.[76] On such a limited energy budget, alpine plants cannot afford the luxury of producing big woody stems, so competition with neighboring plants is only a minor issue. In a forest, many layers of leaves shade an average patch of ground, but in alpine heaths and meadows, the low-growing plants are all in direct sun.[77] Most alpine plants have small, tightly packed leaves that trap and conserve the precious heat of the sun, allowing them to warm above surrounding air temperature and grow a little faster.

Wind is also a nearly constant factor in the alpine zone. The dwarf tree and shrub communities, called krummholz, can grow in areas where the topography gives some protection from wind.[78] A well-developed krummholz community builds a dense canopy, usually no more than 0.5 meters above the ground surface. In winter this canopy is usually buried in a protective layer of snow. Any branches that grow above the snow are "sandblasted" by windborne snow and ice crystals, a brutally effective pruning that keeps the canopy of the krummholz community close to the ground.[79] Wind does not, however, break or uproot whole stems, as it does in forests.

Low temperature also slows decomposition, causing alpine soils to typically develop a layer of partially decomposed, acidic organic matter at the soil surface. The soil that develops over bare rock is often nearly 100 percent organic but even if soils develop over sand or other deposits, most of the roots and nutrient storage occur in the surface organic layer. In the alpine environment as well as in the forest

---

75 *Id.* at 353, 359, 362–63, 370.

76 *Id.* at 49, 109, 153.

77 Leaf area index (LAI) is the ratio of the area of canopy foliage to the area of ground, and gives a measure of the amount of stratification in a community. In mature temperate and boreal forests, LAI can be as high as 15; in tundra communities it ranges from 0.5 to 2.5. *Id.* at 36, 152.

78 "Krummholz 'is a German word meaning 'crooked wood'" referring to the twisted, much-pruned shape of the trees. Getting on hands and knees and peering under the canopy of a krummholz community reveals a detailed forest in miniature. THOMPSON & SORENSON, *supra* note 6, at 108.

79 *Id.*

soils, organic matter accumulates slowly,[80] and the organic layer can rapidly erode if disturbance kills its sheltering plants and their roots.

Alpine communities are usually characterized as fragile because they are slow to recover from disturbance, yet alpine plants are able to live in some of the most extreme growing conditions on the planet. Forest community plants evolved strategies to compete for light and to capitalize on disturbance events. Additionally, these forest communities can achieve long-term stability through resilience, the ability to recover from even major disturbances.[81] In contrast, the survival strategies of alpine plants center on enduring continuous stress (resistance), and they can withstand the effects of minor disturbances. The alpine plants, however, recover very slowly from major natural disturbances, which are rare in alpine communities. Consequently, alpine plants do not tolerate the effects of human trampling.[82] Summer and winter visitors who wander off established trails can rapidly expose thin alpine soils to erosion. Concerted efforts to educate and control summer visitors resulted in the gradual and partial recovery of alpine communities in places like the Presidential and Franconia Ranges in New Hampshire and Mount Mansfield in Vermont.[83] While few northeastern ski areas deliver skiers directly to alpine zones, those in search of "wild snow" will climb above the lifts and trample alpine vegetation that is exposed or only thinly protected by snow. Pruning by skiing and sideslipping over plants hidden in or exposed above the snow is another potential impact. At resorts like Mount Mansfield and Whiteface Mountain, ski lifts and roads also give many more summer visitors access to the alpine zone.[84]

---

80 In a study of alpine soil development on dated moraines in Norway, long-term average organic carbon accumulation rates varied widely from about 0.02 grams per square centimeter per year on 9,000 year-old moraines to 0.31 grams per square centimeter per year on 250 year-old moraines. R.G. Darmody et al., *Soil Topochronosequences at Storbreen, Jotunheimen, Norway*, 69 Soil Sci. Soc. Am. J. 1275, 1283 (2005).

81 C.S. Holling, *Resilience and Stability of Ecological Systems*, *in* 4 Annual Review of Ecology and Systematics 14-15 (Richard F. Johnston et al. eds., 1973).

82 David N. Cole, *Trampling Effects on Mountain Vegetation in Washington, Colorado, New Hampshire and North Carolina*, USDA Forest Service Res. Pap. INT 464 (1993); *see generally* M.J. Liddle, *A Selective Review of the Ecological Effects of Human Trampling on Natural Ecosystems*, 7 Biological Conservation 17 (1975).

83 J.E. Doucette, & K.D. Kimball, *Passive Trail Management in Northeastern Alpine Zones: A Case Study*, in Proceedings of the 1990 Northeastern Recreation Research Symposium, U.S. Forest Service, General Technical Report NE-145, at 195 (T.A. More et al., eds., 1990).

84 The 2001 caretaker's report indicates that between 30,000 and 40,000 people a year visit the summit ridge of the mountain. Timothy J. Sullivan, Green Mountain Club, Mt. Mansfield Lead Caretaker's Report 11, November 2001 (on file with author). A 1992 University of Vermont natural areas study found that over 60 percent arrived via the toll road. *Assessing the Nature of Visitor Use on Mount Mansfield Leads to Programs for Protection*, Natural Areas Notes (University of Vermont Natural Areas), Autumn 1992, *available at* http://www.uvm.edu/~envprog/ naturalareas/nanews92.html. People riding up

Invasive Species

Biological invasion is an increasingly important threat to the integrity of natural communities throughout the Northeast, as well as many other areas of the world.[85] The threat is most serious in wetlands and other lowland communities, but mountainsides are not immune. Japanese knotweed (*Polygonum cuspidatum*) is a beautiful plant, two meters tall, with jointed, bamboo-like stems, big heart-shaped leaves, and curved sprays of tiny white flowers in late summer. A patch of it grows alongside the Toll Road atop Stowe Mountain Resort on Mount Mansfield, just above the top of the high-speed quad ski lift and below the stake where the National Weather Service measures snow depth. It is an aggressive invasive species that spreads rapidly along roadsides and rivers throughout the northeastern region.[86] It is ubiquitous along the West Branch of the Little River in Stowe, just a few miles from and less than a thousand meters below the patch on the mountain. It colonizes sandy or gravelly open patches along the rivers and roadsides where there is little competition. Once established, it grows luxuriantly and spreads by rhizomes, producing a dense, ever-widening thicket of stems and a deep shade under which no native plant can establish, and it is very difficult to eradicate.

Japanese knotweed has grown for at least ten years, at an elevation of 1100 meters, in a subalpine climate where few would suspect it could survive. It most likely arrived in a load of fill used to repair the road. Its distribution along streams and roadsides suggests that it spreads best downhill, because running water transports rhizome fragments. From its perch high on the Toll Road, it is in a position to move downwards over the entire mountain and base area, eventually joining up with the already burgeoning population along the West Branch and expanding its overall presence in the landscape. In fact, another patch is already established lower down on the Toll Road. While Japanese knotweed is unable to invade most well-established natural communities, especially forests, it is displacing native river shore communities along the rivers.

This patch of Japanese knotweed is just one example of the potential invasion of aggressive species along maintenance roads and ski trails.[87] The invasive Tartarian and Morrow's honeysuckles (*Lonicera tatarica* and *L. morrowii*) and common and glossy buckthorns (*Rhamnus cathartica* and *R. frangula*) have berries and

---

the gondola and hiking the rest of the way up the Cliff Trail in both summer and winter must also account for a significant percentage.

85 *See generally* Julie Lockwood et al., Invasion Ecology (2006).

86 The Nature Conservancy, *Invasive Plant Fact Sheet/Japanese Knotweed*, Where We Work: Connecticut, at http://nature.org/wherewework/northamerica/states/connecticut/science/ art323.html (last visited May 31, 2005).

87 For current summaries of invasive species in the region, see U.S. Forest Service, *Noxious Weeds and Non-Native Invasive Plants,* http://www.fs.fed.us/r9/weed/ (Sept. 1998), and the National Biological Information Infrastructure pages on invasive species, http://www.invasivespecies.gov/ (last visited May 31, 2005).

bird-dispersed seeds that can spread in old fields. These species are mostly found in warmer areas, such as the lower slopes of Mount Equinox in southern Vermont. The edges of ski trails, roadsides, and parking lots may represent opportunities for these species to expand their presence in the landscape. Roadside ditches and any disturbances in natural wetlands associated with development may present similar opportunities for expansion of purple loosestrife (*Lythrum salicaria*) and common reed (*Phragmites australis*).

More generally, numerous non-native species have been consciously introduced into the region, often by deliberate planting in seed mixes used along roadsides, in clearing after logging operations, and of course on ski trails. These include grasses and various kinds of wildflowers originating from Europe or elsewhere in North America. Ski trails, roadsides, lawns, and pastures are maintained by regular mowing and sometimes fertilization, allowing these species to persist in more or less permanent communities.[88] While many of these species are not as aggressive as those discussed above, their broad presence and persistence in the mountain landscape may put them in a position to invade and compete with native plants in suitable habitat patches, whether they are formed by disturbance or local soil conditions.

Summary

As the focus of biological conservation shifted from species to communities, ecosystems, and landscapes, ecologists have identified a need to recognize and conserve the dynamic ecological processes that shape and maintain ecological systems across all spatial scales.[89] Individual organisms, populations, communities, ecosystems, and landscapes are the building blocks of ecological systems, united by their functioning processes that produce useful ecosystem services. Large-scale ecological processes include hydrological cycles, energy flow, and nutrient cycling, but the regulation of these processes is often achieved by the actions and interactions of organisms in the system. While climate, geology, and other abiotic influences may constrain the development of communities and landscapes, individual organisms and populations interact with the environment and with each other to influence the trajectory and details of ecosystem development.

Mountain resort development, from the tops of ski lifts to the base areas and villages, potentially affects the ecological processes that knit communities and ecosystems together into a landscape (Table 3.1). After much of the region was logged over in the nineteenth and early twentieth centuries, the forests that form the matrix of the mountain landscape reestablished more or less continuous cover,

---

88 J.H. Titus & S. Tsuyuzaki, *Ski Slope Vegetation at Snoqualmie Pass, Washington State, USA, and a Comparison with Ski Slope Vegetation in Temperate Coniferous Forest Zones*, 13 Ecological Research 97–104 (1998).

89 *See, e.g.*, R.E. Ricklefs et al., *supra* note 1, at 8.

Table 3.1 Community and Landscape Processes Affected by Mountain Resort Development

Process	Scale	Function	Effects of Resort Development
Competition	Community	Controls forest community composition and physical structure.	Largely unaffected.
Disturbance	Landscape	Creates landscape patches of heterogeneous size and age.	Some potential for alteration of scale and pattern of disturbance within and near developed area.
Secondary Succession	Community	Reestablishes forest cover in disturbance patches.	Reestablishment of the coarse structure of forest ecosystems largely unaffected, but establishment of late-succession composition inhibited.
Seed Dispersal	Landscape	Controls movement of plants between patches.	Dispersal of late successional plant species is inhibited by ski trail systems and other open corridors. Seed dispersal links in metapopulations may also be disrupted.
Seed Predation	Community	Primary effect on reproductive success of plants and secondary effect on community composition.	Reduced predator activity on edges and in small patches leads to increased seed predation within and near developed areas.
Herbivory	Community to landscape	Selective and intensive grazing and browsing affects establishment and survival of trees and understory species.	If development restricts activity of predators, including human hunters, it may affect density of deer, moose, or other herbivores, with secondary effects on forest composition and structure.
Soil Development	Community	Accumulation of organic matter, leaching and accumulation of soluble substances over long term results in development of distinctive characteristics. Also affects nutrient cycling.	Trampling causes soil erosion in alpine zone, with extremely slow recovery.
Biological Invasion	Community to landscape	Modifies community development and structure via competition.	Development creates opportunities for spread of invasive species

but have not yet recovered their complete structure and biodiversity. The dominant ecological processes of competition, disturbance, and secondary succession can continue to function as long as forest cover is continuous over large areas. Because northeastern resorts are usually surrounded by expanses of recovering forest, resort development may locally fragment forests, but will not, in and of itself, disrupt continuity at larger scales. The effects of ski trails may extend many meters beyond the visible edge in the form of altered microclimate and increased damage, and developed glade and out-of-bounds skiing may further extend the ecological footprint of a resort area.

Some late-successional understory and epiphytic species, characteristic of old-age forests, which include many rare, threatened, and endangered species, are confined to remnant old-age stands. Many of these species have limited dispersal abilities. Therefore, their ability to locate and spread into small and widely spaced patches of appropriate habitat is limited. Ski trails, roads, and large open areas may further slow recovery of these species by creating barriers to dispersal.

Patch communities, such as outcrops, seeps, and wetlands, are important reservoirs of biodiversity. Populations in patches may be insular or linked into metapopulations by immigration and emigration. Periodic immigration from neighboring patches may maintain populations of some species in small patches. Resort development may affect patch communities by removing entire patches, degrading them via altered hydrology, or disrupting movement between patches.

Alpine plant communities are adapted to low-temperature stress and wind pruning, but natural large-scale disturbance is rare. Human trampling can rapidly kill off alpine plants, resulting in soil erosion from which alpine communities are very slow to recover. Some resorts give skiers and summer visitors access to the alpine zone, exacerbating disturbance and erosion problems.

The openings and exposed soil created by development may also give populations of invasive species an opportunity to expand in the landscape. While most upland invasive species will not readily spread into well-established communities of native plants, they can move into disturbed areas and delay or prevent establishment of native plants. Maintenance of ski trails and other openings by mowing allows a mixture of less aggressive non-native species to persist in the landscape, increasing the risk that they will move into, and compete with native plants in, some natural community types.

Chapter 4
Water Quantity and Quality in the Mountain Environment

James B. Shanley and Beverley Wemple

Introduction

Mountain streams[1] provide habitat for fish, amphibians, and macroinvertebrates, as well as clean water for human consumption. A healthy mountain stream with clean water, a stable channel, a gravel substrate, and abundant aquatic life reflects a healthy ecosystem. The water comprising the stream must first pass through the adjacent terrestrial ecosystem, whose vegetation and soil system buffers extremes in flow and limits erosion.[2] A healthy terrestrial ecosystem acts as a filter, preventing some types and amounts of contaminants from reaching the stream.

Mountain stream systems have pronounced and abrupt variations in gradient, valley width, channel pattern, and grain size of the bed.[3] The upper reaches, or headwaters, commonly have a step-pool structure,[4] in which the stream drops steeply between less rapidly flowing pools.[5] This structure is fairly stable through time due to the bedrock and/or large rocks making up the channel boundaries.

---

1 A mountain stream is defined as a stream in a mountainous region that has a gradient of 0.02 meter/meter (a .02 meter fall for each meter of length) or more along the majority of its channel. *See* E. Wohl, Mountain Rivers, 1–3 (American Geophysical Union, Water Resources Monograph 14, 2000).

2 *See generally* P.S. Giller & B. Malmqvist, The Biology of Streams and Rivers 3–6 (1998); P.E. Black, Watershed Hydrology 91–206 (1996).

3 Wohl, *supra* note 1, at 1–3.

4 Flowing water ecosystems are a series of interrelated habitats, including the turbulent riffle and the quiet pool. Riffles are the primary production sites for algae and other invertebrates, while the pools—above and below the riffles—act as catch basins, in which the chemistry, the intensity of the current and the depth are different. Without either habitat, a stream could not maintain proper chemical equilibrium. The overall productivity of a stream is influenced by the substrate (stream bottom material). Gravel and rubble substrates support the most abundant life, as organisms attach to and move on loose gravel, which also provides protective crannies for insect larvae. *See generally* P.S. Giller & B. Malmqvist, The Biology of Streams and Rivers 30–70 (1998); L.B. Leopold, A View of the River 21–29 (1994).

5 *See* A. Chin, *The Periodic Nature of Step-Pool Mountain Streams*, 302 Am. J. Sci. 144–167 (2002).

At lower elevations the streams phase into a less steep pool and riffle structure, typical of broad mountain valleys. This pool and riffle structure is inherently less stable and thus more vulnerable to physical and biological effects of watershed development, which may alter flow and sediment inputs.

The mountain stream is an indicator and integrator of processes and activities occurring within the stream's watershed, defined as the land area that contributes runoff to the stream. This means that the condition of the stream (i.e., biology, chemistry) at a given point reflects the net effects of all activities upstream. A stream reach, or segment, may be degraded as a result of disturbance upstream even when the adjacent watershed is healthy. Too much disturbance in the watershed of a stream can destabilize the stream, and this is a major concern in mountain development.[6] Several types of disturbances, including forest clearing, soil compaction, and the creation of impervious surfaces, such as roofs and roads, may lead to increased storm peak flows and erosion.[7] Stream channels adjust to higher flood peaks by incising or widening, which may cause stream banks to fail and trees to fall.[8] Sediment carried by runoff over impervious surfaces, combined with sloughing stream bank material, fills in stream pools and deposits fine-textured material on the gravel stream bed, thus degrading critical fish spawning habitat[9] and altering the abundance of stream macroinvertebrates, which are the food source for many stream organisms.[10] This is the worst-case scenario, where the fabric of the stream ecosystem is said to "unravel."

Despite these concerns, there is a notable lack of research on the effects of ski resort and mountain development on hydrology and water quality.[11] Thus, policymakers and agencies that issue permits have little scientific information on which to base their decisions. Instead, mountain resort plans may be approved based on the implementation of standard erosion control measures, such as stormwater runoff control practices and the retention of forested buffers along stream channels. Permit applicants attempt to predict the effects of these measures with hydrologic models that are rarely, if ever, calibrated with site data. Whether these standard erosion control measures are truly appropriate for high-elevation environments has not been adequately tested.

---

6 T. Dunne & L.B. Leopold, Water in Environmental Planning 510 (1978) ("Human occupance of land almost always increases the rate of hillslope erosion by significant and sometimes catastrophic amounts.").

7 *Id.* at 507–17 (describing geological normal and accelerated rates of erosion due to human activity); Giller & Malmqvist, *supra* note 2, at 229–30.

8 Dunne & Leopold, *supra* note 6, at 695; *see also* Leopold, *supra* note 4, at 126–31.

9 Dunne & Leopold, *supra* note 6, at 714.

10 K.H. Nislow & W.H. Lowe, *Influences of Logging History and Riparian Forest Characteristics on Macroinvertebrates and Brook Trout* (Salvelinus fontinalis) *in Headwater Streams (New Hampshire, USA)*, 51 Freshwater Biology 388–397 (2006).

11 B. Wemple et al., *Hydrology and Water Quality in Two Mountain Basins of the Northeastern US: Assessing Baseline Conditions and Effects of Ski Area Development*, 21 Hydrological Processes 1639–1650 (2007).

This chapter begins with an overview of hydrology and water quality of undisturbed mountain streams in the natural ecosystem, then turns to the effects of development in mountainous terrain on stream flow and water quality. Special consideration is given to the effects of snowmaking, a practice of increasing importance to the economic viability of mountain resorts. Later in the chapter we present findings from a scientific study at a Vermont mountain resort, designed to help fill the current gap in scientific understanding. The chapter concludes with a discussion of the role of scientific information in the formulation of policy regarding mountain resorts.

Basic Mountain Hydrology Concepts

Put simply, streamflow is the water left over after natural processes consume water that originally fell as precipitation.[12] In cold-climate mountainous watersheds, including the forested mountains of northeastern North America (northeastern United States and eastern Canada), annual streamflow amounts to roughly half of the annual precipitation.[13] The other half evaporates or is transpired by vegetation.[14] Transpiration is the movement of water from the plant roots up though the plant to the atmosphere via microscopic openings in the leaf surface called stomata.[15] A small fraction of this water is consumed in the process of photosynthesis, in which the plant uses the energy in sunlight to combine water and carbon dioxide to create new biomass;[16] the bulk of the remaining water is evaporated from leaf

12 This section provides a basic introduction to hydrology. For further reading on basic hydrology we recommend the following: K.N. BROOKS ET AL., HYDROLOGY AND MANAGEMENT OF WATERSHEDS (1991); J.M. Buttle, *Fundamentals of Small Catchment Hydrology*, *in* ISOTOPES IN CATCHMENT HYDROLOGY 1 (C. Kendall & J.J. McDonnell eds., 1998); S. LAWRENCE DINGMAN, PHYSICAL HYDROLOGY (2002); DUNNE & LEOPOLD, *supra* note 6; G.M. HORNBERGER ET AL., ELEMENTS OF PHYSICAL HYDROLOGY (1998); L.B. LEOPOLD, WATER, RIVERS AND CREEKS (1997); M. Bonnell, *Progress in the Understanding of Runoff Generation Dynamics in Forests*, 150 J. HYDROLOGY 217 (1993); M. Bonnell, *Selected Changes in Runoff Generation Research In Forests From the Hillslope to Headwater Drainage Basin Scale*, 34 J. AM. WATER RESOURCES ASS'N 765 (1998). A monograph geared toward mountain hydrology is E. WOHL, MOUNTAIN RIVERS (American Geological Union, Water Resources Monograph 14, 2000). For a very readable and comprehensive treatment of fresh water hydrology for those with a limited science background, please see E.L. PIELOU, FRESHWATER (1998).

13 G.E. LIKENS & F.H. BORMANN, BIOGEOCHEMISTRY OF A FORESTED ECOSYSTEM 16, 22–23 (2d ed. 1995) (summarizing results from a long term study at Hubbard Brook in New Hampshire).

14 *Id.*

15 DINGMAN, *supra* note 12, at 275, 277.

16 *Id.* Biomass is any biological material. In ecological studies, the dry mass of living organisms in a specified area is often expressed as grams of biomass per square meter. B.

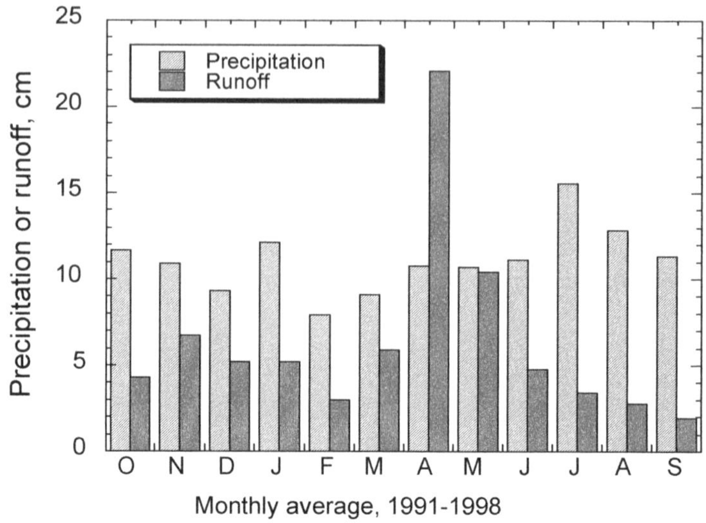

Figure 4.1 Typical Annual Cycle of Precipitation and Streamflow

Note: Based on eight years of data (1991–98) from Sleepers River Research Watershed, Danville, Vermont.

surfaces.[17] Trees act as giant wicks that transfer water from the soil to the atmosphere.[18] When water is scarce, some trees, especially conifers, can close the stomata in leaves and needles to limit water loss[19] but sacrifice acquiring the carbon dioxide needed for photosynthesis in the process. Evaporation and transpiration have the common result of returning precipitation to the atmosphere, and are often lumped in the term "evapotranspiration."

The annual climatic cycle drives the precipitation and plant growth cycles, which in turn drive streamflow (Figure 4.1). In northeastern North America, precipitation is distributed relatively uniformly throughout the year; there is no distinctive dry season or rainy season.[20] In the fall, the vegetation demand for water decreases sharply, allowing streamflow to recover from its summer minimum.[21] In winter, most

Wyman & L.H. Stevenson, The Facts on File Dictionary of Environmental Science 47 (2000).

17 Dingman, *supra* note 12, at 275.

18 *Id.* at 275–77.

19 E.D. Schulze et al., *Plant Water Balance*, 37 Bioscience 30, 34 (1987); *see also* B.J. Yoder et al., *Evidence of Reduced Photosynthetic Rates in Old Trees*, 40 Forest Sci. 513, 524–25 (1994).

20 Leopold, *supra* note 4, at 185.

21 Likens & Bormann, *supra* note 13, at 22; *see also* Dunne & Leopold, *supra* note 6, at 466.

of the precipitation falls as snow and is stored in the snowpack, causing streamflow to decrease again until snowmelt, punctuated by occasional midwinter thaws.[22] In spring, several months of accumulated snow is released in a relatively short period, causing sustained high flow.[23] Through the summer, flow gradually decreases as high vegetative demand consumes most rainfall and depletes soil water storage.[24] Rainfall intensity is highest in summer[25] and intense storms can cause high peak flows, but soils are typically dry in summer and can absorb considerable rainfall.

An important aspect of mountain hydrology is the abundance of water compared to the adjacent lowlands. Precipitation increases with elevation, on average about twenty centimeters per 300 meters (eight inches per 1,000 feet) on an annual basis.[26] For example, the summit of Mt. Mansfield, Vermont (1,340 meters elevation) receives about two times as much annual precipitation compared to Burlington (61 meters elevation): 198 centimeters (78 inches) compared to 91 centimeters (36 inches).[27] Another important difference is that a much higher percentage of the precipitation falls as snow in the mountains, which delays and amplifies the spring runoff peak.[28] While precipitation increases with elevation, evapotranspiration decreases with elevation, because the growing season becomes shorter and forest growth is less vigorous due to climatic stress and poor soil conditions. With relatively higher precipitation and lower water demand by trees, mountain environments yield a considerably higher amount of streamflow for a given area of land relative to lowland areas,[29] an important consideration in managing mountain watersheds for water quality and water yield.

Mountain streams are generally "flashy," a term hydrologists use to denote a rapid response to precipitation, a high peak flow, and a quick return to base flow (the flow between storms that is sustained by groundwater). This flashy behavior results from water moving quickly down steep slopes with thin soils. The hydrology of a mountain stream system, however, is not all at the surface; water movement in the subsurface is an integral part of the hydrologic cycle. Rain and

---

22 *See, e.g.*, Black, *supra* note 2, at 251–52 (discussing seasonal runoff patterns in the Mohawk River valley of New York). In northern Vermont, 25 to 35 percent of the annual precipitation occurs as snow. Dunne & Leopold, *supra* note 6, at 465.

23 Black, *supra* note 2, at 251–52.

24 *Id.*; *see generally* Dunne & Leopold, *supra* note 6, at 126–28.

25 Nat'l Weather Service Forecast Office, Detailed Climatological Information for Burlington: Top 10 Seasonal Precipitation Totals, http://www.erh.noaa.gov/er/btv/climo/seapcpn.txt (showing largest and smallest precipitation totals for each season, by year) (last visited Sept. 13, 2002).

26 Dingman, *supra* note 12, at 104.

27 Nat'l Weather Serv. Forecast Office, Average Annual Precipitation Map: Vermont, http://www.erh.noaa.gov/er/btv/images/vt_pcpn.gif (last visited Sept. 13, 2002).

28 Dunne & Leopold, *supra* note 6, at 481.

29 Dingman, *supra* note 12, at 95; S. Lawrence Dingman, *Elevation: A Major Influence On the Hydrology of New Hampshire and Vermont*, 26 Hydrological Sci. Bull. 402, 405–06 (1981).

snowmelt infiltrate the soil and move both vertically and laterally downslope.[30] The underlying bedrock surface often forms a barrier to the downward movement of this water, creating a zone of saturation, called groundwater.[31] In saturated soils, water moves more rapidly downslope by the force of gravity.[32] On steep mountain slopes, this saturated groundwater layer may be transient, dissipating nearly as quickly as it forms, but nonetheless providing a means of rapid downslope water transit through the soil. Groundwater tends to persist in flatter areas, particularly along stream channels, where it is important in sustaining streamflow between storms. High-flow episodes are the important channel-forming events.[33] This is why mountain stream channels often appear oversized, with a trickle of water in a voluminous channel; but at different times of the year, that channel must accommodate the occasional "gullywasher."

Above the groundwater, or saturated zone, is the unsaturated zone of the soil, through which water moves more slowly in response to gradients of soil water potential driven by gravity, surface evaporation, and soil water uptake by roots.[34] In summer, water uptake by tree roots progressively dries out the unsaturated zone through the growing season. The unsaturated zone wets up in the fall as vegetative demand for water drops off, and this rewetting is a key factor in increased streamflow in the fall. As soil moisture increases, groundwater levels rise to the land surface in stream channel areas. Rain or snowmelt on these now saturated areas then flows directly to the stream channel. The soil is analogous to a sponge; in the summer it is dried out and can absorb most of the water applied. In late fall and early spring, the soil is nearly saturated, causing additional water to run off immediately to streamflow. In the mountains, this sponge is smaller yet subjected to greater water input than in the adjacent lowlands, thus the tendency for high and variable runoff in mountain streams.

Bedrock is not always a barrier to water movement. Some rocks, such as sandstone and limestone, have intrinsic permeability—pore space within the rock through which water can flow.[35] Other rocks lack intrinsic permeability, but may

---

30 *See* Dunne & Leopold, *supra* note 6, at 262–72 (describing how water infiltrates soil, which eventually becomes saturated, causing water to emerge from the ground downslope).

31 *Id.* at 192–93.

32 *Id.* at 179–80. Groundwater movement is expressed by Darcy's Law, an equation that relates groundwater velocity to the product of the permeability of the aquifer and the slope of the water table. *Id.* at 204.

33 Leopold, *supra* note 4, at 126–31.

34 Dunne & Leopold, *supra* note 6, at 194. A saturated zone is the zone in the earth's crust extending from the water table downward, in which pore spaces in the soil or rock are filled with water at greater than atmospheric pressure. Wyman & Stevenson, *supra* note 16, at 338. Conversely, the unsaturated zone consists of the upper layers of soil in which pore spaces in soil or rock are filled with water and air at less than atmospheric pressure. Dunne & Leopold, *supra* note 6, at 194. This zone is also called the zone of aeration.

35 Dunne & Leopold, *supra* note 6, at 206 (showing table of values of permeability for geologic materials).

be fractured.[36] Water entering bedrock fractures on a mountain slope may follow those fractures all the way to the valley below and bypass the mountain stream network altogether. Researchers found evidence of fracture flow on the west slope of Mt. Mansfield in Vermont.[37] Alternatively, water entering fractures on one side of a mountain may issue from fractures on the other side, or more commonly on the same side. Gains or losses of water from mountain streams that result from flow through bedrock fractures are generally minor, but may be important in some settings.

Snow—its accumulation in the snowpack and subsequent release in melting—plays an important role in streamflow in many mountain environments. Up to one-third of the annual precipitation in the mountains of northeastern North America is stored in the snowpack.[38] The snowpack depth and stored water content increases as elevation increases because of greater precipitation, higher percentage of snow relative to rain, and colder temperatures that limit melting.[39] In the spring, snowmelt releases this stored precipitation relatively quickly, causing about one-half of the total annual streamflow during just six weeks of snowmelt.[40] In the more alpine mountains of western North America, Europe, and elsewhere, snow and snowmelt dominate streamflow to an even greater extent. Nearly all of the annual streamflow in these areas is derived from snowmelt, and peak flow in some locations may not occur until mid-summer.

Considerable energy is required to melt snow.[41] This energy may be supplied by various sources, including incoming shortwave solar radiation,[42] longwave radiation,[43] advected energy from rain,[44] and the latent heat of vaporization.[45] Shortwave radiation is generally the most important energy source, but under the right conditions latent heat can provide even more energy. The energy that latent

---

36 *See id.* at 215 ("Fracture zones may provide valuable locations in rocks that otherwise provide relatively poor opportunities for groundwater development.").

37 *See generally* M.D. Abbott et al., *δ180, δD, 3H Measurements Constrain Groundwater Recharge Patterns in an Upland Fractured Bedrock Aquifer, Vermont, USA*, 228 J. Hydrology 101–12 (2000).

38 *Id.* at 465.

39 *See id.* at 466 (describing the parameters affecting snow cover and snow measurements).

40 *See* Likens & Bormann, *supra* note 13, at 48 ("[D]uring the spring snowmelt, stream water is composed of nearly pure snowmelt water.").

41 *See* Dunne & Leopold, *supra* note 6, at 470 ("To melt one gram of ice at 0 degrees Celsius, 80 calories of heat must be transferred to the snowpack.").

42 *Id.* at 471–72. Shortwave radiation is part of the range of wavelengths of energy emitted by the sun. Wyman & Stevenson, *supra* note 16, at 349.

43 Dunne & Leopold, *supra* note 6, at 472–74. Longwave radiation is energy radiated by terrestrial objects or surfaces. *See id.*

44 Advection is transport by moving liquid or gas. Wyman & Stevenson, *supra* note 16, at 8.

45 Latent heat of vaporization is the energy released by condensing vapor as warm, moisture-laden air passes over the snowpack. Dunne & Leopold, *supra* note 6, at 475–76.

heat releases can be observed in the formation of fog-condensed vapor droplets over the snowpack. Because of the high energy requirements, it is difficult to generate high streamflow rates by snowmelt alone; a high snowmelt rate is equivalent to a light to moderate rainfall rate. When rainfall is added to a melting snowpack, however, the potential for very high streamflow peaks develops, especially when significant melt is occurring from latent heat.[46]

Before the snowpack can produce meltwater, it must ripen.[47] First, energy must be supplied to warm the entire snowpack up to zero degrees Celsius (32 degrees Fahrenheit).[48] Additional energy begins to melt the snow, but the remaining snowpack absorbs the meltwater in its pore space until it attains a critical level. At this point, the snowpack is said to be ripe, and only after this point will further energy inputs cause meltwater to leave the snowpack (the sponge analogy applies here as well).[49] Two factors conspire to accelerate the snowmelt process once it begins. First, the aging snowpack becomes less reflective because crystals change form, and dark organic debris emerges from the pack as it melts down. This decrease in reflectivity, or albedo, causes more of the sun's shortwave radiation to be absorbed by the snowpack rather than reflecting back to space.[50] Secondly, as patches of bare ground and ablation (melt) rings around trees open up, these areas generate increased longwave radiation that is absorbed by the adjacent snowpack, increasing melt.[51] These interactions create a positive feedback that hastens the melting of snow.

In the western U.S. mountains, snowmelt typically produces the highest streamflow peak of the year, but in northeastern North America the annual streamflow peak sometimes occurs in other seasons. The snowmelt peak is broad, and high flow is sustained over several weeks. The lengthy snowmelt period creates wet soils, high groundwater levels, and expanded areas of surface saturation that rapidly shed subsequent rain and meltwater. These conditions can cause the annual peak flow to occur in late winter or spring from a combination of snowmelt and rainfall. The annual peak flow may occur during the higher intensities of summer storms. Summer convective storm cells sometimes stall in the mountains, producing extremely high rainfall amounts.[52] Such storms have caused extensive

46 R.D. Harr, *Some Characteristics and Consequences of Snowmelt During Rainfall in Western Oregon*, 53 J. Hydrology 277, 281–82 (1981).

47 Dunne & Leopold, *supra* note 6, at 470–71.

48 *Id.* at 471.

49 *Id.* at 470–79.

50 *Id.* at 472.

51 J.P. Hardy et al., *Snow Ablation Modeling at the Stand Scale in a Boreal Jack Pine Forest*, 102 J. Geophysical Res. 29397, 29403–04 (1997).

52 *See* Wyman & Stevenson, *supra* note 16, at 272. Orographic lifting is the upward movement of air when currents in the atmosphere encounter mountains. As the air expands and then cools, the result is precipitation. *Id.* "Orographic precipitation is more likely to be general and prolonged than showery and brief because there is a relatively steady upslope flow of air [traveling over the mountains]." T.L. McKnight, Physical Geography: A Landscape Appreciation 155 (1993).

flooding in Vermont in recent years.[53] However, summer storms usually occur on dry soils, which absorb much of the rain and limit runoff. The annual peak flow can also occur in the fall during prolonged rainfall events, such as hurricanes.

Water Quality in Mountain Streams

To many people, the image of a mountain stream is one of clean water cascading over rocks and through a forest. For the most part, this image is realistic; the mountain stream rises from rain or snowmelt that has filtered through forest soils. Apart from atmospheric contaminants in the precipitation or accumulated in the soils,[54] there is little to degrade the water quality. Extreme rainfall can erode steep slopes and clog streams with sediment, but under natural conditions stream channels have adapted to all but the most extreme high-flow events and sedimentation is usually minimal.

Streamwater, however, is never free of impurities. There are two general classes of substances carried by water—dissolved constituents and particulate matter.[55] Dissolved substances consist of both inorganic and organic solutes.[56] Inorganic solutes, such as calcium and sulfate, may either be deposited from the atmosphere or derived from the weathering (i.e. slow chemical breakdown) of minerals in the soils and rocks.[57] Decomposing organic matter, such as leaves and wood, releases both dissolved organic and inorganic material.[58] Dissolved organic matter often exhibits a yellow or brown color in natural waters. Particulate matter carried by streams consists of soil particles and organic debris.[59] Some substances, such as lead and phosphorous, have a strong chemical affinity for these particles (mainly clays) and will only be present in significant amounts when particles are moving.[60] Controlling soil erosion associated with resort development is important for protecting streams and lakes from these pollutants.

---

53 Vermont Agency of Natural Resources, Options for State Flood Control Policies and a Flood Control Program 2 (1999).

54 Atmospheric deposition places solids and/or liquids from the atmosphere into mountain streams. "Snow, rain and dust are natural examples, whereas, acids, metallic dust, rock dust, and toxic organic compounds are deposits caused by human activities." Wyman & Stevenson, *supra* note 16, at 29.

55 Dunne & Leopold, *supra* note 6, at 5–6, 728.

56 *Id.* at 727–33, 739–50. A solute is a substance dissolved in a solution, Wyman & Stevenson, *supra* note 16, at 358, in this case stream water.

57 Dunne & Leopold, *supra* note 6, at 728–29.

58 *Id.* at 728.

59 *See* H.B.N. Hynes, The Ecology of Running Waters 49 (1970) ("All natural surface waters contain dissolved and particulate organic matter . . . .").

60 Dunne & Leopold, *supra* note 6, at 735. The absorption of lead, phosphorous and other substances by particulate matter, such as soil particles, is part of a chemical process known as ion exchange. Wyman & Stevenson, *supra* note 16, at 64.

Mountain streams generally have low concentrations of dissolved substances. Concentrations tend to increase downstream as water has more time to react with soil particles and dissolve soil minerals. The forest exerts an important influence on stream chemistry through its nutritional requirements.[61] For example, uptake of nitrate and phosphate by trees limits the concentrations of these ions in streamwater.[62] Because it involves both geologic and ecosystem considerations, the study of the movement of chemical substances in forested ecosystems is known as "biogeochemistry."[63] Pioneering research in biogeochemistry began in the 1960s by faculty at Dartmouth College and colleagues with the U.S. Forest Service and continues today at Hubbard Brook Experimental Forest in New Hampshire.[64]

High-flow events are an important aspect of mountain stream water quality. The rain or snowmelt causing a high-flow event is typically high quality water that is low in dissolved material. As streamflow increases from inputs of this dilute, high quality water, concentrations of major solutes, such as calcium, chloride, and sulfate, generally decrease. Concentrations of other solutes, such as nitrate and dissolved organic carbon, increase because their source is the organic-rich forest floor, or topsoil, which is flushed by infiltrating rain or snowmelt. Solutes that impair water quality, including phosphate and pesticides from development and landscaping, or metals such as lead and mercury which enter in precipitation, also are bound to organic matter in the forest floor and may be introduced to the stream during high flow.

One of the primary water quality concerns during high-flow events is sediment mobilization. Sediment moved by streams is classified either as suspended sediment or bedload.[65] Suspended sediment is carried along with the water.[66] Concentrations are generally very low or negligible at low flow, but may increase dramatically at high flow. Sediment begins to move at a certain flow threshold, which is dependent on the particle (grain) size, and requires a certain flow velocity to keep it in suspension.[67] Sources may include upland areas (especially where the land surface has been disturbed), the near-stream zone, the stream banks, or the channel itself. Sediment may be deposited and resuspended repeatedly as stream velocities adjust to the steps, pools, and riffles of a mountain stream.[68] Bedload consists of large particles (sand, gravels, cobbles) generally too heavy to be suspended but which are mobilized by extreme high flow and skirt along the channel bottom,[69] altering the geomorphology of the streambed and its suitability as a habitat for stream organisms.

---

61 Likens & Bormann, *supra* note 13, at 3.

62 *Id.* at 2–4.

63 *Id.* at 1–2.

64 *Id.* at 122.

65 L.B. Leopold et al., Fluvial Processes in Geomorphology 180 (1964).

66 *Id.* at 180–81.

67 *Id.* at 176–77.

68 *See supra* note 4 and accompanying text.

69 *See* L.B. Leopold, *Sediment Size that Determines Channel Morphology, in* Dynamics of Gravel-bed Rivers 297-311 (P. Billi et al. eds., 1992).

Two critical factors in the biological health of a stream are dissolved oxygen concentration and temperature. These factors affect fish populations and plant life. Dissolved oxygen is higher in cooler waters and usually maximized in a mountain stream as the cascading waters incorporate air and continually renew any oxygen that fauna or respiring flora and heterotrophs consume.[70] Trout require cool temperatures in summer, a condition generally met in forest ecosystems of cold mountain regions.

The hallmark of high water quality in a stream is a healthy macroinvertebrate community. Macroinvertebrates, commonly the larval stage of flying insects, live in the sand and gravel beds of flowing streams.[71] They typically thrive if there is adequate oxygen, no adverse chemical or temperature stresses, and no excessive sedimentation in the stream channel.[72] Many states, including Vermont, assess the macroinvertebrate population as a barometer of stream quality.[73] Certain indicator species begin to disappear as stream quality degrades, and tracking the various populations gives an indication of status and trends in water quality. Sediment deposition, in particular, degrades the habitat by filling in the spaces in the sand and gravel with finer sediments,[74] creating a condition known as embeddedness[75] and preventing movement and feeding by these organisms. Macroinvertebrates are the primary food supply for small fish; thus, a healthy macroinvertebrate population is vital to a healthy fish population. A later section of this chapter discusses the ways in which development may potentially degrade water quality and fish habitat.[76]

The Potential Effects of Mountain Development on Hydrology: What Happens to a Mountain Stream When a Resort Is Developed Around It?

As mentioned earlier, there has been little study of the hydrologic effects of development at mountain resorts.[77] Thus, when determining effects of resorts, one

70 Hynes, *supra* note 59, at 40.

71 *Id.* at 112–15.

72 *Id.* at 196–222.

73 U.S. Environmental Protection Agency, Invertebrates as Indicators, http://www. epa. gov/bioindicators/html/invertebrate.html (last visited Feb. 18, 2002); Water Quality Division, Vermont Department of Environmental Conservation, Why Biomonitoring?, http:// www.vtwaterquality.org/ bassabn.htm (last visited Jan. 16, 2002). The macroinvertebrate population is seen as an "indicator" population, or a population whose characteristics show the presence of specific environmental conditions or contamination. *See generally* J. Cairns, Jr. & J.R. Pratt, *A History of Biological Monitoring Using Benthic Macroinvertebrates*, *in* Freshwater Biomonitoring and Benthic Macroinvertebrates 10, (D.M. Rosenberg & V.H. Resh, eds., 1992).

74 Giller & Malmqvist, *supra* note 2, at 242.

75 *Id.* at 40.

76 See text *infra* accompanying note 161 and thereafter.

77 Aside from those studies required by regulatory agencies when resorts apply for development permits, etc.

must rely on information learned from forest clearing and urbanization studies and infer how these results might transfer to the mountain resort setting. This lack of site-specific information is a problem for crafting law and regulation tailored to local to regional scale differences in mountain ecosystems and environments. The lack of study in eastern North America is particularly notable. While some studies have been made at western and overseas mountain resorts, they require assumptions and extrapolation to apply to the landscape of New York, New England, and Quebec. This section addresses the effects of development on water flow in streams. Succeeding sections take up the special case of snowmaking, the effects of development on water quality, and finally a short discussion of the transferability of these studies to the mountain resort setting.

In general, removal of a significant amount of the forest cover causes an increase in streamflow.[78] Land development, which leads to compacted soils and impervious surfaces such as roads and roofs, has a similar effect.[79] Impervious surfaces force precipitation to flow over the surface, rather than percolate into the soil.[80] Tree clearing allows more of the precipitation to reach the ground, and the lack of vegetative demand makes more water available to run off to streams.[81] Removal of trees may also result in increased snow accumulation in high-elevation environments, leading to increased runoff during melt or rain-on-snow events.[82] The net result of forest clearing and soil compaction is a tendency for higher and earlier peak flows and greater water yields from cleared landscapes than from standing forests.[83]

The classic experimental approach to quantify the effects of forest clearing on water runoff is the paired watershed study. In this approach, researchers select two watersheds with similar characteristics. Theoretically, if the watersheds are near each other and have similar size, soils, slopes, elevation, aspect, and forest cover, they should have similar hydrology. Flow is measured at both sites, preferably for several years, to quantify natural differences in the hydrology.[84] One basin is then harvested. The difference in flow in the two basins is corrected for any natural differences determined during the pre-harvest period; any remaining difference is ascribed to the harvest. These measurements are also continued for many years to observe the initial effect and the recovery. Simultaneous water quality monitoring can likewise determine the effects on water quality.

78 Dunne & Leopold, *supra* note 6, at 152.

79 *Id.* at 275.

80 J.A. Jones, *Hydrologic Processes and Peak Discharge to Forest Removal, Regrowth, and Roads in Ten Small Experimental Basins, Western Cascades, Oregon*, 36 Water Res. Research 2621, 2623 (2000).

81 *Id.* at 2622.

82 Harr, *supra* note 46, at 296–300.

83 Black, *supra* note 2, at 124. *See generally* I.R. Calder, *Hydrologic Effects of Land Use Change*, *in* Handbook of Hydrology 1–99 (D.R. Maidment ed., 1993).

84 See the start of this chapter for a general explanation of the influences on hydrology.

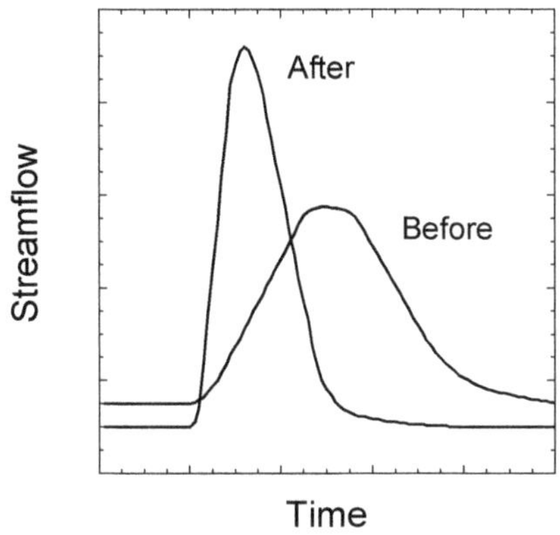

Figure 4.2 Theoretical Shift in Storm Hydrograph to Earlier and Higher Peak Flows as a Result of Land Disturbance and/or Development

Bosch and Hewlett reviewed nearly one hundred paired catchment studies.[85] The collective results indicated that forest clearing increases water yield, due to the reduction in evapotranspiration.[86] For example, at Hubbard Brook, New Hampshire, Hornbeck and others found a 310 millimeter per year (34 percent) increase in flow in the first two years after clearcutting.[87] In a wider regional analysis of 11 paired catchment studies in the northeastern United States, Hornbeck and his colleagues found initial water yield increases up to 350 millimeters per year (41 percent) where regrowth was suppressed, and up to to 250 millimeters per year (40 percent) where regrowth was allowed.[88] Although these initial runoff gains were similar, the excess water yield diminished relatively quickly as the forest grew back and disappeared in ten years.[89] Most of the flow increase occurred in the dry summer months.[90] In ten Oregon catchments, Jones also found the largest flow increase during the dry season.[91] Brown et al. confirmed these results in a review of the more recent literature, reporting that proportionately greater water yield changes

85 J.M. Bosch & J.D. Hewlett, *A Review of Catchment Experiments to Determine the Effect of Vegetation Changes on Water Yield and Evapotranspiration*, 55 J. Hydrology 3, 3 (1982).

86 *Id.* at 4.

87 J.W. Hornbeck et al., *Streamflow Changes After Forest Clearing in New England*, 6 Water Res. Research 1124, 1126 (1970).

88 J.W. Hornbeck et al., *Long-Term Impacts of Forest Treatments on Water Yield: A Summary for Northeastern USA*, 150 J. Hydrology 323, 323 (1993).

89 *Id.* at 337–38.

90 *Id.* at 330.

91 Jones, *supra* note 80, at 2635.

occurred in the drier seasons.[92] Hewlett and Helvey, working at the Coweeta watershed in western North Carolina, found 11 percent greater stormflow volume, 7 percent higher peaks, but no change in peak flow timing after clearcutting.[93] They likewise attributed the increased water yield to reduced evapotranspiration.[94] Troendle and King found that flow increases persisted thirty years after partial cutting in the Colorado Rockies.[95] Unlike logging operations, forest clearing at mountain resorts is a permanent alteration to the landscape, so hydrologic changes and associated changes in stream biota would tend to endure.

The effects of forest roads on hydrology are related to the effects of forest clearing. Most logging requires road access, and the roads often remain after the logging, so there are both short and long-term effects.[96] Forest road surfaces are relatively impermeable. Water readily runs over the road surface and associated roadside ditches, often directly to a stream channel, with the net effect of extending channel networks and increasing drainage density (the total stream length for a given land area).[97] In addition to providing conduits for overland flow, forest roads involve slope-cuts and ditching that may intersect the water table and interrupt natural subsurface water movement.[98] This diversion of subsurface water may be quantitatively more important than the overland flow of stormwater in some watersheds.[99] The importance of roads in altering basin hydrology has been underscored in paired watershed studies and recent modeling studies.[100]

---

92 A.E. Brown et al., *A Review of Paired Catchment Studies for Determining Changes in Water Yield Resulting from Alternations in Vegetation*, 310 Journal of Hydrology 28, 28 (2005).

93 J.D. Hewlett & J.D. Helvey, *Effects of Forest Clear-felling on the Storm Hydrograph*, 6 Water Res. Research 768, 774–75 (1970).

94 *Id.* at 778.

95 C.A. Troendle & R.M. King, *The Effect of Timber Harvest on the Fool Creek Watershed, 30 Years Later*, 21 Water Res. Research 1915, 1915 (1985).

96 *See generally* Beverly C. Wemple et al., *Channel Network Extension by Logging Roads in Two Basins, Western Cascades Oregon*, 32 Water Resources Bull. 1195 (1996).

97 *Id.* at 1201–02.

98 B.C. Wemple & J.A. Jones, *Runoff Production on Forest Roads in a Steep, Mountain Catchment*, 39(8) Water Resources Research 1220 (2003).

99 *Id.*

100 *See, e.g.*, R.D. Harr et al., *Changes in Storm Hydrographs After Road Building and Clear Cutting in the Oregon Coast Range*, 11 Water Res. Research 436 (1975); Jones, *supra* note 80, at 2638; J.G. King & L.C. Tennyson, *Alteration of Streamflow Characteristics Following Road Construction in North Central Idaho*, 20 Water Res. Research 1159 (1984); J.L. LaMarche & D.P. Lettenmeier, *Effects of Forest Roads on Flood Flows in the Deschutes River, Washington*, 26 Earth Surface Processes & Land Forms 115 (2001); W.T. Swank et al., *Streamflow Changes Associated With Forest Cutting, Species Conversions and Natural Disturbances*, *in* 66 Forest Hydrology and Ecology at Coweeta 297, 312 (W.T. Swank et al. eds., 1988) (finding that carefully located and designed forest roads only increase mean streamflow volumes and peak flow rates by approximately 15 percent);

Only one scientific study specifically addresses the hydrologic or water quality effects of ski areas in New England.[101] Hornbeck and Stuart did not have the benefit of direct data from a ski area; instead, they extrapolated from results of a strip cutting study at Hubbard Brook Experimental Forest, New Hampshire, to simulate ski trail clearing. They found that at Hubbard Brook, where one-third of the trees were removed, runoff increased several centimeters per year, but mainly during the summer low-flow period.[102] They argued that this was not a concern, as an increase in low flow did not tax the existing capacity of the stream channel. They noted, however, that ski trail clearing involves considerably more disturbance, including soil removal and soil compaction, which may lead to impervious surfaces and potentially more runoff in the short term. If care is taken, these problems can be minimized. Vigorous herbaceous growth on the trails can match the water demand of the original forest and thereby eliminate any effects on runoff once the ground cover is well established.[103]

Ski trails act as gaps in the canopy with a high efficiency of precipitation capture. The simple presence of an opening in the forest is known to increase the amount of precipitation falling there. There are two reasons for this increase. First, rain or snow falling on the forest canopy is intercepted by leaf or needle surfaces, and some of it evaporates back to the atmosphere without ever reaching the ground.[104] Second, the reduced wind in forest clearings favors increased deposition of snow.[105] The latter effect has spurred efforts to increase snowpacks by strategic forest clearing in western North America.[106]

Ski trails, like forest roads, frequently involve slope cutting and grading, and, once created, the trails are designed to be a permanent feature on the landscape.[107] Ski trails are more pervious than forest roads, but their infiltration capacity is frequently lessened by compaction and soil disturbance. To minimize erosion, ski trails have ditches and water bars to divert water off the trail, but these measures focus water for more rapid runoff elsewhere.

In addition to ski trails, most mountain resorts have one or more service roads leading up the mountains for maintenance vehicles in summer and snow grooming equipment in winter. Some resorts also have toll roads to their summits for tourist

---

C. Tague & L. Band, *Simulating the Impact of Road Construction and Forest Harvest on Hydrologic Response*, 26 Earth Surface Process & Land Forms 135, 149 (2001).

101 S. Hornbeck & G. Stuart, *When Ski Trails Are Cut Through Forestland, What Happens to Streamflow?*, Ski Area Mgmt. 34 (1976).

102 *Id.* at 35.

103 *Id.* at 34–36.

104 Dingman, *supra* note 12, at 399–413; Dunne & Leopold, *supra* note 6, at 152.

105 H.G. Wilm & E.G. Dunford, *Effect of Timber Cutting on Water Available for Streamflow From a Lodgepole Pine Forest*, USDA Tech. Bull. 968 (1948); Hornbeck et al., *supra* note 88; Troendle & King, *supra* note 95, at 1917.

106 *See generally* C.A. Troendle & J.R. Meiman, *Options for Harvesting Timber to Control Snowpack Accumulations*, 52 Proc. Western Snow Conf. 86 (1984).

107 Hornbeck & Stuart, *supra* note 101, at 36.

use in summer.[108] Often doubling as ski trails, these roads are more likely than ski trails to have side cuts and ditching as they switchback up the mountain. Roads are also likely to have a more compacted surface capable of generating overland flow compared to standard ski trails.

Several competing factors affect the timing and quantity of runoff from ski trails. In theory, the studies discussed above suggest that ski trails would receive more snow than adjacent forested areas. Moreover, increased solar radiation in forest openings would tend to increase snowmelt rates. In the New Hampshire strip cut experiment, Hornbeck and Stuart found that the cleared strips melted four to eight days sooner than the adjacent forest.[109] Further, ski trails and service roads delivered rain and snowmelt more efficiently to stream channels than adjacent permeable forest soils. On the other hand, compaction of snow on ski trails by skiers and by trail grooming activity may have offsetting effects, causing snow to melt more slowly and delaying runoff.[110] In addition, machine-made snow is intrinsically more dense and also tends to melt more slowly. For example, at a ski area in New Hampshire, complete snowpack loss occurred nineteen days later on slopes with snowmaking than without snowmaking.[111] Similarly, at a ski area in Montana, snow compaction delayed snowmelt runoff for seven to fourteen days.[112] In contrast, Chase's study found that there was little difference in the timing of runoff in streams draining a ski area and an adjacent watershed in Maine, though runoff amounts were not measured.[113] He attributed the synchronous melt to offsetting factors, presumably a balance between the greater solar radiation on the open ski trails and the slower melt rate of the compacted snow.[114] Because of these potentially offsetting effects, it is difficult to predict the timing and magnitude of the spring runoff in watersheds where alpine ski trails make up most of the forest openings.[115]

---

108 For example, Stowe Mountain Resort on Mount Mansfield allows visitors to travel near to the summit by way of a toll road, and Whiteface Mountain, one of the case studies in this book, also has a road to the summit.

109 Hornbeck & Stuart, *supra* note 101, at 35.

110 K.S. Fallon & P.K. Barten, A Study of the Natural and Artificial Snowpacks at a New Hampshire Ski Area 8–10 (1992) (unpublished M.F.S research project, Yale School of Forestry and Environmental Studies) (on file with author).

111 *Id.* at 9–10.

112 T.R. Grady et al., The Effects of Snow Compaction on Water Release and Sediment Yield, Bridger Bowl Ski Area Gallatin County, Montana, Montana University Water Resources Center Report No. 124, at 9 (1982).

113 J.E. Chase, The Physical Characteristics and Meltwater Output from a Show Cover Compacted By Ski-Area Operations 60 (1997) (unpublished M.Sc. Thesis, University of New Hampshire) (on file with author).

114 *Id.* at 77.

115 K.W. Birkeland, *The Effect of Ski Run Cutting and Artificial Snowmaking on Snow Water Accumulation at Big Sky Area, Montana,* PROC. WESTERN SNOW CONF. 137, 146 (1996).

The mountain environment presents additional complexities that influence water quantity. Some mountains receive a significant percentage of their precipitation as cloud water interception.[116] The effectiveness of cloud water interception decreases sharply when trees are removed.[117] In the Cascade Range in Oregon, loss of cloudwater interception balanced the decrease in evapotranspiration after logging at two catchments.[118] Another influence on water quality is topographic complexity in the mountain environment, which affects the capture and redistribution of snow. In a mountain watershed in southwestern Idaho, the snow-water equivalent varied substantially among various topographic settings that represented zones of snow accumulation or depletion through drifting.[119] High winds in an alpine environment may also affect water quantity, but little is known about the effectiveness of snow capture on ski trails that tend to be aligned along steep vertical gradients, with openings at either end that may serve as "wind corridors." In the windy alpine environment, the "lay of the land" relative to prevailing winds may outweigh forest opening patterns in dictating snow deposition; snow is scoured from the windward side and deposits on the leeward side. Tuckerman's Ravine in New Hampshire provides a classic example of this phenomenon. Snow from windswept Mt. Washington accumulates to great depth in the ravine and may remain until late summer.[120]

A final aspect of hydrological effects to consider is stream water extractions. The mountain resort usually turns to its own streams and/or ponds to supply its operational water needs.[121] Much of this water demand comes during winter and summer periods of the year, when supply is most limited.[122] Snowmaking is the most publicized water demand and will be discussed in the next section. Increasingly, mountain resorts are becoming four-season facilities and water demands are becoming year-round as well.[123] Water use for residential and resort facilities may be small compared to demand for snowmaking in winter, but summer water use is on the rise for landscaping, swimming pools, and in particular, golf

116 Black, *supra* note 2, at 100–01.

117 Jones, *supra* note 80, at 2623.

118 *Id.* at 2622–23.

119 D. Marks et al., *Simulating Snowmelt Processes During Rain-on-Snow over a Semi-Arid Mountain Basin*, 32 Annals Glaciology 195 (2001).

120 *See* L. Waterman & G. Waterman, Forest & Crag (1989) (discussing conditions on Mt. Washington); *see also* Tuckerman Ravine, http://www.tuckerman.org/tuckerman/tuckerman.htm (last visited Apr. 16, 2002) ("This large glacial cirque, with its bowl-like form, collects snow blowing off the Presidential Range. Snow averages 55 feet in the deepest spot . . . .").

121 OnTheSnow.com, It's Our Turn, Jan. 4, 2002, http://www.onthesnow.com (no longer available, copy on file with author).

122 *Id.* ("Killington . . . used to consume so much water from Roaring Brook that the stream would dry to a trickle.").

123 *See* J. Pelley, *States Combat Ski Resort Pollution*, 35 J. Envtl. Sci. & Tech. 60 A (2001) (discussing the expansion of ski resorts to encompass condominiums, golf courses, and second homes).

courses.[124] These summer water demands stress small mountain streams that are already at their lowest flows of the year.[125]

Although the mountain environment is the primary focus of this chapter, it is important to keep in mind that activities in the mountains have repercussions downstream. The mountain environment is the headwater environment. Perturbations to the hydrologic cycle in the mountains are transmitted to the landscape downstream, whether it be increased flood peaks, increased frequency of high-flow events, or excessive winter water withdrawals. The environment downstream of a mountain resort is often a resort community, which may have development issues of its own. Flood peaks that may be enhanced by mountain development could cause or exacerbate flooding in mountain valleys.[126]

Snowmaking

Machine-made snow has unique effects on the hydrology of mountain streams. The earliest attempts at snowmaking were in the late 1940's, and the practice became common by the 1960's as a means to ensure snow cover for an increasingly popular ski industry. Improvements and efficiencies were continually realized as the art of snowmaking spread. Even resorts located in usually reliable snow areas like the Rocky Mountains and the Alps have recently made large investments in snowmaking. In northeastern North America snowmaking is a mainstay of the business.[127] Snowmaking starts in October or November to allow early season skiing and ensure good snow conditions during the December holiday period. In February, snowmaking activity usually drops off, but the accumulated snow allows the ski season to extend well into April and sometimes May or June.[128]

Machine-made snow is produced when compressed air is introduced to a stream of pumped water, breaking the water into fine droplets and forcibly ejecting it through a nozzle.[129] The fine mist of water droplets readily freezes into fine, dense crystals.[130] Because water needs a nucleus to induce the formation of ice crystals, early snowmaking relied on impurities in the water or air, or existing ice crystals

---

124 *Id.*

125 *See id.*

126 For an overview of secondary development issues, see Jonathan Isham & Jeff Polubinski, *Killington Mountain Resort: A Case Study of 'Green' Expansion in Vermont*, 26 VT. L. REV. 565 (2002).

127 *See* Vermont Ski Area Association, Vermont Snowmaking Facts, http://www. skivermont. com/environment/Snowmkg.html (last visited Apr. 16, 2002).

128 *See, e.g.*, Killington, Ltd., Killington has the longest season in eastern North America, http://www.killington.com (last visited Sept. 12, 2002).

129 Laurie Lynn Fischer, *There's No Business Like Snow Business*, RUTLAND HERALD, Jan. 8, 2001.

130 GoSki.com & American Skiing Company, Everything You Ever Wanted to Know About Snowmaking, http://www.goski.com/news/snowmake.htm (last visited Apr. 1, 2002).

to serve as the nucleus.[131] Snowmakers have found they can increase the efficiency of the process, and make snow at higher temperatures (up to minus 0.5 degrees Centigrade, or 31 degrees Fahrenheit), by adding nucleating material to the water at the source. Commonly, the nucleating material is a protein isolated from cultured bacteria. The structure of the protein offers a high density of nucleation sites.[132]

Snowmaking in Northeastern North America

Snowmaking has become such an integral part of mountain resort operations in northeastern North America that the water source for snowmaking is often at the heart of resort development or expansion plans. The water source is generally at the bottom of the mountain, so considerable pumping capacity is required. Typically, the streams at the base of mountain developments are too small to serve this demand easily, yet the cost of pumping water from a larger source down-valley is at times prohibitive.[133] One of the primary concerns in snowmaking water withdrawals is maintaining sufficient streamflow to protect overwintering fish eggs and macroinvertebrates. Some fish, including trout, spawn in the fall and deposit their eggs in gravel stream bottoms.[134] If flows become too low, the eggs are at risk of freezing. Most states, including Vermont, make new development or expansion contingent upon maintaining a minimum streamflow, typically the February Median Flow (FMF).[135] Winter streamflow generally reaches its lowest level in February, so biologists assume that fish habitat and spawning grounds are adapted to these low levels.[136] Snowmaking is prohibited if flow falls below the FMF.[137]

To help meet snowmaking water demands from small mountain streams, mountain resorts commonly construct storage reservoirs in order to continue snowmaking when streamflow falls below the FMF.[138] Siting of storage reservoirs

131 York Snow, Inc., The Science of Making Snow, http://www.snowmax.com/education/ index.htm (last visited Apr. 16, 2002).

132 *Id.*

133 *See* OnTheSnow.com, Daily New England News, Jan. 4, 2002, http://www.onthesnow.com. ("Nearly two decades of battling over snowmaking and land development eventually lead to a $5 million solution. The resort [Killington] completed construction of a 1.8 mile pipeline for snowmaking water in Sept. 2000.") (no longer available, copy on file with author).

134 C.E. Cushing & J.D. Allan, Streams: Their Ecology & Life 69 (2001).

135 Isham & Polubinski, *supra* note 126, at 571 n.48; *see also* Vermont Ski Area Association, *supra* note 127 ("The February median Flow (FMF) standard was adopted as part of the water withdrawal rules by the [Vermont] Legislature in 1996 and is the strictest in the nation.").

136 Vermont Ski Area Association, *supra* note 127.

137 *Id.* ("Vermont ski areas now either comply with FMF or must meet FMF when expanding snowmaking operation.").

138 See the discussion in chapter 17 *infra* about Killington's use of Woodward Reservoir.

can be a problematic issue in mountain resort permitting,[139] due to aesthetic considerations, the need to avoid wetlands and the stream corridor itself, and the scarcity of suitably flat terrain away from the channel.[140] Storage reservoirs also may contribute to water quality problems, an issue addressed in the next section.[141] Where economically practical, water for snowmaking may be pumped from a reservoir outside the basin. This interbasin transfer of water increases the overall amount of water the mountain stream system must ultimately convey, and thus may exacerbate the effects of development on spring peak flows.

As noted in the previous section, snow compaction from skier traffic delays snowmelt. Unlike natural snow, machine-made snow is intrinsically more dense, and thus tends to melt more slowly.[142] The greater depth and density of snow on the trail increases the time necessary for the snowpack to ripen, also delaying the onset of melt.[143] As spring progresses, the melting snow receives increased solar radiation and melts more rapidly.[144] These rapid melt rates and large snow packs should lead to greater flow peaks. However, because ski trails typically comprise 20 percent or less of a watershed, and only some of the trails have snowmaking, the effect on the magnitude and timing of peak flows may be difficult to discern. As mentioned, Chase found no difference in the timing of runoff, but he did not measure flow rates.[145] There have been no definitive studies that address this question.[146]

Snowmaking in the Western United States

In western North America, snowmaking covers a lower percentage of the terrain but resorts are larger, so overall water use for snowmaking may rival usage in the East. In the West, water withdrawals are subject less to environmental regulations than to local water rights provisions.[147] Water rights are needed only for consumptive use, i.e. water withdrawn from a stream and not returned.[148] To determine the consump-

---

139 *Id.*

140 For an example of a legal struggle over the potential for such an effect, see *Killington, Ltd. v. State*, in which Killington challenged a ruling by the Vermont Environmental Board which denied an application to build a snowmaking pond in a fragile area. Killington, Ltd. v. State of Vermont and Town of Mendon, 164 Vt. 253, 668 A.2d 1278 (1995).

141 See *infra* note 190 and accompanying text.

142 See *supra* notes 111–13 and accompanying text.

143 Chase, *supra* note 113, at 80.

144 Fallon & Barten, *supra* note 110, at 10.

145 Chase, *supra* note 113, at 60.

146 *See* Birkeland, *supra* note 115, at 146.

147 For a general discussion of water issues in the western United States, see M. Reisner, Cadillac Desert, the American West and Its Disappearing Water (1993).

148 L.M. Eisel et al., *Estimated Consumptive Loss From Man-Made Snow*, 24 Water Resources Bull., 815, 815 (1988) (finding that ski areas reduce the amount of water rights needed by calculating consumptive loss from snowmaking).

tive loss from snowmaking, Colorado researchers performed two assessments.[149] The first study determined that about a 6 percent consumptive loss occurred during the snowmaking process.[150] This initial loss represents water that left the snowmaking gun but evaporated or sublimated before reaching the ground.[151] The second study combined hydrologic modeling and measurements at six Colorado ski areas to determine that an additional 7 to 33 percent consumptive loss occurred from the watershed.[152] This watershed loss represents water that evaporated or sublimated from the snowpack or, as the snow remained into the growing season, was consumed by evapotranspiration.[153] In northeastern North America, the humid climate and frequent rainfall limits all categories of these consumptive losses. Therefore, in the East, most of the water withdrawn from streams in the winter will add to runoff in the spring, increasing the potential for high spring flow peaks.

The Potential Effects of Mountain Development on Water Quality

As with hydrologic effects, there has been limited study of the water quality effects of mountain resorts. To estimate water quality effects, it is necessary to draw from the results of forest clearing, and urbanization studies. Many studies have linked the soil disturbance associated with forest clearing to increased soil erosion and sediment loading to streams.[154] In extreme cases, poorly-managed forest clearing and road construction on steep slopes, followed by heavy rains, may result in landslides.[155] Direct runoff over impervious forest road surfaces is another mode of

---

149 *Id.*; L.M. Eisel et al., *Estimated Runoff From Man-Made Snow*, 26 Water Resources Bull. 519, 519 (1990) (studying the consumptive loss that occurs to man-made snow particles while they reside in the snow pack until spring snowmelt).

150 Eisel, *supra* note 148, at 818.

151 *Id.* at 815.

152 Eisel, *supra* note 149, at 520, 525.

153 *Id.* at 519.

154 R.C. Sidle et al., Hillslope Stability and Land Use 9, 73–74 (1985).

155 D.R. Montgomery, *Road Surface Drainage, Channel Initiation, and Slope Instability*, 30 Water Res. Research 1925, 1931–32 (1994); J. Sessions et al., *Road Location and Construction Practices: Effects of Landslide Frequency and Size in Oregon Coast Range*, 2 W. J. Applied Forestry 119, 121–22 (1987); F.J. Swanson & C.T. Dyrness, *Impact of Clear-Cutting and Road Construction on Soil Erosion by Landslides in the Western Cascade Range*, Oregon, 3 Geology 393, 394–95 (1975) (focusing on the H.J. Andrews experimental forest in the Western Cascade Mountains, and finding that roads contribute "about half of the total management impact" and that those impacts were most severe during the first few storms after the initial road construction). Studies have also found that forest removal can release nutrients such as nitrate and calcium due to interruption of biological uptake. *See, e.g.*, M. Liddle, Recreation Ecology 82 (1997) (citing a 1974 study that found a significantly higher level of nitrogen and potassium in areas trampled by a pathway). *See also* C.W. Martin et al., *Effects of Forest Clear-cutting in New England Stream*

sediment movement.[156] However, the water quality problems specifically linked to mountain resort development are not limited to sediment production, transport and deposition. They also include septic system leakage or failure, salt contamination from roadway de-icing, heavy metals and petroleum derivatives from vehicles, and contamination from fertilizers and pesticides, especially if the resort operates a golf course or has extensive landscaping.[157]

Mountain environments, with steep slopes and thin soils, have limited capacity to counter water quality degradation caused by development. An activity or disturbance that may have little or no environmental effect in flat or gently sloping terrain may have a large effect in the mountains.[158] A common water quality problem at mountain resorts is sediment transport and deposition.[159] Some mountain resort managers feel that if they can solve their sediment problem, they have solved their water quality problem. Why is this mostly true, and what is so harmful about sediment? Regardless of whether the sediment source is erosion of disturbed surfaces within the watershed, sloughing of stream banks as a channel adjusts to a new flow regime, or entrainment of sand applied to roadways and parking areas after snow clearing, sediment deposition negatively affects aquatic communities by degrading habitat on the stream substrate.[160] Fine sediments tend to settle in the slower-moving waters of stream pools, effectively clogging the gravel substrate, which provides refuge for macroinvertebrates and amphibians, and shelter for fish eggs after spawning.[161] One study clearly demonstrated the interrelationship among impervious surface, sediment concentrations, and species richness.[162] The study found that as the percentage of impervious surface in a watershed increases, species richness declines.[163] Further study of lowland environments has shown that increasing development of a watershed leads to

---

Chemistry, 13 J. Envtl. Quality 204, 204–08 (1984); C.W. Martin & R.S. Pierce, *Clear-Cutting Patterns Affect Nitrate and Calcium in Streams of New Hampshire*, 78 J. Forestry 268, 271–72 (May 1980).

156 L.M. Reid & T. Dunne, *Sediment Production From Road Surfaces*, 20 Water Res. Research 1753, 1753 (1984); A.D. Ziegler & T.W. Giambelluca, *Importance of Rural Roads as Source Areas for Runoff in Mountainous Areas of Northern Thailand*, 196 J. Hydrology 204, 205–06 (1997).

157 *See* Pelley, *supra* note 123, at 60 A.

158 See *supra* notes 26–40 and accompanying text, describing hydrologic factors associated with mountain/high slope runoff.

159 *See* R.A. Smith, R.B. Alexander & M. Gordon, *Water Quality Trends in the Nation's Rivers*, 235 Science 1607–15 (1987).

160 *Id.*

161 See *supra* note 4 and accompanying text, discussing pools and riffles in running streams.

162 T.R. Scheuler, *Minimizing the Impact of Golf Courses on Streams*, 1(2) Watershed Protection Tech. 73 (1994).

163 *Id.* at 75.

degradation of fish habitat.[164] Sediment also may carry phosphate, metals, and organic contaminants such as pesticides into streams.

Construction of resort facilities, ski trails, and service roads disturbs the land and creates the potential for sediment transport.[165] Sediment production can be minimized by implementing measures such as sediment fencing, water bars, ditching, and soil stabilization through vegetation.[166] Nonetheless, the steep slopes and frequent storms in the mountains make some erosion, which is a natural process, unavoidable.[167] The potential for erosion is greatest immediately after disturbance and declines rapidly with revegetation. However, this threat endures with the creation of impervious or compacted surfaces, which allow more overland flow, and thus a greater potential for erosion, compared to the undeveloped landscape.

One method used to assess watershed disturbance and sedimentation potential is the Cumulative Watershed Effects (CWE) approach.[168] This approach has been applied at mountain resorts, most notably in the Lake Tahoe region.[169] The CWE approach characterizes development activity within a watershed and gives each activity a relative rating of its potential to generate overland flow and sediment. For example, a given area of ski trail might be assigned one-half the effect of the same area of parking lot. The land area of each activity is weighted by its effect factor, and they are all summed to yield an overall effect factor for the watershed. Certain threshold values of this factor are regarded as an upper limit of what a watershed can withstand and are used as a guide for planning purposes. Variability in site conditions and uncertainty in the outcome of management activities, however, often limit the effectiveness of the CWE approach.[170]

Some researchers have studied erosion and sediment production at mountain resorts. Ries studied erosion damage on ski trails in the Black Forest of Germany, a glaciated landscape with topography, elevations, and climate similar to the

---

164 A.L. Moscrip & D.R. Montgomery, *Urbanization, Flood Frequency, and Salmon Abundance in Puget Low Streams*, 38 J. AMER. WATER RESOURCES ASSN. 1289, 1295 (1997).

165 *See, e.g.*, *In re:* Killington, Ltd., No. 1R0813-5, Findings of Fact and Conclusions of Law and Order (Vt. Dis. Env. Comm. #1, Aug. 25, 1997) (discussing concerns associated with mountain development).

166 See text following note 11 *supra*.

167 C.A. Troendle & W.K. Olsen, *Potential Effects of Timber Harvest and Water Management on Streamflow Dynamics and Sediment Transport*, USDA FOREST SERVICE GEN. TECHNICAL REP. RM-247, 34–41 (1993).

168 L.H. MacDonald, *Evaluating and Managing Cumulative Effects: Process and Constraints*, 26 ENVTL. MGMT. 299, 300–01 (2000).

169 *See generally* J. Cobourn, *An Application of Cumulative Watershed Effects Analysis on The Eldorado National Forests in California*, PROC. OF SYMPOSIUM ON HEADWATERS HYDROLOGY AMER. WATER RES. ASS'N 449 (1989); J. Cobourn, *Using Cumulative Watershed Effects Analysis for Land Use Management in Ski Areas*, PROC. ANNUAL SUMMER SYMPOSIUM OF THE AMER. WATER RES. ASS'N 197 (1994).

170 L.H. MacDonald, *supra* note 168, at 299.

mountainous areas of New York and New England.[171] Grading and hollow filling during original trail and lift construction, combined with the action of trail grooming equipment and skis traversing slopes with minimal snow cover, caused erosion and downslope creep of soil material. The main mechanism of creep was needle ice solifluction, whereby moisture freezing in the soil pushes soil grains up and out, followed by redeposition in a lower slope position. This downslope movement reached a maximum of five to seven centimeters per year in artificial fill areas that were poorly vegetated and subject to the additional disruption of cattle grazing in summer.[172] At ski areas in northern Japan, downslope soil movement also has been a problem, because grasses sown after trail construction fail to establish, leaving unvegetated patches.[173] Soil movement in Japan is attributed to erosion during snowmelt. Titus and Tsuyuzaki contrasted the Japanese condition with a ski area in Washington State, where trail construction involved less mechanical slope contouring. Grassy vegetation has established itself well on the Washington ski slopes, and erosion has been minimal.[174] During spring snowmelt, Chase made qualitative observations of sediment-laden streamwater running off a mountain resort in Maine, compared to clear water in a nearby stream.[175]

As mountain resorts move toward greater four-season use, fertilizer applied to lawns around condominiums and resort facilities may lead to increased concentrations of nitrate and phosphate in streams.[176] Naturally occurring nitrate is also released from soils following soil disturbances, such as logging.[177] Fertilizer containing nitrogen and phosphorus may also be applied to ski trails to maintain the herbaceous cover.[178] Nitrogen and phosphorus are limiting nutrients in aquatic ecosystems. Increased nitrogen and phosphorus supplied to streams and ponds promotes unsightly algal growth.[179] As excessive amounts of algae accumulate on stream or lake bottoms, the breakdown of this material by microrganisms consumes oxygen and may lead to dissolved oxygen levels unacceptably low for desired macroinvertebrates and fish.[180] Lawns and golf courses, in particular, may be sources of nutrient runoff from fertilizer and also may be sources of pesticide

---

171 J.B. Ries, *Landscape Damage by Skiing at the Schauinsland in the Black Forest, Germany*, 16(1) MOUNTAIN RES. & DEV. 27, 27 (1996).

172 *Id.* at 30.

173 S. Tsuyuzaki, *Species Composition and Soil Erosion on a Ski Area in Hokkaido, Northern Japan*, 14 ENVTL. MGMT. 203, 204–06 (1990).

174 J.H. Titus & S. Tsuyuzaki, *Ski Slope Vegetation at Snoqualmie Pass, Washington State, USA and a Comparison with Ski Slope Vegetation in Temperate Coniferous Forest Zones*, 13 (2) ECOLOGICAL RES. 97 (1998).

175 Chase, *supra* note 113, at 60, 77.

176 DUNNE & LEOPOLD, *supra* note 6, at 757–58.

177 Martin & Pierce, *supra* note 155, at 278; Martin et al., *supra* note 155, at 209.

178 Hornbeck & Stuart, *supra* note 101, at 36.

179 DUNNE & LEOPOLD, *supra* note 6, at 755–60.

180 *Id.* at 756.

runoff.[181] Recently, the town of Stowe, Vermont conditioned approval for a new golf course at the Stowe Mountain Resort on a very low pesticide application rate.[182] Conservation organizations such as Audubon International[183] have developed certification programs for golf courses that aim to protect the environment and provide wildlife habitat. Certification gives consumers information about the standards of environmental management met by the resort.

As mentioned earlier, the two most important water quality factors that affect fish habitat, aside from sediment load, are dissolved oxygen and water temperature. These two factors are related, in that colder water can hold more oxygen.[184] Some fish species, including brook trout, brown trout, and slimy sculpin, require cold, well-oxygenated waters.[185] Forest clearing for ski trails and other development allows sunlight to penetrate to the ground surface. Sunlight directly on a stream channel can have a dramatic heating effect.[186] When forested buffer strips are left along the stream channels, the temperature increase associated with forest clearing will be on the order of 1degree Centigrade, as opposed to up to 5 degrees Centigrade in an unbuffered clear cut.[187] The cascades and riffles of a mountain stream tend to keep it well aerated, which incorporates oxygen. A warming alone would threaten the trout population, but only a large input of nutrients could cause an oxygen-depleting algal bloom.[188] This could happen in a snowmaking reservoir, but it is unlikely in a mountain stream.[189]

De-icing salts applied to parking lots and resort roads readily run off to streams, and they also mobilize heavy metals,[190] as documented at a mountain resort in New Mexico.[191] Road and parking lot sanding provides a ready source of sediment to runoff waters.[192] Mountain resorts often must treat their own sewage, either with a wastewater treatment facility that discharges to a stream or a septic system that

181 Scheuler, *supra* note 162, at 73–75.

182 J. Dillon, *Stowe Deal Signed*, MONTPELIER TIMES ARGUS, June 13, 2001, at 1.

183 Audubon International, Audubon Cooperative Sanctuary Program for Golf Courses, http://www.auduboninternational.org/programs/acss/golf_certoverview.htm (last visited Feb. 18, 2008).

184 DUNNE & LEOPOLD, *supra* note 6, at 719.

185 CUSHING & ALLAN, *supra* note 134, at 68–69.

186 Hornbeck & Stuart, *supra* note 101, at 36.

187 *Id.*

188 *See* DUNNE & LEOPOLD, *supra* note 6, at 756.

189 *See id.* at 746 (discussing the importance of "turbulent mixing" in reaereation of oxygen depleted water).

190 *Id.* at 735–36 ("[T]he effects of several metals can be synergistic, and their effects can be aggravated by other ions in solution.").

191 J.R. Gosz, *Effects of Ski Area Development and Use on Stream Water Quality of the Santa Fe Basin, New Mexico*, 23 FOREST SCI. 167, 176–77 (1977); D.I. Moore et al., *Impact of a Ski Basin on a Mountain Watershed*, 10 WATER, AIR, & SOIL POLLUTION 81, 92 (1978).

192 *Id.*

discharges to ground water. Isolated mountainside or mountaintop facilities often have independent septic systems. Wastewater effluents pose the threat of leaking nutrients, *E. coli*, and other bacteria into adjacent streams.[193] White and Gosz, however, found no difference in bacteria counts in a stream above and below a mountain resort in New Mexico.[194] Some resorts apply treated effluent to forested slopes to allow assimilation of the waste by natural processes.[195] Proposals at some mountain resorts to use sewage effluent as snowmaking water have not gained enough public acceptance to implement.

Another commonly cited environmental issue at mountain resorts is the so-called "iron seep," caused where groundwater containing dissolved iron seeps from the ground. When the iron is exposed to oxygen it deposits as a red stain. Although not in itself harmful, the iron staining is an aesthetic issue, and is often treated with crushed limestone. Iron seeps commonly occur where fill that contains iron is added and terrain is altered to induce a rise in groundwater levels, such as in the construction of a snowmaking pond. Depleted oxygen in the groundwater zone promotes the mobilization of iron.

Mountain resort streams and undeveloped streams alike share the water quality effects of regional air pollution. Eastern North America receives inputs of acidic compounds and mercury as a result of long-range transport from industrial areas further south and west.[196] Forested mountain environments are particularly susceptible to these pollutants, because mountains receive higher rainfall and cloud water interception, and the forest canopy is effective at scavenging pollutants from the atmosphere. The snowpack and falling snowflakes also are effective at scavenging pollutants from the air. Similarly, atmospheric mercury becomes incorporated in forest floor material, and when soil erosion occurs, high concentrations of mercury may be released to streamflow, especially during high-flow episodes.[197] A study on an acid-rain impacted stream in the Laurel Highlands of Pennsylvania showed that a mountain resort had no exacerbating effect on stream acidity.[198]

---

193 Gosz, *supra* note 191, at 170 (discussing nutrients leaking from area septic systems).

194 C.S. White et al., *Impact of Ski Basin on a Mountain Watershed*, 10 Water, Air & Soil Pollution 71, 78 (1978).

195 W. Forney et al., U.S. Geological Survey, Land Use Change and Effects on Water Quality and Ecosystem Health in the Lake Tahoe Basin, Nevada and California 7 (2001) (discussing the effects of "spray disposal of secondary-treated sewage effluent" on Heavenly Valley Creek), *available at* http://pubs.usgs.gov/of/of01-418/of01-418.pdf.

196 Black, *supra* note 2, at 320–21.

197 T. Scherbatskoy et al., *Factors Controlling Mercury Transport in an Upland Forested Catchment*, 105 Water, Air & Soil Pollution 427, 435–37 (1998).

198 W.E. Sharpe et al., *Causes of Acidification of Four Streams on Laurel Hill in Southwestern Pennsylvania*, 13(4) J. Envtl. Quality 619, 624–25 (1984).

Case Study: Mt. Mansfield

In September 2000, the U.S. Geological Survey, in collaboration with the Vermont Monitoring Cooperative and the University of Vermont, began a study to investigate the possible effect of a mountain resort on the timing and amount of runoff and sediment yield.[199] The study was modeled after the paired watershed approach, discussed earlier as the approach used in forest clearing studies. Researchers set up stream gages and sampling stations at two watersheds. (See Figure 4.3).

The West Branch watershed (11.7 square kilometers) contains the entire Stowe Mountain Resort. The adjacent Ranch Brook watershed (9.6 square kilometers) is nearly undeveloped. The two watersheds have similar climate, vegetation, topography, aspect, soils, and geology, but differ in land use. A state highway bisects the West Branch watershed (closed above the resort parking lot in winter), with part of the mountain resort on either side of the road. About 17 percent of the watershed has been cleared for ski trails, two base lodge facilities, and some vacation homes. The Ranch Brook watershed is completely forested, except for a network of cross-country ski trails and a short section of the auto toll road to the Mt. Mansfield summit ridge. The ski area was established in the 1940s, so the land use change was well-established prior to this study. However, the first three years of data collected by Wemple et al. serve as a baseline from which to evaluate effects of a major expansion of the resort which started in 2004.[200]

Streamflow is recorded every five minutes at the two gages. Samples are collected periodically for analysis of water chemistry and suspended sediment, particularly during high-flow periods such as snowmelt. Precipitation is measured at the West Branch gage and at other points along elevational transects, including the summit ridge (National Weather Service station).

Annual streamflow per unit area was 18 to 36 percent greater in the West Branch basin.[201] Although this difference supports the hypothesis that development could increase runoff, the magnitude is too great to be attributed solely to the mountain resort. The Mount Mansfield runoff is anomalously high on a plot of water yield changes from paired watershed studies examining forest harvesting in the eastern U.S. (See Figure 4.4).

---

199 James Shanley is principal investigator of this project for the USGS on the initial Vermont Monitoring Cooperative grant, and has been investigating hydrology and water quality. Beverley Wemple is principal investigator on subsequent grants from the Vermont Water Resources and Lake Studies Center for suspended sediment research and hydrologic modeling, and from EPSCoR (the U.S. government's Experimental Program to Stimulate Competitive Research) for evaluating the impacts of high elevation development on watershed processes.

200 B. Wemple, J.B. Shanley, J. Denner, D. Ross, and K. Mills, *Hydrology and Water Quality in Two Mountain Basins of the Northeastern US: Assessing Baseline Conditions and Effects of Ski Area Development*, 21 HYDROLOGICAL PROCESSES 1639 (2007).

201 *Id.*

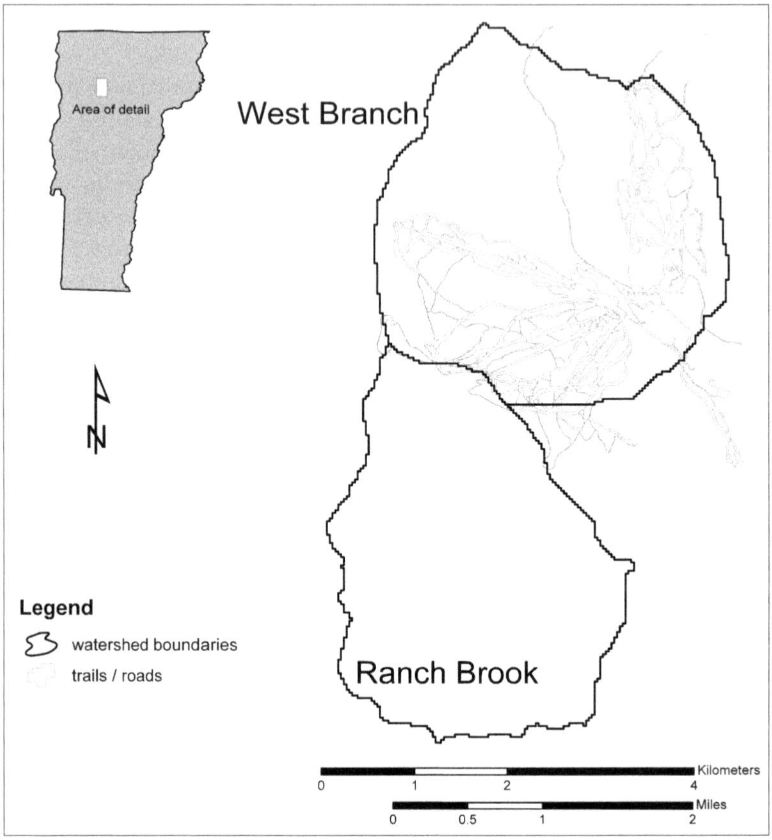

Figure 4.3 Outline of Study Watersheds on the East Slope of Mt. Mansfield, Vermont

Note: West Branch contains the entire Stowe Mountain Resort, while Ranch Brook is relatively pristine.

The large difference may be caused by natural differences in precipitation patterns, snow redistribution, groundwater contributions from outside the surface topographic boundary of the watershed, and other factors. Apart from the greater runoff at West Branch, the streamflow characteristics of the two watersheds are quite similar. The shapes of the hydrographs (graph of streamflow versus time) are similar, and the timing of initial rise and peak flow are relatively synchronous.

During the 2001 snowmelt period, unit area flows were higher for West Branch than for Ranch Brook during the initial melt, but became nearly equal for the two sites as snowmelt progressed toward peak flow. (See Figure 4.5).

Late in the snowmelt period, after the peak, flow at West Branch again became greater than that at Ranch Brook. The high diurnal peaks on May 1–4 and the

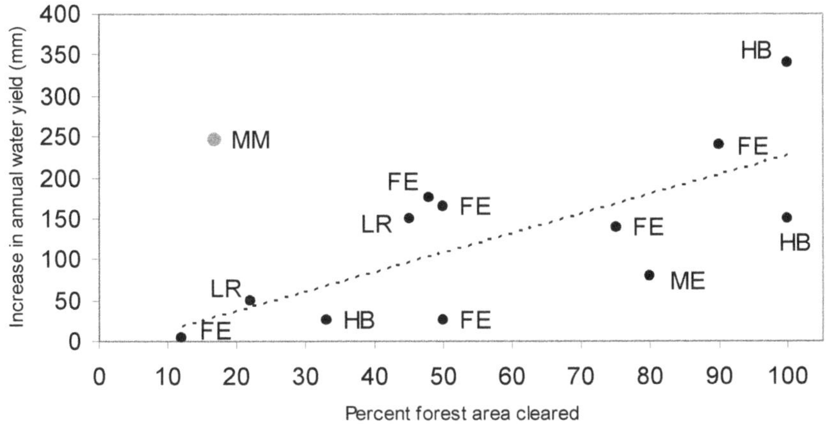

Figure 4.4 Water Yield Increases Following Forest Harvest in Paired Watershed Studies in the Northeastern U.S., with Water Yield Difference in Mt. Mansfield Case Study (MM) Described Herein

Note: As summarized in Hornbeck et al. (1993): HB, Hubbard Brook Experimental Forest, NH; LR, Leading Ridge, PA; FE, Fernow Experimental Forest, WV; ME, Marcel Experimental Forest, MN. Some studies have multiple watersheds.

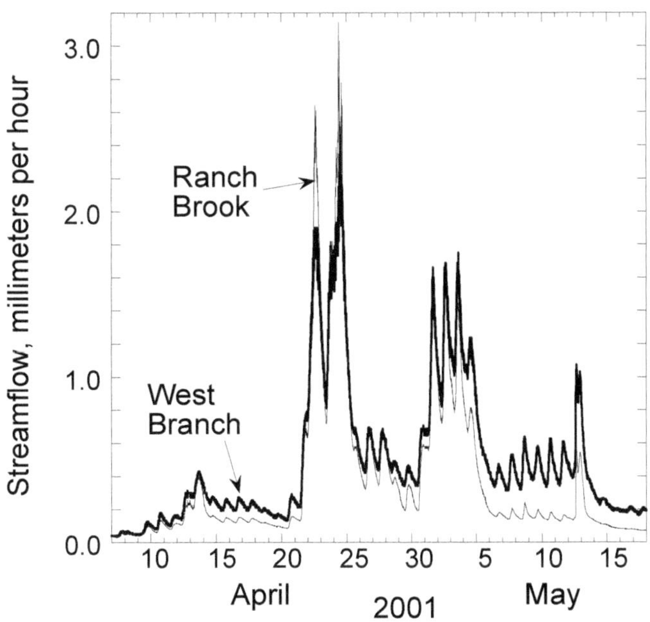

Figure 4.5 Comparison of West Branch and Ranch Brook Streamflow Hydrographs During Snowmelt, 2001

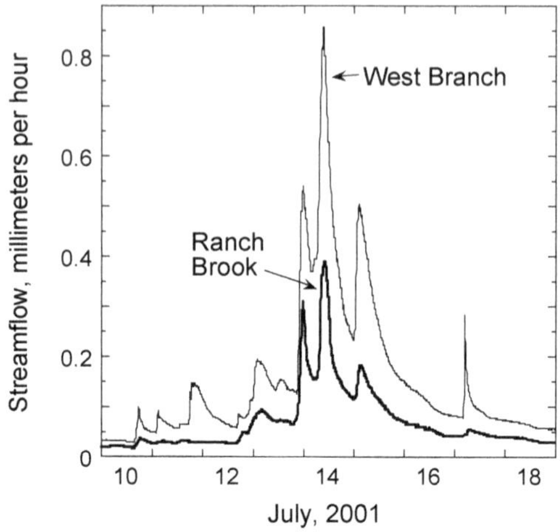

Figure 4.6 Comparison of West Branch and Ranch Brook Streamflow Hydrographs During a Series of Rainstorms, July 2001

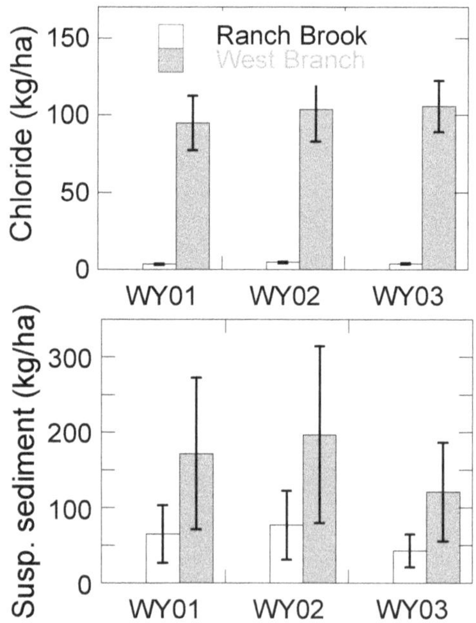

Figure 4.7 Stream Fluxes of Chloride and Suspended Sediment at West Branch and Ranch Brook Gages, Water Years 2001, 2002, and 2003

Note: WY stands for water year, which starts in October (e.g., WY 2001 runs from October 2000 through September 2001).

sustained flow differential throughout May clearly showed that the snowpack persisted at West Branch and contributed meltwater to streamflow for a much longer time than at Ranch Brook, probably due in part to machine-made snow on the mountain resort trails. These results are consistent with the findings of Chase, discussed earlier, of synchronous hydrograph peaks (both watersheds peaked on April 24), and those of Fallon and Barten, who found sustained melt runoff from machine-made snowpacks, which lasted nearly three weeks later into spring than compacted natural snowpacks.[202]

There was somewhat more variability in the response to summer storms. Although some of this difference may result from different rainfall patterns in the two basins, there was a consistent tendency for a sharper and more rapid response at the developed West Branch basin. Summer rains tend to be high-intensity storms that produce relatively small amounts of streamflow because most of the rain is absorbed by dry summer soils; this was especially true during the drought-like summer of 2001. The larger and more rapid response to small storms at West Branch, most notably on July 10, 11, and 17, may be a result of rapid runoff over near-stream impervious surfaces associated with development in that basin. (See Figure 4.6).

One clear effect of the development in the West Branch watershed was the presence of elevated sodium and chloride concentrations in streamwater. The annual amount of chloride passing through the West Branch gage was more than 10 times that at the Ranch Brook gage, and can be attributed to de-icing salt application to the access road at the resort. (See Figure 4.7).

Concentrations are elevated year-round, implying the salt has entered the groundwater aquifer which provides base flow. Suspended sediment moving off the West Branch basin was about double the amount moving off the Ranch Brook basin. This difference is also in the direction one might expect, implying more sediment is mobilized from the mountain resort compared to the natural forest, but the difference was not statistically significant.

Long-Term Research and Monitoring on Mt. Mansfield

What has drawn scientific researchers to Mount Mansfield? As the highest mountain in Vermont, and centrally located between its largest city and the state capital, Mt. Mansfield is a highly visible icon to an outdoor-loving and environmentally aware population. Since 1993, the Vermont Monitoring Cooperative (VMC) has provided a framework for research on State forested lands on Mt. Mansfield. The VMC fosters research on the dynamics of forested ecosystems and how they are affected by both natural change and human management. VMC collaborators include scientists and students from universities and colleges in Vermont and other northeastern states, state- and federal-agency resource specialists, and scientists from independent research institutes.

202 *See* Chase, *supra* note 113, at 60; Fallon & Barten, *supra* note 110, at 10.

Long-term monitoring and research is critical to understanding ecosystem processes and the role of changing climate conditions, natural disturbance, and human management on the structure and function of ecosystems (Lovett et al., 2007). The existence of long-term monitoring and research support through VMC and the presence of an alpine ski resort on the eastern slopes of Mt. Mansfield have led to a number of research and educational efforts focusing on the alpine ski resort development and operations. Research studies include the UVM-USGS study on mountain development effects on streamflow and water quality described in this chapter, as well as studies of the effects of the ski area on habitat fragmentation and biological resources, including salamanders and birds (described in Chapter 5). Educational efforts build on the synergy afforded by long-term research and monitoring and the existence of the ski resort and include regular courses offered through the University of Vermont in mountain geomorphology and ecology and alpine resource management and periodic field intensives by regional high school and college students and educators.

Sources: G.M. Lovett et al., Who Needs Environmental Monitoring? 5(5) FRONTIERS IN ECOLOGY AND THE ENVIRONMENT 253–260 (2007). For more information on the Vermont Monitoring Cooperative, visit http://sal.snr.uvm.edu/vmc/ .

Figure 4.8 Eastern Slopes of Mt. Mansfield, Vermont, and Ski Trails of the Stowe Mountain Resort

Photo: B. Wemple

Science as a Basis for Management Practice and Public Policy

This chapter has reviewed scientific studies on the hydrology of mountain streams, the effects of forest clearing on streamflow, the effects of forest roads on hydrology and sediment production, and the effects of impervious surfaces in a watershed to the biological health of its stream. Few of the studies discussed were conducted at mountain resorts, thus there is some question as to their applicability to the mountain resort setting. Studies based on logging operations or urbanization cannot fully represent the situation at a mountain resort, but study results provide guidelines that can be used by regulatory officials and land- and water-resource managers. In the absence of more specific data, extrapolating the results of these studies to mountain resorts is a reasonable next step. For example, study after study shows that forest removal increases water yield and causes an initial flush of sediment and nutrients to streams.[203] These changes lead to degradation of aquatic habitat, water quality, and stream aesthetics. With this awareness as a starting point, a resort can take measures to minimize, mitigate, and possibly eliminate these adverse effects.

We conclude with two brief examples of scientific considerations that have been useful to regulators. These examples involve Total Maximum Daily Load (TMDL) limits[204] set by states in cases affecting mountain resorts. A TMDL is set for a given pollutant based on scientific understanding of the maximum amount of the pollutant that an ecosystem can withstand. A mountain resort in Vermont has had recurring violations of state water quality standards due to excessive sediment and nutrient runoff, and high stream flow caused by removal of streamside vegetation. As a condition of its permit to expand, the resort must implement a TMDL for sediment. This marks the first time a TMDL has been set for a mountain resort.[205] A second TMDL case indirectly involves the ski industry—a TMDL for phosphorous in a reservoir near Frisco, Colorado. As a result, mountain resorts wishing to expand are held to their existing levels of phosphorous runoff.[206] The National Ski Area Association is advocating a voluntary approach to meet this type of water quality standard.[207]

Conclusions

High-elevation mountain environments are among the world's least resilient ecosystems. The very qualities that draw people to mountain ecosystems render them susceptible to adverse effects from development. These characteristics include: the steep slopes that attract skiers and hikers, but promote erosion; the cool temperatures that bring abundant snows, but which create a harsh environment for vegetation; the thin soils that give way to spectacular rock outcrops, but provide little buffering capacity to store water or pollutants; and the beautiful mountain streams, whose balance of pools and riffles is easily upset by inputs

---

203 *See, e.g.*, Hewlett & Helvey, *supra* note 93; Hornbeck et al., *supra* note 88.

204 Total Maximum Daily Loads. U. S. Environmental Protection Agency, http://www.epa.gov/owow/tmdl/ (last visited Feb. 19, 2008).

205 Pelley, *supra* note 123, at 60A–61A.

206 *Id.* at 61A.

207 *Id.*

of too much water, or too much sediment, or both. In some regions, such as the Rocky Mountains of the western United States, alpine areas are the prime source of water for downstream use by wildlife and humans, and maintaining its quantity and quality is imperative.

Despite the importance of mountain stream systems and their vulnerability to mountain development, the effect of mountain development on hydrology is under-studied and poorly understood. In compiling this chapter, the authors have made numerous inferences from research on the effects of forest harvesting and the effects of urbanization on streamflow, sediment export, and water quality. Research on mountain development *per se*, with a few notable exceptions, simply does not exist. Therefore, this overview is primarily a qualitative treatment, supported where possible by research of the authors and others. As the pressure on mountain resources continues to grow rapidly, the need for more rigorous scientific study grows along with it. Lawmakers, policy makers, and land managers all need a greater scientific foundation on which to base their decisions on development in the mountain environment.

Chapter 5
Effects of Mountain Resorts on Wildlife

Allan M. Strong, Christopher C. Rimmer, Kent P. McFarland
and Kimberly Hagen[1]

Introduction

Mountain ecosystems are characterized by harsh climatic conditions, low productivity, low species diversity, and high endemism. These ecosystems are increasingly subject to a wide range of anthropogenic disturbances such as mercury deposition, acid precipitation, construction of wind and communication towers, and climate change. Although few data exist concerning the resilience of these ecosystems, thin, poorly buffered soils suggest that these are fragile environments. Consequently, overlaying additional development pressure on an already sensitive ecosystem would be expected to produce substantial changes in species composition and ecosystem processes.

This chapter begins with a review of selected species' responses to natural disturbances and a discussion of whether or not these cases enable predictions of wildlife responses to anthropogenic disturbances. It examines anthropogenic disturbances in the context of the three most important effects of mountain resorts on wildlife habitat: habitat loss, habitat fragmentation, and habitat modification. These three aspects of human-induced habitat change are by no means mutually exclusive, but provide a convenient means for subdividing our review. The chapter then discusses a spatial analysis of the effects of habitat fragmentation in two ski areas in Vermont, quantifying the hypothetical population declines associated with habitat loss, fragmentation, and modification. In the next section, we assess certain species for risk of population decline based on three life history characteristics: home range size, gap-crossing ability, and edge sensitivity. We evaluate the broad effects of mountain resorts on wildlife populations at a landscape level, then analyze the cumulative effects of mountain resort development on certain wildlife populations. Finally, we recommend local management practices that may mitigate the negative effects of ski trails on high elevation wildlife populations. We conclude that careful long-term and landscape scale planning may minimize conflicts over

---

1 The authors would like to thank the Stratton Mountain Corporation and Stowe Mountain Resort for allowing us to conduct ecological studies on Bicknell's thrush and other forest birds. Our studies have been assisted by numerous field assistants, and we greatly appreciate their contributions to our work.

expansion and development in and around mountain resorts. Although most of our examples are Vermont-based, the issues and management recommendations are broadly applicable to the northeastern forest region as we focus on the generic concepts of life history strategies, habitat loss, and habitat fragmentation.

Extreme weather fluctuations are the primary natural disturbance in high elevation ecosystems. Some of these variations, such as temperature and water availability, show strong seasonal trends, whereas others, such as wind, are less predictable. Elevational gradients in environmental conditions lead to well-developed distributional patterns of high elevation fauna. For example, thrushes in the northeastern United States and Quebec show distinct zonation in elevational distribution, with the wood thrush (*Hylocichla mustelina*) and veery (*Catharus fuscescens*) found below 2,460 feet (750 meters), the hermit thrush (*Catharus guttatus*) around 2,625 feet (800 meters), the Swainson's thrush (*Catharus ustulatus*) at 3,450 feet (1,050 meters), and the Bicknell's thrush (*Catharus bicknelli*—shown in Figures 5.1 and 5.2) at 3,940 feet (1,200 meters).[2] These distributions are presumably a result of both interspecific competition as well as responses to distinct environmental features of the habitat. For species such as the Bicknell's thrush or the blackpoll warbler (*Dendroica striata*), which are largely restricted to high elevation balsam fir (*Abies balsamea*) forests, the patchy distribution of their habitat results in a restricted range that is naturally fragmented to include only high mountain peaks in the northeastern U.S.

This patchy species distribution has both costs and benefits. These habitat specialists (especially migratory species) may require an increased propensity for natal dispersal[3] because their naturally fragmented distribution of widely isolated small populations necessitates widespread exploratory movements to find suitable habitat.[4] Thus, these species may on the one hand be better able to cope with anthropogenic habitat fragmentation because of their inherently strong dispersal abilities.[5] On the other hand, high elevation habitats have increasingly been subjected to multiple environmental perturbations, such as acid precipitation,[6] mercury deposition,[7] construction of wind turbines and communication

---

2 Barry R. Noon, *The Distribution of an Avian Guild Along a Temperate Elevational Gradient: The Importance and Expression of Competition*, 51 Ecological Monographs 105, 108 (1981).

3 Keith A. Hobson et al., *Linking Breeding and Wintering Grounds of Bicknell's Thrushes Using Stable Isotope Analyses of Feathers*, 118 Auk 16, 21 (2001).

4 Gary S. Miller et al., *Habitat Selection by Spotted Owls During Natal Dispersal in Western Oregon*, 61 Wildlife Mgmt. 140, 140 (1997).

5 William Z. Lidicker, Jr. & Walter D. Koenig, *Response of Vertebrates to Habitat Edge and Corridors*, *in* Metapopulations and Wildlife Conservation 85, 89–90 (Dale R. McCullough ed., 1996).

6 Donald DeHayes et al., *Acid Rain Impacts on Calcium Nutrition and Forest Health*, 49 BioScience 789 (1999).

7 Vincent L. St. Louis et al., *Importance of the Forest Canopy to Fluxes of Methyl Mercury and Total Mercury to Boreal Ecosystems*, 35 Envtl. Sci. & Tech. 3089 (2001).

Figure 5.1 Bicknell's Thrush (Stratton Mountain, Vermont)
Photo: Courtesy of Vermont Center for Ecostudies

Figure 5.2 Bicknell's Thrush Nest with Nestlings (Mt. Mansfield, Vermont)
Photo: Courtesy of Vermont Center for Ecostudies

towers,[8] ski area development, and global climate change.[9] These habitats typically have shallow soils with poor buffering capacities[10] and may recover slowly, even from natural disturbances.[11] Therefore, species with specialized habitat requirements may find increasingly degraded conditions due to human habitat modification.

Much of our understanding of the effects of human disturbances on natural communities has come through studies of agricultural landscapes, forest clearcutting, expansion of suburban habitat into forested landscapes, and the impacts of roads on habitat fragmentation.[12] The influences of mountain resorts have been poorly documented, partly because resorts represent relatively small-scale ecological perturbations and partly because ski trails appear to cause relatively benign habitat changes compared to, for example, extensive clear cuts or the construction of a large shopping mall.

Effects of mountain resorts may, however, be relatively severe in concentrated areas, especially for species that are restricted to fragile subalpine or true alpine habitats.[13] A unique aspect of mountain resorts is that the traditional pattern of development maximizes the degree of habitat fragmentation over a relatively small proportion of a mountain slope. Within a ski area, trails are designed to enhance visual isolation among trails and to provide skiers with a diverse set of trails with varying degrees of difficulty. Further, to "sell" the diversity of runs available, mountain resorts typically advertise the total number and length of trails, creating competition to increase the amount of habitat fragmentation. The result is

---

8 Robert L. Crawford, *Weather, Migration and Autumn Bird Kills at a North Florida TV Tower*, 93 Wilson Bull. 189 (1981).

9 Felix Kienast et al., *Potential Impacts of Climate Change on Species Richness in Mountain Forests—An Ecological Risk Assessment*, 83 Biological Conservation 291 (1998); Louis R. Iverson & Anantha M. Prasad, *Predicting Abundance of 80 Tree Species Following Climate Change in the Eastern United States*, 68 Ecological Monographs 665 (1998).

10 *See* Charles W. Johnson, The Nature of Vermont 61 (1980) (describing soils as acidic, porous, and with a tendency to lose minerals).

11 *See generally* Kristina M. Urbanska, *Restoration Ecology Research Above the Timberline: Colonization of Safety Islands on a Machine-Graded Alpine Ski Run*, 6 Biodiversity and Conservation 1655 (1997) (describing a study that evaluated the extent of environmental damage caused by ski trails in high-alpine sites).

12 *See, e.g.*, Craig L. Shafer, Nature Reserves: Island Theory and Conservation Practice (1990).

13 Antonio Rolando & Ian James Patterson, *Range and Movements of the Alpine Chough Pyrrhocorax Graculus in Relation to Human Developments in the Italian Alps in Summer*, 134 J. Fuer Ornithologie 338 (1993); S. Tsuyuzaki, *Environmental Deterioration Resulting from Ski-Resort Construction in Japan*, 21 Envtl. Conservation 121, 121–25 (1994); *Johanne B. Ries, Landscape Damage by Skiing at the Schauinsland in the Black Forest, Germany*, 16 Mountain Res. & Dev. 24, 24–40 (1996); *see also* Urbanska, *supra* note 11, at 1655 (discussing effects of mountain resorts on plant species).

a landscape in which incentives exist to maximize habitat fragmentation. Thus, a more detailed evaluation of the effects of mountain resorts on animal populations and their habitats is required.

Species Responses to Disturbances

The classic approach to understanding species' responses to disturbance is through an assessment of life history strategies along the *r*- and *K*-selection[14] spectrum.[15] *r*-selected species are highly adapted to disturbance. These species typically show extreme variation in population size as new colonizers disperse to recently disturbed sites and show immediate, but temporary, exponential population growth. These high population growth rates are short-lived because *r*-selected species allocate most of their energy to reproduction, with large cohorts, mobile offspring, and minimal parental care. Biotic and abiotic changes in the environment decrease the quality of a disturbed site for *r*-selected species as more species begin to colonize the site and per capita resources decrease. Because newly-disturbed sites are temporally ephemeral, these species show relatively rapid changes in distribution and population size.

In contrast, *K*-selected species are those that are better adapted to more constant, stable environments. They are long-lived, better competitors, and put less energy into reproductive output and more into parental care. Reproductive events are small and less frequent and substantial energy is invested in each offspring. These species are poor dispersers, and individuals may move only a few home ranges from their parents before settling into a new site. Therefore, their populations are relatively constant in size and slow to recover when disturbed.

Few species show the extreme variation in life history traits described here. In fact, species that occupy the extremes of the r/K continuum are often habitat specialists, and therefore are at risk from human modification of the environment.[16] Most species fall somewhere between these two endpoints and show a mixture of life history traits, complicating our ability to predict how a species will respond to disturbance. Our understanding of a species' response to development activities is

---

14 The symbols "*r*" and "*K*" refer to variables in widely used mathematical expressions describing population dynamics. "*r*" refers to the growth capacity or exponential growth rate of a population while "*K*" refers to the carrying capacity or specific resource limit of the environment for a population. Robert E. Ricklefs, Ecology 565 (1990). *K*-selected species express traits that enable adaptation to low-resource or overcrowded environments, while *r*-selected species express traits such as early maturity and increased reproductive capacity that enable rapid population growth. *Id.* at 577–78.

15 *See generally* Eric R. Pianka, *On r and K selection*, 104 Am. Naturalist 592 (1970).

16 *See, e.g.*, Deborah Rabinowitz et al., *Seven Forms of Rarity and their Frequency in the Flora of the British Isles*, *in* Conservation Biology and the Science of Scarcity and Diversity 182 (Michael E. Soulé ed., 1986).

often limited to that resulting from the study of natural disturbances or relatively common land use practices, such as succession following hurricanes, forest clearcutting, or abandonment of agricultural fields. Predictions about responses to human-caused disturbances based on studies of natural disturbance events are limited in that anthropogenic disturbances have only recently begun to be studied in earnest. Thus, our predictive ability is hampered by a lack of empirical data, particularly over longer timescales. Further, there are frequently secondary, or even tertiary, effects and interactions that extend beyond the immediate human-induced disturbance, which complicate understanding causality and making predictions.

For example, land clearing for a ski trail necessarily eliminates some amount of forested habitat. The resulting ski trails are used primarily in winter when most animals are either dormant or have migrated away from the area, minimizing the immediate effects of disturbance. Increasingly, however, economic pressures to make mountain resorts attractive to visitors during all four seasons opens ski trails to hiking and mountain biking during the summer breeding season, when adults are under the energetic constraints of reproduction.[17] Thus, these complex interactions complicate our ability to predict accurately how species will respond to human-induced habitat modifications. Only now are we beginning to realize the ecological pervasiveness of some of these land use changes.

Habitat Loss

Species vary in their degree of specialization. Habitat specialization is one life history trait of extreme *r*- or K-selected species that increases their susceptibility to habitat loss. However, specialization can also characterize other aspects of a species' life history, such as feeding habits, den sites, temperature limits, or mating strategies. For those species that are specialized in at least one component of their annual cycle, habitat loss can critically limit their populations.

The Bicknell's thrush is a migratory songbird that is extremely specialized in its habitat requirements during the nesting season, breeding in montane fir habitat above approximately 2,950 feet or 900 meters (varying with latitude).[18] This habitat specialization limits the species to about 136,000 hectares (336,000 acres) in New York, Vermont, New Hampshire, and Maine, which constitute just 0.4 percent of the total area of these states.[19] Suitable habitat for the Bicknell's thrush is distributed across about 720 discrete mountaintops, which are naturally

---

17 *See* Hans Gander & Paul Ingold, *Reactions of Male Alpine Chamois* Rupicapra r. rupicapra *to Hikers, Joggers and Mountainbikers*, 79 Biological Conservation 107 (1997) (observing that alpine chamois abandon pastures near hiking and biking trails); Don White, Jr. et al., *Potential Energetic Effects of Mountain Climbers on Foraging Grizzly Bears*, 27 Wildlife Soc'y Bull. 146, 150 (1999).

18 J. Daniel Lambert et al., *A Practical Model of Bicknell's Thrush Distribution in the Northeastern United States*, 117 Wilson Bull. 4, 6 (2005).

19 *Id.*

fragmented as disjunct habitat "patches." Within these high elevation forests, the distribution of Bicknell's thrush is further limited by the specificity of its breeding habitat. Birds select forested sites with high stem densities of balsam fir that have been recently disturbed.[20] Under natural conditions, these sites regenerate every 80 to 100 years in a process known as fir wave migration,[21] where mortality of the exposed portions of the overstory due to high winds releases successive areas of dense understory fir regeneration. In certain situations, clearing of mountain fir forests for ski trails and associated infrastructure can mimic this regeneration process as the windward side of ski trails are similarly characterized by high mortality of the overstory trees and dense regeneration below. However, suitable habitat created by ski trails rarely extends more than 10 meters into the forest, and the cleared portion of the ski trail is habitat that the Bicknell's thrush will rarely, if ever, use. In fact, observations of radio-tagged individuals (34 individuals over three breeding seasons 1997–1999) on Stratton Mountain have shown that during daily crossings of their home ranges, individuals will take circuitous paths to avoid ski trail openings wider than 165 feet or 50 meters.[22] Thus, for a habitat specialist such as the Bicknell's thrush, forest clearing above 900 meters elevation may regulate the long-term carrying capacity of the mountain for this species.

Bicknell's Thrush

The Bicknell's thrush occupies one of the most restricted ranges of any bird species in North America, breeding exclusively in high elevation forests of the northeastern U.S. and southeastern Canada. The species' wintering range is even more contracted, with nearly the entire global population inhabiting the island of Hispaniola. The species' small population size (estimated at fewer than 50,000 individuals) and limited geographic distribution underscore a critical need for research into its habitat requirements and natural history. Although the Bicknell's thrush has proven to be an elusive study subject, ornithologists at the Vermont Institute of Natural Science (VINS), now at the Vermont Center for Ecostudies (VCE), have learned a great deal about the species since undertaking research in 1992.

One fascinating discovery involves the species' mating strategy, in which multiple males mate with multiple females, and vice versa. Although that system is not unusual in birds, the Bicknell's thrush adds its own twist, with individual males providing parental care at more than one nest—data from video cameras have shown as many as four males feeding young at a single nest. Another remarkable finding has been documentation of direct linkages between the species' breeding grounds in Vermont and its Dominican Republic wintering grounds. In 1995, an adult male banded on Mt. Mansfield was

---

20 *Id.*

21 Douglas G. Sprugel, *Dynamic Structure of Wave-regenerated* Abies balsama *Forests in the North-Eastern United States*, 64 J. Ecology 889, 906 (1976).

22 Christopher C. Rimmer et al., Evaluating the Use of Vermont Ski Areas by Bicknell's Thrush: Applications for Whiteface Mountain, New York (unpublished report submitted to the Olympic Regional Development Authority) (2004).

recaptured six months later by the VINS, now VCE, researchers in the remote Sierra de Bahoruco. A second north-south recovery involved a nestling banded on Stratton Mountain in 2002 and recaptured in 2003 in the Sierra de Neiba. These recoveries underscore the crucial conservation connection between different regions of this vulnerable species' annual cycle. These researchers have also documented an intriguing ecological cycle that appears to dominate the population dynamics of the Bicknell's thrush. Balsam fir show a strong two-year cycle in cone production, with heavy fruiting in one year and little, if any, cone production the following year. The high cone years promote major increases in red squirrel populations, leading to heavy nest losses from this predator in the following summer.

Despite dramatic gains in our understanding of the species' natural history, many serious threats face the Bicknell's thrush. Foremost among these are climate change and atmospheric pollution. VCE researchers recently documented the existence of mercury in thrush tissue samples. Previously thought to only threaten species in aquatic food webs, researchers are now trying to pin down the sources, pathways, and impacts of mercury in mountain terrestrial ecosystems.

Another group of habitat specialists are the aquatic salamanders. Unlike the Bicknell's thrush, these species appear to be affected more by modification of habitat within the ski area, rather than by direct habitat loss. Three species of aquatic salamander exist in the mountain forests of Vermont: the two-lined salamander (*Eurycea bislineata*), the northern dusky salamander (*Desmognathus fuscus*—shown in Figure 5.3), and the northern spring salamander (*Gyrinophilus porphyriticus*—shown in Figure 5.4). Rather than undergoing both terrestrial and aquatic stages as do several other salamanders, these species inhabit streams or stream banks during all phases of their life cycle. Because these species respire through their skin, they require highly oxygenated streams.

The abundance and body sizes of the above three salamanders in streams were quantified within the boundaries of seven Vermont ski areas and streams in adjacent undisturbed areas.[23] Hagen used timed counts in each stream to sample salamanders, turning over all rocks greater than 10 centimeters in diameter. All salamanders encountered were then tallied and measured. Her results revealed significantly lower populations of spring salamanders and northern dusky salamanders within ski area streams, and shorter body lengths of northern dusky salamanders within ski areas. In contrast, ski area development did not appear to affect two-lined salamanders. Hagen speculated that the observed changes in species' distributions were a result of clearing streamside vegetation and resulting increased siltation rates in streams within ski areas. These disruptions of the ecological integrity of streams may negatively affect salamanders because of higher water temperatures, lower dissolved oxygen concentrations, siltation of refugia under rocks, and a

23 Kimberly Hagen, The Effects of Ski Area Development on Populations of Stream Salamanders in Central Vermont 7 (1999) (unpublished M.S. thesis, Antioch University) (on file with author). Research sites included Killington and Pico.

Figure 5.3 Northern Dusky Salamander (Smuggler's Notch, Vermont)

Photo: Courtesy of Kimberly Hagen

Figure 5.4 Spring Salamander (Smuggler's Notch between Stowe and Cambridge, Vermont)

Photo: Courtesy of Kimberly Hagen

decreased prey base.[24] Because these species are highly specialized in their habitat requirements, they may serve as useful bioindicators of stream habitat quality.

The American black bear (*Ursus americanus*) is a species that has more general habitat requirements than either the Bicknell's thrush or aquatic salamanders, inhabiting most forested landscapes in the Northeast. However, this species is fairly intolerant of disturbance and can create management conflicts if it becomes habituated to human presence or is forced into areas with high human population densities (because of food shortages).[25] Additionally, the species goes through an energetic bottleneck in the fall and must consume substantial quantities of high energy food (mast crops such as beech (*Fagus grandifolia*), hickory (*Carya*), and acorns (*Quercus*)) to deposit sufficient fat prior to hibernation[26] and to provide females giving birth during winter with adequate energy stores for fetus development.[27] During this critical autumn period, black bears' preferred food source is beech nuts, which are often temporally variable in their production, and each fall individuals may travel 40 to 80 kilometers from their normal home ranges to forage in traditional mature beech stands.[28] Because of these energetic constraints, human disturbance or development of key mast areas can have a significant negative effect on bear populations. Therefore, although bears are generalists in their habitat requirements, their specialized food habits during a crucial period of the annual cycle make habitat loss a critical limiting factor in their population dynamics.

Habitat Protection and Vermont's Act 250

The Vermont Environmental Board has denied building permits under Act 250, the state development permit mechanism, where the applicants failed to demonstrate that the proposed development would not destroy or harm habitat for both the Bicknell's thrush and black bears. (See Chapters 15 through 18 for a full discussion of Act 250.) Criterion 8A of the Act evaluates a proposed development on the basis of whether or not it "will destroy or significantly imperil necessary wildlife habitat." The Act defines "necessary wildlife habitat" as "concentrated habitat which is identifiable and is demonstrated as being decisive to the survival of a species of wildlife at any period in its life including breeding and migratory periods." Long-lasting claw marks on beech trees and the ability to age these scars permit ready identification of key mast areas

24 *Id.*; Manuel C. Molles, Jr., & James R. Gosz, *Effects of a Ski Area on the Water and Invertebrates of a Mountain Stream*, 14 WATER, AIR & SOIL POLLUTION 187, 203–04 (1980).

25 Serge Larivière, Ursus americanus, 647 MAMMALIAN SPECIES 1 (2001).

26 Kenneth D. Elowe & Wendell E. Dodge, *Factors Affecting Black Bear Reproductive Success and Cub Survival*, 53 J. WILDLIFE MGMT. 962, 963–966 (1989).

27 *Id.*

28 George B. Kolenosky & Stewart M. Strathearn, *Black Bear*, *in* WILD FURBEARER MANAGEMENT AND CONSERVATION IN NORTH AMERICA 442, 446 (Milan Novack et al. eds., 1987).

for black bears. Bicknell's thrush habitat is readily identifiable based on elevation, latitude, vegetation type, and structure, and due to its limited areal extent, fulfills the concentrated habitat requirement of the definition. (Further, nearly all Bicknell's thrush habitat in the U.S. is above 2,500 feet (763 meters) which is also protected under Act 250.)

Could Act 250 be used to protect habitat for other species? Most species with specialized habitat requirements by definition require concentrated habitat. Thus, perhaps Act 250 could be invoked to protect habitat for species that require distinct sites for reproduction (such as rocky outcroppings for bobcats), species with specific breeding areas (such as amphibians and vernal pools), or species such as aquatic salamanders that require highly oxygenated streams. Modifying the interpretation and application of this law to cover additional species with specialized habitat requirements may, however, depend on Vermont's political and economic climate.

Sources: Act 250, Vt. Stat. Ann. Tit. 10 §§ 6001(12), 6086(a)(8)(A); Robert F. Gruenig, *Killington Mountain and Act 250: An Eco-Legal Perspective*, 26 Vt. L. Rev. 544, 554–46 (2002).

Note: Identifying Bicknell's thrush habitat is somewhat more complicated than depicted here. The species prefers early- to mid-successional montane fir forest, which is ephemeral by nature. Therefore, although it is relatively straightforward to identify current Bicknell's thrush habitat, over longer time scales, all montane fir habitat is likely to eventually provide high quality habitat for this species.

Habitat Fragmentation and Modification

Habitat fragmentation is the division of large patches of continuous forest into smaller, more isolated patches. In the strictest sense, the issue of fragmentation is distinct from that of habitat loss, in that it addresses the spatial distribution, configuration, and size of remnant patches.[29] The breakup of continuous forest into small patches has the greatest effects on area-sensitive species which require areas of continuous habitat that are substantially larger than the size of their home range. Mountain resorts exert a unique form of fragmentation because the area of habitat loss is not particularly large, but fragmentation is extreme. For example, the east slope of Mount Mansfield (Stowe Mountain Resort, west of Route 108) has been fragmented into 123 discrete forest patches, each with potential changes in biodiversity and ecological processes, but with relatively minimal forest clearing as 77 percent of the original forest acreage is still intact.[30]

In considering the effects of habitat fragmentation on wildlife populations, two components are important. First, individuals within isolated remnant habitat patches are separated over time from populations in adjacent patches. This leads to spatially-structured metapopulations: populations that are spatially separated,

29 *See* Richard T.T. Forman & Michel Godron, Landscape Ecology 83–120 (1986).

30 Data gathered by the authors. See the discussion in the next section.

but linked demographically and genetically by occasional dispersal of individuals between patches.[31] This spatial separation of populations is of management concern because over time, small isolated populations, coupled with reduced gene flow, may lead to decreased genetic diversity, decreased fitness of isolated populations, and local extinction.[32]

Second, habitat modification along the edges of remaining fragments may result in patch edges that no longer provide suitable habitat for forest interior species, or which allow penetration into forest habitat by edge-adapted species. Scientists have long considered edge effects to be a significant negative consequence of habitat fragmentation because abiotic effects, such as wind and solar radiation, create light, dry microclimates along the edges of isolated patches.[33] Research has shown that edge effects may penetrate as far as 1,640 feet (500 meters) into forest fragments, depending on the species or parameter in question.[34] Edge effects may also affect biotic interactions, as species that are more tolerant of disturbances may find that edges provide high quality habitat. This, in turn, can change the species composition of forest fragments, often increasing species richness, but also changing the realm of biotic interactions for forest interior species.[35]

Spatial Analysis of Wildlife Habitats

To quantify the relative effects of habitat loss, fragmentation, and edge effects on wildlife populations in Vermont, we measured the size and extent of the forest patches on Stowe Mountain Resort and Stratton Mountain. We used digital orthophotography available through the Vermont Mapping Program.[36]

---

31 Jekka Hanski & Michael Gilpin, *Metapopulation Dynamics: Brief History and Conceptual Domain*, 42 Biological J. Linnean Soc'y. 3, 7 (1991).

32 F. Thomas Ledig, *Heterozygosity, Heterosis, and Fitness in Outbreeding Plants*, *in* Conservation Biology: The Science of Scarcity and Diversity 77, 104 (Michael E. Soulé ed., 1986).

33 Dennis A. Saunders et al., *Biological Consequences of Ecosystem Fragmentation: A Review*, 5 Conservation Biology 18, 20 (1991).

34 Jiquan Chen et al., *Vegetation Responses to Edge Environments in Old-Growth Douglas-Fir Forests*, 2 Ecological Applications 387, 395 (1992).

35 *See generally*, Kevin R. Crooks & Michael E. Soulé, *Mesopredator Release and Arifaunal Extinctions in a Fragmented System*, 400 Nature 563 (1999) (describing a study of a predator, the coyote, its decline in a fragmented landscape, and the effect of fragmentation on smaller carnivores).

36 Vermont Mapping Program, Vermont Dep't of Taxes, http://www.state.vt.us/tax/Vermont%20ortho%20 Program.htm (providing both online digital images and information for ordering printed images and CD-ROM's). Orthophotographs consist of a "pair of [overlapping] aerial photographs mathematically and optically corrected…to meet national map accuracy standards, but still have the readability of an aerial photograph." *Id.* Vermont imagery is available at 1:5,000 scale with 0.5 meter^2 pixels.

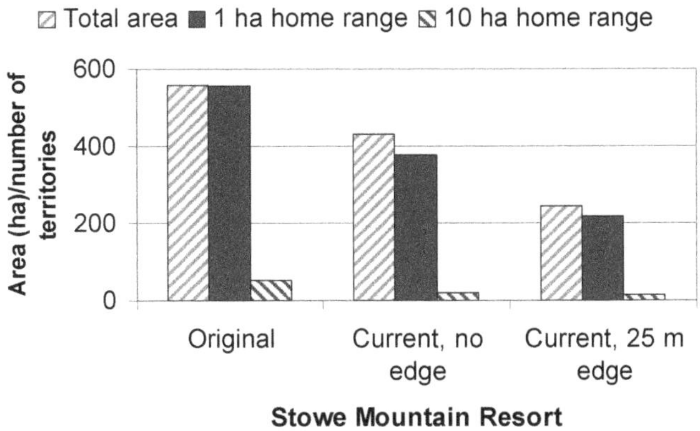

Figure 5.5 Effects of Fragmentation and Edge Effects on Forest Area and Populations of Two Hypothetical Species with Limited Gap-Crossing Abilities on Stowe Mountain Resort

Note: One species occupies a territory of 1.0 hectare (ha) , and the second, a territory of 10.0 hectares.

Interpretation of these aerial photos is fairly straightforward, particularly when identifying ski trails and developed areas versus forested habitat. However, to keep our results conservative, we assigned areas that could not be classified unambiguously as forest.

We modeled the response of two hypothetical species to assess the effects of forest loss, fragmentation, and edge effects on wildlife populations (Figures 5.5 and 5.6). Both species were forest generalists (i.e., present throughout all forest habitat types) with limited gap-crossing abilities such that their home ranges could not extend outside a single forest fragment. We selected one species with an assigned territory size of 1.0 hectare or 2.47 acres (e.g., a typical forest-dependent songbird, such as blackpoll warbler) and a second species with an assigned 10.0 hectare territory (e.g., a small mammalian predator such as the ermine (*Mustela erminea*)).[37] We consider these occupied areas to be territories rather than home ranges because we are assuming that once an area is occupied by an individual (or a breeding pair), the area will no longer be available to conspecifics. We assumed that all available habitat was fully saturated prior to habitat loss and fragmentation; that is, there was no unoccupied habitat.

We also investigated how our estimates of population size might be affected if each species were sensitive to edge effects that extend 25 meters (82 feet) into the interior of each fragment (Figure 5.5). Twenty-five meters is an underestimate of the extension of edge effects for some species (e.g., the ovenbird (*Seiurus*

37 Richard M. DeGraaf & Mariko Yamasaki, New England Wildlife: Habitat, Natural History, and Distribution 349 (2001).

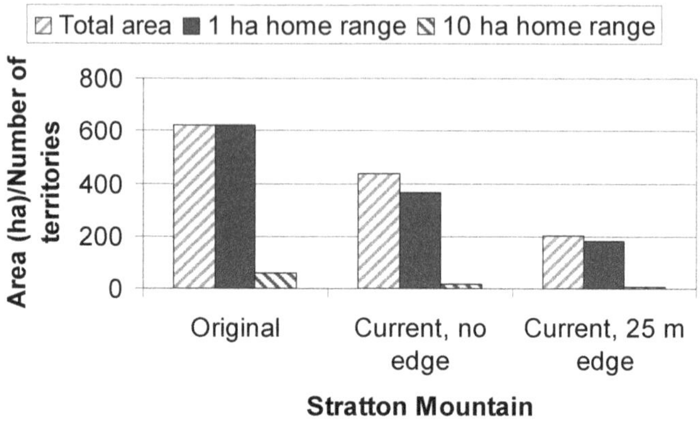

Figure 5.6 Effects of Fragmentation and Edge Effects on Forest Area and Populations of Two Hypothetical Species with Limited Gap-Crossing Abilities on Stratton Mountain Resort

Note: One species occupies a territory of 1.0 hectare (ha), and the second, a territory of 10.0 hectares.

aurocapilla)),[38] but may be an overestimate for some edge-tolerant species. Consequently, the value is simply illustrative of how edge effects can magnify the impacts of forest fragmentation resulting from ski trail construction.

The results of this analysis showed that the slope of Mount Mansfield (west of Route 108) occupied by Stowe Mountain Resort originally supported 557 individuals of the 1.0 hectare territory species, and 55 individuals of the 10.0 hectare territory species (Figure 5.5). These values decreased to 376 and 20 individuals, respectively, with the current levels of fragmentation. Incorporating edge effects of 25 meters, these values further declined to 217 and 14 individuals. This is a population decrease of 61 percent and 75 percent, respectively, compared to the mountainside in an undisturbed condition. Perhaps the most important finding is that these predicted decreases in population size occur with only a 23 percent decrease in the total forest area.

The results are more extreme for Stratton Mountain. We predicted an original population of 621 individuals with a 1.0 hectare territory and 62 individuals with a 10.0 hectare territory (Figure 5.6). With the current levels of fragmentation these values decreased to 367 and 17 individuals, respectively. Incorporating edge effects into the analysis resulted in a further decline to 180 and 7 individuals, with respective population decreases of 70 percent and 89 percent. Compared to Stowe,

38 Yvette K. Ortega & David E. Capen, *Effects of Forest Roads on Habitat Quality for Ovenbirds in a Forested Landscape*, 116 Auk 937, 937–38 (1999); David Flaspohler et al., *Effects of Forest Edges on Ovenbird Demography in a Managed Forest Landscape*, 15 Conservation Biology 173, 173 (2001).

Stratton Mountain has a greater loss of total forest (30 percent) but again, this is proportionately small compared to the declines in population size.

Species Risk Analysis

The results of this spatial analysis suggest that the percent of total forest area lost can be a misleading indicator of total habitat availability, particularly under conditions of high fragmentation. Recall, however, that this analysis is for hypothetical species that are intolerant of edge effects and have no gap crossing ability. Thus, the actual pattern of fragmentation and subsequent decline in population size will vary depending upon a species' tolerance of these factors. Certainly, many species will be affected less severely than others, but ecologically sensitive species will be impacted more drastically. Most importantly, this analysis provides a framework by which to more thoroughly evaluate the effects of ski area development on animal populations. Modifying the parameters used in this modeling exercise is relatively simple and could allow us to examine species that vary in their life history traits and their sensitivity to habitat fragmentation. For example, would results change if a species is able to cross gaps, but only those that are less than or equal to ten meters wide? What if a species is sensitive to edges within one hundred meters of a ski trail edge? What if a species has a thirty-five hectare territory, but is able to cross gaps greater than or equal to fifty meters in width?

Our modeling results explicitly take into account home range size and edge sensitivity, and make an implicit assumption about a species' gap-crossing ability. Although our model does include the latter parameter, a species with gap-crossing abilities will experience fewer constraints on its territory placement, thereby mitigating the effects of fragmentation. Of these three variables, most studies have focused on home range size because radio telemetry or mark-recapture studies can document this parameter with relative ease. As our results show, species with larger home ranges, generally larger-bodied animals, will be more sensitive to fragmentation.[39] A plethora of studies documenting the loss of large carnivores from most of North America's fragmented landscapes support this finding.[40]

Certainly social behavior will mitigate the effects of home range size. Strictly territorial species are likely more susceptible to fragmentation, as conspecifics will not be tolerated within the same area. However, lack of territoriality does not necessarily make a species less susceptible to fragmentation. For example, ski area development in the western United States has negatively affected elk (*Cervus*

---

39 Douglas A. Kelt & Dirk H. Van Vuren, *The Ecology and Macroecology of Mammalian Home Range Area*, 157 AM. NATURALIST 637, 639 (2001).

40 *See, e.g.*, Paul Beier, *Determining Minimum Habitat Areas and Habitat Corridors for Cougars*, 7 CONSERVATION BIOLOGY 94 (1993); Reed F. Noss et al., *Conservation Biology and Carnivore Conservation in the Rocky Mountains*, 10 CONSERVATION BIOLOGY 949, 957 (1996).

elaphus).[41] Similarly, forest loss and fragmentation may negatively affect wide-ranging irruptive seed-eating birds that follow coniferous cone crops.[42]

Edge sensitivity is more difficult to assess because it can be measured in a variety of ways, some of which (i.e., reduced reproductive success along edges) may have substantially greater effects on demographic processes than others (e.g., edge avoidance). Edge effects have been studied most thoroughly in songbirds, where the attraction of generalist predators such as raccoons (*Procyon lotor*), skunks (*Mephitis mephitis*), blue jays (*Cyanocitta cristata*), American crows (*Corvus brachyrhynchos*), and nest parasites (e.g., brown-headed cowbirds (*Molothrus ater*)) often reduce nesting success along forest edges.[43] Studies on ski areas in the Italian Alps have shown decreased density and diversity of birds along ski trail edges.[44] However, on Mount Mansfield and Stratton Mountain, analyses for 1994–2002 show that Bicknell's thrush do not experience significantly different nest survival rates along ski trail edges than in forests farther from human-caused forest openings.[45] To our knowledge, this is the only study to examine the effects of ski trail openings on avian productivity.

Although studies of other taxa have been less systematic, research on root voles (*Microtus oeconomus*) demonstrates that habitat connectivity is critical to maintaining population processes and genetic structure in an experimentally fragmented ecosystem.[46] Dispersing juvenile amphibians avoid open areas.[47] Generally, species that require humid microclimates, species that feed on leaf litter fauna or use the leaf litter for cover, and species that are sensitive to human

---

41 James R. Morrison et al., *The Effects of Ski Area Expansion on Elk*, 23 WILDLIFE SOC'Y BULL. 481, 485–87 (1995) (finding a decline in elk inhabitation of ski areas).

42 ROBERT ASKINS, RESTORING NORTH AMERICA'S BIRDS: LESSONS FROM LANDSCAPE ECOLOGY 103–105 (2000).

43 J. Edward Gates & Leslie W. Gysel, *Avian Nest Dispersion and Fledgling Success in Field-Forest Ecotones*, 59 ECOLOGY 871, 875–76 (1978); David S. Wilcove, *Nest Predation in Forest Tracts and the Decline of Migratory Songbirds*, 66 ECOLOGY 1211, 1213 (1985).

44 Paola Laiolo & Antonio Rolando, *Forest Bird Diversity and Ski-runs: A Case of Negative Edge Effect*, 7 ANIMAL CONSERVATION 9, 12 (2005); Anotonia Rolanda, Enrico Caprio, & Ivan Ellena, *The Impact of High-altitude Ski-runs on Alpine Grassland Bird Communities*, 44 J. APPLIED ECOLOGY 210, 213–214 (2007).

45 *See* note 21.

46 Harry P. Andreassen & Rolf A. Ims, *The Effects of Experimental Habitat Destruction and Patch Isolation on Space Use and Fitness Parameters in Female Root Vole* Microtus oeconomus, 67 J. ANIMAL ECOLOGY 941, 950 (1998); *see generally* Jon Aars & Rolf A. Ims, *The Effect of Habitat Corridors on Rates of Transfer and Interbreeding Between Vole Demes*, 80 ECOLOGY 1648 (1999) (describing an experimental study of the effects of corridors in 12 experimentally fragmented root vole populations).

47 *See, e.g.*, Philip G. deMaynadier & Malcolm L. Hunter, Jr., *Forest Canopy Closure and Juvenile Emigration in Poolbreeding Amphibians in Maine*, 63 J. WILDLIFE MGMT. 441, 446 (1999).

disturbance or predation show a greater degree of edge sensitivity. For example, forest fragmentation negatively affects the ovenbird, a ground-foraging and ground-nesting migratory songbird, because of increased nest predation and parasitism rates.[48] However, ovenbirds also show avoidance of forest edges, a behavior that appears to be influenced by the abundance of insects, their primary food source, which are present in lower numbers near the dry edges of forest fragments.[49]

Gap-crossing ability is the least well-studied trait affecting sensitivity to fragmentation, and most species probably show extreme variation based upon life cycle stage. Traits that increase species' vulnerability to gaps in forest cover are strict habitat requirements, complex life cycles that entail seasonal movements between different habitat types, susceptibility to predation, limited mobility, and sensitivity to disturbance.[50] Because birds are highly mobile, they are rarely limited by gap-crossing ability. However, this trait may vary throughout the annual cycle. For example, an individual Bicknell's thrush, which will cross thousands of forest gaps while migrating from Vermont to the Dominican Republic, will situate its home range to minimize the number of wide ski trails it must cross during its daily foraging activities.[51] Many species of amphibians make seasonal movements from breeding ponds to terrestrial foraging sites.[52] Because these species have relatively limited rates of movement, they are susceptible to predation during their seasonal migrations. The attributes of ski trail gaps probably make them less formidable obstacles than roads, suburban subdivisions, or agricultural fields. For most species, however, it seems reasonable to assume that mortality rates will likely increase in ski trail openings compared to within forested habitats.

Given these life history characteristics, we can make some preliminary predictions about which species may be susceptible to population declines near mountain resorts, based on home range size, gap-crossing ability, and edge sensitivity (Table 5.1). Numerous species will experience susceptibility to population declines from the development of mountain resorts due to only one aspect of their life history strategy. We have, however, limited the results in Table 5.1 to species that are sensitive to fragmentation through at least two of the attributes listed above.

---

48 Scott K. Robinson et al., *Regional Forest Fragmentation and the Nesting Success of Migratory Birds*, 267 SCIENCE 1987, 1989 (1995).

49 Dawn M. Burke & Erica Nol, *Influence of Food Abundance, Nest-Site Habitat, and Forest Fragmentation on Breeding Ovenbirds*, 115 AUK 96, 101 (1998).

50 GARY K. MEFFE & C. RONALD CARROLL ET AL., PRINCIPLES OF CONSERVATION BIOLOGY 291–94 (2d ed. 1997).

51 Christopher C. Rimmer et al., *supra* note 22.

52 Kenneth C. Dodd & Brian S. Cade, *Movement Patterns and the Conservation of Amphibians Breeding in Small, Temporary Wetlands*, 12 CONSERVATION BIOLOGY 331, 332 (1998).

Table 5.1 Species that May Suffer Population Declines as a Result of Habitat Fragmentation Associated with Mountain Resorts

Species	Edge Sensitive	Large Homerange	Poor Gap-Crossing Ability
Jefferson salamander (*Ambystoma jeffersonianum)*	X		X
Red-spotted newt (*Notophthalmus viridescens*)	X		X
Northern spring peeper (*Pseudacris crucifer*)	X		X
Wood frog (*Rana sylvatica*)	X		X
Northern goshawk (*Accipiter gentiles*)	X	X	X
Northern saw-whet owl (*Aegolius acadicus*)	X	X	
Barred owl (*Strix varia*)	X	X	X
Migratory songbirds (*Passeriformes*)	X		X
Shrews (*Sorex* spp.)	X		X
Southern red-backed vole (*Clethrionomys gapperi*)	X		X
Woodland jumping mouse (*Napaeozapus insignis*)	X		X
Black bear (*Ursus americanus*)		X	X
Bobcat (*Felis rufus*)		X	X
Fisher (*Martens pennanti*)		X	X

Note: For many species of wildlife, many of these parameters have not been fully investigated. For most species, the response to fragmentation may be situation specific. However, we have tried to categorize threats to these species so that managers and developers can assess effects on high-elevation fauna.

Two species that appear to be at risk as a result of all three habitat factors are the barred owl (*Strix varia*) and the northern goshawk (*Accipiter gentilis*). Both species occupy home ranges larger than 150 hectares and are sensitive to forest fragmentation and human disturbance.[53] The assessments presented here are preliminary, and further research is necessary to test these species' responses to

53 John R. Squires & Richard T. Reynolds, *Northern Goshawk* (Accipter gentilis), *in* Birds of North America, No. 298, at 21, 23 (Alan Poole & Frank Gill eds., 1997); Kurt M.

high elevation developments. More refined spatial databases with special habitat features, such as rock ledges, vernal pools, snags, or mast trees, would further enhance risk assessments for species of concern. But, our analysis indicates that general effects of further ski trail construction can be assessed remotely, and that the impacts on particular species can be modeled and predicted given basic knowledge of their life history traits.

Applying the results of these modeling analyses to an actual landscape presents several difficulties. The most significant obstacle is that in frequently-studied fragmented landscapes, the fragment of interest is nested in a matrix of dissimilar habitat (for example, forest fragments surrounded by agricultural habitat). Few studies have investigated forest fragments within a predominantly forested landscape,[54] exactly the situation found surrounding most mountain resorts. The degree to which fragmentation alters connectivity will depend on the spatial scale of the investigation: a single, isolated forest patch, a series of fragments along a ski slope, an entire mountain, or a mountain ridgeline. A forest-dwelling flightless carabid beetle may be unable to move from one forest patch to another, and consequently its populations may be rapidly extirpated from isolated forest patches within a ski area.[55] A red-backed salamander *(Plethodon cinereus)* might easily be able to move from one forest patch to another, but will be forced into suboptimal habitat (ski trails) to accomplish such movements across the landscape. In contrast, a black bear that chooses to avoid ski trails can more easily cross from one part of a mountain to another by simply moving around the perimeter of the resort, perhaps in a matter of hours. Because gap-crossing ability remains a poorly understood component of most species' life histories, an improved understanding of how such species respond to fragmentation will require additional detailed studies.

Disruption of Ecological Processes

It is naïve to believe that we can manage for all species simultaneously, and unrealistic to try, even over relatively large landscapes. Because mountain ecosystems support a unique suite of species, management simply for biodiversity or species richness is inappropriate. In fact, biodiversity in these forests may be

---

Mazur & Paul C. James, *Barred Owl* (Strix varia), *in* BIRDS OF NORTH AMERICA, NO. 508, at 7, 12, 13 (Alan Poole & Frank Gill eds., 2000).

54 *See, e.g.*, David I. King et al., *Effects of Clearcutting on Habitat Use and Reproductive Success of the Ovenbird in Forested Landscapes*, 10 CONSERVATION BIOLOGY 1380, 1383–1384 (1996).

55 Hank H. De Vries & Pieter L. Den Boer, *Survival of Populations of Agonum Ericeti Panz.* (Col., Carabidae) *in Relation to Fragmentation of Habitats*, 40 NETHERLANDS J. ZOOLOGY 484, 486 (1990); Allan M. Strong et al., *Ski Trail Effects on a Beetle* (Coleoptera: Carabidae, Elateridae) *Community in Vermont*, 6 J. INSECT CONSERVATION 149–159 (2002).

naturally low as a result of the extreme environmental conditions.[56] Consequently, artificial increases in biodiversity through inadvertent species introductions or anthropogenic habitat modifications may lead to population declines of habitat specialists through competition and habitat degradation.[57] Many species whose life history traits lie to the *r*-side of the continuum have populations that are stable or expanding as a result of human habitat modification at all elevations. Thus, increases in American robins (*Turdus migratorius*) or indigo buntings (*Passerina cyanea*) on a ski area may increase the total number of species present, but should not be interpreted as an overall increase in habitat quality. In fact, increases in these habitat generalists could be construed as an indication of declining habitat quality for many forest interior species through the modification of ecological processes. Further, increases in species with general habitat requirements may lead to increases in generalist predators and nest parasites, which have been shown to negatively affect high elevation species nesting in European ski areas.[58] This result primarily from direct habitat modification, but also indirect effects, such as increased food waste, that attract nest predators such as gulls (*Larus* spp.) and corvids (ravens, crows, and jays) to areas in which they had not previously been present.

White-tailed deer (*Oidocoleus virginianus*) are "keystone herbivores" in many forested ecosystems, in that their consumption of plant material influences forest structure to such a degree that the abundances of other species are affected.[59] The composition of the landscape around mountain resorts has created excellent habitat for white-tailed deer, with forested habitat punctuated by ski trail openings. Abundant white-tailed deer populations negatively affect forest songbird populations through their effect on vegetation structure.[60] The impact of white-tailed deer on forest songbird populations could conceivably have additional

---

56 John G. Blake & Bette A. Loiselle, *Diversity of Birds Along an Elevational Gradient in the Cordillera Central, Costa Rica*, 117 Auk 663, 663 (2000) (noting that "[d]eclines in bird-species richness with elevation are common"); Erica Fleishman et al., *An Empirical Test of Rapoport's Rule: Elevational Gradients in Montane Butterfly Communities*, 79 Ecology 2482 (1998). "Monotonic declines in species richness with increasing elevation have been documented in both temperate and tropical regions for" a variety of species. *Id.* at 2489.

57 Robert A. Garrott et al., *Overabundance: An Issue for Conservation Biologists*, 7 Conservation Biology 946, 946 (1993).

58 *See* Adam Watson, *Bird and Mammal Numbers in Relation to Human Impacts at Ski Lifts on Scottish Hills*, 16 J. Applied Ecology 753, 759, 763 (1979); Roy Dennis, *Birds and Conservation Problems of the High Tops*, 4 Royal Soc'y Protection Birds Conservation Rev. 48, 50–51 (1990) (asserting that development of ski areas has brought increased visitor use to the Scottish Highlands negatively impacting bird habitat).

59 Donald M. Waller & William S. Alverson, *The White-Tailed Deer: A Keystone Herbivore*, 25 Wildlife Soc'y Bull. 217 (1997).

60 David S. deCalesta, *Effect of White-Tailed Deer on Songbirds Within Managed Forests in Pennsylvania*, 58 J. Wildlife Mgmt. 711, 715 (1999) (finding negative effect on

ecosystem effects. Recent research has shown that songbirds can indirectly affect forest growth rates through their consumption of herbivorous insects.[61] Thus, as songbird populations decline, herbivorous insect populations increase, and biomass production by understory trees and shrubs further decreases. Clearly, additional fragmentation could negatively impact forest productivity through such multiplier effects.

At the landscape level, an important factor in evaluating the contribution of mountain resorts to ecosystem function is the infrastructure surrounding the base of the mountain. For example, does the resort-generated clientele lead to sprawl and the construction of new hotels, bed and breakfasts, restaurants, condominiums, gas stations, convenience stores, golf courses, and gift shops? Further, what effect does this secondary development have on landscape-level processes? One effect of these associated businesses is the creation of habitat that is suitable for synanthropic species, which can have negative consequences for native wildlife. Eurasian starlings (*Sturnus vulgaris*) and house sparrows (*Passer domesticus*) are rarely found far from human habitation and often outcompete native species for nest cavities.[62] Brown-headed cowbirds are nest parasites that have been implicated in the declines of forest nesting songbirds, particularly in the midwestern United States.[63] Their populations have been increasing in the eastern United States[64] and although they do not inhabit high elevations, grassy slopes at low elevations provide suitable habitat that, if not currently occupied, may be in the future. Other species attracted to human refuse, such as American crows, raccoons, skunks, and gulls, are avian nest predators and may reach artificially high densities in human-modified habitats.[65] A related concern is the habituation of bears to human refuse, which continues to hinder grizzly bear (*Ursus arctos horribilis*) recovery in the lower 48 states,[66] because bears that threaten human safety are quickly removed from the population.[67] Thus, secondary effects of mountain resorts will likely continue to have substantial impacts on wildlife populations.

One challenge of a legal approach to maintaining the ecological integrity of a mountain resort area is our limited understanding of how individual species

---

intermediate canopy-nesting songbirds, but no effect on upper canopy-nesting or ground-nesting songbirds).

61 Robert J. Marquis & Christopher Whelan, *Insectovorous Birds Increase Growth of White Oak through Consumption of Leaf-Chewing Insects*, 75 Ecology 2007, 2012 (1994).

62 Patricia A. Gowaty & Jonathan H. Pilsner, *Eastern Bluebird (*Sialia sialis*)*, *in* The Birds of North America No. 381, at 24 (Alan Poole & Frank Gill eds., 1998).

63 Robinson et al., *supra* note 48, at 1987.

64 Margaret Clark Brittingham & Stanley A. Temple, *Have Cowbirds Caused Forest Songbirds to Decline?*, 33 BioScience 31, 31 (1983).

65 John W. Terborgh, Where Have All the Birds Gone? 49–51, 67 (1989).

66 Matthew M. Reid & Richard Meis, *Ski Yellowstone and Grizzlies: A Case Study of Conflict*, Western Wildlands, Winter 1985, 5, at 6.

67 *Id.*

contribute to ecosystem processes such as predation, herbivory, or competition. As Aldo Leopold noted with his usual foresight, "to keep every cog and wheel is the first precaution of intelligent tinkering."[68] Currently, however, we have no legal mechanism to monitor or maintain natural ecological processes that are critical to ecosystem integrity.

Cumulative Effects of Development

A crucial issue regarding development in and around mountain resorts concerns the cumulative effects of such development. Habitat fragmentation occurs in a landscape context, such that ski trail construction is not simply a loss of 1.0 or 2.0 hectares, but adds to the current amount of habitat that has already been altered. This factor may not necessarily be considered in development permits.[69] The behavioral properties of ecosystems have been studied by modeling random landscapes, which have led to some useful theoretical results, some of which have been supported through empirical studies.[70] Modeling results indicate that when a landscape is fragmented to the point at which less than 58 percent remains forested, the landscape no longer percolates or retains connectivity.[71]

This result implies the existence of a threshold at which the landscape will no longer be perceived as connected, at least for certain species. This "percolation threshold" will vary depending upon the species' home range size, its ability to cross habitat gaps, and its tolerance of habitat edges.[72] Evidence of threshold effects on distribution come primarily from large-scale studies or meta-analyses where regional differences in habitat cover vary widely. For instance, a study of the occurrence of scarlet tanagers (*Piranga olivacea*) across North America found that "sensitivity to fragmentation varies geographically and may be lower in regions with greater overall forest cover."[73] Similarly, a review of studies on birds and mammals in habitat patches in landscapes with different proportions of suitable habitat concluded that patch size and isolation are not important when

---

68 Aldo Leopold, Round River: From the Journals of Aldo Leopold 147 (Luna Leopold ed., 1953).

69 Act 250, Vt. Stat. Ann. tit. 10, § 6086 (2001).

70 *See generally* Therese M. Donovan & Allan M. Strong, *Linkages Between Theory and Population Dynamics: A Review of Empirical Evidence*, *in* Landscape Theory and Resource Management: Making the Match (John A. Bissonnette ed., 2002).

71 R.H. Gardner et al., *Neutral Models for the Analysis of Broad-Scale Landscape Pattern*, 1 Landscape Ecology 19, 25–27 (1987).

72 *See generally* Kimberly A. With, *Is Landscape Connectivity Necessary and Sufficient for Wildlife Management?*, *in* Forest Fragmentation: Wildlife and Management Implications 97 (Rochell et al., eds., 1999) (discussing a study of species' perceptions of landscape connectivity in forests with different levels of fragmentation).

73 Kenneth V. Rosenberg et al., *Effects of Forest Fragmentation on Breeding Tanagers: A Continental Perspective*, 13 Conservation Biology 568, 568 (1999).

landscapes consist of greater than 30 percent habitat, but that in landscapes with less than 30 percent habitat, patch size and isolation compound the effect of habitat loss, resulting in cumulative effects greater than that of habitat loss alone.[74] The existence of these thresholds suggests that the loss of an additional few hectares could have dramatic effects on ecosystem function. These thresholds will be greater for species that have large home ranges, poor gap-crossing abilities and are intolerant of habitat edges, such that fragmented landscapes will deteriorate faster for species with those life history traits.

Our own modeling results indicate that for Stowe and Stratton Mountains, the landscapes are well above current predicted thresholds at which percolation no longer exists. However, as discussed above, landscapes surrounding ski areas are not fragmented randomly but are designed to maximize habitat fragmentation. Consequently, in these unique landscapes, additional studies will be required to evaluate the effects of relatively small incremental habitat losses on populations of species of management concern.

Population Viability Analysis

Is it possible to assess how much development can be permitted before wildlife populations are adversely impacted? One means of evaluating such effects is by using population viability analysis (PVA).[75] This method seeks to determine the effects of a specified management practice on population persistence through some predetermined length of time. PVAs allow managers to determine the discrete stages in a species' life cycle that make it vulnerable to extinction and how a particular management action might influence this risk. For example, a proposed ski trail cuts through an area that supports nesting Bicknell's thrush. Will the decrease in carrying capacity affect the viability of the population on the mountain, or in the region, or across its range? A PVA would examine the current temporal variation in population size and use those data to examine the effects of the loss of a local breeding subpopulation. Thus, in theory, the analysis could help determine the effects of decreased carrying capacity at a breeding site on the probability of population persistence in relation to other factors such as adult survival or reproductive success.

Although PVAs provide a useful means of determining the effects of habitat loss or modification on the population of a species of concern, detailed information is necessary to produce a PVA with reasonably certainty (i.e., narrow confidence intervals). Consequently, an inevitable question will be who should

---

74 Henrik Andren, *Effects of Habitat Fragmentation on Birds and Mammals in Landscapes with Different Proportions of Suitable Habitat: A Review*, 71 Oikos 355, 362 (1994).

75 *See generally* Mark S. Boyce, *Population Viability Analysis*, 23 Ann. Rev. Ecology & Systematics 481 (1992).

pay for data collection and the PVA itself? Should the burden of proof be on those with economic interests, ecological concerns, or impartial third parties? More contentious discussions may result from the interpretation of PVAs. Even if sufficient data were available to conduct a rigorous PVA, results may defy clearcut interpretation and application. Is a 10 percent increase in the probability that a species will be extirpated from a mountain in the next one hundred years an acceptable risk, given the economic and recreational benefits of mountain resorts to society? These are difficult and complex issues for which resolution can come only through cooperative dialogue among stakeholders.

Management Recommendations

Fragmentation on ski areas may be addressed through careful design and maintenance of ski trails and management of skier traffic across the mountain. Below, we present several management recommendations to minimize the impacts of ski area expansion on wildlife habitat. Most importantly, ski trails should be located to minimize the creation of new forest islands and to avoid bisecting large patches of intact habitat. In situations where one or more islands can be combined into a single, larger island, habitat will be improved for forest interior species.

Buffering of edge effects is possible by managing vegetation to create a "feathered" edge along ski trails, gradually decreasing vegetation height from the forest interior to the trail edge. For Bicknell's thrush (and other passerines found at high elevations), vegetation management is warranted mainly in areas where the adjacent forest is conifer-dominated and characterized by a high stem density in the understory, often forming a dense thicket. Taller trees (greater than five meters or 16 feet in height) may be present, but these are often damaged by wind, ice, and/or insects and do not form a complete canopy, thus promoting understory growth. In these areas, which may include only one (usually the wind-exposed) side of a ski trail, low fir-spruce can be allowed to extend along the edge outward for six to seven meters or 20 to 23 feet (or wider) at heights of 0.3–1.0 meters (or higher). An attempt should be made to gradually decrease tree height from the forest to the grassy trail edge. When these areas are cut back, woody vegetation should be maintained at heights of 0.3 meters (one foot) or more. This management practice maintains a wider ecotone of dense vegetation, creating more habitat for nesting birds while decreasing the ease of search for predators that use edge habitats.

Buffer zones should also be created around streams to maintain the integrity of habitat and water quality. Although this may be difficult within ski trails, recent advances in stream restoration[76] may suggest suitable plant species that provide adequate cover and erosion protection without the subsequent structure that interferes with ski trail maintenance. Care must be taken, however, not to

76 *See generally* Catherine Kashanski, Vermont Agency of Natural Resources, Native Vegetation for Lakeshores, Streamsides and Wetland Buffers (1994).

introduce aggressive exotics that may preserve stream quality at the expense of native species.

To minimize adverse impacts to Bicknell's thrush and other forest-nesting birds, existing gladed trails in suitable habitat should be kept as narrow as possible. Patches of low, dense balsam fir should be left intact or minimally altered, while still allowing the trails to function for their intended recreational purpose. Annual maintenance should ensure that some tree saplings are retained so there is continual recruitment to older age classes. This will help to prevent tree mortality events that could cause the longer-term conversion of gladed trails to completely open trails, degrading special habitat features such as low dense vegetation, vernal pools, or rock ledges.

Concerted efforts should also be made to prohibit any unauthorized gladed trail establishment or maintenance, or unauthorized habitat alteration (cutting) of any kind. The proliferation of trails illicitly cut by recreational, off-trail skiers, and recently documented on some Vermont ski areas, must be actively discouraged.

In instances of habitat removal or alteration for ski trail establishment or expansion, we recommend a minimum one-to-one mitigation process, such that an area of currently developed habitat equal to (or greater than) that to be altered will be actively restored or passively allowed to recover to conditions suitable for occupancy by wildlife. Further, the timing of vegetation management (including mowing) in areas of high elevation songbird breeding habitat is important and should be delayed until after August 1, when the majority of nesting activities are complete. Disturbance of any kind around key mast areas should be entirely eliminated during the late summer and fall.

The Impact of Societal Values and Economic Practices

The values, ethics, and biases of society all play a significant role in the management and conservation of wildlife populations. For example, there may be widespread support for the creation of buffer zones to minimize disturbance to black bears in key mast areas and moderate support for conservation of high elevation Bicknell's thrush habitat. However, societal support may be minimal for preservation of salamander habitat, and nearly nonexistent for ground beetle habitat conservation. As interest and funding levels for non-game wildlife management are often negligible, the best-case scenario may be to integrate the management of keystone species (species whose populations or ecological role affect the abundance of numerous other species) or indicator species (species whose presence signifies some measure of habitat quality) into the management of mountain resorts as ecosystems. No matter how strong the supporting scientific evidence, societal values will need to be incorporated into habitat management plans. Consensus will be reached far more easily on charismatic species than on species for which there is little perceived value to society.

Recently, ecologists have attempted to elevate public perception of wildlife and ecosystems by documenting the economic value that both provide, either through the generation of tourism dollars or through ecosystem services. Although the field of ecological economics is in its infancy, data suggest that economic benefits are far from trivial. For example, national hunting expenditures were estimated to generate $23 billion in 2006; some of these were directly or indirectly returned to local economies.[77] Wildlife watching has been estimated to provide substantial returns to local economies (greater than $45 billion per year), with birdwatching generating over 67 percent of the total number of participants.[78] In 1999, it was estimated the ski industry added $722 million to Vermont's economy,[79] compared to $123 million spent on wildlife watching in Vermont in 2006.[80] Thus, both provide substantial tourism benefits to the region. In areas that feature rare or endemic species, or that offer other special wildlife spectacles such as migratory concentrations, dollars generated by wildlife watching for the local economy can be substantial.[81]

The benefits that ecosystems provide to humans through nutrient cycling, regulation of disturbances, waste treatment, food production, recreation, and other services have been estimated at over $33 trillion per year.[82] Although the tools used to estimate these services are still being developed, the total estimate in 1997 dollars was 1.8 times greater than the world's gross national product, suggesting that it would be impossible for the world's economies to accurately account for ecosystem goods and services.[83] However, applied to the conservation of biodiversity, some authors have argued that species may still be driven to extinction through optimal behavior in a traditional economic market.[84]

In contrast, ecological economics argue for limiting market substitutions (for example, substituting aquatic systems for aquaculture), maintaining minimum stocks of natural capital, and preserving ecosystem function.[85] In this way, the values that ecosystems provide to humans would be explicitly taken into account

77 U.S. Fish & Wildlife Service, U.S. Dep't of Interior & Bureau of the Census, U.S. Dep't of Commerce, 2006 National Survey of Fishing, Hunting, and Wildlife-Associated Recreation, 2006, at 45.

78 *Id.*

79 Vermont Tourism Data Center, UVM & Vermont Department of Tourism and Marketing, The Vermont Ski Industry 1999, http://www.uvm.edu/~snrvtdc/publications/vt%20ski%20industry.pdf (last visited Feb. 23, 2008).

80 U.S. Dep't of the Interior, Fish and Wildlife Service & U.S. Census Bureau, U.S. Dep't of Commerce, 2006 National Survey of Fishing, Hunting, and Wildlife-Associated Recreation.

81 *Id.*

82 Robert Costanza et al., *The Value of the World's Ecosystem Services and Natural Capital*, 387 NATURE 253, 259 (1997).

83 *Id.*

84 Colin W. Clark, *Profit Maximization and the Extinction of Animal Species*, 81 J. POL. ECON. 950, 950–51 (1973).

85 *See generally* ROBERT COSTANZA ET AL., AN INTRODUCTION TO ECOLOGICAL ECONOMICS (1997).

in plans for development of natural areas. Currently, economic incentives are insufficient to favor a shift from a traditional economic paradigm to an ecological economic system. Until we can realistically assess the current impact of human actions on wildlife and their habitat, we will continue to rely on a legal framework that protects the few charismatic species which society deems to have inherent value.

Can a shift in societal values emerge from within the resort industry and its clientele? Although it is typically the purview of land managers, biologists, and planners to provide best management practices for these sites, management recommendations are necessarily given in the context of what society deems to be acceptable or appropriate uses. Thus, no matter what the scientific evidence for the persistence of a population, or the healthy functioning of an ecosystem, societal values must be entered into the equation. These demands and decisions will to a large part depend on the information users are given. Assuming factors of price, quality of experience, and ease of access to be equal, most skiers likely prefer to use mountain resorts that leave the least ecologically damaging footprint. However, the way in which these footprints are measured must be standardized so that resort users have the necessary information to make informed decisions. For example, if regional ski reports stated the number of trails open, snow depth, lift ticket price, and a "green index" rating, skiers could use this information to weigh resort land and energy use policies against cost and ski experience.[86] EPA's Sustainable Slopes program was a first step toward this goal, but with no current federal support for the program and no consistent evaluation protocol across resorts, the indices generated will probably be of limited value to resort users.[87]

A key ingredient that enhances quality of the skiing experience is the scenery associated with high elevation environments. As such, mountain resorts have a vested interest in maintaining the aesthetic quality of mountainous areas. Unfortunately, the combined effects of habitat loss, modification, and fragmentation, particularly on wildlife populations, may not be readily apparent to skiers. Armed with information about the ecological impacts of the resort, economic pressures may allow resort users to indirectly influence land use changes that positively impact wildlife populations. Substantial opportunities exist for biologists and resort managers to collaborate on sound conservation practices. In the Northeast, global warming may pose the greatest long-term threat to the ski industry and is thus an obvious common rallying point for conservationists and business owners. Further, mountain resorts represent a unique entry point into alpine ecosystems; both biologists and resort managers should capitalize on the myriad opportunities to educate visitors.

---

86 *See, e.g.,* Ski Area Citizen's Coalition, http://www.skiareacitizens.com/ (last visited Feb. 23, 2008).

87 Assessment and Watershed Protection Division, Office of Wetlands, Oceans & Water, U.S. Envtl. Protection Agency, *Notes on Watershed Management: Ski Resorts Pledge to Protect the Environment*, NONPOINT NEWS-NOTES, Dec. 2000, at 1, 23.

Summary and Conclusion

The effects of mountain resorts on wildlife habitat and populations have been poorly studied, despite widespread concern over the ecological effects of development and habitat modification in high elevation ecosystems. Habitat loss, habitat modification, and habitat fragmentation are the three primary means by which mountain resorts affect wildlife populations. Habitat loss will have the greatest effect on species with specialized habitat requirements. For example, Bicknell's thrush (*Catharus bicknelli*) are restricted by habitat structure and elevation, aquatic salamanders by stream quality, and black bears (*Ursus americanus*) by loss of key mast areas. The effects of habitat fragmentation are most severe for species that have large area requirements, poor gap-crossing ability, and low tolerance of edge effects.

Our spatial analysis of development at the Stowe and Stratton ski areas suggests that under current management scenarios, populations have theoretically declined by a range of 32 percent to 41 percent for species with approximately 1.0-hectare territories, while species with approximately 10.0-hectare territories have experienced population declines ranging from 64 percent to 73 percent. For a species with a 10.0-hectare territory, edge sensitivity of 25 meters could increase population declines from 75 percent to 89 percent. The results of our spatial analysis further suggest that species such as barred owls (*Strix varia*) and northern goshawks (*Accipiter gentilis*) may be particularly vulnerable to fragmentation on ski areas because multiple components of their life history make them vulnerable to development on mountain resorts. Other species may be similarly vulnerable to mountain development.

Life history traits such as complex life cycles, susceptibility to predation, limited mobility, sensitivity to disturbance, use of humid microclimates, and dependency on leaf litter fauna will also increase species' risk of local extinctions. As a fragmenting mechanism, ski trails are relatively benign in comparison to roads, agricultural fields, and urban development. However, most resorts maximize recreational benefits by dispersing trails across the mountain slope, thereby greatly increasing forest fragmentation. Consequently, management practices that minimize disturbance, edge effects, and additional fragmentation will have the fewest negative effects on wildlife populations.

A primary concern regarding high elevation development is the failure to account for long-term cumulative effects of development. Percolation theory predicts that small changes in the amount of forest clearing can have significant impacts on habitat connectivity. Additional losses of 1.0 or 2.0 hectares may cause abrupt declines in habitat quality for a particular species. Cumulative effects of habitat loss can be modeled through existing spatial databases and should be explicitly considered in the planning process for developments in and around mountain resorts. Unfortunately, existing legal and regulatory mechanisms provide little recognition of the importance of key ecological processes (e.g., predation, competition, or herbivory). Therefore, our current species-based approach to conservation may limit our ability to maintain these processes, which are integral to protecting wildlife and their habitat.

PART II
Loon Mountain, New Hampshire

United States Federal Law and Mountain Resort Development in the National Forest

Roger Fleming

Chapter 6
An Introduction to Loon Mountain and the Loon Resort

Introduction

The world's forests have always occupied our consciousness. This has resulted in a rich cultural history that continues to affect how we regard the forest today.[1] The place the forest has occupied in our consciousness and eventually our law has evolved through many stages, often in contradictory ways. For example, views of the forest have ranged from the primitivist standard of the "natural" in contrast with civilization, to both a lawless place and a haven for the unjustly treated, and to a place of both darkness and revelation.[2] More modern views of the forest tend to be less romantic and include the forest as an economic machine, an ecosystem or home of biodiversity, and a wilderness for solitude or recreation.[3] These modern visions of the forest were first evident in the law in the United States at the state and local level dating back to colonial times when forests were viewed as a resource for wood, water, recreation, and game.[4]

For over a century now, federal laws in the United States have reflected the view of the forest as an aggregate of goods and services, with emphasis on the production of timber.[5] The differing views of the forests, however, have continued to compete for primacy in United States culture and equal footing in the law. Built upon the foundation of several preceding federal statutes, the National Forest Management Act of 1976 is designed to promote the long-range planning of our national forests for multiple use and sustained yield of the forest's renewable resources.[6]

National forests today total some 188 million acres, or about 8.5 percent of the total land area in the United States.[7] More than one-tenth of these lands are in

---

1 *See* Richard O. Brooks et al., Law and Ecology: The Rise of the Ecosystem Regime 207 (2002).

2 *See id.*

3 *See id.* at 207–08; U.S. Dep't of Agric., Forest Service, White Mountain National Forest Final Environmental Impact Statement Land and Resource Management Plan, Record of Decision 2 (1986).

4 *See* Brooks et al., *supra* note 1, at 208.

5 *See id.* at 208–09.

6 *See* 16 U.S.C. §§ 1601–1614 (2007), Pub. L. No. 93-378, 88 Stat. 476 (1974).

7 *See, e.g.,* 36 C.F.R. § 200.4b(2)(ii) (2007); U.S. Dep't of Agric., Forest Service, 2006 Performance and Accountability Report D-7 (Nov. 2006); *see also* http://www.fs.fed.

Alaska; thus, national forests in the contiguous 48 states total about 166 million acres, or about 7.5 per cent of the land.[8] Under the original legislative mandate in 1897, the national forests were conceived as a source of timber and water, but during the 1900s, management objectives were broadened to include recreation, wilderness areas, fish and wildlife management, and mineral extraction.[9] In many instances, the Department of Agriculture's National Forest Service (Forest Service), which is charged with managing the national forests, has issued use permits and leased rights to private entities as allowed by law. Despite the years of management for the production of timber, the fact that this relatively small amount of public forest land is so heavily managed for the production of goods and services by private entities remains antithetical to the strongly held views of many citizens.[10] These citizens argue that our national forests should be held for either nonconsumptive recreation like snowshoeing and hiking or as reserves for the protection of the forest, the waters that flow through it, and the wildlife and biodiversity it supports.[11] And some citizens who are aware of the nation's long history of using public forest lands for timber production are surprised to learn that our national forests are also subject to development for consumptive forms of recreation ranging from trail riding on all-terrain vehicles and snowmobiles to development as privately-held four-season resorts for skiers, snowboarders, and mountain bikers.

In 2002, the Forest Service recommitted itself to the Loon Mountain Ski Resort (Loon Resort), located in the White Mountain National Forest near Lincoln, New Hampshire, with the approval of further development of the existing resort and expansion onto adjoining national forest lands on South Mountain (together the South Mountain Expansion). This resort is operated on national forest lands under permits issued first in 1965 to a private, for-profit corporation, the Loon Mountain Recreation Corporation. In retrospect, the arguments justifying the occupation of national forest lands in Lincoln probably seemed very different when the resort was initially approved, since like so many other ski areas in New England it was

---

us/aboutus/meetfs.shtml (last visited Feb. 8, 2008). The Forest Service also manages over 4 million acres of national grasslands.

8 *See* http://www.fs.fed.us/r10/ro/about/ (last visited Feb. 8, 2008). Hawaii has no national forest lands.

9 *Compare* the Forest Service Organic Administration Act of 1897, 16 U.S.C. § 475 (2007), *with* the Multiple Use Sustainable Yield Act of 1960, 16 U.S.C. § 528 (2007).

10 *See, e.g.,* U.S. Dep't of Agric., Forest Service, Loon Mountain Ski Resort Development and Expansion: Final Environmental Impact Statement D-30–45 (Feb. 2002) [hereinafter South Mountain Expansion FEIS] (containing public comments stating, for example, that private, for-profit companies should not be allowed to operate on public land, and that the Forest Service has a mission to protect the forest and the waters that run through the forests, and not to act as facilitators of resources consumption by industries).

11 *See id.* Note that the Wilderness Act of 1964, 16 U.S.C. §§ 1131–1136 (2007), provides for the establishment and administration of lands as unimpaired wilderness. See Chapter 10 *infra* at note 3 and accompanying text.

relatively small and the Lincoln area, including the national forest, was transitioning from the end of a long history of heavily industrialized timber operations. The year of the decision, 1965, also seems to have narrowly preceded the full blossoming of the environmental movement in the United States.

The Loon Resort has grown incrementally over the years into a four-season resort that today is significantly different from the initial modest ski operation approved by the Forest Service to provide recreational skiing opportunities on national forest lands. It is evident from this transition that the concept of recreation and what it means to recreationally ski has also significantly changed. The changes at the Loon Resort are typical of those that are taking place throughout the ski industry, and as an increasing amount of the nation's privately held forest lands also yield to the developers' bulldozer and the environmental stresses on the nation's mountain ecological systems mount, objective reexamination of our forest management laws and the way they are implemented may be warranted. Thus, to examine some of the important issues arising at a national scale from decisions to develop federal forest lands into mountain resorts, this case study considers the decision made by the Forest Service in 2002 to authorize the Loon Resort South Mountain Expansion. Although the decision involved an existing resort, the new development and expansion onto additional national forest lands provide an excellent analytical focal point because the potential impacts were determined to be significant and triggered review under several core federal statutes. Specifically, this case study examines whether federal law causes decision-makers to take an ecosystem-based approach when making decisions related to mountain resort development on federal lands.

This chapter provides an introduction to the Loon Mountain area and the Loon Resort, and it describes the South Mountain Expansion proposal. The next chapter (Chapter 7) introduces the federal legal regime governing mountain resort development on national forest lands by reviewing the history of the regulatory approvals and related events that led up to the penultimate South Mountain Expansion proposal. Chapter 8 analyzes whether the law caused decision-makers to take an ecosystem-based approach when deciding to approve the Loon Resort's South Mountain Expansion proposal, focusing primarily on the National Forest Management Act and the National Environmental Policy Act. The chapter concludes by discussing the related question of whether the existing law *could* cause, or at least allow for, an ecosystem-based approach. Chapter 9 discusses whether other federal laws contribute to an ecosystem-based approach to resort development, in particular the Clean Water Act and the Endangered Species Act. The final chapter in the case study (Chapter 10) discusses several overarching conclusions drawn from the Loon Resort experience, and briefly discusses some legal and policy changes that could be considered in order to improve the likelihood of an ecosystem-based approach to decision-making for mountain resort development on federal lands. Although federal law plays a dominant role in this case study, given the location of the resort primarily on federal land, this case study also briefly illustrates how federal laws relate to certain state and local laws.

The White Mountain National Forest and Lincoln, New Hampshire

Loon Mountain and the Loon Resort are located along the East Branch of the Pemigewasset River in the town of Lincoln in central New Hampshire. Lincoln sits at the intersection of Interstate 93 and the western end of the Kancamagus Highway, which runs east to the town of Conway in eastern New Hampshire. Less than three hours' drive from both Boston, Massachusetts, and Montreal, Canada, Lincoln and its neighboring towns are ensconced within a pocket of privately held land that is carved out from lands making up the western part of the White Mountain National Forest. (See Figure 6.1).

The White Mountain National Forest encompasses nearly 800,000 acres in north-central New Hampshire and western Maine.[12] The forest lies in the transitional zone between the boreal, conifer-dominated woodlands of northern New England and the deciduous woodlands of southern New England's more temperate climate.[13] This area is part of what geologists call the Central Highlands physiographic province,[14] which is characterized by rugged mountain peaks and the largest alpine zone in the eastern United States.[15] The White Mountains themselves are part of the Appalachian Mountains.[16] The White Mountain National Forest contains 48 summits above 4,000 feet with several rising above 5,000 feet, including Mount Washington at 6,288 feet—the highest peak in the northeastern United States.[17] The White Mountain National Forest was established by Presidential Proclamation on May 16, 1918, following the purchase in 1914 of 7,000 acres of land in the town of Benton, New Hampshire, under the provisions of the Weeks Act of 1911.[18] The base of the Loon Resort is about 1,200 feet above sea level and the ski slopes, located within the White Mountain National Forest, rise to the summit of Loon Mountain at about 3,300 feet.[19]

The town of Lincoln can trace its cultural history as a tourist destination back to 1802 when the home of Jeremiah Stuart in Lincoln was licensed as a public inn and tavern.[20] In the 1800s, the Lincoln inns catered to summer crowds on their

---

12 *See* U.S. Dep't of Agric., Forest Service, White Mountain National Forest Final Environmental Impact Statement Land and Resource Management Plan, Record of Decision 8 (2005) [hereinafter 2005 Forest Management Plan ROD].

13 *See* South Mountain Expansion FEIS, *supra* note 10, at 3-2.

14 *See id.*

15 *See* 2005 Forest Management Plan ROD, *supra* note 12, at 8.

16 *See* Encyclopedia Britannica Online, Appalachian Mountains, http://www.britannica.com/eb/topic-30353/Appalachian-Mountains (last visited Apr. 25, 2008).

17 *See* 2005 Forest Management Plan ROD, *supra* note 12, at 8.

18 *See infra* notes 31–34 and accompanying text; U.S. Forest Service, History of the White Mountain National Forest, http://www.fs.fed.us/r9/forests/white_mountain/about/history/index.php, (last visited Apr. 25, 2008).

19 *See* South Mountain Expansion FEIS, *supra* note 10, at 3-2, 66.

20 *See* Loon Mountain's Beginnings, http://www.loonmtn.com/info/loon_history.asp (last visited June 2, 2008).

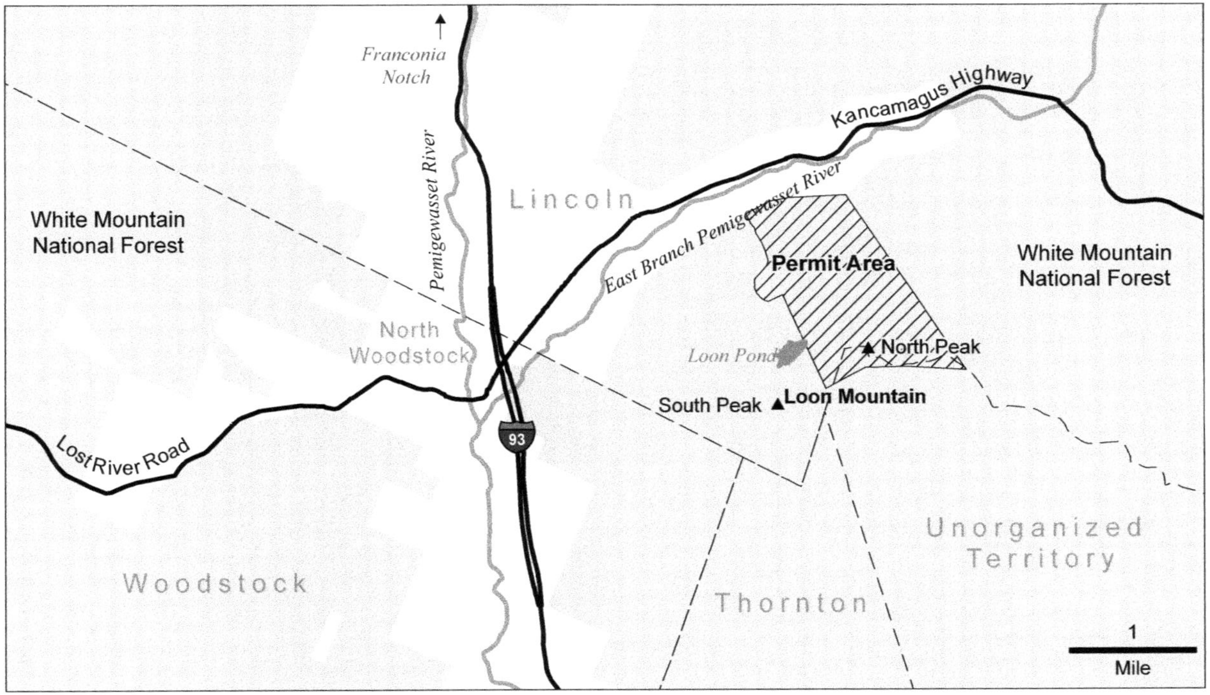

Figure 6.1 Loon Mountain and its Regional Setting

Note: The Permit Area indicates the land Loon Resort was permitted to use in the White Mountain National Forest before the South Mountain Expansion.

Data Sources: US Geological Survey in cooperation with US Environmental Protection Agency, USDA Forest Service, and other federal, state and local partners; Society for the Protection of New Hampshire Forests; Tele Atlas North America, Inc.; ESRI; Loon Mountain Ski Resort Alternative B Proposed Action (Jan. 15, 2002) (Pioneer Environmental Services)

way to see the natural wonders in nearby Franconia Notch where they could stay in grand hotels like the Flume House, first built in 1848.[21] While this era of tourism in Lincoln allowed local residents to augment what were mostly hard-earned farm incomes, it did not lead to significant growth—from 1800 to 1890 population in Lincoln grew by only 24 people, from 41 to 65.[22]

Historical references from this era suggest that the physical environment in the area was a factor in the slow development of the town. In 1856 one person wrote that, "Many portions of the town seem to have been designed by Nature as a residence for creatures of habit different from those of man."[23] There is also no evidence of permanent settlement by Native Americans in the area, whose views may be reflected in the name they gave the river—Pemigewasset, which literally means "the crooked mountain pine place."[24]

The town of Lincoln grew in the early 1890s as a result of efforts to tap the huge timber resources in the Pemigewasset River valley and surrounding mountains. In 1892, J.E. Henry and his sons began construction of a mill, railroad, homes, stores, and other structures necessary to create an industrial town about a mile east of the junction of the East Branch and the main stem of the Pemigewasset River.[25] They transformed the forest and small community of Lincoln into a "company town" that became the heart of one of the largest industrial complexes in the region. While the Henrys began the company as a timber and sawmill operation, the potential for manufacturing pulp and paper from the massive amounts of spruce in the area was soon recognized. The Henrys built a pulp and paper mill in 1902 that took advantage of the abundant supply of river water for processing the spruce and generating electricity from dams they built along the river.[26] Several large hotels were built in Lincoln during this era and as a result of the combination of industry and tourism Lincoln's population grew to 1,278 by 1910.[27]

In 1917 the Henrys sold the entire complex, including the mill, homes, store, railroad and timberland, to the Parker Young Company which carried on the operation for another four decades.[28] Unlike other industrial scale timber operations of this era that relied on rivers to move logs to their mills, between 1892 and 1948 these operations developed and relied upon the East Branch & Lincoln Railroad, which ran throughout much of what today appears to be untouched forest.[29] As the

21 *See* William L. Taylor, Railroad in the Wilderness: The East Branch & Lincoln Railroad, 1892–1948, at 7–8, *available at* http://wac.colostate.edu/journal/vol7/taylor.pdf (last visited Feb. 9, 2008).

22 *See* Loon Mountain's Beginnings, *supra* note 20.

23 *Id.*

24 *Id.*

25 *See* Taylor, *supra* note 21, at 7–8.

26 *See id.* at 9.

27 *See* Loon Mountain's Beginnings, *supra* note 20.

28 *See* Taylor, *supra* note 21, at 9.

29 *Id.* at 7, 11.

1940s drew to a close, however, virtually all of the old growth timber accessible by railroad had been cut and trucks began to take over as the more efficient means of hauling wood from new cutting areas.[30]

The intense timber harvesting taking place around Lincoln was occurring throughout the White Mountains and, but for enactment of the Weeks Act in 1911,[31] would likely have destroyed the White Mountain forests and the forests in many other parts of the East.[32] The Weeks Act authorized the Secretary of Agriculture to purchase "forested, cut-over, or denuded" lands for the purposes of watershed protection and timber production.[33] The Act represented a significant turning point for conservation and the establishment of national forests in the United States, as for the first time it provided the federal government with the authority and resources to acquire private forest lands for the purposes of management and conservation.[34]

In 1936 the Forest Service used its authority under the Weeks Act to purchase more than 68,000 acres of land from Parker Young for addition to the White Mountain National Forest, signaling the beginning of a new era in Lincoln. While the company retained cutting rights on 8,700 acres of this land for 20 years, the Forest Service was anxious to have railroad operations cease on the new government land and sought to end all logging in the area.[35] In time, the government would seek to have the area designated as a wilderness tract.[36]

In the late 1950s and 1960s, while summer tourism steadily increased, the paper industry faltered under increased operating costs and environmental pressures. Although Lincoln continued on largely as an industrial community into the 1970s, the combination of these circumstances brought an end to the one hundred year era of logging activity near Lincoln. Decreased employment forced some residents to leave town and a new economic base was sought.

The Birth and Growth of the Loon Resort

The Loon Resort was first conceived in the early 1960s as a result of one man's vision.[37] Immigrant lumber and railroad workers from Scandinavia introduced skiing to New England in the early 1870s. The first ski club in New England was

---

30 *See id.* at 15.

31 16 U.S.C. §§ 515, 521 (2007).

32 *See* Christopher Johnson, This Grand & Magnificent Place: The Wilderness Heritage of the White Mountains 171–72 (2007).

33 *See* 16 U.S.C. §§ 515, 521.

34 *See* Johnson, *supra* note 32, at 171–72.

35 *See* Taylor, *supra* note 21, at 15.

36 *See id.* at 20–21.

37 History of Loon, Loon Mountain NH, Loon History, http://www.loonmtn.com/info/winter/history.asp (last visited Jan. 30, 2008).

formed in Norway Village, New Hampshire, and though membership in this club was limited to Scandinavians the sport's popularity grew. By the early 1900s most New England colleges had ski clubs, such as the Dartmouth College Outing Club formed in 1909.[38] Sherman Adams was the ninth president of the Outing Club and went on to become governor of New Hampshire and Chief of Staff to President Eisenhower. Adams is remembered for setting the standard as perhaps the nation's strongest Chief of Staff in history; however, he was forced to resign in 1958 as a result of the "Vicuna Coat Affair," resulting from his acceptance of a vicuna coat and oriental rug from a prominent Massachusetts textile manufacturer with business before the government.[39] As a result, Adams retired and led a quiet, non-public life with his wife Rachel from his home in Lincoln, with a view of Loon Mountain.[40]

As construction of the Kancamagus Highway neared completion in 1961, thereby opening up access to over 100 square miles of White Mountain National Forest, Adams set out to find a good ski mountain somewhere along the route. He was familiar with the White Mountains from his college years with the Outing Club and his work during summer school vacations with the Appalachian Mountain Club, when he helped to locate, cut, and maintain the extensive trail system throughout the White Mountains. Later, in the 1920s, Adams worked as Director of Lumber Operations for the Parker Young Company where he was responsible for maintaining a steady flow of wood for the mill in Lincoln. As a result, he knew the mountains surrounding Lincoln well. In February of 1964, Adams snowshoed onto Loon Mountain not far from his home and concluded that the fairly gentle inclines made it suitable for intermediate skiers. It was well sheltered with a northeast-facing slope and only scattered glacial boulders. His views were confirmed by Sel Hannah, a former Olympic skier and fellow Dartmouth graduate, who had planned over a hundred ski areas across the United States. Hannah spent a week in the woods on Loon Mountain and concluded that while it would "not be an Olympic mountain, the kids and the mothers and fathers would love it."[41] It was also close to town and the soon-to-be-built interstate highway (Route 93).[42]

Because the area identified for the ski mountain was on White Mountain National Forest lands, Adams needed a permit to use the land. In 1965 his corporation, the

---

38 *See* U.S. Dep't of Agric., Forest Service, Loon Mountain Ski Area South Mountain Expansion Project: Final Environmental Impact Statement 10–11 (1992) [hereinafter 1992 South Mountain Expansion FEIS].

39 Russell Baker, *Aide Goes on TV, Tells Nation He Was Innocent of Wrong in Goldfine Case*, N.Y. Times, Sept. 23, 1958, at 1. Adams was also referred to by political commentators as the "abominable 'no' man" for his blunt-spoken style. At the height of Adams' power, it was famously joked, "What if Adams should die and Eisenhower becomes President of the United States?" *See also* James Brooke, *Sherman Adams is Dead at 87: Eisenhower Aide Left Under Fire*, N.Y. Times, Oct. 28, 1986.

40 Associated Press, *Adams Occupied With His Memoirs, Works in New Hampshire Seclusion on Review of His White House Days*, N.Y. Times, July 26, 1959.

41 *See* History of Loon, *supra* note 37.

42 *See id.*

Loon Mountain Recreation Corporation (LMRC), sought and quickly received a "special use permit" for a ski facility from the Forest Service.[43] Thus began the long and intertwined public-private relationship between the Forest Service in its management responsibilities for the White Mountain National Forest and the operator of the ski area imbedded in the national forest on Loon Mountain.

The ski area opened for business on December 27, 1966, and over 30,000 skier visits were recorded that first ski season. Though successful, even some of Adams' friends nicknamed Loon "Medicare Mountain" because its terrain was suited to intermediate skiers, a label Adams said was "both compliment and insult."[44] The lack of expert terrain was later addressed with the development of East Basin in 1968, a challenging area Sel Hannah had originally thought too steep for skiing.[45] The Loon Resort carved a steady growth trail over the years. In the 1970s, Loon invested significantly in snowmaking capacity and by the mid-1980s Loon had roughly doubled its skiable terrain with the addition of more novice and intermediate trails in the West Basin, along with additional expert trails on North Peak.[46] In terms of skier visits, by the mid-1980s the Loon Resort had grown tenfold from its first season to over 340,000.[47] Figure 6.2 later in this chapter shows the configuration of the trails as of 1986.

Over the years, the growth at the Loon Resort anchored one of New England's more explosive real estate booms.[48] The Loon Resort "product" was marketed to an affluent, primarily New England clientele who were offered dependable skiing, competitive prices, limited ticket sales to keep crowds reasonable, and quality base amenities and surrounding real estate opportunities.[49] Although it was located within a reasonable drive from Boston or Montreal, the Loon Resort's clients were primarily second-home owners, and 80 percent of the skiers stayed overnight in condominiums, second homes, or local motels and inns.[50] Lincoln's transition to a resort community was also reflected through commercial real estate development, with even the former mill complex and railroad yards converted to retail properties.

The LMRC itself got into the real estate development business in the 1980s by cutting up its old 45-room inn, shipping it to town for employee housing, and replacing it with a luxury condominium hotel called the "Mountain Club at Loon,"

---

43 *See* U.S. Dep't of Agric., Forest Service, Term Special Use Permit 70-09-22-04-4008-161-33-009-1 (Jan. 7, 1976).

44 *See id.*

45 *See id.*; *see also Renting a Slope in New Hampshire*, N.Y. TIMES, Dec. 1, 1968.

46 *See* History of Loon, *supra* note 37; Michael Strauss, *Ski Areas: What's New,* N.Y. TIMES, Nov. 8, 1970, at 1, 10.

47 *See* 1992 South Mountain Expansion FEIS, *supra* note 38, at 10.

48 *See* L. Dana Gatlin, *Good Mountain, Good Value*, 27 SKI AREA MANAGEMENT 83 (May 1988).

49 *See id.*

50 *See id.* at 84 (noting the bed base had grown from 3,000 to 13,000 in the years 1983–1987).

located slopeside on private land just outside the northern edge of the forest boundary.[51] The LMRC also prepared to take advantage of its plans to expand onto South Mountain (also known as "South Peak") by purchasing the private land running between the national forest on South Mountain and the East Branch of the Pemigewasset River from the family trust of a former paper mill tycoon who had backed Adams' original efforts.[52] Much of the LMRC's work during this period was facilitated by Sherman Adams' eventual successor, who as vice-chairman of the Lincoln town planning board helped make necessary planning and zoning changes, and negotiated a deal with Lincoln's other big developers to join the LMRC in guaranteeing town infrastructure improvements through impact fees assessed on new condominiums.[53]

The Evolution of the South Mountain Expansion Proposal

The approval of the South Mountain Expansion in 2002 was preceded by years of planning, proposals, reviews, litigation, and revised plans that influenced the shape of the final project. These are summarized here but the important pieces are explored in greater detail in the following chapters.

In November of 1986, the LMRC took its first formal step to significantly expand the Loon Resort onto South Mountain. It submitted to the Forest Service its South Mountain Expansion plan, which proposed to expand onto an additional 930 acres of forest on South Mountain,[54] more than doubling the size of the resort from its then-785 acres.[55] This proposal was based on the LMRC's conclusion that there was increased demand for additional skiing in the national forest and that additional guest capacity was needed at the Loon Resort.[56]

As the Forest Service analyzed the proposal, concerns surfaced about the capacity of the Town of Lincoln's water treatment facilities and the impacts of the LMRC's proposed water withdrawals for snowmaking from the ecologically fragile Loon Pond, located near the summit of Loon Mountain. (See Figure 6.2). The plan sought authorization to withdraw up to 15 feet of water from Loon Pond for snowmaking which, when combined with an existing authorization for a drawdown of five feet by the Town of Lincoln for its drinking water supply, would have drained Loon Pond by approximately 63 percent.[57]

51 *Id.* at 85.

52 *Id.*

53 *Id.* at 117.

54 *See* 1992 South Mountain Expansion FEIS, *supra* note 38, at 10–11.

55 *See* South Mountain Expansion FEIS, *supra* note 10, at 1-1–2.

56 1992 South Mountain Expansion FEIS, *supra* note 38, at 1, 11.

57 The Loon Resort at this time drew its water for snowmaking from Boyle Brook, a brook on Loon Mountain, the Pemigewasset River, and Loon Pond. New Hampshire's Department of Environmental Services classifies Loon Pond as a "Class A waterbody,"

Despite these concerns, the Forest Service eventually approved the proposal in March 1993. This approval was challenged in federal court by a member of the public named Roland Dubois, who was later joined by an environmental organization named RESTORE: The North Woods (RESTORE).[58] After three years of litigation, in 1996 the United States Court of Appeals for the First Circuit sided with Dubois and RESTORE, holding that the environmental analysis related to the water withdrawals from Loon Pond was inadequate.[59] Pursuant to that decision, the federal District Court in New Hampshire issued an order on May 5, 1997, invalidating the 1993 Forest Service decision and prohibiting any further development activities related to the expansion until additional environmental analysis was completed.[60] As this court battle was concluding, the LMRC on May 12, 1997, separately proposed construction of a new 16-inch snowmaking pipeline to improve snowmaking capacity and snow coverage for its existing trail system. This proposal was also approved by the Forest Service, litigated by Dubois and RESTORE, and again the approval was invalidated by the federal court pending additional environmental analysis.[61]

In the wake of these court decisions, on January 26, 1998, the LMRC submitted a letter to the Forest Service reaffirming its need for the expansion project, and it included several modifications intended to address the court decisions and changes in skier preferences and industry technology that had emerged since the original proposal. In response, the Forest Service began to analyze the revised proposal by supplementing its earlier environmental analysis; however, after receiving an initial round of public comments, it decided in December 1999 that the proposal had changed significantly enough that it needed to initiate a completely new analysis.[62] During this period, Booth Creek Ski Holdings Inc. purchased the Loon Resort, though the LMRC remained in place as a subsidiary of Booth Creek and the Loon Resort's operating entity.[63]

---

protected against measurable long-term degradation as an "Outstanding Resource Water" and describes it as unusual for its pristine nature. The pond is ranked in the upper 95th percentile of all waterbodies in New England for its high clarity and overall biological production, and it serves as a major source of drinking water for the Town of Lincoln. *See* Dubois v. U.S. Dep't of Agric., 102 F.3d 1273, 1277–78 (1st Cir. 1996). For additional discussion of the issues related to the proposed Loon Pond water withdrawals and related litigation, see the discussion in Chapter 9.

58 *See* Dubois v. U.S. Dep't of Agric., No. CIV.A.95-50-B, 1995 U.S. LEXIS 16608 (D.N.H. Nov. 2, 1995).

59 *See* Dubois v. U.S. Dep't of Agric., 102 F.3d 1273, 1277–78 (1st Cir. 1996).

60 *See* Dubois v. U.S. Dep't of Agric., CV-95-50-B (D.N.H., May 5, 1997).

61 RESTORE: The North Woods v. U. S. Dep't of Agric. et al., CV-97-435-B, 28 (D.N.H., Jan. 20, 1998).

62 *See* South Mountain Expansion FEIS, *supra* note 10, at 1-1–2.

63 Garry Rayno, *Loon Mountain Gets New Owners*, New Hampshire.com (Dec. 10, 2006), http://www.newhampshire.com/article.aspx?headline=Loon+Mountain+gets+new+owners&articleid=311 (last visited June 2, 2008).

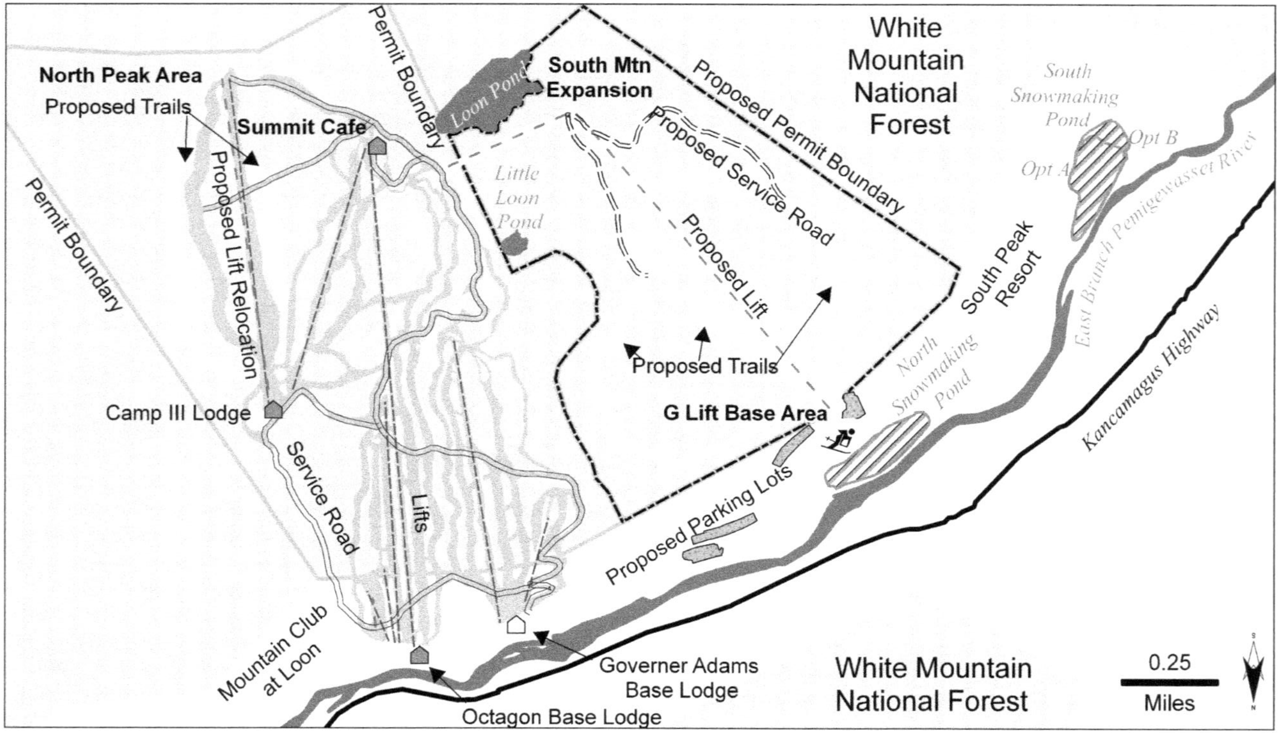

Figure 6.2 Loon Resort and the Proposed South Mountain Expansion, as proposed in 1999

Data Sources: US Geological Survey in cooperation with US Environmental Protection Agency, USDA Forest Service, and other federal, state and local partners; Society for the Protection of New Hampshire Forests; Tele Atlas North America, Inc.; ESRI; Loon Mountain Ski Resort Alternative B Proposed Action (Jan. 15, 2002) (Pioneer Environmental Services)

In response to the Forest Service's decision to initiate a new analysis of its proposal, on December 2, 1999, the LMRC formally submitted a new letter seeking approval for a revised South Mountain Expansion.[64] The revised proposal included further development of the existing national forest special use permit area, expansion onto 581 acres of national forest land on South Mountain, and development of additional private lands adjoining the national forest at the base of South Mountain for base and snowmaking-related facilities. The LMRC described the revised proposal as necessary to ensure a continued high-quality winter recreation experience for existing and future skiers and snowboarders.[65]

In order to accomplish its goal, the LMRC sought to build new trails, expand support facilities such as lodges, lifts, and parking lots, and improve snow conditions through improved snowmaking capacity, all of which would allow it to increase skier comfortable carrying capacity from 5,800 to 9,000 skiers per day. In particular, it proposed:

- Construction of six new ski trails and a freestyle jump (30.9 acres) within the existing special use permit area, widening of many existing ski trails (20.1 acres), reconfiguration of a lower trail system, and construction of six new trails (73.2 acres) on South Mountain;
- Realignment of two existing lifts, upgrade of all existing lifts, construction of two new chairlifts on South Mountain, and construction of one new J-bar lift on private land;
- The expansion of four existing lodges (two within the existing special use permit area) and construction of a new base area and lodge on private land;
- Expansion of existing parking lots and construction of new parking facilities on private land;
- Snowmaking upgrades necessary for complete coverage of 382.3 acres of ski terrain in both the existing and expanded special use permit areas;
- Continued water withdrawals within levels currently authorized from the East Branch of the Pemigewasset River and Boyle Brook, and replacement of water withdrawals from Loon Pond with new water storage ponds on private land;
- Installation of a 16-inch diameter pipeline and associated facilities for the existing special use permit area, installation of a 20-inch diameter pipeline and associated facilities to serve the expansion area, and installation of pipelines and associated facilities from the new water storage ponds necessary to provide complete snowmaking coverage for the entire resort; and
- Construction of the new water storage ponds with a total capacity of 180 million gallons on private land.[66] (See Figure 6.2).

---

64 *See* South Mountain Expansion FEIS, *supra* note 10, at 1–2.

65 *See id.* at 1–6.

66 *See id.* at 2-11–13

The Forest Service completed its environmental review and approved the South Mountain Expansion on February 26, 2002, thereby authorizing the occupation and development of the additional 581 acres of White Mountain National Forest land on South Mountain, bringing the forest occupied by the Loon Resort to a total of 1,366 acres.[67] The Forest Service approval also authorized the further development of ski trails and facilities within the existing Loon Resort boundaries. In addition, the Forest Service's analysis for the South Mountain Expansion was the basis upon which several other authorizations by federal, state, and local regulators were made, including decisions related to water storage and use by the resort and the occupation and development of approximately 180 acres of adjacent private land running along the East Branch of the Pemigewasset River at the base of the new boundary on South Mountain.[68]

Not included in the analysis was development of the nearly 400 acres of privately held slopeside land at the base of South Mountain that began to take place shortly after the Forest Service's approval. First, Booth Creek and the LMRC completed a series of high-stakes financial transactions designed, at least in part, to raise the money needed to complete the South Mountain Expansion. In October 2005, Booth Creek and the LMRC completed a multimillion dollar real estate deal with Centex Destination Properties in which Centex purchased 47 acres of the LMRC's privately held land at the base of the South Mountain Expansion area and announced plans to build 54 single family homes as part of the "South Peak Resort on Loon Mountain."[69] Centex also acquired an option on an additional 340 acres of private land owned by the LMRC running farther west along the East Branch of the Pemigewasset River, setting the stage for Centex to expand the new community through townhouses, condominiums, and a condo-hotel, in all totaling 900 units of new housing, and additional four-season "recreational amenities."[70]

---

67 *See* U.S. Dep't of Agric. Forest Service, Record of Decision: Loon Mountain Ski Resort and Expansion, Final Environmental Impact Statement 3–6 (Feb. 2002).

68 *See id.*

69 *See* Paula Tracy, *Loon Mountain Plan Includes 900 New Units*, UNION LEADER, Jan. 29, 2006; CNL Income Properties Inc., United States Securities and Exchange Commission Form 8-K (Jan. 19, 2007).

70 In advance of this deal, in March 2003 the LMRC successfully had this land rezoned from rural residential to general use zoning, thus allowing for the development of multi-family housing units and greater flexibility for commercial uses. *See* Booth Creek Ski Holdings, Inc., United States Securities and Exchange Commission Form 10-K (Oct. 29, 2004). The LMRC also undertook studies and estimated that over 900 residential units, and substantial related commercial space could be developed on the land, and it received approval of approximately 67 single family lots in November 2004. *See id.* at 10. Before ground was broken on the expansion of the ski area itself, Centex began soliciting buyers for the yet-to-be-approved subdivisions, enticing prospective buyers to become "one of the first to own property at the base of the planned new slopes." The pitch included the argument that this was the first expansion in 25 years and encouraged those interested to

Proceeds from this transaction helped enable the LMRC to initiate work on the South Mountain Expansion in November 2005.[71]

Then in January 2007, CNL Income Properties, Inc., a real estate investment trust specializing in resort and tourism-related properties, acquired the Loon Resort from Booth Creek. As part of the deal, CNL leased the resort back to Booth Creek and the LMRC, and agreed to help finance continuation of the South Mountain Expansion.[72] In addition, in anticipation of the second phase of its real estate purchase and development, in April 2007 Centex agreed to provide a significant advance to the LMRC in order to help fund the South Mountain Expansion.[73] Finally, in September 2007, Booth Creek sold its remaining equity interest in the Loon Resort to Boyne USA, Inc., a four-season resort company specializing in mountain and golf resorts.[74] The LMRC again remained in place as the operator of the Loon Resort.

On December 20, 2007, the Loon Resort opened South Mountain to skiing for the first time.[75] In total, the LMRC spent over $13 million in the summer of 2007 to complete two new chairlifts, three new trails, a new base area, and a new snowmaking system that greatly expands Loon's snowmaking capacity. The new lifts include Loon's fourth high-speed lift, the "Lincoln Express," that runs from the base to the summit of South Peak, and the "Tote Road Quad" that carries skiers and riders between the South Peak summit to the trails and lifts on North Peak. Fifty acres of new terrain were opened, representing about 35 percent of total approved terrain, with further expansion planned in the coming years.[76]

Concurrent with the opening of South Mountain to skiing, the LMRC announced completion of the first phase of the Centex residential development on the private land adjoining the national forest on South Mountain—the "South Peak Resort on Loon Mountain."[77] Phase one included infrastructure development and 67 single-family home sites. The second phase of the development, which Centex began building in 2007, has a projected eight to ten year build-out plan and is described as "an upscale, four-season mountain destination including private ski-in/ski-out

"hurry, or [they] might have to wait another quarter century." *See, e.g.*, Advertisement, Boston Globe, Jan. 19, 2006, at D-7.

71 *See* Press Release, Celebrate 40 Years of Skiing at Loon Mountain (Winter 2006/2007) (on file with author); Booth Creek Ski Holdings, Inc., United States Securities and Exchange Commission Form 8-K (Apr. 14, 2005).

72 *See* CNL Income Properties Inc., United States Securities and Exchange Commission Form 8-K (Jan. 19, 2007).

73 *Id.*

74 Press Release, Booth Creek Ski Holdings, Inc. to Transfer Control of Loon Mountain to Boyne USA Resorts (Sept. 19, 2007) (on file with author).

75 Press Release, Loon Mountain, NH, Opens South Peak, New England's Newest Ski Terrain (Dec. 20, 2007) (on file with author).

76 *See id.*

77 *See id.*

and riverside custom homes and condominiums with premium amenities."[78] The planned amenities include "The South Peak Club," featuring an indoor/outdoor pool pavilion, hot tubs, massage studio, fitness center, theater room, dining facility, and skier services.[79]

Although Sherman Adams originally received approval to use national forest lands for a modest ski area designed to provide recreational alpine ski opportunities to the public, Loon Resort today provides the full range of recreational activities typical of the modern four-season mountain resort. Activities at the Loon Resort remain anchored around alpine skiing. However, in the winter the resort also provides snowboarding, Nordic skiing and snowshoeing,[80] while during the summer months on-mountain activities include hiking, mountain biking, and horseback riding. Related development in or surrounding Lincoln resulting from the presence of the Loon Resort includes numerous hotels, inns, condominiums, restaurants, and retail stores.

The decision to approve the South Mountain Expansion is examined in this case study in an effort to answer the question whether the current United States legal framework causes decision-makers to take an ecological approach when evaluating mountain resort development on federal land, focusing primarily on federal law. However, significant decisions about the Loon Resort and the South Mountain Expansion were made prior to the analysis reflected in the final 2002 approval decision. Chapter 7 traces the evolving federal legal regime that influenced that set of somewhat complex decisions, which began with the original development of the ski area on Loon Mountain and continued through the ski area's incremental growth into a year-round resort. Because the decisions about the South Mountain Expansion are inherently linked to these earlier decisions, it is necessary to briefly review them in order to understand the 2002 Forest Service decision, analyzed in Chapter 8.

78 *Id.*

79 *See id.*

80 Specifically, in winter, Loon now provides the following activities and related amenities: over 23 miles of alpine skiing and snowboarding trails, including moguls and a half pipe, glade (tree) skiing; nordic (cross-country) skiing and snowshoeing (including guided night snow shoeing on base lodge trails); a summit lodge; a mid-mountain lodge; three base lodges and "the Mountain Club on Loon" which together provide numerous dining facilities; twelve lifts (a Gondola and 11 additional lifts); related support facilities and parking; homes and condominiums; "snowplay" facilities including day and night tubing; ice skating and bonfires; an indoor climbing wall; and horseback riding. The base lodges, support facilities, homes and condominiums, and non-skiing or snowboarding activities take place near the base of the resort, located on private lands just outside the Forest Service boundary. *See* Loon Mountain Resort, http://loonmountain.com (last visited June 10, 2008).

Chapter 7
The Legal Foundation for the South Mountain Expansion Proposal: The Early Permits and the Forest Management Planning Regime

Loon Resort's Early Permits

Sherman Adams' vision for a ski mountain along the Kancamagus Highway took shape in 1965 when the United States Forest Service (Forest Service) issued the Loon Mountain Recreation Corporation (LMRC) its original special use permit (SUP) to build and operate a modest alpine ski area on Loon Mountain.[1] From its humble beginning, the ski area grew incrementally over the years, with the LMRC acquiring a new (superseding) 30-year term SUP issued in 1976 and a series of additional annual SUPs and amendments until the Loon Resort occupied a total of 785 acres of national forest land at the time of the original South Mountain Expansion proposal in 1986.[2]

In issuing the original and subsequent permits, the Forest Service relied upon a combination of federal laws to authorize the occupation and development of Forest Service lands, including the Forest Service Organic Administration Act of 1897 (the Organic Act),[3] the Occupancy Act of 1915,[4] and the Multiple Use Sustainable Yield Act of 1960 (MUSYA).[5] The Organic Act set the initial charter for national forests, stating that:

---

1 *See* U.S. Dep't of Agriculture, Forest Service, Term Special Use Permit 70-09-22-04-4008-161-33-009-1 (Jan. 7, 1976) [hereinafter Term Special Use Permit].

2 *See id*; Loon Mountain Ski Resort Development and Expansion: Final Environmental Impact Statement at 1–1–2 (February 2002) [hereinafter South Mountain Expansion FEIS].

3 16 U.S.C. § 475 (2007).

4 *Id.* § 497. The Occupancy Act provided authority to occupy and develop national forests for recreational use of only up to only 80 acres of land for a 30-year term. *See* 16 U.S.C. § 497. As a result, Organic Act authority was used to issue annual permits for the additional use of Forest Service lands within the Loon ski area boundaries. The Occupancy Act limitations were addressed in the National Forest Ski Area Permit Act of 1986, 16 U.S.C. § 497b (2007), discussed *infra* at note 86 and accompanying text.

5 *Id.* §§ 528–531.

> No National Forest shall be established, except to improve and protect the Forest within the boundaries, or for the purpose of securing favorable conditions of water flows, and to furnish a continuous supply of timber for the use and necessities of citizens of the United States.[6]

With the passage of MUSYA in 1960, however, Congress broadened the uses of national forests, providing that they "shall be established and administered for outdoor recreation, range, timber, watershed, and wildlife and fish purposes,"[7] and it specifically strengthened the national forests' multiple-use management mandate for renewable resources by stating that national forests should be managed "for multiple use and sustained yield of the several products and services obtained therefrom."[8] Thus, from the perspective of the Forest Service, the legal justification for the issuance of the permits to the LMRC was to assist the Forest Service in meeting its obligations to provide opportunities for outdoor recreation under MUSYA.[9]

Because the permitting and development of the original ski area at Loon Mountain and the majority of its incremental growth preceded enactment of the National Forest Management Act in 1976 (NFMA),[10] discussed below, it was not subject to NFMA's comprehensive planning requirements. Nonetheless, prior to NFMA, the Forest Service did engage in land and resource planning. The earliest pre-NFMA planning focused on timber production, while after World War I the Forest Service increasingly provided for recreation and wilderness in its planning.[11] This evolution was evident in the White Mountain National Forest surrounding Lincoln, when the Forest Service purchased 68,000 acres of land under Weeks Act authority from the Parker Young Company in 1936 with the intent to end logging in the area and eventually have it designated as wilderness.[12]

---

6 *Id.* § 475. Enactment of the Weeks Act in 1911 provided the Secretary of Agriculture the authority and resources to purchase forested, cut-over, or denuded lands for the purposes of watershed protection and timber production, which represents a significant turning point for conservation and the establishment of national forests in the U.S. *See* Chapter 6 *supra* at notes 31–34 and accompanying text.

7 *Id.* § 528.

8 *Id.* § 529.

9 It became Forest Service policy over the years that winter sports facilities offering outdoor recreational opportunities would be provided by private entities authorized to use national forest lands. *See* U.S. Department of Agriculture, Forest Service Manual, § 2340.2 (Apr. 3, 2006).

10 16 U.S.C. §§1600–1614 (2007) (amending the Forest and Rangeland Renewable Resources Planning Act of 1974, Pub. L. No. 93–378, 88 Stat. 476 (1974)).

11 Charles Wilkerson and H. Michael Anderson, *Land and Resource Planning in the National Forests* 45 (1987) in Richard O. Brooks et al., Law and Ecology: The Rise of the Ecosystem Regime 208 (2002).

12 See *supra* Chapter 6 at notes 31–36 and accompanying text.

As demands for timber steadily grew after World War II, the Forest Service increasingly applied land-zoning principles to try to resolve multiple-use conflicts on forest lands, especially as it sought to implement the multiple-use objectives of the MUSYA after 1960.[13] New uses were added to management plans as they came along, as reflected in the White Mountain National Forest by the introduction of the Loon Mountain ski area in 1965. Thus, while the Forest Service historically applied planning principles in the White Mountain National Forest, the pre-NFMA plans tended to be reactive and were based on applying zoning concepts to resolve multiple-use conflicts and coordinate forest management actions rather than ecological principles.[14]

There is no history to indicate that an ecosystem perspective was applied when considering the applications for the early SUPs for the Loon Resort, and the permits themselves contain only passing references to protecting the natural resources of Loon Mountain. For example, the SUPs include a general prohibition on discharging pollutants in sufficient concentrations that would result in substantial harm to fish and wildlife or human water supplies, a requirement for prior approval before using pesticides, a requirement for an erosion control plan, and a requirement to cooperate with the Forest Service in maintaining the lands covered by the permit.[15] While meeting these conditions would be beneficial to the mountain environment and could flow as conditions from an ecological approach to decision making, there is no evidence to indicate that they were put in place after an ecosystem-based evaluation of the potential impacts of the ski area, or were in response to any specific ecosystem-based concern.

The evolution of the laws and policies affecting the early development of the Loon Resort reflect many of the problems with national forest management that Congress sought to address with the passage of NFMA. While the MUSYA had broadened the uses of our national forests it continued "to treat national forests as an aggregate of products and services requiring that a vague 'due consideration' be given to the values of the various resources."[16] This aggregate approach was reinforced through the Forest Service's practice of breaking the forest down into smaller planning units, often established in response to use demands as they arose.[17] In practice, this MUSYA-based planning process led to dissatisfaction, reflected by concerns that Forest Service management was out of balance and favored some uses at the expense of others, and that there were ineffective opportunities for public participation.[18] These concerns contributed to the passage of NFMA.

---

13 *See* Wilkerson et al., *supra* note 11, at 45.

14 *See* Land and Resource Management Plan: White Mountain National Forest 4–5 (1986) [hereinafter 1986 Forest Management Plan].

15 Term Special Use Permit, *supra* note 1, at 18–19 (Jan. 7, 1976).

16 *See* Brooks et al., *supra* note 11, at 209; 16 U.S.C. § 529.

17 *See* Brooks et al., *supra* note 11, at 209.

18 *See* 1986 Forest Management Plan, *supra* note 14, at 5.

National Forest Management Planning Enters the Picture

Since 1976, the Forest Service's forest management responsibilities have been primarily carried out through forest management planning as outlined within the framework of two principal laws: the National Forest Management Act[19] and the National Environmental Policy Act[20] (discussed below). NFMA provides the comprehensive framework, primary source of direction, and substantive legal obligations of the Forest Service as it fulfills its management mandate for Forest Service lands. The central element of NFMA is the institution of land and natural resource planning as the basic means to achieve the productivity and use objectives for the renewable resources of Forest Service lands.[21] Aside from timber, mineral, and livestock operations, all commercial uses of Forest Service lands are designated as special uses and must be specifically authorized through SUPs.[22] The Forest Service issued its first Land and Resource Management Plan (Forest Management Plans) for the White Mountain National Forest in 1986 (the 1986 Forest Management Plan discussed below), and issued a new SUP for the South Mountain Expansion in 2002.[23]

Forest Management Plans are prepared pursuant to NFMA regulations promulgated by the United States Department of Agriculture within which the Forest Service resides.[24] The purpose of the plans is to provide for multiple use and sustained yield of products and services from national forests and to guide all natural resources activities for the 15 years following plan adoption.[25] Forest Management

---

19 16 U.S.C. §§ 1600–1614.

20 42 U.S.C. §§ 4321–4370f (2007).

21 16 U.S.C. § 1604.

22 36 C.F.R. § 251.50 (2007).

23 See the discussion in Chapter 8 *infra*.

24 36 C.F.R. Part 219 (2000). The National Forest planning regulations contained in Part 219 are a significant source of controversy as this book goes to press. Regulations issued in 1982 clearly guided planning activities for nearly 20 years. *See* 47 Fed. Reg. 43,026 (Sept. 30, 1982) as amended by 48 Fed Reg. 29,122 (Jun 24, 1983) and 48 Fed. Reg. 40,383 and (September 7, 1983) (collectively the 1982 Planning Rule). Although at least two different sets of new planning regulations have been published as final rules since November 2000, efforts by the Forest Service under the George W. Bush administration to prevent the 2000 revisions from going into effect and then litigation by environmental organizations to successfully enjoin implementation of the Forest Service's 2005 final revisions have resulted in the 1982 Planning Rule being applied in most forest planning decisions through 2008. Further, the South Mountain Expansion and the underlying 1986 Forest Management Plan were both completed under the 1982 Planning Rule, and the 1982 Planning Rule remains the standard from which current "reform" efforts are being judged. Therefore, unless otherwise indicated, references to the Forest Service's planning regulations in this text refer to the 1982 Planning Rule. Further discussion of the ongoing efforts to revise the Forest Service's planning regulations is included in Chapter 10.

25 16 U.S.C. § 1604(e)(1), (f)(5).

Plans also provide the direction that the Forest Service will use to manage fish and wildlife habitat and to maintain viable populations of existing species in the habitat area.[26] In accomplishing this, plans must provide for the "coordination of outdoor recreation, range, timber, watershed, wildlife and fish, and wilderness."[27] The statute requires "a systematic interdisciplinary approach to achieve integrated consideration of physical, biological, economic and other sciences."[28]

Though written prior to the time the field of conservation biology emerged and placed a focus on the preservation of biodiversity,[29] NFMA mandates that Forest Management Plans "provide for diversity of animal and plant communities based on the suitability and capability of the specific land area in order to meet overall multiple-use objectives."[30] Regulations established the requirement to maintain populations of existing species and mandated the selection of management indicator species.[31] Management indicator species are important tools for analysis that are used to assess the effects of management alternatives on plants, animals, and biological communities.[32] Planning alternatives must be stated and evaluated in terms of the amount and quality of habitat and of animal population trends for the management indicator species.[33] "Population trends of the management indicator species [are to] be monitored and relationships to habitat changes determined."[34] Regulations also require the use of "quantitative data making possible the evaluation of diversity in terms of its prior and present condition."[35] While the mandate for biodiversity considerations clearly signals a joinder between ecological insights and forest management regulations, no specific scientific methodology was required, thus leaving considerable discretion to the Forest Service.[36]

Citizen participation in the planning process is primarily guided by the procedural framework established through the National Environmental Policy Act,[37] although NFMA itself requires that the Forest Service provide for public participation in the development, review, and revision of Forest Management Plans.[38] This includes making plans or revisions available for public review at convenient locations near the affected forest for at least three months before final adoption of the plan.[39] During this time, public meetings or comparable

---

26 36 C.F.R. § 219.19; *see also* 1986 Forest Management Plan, *supra* note 14, at VII-B.
27 16 U.S.C. § 1604(e)(1).
28 *Id.* § 1604(b).
29 *See* Brooks, et al., *supra* note 11, at 213.
30 16 U.S.C. § 1604(g)(3)(B); *see also* 36 C.F.R. § 219.26.
31 36 C.F.R. §§ 219.19–219.19(a)(1).
32 *See id.* § 219.19(a)(1)–(2).
33 *Id.* § 219.19(2).
34 *Id.* § 219.19(a)(6).
35 *Id.* § 219.26.
36 *See, e.g.*, Sierra Club v. Marita, 843 F.3d 606, 622 (7th Cir. 1995).
37 36 C.F.R. § 219.6(b).
38 *See* 16 U.S.C. § 1604(d).
39 *See id.*

processes must be publicized and held to foster public participation.[40] These public participation provisions are intended to broaden the information base for planning decisions, ensure understanding of the public's needs, concerns and values, and inform the public of planning activities and Forest Service programs and proposed actions.[41] These provisions offer the opportunity for environmental groups, as well as local governments and others groups and individuals, to play a significant role in the forest management planning process.

Any agency actions within the national forest system, including decisions about whether to approve specific mountain resort developments or expansions, must comply with NFMA, its regulations, and the applicable Forest Management Plan.[42] As a result, the decisions made during the forest planning stage can be pivotal in the outcome of future resort decisions—as will be seen in the next chapter. Also critical in the decision-making process is the analysis of the environmental impacts of proposed Forest Management Plans and specific mountain resorts. This analysis, including participation by the public, is guided procedurally through NEPA.

The National Environmental Policy Act's Procedural Framework

The National Environmental Policy Act of 1969[43] is regarded as the United States' environmental charter.[44] In enacting NEPA, Congress authorized and directed that, to the fullest extent possible, federal agencies carry out their regulations, policies, and programs in accordance with NEPA's policies of environmental protection.[45] The Act's purposes are to:

> declare a national policy which will encourage productive and enjoyable harmony between man and his environment; to promote efforts which will prevent or eliminate damage to the environment and biosphere and stimulate the health and welfare of man; to enrich the understanding of the ecological systems and natural resources important to the Nation; and to establish a Council on Environmental Quality.[46]

40 *See id.* The Forest Service must provide at least 30 days' notice for public participation on activities associated with Forest Management Plan development and at least 30 days for filing any written comments on plans. *See* 36 C.F.R. § 219.6(g).

41 36 C.F.R. § 219.6(a).

42 *Id.* § 219.10. The Forest Service's final decisions are subject to appeal to federal court. *Id.* §§ 217 and 251.

43 42 U.S.C. § 4321–4370f (2007).

44 40 C.F.R. § 1500.1(a) (2007).

45 42 U.S.C. § 4322; 40 C.F.R. § 1500.2.

46 42 U.S.C. § 4321. NEPA also declares it the "continuing policy of the Federal Government ... to use all practicable means and measures ... to create and maintain conditions under which man and nature can exist in productive harmony, and fulfill the

While this language contains substantive implications, NEPA is largely considered a procedural statute.[47] At the heart of NEPA lies its requirement that federal agencies produce an environmental impact statement (EIS) containing an objective evaluation of a reasonable range of alternative actions prior to undertaking "major Federal actions significantly affecting the quality of the human environment."[48] This requirement seeks to improve the environmental outcomes of federal agency decisions by forcing comprehensive analysis and disclosure of the expected consequences of agency actions.[49] In addition to the EIS requirement, NEPA requires that agencies, among other things, "utilize a systematic, interdisciplinary approach which will insure the integrated use of the natural and social sciences and the environmental design arts in planning and in decision-making ... ; initiate and utilize ecological information in the planning and development of resource-oriented projects;" and make available to other government entities and individuals advice and information useful in enhancing environmental quality.[50]

Once an agency makes a final decision meeting NEPA's procedural requirements, the judicial role is limited to whether the agency "considered" the environmental consequences of its action.[51] The Act's procedural provisions should not be underestimated, however, as they have been enforced vigorously by courts.

Specifically, NEPA's provisions require that the EIS include analysis of any adverse and unavoidable environmental effects of the proposed action, alternatives to the proposed action, the relationship between the short-term uses of the environment and the maintenance and enhancement of long-term productivity, and any irreversible and irretrievable commitment of resources.[52] Actions that could significantly affect the quality of the human environment must be disclosed and analyzed in terms of the "context and intensity" that makes them significant.[53] Under NEPA's analysis, the relevant effects are wide-ranging. They may be ecological (such as the effects on natural resources and on the components,

---

social, economic, and other requirements of present and future generations of Americans." *Id.* § 4331(a). The Council on Environmental Quality, among other things, issues regulations to assist federal agencies in implementing NEPA. 40 C.F.R. Part 1500.

47 *See* Yankee Nuclear Power Corporation v. NRDC, 435 U.S. 519, 558 (1978). NEPA contains a seldom invoked substantive provision that requires federal agencies to attain the widest range of beneficial uses of the environment without degradation, preserve important natural aspects of the national heritage, maintain an environment which supports diversity, and enhance the quality of renewable resources, and maximize recycling of depletable resources. *See* 42 U.S.C. § 4331(b).

48 42 U.S.C. § 4332(C); 40 C.F.R. § 1502.14.

49 *See generally* Bradley C. Karkkainen, *Toward a Smarter NEPA: Monitoring and Managing Government's Environmental Performance*, 102 Colum. L.Rev. 903 (2002).

50 *See* 42 U.S.C. § 4332(2)(A)(G)(H).

51 *See* Stryker's Bay Neighborhood Council, Inc. v. Karlen, 444 U.S. 223, 227 (1980).

52 42 U.S.C. § 4332(2)(C)(ii)–(iv).

53 40 C.F.R. § 1508.27.

structures, and functioning of affected ecosystems), aesthetic, historic, cultural, economic, social, or health, whether direct, indirect, or cumulative in nature.[54] Indirect effects must be reasonably foreseeable, and may include growth inducing effects and other effects related to induced changes in the pattern of land use, population density or growth rate, and related effects on air and water and other natural systems, including ecosystems.[55]

From a procedural perspective, the federal official responsible for the agency action must consult with and obtain the comments of any federal agency with legal jurisdiction or special expertise with respect to any environmental impact involved, and the EIS must be circulated to interested federal, state, and local agencies and "shall accompany the proposal through the existing agency review processes."[56] NEPA also requires federal agencies to meet minimum standards for public participation throughout the development of the EIS beginning with "scoping," which is a public process designed to determine the scope of issues to be addressed in the EIS.[57] At minimum, additional opportunities for public participation are also provided during the draft environmental impact statement (DEIS) stage and the final environmental impact statement (FEIS) stage of the analysis.[58]

NFMA regulations require that the Forest Service prepare an EIS for each proposed Forest Management Plan according to procedures established to comply with NEPA's statutory requirements and implementing regulations.[59] Consistent with this requirement, the Forest Service prepared an EIS analyzing the environmental impacts of the 1986 Forest Management Plan,[60] and as discussed in Chapter 8, the Forest Service determined that the South Mountain Expansion proposal also triggered NEPA review.[61]

The permitting and development of the original Loon Resort, however, preceded enactment of NEPA.[62] Although later and superceding SUPs were issued to the LMRC for ski operations after the passage of NEPA, it appears that the Forest Service never interpreted the issuance of these permits, and any related approvals for further development of the resort or changes in the existing Forest Service multiple-use plans, as triggering the need for detailed environmental analysis

---

54 *Id.* §§ 1508.25, 1508.27.

55 *Id.* § 1508.8.

56 42 U.S.C. § 4332(C).

57 *See* 40 C.F.R. §§ 1501.7, 1506.6.

58 *See id.* §§ 1502.9(a)–(b), 1506.6, 1506.10. EISs may also be supplemented (SEIS) if the agency makes substantial changes to the proposed action, if there are significant new circumstances or information that are relevant, or if the agency determines the purposes of the act will be furthered by doing so. *See id.* § 1502.9(c).

59 36 C.F.R. § 219.7(c).

60 White Mountain National Forest Final Environmental Impact Statement, Land and Resource Management Plan, Record of Decision, 1 (1986) [hereinafter 1986 Forest Management Plan ROD].

61 See *infra* Chapter 8 at notes 2–6 and accompanying text.

62 42 U.S.C. § 4321–4370f (2007).

under NEPA—until the South Mountain Expansion proposal. The Forest Service could have interpreted the various decisions it made after NEPA's effective date as triggering NEPA's environmental review requirements, but the fact that the ski area already existed, combined with the Forest Service's inexperience with implementing NEPA, likely left those decisions beyond NEPA's reach as a practical matter.

Thus, the EIS provides the framework for analysis of the environmental, social, and economic consequences of proposed Forest Management Plans and significant mountain resort developments, including the framework for communication and collaboration among federal agencies, and between federal agencies and those who will receive the benefits and bear the burdens of the impacts of the decisions made. The heart of the EIS is the presentation and analysis of the environmental effects of a reasonable range of alternative actions, including an alternative that proposes the Forest Service take no-action.[63] The EIS provisions of NEPA have been found by courts to be "action forcing," requiring the agency to not only prepare the EIS, but also to "consider environmental issues just as they consider other matters within their mandate."[64] The details of how NEPA applied to the South Mountain Expansion are explored in Chapter 8, but the 1986 Forest Management Plan and its evaluation under NEPA laid the groundwork for the future expansion.

The 1986 White Mountain National Forest Management Plan: Opening the Door for Future Expansion

On April 30, 1986, ten years after enactment of NFMA, the Forest Service approved the first Forest Management Plan for the White Mountain National Forest.[65] The environmental impacts of the proposed 1986 Forest Management Plan, and several alternative management plans, were analyzed in an EIS,[66] and a "record of decision" was issued explaining the Forest Service's decision.[67] The plan established several management goals, including to protect soil and water

---

63 *See* 40 C.F.R. § 1502.14.

64 Calvert Cliff's Coord. Comm. v. United States Atomic Energy Comm'n, 449 F.2d 1109, 1122 (D.C. Cir. 1971); 40 C.F.R. § 1500.1(a).

65 *See* 1986 Forest Management Plan ROD, *supra* note 60, at 47. The planning approach for the1986 Forest Management Plan was broken into four phases. In phase one the Forest Service identified the resource-related issues, concerns and opportunities to guide the analysis, while phase two determined the forest's ability to supply outputs and uses (goods and services) and estimated demand for those outputs and uses over time. Phases three and four established the management direction of the forest through developing and analyzing alternative plans that sought to take advantage of opportunities for using and developing forest resources and by addressing public issues and management concerns. *See* 1986 Forest Management Plan, *supra* note 14, at I-1.

66 *See* White Mountain National Forest Final Environmental Impact Statement, Land and Resource Management Plan 2 (1986) [hereinafter 1986 Forest Management Plan EIS].

67 *See* 1986 Forest Management Plan ROD, *supra* note 60.

resources, preserve a natural landscape distinct from the man-made environments otherwise dominant in the eastern United States, provide quality recreational opportunities not likely to be provided on other lands, manage for indigenous wildlife species including threatened, endangered and sensitive/unique species, use timber management as a tool to achieve future desired conditions and resource objectives, and feature northern hardwood management over softwood in order to meet the demand for high quality hardwoods in specialty products.[68]

The Forest Service's management goals and planning approach under the 1986 Forest Management Plan reinforce that, with the passage of NFMA, the Forest Service's fundamental goal in managing forests did not change from providing for the multiple use and sustained yield of the products and services derived from national forests.[69] The 1986 Forest Management Plan does indicate, however, that the new planning process introduced through NFMA led the Forest Service to more carefully coordinate the various uses of the forest's natural resources.[70] The process included discussion of some of the impacts of the management alternatives on the habitat necessary to maintain viable populations of wildlife species,[71] and the provision of significant opportunities for the public to participate in the planning process.[72] As was the case elsewhere around the nation, the plan successfully incorporated much of the appropriate terminology characteristic of the then emerging field of conservation biology and helpful for implementing an overall ecological approach to decision making, but many of the Forest Service's key assumptions and use of tools such as indicator species lacked the substantive content of contemporary ecological thought.[73]

Specifically in terms of the 1986 Forest Management Plan's influence on mountain resort development, the Forest Service determined that, although it would not consider developing any completely new ski resorts or phasing out existing resorts, it would consider opportunities for several of the existing resorts in the White Mountain National Forest to expand their ski areas onto adjacent lands.[74] The LMRC responded positively to the Forest Service's solicitation of interest in future expansion and identified suitable adjacent ski terrain, and in response the

68 *See id.* at III-2–3.

69 See *supra* note 8 and accompanying text.

70 *See generally* 1986 Forest Management Plan ROD, *supra* note 60.

71 *See id.* at VII-B.

72 *See* 1986 Forest Management Plan ROD, *supra* note 60, at 9-25; 1986 Forest Management Plan EIS, *supra* note 66, at IX-K.

73 *See* Brooks et al., *supra* note 11, at 295–301 (discussing Sierra Club v. Marita, 843 F.3d 606, *supra* note 36; Sierra Club v. Marita, 843 F.Supp. 1526 (E.D. Wis. 1994); Sierra Club v. Marita, 845 F.Supp. 1317 (E.D. Wis. 1994)).

74 *See* 1986 Forest Management Plan, *supra* note 14, at II-6–7; 1986 Forest Management Plan EIS, *supra* note 66, at I-7, IX-K-67. In addition to the Loon Resort, the Waterville Valley, Attitash, and Cannon/Mittersill resorts were identified for potential expansion, while the Wildcat resort was not. *See* 1986 Forest Management Plan, *supra* note 14, at II-6–7; 1986 Forest Management Plan EIS, *supra* note 66, at III-3.

Forest Service laid the groundwork for the South Mountain Expansion by setting aside approximately 1,000 acres of forest land on South Mountain for Loon's possible expansion as part of its approval of the 1986 Forest Management Plan.[75]

The Forest Service decision to allow for potential ski area expansion was based on its view that, although demand for skiing was growing at a slower rate than in the past, ski areas would market skiing opportunities more actively.[76] In reaching this decision, the Forest Service concluded that this demand could be met through expansion of existing resorts, which it viewed as cost efficient and consistent with the recreational objectives of the forest and with the concept of multiple-use management.[77] The Forest Service reasoned that while the ski areas occupied less than 1 percent of the White Mountain National Forest, their return to the United States Treasury was far greater than its administrative costs—in total a return of $200,000.[78]

During the public comment period on the 1986 Forest Management Plan, members of the public raised concerns about potential ski area expansion, arguing that it would benefit only few people while degrading the forest and surrounding area and burdening local communities, and therefore that it should occur only on private land.[79] The Forest Service acknowledged that ski area development may have physical, biological, social, and economic impacts on the national forest and adjoining lands, but it did not undertake any substantive analysis of the expansion's potential impacts, including the ecological impacts, on the forest or surrounding area.[80] The EIS analysis generally discussed the fact that ski-area development activities, such as tree cutting for trails, water demand for snowmaking, and the spillover effects to the surrounding community, could be potentially significant. However, it concluded that such impacts would be concentrated on specific locations and tied to the scale of any specific, future proposal, and, therefore, that those impacts would be identified and evaluated through the NEPA process when a site-specific expansion project was submitted.[81] The Forest Service also reasoned that the total ski area development in the forest would be a small percentage of the overall forest and concluded, but did not discuss, that any impacts of development from recreation would be temporary.[82] The LMRC submitted its original site-

75 *See* 1986 Forest Management Plan ROD, *supra* note 60, at 5; 1986 Forest Management Plan EIS, *supra* note 66, at II-39, II-48, IX-K-66.

76 *See* 1986 Forest Management Plan EIS, *supra* note 66, at I-7, IV-7.

77 *See id.* at II-39, IV-7, IX-K-66; 1986 Forest Management Plan ROD, *supra* note 60, at 11.

78 *See* 1986 Forest Management Plan EIS, *supra* note 66, at III-3.

79 *See id.* at IX-K-65.

80 *See id.* at IX-K-66.

81 *See id.* at IV-6, III-48, IX-K-66; 1986 Forest Management Plan ROD, *supra* note 60, at 11; 1986 Forest Management Plan, *supra* note 14, at II-7, III-93.

82 *See* 1986 Forest Management Plan EIS, *supra* note 66, at III-3, IV-6; 1986 Forest Management Plan ROD, *supra* note 60, at 45;

specific expansion proposal in November 1986, less than seven months after the approval of the plan.[83]

Thus, the Forest Service's approval of the 1986 Forest Management Plan opened the door for future expansion of the Loon Resort onto South Mountain. In reaching its decision, the Forest Service concluded that the identified area had suitable terrain for skiing and met certain other financial and policy criteria, but never analyzed whether it was suitable for development from an ecological perspective. While it may be reasonable for the Forest Service to note that the impacts of expansion would vary depending upon the scope and intensity of a site-specific expansion proposal, a reasonable range of alternative development scenarios could have been identified and analyzed within the NFMA and NEPA decision-making framework in order to gain the integrated planning perspective sought by NFMA. Further, because this was the first White Mountain National Forest Management Plan to be developed under NFMA, it could have been reasonable for the Forest Service to undertake a comprehensive evaluation of whether the existing ski resorts were compatible with the forest ecology, NFMA's goals, and the specific goals established in the 1986 Forest Management Plan. NFMA, however, leaves significant discretion to the Forest Service to determine the specific methodology and other criteria for its planning analysis, and the courts have shown great deference to the Forest Service's judgment.[84]

Delaying analysis until a site-specific expansion proposal is submitted for approval may also make it more difficult for the public to participate effectively. On the one hand, at the time when the Forest Service considers the Forest Management Plan, the public's concerns may be found to be not yet ripe for analysis, while on the other hand, by the time a site-specific expansion proposal is made, the persuasiveness of the public's concerns may be compromised by the fact that the proposal is for an area already approved as suitable for expansion. Although the South Mountain Expansion proposal triggered analysis under the NFMA and NEPA framework, designation of the expansion area on South Mountain through the 1986 Forest Management Plan played a significant role in the subsequent decision making, and ultimately helped pave the way for the expansion of the Loon Resort—an issue further considered in the next chapter.

The Warming Legal Relationship Between the Forest Service and the Ski Industry

The same year that the Forest Service completed the 1986 Forest Management Plan, Congress responded to ski-industry and Forest Service requests for passage of the National Forest Ski Area Permit Act of 1986 (Ski Area Permit

83 *See* U.S. Dep't of Agriculture, Forest Service, Loon Mountain Ski Area South Mountain Expansion Project: Final Environmental Impact Statement 10–11 (1992).

84 *See* Brooks et al., *supra* note 11, at 301.

Act).[85] The Act was passed in recognition of the long-term construction, financing, and operational needs of modern ski area development.[86] The Ski Area Permit Act extended the maximum length of the term for which ski area SUPs may be issued from 30 to 40 years,[87] and it removed the statutory cap on the total acreage for Nordic and alpine skiing operations, allowing "such acreage .... sufficient and appropriate to accommodate the permittee's needs for ski operations and appropriate ancillary facilities."[88] Mountain resort SUPs were also renewable at the discretion of the Forest Service,[89] with the requirements for renewal defined in each individual SUP.[90] These measures in the Ski Area Permit Act set mountain resorts apart from all other recreational and non-recreational uses of forest land.

In addition to the Ski Area Permit Act, Forest Service policy has evolved over the years into a closer relationship with the ski industry. This closeness is reflected in a memorandum of understanding between the Forest Service and ski industry[91] (Ski Industry Partnership) and the December 2000 Forest Service Recreation Agenda.[92] The Ski Industry Partnership established a "framework of cooperation" between the Forest Service, U.S. Skiing, and the National Ski Areas Association in "partnership to achieve the common goals of managing and promoting active participation in alpine recreation and sports by all people that emphasizes [...] public/private partnerships in developing recreational facilities."[93] The December 2000 Forest Service Recreation Agenda was established by the Forest Service to encourage cooperation between the Forest Service and SUP holders.[94] This cooperation is intended to improve the delivery of economically sustainable recreation and, in turn, provide a quality recreational experience to customers. The Agenda relies on a market research-based approach that assesses customer satisfaction and expectations.[95]

While these changes in law and policy help to provide the increased financial and regulatory certainty desired by the private sector, from the perspective of the

---

85 16 U.S.C. § 497b. The legislation amended the Occupancy Act of 1915. See *supra* note 4.

86 Pub. L. 99-522, § 2(c), Oct. 22, 1986, 100 Stat. 3000; *see also* 36 C.F.R. § 251.56.

87 16 U.S.C. § 497b(3)(b)(1).

88 *Id.* § 497b(3)(b)(3).

89 *Id.* § 497b(4).

90 36 C.F.R. § 251.56(b)(1).

91 *See, e.g.*, Master Service-Wide Memorandum of Understanding Between U.S. Skiing, National Ski Areas Association, and the U.S. Dep't of Agriculture Forest Service (Aug. 3, 1994) [hereinafter the Ski Industry MOU], *available at* http://www.wildwilderness.org/docs/ski-mou.htm (last visited Feb. 8, 2008).

92 *See* U.S. Dep't of Agriculture-Forest Service Recreation Agenda (December 2000) [hereinafter Recreation Agenda], *available at* http://www.fs.fed.us/recreation/programs/strategy/rec_agenda_ht.html. (last visited Feb. 8, 2008).

93 Ski-Industry MOU, *supra* note 91, at 1.

94 *See* Recreation Agenda, *supra* note 92, at 9.

95 *Id.* at 8.

public and other stakeholders, they may call into question whether all interests, including the health of the forest ecosystem, will be objectively evaluated when the Forest Service makes decisions about mountain resort development.

Thus, the legal and policy stage was set for LMRC's South Mountain Expansion proposal. The 1986 Forest Management Plan established an approved area for expansion of the Loon Resort, subject to a proposal-specific environmental analysis. Further, changes in the law and Forest Service policy encouraged continuation of the partnership between the LMRC and the Forest Service, and helped establish the certainty necessary for the significant investment required to redevelop significant amounts of the existing Loon Resort, expand onto South Mountain, and gain the commitment of partners to develop the private lands at the base of South Mountain. All that remained for the South Mountain Expansion to be realized was for the LMRC to submit its formal proposal and for the Forest Service to analyze the site-specific impacts of the proposal through the NFMA and NEPA legal framework and issue the necessary approvals. The next chapter reviews that analysis and the final South Mountain Expansion approval decision.

Chapter 8

The South Mountain Expansion: Did the National Forest Planning and Environmental Impact Statement Framework Cause Decision-Makers to Take an Ecosystem-Based Approach?

Mountain resort development in the United States' national forests triggers a number of federal forest management and related legal authorities. This analysis of the South Mountain Expansion focuses primarily on the federal legal framework provided by the National Forest Management Act (NFMA) and the National Environmental Policy Act (NEPA), which provide the substantive and procedural structure, respectively, for analysis of federal actions on national forest lands.[1] This structure dominated the analysis of the South Mountain Expansion, but as discussed in the next chapter, federal law governing water quality also played a central role, and under different circumstances the NFMA and NEPA legal framework might take a back seat to analyses under other federal laws.

The South Mountain Expansion proposal, through each of its iterations, required the Forest Service to make three key decisions. First and foremost, the Forest Service needed to decide whether to authorize the proposed construction and development on national forest lands and to determine what, if any, mitigation and monitoring measures to require.[2] This decision squarely triggered NEPA's requirement that an Environmental Impact Statement (EIS) be prepared, given the potential for the authorized activities to significantly affect the environment.[3] Second, the Forest Service needed to decide whether to issue a new Special Use Permit (SUP) for the occupancy and use of additional Forest Service lands, which

---

1 The proposal also required other state and federal permits. *See* U.S. Dep't of Agric., Forest Service, Loon Mountain Ski Resort Development and Expansion: Final Environmental Impact Statement, 1-34–35 (Feb. 2002) [hereinafter South Mountain Expansion FEIS].

2 *See id.* at 1-27; *see also* U.S. Dep't of Agric. Forest Service, Record of Decision: Loon Mountain Ski Resort and Expansion, Final Environmental Impact Statement, 3-5 (Feb. 2002) [hereinafter South Mountain Expansion ROD].

3 *See* 40 C.F.R. § 1508.18(b)(4) (2007); 40 C.F.R. § 1508.27.

could also have independently triggered an EIS.[4] Finally, the Forest Service needed to decide whether to approve an amendment to the 1986 White Forest Management Plan for the White Mountain National Forest (1986 Forest Management Plan) in order to accommodate the expansion of the Loon Resort onto South Mountain.[5] As discussed in Chapter 7, the Forest Service had already identified South Mountain as suitable for expansion of the Loon Resort in the 1986 Forest Management Plan, but at that time the Forest Service left final designation of the land for use as alpine skiing until the Loon Mountain Recreation Corporation (LMRC) submitted a site-specific construction and development proposal and an environmental analysis was completed.[6]

This chapter's discussion of the Forest Service's decision to approve the South Mountain Expansion focuses on the LMRC's December 1999 proposal, which revised the original 1986 proposal that triggered more than a decade of litigation. As explained in Chapter 6, the 1999 proposal involved expansion onto 581 acres of national forest land on South Mountain, the construction of new trails and snowmaking facilities for the existing resort and the South Mountain Expansion, and the addition of base facilities at the bottom of the mountain.[7] (See Figure 6.2 in Chapter 6). The Forest Service approved the expansion in 2002.

---

4 *See* South Mountain Expansion FEIS, *supra* note 1, at 1-27; *see also* South Mountain Expansion ROD, *supra* note 2, at 3-5. In the absence of the proposed development activities it is unlikely that the Forest Service would have viewed renewal of the existing SUP alone as triggering the EIS requirement given that prior renewals and even amendments modestly expanding the SUP boundaries did not undergo NEPA analysis. On the other hand, Forest Service regulations do provide that significant new information or circumstances can trigger the need for appropriate environmental analysis to accompany the decision to reauthorize the special use. 36 C.F.R. § 251.64(a) (2007). Thus the need for a new SUP incorporating the significant increase in occupied forest lands could be interpreted as triggering NEPA EIS requirements. *See* 40 C.F.R. § 1508.27.

5 *See* South Mountain Expansion FEIS, *supra* note 1, at 1-27; *see also* South Mountain Expansion ROD, *supra* note 2, at 3-6. Amendments of forest management plans are considered major federal actions triggering NEPA review, thus if an amendment's environmental impacts could be significant it would trigger NEPA's EIS requirement. 36 C.F.R. § 219.20(f)(2007); 42 U.S.C. § 4332(C)(2007); 40 C.F.R. § 1508.27. As discussed in Chapter 7 and below, the change in the approved use of the affected national forest lands for the expansion of the Loon Resort had already been analyzed in the EIS prepared for the 1986 Forest Management Plan, thus NEPA's EIS requirements were not triggered specifically for the proposed plan amendment. *See* U.S. Dep't of Agric., Forest Service, White Mountain National Forest Final Environmental Impact Statement, Land and Resource Management Plan, Record of Decision, 5 (1986) [hereinafter 1986 Forest Management Plan ROD]; *see* U.S. Dep't of Agric., Forest Service, White Mountain National Forest Final Environmental Impact Statement, Land and Resource Management Plan, II-39, 48; IX-K–66 (1986) [hereinafter 1986 Forest Management Plan EIS].

6 *See* 1986 Forest Management Plan ROD, *supra* note 5, at 5; 1986 Forest Management Plan EIS, *supra* note 5, at II-39, 48; IX-K-66.

7 *See* Chapter 6 *supra* at notes 64–66 and accompanying text.

In evaluating the proposed expansion, the Forest Service analyzed at least some of the impacts at three different spatial scales.[8] The Special Use Permit analysis area (SUP analysis area) totaled 1,546 acres and included the 1,366 acres of national forest land that would be occupied by the Loon Resort, plus an additional 180 acres of private land at the base of the existing SUP area, South Mountain, and along the Pemigewasset River corridor that would be used for base-facilities and activities related to water withdrawals for snowmaking.[9] Decision-makers also analyzed the impacts on two broader scales: a more general, or Loon Mountain Project, scale (LMP analysis area), and a regional scale (regional analysis area). The LMP analysis area totaled about 15,000 acres and included the SUP analysis area plus the estimated area of potential impacts to habitat outside the SUP analysis area from activities such as development of the base-facilities and water withdrawals for snowmaking.[10] The regional analysis area comprised approximately 138,000 acres and represented the Forest Service's estimated scale for analyzing the potential impacts to all species that may use the SUP or LMP analysis areas.[11] These differing scales of analysis would appear to provide an adequate basis for an ecosystem-based analysis of the South Mountain Expansion, though as discussed below and in Chapter 10, the Forest Service could consider issues related to scale at a larger policy level that would require a truly regional or even national ecosystems perspective.

The Loon Resort EIS was also significantly shaped by the way in which the Forest Service framed the analysis through the definition of the "purpose and need" for the expansion and the "scope" of the proposed actions and alternatives to be analyzed. The section below discusses the ways in which these definitions affected the Forest Service's review of the South Mountain Expansion under NEPA's procedural requirements and ultimately its ability to take an ecosystem perspective. It also considers how the analysis was influenced by the opportunities provided for participation by the public. Subsequent sections of this chapter examine the extent to which the Forest Service evaluated the ecological impacts of three specific components of the expansion plan—the cutting of trees for the creation of new trails and facilities, the withdrawal and storage of water for snowmaking, and the secondary growth that accompanies resort expansion.

How the Forest Service Framed the South Mountain Expansion Proposal Analysis

The starting point for determining whether federal law led to an ecological approach to the South Mountain Expansion approval decision is an examination

8 *See* South Mountain Expansion FEIS, *supra* note 1, at 3-133.

9 *See id.* at 3-133; S-2.

10 *See id.* at 3-133–34.

11 *See id.* at 3-133–35.

of how the Forest Service framed its analysis of the proposal. The identification of the purpose and need for the project and the determination of the scope of the proposal, two requirements established under NEPA, directly affect the range of issues analyzed and considered through an EIS. Weaknesses in how the Forest Service finally framed the proposal help demonstrate how framing the analysis can affect the ability to use an ecosystem-based perspective for decision making.

The Definition of the Purpose and Need for the South Mountain Expansion

NEPA requires federal agencies preparing an EIS to specify the underlying purpose and need the agency is responding to in proposing its action and alternatives[12]—in this case the proposed action being the authorization of new development activities, the issuance of a new SUP, and the amendment of the forest management plan. The identification of purpose and need is important because it drives the range of alternative actions the EIS will explore, and in turn the scope of public disclosure and comment. A narrowly tailored definition of the purpose and need may substantively limit the range of alternatives and environmental impacts analyzed in the EIS.[13]

On December 13, 1999, the Forest Service issued a notice of intent to prepare a new EIS and initiate scoping for the LMRC's revised December 2, 1999, South Mountain Expansion proposal.[14] The Forest Service defined the purpose and need for the expansion as composed of two parts: 1) the Forest Service's general purpose and need, dictated by its policy and management direction; and 2) the LMRC's specific purpose and need, dictated by skier market demand.[15] More specifically, the Forest Service's direct purpose and need was defined by its "responsibility of providing quality recreational opportunities to the public in an outdoor, natural setting on [Forest Service] lands."[16] The Forest Service added that:

> the basis for determining the types of activities and facilities that are appropriate at winter sports resorts, which are permitted to operate on [Forest Service] lands, is contained in federal laws and Forest Service [policies, the 1986 Forest Management Plan], and ski-area SUPs.[17]

The second part of the purpose and need was defined by the LMRC's need to provide the facilities it viewed as necessary for an enjoyable skiing

12 40 C.F.R. § 1502.13.

13 *See* Ronald E. Bass and Albert I. Herson, Mastering NEPA: A Step-by-Step Approach 67 (1993).

14 *See* South Mountain Expansion FEIS, *supra* note 1, at 1-2. See also Chapter 6 *supra* at notes 56–64 and accompanying text for a discussion of the evolution of the December 2, 1999, proposal.

15 *See* South Mountain Expansion FEIS, *supra* note 1, at 1-5.

16 *See id. See also* Chapter 7 *supra* at notes 7–8 and accompanying text.

17 *See* South Mountain Expansion FEIS, *supra* note 1, at 1-5–6.

experience.[18] The South Mountain Expansion "would accomplish this by addressing the existing shortcomings at the ski resort to meet current skier expectations for a quality winter sports recreation experience, and by positioning Loon Mountain to take advantage of potential future growth in the New England skier market, [which] in turn would allow the ski resort to remain competitively viable within their market niche into the future."[19]

The Forest Service recognized that although there were two parts to the purpose and need for the South Mountain Expansion, divided between the Forest Service and the LMRC, they were "connected through a committed long-term partnership to provide quality recreation opportunities on [forest] lands."[20] Thus, it was the Forest Service's view that the LMRC's ability to satisfy its current and future visitors and to remain healthy and competitive in its market niche was necessary to help the Forest Service to meet its policy, objectives, and direction for ski area management in the White Mountain National Forest,[21] consistent with the 1986 Forest Management Plan.

In establishing this framework for analysis, the Forest Service effectively narrowed the range of alternatives and environmental analysis on the table and, as a result, decreased the possibility for a full ecosystem-based analysis. By defining the purpose and need of the project as so closely dependent upon the LMRC's ability to make improvements to its ski resort in order to satisfy the demands of its current and future visitors, the continued existence of the resort on public lands was effectively made in advance of the analysis, and thus the question of "no Loon Resort"—or in other words an alternative to renewing the Loon Resort's SUP—was never seriously addressed[22] even though the SUP was set to expire in 2006.[23] Further, it could be argued that, although a "no action" alternative was included as required by law,[24] the narrow definition of purpose and need implicitly ruled out the option of rejecting the expansion (one of the alternatives) because expansion was necessary to meet the identified purpose and need.[25]

---

18 *See id.* at 1-6.

19 *Id.*

20 *Id.*

21 *See id.*

22 In fact, several public comments questioned whether the Loon Resort should continue to exist and recommended a "No Permit Alternative;" however, the Forest Service rejected including such an alternative for analysis on the basis that it would not meet the purpose and need for the proposal, conflict with the 1986 Forest Plan goal of expanding the Loon Resort onto South Mountain, cost the Forest Service money to reverse the conditions at the Loon Resort back to the pre-ski environment, and result in economic impacts to the surrounding communities. *See* South Mountain Expansion FEIS, *supra* note 1, at 2-34–35.

23 U.S. Dep't of Agric., Forest Service, Special Use Permit 70-09-22-04-4008-161-33-009-1 (Jan. 7, 1976).

24 *See* 40 C.F.R. § 1502.14(d).

25 *See* South Mountain Expansion ROD, *supra* note 2, at 14–15, 17–18.

This framing of the purpose and need prevented decision-makers and the public from having the opportunity to consider a detailed analysis of the larger issues, such as whether the Loon Resort should, in fact, be further developed and expanded, or whether the resort should continue to exist on federal lands at all—potentially significant questions from an ecosystem perspective but also in terms of balancing the national forest's obligation to serve multiple uses.

For example, important questions such as whether the demand for skiing justified a recommitment to the resort and its expansion could have been answered.[26] This question would seem to have been an important one to consider since the 1986 Forest Management Plan defined its recreational goals in terms of its ability to provide quality recreational opportunities not likely to be provided on other lands.[27] At the time of the South Mountain Expansion proposal, dozens of similar opportunities for skiing and mountain-related recreation existed on privately held or state-owned lands in the surrounding northeastern United States and Canada, and three additional ski areas still existed in the White Mountain National Forest alone.[28] All of these facilities are within easy reach of the same northeastern points of departure; thus, the need for what has developed incrementally into a four-season resort facility in the White Mountain National Forest is unclear. While the Loon Resort remained New Hampshire's most popular mountain resort, the data show that the number of skier visits to the Loon Resort was essentially unchanged in the years leading to the time of the South Mountain Expansion decision,[29] consistent

26 While some public comments on the EIS questioned the need to continue this type of recreational opportunity when it is being offered by private entities on private lands throughout the surrounding area, the Forest Service indicated in response that part of the niche they were targeting here was the destination crowd—skiers who come for several days—as opposed to the day skiers. This argument, however, only suggests that still additional alternatives exist as destination skiers could travel to an even wider variety of resorts in New England, New York, Canada, or beyond. This target niche argues against one of the original reasons, or purposes for the initial Loon development in the 1960s—providing a recreational alpine ski opportunity for those who did not want to travel for great distances or leave for extended periods of time. This again reflects the shell game that can occur within the bounds of the procedural requirements of NEPA and the substantive requirements of the NFMA.

27 See Chapter 7 *supra* at note 68 and accompanying text.

28 These facilities are Waterville Valley (owned by Booth Creek), Attitash/Bear Peak, and Wildcat. Booth Creek also owns Mt. Cranmore in New Hampshire. Booth Creek and the LMRC argued that their New Hampshire resorts compete in the "highly competitive" Northeast ski market that includes all of New England and eastern New York, where skiers can choose from over 50 major resorts/ski areas, seven of which are in New Hampshire alone. *See* Booth Creek Ski Holdings, Inc. Form 10-K, at 13, U.S. Securities and Exchange Comm'n (Fiscal Year Ending Oct. 29, 2004).

29 Filings with the Securities and Exchange Commission allow one to compare the three-year average for the 2001–2002 thru 2003–2004 ski seasons with the three-year average from the 1998–1999 (the first full year Booth Creek owned the LMRC) through 2000–2001 season. Booth Creek Ski Holdings, Inc. Form 10-K, at 23 (Fiscal Year Ending

with the overall trend for the Northeast.[30] A broader definition of purpose and need would have allowed for serious consideration of factors such as these.

Significantly, for purposes of this book, a focus on a broader definition that included the "no resort" alternative would have changed the ecosystem analysis of the alternative courses of action. It would have put on the table the environmental analysis of a "no resort" option, and created a different baseline for analyzing the other alternatives. Without a true no action alternative, it is difficult to understand the natural communities and thus the ecosystem that would exist in the absence of human disturbance. It is essential to know what the composition, structure, and function of the ecosystem would most likely be without human intervention in order to properly document, characterize, and measure the changes that might occur as a result of the decision to modify the use of the landscape. The analysis contained in the EIS, however, compared the proposed alternatives to the Loon Resort as it already existed.[31]

In defining the purpose and need for action narrowly, the Forest Service relied on a combination of legal mandates and policy directives. In the end, the barrier to taking the broader view was, at least in part, one of timing and the failure to coordinate among different, evolving legal regimes. The environmental impacts of the original ski area and the subsequent development and expansions were never subjected to a NEPA analysis, nor were they evaluated as part of a "no resort" alternative during development of the 1986 Forest Management Plan. The 1986 Forest Management Plan laid the foundation for expansion by identifying South Mountain as suitable for expansion, and having done so, it allowed the Forest Service to avoid serious consideration of a "no resort" alternative as it evaluated the specific South Mountain Expansion proposal, which in turn resulted in a 40-year

---

Oct. 29, 2004) and Booth Creek Ski Holdings, Inc. Form 10-K, at 5 (Fiscal Year Ending Oct. 29, 2001). In fact, the average number of skier visits on average for these years, 327,000, was basically unchanged from (slightly less than) the number of skier visits Loon received in 1987. However, the record of decision and supporting analysis argues that "[o]vercrowded trails, long lift line waits, poor skier circulation, inadequate snowmaking ability, and shortages of parking and lodge space have resulted in visitor dissatisfaction with the overall recreational experience." *See* South Mountain Expansion ROD, *supra* note 2, at 10.

30 *See* South Mountain Expansion ROD, *supra* note 2, at 10. Similar comparisons for the Northeast Region were done using three-year averages dating back to the 1995–1996 ski season.

31 The question of what is the appropriate baseline for analysis established through the "no action" alternative has been debated since NEPA's inception, with many arguing that the failure to consider the equivalent of a "no resort" alternative prevents decision-makers from understanding the full, or cumulative, environmental impacts of their decisions over time, while others take the view that such an approach could be a useless academic exercise. *See, e.g.,* Memorandum: Forty Most Asked Questions Concerning CEQ's NEPA Regulations, 46 Fed. Reg. 18026, 18027 (Mar. 23, 1981), as amended, 51 Fed. Reg. 15618 (Apr. 25, 1986).

extension of the SUP set to expire in 2006. In addition, although the Forest Service initiated the process of revising the 1986 Forest Management Plan in 2000, within three months of the submission of the South Mountain Expansion proposal,[32] that planning process was not coordinated with the review of the expansion proposal and the extension of the SUP.

Ideally, all of the decisions about the existence of a resort on national forest lands should have been coordinated and considered at the same time, in the context of a Forest Management Plan review. Alternatively, those appropriate aspects of the Forest Management Plan could be fully reopened when a specific and significant development proposal, such as the South Mountain Expansion, is made. Splitting the Forest Management Plan decisions from the decisions about the specific expansion plans and extension of the SUP resulted in a "shell game" that as a practical matter hid alternatives and potential impacts from analysis, and prevented the decision-makers and public from addressing the full breadth of the issues that are relevant to an ecosystem perspective, in particular the possibility of not expanding the resort or its eventual discontinuation.

The Definition of the Scope of the South Mountain Expansion Actions, Alternatives, and Impacts

The second critical part of framing the EIS analysis was how the Forest Service defined the scope of the South Mountain Expansion under NEPA and its implementing regulations. NEPA seeks to prohibit agencies from avoiding environmental analysis by breaking actions down into smaller component parts,[33] and the relatively broad definition of scope helps reduce the risk of fragmentation. The regulations define "scope" as "the range of actions, alternatives, and impacts to be considered in an [EIS]."[34] This range of actions will center on the principal proposed activities, but it also includes actions that may be "connected," such as those actions that automatically trigger other actions requiring an EIS, that cannot or will not proceed unless other actions are taken, or that are interdependent parts of a larger action.[35] Covered actions may also either be "cumulative," which includes those actions that when viewed with other proposed actions have cumulatively significant impacts, or "similar," which includes actions that when viewed with other reasonably foreseeable or proposed agency actions have similarities, such as in timing or geography, that provide a basis for evaluating their environmental

32 *See* U.S. Dep't of Agric., Forest Service, White Mountain National Forest Final Environmental Impact Statement, Land and Resource Management Plan, Record of Decision, 3 (2005).

33 *See* 40 C.F.R. §§ 1508.25, 1508.27(7).

34 *See id.* § 1508.25.

35 *See id.* § 1508.25(a)(1).

consequences together.[36] The defined scope of an action will derive from the purpose and need for an action and is important because it establishes what will be analyzed in the EIS. A narrow scope may limit opportunities for public disclosure and comment on the potential impacts of the proposal, and would likely substantively limit the analysis of the alternatives and impacts covered by the EIS. Thus the defined scope of the proposal can play an important role in the final decision.

In framing the South Mountain Expansion proposal for analysis, the Forest Service naturally included within the scope of its proposal those actions that would take place in the national forest, and it also considered some actions that would occur on private land. For example, the Forest Service specifically identified as connected actions construction of the new base-facilities that would only occur if the proposed action received approval, including the lodge at the base of South Mountain and some of the new parking lots and snowmaking infrastructure.[37] (See Figure 6.2 in Chapter 6.) It also identified as cumulative actions those activities that would occur regardless of the expansion proposal, such as certain other parking lot and existing lodge construction.[38]

The Forest Service, however, did not identify other resort development on private land at the base of South Mountain, including what would eventually be known as the South Peak Resort at Loon Mountain (South Peak Resort),[39] as either a connected or cumulative action to the South Mountain Expansion proposal even though key decisions about it were made close in time with the South Mountain Expansion. The development of that private land appears to have been under consideration by the LMRC over the years during which the final South Mountain Expansion proposal and EIS was developed.[40] The LMRC eventually sold the land for development by the resort development company Centex beginning in 2005, which helped finance the South Mountain Expansion.[41] The nearly 400-acre residential and commercial development project—an area approximately two-thirds as large as the national forest land slated for development—appears in most important respects to be very similar to the base-facility development activities

36 *See id.* § 1508.25(a)(2).

37 *See* South Mountain Expansion FEIS, *supra* note 1, at 1-12–13. See also Chapter 6 *supra* at note 66.

38 *See* South Mountain Expansion FEIS, *supra* note 1, at 1-12–13.

39 See Chapter 6 *supra* at notes 69–71 and accompanying text.

40 For example, as discussed in Chapter 6 the LMRC purchased the private land running between the national forest land on South Mountain and the East Branch of the Pemigewasset River and secured zoning changes necessary for residential development prior to the first iteration of the South Mountain Expansion proposal in the 1980s. See Chapter 6 *supra* at notes 52–53 and accompanying text. Within months of the final approval decision, further zoning changes and studies supporting plans for intense residential and commercial development were completed. See Chapter 6 *supra* at note 70.

41 See Chapter 6 *supra* at notes 72–73 and accompanying text.

that the Forest Service acknowledged as a connected activity.[42] For example, the development activities on private land for both were closely linked with the South Mountain Expansion and would not have occurred at anywhere near the same scale absent the South Mountain Expansion.[43]

As a result of the omission of these development activities from the scope of the South Mountain Expansion proposal actions, the environmental analysis was limited, and may have contradicted NEPA regulations on defining the scope of the proposal. In addition, this limited scope inherently had the effect of narrowing the focus of the EIS's inquiries into alternative actions and their impacts.

The range of alternatives addressed in the EIS for the South Mountain Expansion included a "No Action Alternative" (Alternative A), defined to mean no further development and expansion of the existing Loon Resort,[44] and the South Mountain Expansion Proposal (Alternative B). The four additional alternatives were: Alternative C, which would have allowed for development within the existing SUP boundaries and the limited development on South Mountain started after the 1993 expansion approval and prior to the court order stopping further construction;[45] Alternative D, which would have allowed development within the existing SUP area only; Alternative E, which was the same as Alternative D but with a new 16-inch pipeline and water storage facilities; and Alternative F, which was the same as Alternative A with only the additional snowmaking infrastructure. The Forest Service ultimately approved Alternative B.

This short description of the alternatives considered for analysis helps to demonstrate that, although the Forest Service discussed several alternatives, their range was heavily influenced by the definitions of the purpose and need for the South Mountain Expansion and its scope. The four alternatives to the No Action Alternative and the South Mountain Expansion proposal may have allowed useful exploration of different development and expansion options. Yet they were relatively narrow variations on the way development and expansion could occur, given that they did not explore the "no resort" alternative or consider the impacts

---

42 *See* South Mountain Expansion FEIS, *supra* note 1, at 1-13 ("Because these activities would occur only if the Proposed Action were implemented, they are connected actions."). It might also be argued that the South Peak Resort was an interdependent part of the larger South Mountain Expansion, as it appears it was necessary to finance the expansion activities. See Chapter 6 *supra* at notes 72–73 and accompanying text.

43 *See* 40 C.F.R. § 1502.14(f). NEPA regulations require agencies to include not only connected and cumulative actions within the scope of their analysis, but also reasonable alternatives not within the jurisdiction of the lead agency. 40 C.F.R. § 1502.14(e). This helps make clear that in cases such as this where some actions are connected but occur on private lands they should be included within the scope of the proposal.

44 *See* South Mountain Expansion FEIS, *supra* note 1, at 4-1. This alternative included some restoration activities that would be necessary as a result of the development started prior to the court order invalidating the 1993 expansion approval.

45 See Chapter 6 *supra* at note 60; see also Chapter 9 *infra* at note 17 and accompanying text.

of actions relating to the South Peak Resort on private land. Inclusion of a broader range of alternatives and associated impacts would have improved the baseline for analysis and increased the likelihood of a broader ecosystem-based analysis. The presentation of the environmental impacts of the proposal and the alternatives in comparative form is fundamental to NEPA, because it can sharply define the issues and provide a clear basis for choice among options by the decision-maker and the public.[46] Consequently, narrowing the range of alternatives can decrease the potential for considering impacts from a broader and more thorough ecosystem perspective. The Forest Service's specific analysis of these alternatives within the context of the two potentially most significant ecological impacts—tree cutting and water demand—under the EIS procedures and the standards established by the NFMA and related authorities are analyzed later in this chapter.

In the end, the failure to identify the full scope of the South Mountain Expansion proposal compromised the EIS analysis by limiting analysis of the full range of direct, indirect, and cumulative impacts.[47] Defining the appropriate scope of the proposed actions is significant not only to the question of which activities and alternatives the Forest Service might analyze and, therefore, the scope of its ecological review under NEPA, but also the ability of the public to understand and comment on the proposed development and its alternatives as contemplated by NEPA.[48]

The Role of Public Participation in the South Mountain Expansion Analysis

According to NEPA regulations, public participation is a cornerstone of NEPA's exploration of the range of alternatives and their impacts on the environment.[49] As discussed in Chapter 7, NEPA and NFMA demand that agencies allow the public to participate,[50] and the site-specific environmental analysis of the South Mountain Expansion proposal provided the public with opportunities to raise issues and concerns about the South Mountain expansion, to shape the analysis through contribution of relevant information related to the impacts of the proposal and its alternatives, and to assist the Forest Service in determining its final course of action.

46 *See* 40 C.F.R. § 1502.14.

47 *Id.* § 1502.25(c).

48 *See* 42 U.S.C. § 4332(c); 40 C.F.R. §§ 1500.1(b), 1500.2(d), 1501.7(a)(1), 1502.1, 1506.6.

49 *See e.g.,* 40 C.F.R. §§ 1500.1, 1500.2, 1502.1, 1506.6. In practice it can be difficult for private citizens to get involved and influence the outcome of federal decisions, given the complexity of federal agencies, the challenge of staying informed of their activities, and the sometimes daunting nature of the forums for participation. *See* Bass et al., *supra* note 13, at 21.

50 Any member of the public may participate in the environmental review process established under NEPA. Comments received by the Forest Service during any scoping period and in response to the draft EIS are regarded as public information, including the names and addresses of commentors.

Public participation, however, must be meaningful and timely.[51] Consequently, it is important that those interested in the proposed action participate during the public comment opportunities so that substantive comments and objections are made available to the Forest Service at a time when it can meaningfully consider them and respond to them in the Final Environmental Impact Statement (FEIS).

Although the proposal and EIS leading to the South Mountain Expansion were technically not initiated until December 1999 when the Forest Service decided that it needed to prepare a new EIS,[52] the Forest Service incorporated comments it had received during the prior 18 months when it had opened a scoping period and conducted three public meetings as it began preparing a "supplement" to the 1992 EIS invalidated by the court.[53] With the initiation of the new environmental review for the South Mountain Expansion, the Forest Service took additional written scoping comments beginning in December 1999, when it identified tentative issues,[54] but determined that no further public scoping meetings were necessary.[55]

After considering the public scoping comments in its draft analysis, the Forest Service in January 2001 released the draft EIS (DEIS) for public comment and held an additional public meeting within the 45-day comment period.[56] In reaching its final decision in 2002, the Service was required to consider the comments received.[57]

51 Courts have held that commentors' participation needs to be meaningful and alert an agency to the reviewer's position and contentions. Vermont Yankee Nuclear Power Corp. v. NRDC, 435 U.S. 519, 553 (1978). A court may waive or dismiss environmental objections that could be raised at the DEIS stage but that are not raised until after completion of the FEIS. City of Angoon v. Hodel, 803 F.2d 1015, 1022 (9th Cir. 1986); Wisconsin Heritages, Inc. v. Harris, 490 F. Supp. 1334, 1338 (E.D. Wis. 1980).

52 See note 7 *supra* and accompanying text.

53 *See* Chapter 7, *supra* note 57; South Mountain Expansion FEIS, *supra* note 1, at 1-29.

54 The tentative issues were based on prior comments from the public and other agencies, many of which were fairly technical. These issues fell into the following major categories: concerns over the size of the development as measured by the skier comfortable carrying capacity and the socioeconomic impacts to the surrounding community; the snowmaking water demand including the source and volume of the withdrawals, and resulting minimum flows for the East Branch and Boyle Brook; water storage options; visual impacts; skier desires for trails; the purpose and need for the proposed action; and impacts to various resources (i.e., wetlands, soils, water quality, wildlife and aquatic habitat, threatened, endangered, and sensitive plants and animals, and cultural sites). The Forest Service also left open the possibility of developing additional alternatives that would meet the purpose and need of the Proposed Action. In addition, issues that were identified in the 1992 EIS were carried forward where the Forest Service determined that they were still relevant to the analysis. *See* South Mountain Expansion FEIS, *supra* note 1, at 1-29.

55 *See id.* Notification of all of these public participation opportunities was primarily accomplished through federal register notices and direct mailing to individuals, organizations, and agencies identified as interested in the proposal. *See id.*

56 *See* South Mountain Expansion FEIS, *supra* note 1, at 1-5; D-1.

57 *See* 40 C.F.R. § 1503.4(b) (requiring agencies to consider all substantive comments). The Forest Service also reviewed and documented comments merely expressing an opinion

These seemingly dull procedures can be significant, because the ability of the public and interested parties to participate in shaping the EIS and final decision creates important opportunities to introduce ecologically oriented perspectives. Eight government agencies, nine organizations, and 84 individuals submitted substantive comments on the DEIS.[58] In addition, there were over 1,500 form letters submitted, most of which were generated by the LMRC from season pass holders and other visitors to the resort in favor of the expansion proposal.[59] This helps to demonstrate that NEPA's open process gives broad opportunities to those who choose to participate, bounded only by relevance and timeliness. It would be difficult to conclude that evidence of impacts on the ecosystem would not be relevant.

During the South Mountain Expansion analysis, the public's opportunity to participate in the process of developing and reviewing the EIS and the choice of alternatives had the potential to significantly influence the ecological scope of the analysis. However, as the discussion above indicates the ability to influence decision makers may be limited by the way the analysis is framed. If the issues important to the public are only addressed in the context of a narrowly defined purpose and need or scope of actions and alternatives, then many of the impacts and alternatives important to the public may not be considered at all. For example, the Forest Service was not swayed by many public comments questioning the continued existence of the resort on public lands,[60] and it found that the No Action Alternative and Alternative F would have made it impossible to meet the stated purpose and need for the project.[61] In addition, although many public comments expressed concern about the secondary growth that could result from the expansion, in the absence of its disclosure through the defined scope of action it appears that none were able to anticipate anything like the South Peak Resort development, and thus no impacts at this spatial scale were analyzed and considered as part of the approval decision.[62]

This review of the Forest Service's definition of the purpose and need, scope, and related opportunities for public participation for the Loon Resort South Mountain Expansion demonstrates the importance of framing the analysis in an EIS. While the final decisions of whether to approve an individual mountain resort

---

for or against the project as providing an indication of the public opinion of the project. *See* South Mountain Expansion FEIS, *supra* note 1, at D-2.

58 *See* South Mountain Expansion FEIS, *supra* note 1, at D-2-9.

59 *See id.* at D-2.

60 *Id.* at 2-34–35 (Forest Service rejecting inclusion of such an alternative for analysis on the basis that it would not meet the purpose and need for the proposal); *see also id.* at D-29–47 (numerous public comments questioning continued need for and/or expansion of the Loon Resort).

61 *See* South Mountain Expansion ROD, *supra* note 2, at 14–18, 35 (rejecting limited development alternatives because they did not meet the purpose and need, especially the defined expectations of visitors); *see also* South Mountain Expansion FEIS, *supra* note 1, at D-29–47 (numerous public comments questioning continued need for and/or expansion of the Loon Resort).

62 *See id.* at D-87–95.

development project ultimately needs to be based upon the substantive provisions contained in NFMA and related authorities, the promise of better decision making resulting from the procedural framework for analysis provided by NEPA may be lost and critical issues may go unaddressed if NEPA is not correctly implemented.

In the case of the South Mountain Expansion, the narrowly defined purpose and need and scope of the analysis appear to have limited the potential for an ecosystem-based approach to the approval decision, and the ability of the public and decision-makers to have a clear basis for deciding whether the proposal should have been approved at all, or whether another alternative may have resulted in a better outcome and should have been selected instead. As the Record of Decision shows, as the Forest Service worked through each of the alternatives to the South Mountain Expansion proposal that were analyzed, each was rejected because the Forest Service determined it did not meet the defined purpose and need for the proposal.[63] As is discussed further below, none of these decisions appears to have turned on the impacts to the ecology of the mountain, though several mitigation measures were included as part of the final decision.

In the end, the decisions made about the critical beginning points for analysis, represented by the definition of the purpose and need and scope of the analysis, resulted in a "shell game" for decision-makers and the public, with many of the most important decisions being made without all of the information necessary for informed decision making. In the absence of such information, in many ways it can be argued that the South Mountain Expansion approval decision relied as much on chance as it did on sound analysis for protecting the long-term health of the mountain ecology.

The Forest Service's Analysis of the Key Environmental Impacts of the South Mountain Expansion

While the preceding discussion emphasized the important role that NEPA's procedural framework for analysis can play in decision making, the final decision of whether to approve an individual mountain resort development project will ultimately turn on the Forest Service's application of the substantive provisions contained in NFMA and related authorities. All Forest Service actions within the national forest system, including decisions about whether to approve specific mountain resort developments, must comply with NFMA, its regulations, and the applicable Forest Management Plan.[64] This section examines the Forest Service's review of the three key ecological issues raised by the South Mountain Expansion proposal: tree cutting; water demand for snowmaking, including both the sources of water and water storage; and the secondary growth triggered by the expansion.

63 *See* South Mountain Expansion ROD, *supra* note 2, at 14–18.

64 36 C.F.R. § 219.10. The Forest Service's final decisions are subject to appeal to federal court. *Id.* §§ 217, 251.

Through the lens of these specific activities, it continues the examination of whether the Forest Service was required by the relevant legal regimes to take an ecological approach to its approval decision for the South Mountain Expansion. The discussion of secondary growth on private land also considers the influence of the relationship between federal and local authorities.

The Tree Cutting Analysis

The South Mountain Expansion proposal included 124 acres of new ski trail terrain, bringing the total ski trail acreage to 382 acres,[65] as well as the creation of glades for skiing and new lifts. The tree cutting associated with clearing for trails, glades, and lifts can trigger a series of ecological consequences as a result of three key changes in the landscape: the fragmentation of forest blocks; the clearing of the trail area itself; and the creation of new forest edges along each side of the trail. As explained in Part I of this book, these changes in turn trigger changes in the wildlife patterns, which often have ripple effects on the pattern of plantlife. At the same time, the changes in the vegetation can result in changes in the quantity and quality of water flows, which in turn affect patterns of plant life and wildlife.[66]

NEPA required the Forest Service to take a hard look at the environmental impacts of the South Mountain Expansion proposal and a reasonable range of alternatives, which the Forest Service explored in the South Mountain Expansion FEIS. As discussed in Chapter 7, however, NEPA is largely a procedural statute, requiring only that agencies consider the environmental consequences of its action pursuant to NEPA's requirements.[67] The Forest Service's substantive obligations for its decisions regarding whether to authorize the proposed development, amend the 1986 Forest Management Plan, and issue a new SUP to the LMRC were guided by NFMA and related authorities.[68]

In considering the ecological impacts of tree cutting, the most relevant NFMA mandate requires the Forest Service to "provide for diversity of plant and animal communities based on the suitability and capability of the specific area in order to meet overall multiple use objectives."[69] To accomplish this goal, the Forest Service must, among other things, manage "fish and wildlife habitat .... to maintain viable populations of existing native and desired non-native vertebrate species in the

65 *See* South Mountain Expansion ROD, *supra* note 2, at 4.

66 For a synthesis of the ecological impacts of tree cutting at mountain resorts, see Chapter 2 *supra* at note 19 and following text. More detailed ecological discussions are contained in Chapters 3 through 5.

67 Stryker's Bay Neighborhood Council, Inc. v. Karlen, 444 U.S. 223, 227 (1980). See also Chapter 7 *supra* at notes 47–49 and accompanying text.

68 *See* Ecology Ctr., Inc. v. Austin, 430 F.3d. 1057, 1062 (9th Cir. 2005) (any Forest Service action in a managed forest must comply with NFMA and must also be consistent with the governing forest plan).

69 16 U.S.C. § 1604(g)(3)(B).

planning area."[70] Under NFMA's implementing regulations, the Forest Service can look to Management Indicator Species (MIS or Indicator Species) to fulfill these obligations as it establishes Forest Management Plans or decides whether to approve clearing activities for resort development. It must select Indicator Species based on the belief that their population changes will indicate the effect of management activities,[71] and planning alternatives need to be stated and evaluated in terms of both the amount and quality of MIS habitat and of the animal population trends of the MIS.[72] Note, however, that the substantive standards for NFMA also cover nonenvironmental considerations, such as the obligation to provide for recreation, so ultimately the Forest Service must balance potentially competing multiple-use objectives.[73]

Determining whether the Forest Service took an ecosystem-based approach to the South Mountain Expansion decision is somewhat difficult since one cannot fully understand what was in the minds of the many individuals involved in the analysis and approval decision. However, the South Mountain Expansion FEIS and Record of Decision (ROD) provide a strong basis for examining the Forest Service's approach to decision making as it evaluated the environmental impact of the proposal and alternatives and reached its decision.[74]

The Forest Service included in the South Mountain Expansion FEIS an "Affected Environment" chapter that identified different spatial scales for evaluating many of the impacts of the proposed development decision—at the SUP scale, the Loon Mountain Project (LMP) scale, and the regional scale. The LMP and regional spatial scales were established primarily to account for physical development impacts outside of the SUP analysis area, and for species that require a larger geographic range for their survival but that use areas impacted by the development.[75] It is important to consider the potential impacts of proposed human activities at a range of spatial scales. The loss of ecosystem components and function associated with trail clearing might impact only a small percentage of land with similar ecosystem characteristics in the immediate vicinity of the ski area development, or only a fraction of a percent in the entire regional analysis area. Thus, for example, if the populations of the organisms at risk are known, it

70 36 C.F.R. § 219.19.

71 *See id.* § 219.19(a)(1). The Forest Management Plan must provide habitat necessary for at least a minimum of reproductive individuals for the MIS. *See id.* § 219.19.

72 *See id.* § 219.19(a)(2). Animal MIS population trends must be monitored and their relationships to habitat changes need to be determined. *See id.* § 219.19(a)(6).

73 *See id.* § 219.21. The Forest Service is also required to provide for diversity of plant and animal communities consistent with the overall multiple-use objectives. *Id.* § 219.26.

74 The South Mountain Expansion ROD specifically stated that it was intended to document the Forest Service's final approval decision and reasoning in accordance with the substantive NFMA standards and after consideration of the environmental impacts identified in the EIS). *See* South Mountain Expansion ROD, *supra* note 2, at 1-3.

75 See *supra* notes 9–12 and accompanying text.

might be possible to determine that at a local scale the local loss of those ecosystem components and related ecosystem function can be tolerated because the impact on the broader mountain ecosystem would be limited. Conversely, the analysis might show that the loss could be of rare organisms and the impact to ecosystem function might not be acceptable.

The Affected Environment chapter described the abiotic and biotic components of the ecosystem that the Forest Service viewed as important to the analysis within the three separate geographic scales of analysis,[76] as well as descriptions of other aspects of the human environment, including socioeconomics, heritage, and visual resources, to enable comparison of the expansion proposal and alternatives.[77] Its discussion of the relevant vertebrate species by community type and defined spatial scales, in particular, provided a reasonable beginning baseline for analysis of the impacts from the alternatives under consideration in the South Mountain Expansion, given the narrow definition of the alternatives. One important weakness in the chapter, however, was its discussion of biodiversity, which was exceptionally brief and general, concluding summarily that "a variety of plants and animals exist within the LMP analysis area" and that "small amounts of certain special habitat components" like snags and coarse woody debris, along with the "high incidence of humans and human-related activities," limit the presence of some wildlife species.[78]

The heart of the Forest Service's analysis was contained in the FEIS chapter on the "Environmental Consequences of the Alternatives."[79] Within this chapter, most of the tree cutting analysis was spread among sections on "Geology and Soils Resources," "Vegetation Resources," "Wildlife Resources," and "Biodiversity," with the Wildlife Resources and Biodiversity sections holding the most promise from an ecological perspective. Overall, the length of the analyses masked the relatively brief amounts of analytical content on the impacts of the tree cutting proposal and, in particular, any ecological impacts. Related to this, the document did a relatively poor job of achieving NEPA's goal of sharply defining the environmental impacts of the alternatives in comparative form in order to provide a clear basis for choice by the decision-maker and public.[80]

---

76 *See* South Mountain Expansion FEIS, *supra* note 1, at Chapter 3. This included descriptions of the soils, water, vegetative, wildlife, and biodiversity resources contained in the three analysis areas, with concise descriptions of the vegetative community and special habitat needs for the vertebrate species that could potentially occur in the LMP analysis area. *See id.* at 3-1–135. Species of high public interest, such as federally or state-listed threatened and endangered species and White Mountain National Forest Management Indicator Species (MIS or Indicator Species), received additional attention. *See id.* at 3-99–109.

77 *See id.*

78 *See id.* at 3-132–35.

79 *See* South Mountain Expansion FEIS, *supra* note 1, at 4-1–328.

80 *See* 40 C.F.R. §§ 1500.1(b), 1500.4, 1502.14.

The analysis of soils and vegetation focused on the impact of clearing activities on erosion and changes in community types.[81] In the FEIS, the Forest Service overlaid the alternatives for trails, lifts, and access roads on the identified soils and vegetation community type to develop a comparison of the acreage disturbed by soil and community type.[82] Although recognizing the presence of some moderately to highly erodible soils and the potential for sedimentation to surface waters, the analysis of erosion found little cause for concern due to mitigating factors, such as rapid revegetation potential, well-distributed rainfall, generally good soil drainage in the area, and post-construction restoration. With regard to the vegetative resources, the analysis concluded that the clearing activities for trails, lifts, and access roads would result in the conversion of these areas from a forested community to the grass-forb ecotone community type.[83] There was little discussion, however, of any linkages between these impacts on soil and vegetation and other resources that might reflect an ecological perspective.

The discussion of the tree cutting impacts on wildlife resources and biodiversity in the FEIS held the most promise for an ecological perspective. The Forest Service relied upon the use of Indicator Species to evaluate the potential effects of the South Mountain Expansion proposal and its alternatives on wildlife in the LMP analysis area, and then evaluated that relationship to the Indicator Species population trends at the forest-wide planning scale to assess the effect of the planned development and the proposed alternatives on specific species.[84] It did a reasonable job of quantifying, in most cases, the species-specific habitat impacts in terms of acreage and as a percentage of the overall habitat at the LMP analysis scale. For example, in the case of the eastern gray squirrel, the Forest Service noted that the cutting of 95 acres of northern hardwood forest would cause a 1 percent reduction in its potential suitable habitat.[85] By tying the conclusions of its analysis only to the forest-wide planning scale,[86] however, the Forest Service discounted the value of assessing impacts at smaller scales of analysis, a vital piece to an ecological approach to decision making. Due in part to this approach, the Forest Service concluded in the FEIS that even where there may be local scale impacts to endangered or Indicator Species, or to biodiversity,[87] the proposal and any of the development alternatives would not adversely affect the Indicator Species population trends at the forest-wide planning level, and therefore would not adversely affect regional ecosystem dynamics or any MIS, rare, or ecologically important species.[88]

---

81 *See* South Mountain Expansion FEIS, *supra* note 1, at 4-4–5, 4-107–17.

82 *See id.* at 4-6–15, 4-107–17.

83 *See id.*

84 *See id.* at 4-129

85 *See id.* at 4-139.

86 *See id.* at 4-129.

87 *See e.g., id.* at 4-135, 4-138, 4-165 (noting impacts to the federally listed endangered Indiana bat, or the MIS small-footed myotis, and biodiversity).

88 *See id.* at 4-135–45, 4-163–64.

While the South Mountain Expansion FEIS discussed most of the significant clearing impacts on Indicator Species, such as those resulting from forest fragmentation, edge effects, and changes in community type, it appears to have overlooked impacts to natural patch communities that could occur as a result of the blasting and leveling activities associated with the trail development. This oversight may be consistent with the emphasis on the forest-wide impacts of the expansion activities, even though important ecological impacts at the local or community scale may result.

The analysis of the tree cutting impacts to biodiversity similarly discounted the local scale impacts in favor of a forest-wide perspective,[89] and although the Forest Service is required to quantify the changes in diversity likely to occur,[90] it only quantified the conversion from mature forest to grass-forb clearing.[91] Perhaps more importantly from an ecological perspective, throughout the analysis of wildlife and biodiversity resources, there was little discussion of the impacts to the linkages and interrelationships among species that would occur as a result of the tree cutting associated with the South Mountain Expansion.

The South Mountain Expansion ROD approving the expansion (Alternative B) contains virtually no mention of the environmental or ecological impacts resulting from the clearing activities.[92] A single paragraph briefly addressed the scenic impacts of the expansion, which hardly indicates an ecological perspective in the decision.[93] While the discussion in the South Mountain Expansion ROD provides little evidence that the decision was based on consideration of ecological impacts, tables containing a number of required and recommended mitigating and monitoring measures[94] hint at ecological considerations, such as sedimentation to surface waters from clearing, reduction of snags or cavity trees, conversion of mature forest cover, loss of quality deer wintering habitat, loss of beech trees as food supply, and abrupt forest/opening edges.[95] The brevity of the tables provides

89 *See id.* at 4-160–64.

90 40 C.F.R. § 219.26.

91 South Mountain Expansion FEIS, *supra* note 1, at 4-160.

92 Even in identifying the environmentally preferred Alternative F, the No Action Alternative eliminating the use of Loon Pond for water storage and withdrawals, the discussion fails to discuss any specific impacts from the clearing activities, stating only general conclusions that the increased impacts from the approval of the South Mountain Expansion would be minimal with the required and recommended mitigation measures. *See* South Mountain Expansion ROD, *supra* note 2, at 35.

93 *See id.* at 12, 22–23. Even if stretched to be considered a loose proxy for the potential ecosystem impacts from tree cutting, this paragraph reaches a cursory conclusion that the potential visual impacts were adequately addressed through mitigation measures such as revegetation of areas graded for trails and lifts, trails cut wherever possible to follow natural fall lines, and buildings designed to blend with the natural environment, none of which take into account ecological impacts.

94 *See id.* at 18–19.

95 *See id.* at 20–21.

little insight into whether the mitigation measures were based on an ecological analysis. Moreover, their ecological effectiveness would turn on whether the potential ecological impacts were appropriately identified and analyzed, and then on whether the specific mitigation measures address the identified impacts effectively, about which the record is silent.

The decision relies on the list of required mitigation measures[96] to conclude that "all potential adverse impacts to all resources disclosed in the Final EIS .... on NFS lands under Alternative B will be avoided or minimized with the implementation of [the] required mitigation measures."[97] In addition, the Forest Service identified a number of recommended mitigation measures that it viewed as under the jurisdiction of other federal, state, and local authorities.[98] Although the Forest Service had no authority for requiring that they be implemented, it concluded that they would "likely be implemented" and therefore viewed them as important in its approval decision.[99] A question that might be asked is whether the identification of mitigating measures by the approving agency is a mere persuasive tool being used to help it justify the decision, regardless of the impacts.

The essence of an ecosystem perspective in land use decisions is considering simultaneously the many effects and resulting cascades of effects that are possible due to the interconnections present in the ecosystem. In the end, the Forest Service analysis of the tree cutting associated with the South Mountain Expansion did not appear to take an ecosystem-based approach, though the final decision did include several mitigation measures for specific environmental impacts that could offset some of the impacts to the mountain ecology. The analysis included valuable information regarding the affected environment, and it applied some of the tools provided under NMFA and the White Mountain National Forest Plan, like the Indicator Species, to document many of the potential environmental impacts that would result from the various alternatives. However, much of the related discussion lacked the robust quantitative or qualitative analysis that could be provided under NFMA's provisions to gain better insight into the ecological impacts resulting from the development. Thus, despite the adoption of much of the language from NFMA that could be associated with an ecological approach such as "communities" and "biodiversity," there is little evidence that the analysis applied fundamental ecological concepts, which would be reflected through discussion of the effects of the development on the critical linkages among the resources on the mountain.

96 The required mitigation measures were included as a means to offset the potential impacts resulting from the construction and operation of the new Loon Resort facilities. *See id.* at 18–23.

97 *See id.* at 18–19.

98 *See id.* at 23–32.

99 *See id.* at 23.

The Water Demand, Sources, and Storage Analysis

Machine-made snow is essential to the success of today's mountain resorts, but making snow triggers a set of human activities with ecological consequences. As with the tree cutting analysis, NEPA helped force the Forest Service to consider the environmental consequences of its water demand-related actions, but the substantive obligations for its approval decisions were guided by NFMA and related authorities. The most important of these NFMA requirements was the Forest Service's obligation to provide for diversity of plant and animal communities and to manage fish and wildlife habitat to maintain viable populations of the animal species in the planning area.[100] However, NFMA also contains requirements specific to protecting water resources in national forests, including that the Forest Service conserve water and soil resources,[101] take into account instream flow requirements, watershed conditions, and other water resource factors that could be affected by its planning and development activities, and comply with the federal Clean Water Act and other federal, state, and local laws related to water and soil resources.[102]

Critical to the South Mountain Expansion proposal was the ability of the Loon Resort to meet the increased water demand necessary to provide complete snowmaking coverage for all 382 acres of ski terrain in both the existing and expanded SUP area. To meet this demand, the proposal sought approval to continue existing water withdrawals from the East Branch of the Pemigewasset River and Boyle Brook up to the existing permitted levels, to replace water withdrawals from Loon Pond with withdrawals from several new water storage ponds on private land with a total capacity of 180 million gallons, and to install a 16-inch diameter pipeline and related infrastructure to serve the existing SUP area and a 20-inch diameter pipeline and related infrastructure to serve the expanded SUP area.[103] (See Figure 8.1 and also Figure 6.2 in Chapter 6).

The potential ecological impacts from snowmaking are typically associated with the water withdrawal, storage of withdrawn water, and the addition of the snow to the slopes. The discussion that follows provides an overview of the types of impacts that can result from the water demands from resort development,[104] and examines the South Mountain Expansion analysis by reviewing the documented

100 *See* 16 U.S.C. § 1604(g)(3)(B).

101 *See* 36 C.F.R. § 219.27(a)(1).

102 *See id.* § 219.23.

103 *See* South Mountain Expansion FEIS, *supra* note 1, at 2-12–13. The four preferred sites for water storage were identified as Connector Pond, Conn Pit, South B Pond, and North Pond. *See id.* at 4-11–14, 4-31. Connector Pond and Conn Pit are ponds formed as a result of gravel pit operations and in the case of Conn Pit is over 3 miles from the Loon Resort. *See id.* at 3-32–34. The South and North Ponds would be constructed on LMRC property at the base of the South Mountain Expansion. *See id.* at 4-11–14; Figure 8.1.

104 The discussion of mountain resort development impacts and ecological interrelationships in this section draws on material in Chapters 3 through 5 of this book.

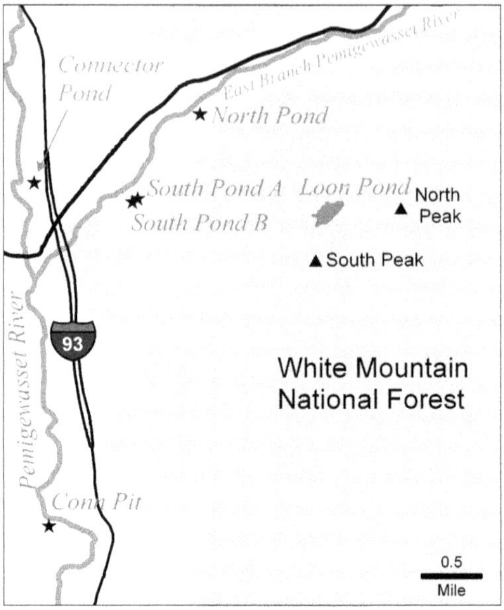

Figure 8.1 Alternative Ponds for Snowmaking

Data Sources: US Geological Survey in cooperation with US Environmental Protection Agency, USDA Forest Service, and other federal, state and local partners; Society for the Protection of New Hampshire Forests; Tele Atlas North America, Inc.; ESRI; Loon Mountain Ski Resort Alternative B Proposed Action (Jan. 15, 2002) (Pioneer Environmental Services)

baseline information and the analysis of the specific ecological impacts likely to occur if the proposal were approved.

Water withdrawals result in the diversion of water from existing sources, such as rivers or ponds. Excessive withdrawals can, as a general matter, threaten macroinvertebrates and overwintering fish eggs from trout or salmon that spawn in the fall by increasing their exposure to freezing. Natural water flows are usually lowest in February when withdrawals for snowmaking can also be high. Manmade storage facilities need to be sited appropriately to avoid construction impacts to wetlands or other ecologically significant features. If the water for storage contains excessive nutrients, algal blooms can occur that in turn deplete oxygen and can threaten the health of the water body.

Adding machine-made snow to slopes can increase the net volume of water in the local basin, or at minimum focus the location of the water in the basin, and increase soil erosion from the mountain slopes. This can also increase the volume of the peak spring flow from the slopes and streams running off the mountain, exacerbating stream bank erosion, sedimentation, and embeddedness in streams and rivers as gravel in quieter parts of streams is filled, eliminating shelter for macroinverebrates, salamanders, and fish in their early stages of life. Issues related to the timing of the snow melt in the spring can also arise from the complex combination of factors associated with the greater than natural volume of snow, compaction, density of machine-made snow, and increased solar radiation as spring arrives.

As with the tree cutting analysis, the FEIS laid the foundation for the environmental analysis of water demand by documenting the water resources the Forest Service viewed as important to the analysis.[105] The Affected Environment chapter included descriptions of rivers, streams, and natural and manmade ponds within the vicinity of the Loon Resort that could be affected by the South Mountain Expansion as a result of water withdrawals, water storage, and increased runoff from infrastructure construction and added snow on cleared areas.[106] Information on stream flows, water volume and storage capacity, existing water demand, and water quality was provided.[107] Because the analysis of the impacts of water demand would also cover impacts to fisheries resources, the chapter included a description of the aquatic species and their habitat within the LMP analysis area, with emphasis on species of high public interest such as federally or state-listed threatened and endangered species and Indicator Species.[108] As with the analysis of the tree cutting impacts, the discussion of the water and fisheries resources provided what appears to be an adequate beginning baseline for analysis, though as noted previously the baseline discussion of biodiversity was exceptionally brief and general.

The Forest Service's analysis of the potential impacts of water demand was contained primarily in FEIS sections on "Water Resources" and "Fisheries Resources." The water resources analysis focused largely on meeting water demand for snowmaking, eliminating Loon Pond as a source for water, addressing potential sedimentation from the addition of snow to the slopes, and maintaining minimum conservation flows essential for fisheries resources.[109] The Water Resources section contained little discussion of potential impacts to the critical ecological linkages that could flow from impacts like increased sedimentation or the failure to maintain minimum conservation flows.[110]

The Fisheries Resources section contained an introductory discussion of some more specific water demand impacts that could occur, covering direct and indirect impacts from sedimentation, water withdrawals, and water quality in general terms in order to set the stage for more specific analysis of the impacts from the different proposed alternatives to aquatic species and their habitat, included MIS species.[111]

---

105 *See* South Mountain Expansion FEIS, *supra* note 1, at 3-9–65

106 *See id.* at 3-9–49

107 *See id.*

108 *See id.* at 3-49–65.

109 *See id.* at 4-20–78.

110 *See e.g., id.* at 4-29–37.

111 *See id.* at 4-78–80. The Forest Service noted that the issues and surface waters specifically addressed in this analysis were determined through review of public and agency scoping comments. *See id.* at 4-78.

Unfortunately, even with this increased focus on aquatic species, there was very little discussion of any impacts to extended ecological linkages. For example, the Forest Service focused on two fish species, the eastern brook trout and the endangered Atlantic salmon, but determined under each of the proposed expansion alternatives that there would be no adverse effects on the Indicator Species based on the cursory conclusion that the LMRC would be required to maintain the specified minimum stream flows and implement best management practices to limit sedimentation consistent with the existing Forest Service handbook.[112] While meeting these existing requirements may result in some protection of the fisheries resources ecology, without more specific discussion of the expansion-specific impacts to that ecology it cannot be said that the outcome was obtained as a result of an ecological perspective.

The discussion of water storage options was somewhat more specific. It recognized that the construction of water storage ponds in general may generate positive impacts to aquatic habitat by providing stored water for peak demand and allowing for smaller withdrawals from surface waters. At the same time, it found that storage ponds could result in the potential outflow of warm water in the summer months that could affect water quality, and the construction of North and South Ponds (see Figure 8.1) could cause sedimentation and loss of some instream and backwater habitats.[113] The analysis concluded, however, that most of the impacts could be addressed by including mitigation measures, and that while there would be some adverse impacts from pond construction to eastern brook trout in portions of the LMP analysis area, there would not be adverse impacts to populations at the forest-wide planning level.[114]

The South Mountain Expansion ROD contained more discussion of its reasoning related to the water demand impacts than it did for the tree cutting analysis. Consistent with the FEIS, however, this discussion focused primarily on the need to meet water demand while maintaining technical conservation flow levels identified through existing policies rather than achieving specific ecological results.[115] Similarly, the additional discussion about the elimination of Loon Pond as a water source and storage option provides no ecological insight.[116] Mitigation tables related to the potential water demand impacts hint at ecological considerations as they provided mitigation measures designed to address water withdrawals, sedimentation from cleared areas, degradation of aquatic habitat, and water quality at storage reservoirs,[117] but nearly all of the water resource impacts were outside the jurisdiction of the Forest Service, and therefore the measures are only recommendations for other entities to implement. The brevity of the

112 *See, e.g., id.* at 4-84–104.

113 *See id.* at 4-93–100.

114 *See id.* at 4-94–100.

115 *See* South Mountain Expansion ROD, *supra* note 2, at 11–12.

116 *See id.*

117 *See id.* at 24–25.

tables again leaves it unclear whether significant ecological considerations went into their development, although this seems unlikely given the limitations of the analysis contained in the FEIS.

The South Mountain Expansion ROD authorized those water demand actions proposed by the LMRC to occur on forest lands, including the changes in the pipeline infrastructure necessary to remove Loon Pond as a source of water.[118] In addition, the Forest Service found that the FEIS provided the information and analysis necessary for the other entities with jurisdiction to make the decisions necessary to approve the use of the proposed storage ponds as shown in Figure 8.1.[119]

Overall, similar to the tree cutting analysis, the analysis of the water demand, sources, and storage demonstrates little evidence that the Forest Service took an ecosystem-based approach despite the adoption of language from NMFA related to communities and biodiversity that could be associated with an ecological approach. The analysis reveals that the Forest Service worked hard to ensure minimum stream flows, to minimize impacts to aquatic habitat from construction and runoff, and to establish water storage options that buffered the need for high-volume withdrawals and eliminated the use of Loon Pond. However, the analysis does not demonstrate that these efforts flowed from any significant consideration of the important ecological impacts that could occur from the expansion activities. The analysis instead was oriented toward fulfilling the more pedestrian requirements of NFMA to comply with federal, state, and local water laws and toward ensuring the use of standard best management practices designed to mitigate environmental impacts to habitat for fish species identified as Indicator Species.

In the end, despite establishing through its baseline resource assessment several building blocks that could allow the Forest Service to approach what would be a fundamentally ecosystem-based decision regarding the tree cutting and water demand impacts from the South Mountain Expansion, the analysis and in turn the approval decision cannot be characterized as informed by an ecological perspective. The Forest Service efforts to satisfy NEPA and NFMA requirements led it to identify essential ecosystem components, conduct some of its analysis at scales that could facilitate an ecosystem approach, and use tools like the MIS in order to help determine whether there would be adverse impacts from the South Mountain Expansion at the White Mountain National Forest-wide scale. However, the primary shortfall from an ecosystem perspective was the failure to analyze the potential impacts from these actions through the extended, critical ecological linkages in order to consider simultaneously the many effects that were possible due to the interconnections present in the natural system. Thus there is little evidence to suggest that the Forest Service took a comprehensive ecosystem-based approach.

---

118 *See id.* at 5.

119 *See id.*

Secondary Growth on Adjacent Private Lands

Resort development triggers new rounds of human development activities, including the creation of facilities, such as ski lodges, restaurants, and other resort support structures, along with lodging and residences on the mountain and at its base. Secondary development is also triggered farther from the resort in the communities that surround mountain resorts, and typically includes additional residential, retail, and recreational development, each triggering ecological consequences. One strength of NEPA is its requirement that agencies consider the cumulative impacts of their actions,[120] and this requirement provided the clearest opportunity for the Forest Service to look at secondary growth impacts.

The Environmental Consequences chapter of the South Mountain Expansion FEIS, however, included only brief discussions of the potential cumulative impacts of the South Mountain Expansion proposal. These noted the potential for additional impacts from other Forest Service activities in the LMP analysis area, generally discussed secondary growth that could occur in the Lincoln area, and briefly mentioned secondary growth that could result if the LMRC were to develop the lands it held adjacent to the resort—including those lands that are now being developed as the South Peak Resort.[121] As discussed above, however, the FEIS did not include any specific analysis of the South Peak Resort. The location of this land, being largely forested and adjacent to both the national forest and the East Branch of the Pemigewasset River, an important component of the area ecosystem, would make such analysis critical to an ecosystem-based approach to decision making.

The only impacts outside of the national forest boundaries that the Forest Service substantively analyzed in the FEIS were those related to that development directly attributable to the Loon Resort base-facilities and snowmaking infrastructure.[122] While the actions of the LMRC before and after the approval decision would appear to indicate a clear intent to develop the South Peak Resort land, it is possible the Forest Service was not specifically aware of the LMRC's development plans as it prepared the EIS. Even so, the FEIS severely discounted the likelihood of any significant residential or commercial growth resulting from the South Mountain Expansion on these lands or more generally in the Lincoln area.[123] Despite Lincoln's market niche with second home owners and overnight

120 *See* 40 C.F.R. §§ 1508.8, 1508.25.

121 *See* South Mountain Expansion FEIS, *supra* note 1, at 4-18–19 and 4-118–19.

122 The failure to consider the appropriate connected growth activities within the scope of the proposal could potentially be remedied by revisiting, or "supplementing," the EIS in view of the clear connection of the South Peak Resort development, however there is no evidence to indicate this has been considered by the Forest Service. *See* 40 C.F.R. § 1502.9.

123 *See, e.g.*, South Mountain Expansion FEIS, *supra* note 1, at 4-119, 4-156–57, 4-166–77, 4-216–20, D-87–88.

guests,[124] the Forest Service concluded that vacation and second homes "would only slightly increase" or noted that such impacts lie outside the jurisdiction of the Forest Service, and therefore did not consider any specific environmental impacts associated with any secondary growth.[125]

The South Mountain Expansion ROD appears to take an ostensibly broader view. It stated that "[a]lthough the decision made by the Forest Service is only for actions that will occur on [National Forest] lands, it is made with the understanding that there are connected actions on private lands and that all the associated environmental effects documented in the FEIS were considered."[126] It also stated that considerable thought was given to adverse impacts outside the jurisdiction of the Forest Service on private lands, and recommended mitigation measures for those impacts that it believed had a high probability of being implemented.[127] Further, two of the three scales of analysis used by the Forest Service were large enough to encompass analysis of growth beyond just the base facilities. However, the FEIS' failure to anticipate and consider the impacts of the South Peak Resort or other secondary growth beyond the base-facilities undermines the promising stated conclusions contained in the South Mountain Expansion ROD. In addition, the recommendations for mitigation measures were weak, such as recommending that in the event secondary growth occurs, there should be enforcement of local zoning laws and effective communications between the LMRC, state officials, Town of Lincoln planners, and local residents.[128]

Another way in which the EIS considered the secondary-growth impacts of the South Mountain Expansion proposal was through the Forest Service's decision to take into account the "[s]ustainability of local communities [a]s one of the components of Forest Service ecosystem-based management, in which social and economic values are considered as important resources along with the physical and biological environment."[129] As noted in Chapter 7, NEPA and NFMA are not limited to an evaluation of environmental impacts, and the Forest Service identified the economic relationship between Lincoln and the Loon Resort as providing the "impetus" for the Forest Service to ensure that the resort remain an attractive recreational offering through the South Mountain Expansion.[130] In the

124 See Chapter 6 *supra* at notes 48–50 and accompanying text. The subsequent, 2003 Town of Lincoln Master Plan anticipated 1,000 to 1,500 additional new housing units being built as a result of the South Mountain Expansion. *See* North Country Council, Town of Lincoln Master Plan (Oct. 2003), at II-7, VII-20. Further development might also have been anticipated based on other similar four season ski resort developments around the country.

125 *See e.g.,* South Mountain Expansion FEIS, *supra* note 1, at 4-119, 4-167, 4-216–20, D-87–95.

126 South Mountain Expansion ROD, *supra* note 2, at 3-4.

127 *Id.* at 23–32.

128 *Id.* at 27, 31.

129 South Mountain Expansion FEIS, *supra* note 1, at 1-7.

130 *See id.*

final analysis, neither the recommended mitigation measures for the secondary growth impacts, nor the consideration of the social and economic impacts to the Lincoln community contributed to a better understanding of the ecological impacts caused by the secondary growth related to the South Mountain Expansion. The failure to account for and substantively analyze a reasonable level of secondary growth impacts from the South Mountain Expansion proposal represents a major gap in the South Mountain Expansion analysis, thereby significantly diminishing the possibility that the Forest Service took an ecological approach to the South Mountain Expansion decision.

This gap in the analysis also undermined the potentially valuable role of the EIS in coordinating or informing the necessary federal, state, and local reviews.[131] The substantive provisions of local planning and development laws, state permits, and other approvals required for secondary growth provide a potential opportunity to incorporate ecosystem principles and thereby affect decision making. As a general matter, neither New Hampshire's laws nor Lincoln's local master plan, land use plan ordinance, or site plan review regulations appear to contain provisions that require an ecosystem-based analysis for any of the approval decisions related to the secondary growth impacts from the South Mountain Expansion.[132] Nonetheless, the South Mountain Expansion FEIS provided supporting analysis for a number of the federal, state, and town permits or approvals that were required prior to implementation of the South Mountain Expansion for the Loon Resort-related activities on private lands, such as the new base facilities and water demand infrastructure. While this NEPA-driven analysis can contribute to an improved ecosystem-based approach to other agencies' decision making, the restrained approach to secondary growth in this instance limited the potential for infusing an ecological perspective into those other permitting processes.

Could the Forest Service Have Taken a More Ecosystem-Based Approach to Decision Making Under Current U.S. Federal Law?

The current federal legal framework led to analysis of many of the environmental impacts that were likely to result from the South Mountain Expansion; however, based on this analysis one cannot conclude that federal law causes the Forest Service to take an ecological approach to its approval decisions for mountain resorts.

---

131 *See* 40 C.F.R. § 1506.2; *see also,* Bass et al., *supra* note 13, at 16-19.

132 *See generally* North Country Council, Town of Lincoln Master Plan (Oct. 2003); Town of Lincoln, Land Use Plan Ordinance (Mar. 12, 2002); Town of Lincoln, Site Plan Review Regulations (June 12, 2002); Town of Lincoln, Subdivision Regulations (Nov. 18, 1999) (all on file with author). For example, in recognition of its location in the middle of wildlife habitats and the potential benefits of conservation, the Master Plan recommends that the Town of Lincoln should create ordinances to protect habitat. *See* Town of Lincoln Master Plan, at VII-19.

Several factors contribute to this conclusion, beginning with how the Forest Service framed the South Mountain Expansion proposal for analysis in the EIS. The defined purpose and need for the proposal turned on the long-term partnership between the Forest Service and the LMRC, established to help the Forest Service meet its obligations to provide outdoor recreation opportunities to the public through continuation of alpine skiing at the Loon Resort. This contributed to a narrow range of alternatives for analysis. In addition, the defined scope of the alternatives and impacts considered as part of the analysis did not take into account significant actions flowing from the South Mountain Expansion proposal, and thus also narrowed the analysis contained in the EIS. These two important framing decisions also contributed to a "shifted" baseline for analysis that never considered what the ecosystem would be like in the absence of the Loon Resort, an analysis that appears to have escaped review under both NEPA and NFMA since the inception of the Loon Resort. The resulting baseline for analysis limits the ability of decision-makers and the public to gain an understanding of the full ecological impacts resulting from the presence and expansion of the Loon Resort in the White Mountain National Forest. Thus, the South Mountain Expansion proposal analysis shows that federal law allows mountain resort development proposals to be framed structurally in ways that limit or prevent an ecological perspective in decision making.

With regard to the Forest Service's specific analysis of the tree cutting, water demand, and secondary growth impacts of the South Mountain Expansion proposal, the available evidence does not support a conclusion that the Forest Service took an ecosystem-based approach. The NEPA and NFMA framework for analysis led to inclusion of valuable baseline information regarding the affected environment and many of the environmental impacts that would result from an approval decision. However, while NFMA requirements like those obligating the Forest Service to provide for diversity of plant and animal communities and maintain viable populations of wildlife were the impetus for a significant amount of important environmental analysis, they ultimately failed to require an ecosystem-based analysis. For example, NFMA's required use of Indicator Species helps to introduce ecological concepts at a manageable level of analysis, but in the end there was little analysis reflected in the FEIS that focused on the potential ecological impacts of the proposed expansion, which would have been reflected in discussion of impacts to the critical ecological linkages between the ecosystem components and the resulting cascades of effects that were possible due to the interconnections present in the Loon Mountain ecosystem.

Despite these conclusions, the analysis in this chapter indicates that existing federal law provides at least the opportunity for decision-makers to take a fundamentally ecosystem-based approach to decision making. NEPA offers a useful procedural structure for decision making that could enhance the potential for ecological analysis contained in NFMA's provisions. Forest Service decision-makers could take advantage of NEPA's procedural requirements and the discretion it allows to explore a range of alternatives that would ensure that the scope of analysis is sufficient to allow for an ecological perspective. In addition, NEPA provides citizens with relatively robust opportunities to participate in the decision-making process, and through this participation citizens may be able to introduce important information and influence the Forest Service to take a more ecological approach. As discussed however, NEPA is largely a procedural statute—in the hands of the right decision-maker capable of contributing to an ecological analysis; but as demonstrated it is ultimately a relatively toothless tool when it comes to causing decision-makers to undertake an ecosystem-based analysis or make ecologically-based decisions.[133]

At its core, NFMA provides a valuable planning tool for managing our national forests. But NFMA's planning process and the special use permitting requirements for mountain resort development do not mandate a truly ecological approach. NFMA and its implementing regulations allow the Forest Service considerable discretion in the forest management planning process, including in the methods used to establish the plans. The Forest Service could use its discretion to conduct its analysis from a deeper ecological perspective and to design plans with more of an ecological focus, in particular if there are important or highly valued species present or to provide for a specific overall level of plant or animal diversity.

Ultimately, however, NFMA is limited because of its multiple-use underpinnings. The statutory goal is largely about resource development through the production of goods and services, and thus ecosystem health is only one of many purposes that are to be balanced by the Forest Service. The "sustainability" concepts contained in NFMA are fundamentally directed toward ensuring continuing economic returns and not necessarily toward ensuring the long-term health of the ecosystem. Although historically there has been a short-term perspective that can result in biodiversity loss and ecosystem instability, at other times NFMA's multiple-use objectives are consistent with an ecological approach, such as when providing for certain recreational opportunities or even for long-term sustainable yields of certain forest resources. Thus, at times NFMA can result in "accidental ecology" which verges on an ecological approach to decision making. Considerations for

133 NEPA does contain a substantive provision that could also be explored. This establishes a continuing responsibility of the federal government to use all practicable means, consistent with other essential considerations of national policy, to improve plans and programs toward achieving six general ends of environmental excellence. These ends include fulfilling the responsibilities of each generation as trustee of the environment for succeeding generations, assuring productive and esthetically pleasing surroundings, attaining the widest range of beneficial uses of the environment without degradation, maintaining wherever possible an environment which supports diversity, achieving a balance between population and resource use, and enhancing the quality of renewable resources and approaching the maximum attainable recycling of depletable resources. Because the ends to be achieved are generally stated, and the government only needs to use those means that are "practicable" to achieve them, the substantive provisions are not specific and may even be ignored if inconsistent with other essential considerations of national policy. *See* 42 U.S.C. § 4331(b).

increasing the likelihood of an ecological approach to mountain resort decision making are discussed in Chapter 10.

As noted in Chapter 6, federal law governing water quality also played a central role in the debate over the South Mountain Expansion. The next chapter discusses this analysis in order to examine whether other federal laws may contribute to an ecosystem-based approach to resort development.

Chapter 9
Can Other Federal Laws Contribute to an Ecosystem-Based Approach to Resort Development?

Federal laws such as the Clean Water Act (CWA) and the Endangered Species Act (ESA) can affect mountain resort development decisions and, in some cases, may help leverage an increased ecological perspective by decision-makers or at least lead to improved ecological results. The CWA was enacted in 1972 and its objective is to restore and maintain the chemical, physical, and biological integrity of the Nation's waters.[1] Congress enacted the ESA in 1973 as a means to conserve endangered and threatened species and the ecosystems they depend upon to the point where statutory protection is no longer necessary.[2] As discussed in Chapter 6, CWA litigation played a significant role in delaying and ultimately altering the proposed expansion of the Loon Resort.

The Clean Water Act and the Fight to Protect Loon Pond

Congress established several important goals and policies in the CWA, including eliminating all pollutant discharges by 1985[3] and achieving water quality by 1983 that provides for the protection and propagation of fish, shellfish, and wildlife, and for recreation in and on the water—commonly referred to as the "fishable and swimmable" goals of the CWA.[4] The primary means by which the CWA seeks to accomplish its goals and objectives is through a permitting program that makes it unlawful to discharge any pollutant "except as in compliance" with the Act's provisions.[5] The CWA's two most important tools within the permitting

---

1 33 U.S.C. §1251(a) (2007).

2 16 U.S.C. §§ 1531(b), 1532(3) (2007). The Supreme Court has recognized the Act's unparalleled protections for species on the brink of extinction characterizing the ESA as "the most comprehensive legislation for the preservation of endangered species ever enacted by any nation." Tenn. Valley Auth. v. Hill, 437 U.S. 153, 180 (1978).

3 33 U.S.C. § 1251(a)(1).

4 *Id.* §1251(a)(2).

5 *Id.* §1311(a). Notwithstanding the general prohibition on pollutant discharges, the CWA's National Pollutant Discharge Elimination System (NPDES) program regulates the addition of pollutants into navigable waters through issuance of NPDES permits. *Id.*

program for ensuring water quality is protected are effluent limitations, which are promulgated by the Environmental Protection Agency (EPA) and restrict the quantities, rates, and concentrations of pollutants discharged from point sources, and water quality standards, promulgated by states under EPA's oversight, which establish the desired condition of waters.[6]

The successful legal skirmishes over the LMRC's original expansion proposal in 1986 (hereinafter 1986 Expansion Proposal), which called for utilizing Loon Pond as the LMRC's own private "cistern" for snowmaking, and the failure by the Forest Service to adequately consider the public's proposed alternatives to that use[7] influenced the final South Mountain Expansion proposal in 1999 and in turn the analysis in the Final Environmental Impact Statement (hereinafter South Mountain Expansion FEIS). This litigation demonstrates the potential impact that a statute like the CWA containing enforceable standards for environmental protection can have in development decisions, especially within the context of an action requiring analysis under the National Environmental Policy Act (NEPA).[8]

In 1992 the Forest Service completed the Environmental Impact Statement for the 1986 Expansion Proposal (hereinafter 1992 South Mountain Expansion FEIS), which analyzed the anticipated environmental impacts of the proposed expansion along with five additional alternative development proposals.[9] The Forest Service approved the proposed expansion on March 1, 1993 (hereinafter 1993 Approval).

§1342(a). NPDES permits are issued by EPA, unless a state or tribe has been approved by EPA to administer the NPDES program consistent with CWA requirements. Forty-four states and the U.S. Virgin Islands have received approval from EPA to operate the NPDES program; however, New Hampshire has not. The EPA maintains oversight responsibility, including the authority to review, comment on and, where a permit is "outside the guidelines and requirements" of the CWA, object to state draft permits.

6 While federal effluent limitations serve as a minimum, states can adopt more stringent standards. EPA authorities under the water quality standards program are found in sections 303 and 304(a) of the CWA. 33 U.S.C. §§ 1313, 1314(a). EPA regulations governing the administration of the NPDES program are found at 40 C.F.R. Parts 122, 124-125 (2007). Under section 304(a) of the CWA, EPA from time to time publishes recommended water quality criteria that serve as scientific guidance for use by states in establishing and revising water quality standards. 33 U.S.C. § 1314(a). These criteria are not enforceable requirements, but are recommended and states may adopt these or other scientifically defensible criteria as part of their legally enforceable water quality standards. 40 C.F.R. § 131.11(b). All pollutant discharge permits must contain effluent limitations reflecting the application of available water treatment technologies, and in cases where technology-based limitations are not enough to meet state water quality standards, any more stringent limitations necessary to ensure compliance with water quality standards. 33 U.S.C. § 1311(b)(1)–(3).

7 *See* Dubois v. United States Dep't of Agric., 102 F.3d 1273, 1278–79 (1st Cir. 1996) [hereinafter Dubois II].

8 42 U.S.C. §§ 4321–4370f (2007).

9 *See* U.S. Dep't of Agric., Forest Service, Loon Mountain Ski Area South Mountain Expansion Project: Final Environmental Impact Statement 10–11 (1992).

After exhausting the available administrative appeals to the Regional Forester and to the Chief of the Forest Service, Roland Dubois and the environmental group RESTORE: The North Woods (RESTORE) challenged the 1993 Approval and the 1992 South Mountain Expansion FEIS in federal court.[10]

Dubois and RESTORE argued to the court that the proposed 20 foot drawdown of Loon Pond was likely to have a severe impact by increasing its acidity by a factor of two or three times that of its normal pH.[11] This would alter the pond's chemistry and release toxic metals present in the sediment, thereby killing naturally occurring organisms. As a mitigation measure, the Forest Service proposed to refill the pond each year with water pumped up the mountain from the East Branch of the Pemigewasset River. The River, however, is a "Class B" waterway, and thus was less protected than the "Class A" Loon Pond, and contained bacteria, *Giardia lambia*, and other harmful aquatic organisms and pollutants, including phosphorus, turbidity, oil, grease, and heat. While the Forest Service argued it would have required that such water transfers not occur when pollutants exceed certain levels, it failed to provide any plan for alternate means of refilling Loon Pond should the specified pollutant levels exist and the LMRC failed to apply for a pollutant discharge permit.[12]

Dubois and RESTORE specifically alleged that the Forest Service's 1993 Approval of the use of Loon Pond in snowmaking operations (1) violated NEPA by failing to consider the creation of artificial water storage ponds and adequate mitigation measures; (2) violated the CWA because of the failure to obtain a permit for the proposed refilling of Loon Pond by pumping of water from the Pemigewasset River; and (3) violated NEPA by failing to prepare a supplemental EIS (SEIS), even though the expansion proposal had changed substantially in the course of review.[13]

While the federal district court rejected these claims and upheld the Forest Service's approval,[14] on December 19, 1996, the U.S. Court of Appeals for the First Circuit sided with Dubois and RESTORE, holding that the environmental analysis related to the water withdrawals from Loon Pond was inadequate.[15]

---

10 *See* Dubois v. U.S. Dep't of Agric., No. CIV.A.95-50-B, 1995 U.S. LEXIS 16608 (D.N.H. Nov. 2, 1995) [hereinafter Dubois I].

11 *See* Dubois II, at 1278.

12 *See id.* at 1278–79.

13 The suit was brought under the CWA's citizen suit provision and under the Federal Administrative Procedure Act. *See* Dubois II, at 1280*; see also* 40 C.F.R. § 1502.9(c)(1)(I) (2007). The LMRC intervened in the case and sought to have the case dismissed on the ground that the plaintiffs lacked standing. The court found that RESTORE and Dubois had standing because Dubois would suffer an "injury in fact" and that his injuries were "likely to be redressed" by the relief requested in his complaint. Dubois II, at 1281 (citing Lujan v. Defenders of Wildlife, 504 U.S. 555, 560 (1992)).

14 *See* Dubois I, at 60–61.

15 *See* Dubois II, at 1292–93, 1301. The circuit court reviewed the district court's grant of summary judgment *de novo. Id.* at 1283. *De novo* review means that the appellate

The court also held that a pollutant discharge permit issued under the CWA was required for the water transfers from the Pemigewasset River to Loon Pond.[16] On remand from the circuit court, the district court issued an order on May 5, 1997, invalidating the 1993 Approval and prohibiting any further activities related to the expansion until a supplemental environmental impact analysis and a new Record of Decision addressing the identified inadequacies were issued.[17]

In reaching its decision, the circuit court examined the Forest Service's analysis of the environmental impacts from the water drawdowns and transfers contained in its FEIS, which the court noted is designed to serve the "twin aims" of NEPA: (1) ensuring that the agency takes a "hard look" at the environmental consequences of the proposed action; and (2) making this information available to the public, thereby assisting the agency's decision making via the public comment process.[18] The court applied a "rule of reason" noting that while the FEIS would not be found insufficient due to technical and inconsequential deficiencies, there is a statutory duty to comply with NEPA's EIS regulations to the fullest possible extent.[19] The court concluded that the Forest Service breached this duty by failing to address those proposed alternatives that demonstrated the benefits of using alternative water storage facilities.[20] The court found that when an alternative would greatly mitigate the proposed project's environmental harm,

---

court reviews the case from the beginning with no deference owed to the lower court. Because neither NEPA nor the CWA articulate their own standards of review, the court concluded that the appropriate standard for both claims is that set forth in the Administrative Procedure Act (APA): "(t)he reviewing court shall . . . hold unlawful and set aside agency actions, findings, and conclusions found to be arbitrary, capricious, an abuse of discretion, or otherwise not in accordance with law." 5 U.S.C. § 706(2)(A). Although the APA entitles substantial deference to a reviewing agency's actions, the reviewing court must determine if the agency considered the relevant factors and articulated a rational connection between the facts found and the choices made. Dubois II, at 1284–85.

16 *See* Dubois II, at 1299.

17 *See* Dubois v. U.S. Dep't of Agric., No. CIV.A.95-50-B (May 5, 1997) (unpublished order).

18 *See* Dubois II, at 1285–86, 1291.

19 *Id.* at 1287. The Council on Environmental Quality's (CEQ) regulations require the EIS to "(r)igorously explore and objectively evaluate all reasonable alternatives, and for alternatives which were eliminated from detailed study, (to) briefly discuss the reasons for their having been eliminated." 40 C.F.R. § 1502.14(a).

20 *See* Dubois II, at 1288. The Forest Service argued that "if commenters could require agencies undertake detailed comparative analysis merely by asserting the superiority of an alternative site, configuration, or method, only the imaginations of project opponents would limit the length of the EIS and the duration of the NEPA process." *See id.* The court rejected this argument as obfuscating through the specter of catastrophe the real issue: whether the Forest Service adequately considered a range of alternatives to using Loon Pond, with analysis adequately based on the reasonableness and practicality of the alternatives, and whether the Forest Service explained its reasoning and factual basis for refusing to consider a reasonable alternative. *Id.* at 1289–90

the agency is bound to address its implementation or explain the reason for its dismissal.[21] The court acknowledged that an alternative may be so costly that it could be rejected with a brief response, but in this case at least one alternative was presented that indicated the potential location of alternative storage ponds and even listed potential cost-saving benefits to the approach.[22] But rather than rigorously exploring the proposed alternative, the Forest Service in its 1992 South Mountain Expansion FEIS did not even respond to the proposed alternatives.[23] Accordingly, the court found that while NEPA does not mandate any particular results, it does require that the agency adequately identify and evaluate a project's environmental consequences and articulate a rational connection between the facts found and the choice made.[24]

In turning to Dubois and RESTORE's CWA claim, the circuit court rejected the Forest Service claim that because the stream running from Loon Pond eventually connects to the East Branch of the Pemigewasset River, the two bodies of water are "hydrologically connected" and therefore that the pumping of water from the River to Loon Pond was simply a transfer of water within the same body of water not requiring a permit for pollutant discharges.[25] The court reasoned that there was no legal or factual basis for the Forest Service's argument because it ignored a fundamental principle of fluid dynamics: the direction of flow.[26] Though hydrologically connected, the bacteria, phosphorus, oil, heat, and other harmful pollutants could not flow uphill to Loon Pond without being actively transferred by the Loon Resort's pumps and pipes.[27] Therefore, the court held that the water transfers from the Pemigewasset River to Loon Pond for snowmaking would require a CWA discharge permit because of the potential additions of various pollutants from the Pemigewasset River to Loon Pond.[28]

The successful challenges by Dubois and RESTORE in this case suggest that the CWA may provide opportunities for forcing improved analyses of mountain resort development impacts, both directly under CWA provisions with the standards

---

21 *Id.* at 1288–89.

22 *Id.* at 1288. While Dubois proposed costly subterranean storage ponds, the Lincoln Committee of Concerned Citizens proposed using three artificial storage ponds and included a map indicating where they could be located. *Id.*

23 *Id.*

24 Specifically, the court held that the Forest Service's refusal to explore and evaluate an alternative that was both feasible and reasonably apparent was arbitrary and capricious and not in accordance with the law. *Id.* at 1288–90; *see* 40 C.F.R. § 1502.14(a). The court also held that in issuing its FEIS, the Forest Service had so substantially changed the proposed action that a supplemental EIS was required in order to evaluate its environmental consequences and provide the public with an opportunity for comment. *See* Dubois II, at 1292–93.

25 *See* Dubois II, at 1296–98.

26 *See id.* at 1298.

27 *See id.*

28 *See id.* at 1299.

it imposes, and under NEPA by informing an "action forcing" legal challenge that draws upon the CWA's substantive requirements as a framework for analysis of the environmental impacts and consideration of alternatives to the proposed action. Consistent with the analysis of the National Forest Management Act and NEPA framework discussed in Chapters 7 and 8, the substantive CWA requirements establishing the need to meet minimum water quality standards and limit pollutant discharges should have informed the Forest Service's NEPA analysis and provided a substantive framework for the court's analysis. Conversely, while Dubois and RESTORE could have brought challenges focusing on the purely legal claim that the Loon Resort had failed to obtain the required pollutant discharge permit, the examination of the project under NEPA both broadened and deepened the analysis of the water demand impacts, bringing a greater understanding of the potential environmental impacts and viable, ecologically preferable alternatives to light.

It is evident from the subsequent South Mountain Expansion proposal, which eliminated Loon Pond as a source for water and instead proposed the construction of storage ponds to meet snowmaking needs, that the CWA can influence mountain resort development decisions in important ways that may lead to better ecological results. While other changes in the revised South Mountain Expansion proposal may not be directly attributable to the successful litigation and enforcement of related CWA requirements, there appears to be little doubt that the litigation resulted in the LMRC and Forest Service rethinking many critical components of the proposal, which contributed to a more careful approach, including a reduction in the footprint of the expansion onto South Mountain from 930 to 581 acres, improvements to Lincoln's sewer treatment facilities, improved water storage facilities, and additional changes.

Some of these changes were memorialized in private agreements directly addressing some of the potential ecological impacts from the proposed project. For example, Dubois reached agreements with the Loon Resort under which previously approved water withdrawals from Loon Pond were restricted and tightly monitored pending the final decision on the South Mountain Expansion proposal, minimum stream flows for the East Branch of the Pemigewasset River were tightened, erosion control standards were established, and the Loon Resort was obligated to make annual payments to the Town of Lincoln in order to fund capital improvements to the town's wastewater treatment plant.[29] Such private settlement agreements are examples of "bridge documents" which may help bridge the gap between the law and ecology through enforceable contractual agreements.[30]

This litigation also provides valuable insight into the important role courts play in this field. Judicial review provides a partial check on agency discretion. From a legal perspective, the successful NEPA and CWA claims brought by Dubois and

---

29 *See* Dubois v. U.S. Dep't of Agric., No. CIV.A.97-435-B (Feb. 12, 1999) (unpublished order with attachments).

30 Richard O. Brooks et al., Law and Ecology: The Rise of the Ecosystem Regime 379 (2002).

RESTORE are in part notable as reflecting an incremental step away from the "highly deferential" standard applied by courts in cases involving the review of agency decisions. The district court followed the common practice of giving great deference to the Forest Service's judgment, viewing the matters covered in the 1992 South Mountain Expansion FEIS related to assessing the proposed action's environmental impacts, potential alternatives, and mitigating measures as "classic examples" of factual disputes "which implicate[] substantial agency expertise."[31] In according agencies this highly deferential standard, courts often fail, as the district court did, to undertake the thorough, probing, and in-depth review of the record necessary to determine whether a rational connection exists between the facts found and the choices made.[32] While the Administrative Procedure Act standard for review is worded so as to encourage a high level of deference to the agency's decisions,[33] courts have held that this standard should not be construed as providing a rubber stamp.[34] In this case, the circuit court properly fulfilled its review function by analyzing whether the Forest Service based its decisions upon a reasoned evaluation of relevant factors.

While ultimately the successful outcome in the litigation did not require a full ecosystem analysis for decision making by the Forest Service, citizen enforcement of the CWA's provisions resulted in a better ecological outcome for the ecologically fragile Loon Pond, and forced greater consideration of the harmful changes that could result in the interrelationships of its biotic and abiotic components. Used in combination with the twin aims of NEPA, depending upon the surrounding facts the CWA can also help force consideration of improved ecological alternatives and possibly even broader ecological analysis. In this case, the CWA and NEPA requirements likely influenced the quality of the environmental analysis under the project's NFMA and NEPA framework.

The Endangered Species Act

Similar opportunities for achieving ecological results may be achieved through the ESA. In enacting the ESA, Congress expressly declined to protect endangered species only "where practicable," as it had under earlier statutes and earlier drafts of the final act, and instead chose to afford species conservation the highest priority

---

31 Dubois I, at 30–31.

32 *See* Citizens to Preserve Overton Park, Inc. v. Volpe, 401 U.S. 402, 415–17 (1971); *see also* Sierra Club v. Marita, 46 F.3d 606 (7th Cir. 1995); Baltimore Gas & Elec. Co. v. Natural Resources Defense Council, Inc., 462 U.S. 87, 105 (1983); Motor Vehicle Mfrs. Ass'n v. State Farm Mut. Auto. Ins. Co., 463 U.S. 29, 43 (1983).

33 5 U.S.C. § 706(2)(A).

34 Citizens Awareness Network, Inc. v. United States Nuclear Regulatory Comm'n, 59 F.3d 284, 290 (1st Cir. 1995).

regardless of cost.[35] The ESA directs the Secretaries of the Departments of the Interior and Commerce (the Services) to promulgate regulations listing species as "endangered" or "threatened" (Listed Species)[36] and designating their critical habitat.[37] The ESA contains substantive teeth that prohibit actions adversely affecting listed species, making it unlawful for any person to take or harm any listed species.[38] Despite this strict prohibition, certain actions resulting in the incidental taking of listed species can be authorized or permitted under the Act.[39] The ESA also imposes both substantive and procedural obligations on federal agencies, licensees and permittees,[40] requiring that federal agencies, in consultation with the Services, insure that any agency action is not likely to jeopardize[41] the continued existence of any listed species or result in the destruction or adverse modification of its critical habitat.[42] The Services broadly construe the term "action" to mean

35 Shannon Peterson, *Congress and Charismatic Megafauna: A Legislative History of the Endangered Species Act*, 29 Envtl. L. 463, 491 (1999) (citing Endangered Species Preservation Act of 1966, Pub. L. No. 89-669, § 2(d), 80 Stat. 926, 928); *see also* Daniel J. Rohlf, The Endangered Species Act: A Guide to Its Protections and Implementation 24 (1989) (the "where practicable" language was in an early version of the ESA bill but removed prior to passage); Tenn. Valley Auth v. Hill, 437 U.S. 153, 180–81 (1978).

36 Endangered species are species in danger of extinction throughout all or a significant portion of their range. 16 U.S.C. § 1532(6) (2007). Threatened species are species likely to become endangered within the foreseeable future throughout all or a significant part of their range. *Id.* § 1532(20). The Services also maintain a "candidate Species list for species that are actively being considered for listing as endangered or threatened but for which there is not yet a proposed rule." 50 C.F.R. § 424.02.

37 16 U.S.C. §§ 1532(15), 1533; 50 C.F.R. § 424 (1999).

38 16 U.S.C. § 1538(a)(1)(B). The statute broadly defines the term "take" to include "harass, harm, pursue, hunt, shoot, wound, kill, trap, capture, or collect, or to attempt to engage in any such conduct." *Id.* § 1532(19). The Services define "harm" to include significant habitat modification or destruction that actually kills or injures wildlife by significantly impairing essential behavior patterns, including breeding, feeding, or sheltering. 50 C.F.R. §§ 17.3, 222.102. The Supreme Court has upheld this regulatory definition. Babbitt v. Sweet Home Chapter of Communities for a Greater Oregon, 515 U.S. 687, 708 (1995).

39 For example, under section 7, where agency actions might otherwise violate the taking prohibition, the Services can issue an incidental take statement along with a biological opinion so long as the Secretary determines that 1) the taking is incidental to the central purpose of the action, and 2) reasonable and prudent alternatives will minimize taking and avoid jeopardy.16 U.S.C. § 1536(b)(4)(A), (B).

40 *Id.* § 1536. Section 7(a)(1) of the ESA requires federal agencies, in consultation with and with the assistance of the Services, to utilize their authorities to further the purposes of the ESA by carrying out programs to conserve listed species. *Id.* § 1536(a)(1).

41 An action would cause jeopardy if it "reasonably would be expected, directly or indirectly, to reduce appreciably the likelihood of both the survival and recovery of a listed species." 50 C.F.R. § 402.02.

42 16 U.S.C. § 1536(a)(2). During a formal consultation, the Services must issue a biological opinion based on the best scientific and commercial date available. *Id.* If the

all activities or programs of any kind authorized, funded, or carried out, in whole or in part, by federal agencies. Such actions include the granting of licenses, contracts, leases, easements, rights-of-way, permits, or grants-in-aid, or actions directly or indirectly causing modifications to the land, water, or air.[43] Thus, many of the approvals and authorizations by the Forest Service for mountain resort development may trigger ESA jurisdiction.

The South Mountain Expansion decision played out under the ESA as most development projects do and did not give rise to significant issues under the Act. After consultation between the Forest Service and the U.S. Fish and Wildlife Service, it was determined that no federally listed species would be jeopardized by the project.[44] In other mountain resort developments, however, the ESA has played and can continue to play a significant role and lead to improved ecological outcomes and analysis, similar to the role of the CWA in the original Loon Resort expansion proposal.[45]

The CWA and the ESA contain substantive provisions that, unlike NEPA, may directly affect the Forest Service's analysis of mountain resort development. As the *Dubois* cases illustrate, these statutes can provide additional points of leverage for concerned citizens to force decision-makers to consider specific ecosystem-related issues and to potentially affect the scope and depth of the larger analysis. The legal requirements contained in these statutes can also leverage negotiated agreements that can enhance ecosystem considerations and limit the discretion of the Forest Service. Thus, NFMA and NEPA provide the primary substantive and procedural framework for analysis and decision making regarding mountain resort development in our national forests; however, statutes such as the CWA and ESA, though in themselves not capable of forcing an ecosystem-based analysis, are legal

Services conclude that a proposed action is likely to adversely affect a listed species or its critical habitat, they must render a jeopardy opinion and provide "reasonable and prudent alternatives" to the action. *Id.* § 1536(b)(3)(A); 50 C.F.R. § 402.02 (2001). If the Services determine that jeopardy is not likely, they typically issue a no-jeopardy opinion and the action proceeds. 50 C.F.R. §§ 402.13, 402.14(h)(3). Federal agencies must also confer with the Services on any agency action that is likely to jeopardize the continued existence of any species *proposed* for listing, or result in the destruction or adverse modification of proposed critical habitat, 16 U.S.C. §1536(a)(4), and include candidate species in any "biological assessment" required for any federal projects potentially impacting listed or candidate species. *See* 50 C.F.R. § 424.02.

43 50 C.F.R. § 402.02 (2001).

44 Loon Mountain Ski Resort Development and Expansion: Final Environmental Impact Statement 3-62–63, 3-75–90 (Feb. 2002).

45 *See, e.g.*, Colorado Environmental Coalition v. Dombeck, 185 F.3d. 1162, 1166 (10th Cir. 1999) (upholding a Forest Service decision to approve a reduced expansion of the Vail Resort with Canada Lynx habitat protections); Oregon Natural Resources Council Fund v. Goodman, 505 F.3d 884, 890, 898 (9th Cir. 2007) (enjoining Forest Service approval of the Mount Ashland Ski Area expansion in Oregon for failing to properly account for the potential environmental harm to Pacific Fisher habitat).

tools that may be used to ensure critical ecosystem components are protected and to leverage further ecosystem analysis.

Chapter 10
Conclusions from the Loon Resort Experience

The Loon Resort case study demonstrates that United States federal law does not adequately protect the mountain ecology when resort development decisions are made for lands within our national forests. As the first book in this series indicated, the rise of the ecosystemic legal regime has been underway for at least the past 50 years.[1] The events marking the rise of the Loon Resort evolved in tandem with this regime, spanning over 40 years from the day in 1964 when Sherman Adams concluded that Loon Mountain provided suitable terrain for a new ski area to the current South Mountain Expansion. The previous chapters explored in detail the laws, legal proceedings, and decisions that built upon each other and eventually led to the final approval of the South Mountain Expansion in 2002. This chapter brings the case study to a close by looking at some overarching conclusions about the relationship between the law and the mountain ecosystem.

In the late nineteenth and early twentieth centuries, industrial scale logging fed the sawmills and pulp and paper plants in the Lincoln, New Hampshire area and laid bare Loon Mountain and all but the most remote and inaccessible forest land in the area. At about the time this era reached its climax, however, the Forest Service in 1914 began purchasing tracts of these cut-over lands under provisions of the Weeks Act, which authorized such purchases for the purposes of watershed protection and timber management. These lands were soon declared the White Mountain National Forest by Presidential Proclamation in 1918, and were managed under the Forest Service's Organic Act mandate to improve and protect the forest, or to secure favorable conditions of water flows and to furnish a continuous supply of timber for the nation. While the Organic Act provided a relatively narrow forest management mandate centered on protecting the forests' timber and water resources, the Forest Service also read its authority broadly enough to manage some lands as wilderness and for recreation. This early multiple-use style of management was strengthened and expanded with passage of the Multiple Use and Sustained Yield Act in 1960 (MUSYA), which memorialized the view of the forest as an aggregate of goods and services to be managed for the multiple use and sustained yield of its several products and services, including outdoor recreation, rangeland, timber, watersheds, and wildlife and fish.

1 Richard O. Brooks et. al., Law and Ecology: The Rise of the Ecosystem Regime 2–3 (2002).

In the earliest decisions authorizing the ski area on Loon Mountain, an ecosystem perspective played no role in the analysis. The Forest Service's grant of the first Special Use Permit in 1965 preceded later federal laws requiring an environmental impact analysis and a comprehensive planning framework that could inject an ecosystem perspective into the decision making. Instead, the decision looked more narrowly at whether the proposed ski area fell within the statutory requirements to provide for multiple uses on national forest land, and the approval contained only minimal "boilerplate" environmental protections, such as a general prohibition on discharging pollutants in sufficient concentrations that would result in substantial harm to fish and wildlife. This first, non-ecosystem-based decision was in large part a prelude to the future; once authorized, the resort was likely to continue despite officially limited terms on permits given the Forest Service's multiple use mandate, the Loon Mountain Recreation Corporation's (LMRC) investments over time, and the focus on the surrounding community's economic wellbeing.

As the ski area grew into a four-season resort over the years, however, a new dominant legal regime emerged with the passage of the National Environmental Policy Act (NEPA) in 1969 and the National Forest Management Act (NFMA) in 1976. This new legal regime offered opportunities for introducing an ecosystem perspective as planning decisions about the White Mountain National Forest and the expansion of the Loon Resort were made. NFMA established a statutory mandate to provide for diversity of animal and plant communities, and under NFMA the Forest Service developed regulatory requirements to maintain viable species populations and to use analytical tools like management indicator species (Indicator Species) that also helped to inject ecological considerations into Forest Service decision making. In addition, NFMA's comprehensive planning regime provides opportunities for periodic reassessment of activities in the White Mountain National Forest.

NEPA introduced an action-forcing procedural framework through its requirement for preparation of environmental impact statements (EIS), which applies in this context to forest management planning and site-specific development proposals. The requirement that the Forest Service take a hard look at the environmental impacts of its proposed actions and analyze a reasonable range of alternatives is at the heart of the EIS and can allow for extensive evaluation of the ecological impacts of the proposed actions and their alternatives. In addition, requirements for identifying the affected environment and examining the cumulative impacts of the action can be critical, as can the valuable opportunities provided for the public to introduce ecological considerations into the analysis.[2]

---

2 The Loon Resort case study also demonstrates that other federal statutes such as the Clean Water Act (CWA) or the Endangered Species Act (ESA) include legal mandates that can be looked to in some situations to help inform an ecosystems-based analysis or may directly lead to results that help protect important components of the ecosystem. For example, species listed under the ESA are incorporated into Forest Service analysis as Indicator Species, while standards set under the CWA may serve as benchmarks for efforts

Through its implementation of the NFMA and NEPA legal framework for analysis, the Forest Service made it part way to an ecosystem-based approach in its analysis of the South Mountain Expansion proposal. The Forest Service laid a relatively strong foundation for its analysis by including a detailed inventory of the potentially affected environment, establishing a set of useful scales for its analysis, and encompassing some of the connected actions that fell outside the national forest boundaries. The Forest Service also set up its analysis to consider the impacts of the proposal and its alternatives in terms of many apparently useful Indicator Species and the diversity of animal and plant communities in the affected area. Finally, the public appears to have received ample opportunities for public comment. These features illustrate how the NFMA and NEPA regimes provide opportunities for evaluating ecological interrelationships.

The extent to which the NFMA and NEPA legal regime ultimately introduced an ecosystem perspective at Loon, however, was limited by at least three significant factors. First, the legal regime resulted in decision making that was fragmented over time, thereby undermining the ability to fully evaluate ecological consequences before making decisions. The initial permit decision was not ecosystem-based but committed the LMRC to substantial investment; the 1986 Forest Management Plan supported the continued existence of the resort and identified South Mountain as an area for expansion, without specific environmental impact analysis; the evaluation of the LMRC's South Mountain Expansion proposal looked at specific environmental consequences, but was predicated on the assumption that South Mountain was suitable for expansion and that expansion served legitimate and specific purposes and needs geared toward satisfying skier demands for upgrades at the Loon Resort. That analysis then led to approval of the South Mountain Expansion and the issuance of a new 40-year permit. And finally, the Forest Service formally initiated the revision process for the 1986 Forest Management Plan in March 2000—within three months of the submission of the South Mountain Expansion proposal—and completed its plan revision in 2005, yet the Forest Service did not integrate plan revision analysis with its analysis of the South Mountain Expansion decision.

As a result of this "shell game," the Forest Service never, at a single point in time, conducted a thorough analysis of the ecological impacts of the Loon Resort without a prevailing assumption that the resort would operate at Loon. Temporal fragmentation of the legal proceedings inevitably led to analytical fragmentation of ecosystem impacts. The risk of this type of fragmentation is relatively high when planning regimes set broad parameters and subsequent specific permit review procedures are used to make individualized decisions. Nonetheless, within the framework of NFMA and NEPA, the Forest Service could have done more to minimize this risk by using its regulatory discretion to better align and consolidate its decisions temporally and/or by defining the purpose and need for the South

to protect Indicator Species or may rule out the use of some waters altogether due to their ecological fragility.

Mountain Expansion more broadly, thereby allowing for a rigorous examination of a broader range of alternatives.

Second, although the NFMA and NEPA framework allows for considerable discretion in both framing and conducting the analysis of its resort development decisions, the Forest Service did not take full advantage of that discretion as it ventured into the details of its review of the South Mountain Expansion proposal. It did not consider the connected and/or cumulative actions related to the private slopeside development that became the South Peak Resort. It ultimately assessed most of the impacts to Indicator Species and other resources at the forest-wide planning level and not the community or local scale, resulting in conclusions that minimized the significance of the impacts. And though both NFMA and NEPA contain language that reflects ecological concepts, little of the Forest Service's analysis focused on the impacts that would flow through the relationships of the biotic and abiotic resources affected. In each of these examples, the Forest Service could have applied its considerable discretion under the NFMA and NEPA framework to consider the full range of impacts, at the appropriate scale, on the Loon Mountain ecology.

Third, even if the Forest Service were to prepare an exhaustive, ecosystem-based analysis, the ultimate decision may not necessarily protect the ecosystem. The Forest Service is limited by its current statutory mandate of providing for multiple uses of the national forest lands, including recreation, and in furtherance of that goal, its partnership with the ski industry. Further complicating this analysis is the Forest Service's recognition of the social and economic impacts of its resort decisions on the surrounding communities, which appears to flow both formally and informally from the economic underpinnings of NFMA (and as part of this the MUSYA and the Ski Area Permit Act) and the related ski industry partnership. While the partnership helps the Forest Service to carry out its commitment to alpine skiing as a form of winter recreation and helps foster the increased financial and regulatory certainty desired by the private sector in order to provide those services, the partnership and the potential for negative impacts to the local community make it more difficult to rule out mountain resorts *per se* as a legitimate management alternative. In addition, from the perspective of some stakeholders, these factors may call into question whether all interests, including the health of the forest ecosystem, will be objectively evaluated when the Forest Service makes decisions about mountain resort development.

Here the NFMA and the NEPA regimes also intersect with the federal Wilderness Act, not yet discussed in these chapters. Within national forests, some lands have been designated as wilderness under the Wilderness Act of 1964,[3] where human activities are restricted to nonmotorized recreation (such as hunting, fishing, and

3 16 U.S.C. §§ 1131–1136 (2007). *See also* the Eastern Wilderness Act of 1975, 88 Stat. 2096, 16 U.S.C. 1132(note). The Eastern Wilderness Act provides for the designation of wilderness in addition to that allowed by the Wilderness Act of 1964 in the eastern half of the U.S. *Id.*

horseback riding), scientific research, and other noninvasive activities, while generally prohibiting logging, mining, roads, mechanized vehicles (including bicycles), and other forms of development.[4] The Wilderness Act may contribute to a more ecological approach to national forest management, though it is based more on romantic notions of primitivism than on a scientific ecological approach to nature.[5] Where land is not designated as wilderness, however, it is potentially open for recreational development pursuant to the Forest Service's multiple-use mandate and commitment to alpine skiing, as at Loon Mountain.

Based upon the Loon Resort case study, there are at least two broad changes in federal law and policy that could increase the likelihood of an ecosystem-based approach to mountain resort decision making in national forests. Most important among these changes would be to revise the multiple-use approach to prioritize ecological considerations. An amendment to NFMA could require the Forest Service to implement a management approach that places ecosystem health and ecological analysis as the first priority in any management plan, and would be the most direct way to achieve this change. Such an approach could require that management decisions account for the needs of the ecosystem first, and then allow for the balancing of the remaining priorities that incorporate social and economic considerations. As has been suggested, even absent Congressional action there is considerable discretion within the NFMA and NEPA framework that could allow for a greater policy emphasis on ecological sustainability as the priority in planning and project-level decision making.[6]

Alternatively, NFMA or NEPA could be amended and their regulations rewritten to require an explicitly *ecological* impact analysis of forest management planning decisions and other significant actions. Under the George W. Bush administration, however, the trend has been in the opposite direction, as reflected in its repeated attempts to revise NFMA regulations in ways that sound ecosystem-friendly, but in fact substantially weaken existing standards for decision making.

---

4 *See* 16 U.S.C. § 1133. There are some over 660 federal wilderness areas in the U.S. totaling about 106 million acres. This represents about 5 percent of the total U.S. land mass, though only about 2.5 percent of the land in the 48 contiguous states. *See* U.S. Dep't of Interior, *Wilderness*, http://www.doi.gov/issues/wilderness.html (last visited June 2, 2008). While over 400 of the 660 wilderness areas are in national forests, these areas total only about 35 million acres, or about 18 percent of our National Forests. *See id.* It is estimated that states and Tribes have designated about 2.7 million acres of land as wilderness, of which about 1.8 millions acres are in the contiguous states. *See* Chad P. Dawson & Pauline Thorndike, *State Designated Wilderness Programs in the United States*, 8 INT'L J. OF WILDERNESS 21, 26 (2002), *available at* http://www.wilderness.net/library/documents/Dawson1.pdf (last visited June 2, 2008).

5 BROOKS ET AL., *supra* note 1, at 209.

6 Revised NFMA planning regulations promulgated in 2000, but never implemented by the Bush Administration, made it the first priority for national forest management to maintain and restore the ecological sustainability of the national forests. *See* 36 C.F.R. §§ 219.2, 219.19 (2001); *see infra* note 7.

The most threatening of the Bush regulatory revisions are measures that weaken the requirement to maintain "viable populations" of wildlife, exclude most Forest Service planning from NEPA's requirements, allow the best available science to be ignored, and trade in enforceable standards in favor of soft goals for planning and management.[7] Each of these changes not only compromise conventional

7 *See* 73 Fed. Reg. 21,468, 21,472–74 (Apr. 21, 2008). Following an extensive scientific review, the Forest Service's planning regulations were revised in 2000 to reflect its increased understanding of ecosystem management, the role of science in decision making, and new planning tools like geographical information systems. *See* 65 Fed. Reg. 67,514–516 (Nov. 9, 2000). In 2001, the new Bush Administration began efforts to undo the revised regulations culminating in new regulations issued in 2005 (2005 Planning Rule). *See* 70 Fed. Reg. 1,023 (Jan. 5, 2005). The Forest Service stated these revisions were designed to "streamline and improve" the planning process by making plans more "adaptable" to changes in social, economic, and environmental conditions, to "strengthen" the role of science in planning, to "strengthen" collaboration with the public, and to "reaffirm" the principles of sustainable management consistent with the MUSYA. *See id.* However, the 2005 Planning Rule was challenged by a host of environmental organizations who argued it would in fact remove key environmental safeguards and give local Forest Service officials too much discretion by favoring soft goals over enforceable wildlife protections; reducing NEPA's applicability; decreasing resource monitoring, and weakening the role of science in decision making. *See e.g.,* Citizens for Better Forestry v. USDA, 481 F.Supp.2d 1059, 1067, 1073–75, 1082 (N.D. Cal. 2007). The court sided with the environmental organizations, holding that the 2005 Planning Rule was promulgated in violation of NEPA, the ESA, and the Administrative Procedure Act (APA). S*ee id.* at 1100. The court issued an injunction prohibiting the Forest Service from implementing the rule until the statutory violations were cured. *See id.*

Unfortunately, the Forest Service re-promulgated essentially the same regulations (2008 Planning Rule) after undertaking additional procedural steps and analysis that, in its view, met the court's order. *See* 73 Fed. Reg. 21,468 (Aug. 23, 2007). The 2008 Planning Rule continues regulatory changes from the 2005 Planning Rule that would replace the requirement to maintain "viable populations" of native fish and wildlife species in the national forests with an "overall goal" to "provide a framework to contribute to sustaining native ecological systems by providing ecological conditions to support diversity of native plant and animal species in the plan area." *See* 36 C.F.R. § 219.10(b)(2008). The 2008 Planning Rule also eliminates the requirement to prepare an EIS when a forest plan is revised or significantly amended. *See id.* § 219.4(b); 73 Fed. Reg. at 21,473. Forest Service officials are also given broad discretion to reject the best scientific evidence and advice, and need only to "take into account" the best available science, *see* 36 C.F.R.§ 219.11(a), which "is only one aspect of decision making" and that "competing use demands" and other factors can override scientific input. 73 Fed. Reg. at 21,473–74. Further, other regulations would also eliminate the use of mandatory "standards" in forest plans, in favor of discretionary "guidelines." *See* 36 C.F.R.§ 219.12(b).

The environmental organizations returned to court to challenge the new rule on May 6, 2008, arguing that the new regulations suffer from the same flaws as the 2005 Planning Rule, and specifically that approval of the 2008 Planning Rule violated NEPA and the APA because the Forest Service failed to prepare an adequate EIS including, among other things,

environmental analysis and undermine the ability of decision-makers and the public to take a comprehensive perspective on forest planning, but also reduce the likelihood of ecosystem-based decision making. As discussed above, even without amendments to NFMA and NEPA, more modest improvements to the planning regulations could address some of the shortcomings identified in the Loon Resort case study and improve the likelihood of an ecological approach. Such changes could focus on eliminating the temporal and spatial fragmentation that resulted in a shell game for decision-makers and the public, instituting rules that ensure a broader and more accurate framework for analysis, and requiring use of the best available science, which should flow from an ecology-based approach to meeting NFMA's standards.[8]

Finally, from a broader ecosystem perspective that takes us out to the landscape scale, the time may be right to reexamine the underlying purposes of our national forests, instead of focusing on how mountain resort development decisions play out at any particular mountain. Applying this scale would require consideration of not just national forest lands but also the private lands that fill out the landscape scale. From such a perspective, it would be fair to ask whether the federal government should continue to assume that the national forests need to serve the currently defined set of multiple uses, or whether a narrower set of uses, such as those provided through the Wilderness Act, may be more appropriate.[9]

The answer to this question may vary with different landscapes and associated patterns of public and private landownership. But in general the nation could look increasingly to private lands for the consumptive outdoor recreational

---

an analysis of the direct, indirect, and cumulative, impacts of the rule and a reasonable range of alternatives. *See* Defenders of Wildlife, et al., v. Schafer, C.A. C08-2326 (N. D. Cal.) Complaint for Declaratory and Injunctive Relief (May 6, 2008), *available at* http://www.earthjustice.org/library/legal_docs/1750-complaint-final.pdf (last visited June 2, 2008). The environmental groups also intend to challenge the adequacy of the ESA consultation after expiration of the 60-day mandatory notice period. *See* Press Release, Bush Administration Challenged Over Abandonment of Wildlife Protections (May 6, 2008), http://www.earthjustice.org/news/press/2008/bush-administration-challenged-over-abandonment-of-wildlife-protections.html (last visited June 2, 2008).

8 The 2000 planning regulations included several additional provisions that would have contributed to an ecological approach to analysis and decision making, such as the requirement that the planning process include the development, analysis, and use of information regarding ecosystem, and species diversity at a variety of spatial and temporal scales when making forest management decisions. 36 C.F.R. § 219.20 (2001).

9 Such uses might be limited to include wilderness, wildlife habitat, clean water, biological diversity, ecological integrity, scientific research and education, and backcountry recreation. Under this approach, the production of commodities such as timber and minerals would not be allowed to compromise these primary uses. *See, e.g.,* The Wilderness Society, *America's National Forests in the 21st Century: The Forest Society's Vision* 9–13 (1999), *available at* http://www.wilderness.org/Library/Documents/upload/The-Wilderness-Society-s-Forest-Vision.pdf (last visited June 2, 2008).

opportunities provided by mountain resorts. A reevaluation of the role of national forests from an ecological perspective would seem timely. From the time national forests first came into existence, to the time when the Forest Service began to purchase cutover lands to form the White Mountain National Forest, to the time when the Multiple Use Sustainable Yield Act was passed in 1960, policy decisions were not made based on the more sophisticated, landscape ecosystem perspective that has emerged with advancements in science and the rise of the ecosytemic regime in the United States. It may be difficult to uproot existing resorts, but the footprint of existing resorts could be frozen and a more careful consideration of retiring existing resorts as their permits expire would seem to be reasonable starting points for an objective review.[10] Perhaps the time is right to reevaluate fundamental assumptions that have driven the federal law of national forests for the past century.

In the final analysis, it appears that current federal law would allow decision-makers to take a basically ecological approach to mountain resort development decisions; however, the law does not require or strongly encourage them to do so. While the range of options available for increasing ecological considerations is broad, the likelihood of successfully implementing any of them will depend greatly on national politics and the demand for change from the public and other stakeholders.

10 This would recognize the sunk capital investments in existing resorts while also recognizing that each resort was authorized pursuant to term permits that clearly establish the risk of those investments. As was seen with the Loon Resort, these investments create momentum for renewal and expansion of mountain resorts.

PART III
Whiteface Mountain Ski Center, New York

Olympic Legacies and Adirondack Park Plans

John S. Banta[1]

1 The views expressed are solely those of the author and do not necessarily reflect official opinions of the Adirondack Park Agency or the State of New York.

Chapter 11

An Introduction to the Whiteface Mountain Ski Center and the Legal Framework

Introduction

The Whiteface Mountain Ski Center, promoted as the "Olympic Mountain," is part of the Olympic winter sports complex centered on Lake Placid in the state of New York. Whiteface and Lake Placid are located in the heart of the Adirondack Mountains, a disconnected part of the Laurentian Shield that occupies about 20 percent of upstate New York and is separated from its Canadian counterpart by the St. Lawrence River and valley. These mountains are now part of the nationally unique, six million acre Adirondack Park (Park) created by the State of New York. Winter sports in the Park gained international attention when Lake Placid hosted the third Winter Olympic Games in 1932. The Winter Olympics returned to the Park on their thirteenth session in 1980, for which Whiteface Mountain was the alpine event venue. Consequently, the Whiteface Mountain Ski Center has become an important asset in an area with a long history of varied winter sports activities. Although the Whiteface Mountain Ski Center is located wholly in the Town of Wilmington, which provides some tourist accommodations, most of the hotels and other tourist facilities are located in the nearby Village of Lake Placid.

Larger than Yellowstone or other well-known national parks, the Adirondack Park encompasses the 46 "High Peaks" of the Adirondack Mountains, thousands of lakes, and over 100 small communities, including Wilmington and Lake Placid. Although it contains a vast acreage of accessible state-owned land, the Adirondack Park is unusual because its boundaries also include land in private ownership, creating a patchwork that is approximately 50 percent state-owned land and 50 percent privately-owned land. In this unconventional configuration, both the public and private lands are inside the "park." The public land alone, which is known as the Forest Preserve, represents the largest public land area under a single management plan in the lower 48 states.[1]

The Adirondack Park's legal regime, which regulates the activities on Whiteface Mountain and the surrounding resort area, is also unique in the United States. The New York Constitution strictly limits the use of the state-owned land in the Park, including Whiteface Mountain; the Park's master planning process and management process for state lands further regulate the uses on Whiteface on an ongoing basis; and the state's planning process for private lands in the Park, which

1 *See* Adirondack Park Agency website, http://www.apa.state.ny.us/ (2007).

is an overlay on local planning, governs most new development on private lands outside the "hamlets" or long-standing settlements in the Park.

As a result, the Whiteface Mountain Ski Center as a mountain resort is quite different from the other resorts featured in this book. The on-mountain commercial facilities at Whiteface are owned and operated by the State of New York, not a private corporation, and those facilities are all directly related to skiing (or off-season use of ski facilities). At the base of the mountain, there are only two small adjacent private ski lodges not affiliated with the Ski Center, and there are no immediately adjacent stores, hotels or residential developments. The support activities necessary for housing, feeding, and entertaining resort visitors, which are provided by the private sector, are all located off-mountain, primarily in the Village of Lake Placid nine miles away.

The Adirondack Park regime offers a fascinating case study of how state-level land use policy and regulatory decisions influence the evolution of activities on Whiteface and the surrounding resort communities, in particular the villages of Lake Placid and Wilmington. In determining the extent to which this legal regime takes an ecological approach to determining permissible uses, this case study focuses on several major techniques:

- *State zoning* governs uses of the state-owned Forest Preserve (about 50 percent of the Park), the privately owned, commercial forests (about 40 percent of the Park), and the developed settlements (about 10 percent of the Park). This regional scale zoning is the product of the New York Constitution's provisions governing public lands, which create a forever wild preserve surrounding Whiteface, and the Adirondack Park Agency Act, which directs a state land master plan and articulates the Park's private land use plan.
- In addition, a planning and environmental assessment approach for units of public lands and facilities has governed capital improvements at Whiteface Mountain.
- Finally, *state subdivision and development permitting for "regional" development on the private lands,* which constrains municipal planning and zoning, have concentrated new commercial development like lodging, restaurants and services in the traditional village centers in the Park.

The state's land use controls create a very tight frame within which the Ski Center operates, much as a picture frame holds the oil canvas taut. As explored at length in the next chapter, the century-old "forever wild" constitutional principles governing the state-owned land—the Forest Preserve—create in effect an approach akin to the precautionary principle for the entire Park. The constitutional protection was augmented with state public and private land plans in the 1970s and more recently has been significantly enhanced with state purchases of conservation easements to protect working forests from residential development.[2] These framing elements

2 *See generally* Eleanor F. Brown, The Forest Preserve of N.Y. State (1986).

combine to ensure ecosystem protection—as the ongoing planning and impact assessment process regulates growth and improvements at the Ski Center. Therefore, while the operational short-term development decision making in the Adirondack Park may encompass relatively little overt ecological analysis, the large watershed scale of the precautionary environmental legal frame operates to achieve ecosystem outcomes. It restricts options during the public decision-making process, and it also affects private markets and decision making that operate outside the command-and-control public regulatory process.

The frame itself is stabilized by legal and administrative checks and balances: the daunting challenges of amending the Constitution to adjust the "forever wild" parameters; the divisions of administrative responsibility between the State's Adirondack Park Agency and the Department of Environmental Conservation; and the similar division of private land regulatory responsibility between the Adirondack Park Agency and local governments. These legal and procedural constraints can make even obvious changes to the framing principles, both process and substance, difficult to implement, thereby enhancing the precautionary effect of this legal regime. This case study of Whiteface will explore how the legal regime in the Adirondack Park guided the modernization of the Whiteface Ski Center from the 1990s to the presently contemplated "build out" of the constitutionally authorized ski trails (Chapter 12). It will also review the effect of the legal regime on the private lands in the Park that surround Whiteface (Chapter 13). The remainder of this chapter lays the foundation for that analysis, introducing the unique features of this mountain resort, the characteristics and ownership of the Whiteface Mountain Ski Area, plans for the future, and an overview of the legal regime.

The Mountain Resort

Although located deep within New York's Adirondack Park, Whiteface is only a two-hour drive from Montreal and a little over six hours from Boston, Toronto or New York City, making it available to 60 million people who live within a day's drive.[3] Access to the mountain from Interstate 87, the Adirondack Northway, is via a two-lane state highway through Wilmington from the north, or Lake Placid from the south. Scheduled air service is available in Saranac Lake, a few miles to the west, and charter service is available at the Lake Placid airport. (See Figure 11.1).

Whiteface Mountain is the "great loner" of the High Peaks in the Adirondack Park.[4] An anorthosite granite outcrop with an elevation of 4,867 feet, it sits distinct and somewhat apart from the other Adirondack High Peaks that lie about ten miles to the south. Its profile, buttressed by Little Whiteface Peak, presents distinctive

3 Adirondack Park Agency, Planning for the Adirondack Forest Preserve (2000).

4 Paul Schneider, The Adirondacks: A History of America's First Wilderness 152 (1997).

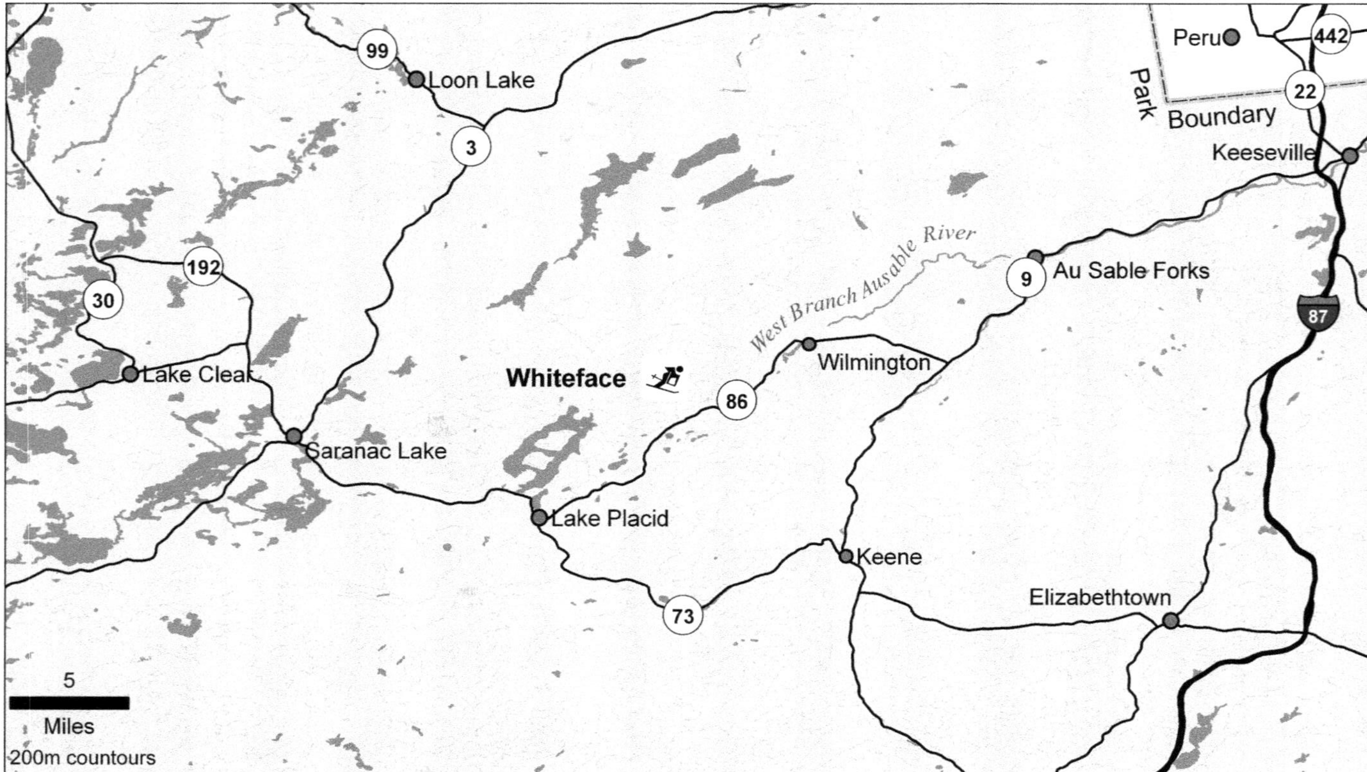

Figure 11.1 Whiteface Mountain and its Regional Setting

Data Sources: New York State Adirondack Park Agency; Tele Atlas North America, Inc.; ESRI

cirque valleys on its east, west and north faces, separated by sharp arêtes,[5] and it rises very visibly and dramatically from the northeastern shore of Lake Placid, an approximately four-mile long lake that has drawn summer residents to their lakeside lodges for over 100 years.

Located in the township of Wilmington, Whiteface Mountain and its Ski Center are midway between the hamlet of Wilmington and the Village of Lake Placid in the township of North Elba. The Village of Lake Placid, nine miles south of Whiteface, is part of a trio of villages at the center of the Adirondack Park that has traditionally served as the primary commercial center for the entire region.[6] The winding two-lane road that connects Lake Placid and Whiteface follows the West Branch of the Ausable River much of the way before continuing north past Whiteface to Wilmington. A state-designated recreational river widely known for its white water and trout fishing upstream, the West Branch flows by the eastern base of Whiteface.[7]

Many mountain resorts integrate the ski slopes, residential development and commercial services into one contiguous development on the mountain, all or most of which is owned or developed by a for-profit corporation. The mountain resort at Whiteface is different. As a result of the state land use controls, Whiteface's on-mountain facilities are limited to the ski slopes on public land, and the off-mountain attractions and residential and commercial support services are primarily located in the Village of Lake Placid.[8] An extremely compact settlement, the village offers diverse opportunities for lodging, restaurants, attractions and winter sports, and activities other than downhill skiing, and although Lake Placid and its immediate

---

5 Brown, *supra* note 2, at 165–66.

6 The three are Lake Placid, long the "toney" resort of the group; Saranac Lake, for many years a tuberculosis cure center and a commercial anchor for the "Tri Lakes;" and Tupper Lake, long the industrial backbone of the region, but emerging as a tourism center with a current proposal for slopeside condominiums and private development of the former municipal ski center, virtually the only location in the Adirondack Park where present land ownership configurations and zoning would allow such a concept to be undertaken. Although Lake Placid is only about ten minutes (on winter roads) from Whiteface, all communities have ready access to the Mountain.

7 *See* N.Y. Envtl. Conservation Law §§ 15-2701–15-2714 (McKinney 2001). The New York State Wild Scenic and Recreational Rivers System was created in 1975 to protect the free flowing character of the State's most significant rivers and also regulates adjacent land uses within the designated river corridor and outside settlement areas zoned hamlet and moderate intensity use by the State. It is administered by the Department of Environmental Conservation for state lands, and by the Adirondack Park Agency for private lands.

8 A few individual commercial properties near the Ski Center itself provide some lodging and dining opportunities. Virtually all winter visitors to the ski area stay in the nearby communities although summer visitors find both public and private campgrounds adjacent to the area. *See* Lake Placid: Forever Adirondack Brochure (2002); *see generally* http://www.lakeplacid.com.

vicinity have only about 8,000 residents,[9] this population swells to several times that number at peak tourist periods. Winter tourism is actually the secondary season; summer activities range from classical cultural offerings to challenging athletic competitions and wilderness outings.

As explained at more length below, the ownership structure of the mountain resort is also different from most. The operations on the mountain are run by a public authority, not a private corporation, while the residential lodging and commercial support facilities in Lake Placid and the surrounding area are owned by unrelated private businesses. The multiplicity of private interests involved and state zoning intervention for large scale development appear to have discouraged any dominant private interest in the mix of private operators, with many smaller scale enterprises providing the diverse winter resort experience for which Lake Placid is known. Thus, given the legal regime, the potential for on-mountain development is limited, and the private, four-season resort activities are tightly integrated around the communities of Lake Placid and, to a lesser extent, neighboring hamlet areas.

The Whiteface Mountain Ski Center

Located in the Park's Forest Preserve, Whiteface Mountain itself is owned by the State of New York and is almost entirely surrounded by other state-owned land. The on-mountain facilities consist of the Whiteface Mountain Ski Center on the east side of the mountain and a paved road constructed in 1927, Veterans Memorial Highway, that climbs the north side of the mountain to its summit and is open to the public during the summer months. Both are operated by the Olympic Regional Development Authority (ORDA), created by the New York legislature after the 1980 Winter Olympics to manage the collection of state and municipal winter sports facilities that hosted the Olympics.[10]

ORDA is a public authority, a special type of New York corporation, created in 1981 to assume responsibility for and manage all Olympic facilities in the vicinity of Lake Placid. The Whiteface Mountain Ski Center operates pursuant to an agreement between the State's Department of Environmental Conservation and ORDA, initially entered into on October 4, 1982, as provided in the Public Authorities Law. ORDA-managed facilities also include the state's bobsled, luge, cross country, and biathlon facilities at Mt. Van Hoevenberg just outside Lake

---

9 United States Census Bureau, 2000 Census, Zip Code Tabulation Area 12946, http://factfinder.census.gov/servlet/SAFFFacts?_event=Search&geo_id=&_geoContext=&_street=&_county=12946&_cityTown=12946&_state=04000US36&_zip=12946&_lang=en&_sse=on&pctxt=fph&pgsl=010&show_2003_tab=&redirect=Y (last visited Mar. 2, 2008).

10 Olympic Reg'l Dev. Auth. and N.Y. State Dep't of Envtl. Conservation, Whiteface Mountain Ski Center Unit Mgmt. Plan Update and Final Generic Envtl. Impact Statement (1996).

Figure 11.2 Whiteface Summit Overlooking Lake Placid
Photo: ©iStockphoto.com/Sebastien Cote

Placid, and municipal facilities owned by the Town of North Elba, including the Olympic Center skating arenas, the speed skating oval, and the Olympic Ski Jumping Complex. In addition, ORDA gained responsibility for the Gore Mountain Ski Center in Johnsburg in the southern Adirondacks in 1984.[11] As a public benefit corporation, ORDA enjoys public privileges in the financial markets and access to some government funds within an operational setting that resembles a private corporation whose board is named at the direction of the implementing legislation. It also has public obligations regarding the management and use of the facilities under its care.

Alpine skiing, assisted by uphill tows or lifts, has been a fixture at Whiteface since the late 1940s,[12] following the state voters' special referendum in 1941 permitting the creation of the Ski Center within the Forest Preserve.[13] The 2,910-

11 *See* N.Y. Pub. Auth. Law § 2605–2611 (McKinney 2001); Dept. of Envtl. Conservation–Olympic Reg'l Dev. Auth. Agreement. (Oct. 4, 1982).

12 Brown, *supra* note 2, at 166. The first ski center on the Whiteface north slope, Marble Mountain, was opened in 1949; it was relocated to its present location on the east slope, opening in 1958. *See* Hal Burton, *Placid's Playgrounds*, Ski Life, Feb. 1961, at 29.

13 Brown, *supra* note 2. at 166.

acre Ski Center operates on a steep-walled cirque marked by major slides and surrounded by flanks where irregular rock surfaces are sufficient to hold the overburden and vegetation in place. The developed ski trails are located on these flanking slopes of Whiteface Mountain and Little Whiteface Peak, with a total vertical drop of 3,166 feet;[14] the slides are open for off-piste skiing when there have been particularly heavy natural snowfalls.[15] The 72 ski trails occupy only approximately 210 acres and totaled approximately 20 miles as the 2007–2008 improvements began.[16]

The base lodge complex for the Ski Center is located within a few yards of the bank of the West Branch of the Ausable River, and five surface parking facilities nearby use approximately 11.15 acres. A second base facility hosts the children's ski center and added parking. One tributary and four sub-tributaries to the river are located within the area dedicated to the Ski Center, and the Ski Center draws water for its snowmaking from the river. The river's designation as a recreational river by the state had little regulatory impact on the creation of the existing base lodge and snowmaking facilities as they were initiated in the 1970's for the 1980 Winter Olympics, before the Rivers Act regulations were implemented for state lands. The river's protection, however, will influence future plans for snowmaking and water storage.

Although somewhat isolated from the surrounding High Peaks of the Adirondacks, the ecology of Whiteface is similar to these other more protected landscapes that offer 100-plus acres of true alpine flora and fauna within the Park. However, there is virtually no undisturbed alpine habitat on the Whiteface summit. Easy access along the summit highway to a wide range of mountain soils and geology attracts tourists and also students and other researchers responsible for pioneering efforts at restoration of Adirondack alpine flora and studies of long-distance transport of air pollutants.[17]

The upper reaches of the ski area include stunted spruce, and "spruce waves" provide an unusual habitat that is occupied by Bicknell's thrush, a neo-tropical songbird whose habitat is specifically recognized by New York State, though not an endangered species. The spruce appear to be in waves progressing from a leading

---

14 Olympic Reg'l Dev. Auth. and N.Y. State Dep't of Envtl. Conservation, 2004 Whiteface Mountain Ski Center Unit Mgmt. Plan Update, Amendment, and Final Generic Envtl. Impact Statement (March 31, 2004) [hereinafter ORDA, 2004 Final Plan and FGEIS]; Olympic Reg'l Dev. Auth. and N.Y. State Dep't of Envtl. Conservation, 2006 Whiteface Mountain Ski Center Unit Mgmt. Plan Update, Amendment, and Final Envtl. Impact Statement (July 19, 2006) [hereinafter ORDA, 2006 Unit Plan Update]; *see also* http://www.whiteface.com/newsite/onmtn/mtnstats.php.

15 ORDA, 2004 Final Plan and FGEIS, *supra* note 14; ORDA, 2006 Unit Plan Update, *supra* note 14.

16 ORDA, 2004 Final Plan and FGEIS, *supra* note 14, at vii, I-3.

17 Whiteface Mountain is the home of the Atmospheric Sciences Research Center, an outpost of the State University at Albany that is deeply involved in weather and climate research and air quality monitoring. As a result, the summit has been intensively observed relative to acid precipitation.

edge of mature spruce, dying because of the prevailing winds, to juvenile and then more mature trees until the next rank of sacrificial trees is reached. This pattern repeats. This phenomenon was considered in the environmental assessment for the Ski Center's most recent build-out strategy, as discussed in the next chapter.

Consistently top-rated among eastern resorts for its off-mountain ambiance, Whiteface has received top ratings for its ski experience as well in recent years.[18] Although it sports the greatest vertical drop in the East, the mountain is mid-sized when measured in terms of skier numbers. With approximately 175,000 winter visitors, Whiteface hosts a significantly smaller number of skiers than either Vermont's Killington Mountain Resort or Quebec's Mont Tremblant.[19] The Ski Center also operates during non-winter months, offering festival events (for example, a Native American festival and Octoberfest), gondola rides up the slopes, and mountain biking. Summer activities at the ski area now integrate wildlife observation and other green-themed considerations consistent with the Adirondack Park setting. As only one of a diverse array of Park activities and facilities administered by ORDA, the Whiteface Mountain Ski Center's past and present are inextricably intertwined with the winter sports and all-season recreation strategies of the Adirondack Park region, including Lake Placid.

Plans for the Future

While privatization of the Ski Center is occasionally discussed, it seems unlikely given the state constitutional issues associated with the Forest Preserve (discussed in the next chapter) and the success to date with ORDA's strategy of balancing traditional recreational skiing, youth education, and training programs with fairly aggressive international competition and integrated community development strategies. ORDA's programs balance and take advantage of public investments in the various competitive venues in order to maximize regional economic benefit.

The 2004 update to the Whiteface Mountain Ski Center Unit Management Plan[20] (the 2004 Unit Plan) lays out plans for expanding the constitutionally

18 *See, e.g.*, *Ski Magazine* ratings, Top Ten in the East, http://www.skinet.com//photogallery.jsp?ID=1000014857&page=3 (Whiteface rated #3 for 2007–08).

19 *See* Technical Assistance Center, SUNY Plattsburgh, Economic Impact of the N.Y. Olympic Regional Development Authority, 2004-2005 Fiscal Year, at 18 (Feb. 28, 2006) [hereinafter Economic Impact]; *see also* Olympic Reg'l Dev. Auth. and N.Y. State Dep't of Envtl. Conservation, Whiteface Mountain Ski Center Unit Mgmt. Plan Update, Amendment, and Draft Generic Envtl. Impact Statement (GEIS) 309 (1995). The ORDA planning process and related documents can be confusing. The ORDA final plan includes all comments to the draft plan and statement, as well as a summary of changes made in response to the comments. The findings statement summarizes the work plan in more detail. The draft management plan and the draft GEIS are the same document, while the final plan and the final GEIS are the same document, which incorporate the draft by reference.

20 ORDA, 2004 Final Plan and FGEIS, *supra* note 14.

permitted ski trails while continuing to adjust the capacity of different elements of the visitor facilities to improve the on-mountain experience for all levels of skiers and boarders. The most ambitious objectives—a new pod of trails, a snowmaking reservoir located mid-mountain, and a mountain top lodge overlooking Lake Placid—remained contingent on funding and further environmental analysis in 2004. As explored in the next chapter, the "Tree Island Pod" has since been authorized through supplemental environmental assessment and resulting Plan adjustments in 2005 and 2006. The mountaintop lodge and snowmaking reservoir remain on hold as of late 2007.

The direct and indirect economic impact of the Whiteface Mountain Ski Center in the Adirondack Region is estimated at about $38 million annually in the 2004 Plan and, according to the 2006 Update of the 2004 Plan, continuing improvements could add approximately $4 million to the Ski Center's operating revenues.[21] The Ski Center plays a critical role in the Lake Placid region during the weaker winter season, as summer visitors traditionally generate greater tourism revenues. The Whiteface contribution can also be viewed as a part of the overall impact of the ORDA programs in the same region, estimated to be $323 million in 2005.[22] ORDA's revenues from Whiteface also help to sustain winter sports at other venues that are less broadly based, like biathalon, ski jumping, luge, skeleton, and bobsled.

The municipalities are also in the process of improving infrastructure for peak seasonal demand, with significant improvements to Wilmington's water supply and Lake Placid's sewer capacity scheduled for completion in 2008, and an electrical grid upgrade for the region scheduled to be complete by winter 2008.

The Legal Regime

The activities at the Whiteface Mountain Ski Center and its supporting communities are directly and indirectly influenced by the legal regime that governs the Adirondack Park. Although subsequent chapters will examine elements of this regime in detail, this section provides an overview of the relevant types of controls contained in this regime, which vary depending on whether the land is owned by the state. The presence of private land intermingled with public land within the Park's boundaries (almost half the total land mass) gives the Park a different fabric than most parks in the United States. The presence of private land necessarily means that the law must deal differently with private land than public land, and it creates a different relationship between state and municipal governmental responsibilities than found in most park settings. At the same time, these various elements must be conceptually integrated in order to yield a coherent plan for the Park as a whole.

21 *Id.* at IV-3; ORDA, 2006 Unit Plan Update, *supra* note 14, at II26.

22 Economic Impact, *supra* note 19, at 4.

What is the Adirondack Park?

The Adirondack Park dates back to the late 1800s. Prior to the creation of the Park, the state designated its state-owned lands in certain counties as "Forest Preserve." In 1892, the state first drew the "Blue Line" on a map, defining a boundary that encompassed state Forest Preserve and private lands at the core of the area that lies within today's Blue Line. The area within the Blue Line served in the early history of the area as a target for state acquisition and protection of the upper watersheds of New York's five great river systems (the Black, Mohawk, St. Lawrence, Champlain, and Hudson).

In 1894 the state's voters adopted a new state constitution that required that the Forest Preserve (the state land existing or thereafter acquired within the Blue Line) remain "forever wild," explicitly prohibiting commercial leasing and removal of timber, effective January 1, 1895. The Blue Line was expanded by the legislature from time to time, resulting in the Park's present area, but no policy was directed at the private lands within the Park until the 1960s.[23] At that time, proposals suggesting reorganization of the area to form a national park at the core of the present Adirondack Park awakened the state and localities to the future of what would become today's Adirondack Park.[24]

After soundly rejecting the idea of a federal presence, the state appointed a Temporary Study Commission on the Future of the Adirondacks in 1968.[25] The Commission's report included numerous recommendations, among them the creation of the Adirondack Park Agency as well as legislation requiring state and private land use plans to guide future development within the Park. The Adirondack Park Agency Act, passed in 1971, authorized the creation of a master plan for the management of state lands (the Forest Preserve) and a land use plan for private lands.[26] The Act created the Adirondack Park Agency to administer the two plans, using a consultative process with the Department of Environmental Conservation for state lands and direct permit regulation for private lands. Consequently, the Park is an amalgam of public and private lands subject to a

23 1892 N.Y. Laws, c. 848; *see also* Philip G. Terrie, *Forever Wild Forever: The Forest Preserve Debate at the New York State Constitutional Convention of 1915*, N.Y. History, July 1989, at 268-69. The "Park" was initially defined as state land only, with minor adjustments until 1912 (L. 1912, c. 444) when the Park was expanded to about 4 million acres and defined to include private lands for the first time. Norman J. Van Valkenburgh, Bureau of Land Acquisition: State of N.Y. Conservation Dep't, The Adirondack Forest Preserve 105 (1968). Additional expansions took place in 1930, to approximately 5.6 million acres, *id.* at 154; in 1956, adding 93,500 acres, and again in 1972, when the legislature adopted most recommendations made by the Temporary Study Commission on the Future of the Adirondacks. 1972 N.Y. Laws, c. 666.

24 Frank Graham, Jr. The Adirondack Park—A Political History 219 (1978).

25 *See generally* Commission on the Future of the Adirondacks, the Future of the Adirondack Park (1970).

26 N.Y. Envtl. Conservation Law § 3-0301 (McKinney 2001).

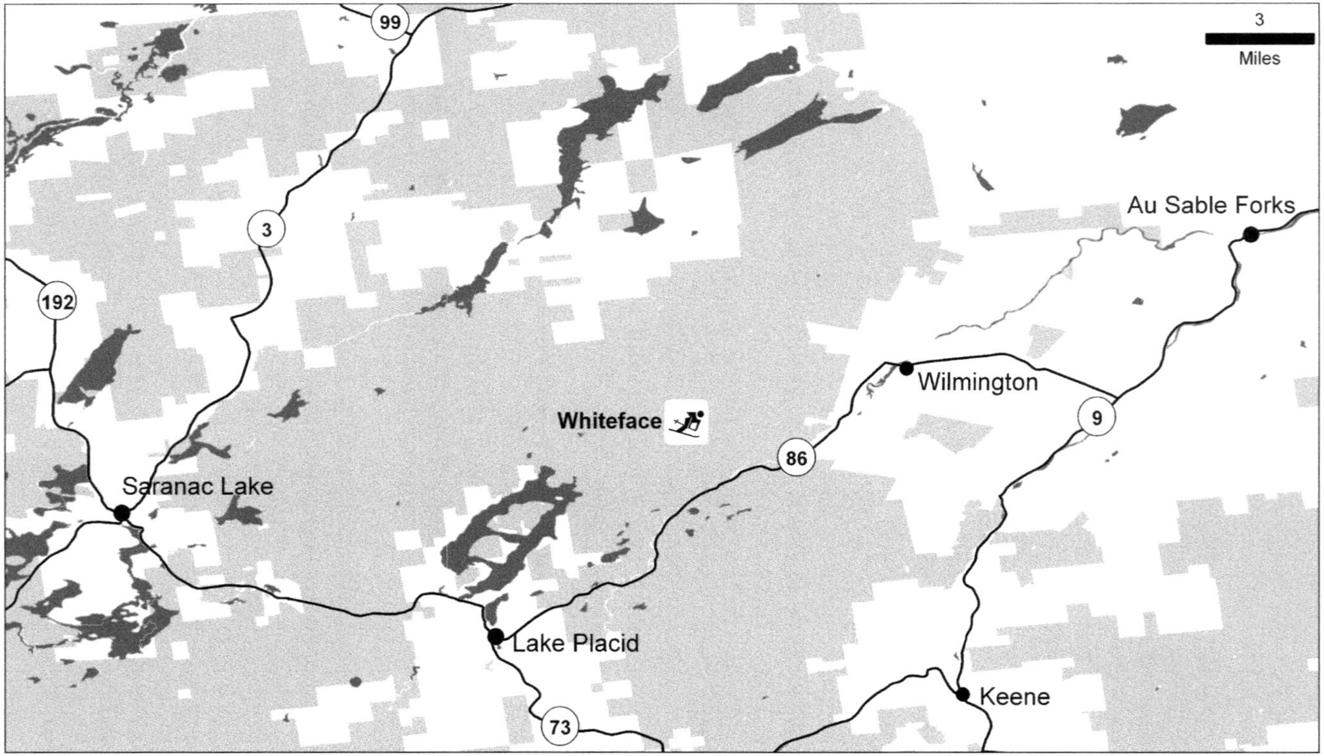

Figure 11.3 The Mix of Public and Private Land in the Adirondack Park

Note: The state-owned Forest Preserve appears in gray and privately owned land in white.

Data Sources: New York State Adirondack Park Agency; Tele Atlas North America, Inc.; ESRI

coordinated system of legal land use mechanisms, as described briefly below and explored at more length in the following two chapters. (See Figure 11.3).

The Law Governing State Land in the Park

Virtually all land owned or acquired by the state within the Park, including Whiteface Mountain, is designated as the Forest Preserve. Since the voters amended the state constitution in 1895, the fundamental legal rule governing the Forest Preserve, now contained in Article XIV of the New York State Constitution, has required that the Forest Preserve remain "forever wild."[27] Consequently, the state has had to obtain constitutional amendments to allow more intensive activities, such as the creation of the Whiteface Mountain Ski Center. As explained in detail in the next chapter, these constitutional provisions serve as the rudder for determining permissible activities within the Forest Preserve and at Whiteface. For three-quarters of a century, this was the primary legal regime for the Park.

In 1971, however, the Adirondack Park Agency Act authorized two zoning-like management plans, one of which directs the management of state activities within the Park. This Adirondack Park State Land Master Plan (Master Plan) must be approved by the Adirondack Park Agency and the Governor.[28] The Master Plan sets the parameters for activities in the Forest Preserve by identifying various intensities of permissible use, ranging from "Wilderness" to "Campground" and "State Administrative," and zoning state-owned lands accordingly. Nevertheless, all uses must be consistent with the "forever wild" principle or any constitutional exceptions, such as the constitutional amendment for the Ski Center. The Master Plan puts the Ski Center into the "Intensive Use" zone.

New facilities and uses allowed under the Master Plan's zoning must be evaluated and authorized in a more detailed unit management plan, which also guides day-to-day management such as the operation of the Whiteface Mountain Ski Center. The unit management plans must be consistent with the governing guidelines of the Master Plan[29] and the Constitution, and they can be adopted only after evaluation pursuant to the State Environmental Quality Review Act.[30] This has resulted in full environmental impact statements for major plans like those for the Whiteface Mountain Ski Center. For the ski area, the environmental impact review process also assists in the integration of other legal regimes, such as new Clean Water Act requirements for storm water management plans for areas of land

27 N.Y. Const. art. XIV, § 1.

28 Adirondack Park Agency Act, N.Y. Exec. Law, §§ 27-800–27-820 (McKinney 2002). Former Section 807 (1971) was renumbered and reworded as Section 816 in the 1973 legislative action, adopting the Adirondack Park Land Use and Development Plan and Map. *Id.* §§ 807, 816.

29 Adirondack Park Agency, State of N.Y., Adirondack Park State Land Master Plan 12 (2001).

30 N.Y. Envtl. Conservation Law §§ 8-0101–8-0117.

disturbance. Thus, activities within the Forest Preserve are subject to overarching constitutional limitations and the planning decisions made through the master planning process and the process of preparing the unit management plans, as well as the normal Clean Water Act, building code and other construction requirements associated with public facilities of this type. The application of these procedures at Whiteface is discussed at length in the next chapter.

The Law Governing Private and Municipal Land

Private and municipally owned lands, such as those in the communities of Lake Placid and Wilmington that support the activities at Whiteface, are governed by a different planning process. They are not subject to any Forest Preserve constitutional provisions, but the Adirondack Park Agency Act established the Adirondack Park Land Use and Development Plan and Map applying to all private and municipally owned land within the Park.[31] The original Plan and related map were presented to the legislature, approved, and signed into law by Governor Rockefeller in 1973, and they remain in effect today.[32] They apply as an overlay on top of any municipal zoning and regulate most new land use and development activities based on a complex set of jurisdictional rules and performance standards. The Park's plan for private land might be thought of as an environmental safety net that is very tight for the undeveloped private forest areas and progressively looser for the pre-existing communities and developed areas.

As with the Master Plan for the Forest Preserve's state land, the Land Use and Development Plan for private and municipal land classifies land into broad zoning-like categories correlating to their suitability for development.[33] Through the private land plan, the state addresses the overall intensity of development on private and municipal land in a given area, and it uses a permit system to prevent "undue adverse impacts" for the specific types of development caught in its safety net of jurisdictional criteria.[34]

31 Adirondack Park Agency Act § 805. The Plan is a sparse legislative document describing the different land use area classifications with policies and objectives for each, not an elaborate package of data and explanation. *See also* Adirondack Park Agency, State of N.Y., Adirondack Park Land Use and Development Plan Map and State Land Map (2001).

32 1973 N.Y. Laws 348.

33 Adirondack Park Agency Act § 805.

34 Adirondack Park Agency Act §§ 809(9), 10(c). Traditional zoning generally seeks to implement a local comprehensive plan, that is, a plan with a specific vision for residential, commercial and industrial development and specific environmental, cultural, and economic objectives for a community. *See, e.g.*, N.Y. Town Law, art. 16, § 261 (2001). The state's private land plan, however, is not traditional "zoning" as it does not prescribe uses or specific lot sizes or configurations. The state's plan seeks out "regional" development with a likelihood of adverse impacts to various purposes, policies and objectives for each of the designated land use areas. Although based on areas delineated on a map, the latter concentrates attention on open areas and minimizing impacts, while the former concentrates

The plan for the Park's private and municipal land not only uses a combination of geographic intensity designations and permitting systems, but it also contains an optional mechanism for coordinating with local land use regulations and plans.[35] A municipality may apply to have its local plan "approved" as consistent with the state plan, a process that amounts to matching local provisions to the jurisdiction and review criteria of the Agency to assure continued Agency review of regional projects. However, after approval, the Agency replaces state plan criteria with the "pertinent criteria" of the local program in Agency decision making (use, density, performance standards), and a number of regional projects are transferred to local review. Eighteen towns have such approvals, which have considerable benefit for local residents who find that most residential decision making by the Agency is transferred to the town. However, a number of larger towns have found it convenient, or politic, to simply administer parallel land use approvals, including the Towns of Wilmington and North Elba (and its Village of Lake Placid) which host Whiteface and the extended resort facilities.

In sum, the Park regime creates two different sets of laws and procedures—one for the state-owned Forest Preserve and one for private and municipally owned land. They operate at different levels of detail. The New York Constitution sets the overarching ground rules for the state's Forest Preserve, including Whiteface; the State Land Plan provides guidelines for activities on these state lands within the terms of the Constitution; and finally the unit management plans offer detailed, day-to-day operational direction. Thus, the nonconstitutional rules governing activities on the state lands in the Forest Preserve periodically are set largely through a planning process, informed by the State Environmental Quality Review Act's environmental impact assessment at the unit management plan level. The private and municipal lands are governed by the terms of the 1973 Plan, which establishes intensity classifications but, unlike the planning procedures for state lands, is heavily reliant on a state permitting process. Finally, the local communities have no direct authority over the plan for state lands, although the State Environmental Quality Review Act's process for an environmental impact assessment process provides access to detailed proposals and alternatives. Nevertheless, they have a significant degree of continuing control over the private and municipal lands, within the confines of the 1973 Plan.

Quite apart from the Park regime, two other types of laws may affect activities at the mountain resort. One is the National Environmental Policy Act,[36] which requires an environmental impact statement for certain federal and federally funded activities, including the Olympic games that have been held at Lake Placid and Whiteface. The other involves the state laws requiring environmental permits

---

on people and services that make up a community. The state plan recognizes this as a local role consistent with the Town and Village law in New York and the Home Rule provisions of the State Constitution.

35 Adirondack Park Agency Act §§ 807.

36 42 U.S.C. § 4331 et seq. (2007).

that apply to state and local activities in the Park but which are not directly linked to the Park's legal regime, such as permits to ensure that activities meet the state's requirements for air and water quality. Although this case study focuses primarily on the laws that are unique to the Adirondack Park as it explores their effect on expansion proposals for Whiteface in the next chapter and activities on private lands beyond Whiteface in Chapter 13, readers should bear in mind that other legal regimes, such as those associated with municipal zoning or federal policy, funding, and environmental assessment, may be relevant as well.[37]

Summary of Adirondack Park Land Use Legal Regime
State-Owned Land
New York Constitution's Forest Preserve—"forever wild"
State Land Master Plan (2001)
Individual Unit Management Plan
Environmental Impact Assessment—State Environmental Quality Review (SEQR)

Private and Municipal Land
Constitutional municipal "home rule"
1973 Adirondack Park Land Use and Development Plan (LUDP)
State permitting implementing LUDP (no separate SEQR)
Local comprehensive planning
Local zoning, subdivision, and other municipal permitting (SEQR unless covered by LUDP permit)

All Land
Federal requirements
Statewide environmental regulations

37 The Federal Energy Regulatory Commission and Department of Energy both wield authority to potentially preempt state law within the Park. The state recently objected to the sweeping designation of the Mid-Atlantic National Interest Electric Transmission Corridor by the Department Of Energy. The designation included eight of the twelve Adirondack Park counties. *See* http://www.energy.gov/news/5538.htm; http://www.ny.gov/governor/press/1105072.html (Nov. 5, 2007).

Chapter 12
The Legal Regime Affecting Whiteface Mountain: Does It Take an Ecological Approach?

As the operator of the Whiteface Mountain Ski Center, the Olympic Regional Development Authority proposed adding a new pod of ski trails to the north of the existing network of trails in its 2004 update to the Whiteface Mountain Ski Center Unit Management Plan (the 2004 Unit Plan)—the Tree Island Pod, now under construction as "Lookout Mountain." This expansion will add significantly to intermediate skiing at the Ski Center, with a long cruising run unlike any presently available, and it will balance skier loads that currently are concentrated around the gondola serving the southern pods, which become quite congested at peak use. The 2004 Unit Plan also proposed a mountaintop lodge and a reservoir for snowmaking and, in early drafts, considered trailside huts and snowmobile rentals. The proposed expansions offer an opportunity to evaluate the extent to which the existing legal mechanisms take an ecosystem approach in evaluating activities at Whiteface. This chapter looks first at the effect of constitutional limits, then the impact of the Adirondack Park State Land Master Plan, and finally, the extent to which the unit management planning process can provide opportunities for an ecosystem perspective.

The Constitutional Limitations

The legal touchstone for all activities at Whiteface is Article XIV of the New York Constitution, which sets specific mileage limits and trail widths for ski trails at Whiteface. It generally authorizes downhill skiing and appurtenant uses, but with only those enumerated exceptions. In all other respects, and for roughly two and one-half million acres of state land of which the ski area is a part, the Constitution establishes broad prohibitions on tree cutting and commercial use of the Forest Preserve, including the portion dedicated to the Ski Center. To understand the effect of Article XIV on the proposals in the 2004 Unit Plan, it is useful to first explore the history of Article XIV and how it has affected the evolution of activities at Whiteface.

Article XIV and Its Interpretation

The language in the New York Constitution governing the Forest Preserve serves as a fundamental constraint on activities at Whiteface Mountain. State-owned lands within certain counties in northern New York have been protected as the "Forest Preserve" since 1885.[1] Some areas were residual colonial lands still held by the state; others came into state ownership after loggers abandoned them to taxes. More recently, lands have been specifically sought for additions to the Forest Preserve. Language characterizing these lands as "forever wild" and prohibiting commercial forestry was added to former Article VII of the New York State Constitution in 1895, now Article XIV.[2] The core language provides:

> The lands of the state, now owned or hereafter acquired, constituting the forest preserve as now fixed by law, shall be forever kept as wild forest lands. They shall not be leased, sold or exchanged, or be taken by any corporation, public or private, nor shall the timber thereon be sold, removed or destroyed.[3]

This language has guided the management of public lands in the Adirondacks for over a century. Interpreted to prohibit any material cutting of trees, it has required a constitutional amendment for such basic objectives as the construction of a state highway, including an amendment passed in 1927 which authorized the construction of the Veteran's Memorial Highway to the summit of Whiteface.[4] Litigation over the meaning of the language clearly indicated that a constitutional amendment would be required before the alpine ski area could be built at Whiteface.[5]

The language of Article XIV early on was interpreted to prevent the cutting of trees to any material extent. In 1930, the highest court in New York, the New York Court of Appeals, considered whether the cutting of 2,500 trees for a bobsled run elsewhere in the Forest Preserve for the 1932 Winter Olympics was a reasonable use, or forbidden by the Constitution. The court concluded:

> However tempting it may be to yield to the seductive influences of outdoor sports and international contests, we must not overlook the fact that constitutional provisions cannot always adjust themselves to the nice relationships of life. The framers of the Constitution, as before stated, intended to stop the willful destruction of trees upon the forest lands, and to preserve these in the wild state now existing; they adopted a measure forbidding the cutting down of these trees to any substantial extent for any purpose.[6]

---

1 Norman J. Van Valkenburgh, Bureau of Land Acquisition: State of N.Y. Conservation Dep't, The Adirondack Forest Preserve 39 (1968).

2 Renumbered as N.Y. Const. art. XIV, § 1, as part of the Constitutional revisions effective Jan. 1, 1939.

3 *Id.*

4 Ass'n for the Pres. of the Adirondacks v. MacDonald, 17 N.E. 902, 904 (N.Y. 1930).

5 *Id.*

6 *Id.* at 905.

This case, which caused the bobsled run to be constructed on land outside the Forest Preserve, established the sparse pattern of strict judicial construction of the "forever wild" clause.[7]

When alpine skiing joined the repertoire of international winter sports competitions after the 1932 Olympics,[8] pressure for an alpine venue began to mount. On the advice of the New York State Attorney General, the Conservation Department authorized forest ski trails (what today would be cross country ski trails).[9] However, the push for an alpine ski area concentrated on an amendment to the state constitution addressing the slopes of Whiteface Mountain that did not face Lake Placid.[10] Virtually all the upper slopes of the high mountains were located within the Forest Preserve, eliminating a private-land alternative in the vicinity of Lake Placid.[11] The amendment process requires two successive legislatures (that is, the legislature after two election cycles) and a statewide referendum ballot to approve an amendment, a five to seven year process. Article XIV amendments are not easily achieved.

After approval in two successive legislatures, the proposed amendment was on the ballot in 1941.[12] The language to be added to the "forever wild" clause was very simple. An exception from the broad "forever wild" prohibitions allowed "constructing and maintaining not more than twenty miles of ski trails thirty to

---

7 Robert C. Glennon, Adirondack Mountain Club, *The Constitution and the Courts: A Review of the Forest Preserve Litigation*, N.Y. State Preserve Centennial Symposium 28–32 (Apr. 27, 1985); *see also* William H. Kissel, Comment, *Permissible Uses of New York's Forest Preserve Under "Forever Wild*," 19 Syracuse L. Rev. 969, 969–99 (1968) (describing the New York Court of Appeals' construction of Article XIV through the lens of *Association for the Protection of the Adirondacks v. MacDonald* and its progeny).

8 Hal Burton, *Placid's Playgrounds,* Ski Life, Feb. 1961, at 29.

9 Eleanor Brown, The Forest Preserve of New York State—A Handbook for Conservationists 162 (1985). Despite sparse judicial construction of Article XIV, there are numerous and sometimes conflicting opinions of the Attorney General.

10 Supporters of the Whiteface Mountain Amendment, Memorandum in Support of the Whiteface Mountain Amendment No. 4: Permitting the Construction of 20 Miles of Ski Trails on the North, Northwest and East Slopes of Whiteface Mountain in the Adirondacks 4, 8 (1941) [hereinafter Memorandum in Support of Amendment No. 4] (available from the Adirondack Room Collection at the Saranac Lake Free Library in Saranac Lake, New York).

11 Brown, *supra* note 9, at 168. One "big mountain" ski area, Big Tupper, was established near Tupper Lake on Mt. Morris within the Adirondack Park about the same time as the Whiteface Mountain Ski Center. Big Tupper is located about 30 miles from Lake Placid. Burton, *supra* note 8, at 54–55. It is currently the subject of a slopeside development proposal under the name "Preserve at Tupper Lake." At Gore Mountain, the other ORDA venue within the Forest Preserve, the legislature recently authorized joint operation with an adjacent municipal ski area to be rehabilitated in conjunction with private development. The objective at Gore is to create links with food, lodging and entertainment in the adjacent hamlet area.

12 Brown, *supra* note 9, at 168.

eighty feet wide … on the north, east and northwest slopes of Whiteface Mountain in Essex county."[13]

A coalition of supporters, representative of the contemporary plethora of not-for-profits and interest groups, organized for the November election. Supporters included the Adirondack Mountain Club and various fish and game interests, but like most successful Article XIV ballots (and there are very few, only 16 in the first century of "forever wild"),[14] the amendment passed by a narrow statewide margin of only about 10,000 votes.[15] The success was credited, in part, to a last minute appeal by radio commentator Lowell Thomas, an avid skier and active member of the Lake Placid Club.[16]

The Whiteface Mountain Ski Center has generally avoided constitutional controversies, although commentators noted that the 1941 amendment failed to provide explicit authority for structures and support facilities,[17] and the 1940s assurances regarding adequate trail widths for the future of alpine skiing did not hold true. With the advent of the 1980 Winter Olympic Games in Lake Placid and changing standards for international competition, the trail width restrictions became unworkable for a mountain at least partly committed to international ski competitions. In 1979, just prior to the Games, the Ski Center recognized that post-Olympic management of the Center must grapple with the constitutional limitation specifying an 80-foot trail width.

During the final summer before the Games, the Adirondack Council, an environmental advocacy group committed to protecting the public and private lands of the Park, joined by three other environmental groups, filed suit arguing that trail widening for the downhill competition run at the Ski Center far exceeded the 80 feet authorized by Article XIV of the state constitution.[18] The course of this litigation differed markedly from its 1932 counterpart, perhaps, in part, because there was no non-Forest Preserve location for the venue. In addition, the Constitution already explicitly authorized the Ski Center, albeit with explicit trail constraints that were exceeded in the preparation for the 1980 Winter Games.

The constitutional challenge was held in abeyance for the duration of the Games, allowing the Games to proceed without a hitch, and late in 1980, the *New York Times* reported that the parties agreed to settle, and discussed a possible amendment to the state constitution:

---

13 N.Y. Const. art. XIV, § 1 (amended 1941).

14 Brown, *supra* note 9, at 201–04.

15 Van Valkenburgh, *supra* note 1, at 179.

16 Frank Graham, The Adirondack Park: A Political History 187 (1978).

17 Brown, *supra* note 9, at 165.

18 Petition for permission to sue pursuant to Article XIV, July 6, 1979, NYS Supreme Court, Appellate Division, Third Judicial Department, David Sive, Counsel for Plaintiffs. Motion granted by Appellate Division, Sept. 26, 1979. In the Matter of The Adirondack Council, Inc., et al., Petitioners v. N.Y. State Dept. of Envtl. Conservation, Supreme Court, Essex County, Docket 35980. The Sierra Club became the fifth plaintiff on October 18, 1979.

> Not arguing the point, the state reached an out-of-court agreement with the plaintiffs, which has not yet been formally signed. But nets have been taken down, plans have been made to restore the trails to the narrower widths they were before the Olympics, and recreational skiers have taken over the trails at Whiteface again.[19]

This settlement reaffirmed the principle of strict construction of the Article XIV constitutional provisions. Strategy for management turned to the creation of an autonomous public authority to manage both the state and municipal facilities created for the Olympics, and to deal with the issues inherent in managing a Ski Center surrounded by wild lands on which development is prohibited by the state constitution. The result was the creation of the Olympic Regional Development Authority (ORDA) in 1981.[20]

The issue of trail width eventually went to the voters of the New York. The 1986 and 1987 legislative sessions passed the necessary authorization for a ballot on trail expansion. In 1987, the voters authorized an increase in the total trail mileage at Whiteface from 20 to 25 miles, increased the maximum trail width to 200 feet, and capped trails wider than 120 feet at no longer than five miles.[21] The amendment further authorized necessary ski trail appurtenances ("constructing and maintaining not more than twenty-five miles of ski trails thirty to two hundred feet wide, *together with appurtenances thereto*, provided that no more than five miles of such trails shall be in excess of one hundred twenty feet wide"[22]) providing a better legal foundation for infrastructure and support facilities, including an extensive snowmaking system. This amendment essentially ratified the situation as it existed at the close of the 1980 Winter Olympics, preserving the competition potential rather than the narrower pre-Olympic configuration. This provided a comfortable margin for continued adjustments to the requirements of international competition, and substantial benefits to the recreational skiing public as well.

The constitutional roadblock to change is not easily modified or removed. Many proposals respecting other developed recreational facilities were also regularly defeated during the period in which the ski area at Whiteface was authorized and expanded.[23] It appears that Whiteface benefited from a general sympathy for skiing, its already developed condition based on the 1927 constitutional amendment authorizing the Veterans Memorial Highway, and strong support from within the Lake Placid community, which had successfully hosted the 1932 Winter Games.[24] In 1947, a comparable amendment for a Forest Preserve ski area at Gore

---

19 Harold Farber, *Report Urges Creation of Authority to Promote Lake Placid Facilities*, N. Y. TIMES, Dec. 21, 1980, at 45.

20 N.Y. PUB. AUTH. LAW § 2605–2611 (McKinney 2001).

21 N.Y. CONST. art. XIV, § 1 (amended 1987).

22 *Id.* (emphasis added).

23 *Id.; see* VAN VALKENBURGH, *supra* note 1, at 188–94.

24 *See generally* Memorandum in Support of Amendment No. 4, *supra* note 10, at 4, 8.

Mountain in the southern Adirondacks, and another at Bellayre in the Catskill Preserve, also won voter approval with a considerably wider margin, bucking the overall opposition the New York voters have shown for relaxing the strict rules for their wild lands in the north.[25]

How Ecological is Article XIV Today?

Today the constitutional limits remain a very real constraint that puts state-owned land off-limits from development or commercial use. Thus, the nineteenth century forest and watershed protection purposes that drove the creation of the Forest Preserve have a contemporary ecological effect at the ecosystem scale. However, they have little effect on the quality and layout of the Ski Center itself from an ecosystem perspective. Article XIV merely blocks certain uses and limits the scale of the ski area. It is fundamentally precautionary, part of a multi-generational strategy to protect the headwaters of the state's major watersheds largely divorced from contemporary issues or the science of ecology.

In the Ski Center context, Article XIV places an upper limit on total trail mileage, provides outer boundaries on trail location and ensures that most surrounding lands will never be developed or have the trees cut for any purpose. The 2004 Unit Plan contemplates an ultimate 37 percent increase in skiable terrain, with the most significant addition the Tree Island Pod. The plan characterizes this addition as a series of weaving, intertwined, and interconnected narrow (40 to 80-foot width) expert trails and a long scenic intermediate run following the primary ridge down towards the base area. With the 2004 Unit Plan's additions and deletions of trails, all trails at the Ski Center would total 24.45 of the 25 miles of designated ski trails allowed under Article XIV.[26] Thus, Article XIV's limits on the degree of trail expansion may have an ecologically positive effect by virtue of limiting human intrusions, but Article XIV does not mandate any ecosystem-based analysis of the placement or design of the trails.

The Constitution also creates interpretive dilemmas, for example, whether clearings for glade skiing are within the constitutional authorization. Among the planned improvements in the 2004 Unit Plan, glade skiing at one point was not characterized as part of the designated trail mileage, but it is now accounted for within the overall trail limit and plays an important role in the final implementation of the Tree Island Pod proposal, as reconfigured in 2006, to shift a concentration of expert glade skiing to this area and create one long intermediate and two new expert trails.[27] Questions have also arisen over what facilities are allowed as

25 Van Valkenburgh, *supra* note 1, at 191–92.

26 Olympic Reg'l Dev. Auth. and N.Y. State Dep't of Envtl. Conservation, 2004 Whiteface Mountain Ski Center Unit Mgmt. Plan Update, Amendment, and Final Generic Envtl. Impact Statement vii (March 31, 2004) [hereinafter ORDA, 2004 Final Plan and FGEIS].

27 Olympic Reg'l Dev. Auth. and N.Y. State Dep't of Envtl. Conservation, 2006 Whiteface Mountain Ski Center Unit Mgmt. Plan Update, Amendment, and Final Envtl.

Figure 12.1 Whiteface Mountain Ski Center's Existing Trails and Proposed Tree Island Pod, 2007

Source: Courtesy of Olympic Regional Development Authority

"appurtenances." For instance, is a trail-side hut a constitutionally permissible appurtenance to skiing, or is it an echo of constitutionally prohibited hiking huts, a Forest Preserve battle dormant for over 75 years but raised by critics of Whiteface's 2004 Unit Plan? Although presented in initial drafts of the Unit Plan, the warming hut concept was dropped after expressions of outrage from Forest Preserve advocates who saw the proposal as the old battle reemerging, not as a harbinger of new concepts for downhill skiing.

Impact Statement I–1-13 (July 19, 2006) [hereinafter ORDA, 2006 Unit Plan Update]. The 2006 update reduces the authorized trail buildout to 24.02 miles from the 2004 proposal of 24.45. *Id.* at. I-6.

Other constitutional questions have surfaced with respect to a summit lodge presented in the 2004 Unit Plan as a concept for Little Whiteface Mountain at the gondola terminus. While a lodge facility would appear to clearly fit within the 1987 amendment's appurtenance allowance, its use for non-ski activities could be severely circumscribed by the general constraints of Article XIV on commercial uses. It now survives as a concept, without specific authorization in the plan. By contrast, proposals for snowmobile rental at the mountain's base lodge provoked concern, in part regarding limits on appurtenant uses to the ski area, and did not survive in the final plan. Off-season activities that do not involve permanent structures, such as festival events, have proved popular and are accepted under these constitutional principles.

Finally, arrangements to extend municipal water service to Whiteface, generally praised as a sensible partnership between the public authority and the Town of Wilmington's water service district, drew constitutional fire because of perceived conflicts between the constitutional prohibition of municipal ownership of facilities in the Forest Preserve, a highly technical property issue that involved the interplay between the requirements for municipal financing and Article XIV. While Article XIV operates as an ecosystem-based precautionary principle at the landscape scale, its interpretation in detail involves technical legal and property principles, not contemporary ecology.

As illustrated above, Article XIV has a significant influence on the geographic scopes and types of activities that can occur at the Ski Center, but its constraints are not governed by any tailored assessment of the ecological impact of the activities. Its effect may in some cases be ecologically positive, and in others negative. As a constitutional principle, operating at a landscape level, "forever wild" lacks any directly associated process outside the courts. The influence of Article XIV rests in citizen suit provisions that are the measure of any contemporary environmental legislation. By creating legal leverage, they empower advocates with a potent influence on administrative policy and decision making, reinforcing the strength of Article XIV.

Ecosystem principles for Article XIV are captured in language carried forward in New York's state constitution from the nineteenth century, a time when the terms "park" and "ecosystem" had yet to be given their contemporary meanings. The discussion of its history gives a sense of process and purpose. A larger environmental question is whether the landscape chosen for the Forest Preserve makes ecological sense. In general, the prevailing view has been that the Forest Preserve exists as the incremental vision of various generations committed to the essentially irreversible "forever wild" principle that state ownership in New York's Adirondack and Catskill Parks represents. In short, the protected landscape of the Forest Preserve reflects political judgments based on the prevailing policy and science or opportunity of different generations. It may be wise, but it is not collectively an application of environmental science. Moreover, as discussed above, the challenges of amending Article XIV enhance its precautionary character but also accentuate its nature as a blunt, but strong instrument.

The following discussion describes the master planning process for these same state lands directed by the Adirondack Park Agency Act in 1971. That process has stayed at a legal arm's length from the underlying constitutional criteria, threading between the broad "forever wild" principle, with its very specific exceptions, and the legislature's varying direction to administrators over the years to provide fire protection, campsites, and other types of forest recreation (and occasionally forest management[28]) within the state-owned lands of the Adirondack Park.

The Adirondack Park's Master Planning Process for Whiteface

The State Land Master Plan

The activities at Whiteface not only must comply with the constitutional provisions, but they also are subject to the terms of the Adirondack Park State Land Master Plan for the Forest Preserve,[29] a document authorized by the Adirondack Park Agency Act, proposed by the Park Agency, and approved by the Governor.[30] First approved by Governor Rockefeller in 1972, the Master Plan provides general guidelines for various land use "classifications" for the Forest Preserve.[31] Under the current plan, adopted in 1987, the designations range from "Wilderness" through progressively less restrictive classifications to "Intensive Use," which includes the Whiteface Mountain Ski Center.[32] Of the roughly 2.4 million acres of state land in the Adirondack Park, only 19,000 acres are classified Intensive Use, with the Whiteface Mountain Ski Center accounting for about 15 percent of the total.[33] The Ski Center is bounded by state lands classified as Wilderness to the west, the

---

28 *See, e.g.*, Finch Pruyn & Co. v. Crotty (Slip Opinion, NY Supreme Court, Ulster County, May 4, 2002) Index No. 6370-01, wherein a landowner, having donated property to the state for forest management pursuant to statutes purporting to authorize the same within the Adirondack Park, sought court direction to allow timber harvest or reverse the sale. The litigation failed.

29 The Master Plan professes constitutional neutrality with respect to Article XIV. Adirondack Park Agency, State of N.Y., Adirondack Park State Land Master Plan 1 (2001) [hereinafter Master Plan]. However, since virtually all the land use classifications contemplated within the Master Plan are also subject to Article XIV's constitutional limitations, the Master Plan's guidelines are intended to be generally consistent with Article XIV.

30 Adirondack Park Agency Act, N.Y. Exec. Law, §§ 27-800–27-820 (McKinney 2002). Former Section 807 (1971) was renumbered and reworded as Section 816 in the 1973 legislative action, adopting the Adirondack Park Land Use and Development Plan and Map. *Id.* §§ 807, 816.

31 Charles W. Scrafford, N.Y. Dep't of Envtl. Conservation, The Adirondack Park State Land Master Plan: Origins and Current Status 32–52 (1990).

32 *See* Master Plan, *supra* note 29, at 14–50.

33 Adirondack Park Land Use Area Statistics, a*vailable at* http://www.apa.state.ny.us/gis/colc0303.htm (last visited Dec. 2, 2007).

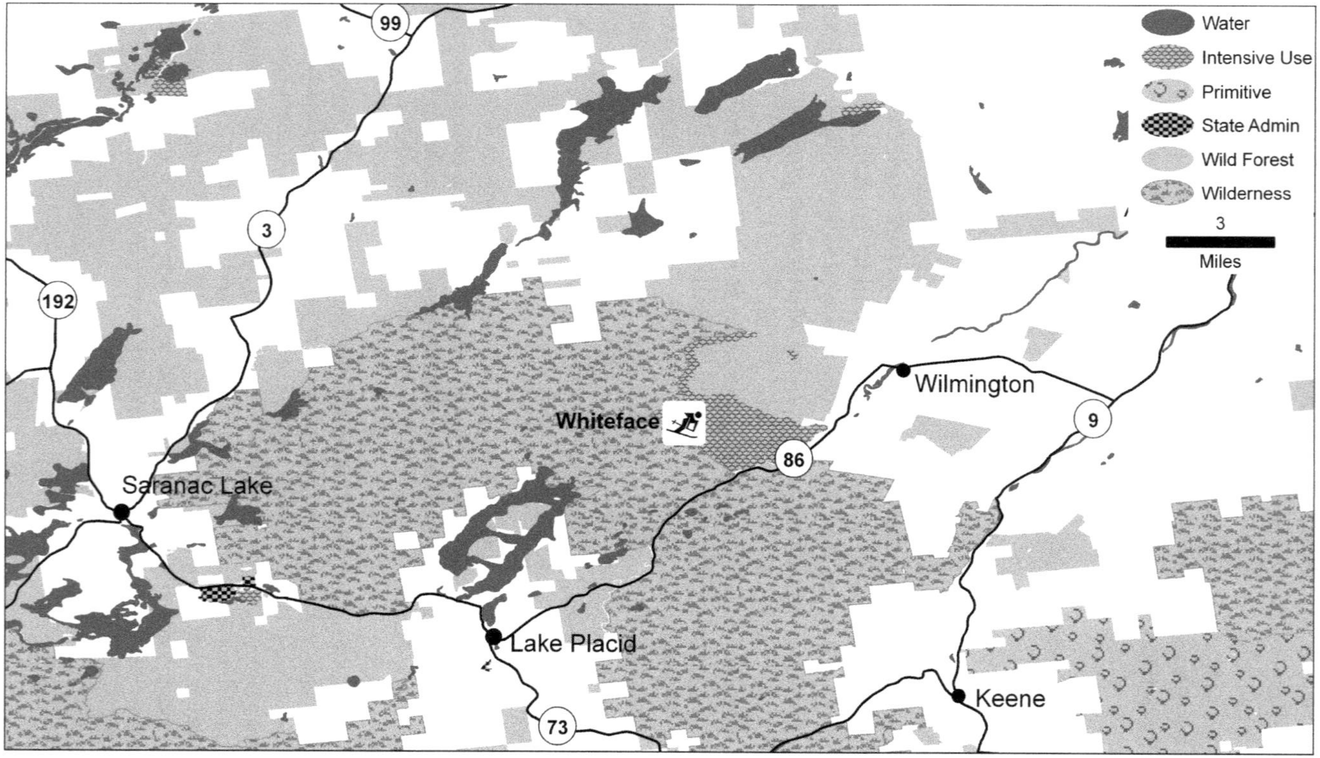

Figure 12.2 Master Plan's Classifications for the Forest Preserve

Note: The white areas represent privately owned land.

Data Sources: New York State Adirondack Park Agency; Tele Atlas North America, Inc.; ESRI

Whiteface Mountain Highway Intensive Use area to the north, and Wild Forest to the east.[34] (See Figure 12.2).

The Master Plan provides basic guidelines and criteria for each land use classification, to be elaborated and specifically implemented by individual unit management plans for land areas such as the Ski Center. Thus, the Master Plan utilizes a two-tier management system: first, general guidelines within the Master Plan, and second, specific management plans elaborated in unit management plans.[35] The legal authorities involved in the development and implementation of the Master Plan and unit management plans are also bifurcated. On the one hand, primary authority for the Master Plan is vested in the Adirondack Park Agency in consultation with the Department of Environmental Conservation pursuant to the Adirondack Park Agency Act, a part of New York's Executive Law.[36] On the other hand, primary authority for care and custody of the state lands lies with the Department of Environmental Conservation, and many specific management objectives are articulated in the Environmental Conservation Law.[37] As the operational manager, the Department is much larger than the Park Agency.

The Master Plan's Treatment of the Whiteface Mountain Intensive Use Area[38]

The Master Plan itself provides guidance for the Whiteface Mountain Ski Center. It states that the Ski Center is a day-use area with no overnight accommodations, and that it is intended to provide downhill skiing "in a setting and on a scale that are in harmony with the relatively wild and undeveloped character of the Adirondack Park."[39] It also provides that:

> Existing downhill ski centers at Gore and Whiteface should be modernized to the extent physical and biological resources allow. Cross country skiing on improved cross country ski trails may be developed at these downhill ski centers.[40]

General guidelines applicable to all intensive uses within the Forest Preserve also provide that construction and development activities will: (1) avoid material alteration of wetlands; (2) minimize extensive topographic alterations; (3) limit

34 *Id.*

35 Master Plan, *supra* note 29, at 1.

36 *Id.* at 12; Adirondack Park Agency Act § 816.

37 Environmental Conservation Law § 9-0105.

38 The Intensive Use Area also includes the Whiteface Mountain Highway for which a separate Unit Management Plan is contemplated. While tourist access to the highway is managed by ORDA, research facilities are managed by the State University at Albany, and other public safety related facilities are managed by the Department of Environmental Conservation and State Police.

39 Master Plan, *supra* note 29, at 38.

40 *Id.* at 41.

vegetative clearing; and (4) preserve the scenic, natural and open space resources of the intensive use area.[41] No new structures or improvements may be constructed except in conformity with a final, adopted unit management plan for the Ski Center.[42] Courts have held that the Master Plan has the force of legislative enactment.[43] Although it is not binding on private individuals' activities on Forest Preserve land, its provisions constrain the actions of the Department of Environmental Conservation and ORDA. However, when operating under its guidance, the Department is excused from special Park regulatory reviews applicable to other state agencies, such as the Department of Transportation.[44]

The Master Plan underwent comprehensive revisions in 1979 and 1987. New land acquisitions also provide an opportunity for more specific revisions, for instance to add and classify new land units to the plan. The addition of the Whitney Wilderness to the plan in 2000 is an example of an individual amendment updating the Master Plan with a new Wilderness unit.

How "Ecological" is the Master Plan?

The Master Plan establishes foundation principles that are based on the capacity of resources to sustain human use. In general, human use is to be subordinated to the health of the resource, a profoundly ecological perspective. The plan itself lays this out in its opening statement of fundamental purpose:

> If there is a unifying theme to the master plan, it is that the protection and preservation of the natural resources of the state lands within the Park must be paramount. Human use and enjoyment of those lands should be permitted and encouraged, so long as the resources in their physical and biological context as well as their social or psychological aspects are not degraded. This theme is drawn not only from the Adirondack Park Agency Act (Article 27 of the Executive Law—"The Act") and its legislative history, but also from a century of the public's demonstrated attitude toward the forest preserve and the Adirondack Park. Fortunately the amount and variety of land and water within the Adirondack Park provide today and will provide in the future, with careful planning and management, a wide spectrum of outdoor recreational and educational pursuits in a wild forest setting unparalleled in the eastern half of this country.[45]

---

41 *Id.* at 39.

42 *Id.*

43 Helms v. Reid, 90 Misc.2d 583, 604, 394 N.Y.S.2d 987 (N.Y.Sup.Ct.1977); *see also* Baker v. Department of Environmental Conservation of State of N.Y., 634 F.Supp. 1460 (N.D.N.Y. 1986).

44 Executive Law (Adirondack Park Agency Act) § 814; NYS Executive Order 150, 9NYCRR 4.150.

45 Master Plan, *supra* note 29, at 1.

The basic principles are then fleshed out for the range of classifications, from Wilderness to Intensive Use. For Wilderness and Wild Forest, the classification guidelines are also profoundly ecological in their precautionary effect, with the Wilderness definition borrowed wholesale from the federal Wilderness Act and the Wild Forest definition echoing the New York constitutional terminology for "wild forest."[46] Wild forest lands are thus off-limits to timber harvest and motorized recreation is strictly limited and not to be "encouraged." The classification category has few parallels in other public land management schemes in the United States, certainly not at the million-plus-acre scale of the State Land Master Plan.

However, the plan also addresses campgrounds, boat launches, state highway corridors, state administrative areas, and a few other developed locations. The ski areas at Whiteface and Gore are permitted under the constitutional exceptions to the "forever wild" principle; other exceptions purporting to authorize specific activities, ranging from timber harvest to campgrounds, exist under other legal rubrics and are given very limited recognition in the Master Plan. For the ski areas which exist under unambiguous constitutional authority, the Master Plan focuses on modernization consistent with the Park setting. This continues to result in an emphasis on services and infrastructure, with larger-scale ecology not a primary focus in the planning process for the developed facilities.

The Master Plan's recognition of the significance of preserving natural resources has helped set the framework for required unit management plans, which must be consistent with the Master Plan's principles. The most recent iterations of unit planning have emphasized Wilderness and Wild Forest areas. Intensive Use area plans in this generation of planning have also given more attention to the foundation principles of the Master Plan with analysis and management responses for vegetation, erosion, and flora and fauna. For instance, as indicated at more length below in the discussion about the Ski Center's 2004 Unit Plan, the Whiteface Mountain Ski Center's plans have recently considered high altitude habitat, particularly for Bicknell's thrush, a species of special concern in New York.

Can a Master Plan be ecosystem-based merely because the macroecology of the Park is anchored by very large islands of wild lands (open to public recreation, including hunting, fishing and trapping), islands of very large forest tracts managed for both timber and recreation, and about 10 to 20 percent of the landscape subject either to special park land development rules for new development or associated with long-standing settlements (like Lake Placid) with much less state regulation? Recent research has begun to attempt to quantify the ecological values of these different elements of the landscape and the impacts of new land use and

46 *E.g.* Wilderness basic guideline 1: "The primary wilderness management guideline will be to achieve and perpetuate a natural plant and animal community where man's influence is not apparent." *Id.* at 20; Wild Forest basic guideline 1: "The primary wild forest management guideline will be to protect the natural wild forest setting and to provide those types of outdoor recreation that will afford public enjoyment without impairing the wild forest atmosphere." *Id.* at 32.

development in this context.[47] The preliminary published literature underscores the paucity of data and analysis, particularly for the northeastern temperate forest that dominates the Adirondack Park. Given the lack of peer-reviewed quantitative analysis, the ecosystem elements of this planning are, at this point, merely expert opinions added to the conventional elements of development decisions—air and water quality, infrastructure for public health and safety, etc.

Nonetheless, the iterative Master Plan/unit plan process provides interesting opportunities to evolve and amplify ecosystem considerations set out in the Master Plan's objectives. However, there are important obstacles. First, resources for planning for rural municipalities and state agencies in New York have been notoriously few since the collapse and closure of the State's Office of Planning Services in the 1970s. The Olympics and subsequent ORDA management of the ski areas are the exceptions rather than the rule with respect to sustained planning. The particular needs of the public authority to garner public funding, and to market, may explain ORDA's early commitment to the process. Benefits provided by well-conceived plans include improvements like the new gondola at Whiteface. However, more than 30 years after the iterative planning concept was framed in the Adirondack Park Agency Act, the Master Plan/unit plan cycle is only in its first iteration for the bulk of the Forest Preserve. Without large capital expenditures to drive planning, either for environmental impact statements or construction details, basic ecosystem data are mostly derived from academic curiosity and the devoted attention of a few not-for-profit groups like the Adirondack Council, National Audubon Society, the Adirondack Mountain Club, The Nature Conservancy, the Wildlife Conservation Society and others.

On the other hand, because it is principle-driven, with details left to the implementing unit plans, the Master Plan continues to afford an economical alternative to ponderous federal planning models. As such, implementing institutions (the Adirondack Park Agency and the Department of Environmental Conservation) can anticipate trends and issues and provide policy guidance that may not come into play for a decade or more. For instance, this was attempted with respect to intrusive back-country recreation using bicycles and all-terrain vehicles in the last comprehensive review of the Plan in 1987.

The Whiteface Mountain Ski Center's Unit Management Plan

In 1972, the Master Plan established the process of developing and adopting the unit management plan to provide the primary mechanism for environmental review

47 *See* MICHALE GLENNON & HEIDI KRETSER, IMPACTS TO WILDLIFE FROM LOW DENSITY, EXURBAN DEVELOPMENT: INFORMATION AND CONSIDERATIONS FOR THE ADIRONDACK PARK (Adirondack Communities and Conservation Program Technical Paper No. 3, Oct., 2005)*; see also* Wildlife Conservation Society, Adirondack Research and Publications, http://www.wcs.org/international/northamerica/Adirondacks/adirondackcommunities/adirondackresearch (last visited Dec. 9, 2007) (posting of research, including the Glennon & Kretser study).

New York State Open Space Plan

The precautionary frame for the Whiteface Mountain Ski Center also includes the statewide plan for land protection, primarily addressing acquisition. The Adirondack Park Agency has a relatively minor role in this plan and the link to the Master Plan avoids inappropriate involvement of the regulatory program of the Agency in specific acquisition objectives of the State. The Open Space Plan sets out statewide policy to guide land acquisition in the context of other actions that protect and enhance valuable open space resources and is prepared by the Department of Environmental Conservation and Office of Parks, Recreation and Historic Preservation, with a parallel effort for agricultural lands overseen by the Department of Agriculture and Markets. Over the last twelve years this plan has framed and implemented a conservation easement strategy with a heavy emphasis on easements outside the Forest Preserve that extinguish development rights but allow commercial forestry and varying levels of public recreation.* This collateral statewide planning effort has been important to balancing the regulatory and non-regulatory tools that provide the environmental frame for the Park. It has targeted acquisition of the most significant ecosystem elements, as well as protecting the "working forests" of the private lands within the Park.

* Unlike much of New England, there is no tradition of uncompensated public use of private forestland in the Park. The easement program has created tensions between traditional users (largely hunting and fishing clubs who lease large tracts year to year) and public recreation which is often a component of public easements that adds value to the compensation package and political support to the larger population interested in access within the Park.

Source: New York State Open Space Conservation Plan & Generic Environmental Impact Statement (Nov. 2006).

of new improvements on all state lands. However, given the limited development possibilities for the "forever wild" Wilderness and Wild Forest land classifications, and lingering disagreements over the specific guidelines of the Master Plan, much of this planning was delayed in the early years of the Master Plan. In 1979, the unit plan became a prerequisite for any new improvement in areas governed by the Master Plan.[48] In the mid-1980's a few Wilderness and Wild Forest unit plans were completed.

The Unit Management Planning Process for Whiteface

The combination of an inherited environmental assessment for the 1980 Olympics and the Master Plan prerequisites to new improvements in Intensive Use areas triggered early attention to unit management planning for the ski area. After an initial unit management plan that laid the preliminary groundwork for the post-Olympic period, ORDA embraced the planning process as the strategic foundation for program development and capital improvements.

48 Master Plan, *supra* note 29, at 33, 39.

Notwithstanding delays for other large land units in the Park, the process has been initiated at close to the recommended five-year intervals for Whiteface (1987, 1995, 2004), with progressively more sophisticated and ambitious objectives for the Ski Center. As indicated above, the unit management plan must be consistent with the guidelines and criteria established in the Master Plan.[49] In addition, the plan is subject to environmental impact assessment under the requirements of the State Environmental Quality Review Act,[50] a process similar to the federal environmental impact review under the National Environmental Policy Act. Once the unit management plan is in place, no separate land use permissions are required to conduct the activities authorized under the plan, although appropriate state environmental permits related to air, water quality, and fuel storage are required before particular development proposals can move forward.[51]

The update of the Ski Center's unit management plan in 1995 illustrates the process for reviewing a plan. In 1995, ORDA published its first unit plan update and generic Environmental Impact Statement in draft form to begin a comprehensive update and lay a foundation for future management strategies at the Ski Center.[52] The plan set out a schedule of anticipated improvements; the generic Environmental Impact Statement ("generic" because it covered the unit plan update as a whole) provided an explanation of those situations that would receive further environmental review with separate environmental assessment after design and engineering were complete, and those for which the generic Environmental Impact Statement concluded the assessment process.

ORDA published the draft Environmental Impact Statement in November of 1995, held a public hearing later that month, and received comments through December 1995.[53] In addition to a Final Generic Environmental Impact Statement, ORDA prepared detailed responses to comments and submitted the completed study to the Department of Environmental Conservation and Adirondack Park Agency in May of 1996.[54] The Park Agency reviewed the unit management plan at its June 1996 monthly board meeting, and forwarded the plan to the Commissioner

49 *Id.* at 12.

50 N.Y. Envtl. Conservation Law §§ 8-0101–8-0117.

51 Adirondack Park Agency Act § 816. The Adirondack Park Agency Act provides a statutory exception to its State Agency and private land use regulatory process applicable to private lands and other state agencies within the Adirondack Park for "land use or development by the department of environmental conservation pursuant to the master plan for management of state lands. . . ." which includes the ski areas at Whiteface and Gore Mountains. *Id.* § 814(1). This exception is carried forward in Executive Order 150, which also directs environmental review of new development within the Park if undertaken by the state. Exec. Order No. 150, N.Y. Comp. Codes R. & Regs. tit. 9 § 4.150 (2002).

52 Olympic Reg'l Dev. Auth. and N.Y. State Dep't of Envtl. Conservation, Whiteface Mountain Ski Center Unit Mgmt. Plan Update and Final Generic Envtl. Impact Statement 3 (1996) [hereinafter ORDA, 1996 Final Plan and FGEIS].

53 *Id.*

54 *Id.*

of Environmental Conservation for implementation.[55] The Park Agency advice determined consistency with the Master Plan, not specific engineering or conditions for the development proposed. Thus, the formal review process took roughly one year, with a little more than a year of preparation for the initial draft.[56] Once approved, the unit management plan became the primary document governing ORDA's activities at the Ski Center.

The 2004 Unit Plan and 2006 Plan Update

The 2004 update of the Ski Center's unit management plan raised issues about the impact of the new Tree Island Pod on Bicknell's thrush habitat, water withdrawal for a proposed reservoir for snowmaking, and storm water runoff. Each reached a different outcome and provides an opportunity for assessing whether or how ecosystem considerations came into play against the backdrop of the general commitments of the Master Plan.

In its broad terms, the 2004 Unit Plan as approved commits:

1. To continue the planning process for Whiteface that is consistent with the Adirondack Park State Land Master Plan and Article XIV of the NYS Constitution. Whiteface is quite unique because it is a designated Intensive Use Area within the Forest Preserve that has received special authorization under Article XIV of the NYS Constitution. As an Intensive Use Area, Whiteface's basic management guidelines include providing facilities for intensive forms of outdoor recreation by the public. At the same time, Whiteface development will blend with the Adirondack environment and have minimum adverse impacts on surrounding state lands. A careful approach to enhancements at Whiteface will provide continued opportunity for the public to enjoy a unique experience, gain an appreciation for sensitive development, and expose large numbers of people to the Forest Preserve.
2. To bring all the facilities into balance in a manner whereby the ski center will comfortably accommodate peak days.

[3.–5. commit to the highest quality recreational and competitive Alpine skiing and boarding]

6. To develop a [Unit Management Plan] that has Management Actions that are consistent with the National Ski Areas Association (NSAA) Environmental Charter.[57]

These commitments illustrate the multiple objectives and constituencies that ORDA must address as a public authority competing within the private ski and boarding industry. The earlier tension between Whiteface as a competitive

55 *Id.*

56 *Id.*

57 ORDA, 2004 Final Plan and FGEIS, *supra* note 26, at v.

venue and recreational skiing is history. Beginning in 1995, the sequence of unit management plans for the Whiteface Mountain Ski Center bridged the interests of the recreational skiing public and the international competitions that keep Lake Placid on the world scene. Similar planning and capital improvement strategies were put in place for the Intervale Ski Jumping Complex and the Mt. Van Hoevenberg Nordic Complex between 1995 and 1999.[58] These programs led to the certification of all winter venues for international competition, and Lake Placid hosted the first "Winter Goodwill Games" in February 2000.[59] The 2004 Unit Plan continues to guide significant community services, cooperating with the New York Ski Education Foundation to deliver youth-oriented skiing programs in addition to its role in other community events related to other facilities managed by ORDA.

The Tree Island Pod and the Bicknell's Thrush In the process of refining the details of the Ski Center's 2004 Unit Plan, the Bicknell's thrush captured a feature role. The 2004 update was initiated with a scoping session in October 2001, and a draft Generic Environmental Impact Statement was accepted in August 2002. A hearing followed in September 2002 but attracted virtually no public or nongovernmental organization attention. It was only after the close of the public comment period that an extended dialog developed regarding the existence and significance of habitat for Bicknell's thrush in the vicinity of the upper mountain ski trails, both existing and proposed (see Figure 12.1). This dialog, and the expert involvement that it entailed, delayed the acceptance of the Final Generic Environmental Impact Statement until March 2004. The discussions about the impact of the Tree Island Pod on Bicknell's thrush habitat began as the Ski Center's own "green" initiative acknowledging its relationship with the Forest Preserve and a commitment to sustainable slopes, but they gathered momentum as other forces came into play, including the inclusion of the upper mountain areas in a separate, state bird-habitat designation highlighting the importance of the area. Environmental advocates coalesced with comments on the draft Generic Environmental Impact Statement and pressed the issue, and with technical assistance from the Wildlife Conservation Society and the Department of Environmental Conservation, ORDA established an analytic protocol to vet the Tree Island Pod proposal.

The Tree Island Pod was removed from the list of projects receiving final clearance in the adopted 2004 Unit Plan, due to the Bicknell's thrush issue. With these and other adjustments (such as the removal of a "warming hut" proposal that triggered constitutional consternation by some constituencies), Adirondack Park Agency advice and approval of the Commissioner of Environmental Conservation followed in May and June 2004. But the work on the Bicknell's thrush issue continued.

58 *See generally* Olympic Reg'l Dev. Auth. (ORDA), Olympic Sports Complex at Mount Van Hoevenberg Final Unit Management Plan and Generic Envtl. Impact Statement (1998–1999).

59 Tim Reynolds, *Persistence Put Lake Placid in Path of TNT*, Times Union (Albany), Jan. 16, 2000, at E9.

ORDA commissioned the Vermont Institute of Natural Science (VINS), which had studied the ecology and population dynamics of Bicknell's thrush at Stowe Mountain Resort (Mt. Mansfield) and at Stratton Mountain ski areas since 1995, to conduct some field work in anticipation of a subsequent update to the plan to address the Tree Island Pod. The Bicknell's thrush report was received in December 2004. The report provided expert advice, but not original research at Whiteface, and therefore was accompanied by disclaimers explaining why research at Stowe and Stratton would not allow VINS to predict specific impacts at Whiteface. The authors recommended four different strategies to minimize impacts:

- Limit construction activity to before May 15 and/or after August 1;
- Shift the proposed trail configuration as far eastward as possible from the exposed western ridge which appears to have the most suitable Bicknell's thrush habitat;
- Avoid trail construction and widening in areas most important for Bicknell's thrush—the west-facing slopes; and
- Site new trails in sheltered areas where natural disturbance is minimal.

The authors also focused on mitigation. They suggested that trail construction and maintenance could achieve a "no net loss" policy for the habitat and encouraged a broad perspective: "We believe that mitigation can best be accomplished by adopting a broadly-based conservation perspective that extends beyond the site of local impacts."[60]

In May 2006, ORDA published a combined draft Environmental Impact Statement and new Unit Plan Update, incorporating various recommendations with respect to the Tree Island Pod and addressing unrelated visitor facility modernization proposals.

> Trail work above 2,800 feet is of particular concern due to impact on the habitat of the Bicknell's thrush. Over the past three years the Olympic Regional Development Authority (ORDA) and Whiteface Mountain Ski Center staff have worked in partnership with the Vermont Institute of Natural Science, the Wildlife Conservation Society, the New York State Department of Environmental Conservation, the Adirondack Park Agency, the Adirondack Council and the New York Audubon Society on the development of the 'Best Management Practices' for the development and maintenance of ski trails above 2,800 feet. The recommendations and processes presented in this amendment are evidence of these efforts and unprecedented achievements in the quest to protect this important species.[61]

---

60 Christopher C. Rimmer et al., Evaluating the Use of Vermont Ski Areas by Bicknell's Thrush: Applications for Whiteface Mountain, New York 2–3 (Dec. 2004).

61 ORDA, 2006 Unit Management Plan Amendment to the 2004 Unit Management Plan and Draft Environmental Impact Statement for Whiteface Mountain Ski Center (May 2006) [hereinafter 2006 Unit Plan].

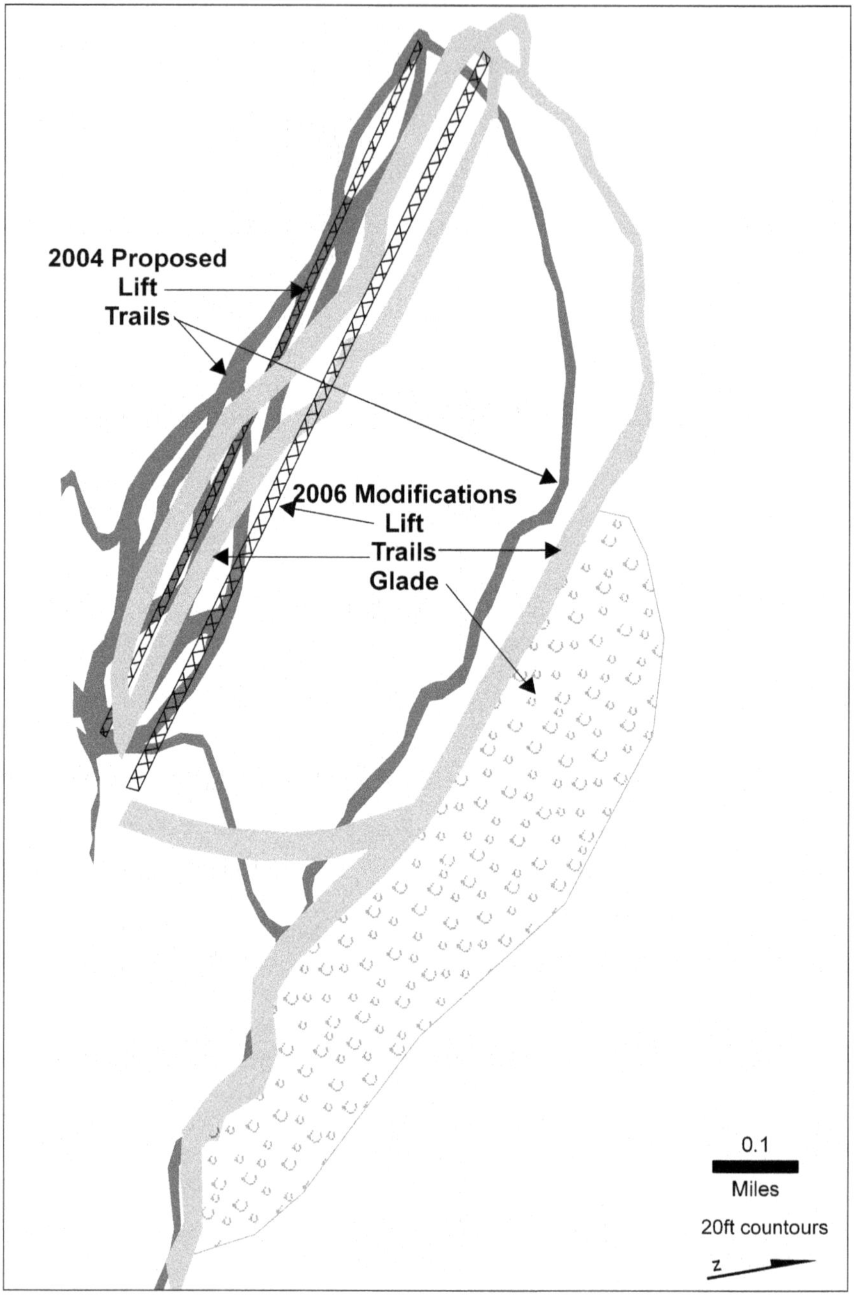

Figure 12.3 The Tree Island Pod, 2004 Proposal and 2006 Modifications

Data Sources: New York State Adirondack Park Agency; Olympic Regional Development Authority; Whiteface Mountain Ski Center; Tele Atlas North America, Inc.; ESRI

Figure 12.4 Whiteface Mountain Trails and the Tree Island Pod, 2008

Note: The Tree Island Pod, under construction, is visible on the right flank of the mountain.

Photo: New York State Adirondack Park Agency

Among the innovations are proposals to engage visitors to the ski area in habitat protection efforts in the winter nesting grounds of the species, as well as the noted best management practices for ski area management.[62]

In addition to the specific design considerations incorporated for the Tree Island Pod to avoid habitat and nesting seasons, in July 2007, ORDA, the Adirondack Community Trust, Adirondack Park constituency organizations, Cornell Lab of Ornithology, and the Vermont Institute of Natural Science celebrated the initiation of the "Bicknell Thrush Habitat Protection Fund." The fund is dedicated to the protection of the thrush's winter habitat in the Caribbean in recognition that protection efforts in the summer range will have no benefit without commensurate efforts in the winter nesting grounds as well.

Figure 12.3 shows the 2004 threaded trail Tree Island Pod proposal, and the 2006 modification with its narrow thrush-friendly expert trails and an extensive glade area relocated from a different 2004 location to open mature forest near the top of the long cruising run featured in both proposals. The trails were being cut in late 2007 and are the distinctive narrower trails on the right in the photo of the upper mountain areas in early January 2008 (Figure 12.4). The existing southern pods that are residual from the 1980 Olympics are to the left in the photo.

62 *Id.* at II-7; *see* "Rare songbird protected through historic partnership included in Whiteface Mountain Unit Management Plan," http://www.apa.state.ny.us/Press/pressrelease.cfm?offset=51&PressReleaseID=236 (last visited Mar. 8, 2008).

Whiteface is now marketing the new pod as "Lookout Mountain," expected to open for the winter of 2008–2009.

The 2006 update to the Ski Center's plan was produced mostly in-house by ORDA, reflecting increased planning and project management capacity within the organization. This shift in responsibility is intended to help ensure follow-through on plan commitments.

The Snowmaking Reservoir The 2004 Unit Plan also included a proposal to construct a snowmaking reservoir to serve the mid-mountain slopes, drawing on water from the Ausable River at the mountain base as well as flow from a tributary. The plain language of the state's Wild, Scenic and Recreational Rivers Act prevents damming the Ausable River, a designated river, to create a reservoir, making it necessary for the Ski Center to rely on water withdrawals. The conceptual proposal outlined in the plan would address most ecological concerns regarding minimum flow in the river if successfully implemented, such as the effects of ice scouring in winter. The proposal builds on an existing program that measures water flow in the river to ensure that water withdrawals for the current snowmaking facilities do not jeopardize fish habitat. However, the existing actions taken to measure flows in the Ausable River have not pleased all constituencies. Trout Unlimited, concerned with the downstream fishery, has applauded the implementation of the protective measures.[63] Others, more interested in the free flow of a designated "recreational" river, have objected.[64] For example, the New York Rivers United organization strongly opposed the 2001 construction of a gauging weir.[65] (See Figure 12.5). Although proposing the concept, the 2004 Unit Plan defers final assessment of a snowmaking reservoir for mid-mountain to a future planning cycle.

ORDA continues to struggle with the tension between restraints on both structures in the main river channel and flow diversions, and problems with ice entering the pump system from the river. The snowmaking reservoir would address both issues and is therefore one practical engineering response to the water supply issue within the constraints on construction of a dam on a free-flowing stretch of a designated "recreational" river. However, the mid-mountain reservoir is not a current priority. ORDA apparently has tentatively concluded that in-stream flows are adequate to support continuing the current snowmaking operation with new technology to address icing within the system. A major energy conservation effort will recycle heat associated with snowmaking to reduce total energy costs and incidentally improve the river withdrawal situation. An ecological outcome would appear to be dictated by the restraints of the Rivers Act more than the unit management planning

63 *See* ORDA, 1996 Final Plan And FGEIS, *supra* note 52, at Appendix 2; *see also id.* at 14–15 (addressing Ausable River issues).

64 John F. Sheehan, *Albany DEC Projects Don't Live Up to "Forever Wild,"* Times Union (Albany) Aug. 23, 2001, at A10.

65 *Id.* at A10; Fred LeBrun, *Watchdog has Bigger Fish to Fry*, Times Union (Albany), Aug. 16, 2001, at C1.

Figure 12.5 Gauging Weir on the Ausable River
Photo: New York State Adirondack Park Agency

process. The run-of-river water supply system has been adequate for the expanding snowmaking operation within the limits set for river flows.

Storm Water Runoff An expanded notion of impact analysis and mitigation was also introduced in the 2004 Unit Plan as a result of Clean Water Act Phase II storm water permit requirements for storm water for all public and private development beginning in 2004 in New York. Anticipating new rules and heightened public concern about compliance, ORDA cooperated with the Department of Environmental Conservation, the Adirondack Park Agency, and others in storm water management training, seeking the most effective solutions for some of the challenges posed at the Ski Center. Customary practices were the initial focus of this effort—the avoidance of materials that risked introducing invasive species, more aggressive re-vegetation of upper mountain trails highly visible from many public vantage points, and improved water bars and erosion control on existing trails.

However, the 2006 update to the 2004 Unit Plan, which refined the details of theTree Island Pod, was subject to the conditions that ORDA obtain specific engineering approvals from the Adirondack Park Agency and the Department of Environmental Conservation, modifying the Phase II "general permit" approach used for New York's implementation of the federal Clean Water Act. The general permit approach would have authorized construction based on the Unit Plan, but the conditions required a specific engineering review by individuals responsible for state land management prior to permit issuance to ensure effective implementation. In most cases specific storm water engineering is not completed at the time of the Unit Plan approval, and the later check point provides an opportunity to verify the general plan commitments against actual design specifications for the trails. Based on the engineering required by the Phase II permits,[66] this additional state land review has improved inter-agency communication among ORDA and the two state agencies. It also has had direct ecological benefit by credibly reducing off-site and cumulative impacts from new trail construction.

How "Ecological" is the Unit Management Plan?

The unit management plan is framed as a conventional environmental impact statement to meet the requirements of New York's Environmental Quality Review Act. As an iterative process, it has been refined and new issues addressed, but there is no core focus on ecology. The bulk of the technical analysis in the 2004 Unit Plan and its 2006 update is devoted to balancing the ski area infrastructure: to match snowmaking to trails; water supply to snowmaking demand; user facilities to the area's design capacity, and so on. Thus, at its core, this unit management plan is a manager's template to deliver the best possible skiing and boarding experience to the public in the most efficient manner possible. The plan lives within its constitutional constraints, and the first order environmental problems it addresses are also conventional—for instance, in-stream flow related to snowmaking, storm water runoff, potable water supply, and sanitary sewers.

Nevertheless, the unit management planning process for the 2004 Unit Plan and the 2006 update show a significantly increased sensitivity to ecologically oriented issues. The 2004 Unit Plan provides the first analysis of the upper mountain Bicknell's thrush habitat, absent in the earlier planning dating back to the Olympics. The research on the habitat impacts and recommended strategies significantly influenced the final configuration of the Tree Island Pod—"Lookout Mountain."[67]

Ecology was injected into the 2004 unit management planning process largely through the interaction between two individuals, Stu Buchanan, then Regional Director for Department of Environmental Conservation who was a biologist and sensitive to all of these issues, and Brian Houseal, chief executive officer of the Adirondack Council with extensive experience in the Caribbean and neo-tropical migratory birds. They also benefited from a group of young scientists, some on the staff of the Department of Environmental Conservation and Adirondack Park

66 Resolution of the Adirondack Park Agency, Resolution and SEQRA Findings Adopted by the Adirondack Park Agency with respect to Whiteface Mountain Ski Center Intensive Use Area Amendment to the 2004 Unit Management Plan, Aug. 10, 2006.

67 *See* Christopher C. Rimmer et al., *supra* note 60.

Agency and some associated with the Wildlife Conservation Society's Adirondack program. Collectively, they wanted to make an ecological point and used the Bicknell's thrush to do so. Technically, the issues were advanced "late" after the close of comments on the 2004 Unit Plan Draft Environmental Impact Statement. Buchanan and Agency staff nonetheless embraced a strategy that turned to the Vermont Institute of Natural Science for help. Buchanan used his role on both the ORDA Board and within the State's Executive decision and policy apparatus to provide the time and analytic space for a more ecologically sensitive review to take shape. Hence, a process in which the 2004 Unit Plan anticipated further analysis on this centerpiece proposal, led to the 2006 update to the 2004 Plan. These events illustrate how the unit management planning process can be flexible enough to take a broader, ecological perspective and how specific individuals can influence whether that happens.

Interestingly, a parallel general shift in tourism marketing for Essex County and the Lake Placid Region to a "forever" Adirondack theme emphasizing the constitutional protection of the landscape and the unique community character of the area occurred in this general time frame. Many in the business community who might have formerly opposed the rigorous and sometimes rigid state policies began to see how they could be turned to the community's benefit. Similarly, ORDA's commitment to implement the National Ski Areas Association's "sustainable slopes" principles, as evidenced in Ski Center's 2004 Unit Plan, indicates a sensitivity to the potential significance of environmental issues.

The 2006 update for the 2004 Unit Plan was approved by the Agency with the engineering conditions noted on August 10, 2006, and subsequently by the Commissioner of Environmental Conservation. Engineers from the Adirondack Park Agency and Department of Environmental Protection signed off on the Phase II plans the first week in August, 2007. As August 1, 2007, is the first date to work on the high altitude trails under the plan to protect the Bicknell's thrush,[68] ORDA crews were waiting for the Phase II engineering signoff with chain saws in hand to get started on the new pod of trails.

Conclusion

In conclusion, one cannot say that the Article XIV of the Constitution, the Park Master Plan, and the 2004 and 2006 Unit Plans for the Ski Center demand a full analysis of the ecosystem impacts of activities occurring at Whiteface. Article XIV severely constrains activity on the mountain, but constitutional amendments that determine changes in uses are based on political consensus rather than a scientific, ecosystem analysis. Within the constitutional limits, the Master Plan sets principles

68 2006 Unit Plan, *supra* note 61, at p. II-4. There is an explicit prohibition of tree cutting above 2,800 feet from May 15 to August 1, and a review of other construction activities proposed during these times above 2,800 feet for potential impacts.

that guide management activities at Whiteface, and the guiding principle of the 1987 Plan requires attention to minimizing impacts on natural resources. Because unit management plans must be consistent with the principles of the Master Plan, the plans in turn should anticipate the natural resource impacts. In addition, under the State Environmental Quality Review Act, the environmental impact statements for the plans should explore those impacts. Yet one cannot go quite as far as saying that the law requires a full ecosystem analysis of these impacts. The more traditional environmental assessments of the first tier of environmental consequences, rather than the assessments of the complex, extended inter-reactions, can satisfy the Master Plan consistency requirement and the environmental impact statement requirements.

Nevertheless, the process offers opportunities to introduce an ecosystem perspective. As the Tree Island Pod situation illustrated, the planning process can allow ORDA to introduce a habitat issue, and the environmental impact assessment process can allow governmental agencies and public interest groups to inject their views, which in turn can provide an opportunity for scientists to prepare significant, new analysis of ecological impacts. The law and its processes, supported by management, government, and citizen initiative, can help force the development of a better understanding of the mountain ecosystem. In addition, the planning and review process provides a mechanism for delaying actions pending further consideration, such as the creation of the snowmaking reservoir and the construction of the mountaintop lodge, thereby encouraging a precautionary approach. As knowledge about the mountain ecosystem improves, these planning and review process offer significant opportunities for evaluating the human impact of the Ski Center's activities on an ongoing basis.

Chapter 13
The Legal Regime Affecting Private Lands Around Whiteface: Does It Take an Ecological Approach?

The Growth Patterns of Whiteface's Resort Communities

Lake Placid and its neighboring communities of Saranac Lake and Tupper Lake provide educational, health, shopping, and core governmental services otherwise found an hour or more away at the periphery of the Park as well as lodging, restaurants, and other tourist facilities. These communities also include important institutions, such as Paul Smith's College, North Country Community College, Trudeau Institute (which conducts immunological research), Cornell's Uhlein research farm, two state prisons and a federal prison, all nestled in the mountain landscape exemplified by the High Peaks, including Whiteface.

The Village of Lake Placid is fundamentally constrained by the state-owned Forest Preserve, which constitutes 75 percent of the surrounding Township of North Elba, including 60,000 acres of designated Wilderness.[1] (See Figure 12.2 in Chapter 12.) It will, therefore, have much the same development pattern for many generations to come. Though Lake Placid is a self-appointed "winter sports capital of the world,"[2] winter is the second tourist season for the region which first entertained summer tourists escaping the East's cities in the late nineteenth century on its shores and mountain slopes. The 1980 Winter Olympics provided invaluable international awareness of the community, but had less impact on local growth than the more recent real estate boom for shoreline property and high-end mountainside vacation homes.

The neighboring community of Wilmington, home to Whiteface, is less constrained by surrounding state land, but has had less ability and fewer opportunities to take advantage of winter tourism, mainly due to lack of public and

---

1 *See* Adirondack Park Agency, Adirondack Park Land Classification Acreage Statistics, http://www.apa.state.ny.us/gis/TownStatResults.cfm?townSelect=North+Elba&townSubmit=Go (last visited Nov. 2, 2007). The township of Wilmington, about half the area of the Town of North Elba and the Village of Lake Placid, is about 63 percent state land designated Forest Preserve. These statistics indicate that the Lake Placid "hamlet" is about 3,500 acres whereas the Wilmington "hamlet" is only about 575 acres.

2 ORDA, Lake Placid Olympic Region: Things to Do, http://www.orda.org/newsite/todo.php (last visited Feb. 5, 2008).

private investments in high intensity tourism. Like Lake Placid, the community has an active planning and zoning program, but its tourist infrastructure remains charmingly rooted in the 1950s. Wilmington's infrastructure improvements in 2005–06 included water system improvements that will link with Whiteface's Ski Center, provide a new potable and firefighting water supply to the mountain's base facilities, and provide some capacity for growth in the community. Perhaps this presages new opportunities to intensify Wilmington's tourism infrastructure. Wilmington also features a summer tourism season perhaps best known for Santa's Workshop (Post Office, North Pole, NY), one of the first theme parks in the US, and one that retains its folksy charm and reindeer in an age of technology. However, Lake Placid's longstanding dominance of the Whiteface neighborhood appears secure.

As a result of the separation of different resort venues, and state or local government ownership of the most significant among them, the pattern of development in Lake Placid and Wilmington is predominantly smaller scale and more locally-based than in the other case studies considered in this volume.

The ecological impact of growth in the communities surrounding Whiteface remains a concern to observers of the Adirondack Park.[3] The Wildlife Conservation Society has published the Adirondack Atlas,[4] intended to engage various concerned constituencies in the culture and ecology of the Park. The broadly-based geographic data sets on which the Atlas is based derive from work by agencies like the Adirondack Park Agency and the Department of Environmental Conservation, as well as regional programs like the Northern Forest Project and the Lake Champlain Basin Program. These data facilitate reconnaissance observations like those associated with the Bicknell's thrush issue by providing quick access to satellite imagery and related terrestrial features.

There is considerable evidence that the second home boom, at best partly related to the winter facilities in the area, is widely dispersed due to the state's "intensity guidelines," described below, which sharply curtail new subdivision and development intensity outside the settlement areas. Lake Placid and its neighbors, such as the hamlet of Keene to the east, have become concerned about disappearing affordable workforce housing. The issue itself illustrates emerging policy concerns at the local level. For many resort communities, housing cost difficulties are seen as involving seasonal labor and impoverished individuals often associated with a seasonal service-based economy. In the area surrounding Lake Placid, however, the tight housing market affects middle-class elements of the communities such as local college professors, hospital staff, state workers and other professionals in the communities forced to struggle with housing availability strained by non-resident demand for second homes. With a short building season and strong demand from

3 *See, e.g.*, Adirondack Council, State of the Park 2007 (2007), *available at* www.adirondackcouncil.org (last visited Jan. 30, 2008).

4 Jerry Jenkins with Andy Keal, Adirondack Atlas (2004).

the high-end slice of the market, neither new construction nor "trickle down" is satisfying the middle and lower segments of this rural housing market.

The legal frame designed to protect the Park landscape plays a role in the demand for housing in the area. Depending on the political perspective, rising costs are attributed to cumbersome regulation, to the constraints of the Forest Preserve, or to construction and land markets that limit access to the available building opportunities within Adirondack communities. Some blame the state's intervention in the land market for purchase of conservation easements and additions to the Forest Preserve, others the boom in residential real estate. Works like the Atlas raise awareness of both the physical resources and cultural factors working on the region. Already local and state initiatives are beginning to address the affordable housing market by creating local and regional affordable housing trusts.[5]

The Interlocking Parts of the Park Land Use and Development Plan: How They Influence Growth Patterns

The Adirondack Park Land Use and Development Plan and Map (Plan and Map) provide a framework for development on private land in the Adirondack Park and, therefore, shape the pattern of development in Lake Placid and Wilmington. Enacted by the legislature in 1973, the Plan and Map form the core of the Adirondack Park Agency Act. The Plan uses three primary mechanisms to guide growth: Adirondack Park Agency administered "intensity guidelines," which govern the average density of development; permit criteria intended to prevent "undue adverse impacts" to the natural and cultural resources of the region, applied to classes of development characterized as "regional" by the Act; and local government land use programs which, once adopted, implement conventional use zoning with standards and conditions for all new uses and existing development, not just "regional" actions addressed by the Plan.[6] These three work in concert to shape private commercial and residential development in the Park.[7]

---

5 *See* Adirondack Community Housing Trust Taking Shape, http://www.senatorlittle.com/45/news/07-11-28/adirondack_community_housing_trust_taking_shape.aspx (last visited Jan. 30, 2008); *see also* New York State Division of Housing and Community Renewal, http://www.dhcr.state.ny.us/ (Governor Spitzer's housing initiative) (last visited Jan. 30, 2008); Adirondack Shelter, http://adirondackshelter.blogspot.com/2007/04/adirondack-community-housing-trust-or.html (last visited Jan. 30, 2008).

6 *See* Adirondack Park Agency Act (N.Y. Exec. Law §§ 27-800–27-820) § 807 (local program approval); § 808 (approved local program administration); § 809(9) (regional permits within municipality with approved local land use program).

7 *See generally* J. Banta & B. Rottier, *The Adirondack Park Agency Act and Related Authorities Administered by the Adirondack Park Agency within the Adirondack Park, in* New York Zoning Law and Practice 9A-1–27 (Patricia Salkin, ed., 4th ed. 2007). The Act also incorporates statutory protection for Adirondack Park shorelines (§ 806) which

The Adirondack Park Land Use and Development Plan for private land operates on top of local zoning and also contains a mechanism for linking state and local planning efforts, so it is useful to start by exploring the local land use element. Under the direction of Town or Village Law and their Home Rule authority,[8] local governments have the authority to create comprehensive plans, regulate subdivision, and administer zoning ordinances concurrently with the Adirondack Park Agency's protections for forests and open spaces.[9] State payment of *ad valorem* property taxes on the Forest Preserve to all municipal taxing jurisdictions is also a significant consideration in the relationship of regional and local policy within the Park.[10]

These local programs can operate with a formal linkage with the Park Agency, or on independent but parallel tracks, depending on the voluntary interest of a given municipality.[11] Eighteen of the 103 municipalities have formally approved local land use programs that are linked to the Adirondack Park Agency's land use permitting responsibilities.[12] Wilmington, Lake Placid and about 60 other municipalities have local land use programs that are not formally linked to the Adirondack Park Agency.[13]

Linkage changes the criteria that the Agency uses in reviewing permit applications, substituting the pertinent criteria of the local program (lot size, use, architectural review) for the Adirondack Park Agency Act's intensity guidelines and its more general statutory purposes and policies that constitute the Plan. While the state's "undue adverse impact" criterion is preserved regardless of linkage, it is administered locally for significant portions of residential development and small-scale commercial development if the municipality has an approved program. The

---

operate independent of the permit process. The Agency also administers the NYS Wild, Scenic and Recreational Rivers Act (N.Y. ENVTL. CONSERVATION LAW Article 15 Part 27) and NYS Freshwater Wetlands Act (N.Y. ENVTL.CONSERVATION LAW Article 24) which strongly influence private land development in the Park in the locations where they apply. These authorities are administered with the primary Adirondack Park Agency Act permit requirement in one integrated permit.

8 New York's Constitution assures municipalities the authority to enact local laws that are not contradicted by express direction from the Legislature. This gives considerable latitude in land use regulation relating to the environment. *See* NYS CONST., art. IX, § 2.

9 *Id.*

10 *See* Dillenburg v. State, No. K1-2003-1208, 2007 WL 4633352 (N.Y.Sup. Ct. Nov. 14, 2007), which has challenged the constitutionality of state tax payments that have been paid for the entire 122 year history of the Forest Preserve. This has reawakened local concerns about the dominant presence of state lands within their jurisdictions. *See, e.g.*, F. Lebrun, *State Tax Payment Loss Threatens Adirondacks, Catskills*, ALBANY TIMES UNION, Feb. 1, 2008.

11 Adirondack Park Agency Act § 807.

12 ADIRONDACK PARK AGENCY, 2000 ANN. REP. 20 (2001).

13 N.Y. LEGISLATIVE COMM'N ON RURAL RESOURCES, LAND USE PLANNING AND REGULATIONS IN NEW YORK MUNICIPALITIES (1999).

state's intensity guidelines and "undue adverse impact" criterion are discussed at more length below.

In addition, with Agency approval and linkage, the locality administers all variances from the state shoreline setback and lot width requirements (also discussed below), subject to review and reversal by the Agency if legal standards are not properly applied. Coordination and reporting requirements between the locality and the Agency assist in administration of the integrated program. The integrated program has significant benefits for landowners but many communities find a separate permitting structure simpler to administer and have not yet sought formal state approval.

Many local plans are quite sophisticated. Some, like those for the Village of Lake Placid and the surrounding Town of North Elba, are tied to local economic development strategies that rely extensively on the environmental qualities of the community's location within the Adirondack Park, but without significant administrative linkages to the Park Agency's land use program.[14] North Elba and Lake Placid have also integrated their local codes with each other for joint administration.

Lake Placid, like some other communities around the country, suffered a minor crisis some years ago when Wal*Mart proposed a store on the outskirts of the hamlet between Lake Placid and Saranac Lake. As the Adirondack Park Agency primarily regulates structures over 40 feet in height in hamlet areas, there were prolonged debates over respective state and local regulatory responsibilities. Ultimately the Town required a detailed environmental impact statement and denied the necessary permit before the matter came before the Park Agency. The debate is illustrative of the division of responsibility between local comprehensive planning and the state. The site is now the Whiteface Lodge, an ultra luxury resort built with local permits and not triggering state review because of the hamlet location and its compact height.

As seen above, the Adirondack Park Land Use and Development Plan creates a permitting system, administered by the Park Agency, which operates on top of or in conjunction with the local permitting. In order to receive a permit for the regulated activities, applicants must demonstrate compliance with five statutory criteria, the most significant being "overall intensity guidelines" and "no undue adverse impact."[15] When a municipality has an approved local land use program,

---

14 Combined Land Use Code, Town of North Elba and Village of Lake Placid, NY (2001).

15 Adirondack Park Agency Act § 809(10) requires: 1) the project would be consistent with the land use and development plan (that is, the statute); 2) the project would be compatible with the character description and purposes, policies and objectives of the land use area (zoning district) wherein it is proposed to be located; 3) the project would be consistent with the overall intensity guideline for the land use area involved; 4) the project would comply with the shoreline restrictions if applicable; and 5) the project would not have an undue adverse impact upon the natural, scenic, aesthetic, ecological, wildlife,

traditional use zoning is engaged and the Agency permit decision criteria are reduced to two, the "pertinent criteria" of the local government program and "no undue adverse impact."[16] Unlike the "permitted" or "prohibited" uses one might find in typical zoning codes, the state criteria do not embed specific use restrictions in the Plan. A specific proposed land use may trigger Agency permit jurisdiction; however, any use may be proposed for any private land location. Because the permit regime applies only to types of development characterized as "regional,"[17] in most instances no permit is required for a typical single family dwelling on a lawful lot, while new commercial uses always require an Agency permit outside "hamlet" areas. These residential and commercial uses may find themselves side by side with only the procedures and "no undue adverse impact" criteria of the Plan to resolve potential conflicts between proposed land uses.

Most new land use and development must show compliance with the "overall intensity guidelines." The Adirondack Park Land Use and Development Plan's "intensity guidelines" are keyed to the legislatively approved Map that depicts six categories suitable for various intensities of development. Statutory guidelines specify the maximum number of "principal buildings"[18] allowable per square mile, often translated into minimum acreage requirements for new subdivision lots or new uses. Though often compared to traditional "lot size" zoning, the intensity criterion is flexible in actual application so long as the intensity "accounting" is consistent with the statutory guideline, which also takes into account how the ownership has evolved since 1973.[19] Agency permits are recorded in special registers in County Clerk's offices to assure intensity accounting over time and long-term enforceability.

One of the primary purposes of the Adirondack Park Agency Act was the protection of an ownership pattern with very large forested tracts in unified private ownerships without significant infrastructure (power, roads) and often with remarkable natural resources such as very large wetlands, small lakes, and flora and fauna in "working forests." These lands form the core of the "resource

---

historic, recreational or open space resources of the park or upon the ability of the public to provide supporting facilities and services made necessary by the project, taking into account the commercial, industrial, residential, recreational or other benefits that might be derived from the project.

16 *Id.*

17 Statutory "purposes," "policies," and compatible use lists which are also part of the "regional project" characterization that may trigger a permit requirement influence permit approval. *Id.* § 805.

18 The term is defined in considerable detail for different uses in the Adirondack Park Agency Act, § 802(50), but roughly equates to a dwelling unit.

19 Banta & Rottier, *supra* note 7, at 9A-5, 9A-25. A municipality with an approved local land use program may apply intensity accounting flexibly within the contiguous state land use area, for instance moderate intensity use, to result in local zoning districts more closely tailored to local needs. Adirondack Park Agency Act § 807; 9 N.Y. Comp. Codes R. & Regs. Part 572.

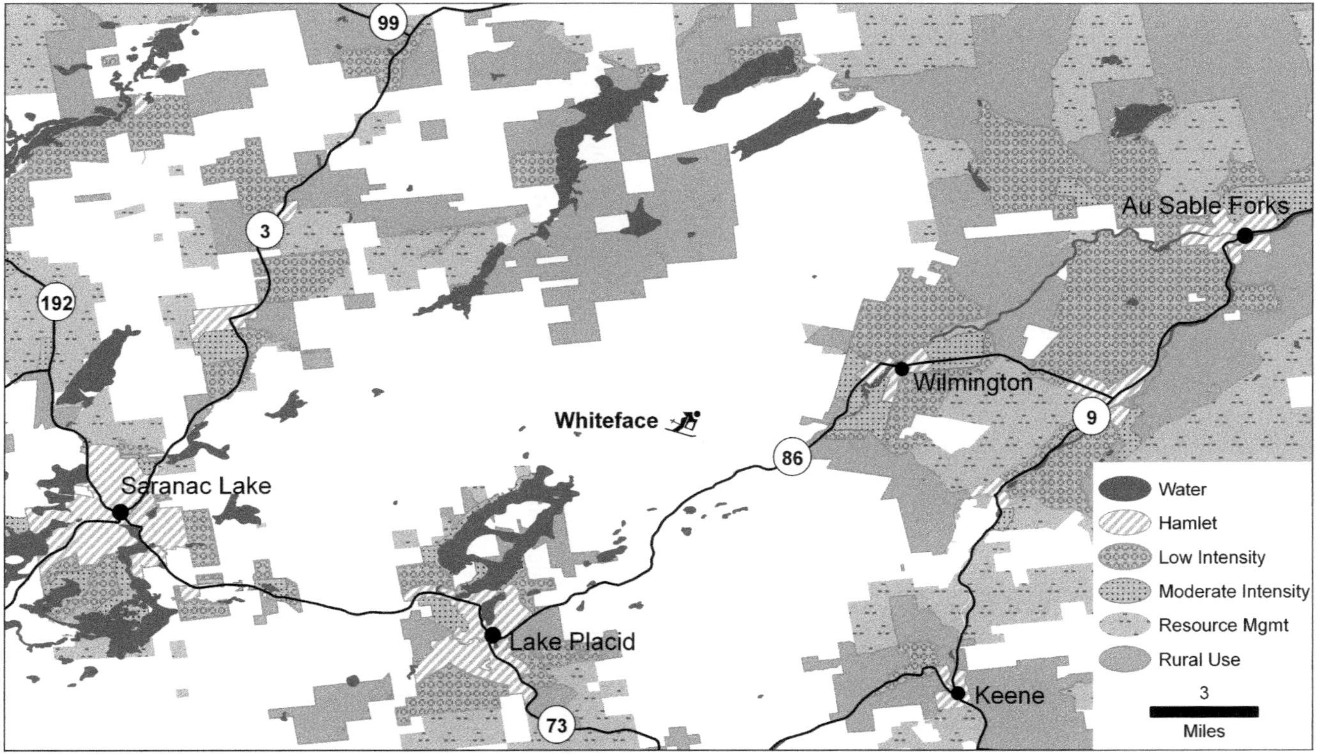

Figure 13.1 Adirondack Park Agency's Intensity Guidelines for Private Land

Note: The white areas represent the state-owned Forest Preserve

Data Sources: New York State Adirondack Park Agency

management" classification. Similarly, former agricultural lands with similar characteristics but an ownership pattern of typically smaller tracts form the core of the "rural use" classification.[20]

A largely unfulfilled aspiration of the Plan is clustering of new development in the most suitable locations, particularly in these two classifications. One reason that reality has fallen short of the goal is the countervailing effect of the exemption from state regulatory review of subdivisions if lots remain larger than statutory minimums. In addition to the state subdivision permit required by the Park Agency for smaller lots, a cluster subdivision may require additional state "consumer protection" filings for common area management. The countervailing effect is most apparent in the more protected "rural use" and the development oriented classifications when smaller subdivisions with lots above the specified average size require no state permit. The opportunity to avoid one or more state permits often outweighs the design advantage of clustering.

Under the Park Agency's intensity guidelines, about 90 percent of the private land in the Park is classified and mapped as "resource management" (15 principal buildings per square mile) or "rural use" (75 principal buildings per square mile) categories where the only exceptions to the requirement of a state permit are forestry, agriculture, and in "rural use," very small subdivisions and single family dwellings.[21] In the absence of an approved local land use program, an Agency permit for all other activities is a second legal layer over any required local zoning and/or building permit to ensure compliance with the regional Adirondack Park Land Use and Development Plan.

The remaining 10 percent of the private land is classified in categories more oriented toward development, and the state's land use permitting role is more restricted.[22] In a simplified view, the Agency jurisdiction is excluded from hamlet areas unless structures are over 40 feet in height, in or affecting wetlands, or include over 100 residential or tourist units. Outside the hamlets, the Agency reviews new commercial uses and larger residential subdivisions. Thus, state review applies to a more limited suite of development decisions than in the 90 percent classified as "resource management" or "rural use." Similarly, the potential for local assumption of permitting responsibilities with local land use program approval by the Adirondack Park Agency is greater in these areas since the Agency retains jurisdiction for many more projects in "rural use" and most, if not all, projects in "resource management." The intensity guidelines and land use classifications do not include specific use restrictions, and as illustrated by the Wal*Mart example, the Agency's permit authority may act as an incentive for smaller scale or location choices to avoid State permit jurisdiction.

---

20 Adirondack Park Agency Act § 805(3)(e), (f).

21 *Id.* § 810.

22 Adirondack Park Land Use Classification Acreage and Percent by County and the Park, http://www.apa.state.ny.us/gis/stats/colc0708.htm (last visited Dec. 22, 2007).

Although the intensity guidelines' designation of geographic areas provides a zoning-like element, the permit review process, in particular the "undue adverse impact" criterion, requires a qualitative assessment of proposed uses. The "undue adverse impact" criterion is defined by a set of statutory "development considerations" which were intended by the drafters to provide a comprehensive evaluation matrix for new development. The statute provides that:

> the project would not have an undue adverse impact upon the natural, scenic, aesthetic, ecological, wildlife, historic, recreational or open space resources of the park or upon the ability of the public to provide supporting facilities and services made necessary by the project, taking into account the commercial, industrial, residential, recreational or other benefits that might be derived from the project.[23]

This criterion is ecological in scope, and procedures for implementation have developed in parallel with New York's environmental impact assessment requirements. The separate and parallel approach for the Park is rooted in a legislative exemption of the Agency-administered permit process from the State Environmental Quality Review Act's requirement for an environmental impact statement that would otherwise apply to significant state decisions.[24]

Overall, the Adirondack Park Agency's relatively comprehensive permit jurisdiction, combined with relatively large average lot size requirements in the "resource management" and "rural use" classifications is intended to protect the open space and environmentally sensitive private lands of the Park. The land use permits administered by the Agency enforce the basic "intensity guideline" or density parameters of its private land plan. Additionally, the permits provide an impact oriented environmental safety net ensuring appropriate on-site wastewater treatment, adequate water supply, appropriate storm water management, and other siting considerations in the absence of underlying local zoning. The jurisdictional net is more porous in already settled areas but relatively restrictive in the largely unsettled and unserviced private forest lands and the old farms that constitute much of the private land within the Park. The dense residential areas existing in 1973 are relatively lightly regulated, whereas forests and more remote areas receive higher levels of protection against uncontrolled development.

In addition, statutory standards for shoreline lot widths and setbacks help to protect private shorelines within the Park.[25] The Adirondack Park Agency Act and New York's Freshwater Wetlands Act provide redundant authority to the Agency to

23 Adirondack Park Agency Act § 809(10)(e)

24 Envtl. Conservation Law § 8-0111(5)(c)

25 Adirondack Park Agency Act § 806. Concurrently, political compromises at passage hobbled the Agency's ability to enforce intensity guidelines on shoreline, by changing the threshold for a permit requirement based on lot size from approximately one acre in the least restrictive classification outside hamlet to approximately one-half acre. Thus shoreline

protect the Park's freshwater wetlands.[26] These are important additional ecological considerations given the extensive wetlands and water bodies in many areas of the Park. Wetland protection is more extensive than in other portions of the state where freshwater wetland protection applies to areas in excess of 12 acres. Within the Park, development is strictly regulated within delineated wetland areas at a threshold of one acre or free interchange with open water. Jurisdiction extends to activities that are likely to impair wetlands, such as on-site wastewater systems within 100 feet of a delineated wetland, but this does not provide significant protection to shoreline vegetation serving as an effective buffer to upland development. Other location-based state jurisdiction applies in "critical environmental areas," which include wetlands, discussed above, areas adjacent to designated state wilderness, elevations above 2,500 feet, and "rural use" and "resource management" state highway corridors.

The pattern of state-local jurisdiction has hundreds of permutations, and a system of jurisdictional advice supplements the permit process to provide landowners with specific legally binding determinations for use in sales, mortgage, and other transactions requiring compliance with all government requirements. A "non-jurisdictional determination" is an important compliance tool, even when a permit is not required from the state, since it sets out the parameters which trigger the need for a subsequent permit if further development is contemplated in the future.[27]

The Ecological Effect of the Park Regime on the Resort Communities

The Adirondack Park creates a nationally unique land use regime for private land, with overlapping state and local controls based on a legislatively adopted plan administered by a state agency attached to the governor's office. As such, it has powerful tools available to shape and implement regional and local land use policies that are ecologically based. At the same time, it has been extremely controversial at points in its history, and controversy has hobbled significant elements of its program. At its core, the Adirondack Park Land Use and Development Plan and the official park plan map acknowledge the spatial component for ecological consequences

---

intensity has become more concentrated without state regulatory oversight that the state "overall intensity guidelines" would suggest. *See id.* §810.

26 *Id.* § 810; *see also* N.Y. Envtl. Conservation Law § 24 (McKinney 2002) (This law was harmonized with the Adirondack Park Agency Act prior to adoption in 1975, and is administered by the Park Agency concurrently with similar jurisdiction conferred by the Adirondack Park Agency Act, § 810.) Unlike the Park Agency Act, which subjects such activities to the Unit Management Planning process only, the Freshwater Wetlands Act regulates activities on state lands such as Whiteface Ski area, otherwise governed by the State Land Master Plan. *See* Adirondack Park Agency Act § 805.

27 *See* Banta & Rottier, *supra* note 7, at 9A-24.

of new development without specifying in advance outcomes for specific areas of private land beyond a gross spatial component keyed to development intensity and their refinement on a site-specific basis when a state permit is required. The analysis underlying the initial zoning reflected a concentrated regional assessment undertaken between 1969 and 1973, reported first by the Temporary Study Commission for the Future of the Adirondack Park, and refined by the Adirondack Park Agency itself in the preparation of the Plan approved by the legislature in 1973. This brought the private lands in the Park within an ecological foundation that was based on spatial and landscape analysis and a common sense instinct to concentrate uses in and near existing settlements.

The state's permit jurisdiction enforces the pattern anticipated by the Plan and adds an impact-reduction component to specific project review. The "undue adverse impact" permit criterion with its statutory "development considerations" empowers ecological considerations in project review, but in practice resources have not been routinely available or demanded for true "ecosystems" analysis focusing on all the ecological interactions. In addition, given the limited spatial context for discrete permits and the scattered and small-scale increments for most development, there are limits to the ecology component of separate permit decisions. Wetlands are given the most prominent protection; less obvious is the degree to which other ecosystem components—alpine habitat, major wetland complexes—are given strong but less documented protection both within the constitutionally protected state-owned Forest Preserve and the extensive "working forests." The Plan provides no magic bullet for cumulative impacts and induced, secondary growth, although a growing consensus seems to be pointing to the need to adjust the framing principles based on the experience of the last 30 years to address shortcomings.

The state role allows land use planning to occur at the regional level, albeit a region so large that disaggregation into meaningful ecological components could be useful to resolving ecological issues. Data remain scarce to support a meaningful retrospective on the ecological impact of the Plan for private lands. The most systematic data target aquatic and wetland ecosystems, thanks to research generated by the pressing need to address the ravages of acid precipitation and a small-scale, ongoing wetland delineation, monitoring and research-oriented relationship between the Park Agency and the federal Environmental Protection Agency's wetlands program. Terrestrial ecology and social and economic parameters important to understanding future directions remain less consistently addressed by the state or localities. Current initiatives to address "smart growth" will frame issues, but profound structural obstacles to comprehensive state or local action lie in local governments' fiscal, property tax and governance systems not susceptible to the "state overlay" strategy injected with the state's private land use plan. For instance, New York's reliance on property and other local taxes to fund education and a significant share of Medicaid expenses gives little room at the local level for spending on long range planning.

Chapter 14
Conclusion

Ecology in the Adirondack Park is largely protected today by stringent precautionary principles imposed on state-owned lands late in the nineteenth century, and augmented and extended with state and private land use plans in the early 1970s. Inherently prospective, the precautionary frame has been very effective in preventing human disruption of the state-owned lands, and 35 years of experience with the plans suggests that large forested tracts have also been shielded from intensive development. However, daily environmental decision making remains conventional, utilizing tools like environmental impact assessment. Remediation of landscape elements that were largely developed when the plans were instituted remains a challenge, whether the object is an abandoned mine, aging settlement infrastructure, or shorelines dotted with "camps" that were given extensive privileges in the legislation establishing the plans that have largely exempted them from remedial regulation. National and global issues—mercury, climate change, acid precipitation—move to different fora, where the Adirondack Park may nonetheless play an influential role, such as when long-range transport of air pollution was killing Adirondack lakes with acid rain in the 1980s and after.

The popular perception is that the "forever wild" status of most of the upper elevations of the Park provides ecological protection for those elements of the landscape, at least from local and regional development pressures. The weakest protections are provided to shorelines of water bodies with predominantly private ownership extensively developed with existing single-family residences. Much of the pattern of uses in these areas predated the Adirondack Park Agency Act, which established the state plans for the area. Yet between the regulations governing the Forest Preserve and the private lands, the mountain resort area of Lake Placid–Wilmington–Whiteface Mountain sits in a unique posture with a rigorously protected landscape that has only modest change possibilities in the foreseeable future. The unique ecological setting is also an important economic asset for Lake Placid and Wilmington, as evident from regional marketing using the theme "forever" followed by the different natural and cultural attributes of the region.

For the most part, the underlying analyses in the nineteenth and twentieth centuries that led to this state of affairs would not be considered ecological by contemporary standards. The consequences of Forest Preserve protection are only beginning to be explored by research addressing the scale and integrity of the regional ecosystem. The policy debate over the Adirondack Park has also resulted in institutions that are often inflexible due to checks and balances of local and statewide interests and of legal regimes embedded in the state constitution, statutes and administrative law. While sensitive to emerging global issues like acid rain and climate change at the policy level, deep institutional responses require remarkable cooperation, like that exhibited at the federal level between Senator Daniel Moynihan, Congressman Sherwood Boehlert, New York's government, and conservation and public utility interests from the 1980s to address acid rain. The region was awakened to the problems of long-range and global environmental pressures on regional ecosystems and then joined in a regional response that has effected meaningful change. Similarly, the Champlain/Adirondack region was recognized as an international biosphere reserve in 1989.[1] Politically charged in some circles, the recognition has yet to be of significant assistance to academic or governmental interests concerned with ecosystem protection. These responses to such threats and policy initiatives are largely outside the reach of the legal regimes discussed here, but the uniqueness of the Park and its vulnerability to global environmental pressures lend weight to the dialogue conducted at the state, national, and international levels.

Mechanisms to redress weaknesses in the legal regime with respect to some elements of the landscape have begun to be discussed, although the subject can be volatile. An aggressive conservation easement program has protected over 600,000 acres of private land in the Park over the last two decades, achieving a higher degree of protection of key lands than is possible under the Park's private land plan.[2] An emerging interest in the Adirondacks as a model for "smart growth" and sustainable development may also frame Park policies in a way that may assist the region in understanding the strengths and weaknesses of the legal and policy regimes guiding the Park relative to the basic ecology of the region.

The Whiteface Mountain Ski Center plays its role in this Park regime as a public recreational facility charged with providing public recreation, youth development programs, international competition and community development in a fiscally responsible manner. It is the flagship for a complex public-private partnership central to the economy of the Lake Placid region. This commitment to community and regional improvement is due in large part to the unique state constitutional provisions that limit the possible land uses at and in the vicinity of the Ski Center and preclude the slope-side condominium development prevalent at other major ski resorts. These factors limit the overall scale of the Ski Center to a comfortable carrying capacity of about 5,000 skiers according to the 2004 Unit Plan. These are the primary motivating concerns, both legally and politically, but they rest within a framework that is, both in theory and increasingly in practice, ecologically based at the planning and decision-making level.

Private development in the neighboring communities of Lake Placid and Wilmington is guided by local government and the Adirondack Park Land Use

1 United Nations Educational, Scientific and Cultural Organization, Biosphere Reserve Information: Champlain Adirondack, at http://www.unesco.org/mabdb/br/brdir/directory/biores.asp?code=USA+45&mode=all (last visited Dec. 23, 2007).

2 New York State Open Space Conservation Plan & Generic Environmental Impact Statement (Nov. 2006).

and Development Plan. The state plan provides relatively few constraints on new development within the hamlet centers of each community, but relatively tight regulation of new land use and development in the open forested areas not under public ownership. An observed result is that area tourist services are generally locally owned and small-to-moderate in scale, and seem destined to remain so. For example, Lake Placid's Main Street bustles with a historic cinema and a diverse array of shops, restaurants, and cultural attractions. Through the two-tiered system of land use regulation, dozens of other communities in the Whiteface region will retain this small-town character for the foreseeable future. Ecology plays less of a role in these development decisions, though the framing plans are based on broad landscape principles, which allowed one of the nation's earliest regional planning efforts to protect the ecologically significant areas by including them in the "rural use" and "resource management" areas identified in the private land use plan. Perhaps no other American community of Lake Placid's scale and accessibility exists in such an intimate relationship with surrounding wilderness.

Whiteface represents a setting where policy commitments made a century ago continue to dominate the landscape. The Ski Center operates in a setting with long policy cycles: from 1932 to 1980 for the Winter Olympics; over a century for the Forest Preserve; a minimum of two legislatures and a vote of the people of New York for any change in the constitutional rules that govern the Ski Center; and so on. The facilities managed by the Olympic Regional Development Authority (ORDA) are a collective resource well-suited to the generic Environmental Impact Statement five-year plan management strategy set up by the Park's State Land Master Plan and implemented through unit management planning. To date this strategy and vision have literally paid off for the community.

ORDA's unit management plans for these different facilities have framed and continue to provide environmental justification for agendas that have required complex economic and political strategies, and considerable will to execute. The result is a full set of winter venues certified for international competition, and at the same time, a string of top ratings among eastern resorts in recent surveys of Whiteface skiers and boarders.

Historically the Adirondack ecological regime was initiated and sustained based on advice from natural resource professionals from multiple generations beginning in the middle of the nineteenth century, each with deep knowledge of the region and its ecology. This is a style of analysis unfamiliar in today's adversarial impact statement environment. From the beginning, the Adirondack Park has reflected a concern for protection of the core natural resources of New York state—its forests and its headwaters. This advice has in turn motivated a precautionary legal regime and deliberately preserved many ecological features using concepts like wilderness and open space, in some ways serving as proxy for the detailed deductive data-based analysis associated with contemporary science. Future planning processes potentially could be built on more thorough ecological analyses—not required by the existing legal regimes, but also not inconsistent with them. New York's multidimensional regulatory regime has resulted in a protected landscape and viable communities that are maintained at a fraction of the research and planning investments for comparable federally managed areas, and with arguably better, though imperfect, integration of local community considerations.

PART IV
Killington Resort, Vermont

Can a Mountain Ecosystem be Protected When the Law Protects its Parts? The Case of Act 250 and Killington Resort

Julia LeMense and Jonathan Isham[1]

1 The authors wish to thank Jeffrey Polubinski and Robert Gruenig for their contributions to earlier articles about Killington Resort that provided the springboard for this case study and Kirk Kardashian for his assistance with the research for this case study. Comprehensive research was completed in 2004, and has been selectively updated through March 2008.

Chapter 15
An Introduction to Killington Resort, its Expansion Plans, and the Issues

Vermonters have always prided themselves on their love of their natural surroundings. Yet at the same time, they understand that these natural surroundings, because of their appeal to tourists, are a critical engine of their economy. The tension between development and environmental protection is pronounced in the case of Vermont's mountain resorts.

We examine the case of Killington Resort[1] to illustrate how Vermont's nationally unique Land Use and Development Law,[2] commonly known as Act 250, addresses mountain resort expansion. This case study reveals how the pressures to expand Killington Resort have encountered both support and opposition from a wide range of Vermont's stakeholders, and how that mixed reception has affected the legal process undertaken to review the Resort's expansion plans. It showcases how Act 250, if applied broadly and in accordance with the spirit of the law, may be able to incorporate an ecosystem perspective, but that accomplishing this is heavily dependent on the type of information that is available to the decision-makers.

We begin with a thumbnail sketch of Killington Resort's expansion plans over the past two decades, with more details in the chapters to follow. Although the owner quietly expanded Killington Resort during the first 30 years of operation, a storm started brewing in 1986, when Killington set its sights on expanding into an area known as Parker's Gore East. Killington Resort, located partially on land in the Coolidge State Forest and leased by Killington from the State of Vermont, is largely dependent upon artificial snow. Adverse weather conditions and inadequate existing water supplies prompted Killington to seek out additional water sources. In 1986, therefore, Killington proposed to dam Madden Brook in an area known as Parker's Gore East and create a pond to be used for snowmaking withdrawals and as a stocked trout pond. (See Figure 15.1). Killington also hoped to expand trails into Parker's Gore East. The battle over Parker's Gore East, led by local

---

1 Killington and Pico Resorts were separate resorts under separate ownership until 1986. Because the discussion in this chapter begins with events taking place in 1986 and going forward, we refer to the combined resort as Killington Resort. Killington Resort has changed ownership a number of times, most recently in 2007. We discuss the changes in ownership, but for simplicity, we refer throughout this case study to the owners of Killington Resort as Killington, unless employing the specific entity name clarifies the text.

2 Act of Apr. 4, 1970, Pub. L. No. 250 (codified as amended at Vt. Stat. Ann. tit. 10, §§ 6001-86 (2007)).

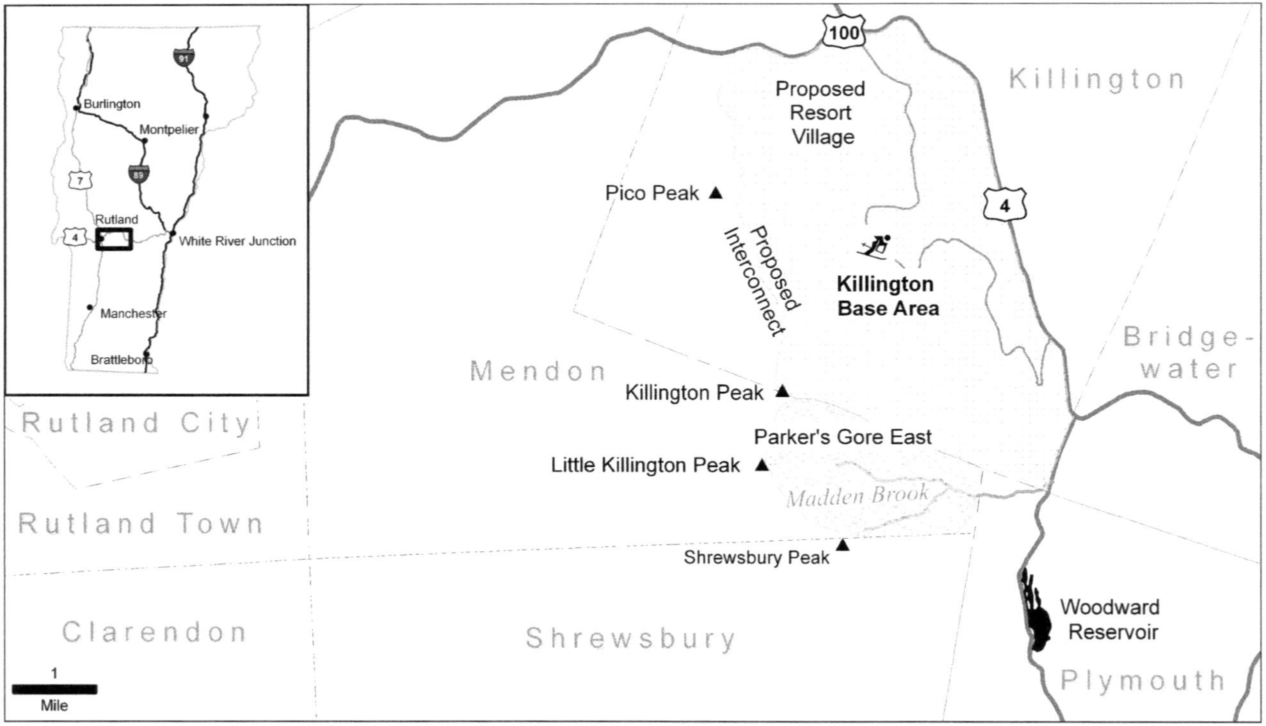

Figure 15.1 Killington Resort and its Regional Setting

Note: This map also shows Killington Resort's expansion proposals.

Data Sources: Appalachian Trail Conference; David Capen; ESRI; Green Mountain Club; VT Center for Geographic Information, Inc.; Tele Atlas North America, Inc.

groups actively participating in Act 250 permitting proceedings, was intense and the project never received the necessary approvals.

In the years following the Parker's Gore East controversy, Killington looked for other ways to expand its trail network, its snowmaking capacity, and its base mountain real estate, lodging, and entertainment offerings. But instead of immediately filing the applications for permits under Act 250, Killington first negotiated with some of the stakeholders that had been involved in the proceedings over the proposal to expand into Parker's Gore East. The resulting Memorandum of Agreement executed in 1996, reached before Killington filed any permit applications, shaped the Act 250 proceedings for the subsequent expansion projects that are the primary focus of this case study, and it continues to shape the future of Killington Resort's expansion and the greater mountain ecosystem.

Collectively, these projects—the proposed 1986 expansions into Parker's Gore East and, a decade later, proposals to build a trail and lift system connecting Killington Peak and Pico Peak (called the Interconnect), to use Woodward Reservoir as a source for water for snowmaking, and to build a new Resort Village—illustrate how both the procedural and substantive provisions of Act 250 function. As Chapter 16 discusses, Act 250 establishes rules governing who may participate in proceedings and what evidence they may introduce. Based on the record created before the Act 250 District Commission, decision-makers then apply ten permitting criteria that must be satisfied before a development permit will be issued, including criteria addressing individual aspects of the environment such as air quality, water quality, wetlands, wildlife, and energy use, as well as the impacts of growth on services such as waste disposal, water supplies, and education. This would seem to suggest, on its face, that Act 250 could adequately protect mountain ecosystems today, because the criteria address many of the individual components of the ecosystem, but this case study explores whether Vermont's Act 250 in fact considers ecological interrelationships.

Chapter 16 also sets the stage for later expansion efforts with a discussion of the pivotal events surrounding Parker's Gore East in 1986. The Parker's Gore East proposal demonstrates that stakeholders can influence the outcome of a proposed project and encourage the decision-makers in Act 250 proceedings to consider the ecological interrelationships among individual elements or aspects of the affected ecosystem. It is against this backdrop that we view later development applications at Killington Resort relating to the Interconnect project, the Woodward Reservoir project, and the Resort Village project, each of which is discussed in Chapter 17.

The Interconnect project highlights how prior agreements among stakeholders can impact the information presented during Act 250 permit hearings for new trails. The Woodward Reservoir project illustrates how other permits, both federal and state, influence the operation of Act 250 as it considers a new source of water for snowmaking, essential for the Killington Resort's expansion. Finally, the Resort Village project reveals how specific guidelines regarding phased development for an expanded base village operate in the context of Act 250. It also emphasizes the importance of the local land use planning process in the context of resort development projects under Act 250, illustrating the critical piece this process can play in the overall effort to protect mountain ecosystems. The conclusion in Chapter 18 offers observations about the ability of Act 250 to take an ecosystems perspective and a suggestion for how Act 250 could be modified to better consider and protect mountain ecosystems. But the tale cannot begin without first introducing Killington Resort.

The Green Mountains, physically and symbolically, are the essence of Vermont. The Green Mountains are part of the vast Appalachian Mountain range and have only five peaks rising above 4,000 feet. Killington Peak, the second highest peak, is located in the center of the state, in the town of Killington (formerly Sherburne), between the towns of Rutland and Woodstock.

Prior to the 1950s, skiing had a relatively small effect on mountain ecosystems and on local economies in the Green Mountains.[3] At that time, ski enthusiasts hiked to mountain summits to ski only one or two runs in a day.[4] The few existing lifts were mostly surface lifts that slowly dragged skiers up long, steep slopes, and ski area operation included limited grooming and no snowmaking.[5]

In the mid-1950s, a young skier from the Killington area named Preston Leete Smith envisioned a unique mountain resort that would attract people from all over the United States to a new recreational experience at Killington Peak.[6] To bring this dream to life, Smith formed the Sherburne Corporation in 1956. On Killington Resort's opening day in 1958, it had seven trails, serviced by four lifts. Since then, the various owners of Killington Resort (see Figure 15.2) have continued to follow expansive business plans: more trails, more lifts, more snow, more guest beds, and the development of a four-season base area to attract more customers.[7]

During Killington Resort's early expansion from the late 1950s to the late 1960s, the owners faced few environmental regulatory constraints.[8] Municipalities in Vermont traditionally were responsible for land use planning; during this time, there were few, if any, environmental laws. But in the late 1960s, extensions to Interstate Routes 89 and 91 increased Vermont tourism by providing easy access from major metropolitan areas in New England and New York.[9] As visitors began to build second homes in high tourism areas, including the Killington area, the pressure on communities to manage these developments became much

3 Karen D. Lorentz, Killington: A Story of Mountain and Men 258–62 (1990).

4 *See generally* Ski Magazine's Encyclopedia Of Skiing 9–45, 69, 102–03, 111–12 (Robert Scharff ed., 1974).

5 Lorentz, *supra* note 3, at 43

6 *Id.* at 27.

7 *Id.* at 69, 102–03, 111–12. Killington conducted tens of thousands of customer surveys on site and online to determine its guests' wants. Pursuant to these surveys, management concluded that additional amenities and variety will increase customer satisfaction. Isham interview with Rich McGarry, Senior V.P. & General Manager, Killington, Ltd. (Mar. 8, 2002).

8 *See* Lorentz, *supra* note 3, at 105-07

9 Robert F. Gruenig, *Killington Mountain and Act 250: An Eco-Legal Perspective*, 26 Vt. L. Rev. 543, 545 n.7 (2002).

greater.[10] The passage in 1970 of a statewide land use permitting law in Vermont, known as Act 250, initially did little to impede Sherburne Corporation's rapid development and grandiose plans for expansion at Killington Resort into the 1980s.

In 1985, Smith restructured Sherburne Corporation and formed a new, public holding company called S-K-I, Ltd. (S-K-I). The Sherburne Corporation (renamed Killington Ltd. in 1985) became a subsidiary of S-K-I. Under S-K-I's ownership, expansion plans continued with the purchase of Pico Ski Area in 1986.[11] Pico lies northwest of Killington Ski Area and can be accessed by driving approximately six miles along the Killington access road and U.S. Route 4.

In 1986, the owners began marketing Killington Resort to a young crowd of advanced skiers, dubbing itself the "the Beast of the East."[12] Killington Resort supplied these skiers with a large amount of challenging terrain as well as nightlife that catered to the Baby Boomer generation.[13] This marketing effort appeared to pay off quickly, generating record skier visits during the 1988–1989 season, which remains the resort's most successful season in terms of the number of skier visits,[14] when Killington Resort reported 1.4 million skier days.[15]

The expansion plans that are featured in this case study were initiated by S-K-I and continued by the next owner of Killington Resort, American Skiing Company (ASC). In 1996, ASC, with a national presence in ski resort operations and real estate development, acquired S-K-I and its assets, including Killington Resort.[16] During the 2002–2003 ski season, Killington Resort had over one million skier visits, the fifth most in the country.[17] The majority of ASC's resort business was generated through the ownership and operation of seven resorts nationwide, which collectively accounted for four million skier visits annually or 6.9 percent of total skier visits in the United States in 2005.[18] But by 2006, Killington Resort reported

10 Cindy Corlett Argentine, Vermont Act 250 Handbook, A Guide to State and Regional Land Use Regulation 2 (2d ed. 1998).

11 Lorentz, *supra* note 3, at 261.

12 *In re* Killington, Ltd., Resort Village Master Plan Application, No. 1R0835, Findings of Fact, Conclusion of Law and Order (Vt. Dist. Envtl. Comm'n #1, Apr. 11, 1999), Exhibit #71 [K-CLH], at 1.

13 *Id.*

14 *Id.*, Exhibit #8 [K-CGS], at 52; *see also id.*, Exhibit #12 [K-CGS], at 12.

15 *In re* Killington, Ltd., Resort Village Master Plan Application, No. 1R0835, Findings of Fact, Conclusion of Law and Order (Vt. Dist. Envtl. Comm'n #1, Apr. 11, 1999), Exhibit #8 [K-CGS], at 52; *see also id.*, Exhibit #12 [K-CGS], at 12.

16 S-K-I, Ltd., a wholly owned subsidiary of ASC, itself had several subsidiaries: Killington, Ltd., Sugarloaf Mountain Corporation, SKI Insurance Company, Mount Snow, Ltd., Pico Ski Area Management Company, and Killington West, Ltd. Several of these, in turn, have their own subsidiaries. American Skiing Company, April 2003 Quarterly Report 7.

17 *See id.*

18 *Id.* As of 2005, ASC owned and operated Killington Resort, Pico Mountain, Sunday River, Attitash, The Canyons, Steamboat Mount Snow, and Sugarloaf, *available at* http://www.peaks.com (last visited June 18, 2005).

Table 15.1 The Changing Ownership of Killington Resort

Entity	Year
Sherburne Corporation	1956
S-K-I, Ltd.	1985
American Ski Company	1996
MBT Killington, LLC, AMSC Killington, LLC, and SP II Resort, LLC (collectively a joint venture of SP Land and Powdr Corp.)	2007

fewer than 800,000 skier visits, making it only the tenth most visited resort in the nation. Struggling under the weight of significant debt,[19] in 2007 ASC sold Killington Resort to a joint venture between SP Land Co. and Powdr Corp.[20] Because S-K-I, and then ASC, owned Killington Resort during the time period covered by this case study (see Table 15.1), they are the prominent players in Chapters 16 and 17, respectively.

After the thwarted attempts to expand in Parker's Gore East in 1986, Killington went back to the drawing board and about a decade later came up with a new vision for Killington Resort, which included trail improvements, increased snowmaking, and additional lodging and lift service.[21] To make this vision a reality, Killington concentrated on three major projects: the Interconnect to connect Killington and Pico,[22] the Woodward Reservoir to provide water for snowmaking,[23] and the expanded Resort Village at the mountain base (see Figure 15.1).[24] ASC's proposed expansion of trails would require an increase in snowmaking capacity, which could only be satisfied by an additional water source since the existing water supplies were already inadequate. After most other water supply options had been exhausted,

---

19 Press Release, American Skiing Company, American Skiing Company Announces Completion of Real Estate Restructuring (May 14, 2004).

20 Karen D. Lorentz, *ASC Parts with Killington, Pico, Mt. Snow Resorts*, Rutland Business Journal, Mar. 8, 2007, *available at* http://vermonttoday.com/apps/pbcs.dll/article?AID=/20070308/RBJ/70308008/-1/RBJ02 (last visited Mar. 2, 2008).

21 *See* Killington Chamber of Commerce, Welcome to The Killington Chamber of Commerce On-Line, http://www.killingtonchamber.com/ (last visited June 25, 2007); *see also In re* Killington, Ltd., Resort Village Master Plan Application, No. 1R0835, Findings of Fact, Conclusion of Law and Order (Vt. Dist. Envtl. Comm'n #1, Apr. 11, 1999), Exhibit #12.

22 *In re* Killington, Ltd., et al., No. 1R0813-2, Findings of Fact, Conclusion of Law and Order (Vt. Dist. Envtl. Comm'n #1, Nov. 24, 1997).

23 Necessary permits included the following: Act 250 permit; an Army Corps of Engineers § 404 permit, pursuant to the Clean Water Act and the Vermont Agency of Natural Resources water quality standards; and an easement from the state to construct the pipeline across a public right of way

24 Lorentz, *supra* note 3, at 105-7; *see also In re* Killington, Ltd., Resort Village Master Plan Application, No. 1R0835, Findings of Fact, Conclusion of Law and Order (Vt. Dist. Envtl. Comm'n #1, Apr. 11, 1999).

ASC pinned its hopes on Woodward Reservoir, which is primarily located on the property of Farm and Wilderness Camps, a series of six Quaker summer camps.[25] Moreover, vital to ASC's efforts to increase skier numbers and attract second home buyers was the Resort Village, an ambitious, three-phased master plan for lodging, additional trails, and off-mountain facilities, which would add to the Killington Resort as many as 4,541 units of housing, 230,000 square feet of commercial space, 118,000 square feet of public assembly and indoor sports facilities, new ski trails, and many other on-mountain improvements.[26] This ambitious plan met with a great deal of opposition, particularly by one prominent New England environmental group, and local and state environmental groups were particularly apprehensive about the Interconnect[27] because of its perceived potential impact on high elevation ecosystems due to significant trail clearing activities.

When Killington was eyeing expansion through these projects it had to wrestle with two (sometimes conflicting) goals among Vermonters: economic development and environmental protection. Each of these projects has tested the capacity of Act 250 to balance economic expansion with protection of the mountain ecology. The Killington Resort has a substantial economic impact on the surrounding community. The largest employer in the Town of Killington[28] and one of the largest employers in the state,[29] as of 2001, Killington employed approximately 2,100 seasonal and year-round workers during the peak ski season.[30] Many small businesses in the Killington area are also dependent on the ski industry, so the success or failure of the Killington Resort can greatly influence the economic well-being of the

---

25 Isham interview with Jean Rosenburg, Farm and Wilderness (Apr. 1, 2001).

26 *In re* Killington, Ltd., Resort Village Master Plan Application, No. 1R0835, Findings of Fact, Conclusion of Law and Order (Vt. Dist. Envtl. Comm'n #1, Apr. 11, 1999), Exhibit #107 [K-NEC-1], at i.

27 Skip King, Vice President Communications, American Skiing Company, A Brief History of the American Skiing Company, http://www.peaks.com/html1/presskit/history.html (last visited Feb. 9, 2002).

28 Killington had an estimated 2005 population of 1,134 and an average annual wage of $24,921. Center for Rural Studies, Information by Town, Rutland County, http://maps.vcgi.org/indicators/cfhome/town_profile.cfm?Call_Program=INDICATORS&ProfileTown=Killington (last visited June 10, 2007). Local historians believe that Killington was named for Killington, Northumberland, England. In 1800, Killington was renamed Sherburne, in honor of one of the original grantees, Colonel Benjamin Sherburne. Because of the popularity of the ski area, locals and visitors have long identified the area as "Killington." Therefore, in 1999 town voters elected to again call the town Killington. About Killington, http://www.virtualvermont.com/towns/killington.html#about (last visited May 14, 2002).

29 *In re* Killington, Ltd., Resort Village Master Plan Application, No. 1R0835, Findings of Fact, Conclusion of Law and Order (Vt. Dist. Envtl. Comm'n #1, Apr. 11, 1999), Exhibit # 108 [K-NEC-1], at 7 (reporting findings of Richard M. Heaps, economist).

30 Bruce Edwards, *Ski Areas Expect to Fill All Jobs,* Rutland Herald, Oct. 15, 2001, *available at* http://rutlandherald.nybor.com/Archive/Articles/Article/35717 (last visited May 14, 2002).

surrounding communities of Killington,[31] Rutland,[32] and Woodstock,[33] as well as other smaller towns and villages in the area that provide housing and services to tourists and resort employees.[34] Unsurprisingly, the local Chambers of Commerce, the Vermont Ski Area Association and most local businesses have consistently supported expansion at Killington Resort.[35]

Before turning to the individual expansion projects at Killington Resort, Chapter 16 introduces Vermont's unique legal regime—Act 250—and chronicles Killington's failed expansion efforts at Parker's Gore East. With that background in place, the remaining chapters will examine whether Act 250 considers the ecological interrelationships in the mountain ecosystem.

31 *In re* Killington, Ltd., Resort Village Master Plan Application, No. 1R0835, Findings of Fact, Conclusion of Law and Order (VT. DIST. ENVTL. COMM'N #1, Apr. 11, 1999), Exhibit # 108 [K-NEC-1], at 7 (reporting findings of Richard M. Heaps, economist).

32 *See id.*

33 The estimated population of the Town of Woodstock as of 2005 is 3224, and the average annual income is $29,603. Center for Rural Studies, http://maps.vcgi.org/indicators/cfhome/village_profile.cfm?Call_Program=INDICATORS&ProfileTown=Woodstock+Vil lage (last visited June 10, 2007).

34 For example, the towns of Pittsfield (pop. 427), Stockbridge (pop. 683), Bethel (pop. 1980), Pittsford (pop. 3214), Plymouth (pop. 580), Bridgewater (pop. 956), Chittenden (pop. 1,227), Castleton (pop. 4,368), and Mendon (pop. 1,068) all offer lodging facilities, which house both visitors to the region and employees of the resort. *See id.*

35 *In re* Killington, Ltd., Resort Village Master Plan Application, No. 1R0835, Findings of Fact, Conclusion of Law and Order (VT. DIST. ENVTL. COMM'N #1, Apr. 11, 1999), Exhibit # 108 [K-NEC-1], at 7 (reporting findings of Richard M. Heaps, economist).

Chapter 16

Vermont's Act 250 and the Early Battles at Parker's Gore East

In 1968, as Deane Davis traveled through Vermont's rural towns during his gubernatorial campaign, he discovered that Vermonters were forming dozens of environmental groups.[1] As the environmental movement began to coalesce nationwide, Vermonters were beginning to put their own stamp on the face of environmentalism in their state. One of their chief concerns, Davis learned, was the unintended consequence of development, and the most notable development was occurring in and around ski resorts. Listening to the concerns of fellow Vermonters, Davis and other political and civic leaders rapidly concluded that the lack of planning associated with the development boom of the late 1960s was threatening Vermont's environment.

At this critical juncture, Vermont's Act 250 was born. In 1970, with the support of the newly inaugurated Governor Deane Davis, the Vermont General Assembly passed Act 250, Vermont's Land Use and Development Law,[2] which attempts "to protect and conserve the lands and the environment of Vermont ...."[3] In passing the Act, the legislature stated that

> it is necessary to regulate and control the utilization and usages of lands and the environment to insure that, hereafter, the only usages which will be permitted are not unduly detrimental to the environment, will promote the general welfare through orderly growth and development and are suitable to the demands and needs of the people of this state.[4]

What emerged at the culmination of this political process is a unique, state-level permitting system. Although Vermont's leaders recognized a lack of planning as a threat, they never implemented the state-level planning component that was

---

1 Joe Sherman, Fast Lane On A Dirt Road 87 (2000).

2 Act of Apr. 4, 1970, Pub. L. No. 250 (codified as amended at Vt. Stat. Ann. tit. 10, §§ 6001-86 (2007)).

3 Findings and Declaration of Intent, 1969, No. 250 (Adj. Sess.), § 1, Eff. Apr. 4, 1970, *available at* http://www.state.vt.us/envboard/statute.htm#dec_of_intent (last visited, Feb. 11, 2002).

4 State of Vermont Environmental Board, *Act 250: A Guide to Vermont's Land Use Law* 6 (Nov. 2000) (quoting Findings and Declaration of Intent, 1969, No. 250 (Adj. Sess.), Section 1, effective Apr. 4, 1970).

originally intended to complement the state-level permitting system for specific developments. Instead, the only component of Act 250, as originally conceived, to become law was the permitting system.[5]

The Act 250 Permitting Process

As described in more detail below, parties proposing to develop or subdivide land must file an Act 250 permit application with the District Environmental Commission (District Commission)[6] unless an exemption applies.[7] After assessing a proposed development project's compliance with Act 250's ten substantive criteria, including whether the proposed project complies with local and regional plans,[8] decision-makers must make one of three choices: (1) grant the application; (2) grant the application with conditions; or (3) deny the application.[9] In most instances, permit decisions are issued expeditiously[10] and are rarely appealed[11] to the Environmental Board (Board) or the Vermont Supreme Court.[12] Since the completion of the four Act 250 proceedings that are at the center of this

5 *Id.*

6 Vermont is divided into nine district commissions with each one composed of three lay individuals who are appointed by the Governor and either serve a two- or four-year term. Vt. Stat. Ann. tit. 10, § 6026(a)–(b) (1999).

7 *Id.* § 6081. An applicant for an Act 250 permit first applies to the District Environmental Commission. After the District Commission issues or denies permits, parties may appeal the decision. Vermont Natural Resources Board, http://www.nrb.state.vt.us (last visited June 14, 2007). During the period of time that is the focus of this case study, appeals from the Commission were directed to the Vermont Environmental Board, whose decisions were reviewable by the Vermont Supreme Court. Since 2005, appeals of Commission decisions are directed to the Environmental Court, whose decisions are reviewable by the Vermont Supreme Court. Vermont Natural Resources Board, http://www.nrb.state.vt.us (last visited June 14, 2007).

8 Before granting a permit, "the board or district commission shall find that the subdivision or development ... (10) is in conformance with any duly adopted local or regional plan or capital program under chapter 117 of Title 24." Vt. Stat. Ann. tit. 10, § 6086(a)(10). For additional requisites of compliance with local and regional plans, see *id.* § 6086(a)(9).

9 *Id.* §§ 6086(a), 6087.

10 During the pendency of the various Killington Resort development applications, the approximately thirty-six full-time staff members who oversaw the Act 250 permitting process normally issued 70 percent of their permit decisions within 90 days after the application was filed. Vt. Natural Resources Council, The Valuable Role of Citizens in Act 250 4 (2d ed. 1999).

11 Appeal percentages during the time period that is the focus of this section include 2 percent for 1997 and 4.2 percent for 1998. *Id.* at 9.

12 Vt. Stat. Ann. tit. 10, § 6089(b). "An appeal from the board will be allowed for all usual reasons, including the unreasonableness or insufficiency of the conditions attached to

chapter, the Vermont Legislature has amended Act 250, and the Environmental Court has replaced the Environmental Board in hearing appeals from the District Commission's decisions.[13] Because Killington's expansion plans were reviewed under Act 250 before this change occurred, our analysis of Act 250's impact on Killington's plans occasionally refers to decisions of or actions taken by the Environmental Board, but we will revisit these and other changes to Act 250 in the final chapter of this case study and speculate how they might have altered the analysis of the projects discussed in this case study.

Act 250 requires a permit for many types of development and subdivisions.[14] As is the case with most laws, the triggering events that give rise to Act 250 jurisdiction are not easily expressed in a tidy list. Generally speaking, and of particular interest in the context of mountain resorts, any construction of improvements for any purpose above the elevation of 2,500 feet is subject to Act 250 review. Projects at any elevation involving the construction of improvements for any commercial or industrial purpose (excluding farming, logging and forestry projects) involving more than ten acres of land (or involving one acre of land if the municipality in which the activity occurs does not have both subdivision and zoning laws) also trigger Act 250 review. A developer constructing ten or more housing units within a five-mile radius must also obtain an Act 250 permit prior to construction. In addition to development activities, the subdivision, or partitioning, of land into ten or more lots within a five-mile radius (or within a particular Act 250 District)

---

a permit." *Id.* § 6089(d). Furthermore, "[t]he finding of the board with respect to questions of fact . . . shall be conclusive." *Id.* § 6089(c).

13 As of February 1, 2005, appeals from District Commission decisions no longer go to the Environmental Board. Act 115 of the Vermont Legislature abolished the Environmental Board, and in its place vested the Environmental Court with jurisdiction over appeals from District Commissions and also created the Natural Resources Board. Prior to February 1, 2005, the Environmental Board was primarily responsible for overseeing the permitting process and also ruling on appeals from the Commissions. Vt. Stat. Ann. tit. 10, § 6089. The Board consisted of nine lay individuals who were appointed by the Governor for four-year terms. *Id.* § 6021(a). Appeals regarding Commission decisions were "de novo hearing[s] on all findings requested." *Id.* § 6089(a)(3). When issues are reviewed *de novo*, previously presented facts and evidence "must be re-established" once again, and new information may be presented for the first time with respect to any issues being addressed by the Board. Cindy Corlett Argentine, Vermont Act 250 Handbook, A Guide to State and Regional Land Use Regulation 2 (2d ed. 1998). Since 2005, the Environmental Court conducts *de novo* hearings of the issues on appeal. Vt. Stat. Ann. tit. 10, § 8504(h). The Natural Resources Board consists of one full-time chairperson and two four-person citizen panels—the Land Use Panel and the Water Resources Panel. The Land Use Panel assumes the Act 250 rulemaking function formerly exercised by the Environmental Board, and is expected to manage the process pursuant to which Act 250 permits are issued. The Land Use Panel may also initiate enforcement actions or petition the Environmental Court to revoke Act 250 permits.

14 *Id.* § 6001(3). *See generally* State of Vermont Environmental Board, Act 250: A Guide to Vermont's Land Use Law 6 (2000), *available at* http://www.state.vt.us/envboard/publications/act250.pdf (last visited Feb. 7, 2002) [hereinafter Act 250 Guide].

and within a five year period will also trigger Act 250.[15] While Act 250 is not retroactive, substantial changes to projects in existence prior to 1970 are subject to review, and if the proposed change triggers Act 250, the developer must obtain an Act 250 permit prior to proceeding.[16]

In light of the fact that Killington Resort encompasses Killington Peak, which rises to an elevation of 4,241 feet, and that Killington Resort is a commercial endeavor, development projects involving construction undertaken by S-K-I and ASC triggered Act 250 jurisdiction. However, because Act 250 is geared toward permitting *subdivision and development activities* and not daily operational or management activities, one can imagine Killington Resort taking ecologically significant actions that do not trigger Act 250 and that, as a result, may be completely unregulated, or regulated in a manner that fails to take into consideration the interaction between development and management activities. We explore this aspect of Killington Resort in Chapter 17 in an effort to explain why Act 250, itself an important aspect of ecosystem protection in Vermont, cannot be the only line of defense against activities that cause ripple effects throughout the mountain ecosystem.

Act 250's Ten Criteria

Under the Act, ten criteria establish a framework that the District Commission and the Board (the Environmental Court post-2005) use to evaluate land use permit applications.[17] Table 16.1 identifies each criterion by number and the focus of that criterion. Together, the ten criteria aim to protect natural resources, environmental quality, and scenic beauty, while striving to ensure that development plans can be absorbed by Vermont communities without causing unnecessary damage.[18]

As Table 16.1 shows, within several of the enumerated criteria are subcriteria that further focus the analysis under Act 250, and some of these subcriteria may be particularly relevant to applications for mountain resort activities. For example, criterion 1 requires the District Commission or the Board to affirmatively find that the project "will not result in undue water or air pollution."[19] To make this determination, at a minimum, the decision-makers must consider the elevation of the land, the ability of soil to support waste disposal, "the slope of the land and

15 Vt. Stat. Ann. tit. 10, § 6001(3) (defining "development," and the jurisdictional limits of Act 250).

16 Under Act 250, "[n]o person shall sell or offer for sale any interest in any subdivision located in this state, or commence construction on a subdivision or development, or commence development without a permit." *Id.* § 6081(a). Based on the exemptions, Act 250 provides a large umbrella of protection for those communities without zoning by maintaining jurisdiction over proposed development projects greater than one acre in size). *Id.* § 6081.

17 Argentine, *supra* note 13, at 73–76.

18 *See* Act 250 Guide, *supra* note 14, at 6.

19 Vt. Stat. Ann. tit. 10, § 6086.

Table 16.1 The Ten Act 250 Criteria

Criterion Number	Focus of Criterion
1	Prevent undue air and water pollution, looking in particular at: • 1(A) Headwaters • 1(B) Solid waste disposal • 1(C) Water conservation • 1(D) Floodways • 1(E) Stream condition • 1(F) Access and erosion control • 1(G) Wetlands
2	Evidence of sufficient water supply for the needs of the project
3	Prevent unreasonable burden on existing water supply
4	Prevent unreasonable soil erosion
5	Prevent unreasonably dangerous or congested traffic conditions
6	Prevent unreasonable burden on educational services
7	Prevent unreasonable burden on municipal or government services
8	Prevent undue, adverse effect on aesthetics, historic sites, or rare and irreplaceable areas • 8(A) Avoid imperiling endangered species and necessary wildlife habitat
9	Conformance with capability and development plan (never adopted), plus other subcriteria • 9(A) – 9(L)
10	Conformance with local and regional plans

Source: Vt. Stat. Ann. tit. 10, §6085

its effect on effluents," "the availability of streams for disposal of effluents," and applicable health and environmental regulations.[20] The applicant must show that the project's effects on ground and surface water quality in areas that have certain characteristics (headwaters, recharge zones, high altitudes, small drainage basins, for example) will meet applicable laws and regulations. This aspect of the first criteria is referred to as "criterion 1(A)–Headwaters." Projects must also comply with applicable waste disposal requirements (criterion 1(B)). The applicant must demonstrate that the project design incorporates water conservation measures, where technically and economically feasible (criterion 1(C)). If the project is located within a floodway, the applicant must also demonstrate that the project will not alter floodwater flows or significantly increase the peak discharge of streams or rivers during flooding that endangers the health, safety, or welfare of the public or riparian owners (criterion 1(D)). When riparian lands are involved, the applicant must further demonstrate that the project will, "whenever feasible, maintain the natural condition of the stream" or will not endanger public or adjoining landowner

20 *Id.*

health, safety, or welfare (criterion 1(E)). Additionally, if the development affects shorelines, the applicant must demonstrate that development on the shore is a necessity and, where possible and reasonable, retain the shoreline and waters in their natural condition, allow continued access, retain or provide screening vegetation, and prevent erosion (criterion 1(F)). Finally, the applicant must show that the project will not violate the state's wetlands rules (criterion 1(G)).[21]

Criterion 8, relating to the impact on "the scenic or natural beauty of the area, aesthetics, historic sites or rare and irreplaceable natural areas," also contains criterion 8(A). Criterion 8(A) allows opponents to a proposed project to defeat the issuance of a permit if they can show it "will destroy or significantly imperil necessary wildlife habitat or any endangered species," *and* the benefit of the proposed project will not outweigh the burden to the public from the destruction of species or habitat, the project does not employ reasonable and feasible means to prevent such loss, or the applicant has an acceptable alternative site. Criterion 9 also contains several subcriteria. These subcriteria focus more on the impacts a project may have on agricultural soils, the mineral extraction industry, and the infrastructure of existing towns.[22]

Having introduced the ten criteria, which perhaps give the appearance of providing a comprehensive review of all aspects of any given ecosystem, we note that the word "ecosystem" does not appear anywhere in Act 250. As a result, if elements of the ecosystem are not specifically identified in these ten criteria, applicants are not affirmatively obligated to demonstrate that the proposed project will not have repercussions on other aspects of the ecosystem. Further, decision-makers are not required to look past the impact being assessed under a particular criterion to determine what other ecosystemic consequences may flow from that action. In addition, several of the criteria contain a "feasibility" or "cost-benefit" analysis component, which further undercuts the force of an ecosystem analysis. For example, criterion 1(E) (streams) requires applicants to maintain stream beds "whenever feasible."[23] Criterion 8(A), addressing necessary wildlife habitat, expressly requires a cost-benefit analysis.[24] Finally, there is no explicit authority in Act 250 to allow parties participating in the process to point out ecological interrelationships. As we discuss in Chapter 17, this void is not a complete barrier to an ecosystem analysis. The void, however, coupled with certain procedural aspects of Act 250, can make the incorporation of an ecosystem perspective a difficult challenge.

Navigating Act 250's Rules

Because the procedural aspects of Act 250 also play important roles in each of Killington Resort's projects, we briefly discuss certain rules that feature

21 *Id.*

22 *Id.*

23 Vt. Stat. Ann. tit. 10, §6086(a)(1)(E).

24 *Id.* § 6086(a)(8)(A).

prominently in each of the permit applications at issue here. As we noted at the outset, an applicant must submit an application for a project to the District Commission office for review to determine whether the proposed project satisfies the ten Act 250 criteria. However, before a proceeding takes place, decision-makers must establish who will be a party to the proceeding. Act 250 also establishes the burden that parties to a proceeding bear to satisfy the criteria, or show that certain criteria have not been met. Finally, Act 250 contains certain presumptions, so that an applicant that meets its burden may be in a position to tip the scales in its favor, thereby leaving it up to the other parties to prove that the applicant's proposed project does not satisfy the ten Act 250 criteria.

Seeking and finally obtaining party status, or "standing" as it is known in most legal contexts, under Act 250 is as critical to an individual or group as a lift ticket is to skiers and boarders. Party status may be obtained by "right" or "petition," but status is restricted in the first instance to those individuals or entities having "issues in which [they have] demonstrated an interest."[25] Party status by "right" is statutorily granted to the applicant, landowner, local municipality, adjoining landowners, and other parties demonstrating a specific interest directly affected by the Act 250 proceeding.[26] Party status by "petition" is granted to those individuals and entities not meeting the statutory requirements for parties by right,[27] but only if the Act 250 decision-makers determine that their involvement will help build a better basis for a decision. This discretionary determination is likely to depend on "the public's general understanding of the matters at issue" and whether the

25 Envtl. Bd. Rule 14(D). With respect to an adjoining landowner, for example, "if a project will degrade water quality in a nearby stream, but a neighbor has no property interest in that stream and the water will not run onto her land, then she cannot participate in the discussion of that effect as an adjoiner." Argentine, *supra* note 13, at 37.

26 Envtl. Bd. Rule 14(A). With respect to adjoining landowners and other parties with a specific interest, new Board rules have raised the bar requiring that such landowners and parties be directly affected by the "proceeding" whereas the former rules required only an effect as a result of the "development." *Id.* This change may reduce the number of parties eligible to participate in Act 250 proceedings and ultimately prevent important information concerning proposed development projects from coming before Act 250 decision-makers.

27 For example, "[t]he Vermont Natural Resources Council has received party status [by petition] on water quality issues in several cases because of its stated purpose of protecting Vermont's environment." *See* Argentine, *supra* note 13 at 40. To acquire petition party status, however, an individual or entity (petitioner) must provide the following: (1) a "detailed statement of the petitioner's interest in the proceeding" based on the appropriate Act 250 criteria; (2) an overview of the organization if an organization is petitioning for party status; (3) the reasons why the petitioner should be granted party status; (4) for adjoining property owners, a map of the location of the adjoining property in relation to the proposed project; and (5) for non-adjoining property owners, a map of the petitioner's location in relation to the proposed project and the project's potential effect of said location. Envtl. Bd. Rule 14(B).

decision-makers already have expertise in the relevant field.[28] Once party status is granted, parties must limit their involvement to providing "personal observations, knowledge, or experience and information" related to the particular substantive Act 250 criterion for which party status has been granted.[29]

Although parties by right and petition presumably have specialized insight or expertise on proposed development projects, Act 250 decision-makers also have the option to grant party status to "non-party" participants who can "materially assist in the review of the application."[30] In this way, "non-party" participants are similar to another legal actor—the *amicus curiae* (friend of the court)—who is allowed to participate but does not have all the rights or responsibilities of parties and whose role is more limited. Once such participation is granted, these "non-party" participants are allowed to file memoranda, offer "proposed findings of fact and conclusions of law," and provide arguments on legal issues.[31] This expertise, however, may be subject to close scrutiny by others involved with the proceeding, who may voice their objections to the request for party status.

The concept of the "burden of proof" is known to just about anyone who has ever read a John Grisham novel or watched *12 Angry Men*, or *Law and Order*. In the context of Act 250, there are two burdens, but much less drama: the burden of production (or going forward) and the burden of proof (or persuasion). The burden of production is simple in Act 250 proceedings: if an applicant seeks a permit, the

28 *See* Argentine, *supra* note 13, at 41. Public knowledge and Board expertise grows with each case and sometimes limits subsequent participation by past hearing participants. In Pico Peak Ski Resort, Inc., #1R0265-12-EB (1995), the Conservation Law Foundation was denied party status concerning snowmaking and stream flow issues although it had been granted such status for a similar case. The Board held that the public awareness of the issues had increased since the previous case, and that the Board now had enough experience that it no longer required assistance from the Conservation Law Foundation. *Id.*

29 Robert F. Gruenig, *Killington Mountain and Act 250: An Eco-Legal Perspective*, 26 Vt. L. Rev. 550 (2002) (citing Cindy Corlett Argentine, Vermont Act 250 Handbook, A Guide To State And Regional Land Use Regulation 5 (2d ed. 1998)). The Environmental Board Rules also encourage "administrative efficiency" by having parties granted status statutorily or by permission join together on issues related to representation, evidence or other related matters. Envtl. Bd. Rule 14(D). Such a practice runs the risk of diluting a party's claim and its proffered expertise at the expense of uniformity among all of the pertinent parties involved with an Act 250 proceeding. If party status is denied, individuals and entities must appeal within 15 days of their respective denial or they will be forever barred from proceedings related to the matter in question. Envtl. Bd. Rule 31.

30 Envtl. Bd. Rule 14(E). Act 250 decision-makers must provide the following information in affirming the use of such participants: (1) description of information or argument that the party will provide in the proceeding; (2) the "desired scope of participation"; and (3) the reasons why the party's participation will be helpful to Act 250 decision-makers. *Id.*

31 *Id.* Act 250 decision-makers may use their discretion in expanding the role of the party's participation to include "provision of testimony, filing of evidence or cross-exam of witnesses." *Id.*

applicant must provide enough information to the District Commission to allow it to make a finding under each criterion.

The burden of proof in Act 250 proceedings is more complicated, because it varies from criterion to criterion, and even then the facts of the proceeding may change it yet again. For instance, under criteria 1, 2, 3, 4, 9(B)–9(L), and 10, the *applicant* bears the burden of proof—it must persuade the Commission that the project satisfies the criteria and is entitled to a permit. For criteria 5, 6, 7, and 8, the burden shifts: once the applicant has met its burden of production by presenting evidence relating to each of the criteria, it is up to *opposing parties* to prove that the proposed project does *not* meet the criteria. In those instances, it becomes apparent why eliminating opposing parties, or curtailing their ability to introduce evidence relevant to these criteria, is a powerful tactic. In the absence of opposition, an application will satisfy those criteria so long as the applicant has met the burden of production. Criterion 9(A) is even more complicated, because the actions taken by the municipality in which the project is located dictates whether the burden of proof shifts. Additionally, the District Commissioners have the authority to probe the evidence and make inquiries to determine that the project satisfies the criteria, but the exercise of this authority is discretionary and the Commissioners are entitled to rely on the information presented by an applicant. Because heightened scrutiny is not required, the review conducted by one Commission in connection with one application may differ from that conducted by another Commission in connection with a different application. This possibility illustrates the point that the human element of Act 250 and the manner in which decision-makers conduct reviews is important.

The last of the seemingly arcane, yet relevant, legal concepts applicable to the Killington Resort case study is the rebuttable presumption.[32] A rebuttable presumption comes into play when state and federal agencies have issued other permits required for a project and it can be seen operating in the context of the Resort Village proposal discussed in Chapter 17. In some cases, presenting the District Commission with evidence that another state or federal agency has issued a permit can fulfill the applicant's burden of production under one of the Act 250 criteria. Those same permits may also satisfy the applicant's burden of proof, provided that there is no contrary evidence. The mere existence of another permit, however, does not foreclose opposing parties from challenging the agency approval and arguing that the project will have an undue adverse effect. It does, however, give the project a regulatory head start—the presumption of success—if the applicant submits permits from other agencies as part of its Act 250 application.

The District Commission ideally should base its decision on all material facts concerning how a proposal will affect the surroundings. Under the rules governing the burdens of production and proof, the applicant, state agencies, and other parties will provide information and possibly testimony and exhibits.[33] As explained

32 Vt. Stat. Ann. tit. 10 § 6086(d); Envtl. Bd. R. 19.

33 *See* Vermont Natural Resources Board, http://www.nrb.state.vt.us (last visited June 14, 2007).

above, however, the District Commission can expand this pool of facts by granting non-party status to other individuals or entities. Whether by statutory right or by petition, these rules can provide for potentially important contributions from stakeholders who are concerned about environmental impacts (or other aspects of affected community, such as schools or the local infrastructure), who oppose all or some aspect of a project, or who otherwise provide information overlooked or not presented by the developer. Killington's attempts to expand the Resort into the area known as Parker's Gore East were met with opposition from local and state environmental groups who used the rules to introduce new information and significantly change the course of events.

Parker's Gore East and Act 250

Since at least the 1960s, the operators of Killington Resort have been withdrawing water from local streams, rivers and ponds to make artificial snow. Because Killington Resort is largely dependent upon artificial snow, adverse weather conditions and inadequate existing water supplies prompted Killington Resort's owners to seek out new water sources in the 1980s. S-K-I set its sights on Madden Brook in an area near Killington Resort known as Parker's Gore East as the solution to its snowmaking water demands. (See Figure 16.1).

Parker's Gore East, located in the Town of Mendon, lies along the spine of the Green Mountains and is a mostly forested area of approximately 1,500 acres located at elevations between 2,100 and 3,900 feet. The forest, interspersed with natural wetlands, transitions from a hardwood forest of beech, birch, and maple trees at lower elevations, to a mixed forest of beech and spruce-fir trees at mid-level elevations, to spruce-fir trees near the summit. It provides a link between bear habitat on federal Green Mountain National Forest land to the north and the Coolidge State Forest to the south. In addition, Parker's Gore East is situated within a 70 square mile area that has been identified by the Vermont Agency of Natural Resources (ANR) as optimal black bear habitat. Because black bears and their needs proved to be pivotal to the analysis and ultimate denial of the development proposal for Parker's Gore East, we take a moment to provide some background on black bears.[34]

Black bears have large home ranges and need extensive tracts of remote, intact habitat. They are wary of humans and generally avoid roads, choosing instead to travel through forested areas that provide cover. Fragmentation of black bear habitat, like that located in Parker's Gore East, by trails, logging clear cuts, and roads could prevent bears from reaching other necessary areas of their ranges, which in turn can endanger essential activities such as feeding and breeding.

34 The discussion below draws on material contained in the Vermont Envtl. Bd., Findings of Fact, Conclusions of Law, and Order, Land Use Permits #1R0593-1-EB and #1R0584-EB-1 (May 11, 1989) (discussing the relationship of black bears to beech forests and wetlands).

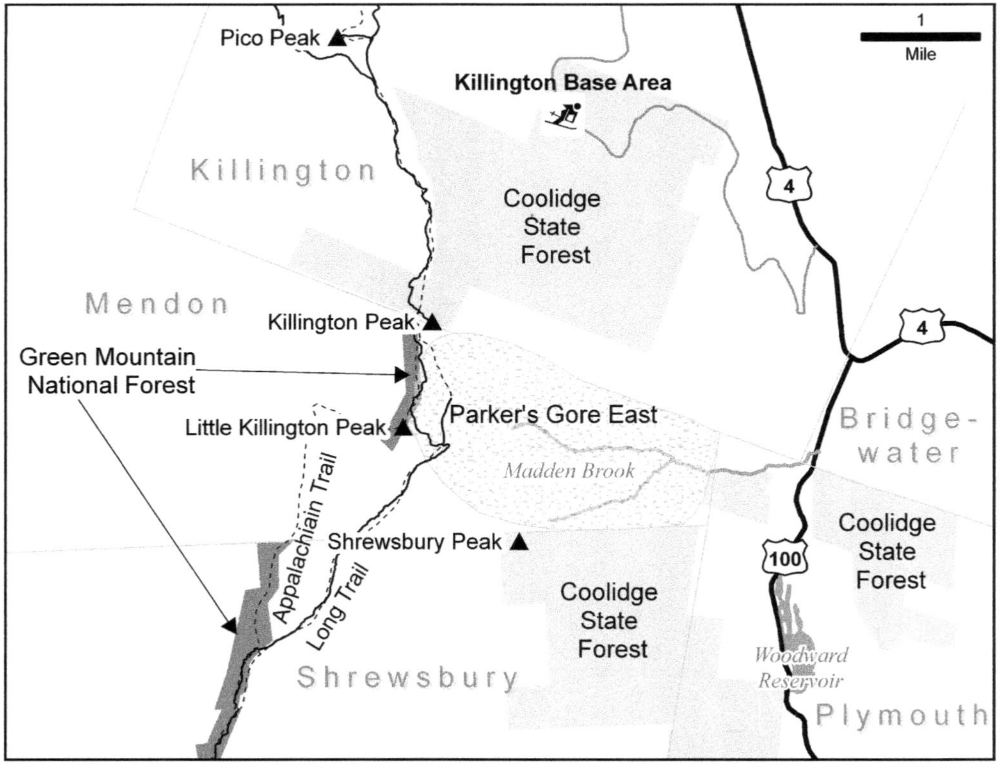

Figure 16.1 Killington Resort and Surrounding Area, 1985

Data Sources: Appalachian Trail Conference; David Capen; ESRI; Green Mountain Club; VT Center for Geographic Information, Inc.; Tele Atlas North America, Inc.

Black bears are primarily vegetarians, feeding on grasses and other emergent vegetation in early spring found most often in and around wetlands. During the spring, when bears emerge, weak and emaciated from their dens, they rely heavily on the nearby wetlands for the nourishing vegetation they provide. Spring wetland vegetation is also the primary source of food for yearling cubs, which cannot store fat reserves as large as adults and thus are entirely reliant on this food source. After gaining strength in the summer, black bears feed on "soft mast," consisting of fruits like berries, cherries, and apples. In the late summer and early fall, they prepare to breed and then hibernate. They build up their fat reserves, on which they rely from mid-November through mid-April, by eating "hard mast" that almost exclusively consists of beechnuts. Female black bears that do not have sufficient fat reserves by winter often cannot produce cubs, or produce weak or fewer cubs; therefore, the availability of hard mast is crucial to the survival of black bears.

The presence of vast tracts of mature beech trees makes Parker's Gore East optimal black bear habitat. Beech trees do not produce beechnuts, however, until they are approximately 50 years old. Even then, all mature beech trees do not produce nuts, and those that do produce beechnuts do not necessarily produce them every year. Therefore, concentrated stands of mature beech are highly valuable to black bears, which come to rely on a particular stand of trees because of its reliability and may not readily shift to other sources, even when their own survival is in jeopardy.

As of 1986, Killington Resort operated in part on land in the Coolidge State Forest that it leased from the State of Vermont, but it also owned land in the adjacent Parker's Gore East, where it also leased land owned by International Paper Realty Corporation. That year S-K-I proposed to dam Madden Brook and create Madden Pond in Parker's Gore East. Due to the number of acres the proposed project would involve, the application triggered Act 250 review. When S-K-I filed its 1986 Act 250 application for the Madden Pond project, which appeared to relate only to the snowmaking pond project, residents and the Town of Mendon were already aware of rumored development plans for additional trails in the area because S-K-I had already unsuccessfully approached the Town of Mendon about changing the Mendon Town Plan to allow for ski-related development in Parker's Gore East. Because of this history, S-K-I's snowmaking proposal fueled understandable suspicion in the local community that S-K-I had more in store for Parker's Gore East than simply the creation of Madden Pond.

After hearing arguments that the Madden Pond project application was incomplete because it was actually part of a larger plan to develop Parker's Gore East, the District Commission denied the permit application in 1987. The District Commission agreed that the pond project was part of a larger plan not adequately described in the application, and thus S-K-I did not meet its burden to produce evidence that the larger project satisfied the ten Act 250 criteria. The District Commission also found that the "construction and operation of the pond would destroy or significantly imperil the necessary habitat of black bear" under criterion 8(A), because of the impact the project would have on the bear travel corridors and the beech tree stands.[35] S-K-I appealed these findings to the Environmental Board, arguing that the District Commission erred in its finding regarding the scope of the project, as well as the adverse finding regarding wildlife habitat.

While this debate over Madden Pond raged, S-K-I and a private logger had separately applied for a different Act 250 permit to harvest timber from Parker's Gore East land owned by S-K-I and lying at an elevation in excess of 2,500 feet. Due to the elevation of the land involved, the project triggered Act 250 review. The District Commission denied the logging application, citing criterion 8(A) (necessary wildlife habitat), because "it found that the logging would significantly imperil necessary black bear habitat."[36] Also implicated were the aesthetics of the area and the impact on the Appalachian Trail under criterion 8, which the District Commission found would need to be protected through the imposition of conditions in the permit, if one were to issue.[37] S-K-I appealed these findings to the Environmental Board.

The Board first found that Madden Pond, as a snowmaking source, would serve existing trails and was not necessarily being constructed for future development. Therefore, it did not consider as relevant to the proceedings other components of a possible larger development project proposed at Parker's Gore and their impacts. The Board acknowledged that phased reviews were not uncommon, but that a review of future applications for development in Parker's Gore East should consider the cumulative impacts of the project in its entirety, including the impacts of damming the pond.[38] There is nothing in the text of Act 250, however, that would require the District Commission when reviewing a future application to consider the cumulative impacts. Because there is nothing in the text that requires this type of review, and the Board's acknowledgment is not binding on future applications, it is possible that any party or non-party seeking to make a cumulative impacts argument would be unable to do so unless they could make the argument under one of the individual Act 250 criterion.

The Board then consolidated the remaining issues on appeal from the Madden Pond decision and the logging decision, ranging from who could participate in the appeal to what issues they could raise. These issues were important to the outcome of the proceedings, because they determined who could present evidence to the Board and what that evidence might look like. The Board also heard arguments about what "necessary wildlife habitat" is and whether the proposed projects would destroy or imperil necessary habitat under Act 250's criterion 8(A).[39] Because

35 *See* Vermont Envtl. Bd., Findings of Fact, Conclusions of Law, and Order, Land Use Permits #1R0593-1-EB and #1R0584-EB-1, at 4 (May 11, 1989).

36 *See id.*

37 *See id.*

38 Vermont Envtl. Bd., Findings of Fact, Conclusions of Law, and Order, Land Use Permit #1R0584-EB (Apr. 19, 1988).

39 Vermont Envtl. Bd., Findings of Fact, Conclusions of Law, and Order, Land Use Permits #1R0593-1-EB and #1R0584-EB-1 (May 11, 1989).

appeals to the Board were *de novo*, meaning the Board was not confined to the evidence submitted to the District Commission or the record created during the lower proceeding, new parties and new information were allowed.

At this point, it is also important to note two things about the Board's proceedings on the Madden Pond application. First, the Shrewsbury Land Trust (which later adopted the name Friends of Parker's Gore), led by a local resident, Nancy Bell, who became an important stakeholder in the debate about Killington Resort's expansion by educating herself about the fragility of black bear habitat and the economics of ski resorts,[40] did not participate in the District Commission proceeding regarding Madden Pond. However, under the Board rules in effect at that time, the Shrewsbury Land Trust petitioned for and was granted party status in the appeal. S-K-I actively challenged the participation of the Shrewsbury Land Trust, arguably in an effort to keep new information out of the proceeding. Second, the Agency of Natural Resources (ANR) had, during the District Commission proceeding, taken the position that damming Madden Brook to create Madden Pond would have no undue adverse impact on necessary wildlife habitat. The ANR later changed its position on appeal, and S-K-I attempted to prevent the Board from considering any new evidence that was contrary to the ANR's earlier position.

The participation of the Shrewsbury Land Trust and the ANR in the Environmental Board proceedings had a decisive effect on the Board's analysis of the applications for development in Parker's Gore, and arguably led to a more thorough analysis. During the evidentiary phase of the Board's review, the ANR, the Town of Shrewsbury, the Shrewsbury Planning Commission, and the Shrewsbury Land Trust submitted evidence for the first time to the Board for its consideration of necessary wildlife habitat under criterion 8(A). The evidence addressed not only of the importance of the beech trees, but also the significance of the wetland as a source of spring food to black bears emerging from hibernation. The prior proceedings before the District Commission made no mention of the wetland or the effect that damming Madden Brook might have on the wetland. S-K-I objected to the admission of this evidence about the wetland on a number of procedural grounds: that the issue of the wetland as bear habitat had not been raised before the District Commission; and that the wetland issue was not included in S-K-I's notice of appeal and was therefore not properly the subject of an appeal (recall that S-K-I appealed the District Commission's findings, not the other parties, so S-K-I had framed the issues for the Board's consideration on appeal). S-K-I attempted to confine any evidence of analysis of the wetlands to the parameters of criterion 1(G) governing wetlands.[41] By limiting the Board's review

40 Isham interview with Nancy Bell (Feb. 9, 2004).

41 The text of criterion 1(G) is as follows:

> (G) Wetlands. A permit will be granted whenever it is demonstrated by the applicant, in addition to other criteria, that the development or subdivision will not violate the rules of the board, as adopted under this chapter, relating to significant wetlands. Vt. Stat. Ann. tit. 10, §6086(a)(1)(G) (2007).

of the wetland to criterion 1(G), S-K-I attempted to steer the discussion away from what constituted necessary wildlife habitat and toward a more traditional wetland analysis that would not have taken into consideration the role the wetland played in the bear's life cycle. Under S-K-I's argument then, criterion 1(G) was not before the Board; therefore, the wetland evidence should not have been allowed. The Board disagreed, finding that the issue of wetlands as bear habitat was properly considered in the appeal as part of the necessary wildlife habitat criterion (criterion 8(A)) and allowed the evidence. Thus, stakeholders who were not parties to the earlier District Commission proceedings were able to participate on appeal and raise new issues relating to necessary wildlife habitat. In response, the Board expanded the scope of its review to go beyond issues included in the notice of appeal and considered how the impact to a wetland, traditionally considered under a different criterion (criterion 1(G)), would affect wildlife habitat.

Once the Board dispensed with the applicant's procedural arguments designed to keep out information about the importance of both the beech trees and the wetlands to the bears, it reached the substantive issue regarding the meaning of "necessary wildlife habitat" under criterion 8(A). The Board recognized the bears' dependence on both the wetlands and the concentrated beech stands that were in the vicinity of Madden Pond. It also acknowledged that the proposed logging activities were likely to fragment the large bear habitat and might remove the mature, productive beech trees upon which the bears relied. The Board also noted that logging in a mature forest may expose stands of trees to increased wind speeds, because the natural windbreaks would be gone, which in turn would lead to more downed trees and thus more habitat fragmentation and loss of beech trees. In addition, both projects would involve construction activities (primarily for roads) and would reduce the amount of tree cover that is essential for bear movement from one area to another. In light of the evidence, the Board found that both projects would destroy or significantly imperil necessary black bear habitat.

The Board reached this conclusion by considering how the proposed projects would collectively affect the area, and how those effects would in turn impact the black bears. Arguably, if the Board had been limited to considering testimony about the wetland only under the wetland criterion (criterion 1(G)) and not as a component of wildlife habitat, with no introduction of the ecological interrelationships between early spring wetland vegetation and its importance to bears emerging from hibernation or to yearling bears, then it may not have reached the same conclusion. Similarly, if S-K-I had successfully kept out all evidence regarding the wetland, under the theory that it had not been raised below and was not an issue on appeal, then the Board would not have been able to draw the interrelationships between the wetlands and the bears.

In the case of Parker's Gore East, the result could have been different had the decision-makers taken a different tact. For example, the plenary nature of the Board's review allowed it to consider both the Madden Pond and the logging applications together and discuss cumulative impacts to the area. This broader view also allowed for a more informed review of the black bear and its habitat needs.

Additionally, the Board's interpretation of the wetland as part of habitat, instead of the wetland in isolation, allowed for a more probing consideration of habitat. Finally, the ability of Nancy Bell and the other groups to participate in the appeal before the Board, even though they had not participated at the Commission level, was critical and was a function of the rules in place at the time. The participation rules have since changed, as discussed in more detail in Chapter 18, and arguably Nancy Bell and the others would not be allowed to participate at the appellate level if they had not participated at the Commission proceedings under today's rules.

After losing appeals to the Board and the Vermont Supreme Court, the writing was on the wall about Killington's plans for Parker's Gore East. Killington's leaders changed their tactics and began negotiating with various groups for an alternative to developing Parker's Gore East. These negotiations culminated almost a decade later, in 1996, with an agreement that would allow S-K-I's successor—American Skiing Company (ASC)—to proceed relatively unimpeded in its plan to expand its trails and snowmaking capacity, as well as to build its Resort Village in phases.

The Memorandum of Agreement

According to Carl Spangler, then-Vice President of Planning and Development at Killington Resort, after ASC acquired Killington Resort from S-K-I, it worked extensively with environmental groups and other stakeholders prior to filing each of the three major Act 250 applications to put ASC in a position to receive its permits.[42] ASC's first major step in acquiring these permits was the execution of a Memorandum of Agreement. On July 2, 1996, ASC, the ANR as the relevant state agency, and the Farm and Wilderness Foundation, Inc.[43] entered into a Memorandum of Agreement (Agreement).[44] The signed Agreement is a conceptual agreement among the parties and covers three separate areas: water, land and "other."[45]

Under the terms of the Agreement, ASC agreed to bring its water withdrawals for snowmaking into compliance with state water quality standards regarding stream flows. In exchange for this compliance, which is arguably not much of a concession because ASC was merely agreeing to comply with the law, the parties supported ASC's use of the Woodward Reservoir as a new water supply. In

42 Isham interview with Carl Spangler, V. P. Planning and Development, American Skiing Co. (Mar. 8, 2002).

43 See Chapter 17 of this case study for a discussion of the Woodward Reservoir project and the role played by Farm and Wilderness. Farm and Wilderness Camps is an association of six Quaker summer camps, located on land bordering Woodward Reservoir. Isham interview with Jean Rosenburg, Farm and Wilderness Camps (Apr. 1, 2001).

44 Memorandum of Agreement (1996) (on file with author) [hereinafter (MOA 1996)]. The MOA 1996 replaced an earlier agreement between S-K-I and the ANR. *Id.*

45 *Id.*

exchange for money, Farm and Wilderness (the owners of the site on which ASC would construct its water withdrawal infrastructure) granted to ASC an easement over and across Farm and Wilderness land adjacent to the Woodward Reservoir to access the reservoir and construct the necessary improvements to withdraw water.

With respect to land issues, the parties (principally the ANR and ASC) agreed that a growth center concept, "where development is concentrated and large areas of open space protected from future development for conservation purposes," should direct the future planning process at Killington Resort.[46] To effectuate this process, ASC agreed to exchange 3,000 acres of high elevation land in Parker's Gore East for 1,070 acres of land lying below 2,500 feet owned by the State of Vermont as part of the Coolidge State Forest. (See Figure 16.3.) The State of Vermont further agreed to transfer development rights on the newly acquired high elevation land in Parker's Gore East to a third party for protection in perpetuity. ASC also agreed to contribute $375,000 to the acquisition of additional conservation lands to protect the "western bear corridor."[47] In exchange for the protection of bear habitat, the ANR agreed to support future development of the lower elevation lands in the newly identified growth center and specifically agreed to "not oppose any future development within the growth center in connection with necessary wildlife habitat of black bears,"[48] which would allow portions of the Interconnect to proceed without a recurrence of the black bear issues with which Killington struggled at Parker's Gore East. In addition, the parties agreed on the necessity of a 900-acre scenic and wildlife conservation easement and forest management plan to protect forest land in the city of Rutland.[49] ASC agreed to limit its annual use of the only existing ski trail[50] near Parker's Gore East to December 1 through April 1 during bear hibernation and, along with the ANR, developed a plan to restrict access to Parker's Gore East over the trail for the rest of the year.[51]

The last section of the Agreement, titled "other," required the signatories to solicit support for the land swap from the groups that had been on the periphery

46 *Id.* at II.

47 Isham interview with Carl Spangler, V. P. Planning and Development, American Skiing Co. (Mar. 8, 2002); *see also* MOA 1996, *supra* note 44, at II.B. Bear corridors are stretches of land that connect two important areas. They are generally contiguous and remote forestland, frequently traveled by bear. They contain habitat critical to bear survival and reproduction. *See* Charles W. Johnson, The Nature of Vermont 121–122 (1998).

48 MOA 1996, *supra* note 44, at II.D.

49 *Id.* Rutland, the second largest city in Vermont, next to Burlington, is located several miles west of Killington Resort. As of 2002, Rutland City had a population of 17,292 and an average annual wage of $28,420. Center for Rural Studies, Information by Town, Rutland County, http://maps.vcgi.org/indicators/cfhome/town_profile.cfm?Call_Program=INDICATORS&ProfileTown=Rutland+City (last visited June 14, 2007).

50 Juggernaut trail, one of the older trails at Killington, winds down near the edges of Parker's Gore. Killington Trail Map, *available at* http://www.killington.com/images/trailmap/Sunrise_final.jpg (last visited May 14, 2007).

51 MOA 1996, *supra* note 44, at II F.

of the predecessor agreement between S-K-I and the ANR, although the land swap would ultimately require approval by the Vermont Legislature. As a result, the Conservation Law Foundation, Nancy Bell of the Friends of Parker's Gore (formerly the Shrewsbury Land Trust), the Green Mountain Club, and the Appalachian Trail Club were asked to indicate, by signature, that they supported the Agreement, and that they promised to work to resolve outstanding issues as the Killington Resort development process progressed.[52] While the Interconnect was not explicitly covered by the Agreement, the issues addressed in the Agreement and the concessions made by the parties and to the signatories acknowledging their approval, had an impact on the Interconnect proceeding, which is discussed in more detail in Chapter 17.

Once the Agreement was in place, and with legislative approval and the support of then-Governor Howard Dean, ASC completed the land swap with the State of Vermont in December 1997.[53] (See Figure 16.2). As will be discussed in more detail in Chapter 17, Killington sought permits from the local, state, and federal governments to connect the ski trails at Killington Mountain to the trails at Pico Mountain with an interconnect chairlift, to add snowmaking capacity through the installation of a water withdrawal system at Woodward Reservoir, and to make various on-mountain trail improvements and build a resort village at the base of Killington Peak.

The events that started with Parker's Gore and ended with the Agreement illustrate how the stakeholders can use the Act 250 review process as leverage. During the Parker's Gore East phase, opponents of the project used Act 250 to influence the decision-makers and ultimately preserve bear habitat. The stakeholders became familiar with one another and more adept at participating in Act 250. Arguably, in recognition of the effectiveness of the various environmental and conservation groups, S-K-I, and later its successor ASC, were motivated to bring the various stakeholders to the table early to get their input and reach an agreement to avoid the type of protracted legal battles that had ended badly for S-K-I at Parker's Gore East.

In the case of side agreements, like the Agreement, whether an ecosystem perspective will infuse the process depends in large measure on the parties invited

52 MOA 1996, *supra* note 44, at III. The copy of the MOA on file in the District Commission #1 office indicates that only Nancy Bell, the Conservation Law Foundation, Green Mountain Club, and Appalachian Trail Club signed to indicate support. Signature spaces for the Vermont Natural Resources Council, Rutland, National Park Service and Sierra Club are blank.

53 *Bear Habitat Saved in Ski Resort Swap*, Christian Sci. Monitor, Jan. 21, 1998, http://csmonitor.com/durable/1998/01/21/us/us.8.html (last visited June 2, 2007); *see also* Killington, Ltd. v. State of Vt. & Town of Mendon, 164 Vt. 253, 668 A.2d 1278 (1995) (upholding the District Commission's decision to limit Killington's use of the land in Parker's Gore for snowmaking). *See also* Isham interview with Carl Spangler, V. P. Planning and Development, American Skiing Co. (Mar. 8, 2002). See Figure 16.3 for a depiction of the Killington Resort area after the completion of the land swap contemplated by the MOA.

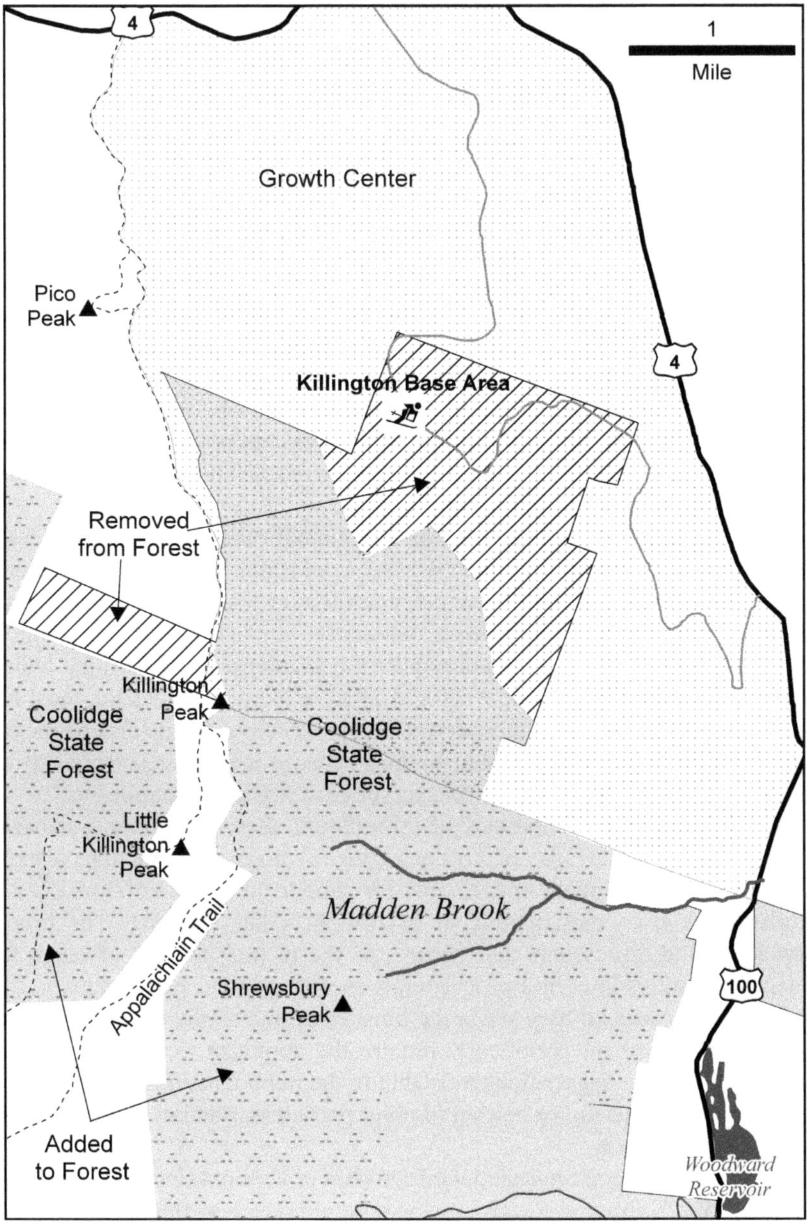

Figure 16.2 Killington Resort and Surrounding Area, 1997

Note: This map shows the impact of the 1996 Agreement on the boundaries of the Coolidge State Forest and the identification of the growth center for Killington Resort.

Data Sources: Appalachian Trail Conference; David Capen; ESRI; VT Center for Geographic Information, Inc.; Tele Atlas North America, Inc.

to the negotiating table. In any context (individual or group participation in a permitting process, hearing, or other negotiation), the cost of compiling, preparing, or analyzing information from an ecosystems perspective may be prohibitive. It is arguably for this reason that parties to negotiations or proceedings focus on single-medium studies, and it is one of several reasons why ecologists use surrogates, such as indicator or keystone species, for measuring ecosystem health and function. The timing of these negotiations also plays a role, because often negotiations occur at preliminary stages before much data are known. In these instances, it is less likely that parties can fully or intelligently discuss impacts on the ecosystem, because those impacts are simply unknown. For example, in the case of Killington, the negotiations occurred before Killington Resort applied for any Act 250 permits for the three projects discussed in Chapter 17. While it is the case that several groups had been active on the Parker's Gore East issues since the 1980s, without having an application that identified the project, its scope, its potential impact, and its location, it is possible that an agreement could be reached that makes later inquiry, when the facts are better known, more difficult.

One possibility is that the parties can negotiate for the inclusion of ecosystem studies, monitoring or conditions in the absence of actual information. To interject an ecosystem perspective in this manner requires a level of sophistication, because it is insufficient to simply require a cumulative impacts study examining the ecological interrelationships but not require the developer to do anything with the information. While this type of front-end process likely provides the most hope for coloring future activity with an ecosystem perspective, it may also be the most difficult due to its prospective nature—and because it has the potential to strip away some of the certainty the permitting process provides to applicants.

In addition to cost and the lack of information, there is another drawback to parties with an ecosystem perspective engaging in informal negotiations to extract conditions from developers in exchange for support in later formal proceedings or forbearance from participating as a party in a later hearing. The process, information, and discussions that occur "off the record" are out of reach from the decision-makers in permit proceedings, as well as other participants in those proceedings, because all they see is the finished product—the agreement. Unless parties to an agreement specifically require the applicant to make information generated during the negotiations available to the public, that information, which might otherwise be useful or helpful to other participants and decision-makers, is essentially locked away.

The rise of grassroots environmental activism in Vermont since the mid-1980s[54] guaranteed that Killington Resort's owners would face a significant challenge to

54 *See* Savage et al., *The Greening of Social Capital: An Examination of Land-Based Groups in Two Vermont Counties*, 70 Rural Sociology 1 (2005); and Savage et al., *How Do Local Environmental Groups Create Social Capital and Affect Environmental Policy? Empirical and Case Study Evidence from Vermont*, 19 Society and Natural Resources 10 (2006).

their desire for expansion. Although some have criticized the inclusion of citizen participation under Act 250,[55] such participation provides valuable oversight of proposed development projects and their likely effects on Vermont's ecology. Chapter 17 further illustrates the key role that environmental groups and other stakeholders played in trying to introduce an ecosystem perspective into the review of Killington's expansion proposals under Act 250, within the confines of the 1996 Agreement.

---

55 Unsubstantiated claims have been made about the cost and delay caused by citizen participation. Vt. Natural Resources Council, *supra* note 10, at 1. Most delays, however, can be attributed to the: (1) size and experience of the program staff; (2) application numbers; (3) complex nature and amount of material to be reviewed; (4) application completeness; (5) issuance of other agency permits which must precede the Act 250 permit decision; and (6) applicant's response time in providing additional information after a hearing. *Id.* at 14. Notwithstanding the questionable validity of these concerns, the changes to Act 250 that became effective in 2005 make significant changes to party status under Act 250.

Chapter 17
Expansion in the Wake of Parker's Gore East: The Interconnect, the Woodward Reservoir, and the Resort Village

The execution of the Memorandum of Agreement in 1996 (Agreement) and the resulting land swap discussed in Chapter 16 were important first steps in Killington Resort's expansion strategy. American Skiing Company's (ASC) next step was to file the Act 250 applications for the Interconnect, Woodward Reservoir, and the Resort Village.

The Interconnect Project and the Effect of Prior Agreements on Act 250

The Interconnect project showcases how prior agreements among stakeholders can affect the Act 250 permit process. First, the Agreement entered into by ASC, Farm and Wilderness, and the Vermont Agency of Natural Resources (ANR), which received support from the other groups that participated in the negotiations leading up to the Agreement, influenced which parties participated in the proceeding. Second, the Agreement affected the roles of those parties participating in the Act 250 proceedings by narrowing the focus to subject matter that was not covered by the Agreement.

Through the proposed Interconnect, Killington sought to create a corridor in which skiers could access Killington Resort's trail network from Pico and vice versa.[1] Conceptually, stakeholders had known about the Interconnect project for nearly a decade before ASC filed its Act 250 permit application with the District Commission on July 22, 1997. The application described the project as consisting of four chairlifts and 110 acres of ski trails with snowmaking and firefighting facilities, and a mid-mountain restaurant.[2]

Initially, representatives of local environmental groups and state-level groups were apprehensive about the Interconnect's potential impact on high elevation

---

1 *In re* Killington, Ltd., et al., No. 1R0813-2, Findings of Fact, Conclusion of Law and Order, at 1 (Vt. Dist. Envtl. Comm'n #1, Nov. 24, 1997) [hereinafter Interconnect Permit Decision].

2 At the same time, ASC sought to amend three existing permits, relating to the deadline to construct a previously approved parking lot, the deadline to decommission 51.5 acres of snowmaking, and the approval of converting a previously approved wastewater pipeline corridor route to ski trails with snowmaking facilities. *Id.*

ecosystems. As noted in the preceding chapter, the Agreement addressed bear habitat, snowmaking water supplies, and the areas in which future growth should occur. As a result, the several groups that had historically been opposed to the Interconnect project on those grounds prior to the Agreement (for example, the Conservation Law Foundation, the Vermont Natural Resources Council, and the Friends of Parker's Gore) did not seek party status from the District Commission when Killington Resort finally submitted its Interconnect Act 250 application.[3]

The Agreement, however, did not cover all issues raised in the Interconnect project proceeding, leaving the ANR, as a statutory party to all Act 250 proceedings, to play an important role in the remaining issues in the Interconnect proceeding. The ANR is also very often in the position to review other permit applications and supporting information, which arguably puts the agency in the best position to infuse Act 250 with an ecosystem perspective. The ANR's participation brought a modest ecosystem approach to the Interconnect proceeding and ultimately affected the conditions in ASC's permit with respect to criterion 8(A), governing wildlife habitat.

The potential impact on the Appalachian and Long Trails (see Figure 16.3) was cause for concern for the National Park Service, the Appalachian Trail Conference, and the Green Mountain Club. These three parties had been working on Appalachian Trail protection issues for several years, and trail protection issues had been raised and partially addressed in the Agreement. The District Commission granted statutory party status to the National Park Service due to its ownership of land along the Appalachian Trail. In addition to the statutory parties, the District Commission granted party status to the Appalachian Trail Conference and the Green Mountain Club. All three entities participated in the proceeding solely for the purpose of protecting the historic and aesthetic values of the trails under criteria 8 and 9K.[4] In a process that paralleled the negotiations surrounding the Agreement, ASC, the Appalachian Trail Conference, the Green Mountain Club, and the National Park Service had negotiated a conservation easement protecting the trails, a draft of which they introduced into the proceedings and ultimately became a condition of the permit.

The Agreement not only affected the parties who participated in the Interconnect Act 250 proceeding and the subject of their focus, but it also heavily influenced the District Commission's findings about the impact of the Interconnect on bear habitat under criterion 8(A). The ANR and the District Commission deemed the black bear habitat protections that would result from the Agreement, including the anticipated land swap, to be sufficient to mitigate impacts of future development in the area identified in the Agreement as the growth center. The Interconnect project was located in the growth center area, and as a result no additional bear habitat protection was required. The District Commission incorporated into the Interconnect permit the terms of the Agreement as conditions precedent that must

3 *Id.* at 2.

4 *Id.*

be completed or satisfied prior to commencement of any Interconnect project construction. Therefore, if the entire deal outlined in the Agreement had fallen apart and the Vermont Legislature had not approved the land swap in 1997, then ASC's permit would have been void.

As noted earlier, not all habitat issues under criterion 8(A), however, were determined primarily by the Agreement. Perhaps unexpectedly, the endangered and threatened species studies performed by ASC to meet its burden of proof under Act 250, and reviewed by the ANR, revealed the presence of Bicknell's thrush habitat (a species of special concern) and squashberry (a state threatened-plant species). These species became a focal point for the District Commission. As a result of the information submitted by ASC and the positions taken by the ANR during the proceeding, the District Commission ultimately took a modest ecosystem perspective. The analysis led to several conditions in ASC's permit, ongoing responsibilities, and continuing District Commission jurisdiction.

After finding that the Interconnect's proposed trails, which were wider than the existing trails, would adversely fragment the habitat of Bicknell's thrush, the District Commission limited trail width. It also limited construction activities to mid July through early October so as not to interfere with breeding and rearing activities. Because the District Commission found that crows and jays are attracted to trash, and those birds depredate on Bicknell's thrush nests, the District Commission also required that ASC utilize wildlife-proof trash receptacles during construction periods to reduce food waste that might attract crows and jays. With respect to squashberry, the District Commission conditioned the permit on the incorporation of mitigation measures to protect the habitat as the construction of the project proceeded. Finally, the District Commission required ASC to prepare and present to the District Commission a proposal for a study to evaluate the effects of ski trail construction on Bicknell's thrush and other high-elevation birds.[5] The permit stated that the study proposal was to be submitted to the District Commission by March 1, 1998, and the District Commission reserved the right to reopen the proceedings and impose new conditions if necessary to ensure compliance with the permit condition. These findings reveal an ecosystem perspective, because they take into consideration the interconnectedness of trail width and habitat fragmentation, and the connection between increased human contact and trash generation and nest predation.

The District Commission also imposed conditions relating to other criteria that could allow it, in the future, to develop a better understanding of and ability to monitor the ecological impacts of the Interconnect. For example, in considering the impact to streams under criterion 1(E), the District Commission required ASC to perform "an upland stream study to develop baseline scientific data to better understand the effects of ski area development in upland watersheds."[6] This study was not, however, a condition precedent to construction. The District Commission also retained jurisdiction under criterion 1 and reserved the right to impose

5 Interconnect Permit Decision, *supra* note 1, at 9.

6 *Id.* at 5.

additional conditions and halt construction if undue water pollution resulted. These findings and conditions also suggest a modest ecosystem perspective, because the District Commission was aware of the connections among trail construction, stream crossings, and erosion.

Thus, the District Commission's findings regarding impact on wildlife habitat and water quality evidence both the desire and the ability of District Commissioners to consider ecological interrelationships. While the interrelationships that the District Commission recognized in the case of the Interconnect are fairly limited and do not evidence the greater understanding of the interdependencies discussed by the ecologists in the earlier chapters of this book, it is a good start. Further, the fact that the District Commission was willing to retain jurisdiction under certain criteria to ensure compliance as construction progresses or even after the project is completed is a positive step.

The weakness of this approach, however, is the fact that conditions and retained jurisdiction are only effective if projects are monitored and noncompliance is enforced. If the District Commission requires the applicant to conduct a study, for instance, then the District Commission must be willing to ensure that the study is completed and that it provides useful information, and willing to enforce failures to satisfy conditions. It is with respect to this set of responsibilities that there is significant room for improvement.

In making findings about the potential effects on bird habitat, for example, the District Commission required the applicant to prepare a study proposal by March 1, 1998. On March 10, 1998, Killington requested that the District Commission either eliminate the requirement, under the theory that the completed land swap mitigated any effect on high-elevation avian species, or extend the deadline. The ANR weighed in and informed the District Commission that the Agreement and completed land swap provided mitigation for bear habitat only, not high-elevation birds. Therefore, ASC only received an extension to complete the study proposal. The District Commission records are inconclusive as to whether ASC ever completed and submitted the study proposal or the actual study that would have logically followed from any proposal. In addition, the District Commission's requirement did not expressly require ASC to use the proposal or any resultant study as a guide to address future impacts on the ecosystem. The District Commission retained jurisdiction over the Act 250 permit under criterion 8(A), but the onus then falls on the Commission to require additional hearings or evidence. In the absence of any mandatory inspections or reporting requirements, it is debatable whether the retention of jurisdiction is meaningful. Thus, while a study may have had the potential to provide additional information to ASC and the District Commission, and the completion of the study proposal was itself a condition of the Act 250, the inclusion of the condition with no requirement that it be satisfied or consequences for not fulfilling it arguably falls short of Act 250's stated goals to provide necessary protection and preservation of the environment.

With respect to the condition that ASC prepare an upland stream study that assessed the impact of ASC's Interconnect ski trail development on upland watersheds, the results of the study were not due to the District Commission until after the Act 250 permit had been issued. The District Commission, therefore, permitted the project before it had relevant information about the effect of the Interconnect on the watershed. While not labeled an "ecological study," many of its elements were to address the interrelationships between animal and plant species within the natural environment.[7] The criterion (criterion 1(E)) under which this study was imposed, however, only necessitates that the development project not compromise the "natural condition" of any streams.[8] Because the District Commission found in this proceeding that the Interconnect would maintain the natural condition of streams wherever feasible, it did not require Killington to assess the ecological impacts of its development activities on the current condition of the streams to arrive at any meaningful baseline for information against which later changes in the ecosystem could be measured.[9] Instead, the District Commission required the study so that immediate impacts from construction activities could be monitored—arguably a much narrower focus.

In conclusion, the Agreement changed the course of the Interconnect Act 250 proceeding. Because the Agreement addressed many of the concerns of the most outspoken opponents to Killington Resort's expansion plans by protecting bear habitat, preserving high altitude lands and other open space, and designating a growth area, many of the groups one would have expected to seek party status in later proceedings either did not seek that status or limited their participation to other issues. By agreeing to the land swap for the protection of Parker's Gore East and its black bear habitat and fragile wetlands, the ANR had essentially agreed to allow Killington's plans to construct the Interconnect and Resort Village in the growth center, and to use Woodward Reservoir for snowmaking, to proceed unimpeded. The ANR pushed back only when Killington asserted that the Agreement, which was designed to mitigate black bear habitat losses, also provided mitigation for all habitat impacts. Conservation-oriented groups that might otherwise be inclined to offer testimony and information on the ecological effects of future resort development had also agreed, in large measure, to stay out of the Act 250 process. By negotiating the Parker's Gore East land swap in advance and identifying a growth center in which future development could occur, Killington Resort was able to streamline the Act 250 process. Nowhere is the success of this approach more noticeable than in the fact that unlike the District Commission's decisions on the Woodward Reservoir project and the Resort Village proposal (discussed in later in this chapter), no party appealed the District Commission's issuance of a permit to ASC for the Interconnect. Interestingly enough, Killington has not yet constructed the Interconnect.

---

7 Interconnect Permit Decision, *supra* note 1, at 5. Killington Resort completed the upland stream study in 1998.

8 Vt. Stat. Ann. tit. 10 § 6086(a)(1)(E).

9 Interconnect Permit Decision, *supra* note 1, at 5.

The Woodward Reservoir and the Role of Other Permits in Act 250

The Woodard Reservoir project illustrates the effect of other, parallel proceedings, such as an encroachment permit, a dredging permit, and a Water Quality Certification, on an Act 250 proceeding. We conclude that the existence of the Agreement and the other proceedings influenced the manner in which the District Commission conducted the Act 250 permit proceeding, the parties that participated, and the roles that they played in the proceedings.

Additional snowmaking capacity was necessary for Killington's Interconnect project to succeed, as well as to improve conditions of existing trails. ASC had identified the Woodward Reservoir as its best source of water for snowmaking. When ASC bought Killington Resort from S-K-I, Farm and Wilderness, a local organization and the owner of property needed to access the Reservoir, watched with great interest how the new owners appeared to be willing to work with other local stakeholders to negotiate compromises, such as in the case of the Parker's Gore East dispute and the ultimate protection for black bear habitat.[10] Farm and Wilderness was initially opposed to ASC's water withdrawal plans for Woodward Reservoir. It later reassessed its position after reviewing the information prepared by ASC regarding the impact the project would have on the Reservoir.[11] Farm and Wilderness ultimately granted Killington Resort an easement over its property to access the Reservoir, in exchange for an annual payment and the promise to implement monitoring techniques for environmental protection. Once that understanding was reached, it was incorporated into the Agreement, and Farm and Wilderness no longer objected to the project—in fact, it joined in the Act 250 permit application with Killington.

The Effect of the 1996 Memorandum of Agreement

Before discussing the role of other permits in the Woodward Reservoir Act 250 proceeding, it is necessary to revisit the Agreement because it clearly affected the outcome in this case.[12] The Agreement covered a number of aspects of the proposed Reservoir project. All of the parties acknowledged an understanding that, to improve the flows on intake streams from which ASC had been withdrawing water and to provide for additional snowmaking coverage, ASC needed an additional water source. Accordingly, the parties agreed to permit water use from Woodward Reservoir, provided Killington minimized biological impact to the greatest extent possible after a "needs and alternatives" analysis.[13] Killington also

---

10 Isham interview with Jean Rosenburg, Farm and Wilderness (Apr. 1, 2001).

11 *Id.*

12 Memorandum of Agreement (1996), at I.B. (on file with author) [hereinafter MOA 1996].

13 *Id.*

agreed to bring *all* of its water withdrawals[14] to February Median Flow standards by the 1997–1998 ski season. The February Median Flow is a specific amount of water in a particular river, below which fish and other organisms cannot survive.[15] In exchange, the ANR agreed to expedite required permitting reviews and approvals as appropriate.[16] Additionally, the ANR agreed to assist Killington in implementing its snowmaking construction plans and in increasing waste disposal capacity, which the ANR deemed to be "both economically reasonable and environmentally sound."[17] Subsequent to the signing of the Agreement, ASC, together with Farm and Wilderness and the Vermont Department of Forests, Parks and Recreation, filed the Woodward Reservoir Act 250 Permit Application with the District Environmental Commission on August 26, 1997.[18]

The Effect of Other Approvals

As noted earlier, the Woodward Reservoir project required not only an Act 250 permit, but other approvals as well. Because the Woodward Reservoir project involved the construction of snowmaking water and fire hydrant intake structures in a public water resource, the ANR required ASC to obtain what is referred to as an encroachment permit. In addition, section 404 of the federal Clean Water Act[19] required ASC to obtain from the United States Army Corps of Engineers a permit to dredge a portion of the Woodward Reservoir to construct the water withdrawal structures. As part of the section 404 permit proceeding, the State of Vermont was required to certify to the Army Corps of Engineers under section 401 of the Clean

14 *Id.* Water withdrawals are areas on brooks, ponds, reservoirs, etc., where ski areas intake water for snowmaking. At Killington, the withdrawals include Falls Brook, Roaring Brook, the Ottauquechee River, and since 2001, Woodward Reservoir.

15 In February, rivers in Vermont are typically at their lowest levels. The February Median Flow (FMF) is a specific amount of water in a particular river, below which fish and other organisms cannot survive. In November of each year the State of Vermont calculates the FMF for specific rivers. Ski resorts that withdraw water from these bodies are required to halt all withdrawals below the FMF—unless "grandfathered" withdrawal permits apply. The resorts affected by FMF requirements must report stream flow data to the State on a monthly basis as part of the compliance procedure. Generally, the resorts not bound by FMF have not applied for water withdrawal permits since the 1950s and 1960s, when standards were more lenient. Isham interview with Ted Williamson, snowmaking manager, Sugarbush Resort (Mar. 26, 2002).

16 MOA 1996, *supra* note 12, at I.A.

17 *Id.* at I.D–E.

18 *In re* Killington, Ltd., Permit Application, No. 1R0813-5, Findings of Fact, Conclusion of Law and Order (Vt. Dist. Envtl. Comm'n #1, Jan. 13, 1998) [hereinafter Woodward Reservoir Act 250 Permit Decision].

19 Federal Water Pollution Control Act of 1972 (Clean Water Act), § 404, 33 U.S.C. §1344 (2006).

Water Act[20] that the issuance of the section 404 permit would not violate Vermont Water Quality Standards—known as a Water Quality Certification.

Each of these three interwoven processes—the state encroachment permit, the federal dredging permit, and Vermont's Water Quality Certification—involved its own set of standards and procedures. As a result, there were opportunities for state and federal agencies to make findings and for interested members of the public to participate. Because the District Commission ultimately incorporated into the Act 250 permit the terms of these other permits, it is useful for our analysis to determine whether these processes, in turn, lend an ecosystem perspective to the Act 250 process.

The struggle of local resident Nicholas Lenge to imbue the various permitting processes regarding Woodward Reservoir with a broader perspective illustrates the potentially limiting role that prior agreements and rules governing participation in both Act 250 and non-Act 250 permit proceedings can have on the type of information considered by decision-makers. Since 1995, Lenge lived on land abutting Woodward Reservoir. He enjoyed swimming and recreating in the Reservoir and enjoyed the plant and animal life at the Reservoir. He was concerned that Killington's proposed use of the Reservoir for snowmaking would not only adversely affect his use of the Reservoir, but also the vegetation and animal life.[21] It does not appear that Lenge was included in any negotiations leading up to the Agreement.

On December 1, 1997, Lenge filed an appeal from the ANR's issuance of the encroachment permit with the Vermont Water Resources Board, alleging that the shoreline encroachment authorized by the permit did not meet the test for that permit: to serve the public good and comport with the public trust doctrine.[22] Importantly, Lenge did not participate in the public process surrounding the issuance of the permit at the agency level. He also filed a related appeal with the Water Resources Board challenging the section 401 Water Quality Certification issued by the ANR, which certified that the dredging permit issued by the Army Corps of Engineers under section 404 of the Clean Water Act would not result in activities that would violate Vermont Water Quality Standards.[23]

The Water Resources Board consolidated Lenge's appeals into one action and conducted simultaneous hearings. Based on the information presented to the Water Resources Board during the *de novo* review of the ANR's issuance of the encroachment permit, the Water Resources Board found that the proposed

20 *Id.* § 401, 33 U.S.C. § 1341.

21 *In re* Killington, Ltd., Permit Application, No. 1R0813-5, Nicholas Lenge Proposed Findings of Fact and Conclusions of Law (June 18, 1998).

22 Vermont Water Res. Bd., Mem. of Decision, Docket Nos. MLP-97-09 and WQC-97-10, at 1 (Mar. 20, 1998). In March 1998, the Vermont Natural Resources Council filed an *amicus curiae* brief with the Board in support of Lenge's appeal.

23 Vermont Water Res. Bd., Prehearing Conf. Rpt. and Order, Docket No. WQC-97-10, at 1 (Apr. 7, 1998).

encroachment would not adversely affect the public good. Additionally, given the fact that Woodward Reservoir had been altered by humans over the years, with successive drawdowns and later floodings, the Water Resources Board found that the proposed project and the conditions placed on Killington's water withdrawal practices would actually provide a benefit to the public by improving the aesthetics, recreational opportunities, and the aquatic and shoreline vegetation.[24] Although this proceeding did not involve a pristine landscape, it nonetheless provides a useful example of the freedom to participate at the appellate level only and a broad substantive standard of public good that could be influential in other settings.

In the context of the 401 Water Quality Certification, the Water Resources Board examined the claims relating to the aesthetics of the Reservoir and "Associated Waterbodies" (waterbodies that had a hydrologic connection to the Reservoir as determined by the Board) and found that in each instance the aesthetics would be neither impacted nor improved by virtue of the projects. The Water Resources Board also found that the conditions imposed on Killington in the 401 certification regarding drawdowns would ensure high quality habitat for biota, fish, and wildlife in the Reservoir and the Associated Waterbodies. Like the ANR, the Water Resources Board found in some cases that the habitat would be improved by the projects. Similarly, the Water Resources Board found that background conditions would be either unaffected or improved as a result of the projects. The fact that the Reservoir had a long history of human manipulation played a major role in these findings.[25]

In addition to public policy goals that inherently favor the ski industry, Lenge also met with obstacles involving the rules and procedures that govern appeals of agency actions. The Water Resources Board rules regarding party status require that a party must have a demonstrated interest in the Reservoir or an Associated Waterbody. As a result of this limitation, Lenge was unable to present evidence about the effects of the proposed project on the entire watershed. Instead, his testimony was limited only to those waterbodies in which he had demonstrated an interest, which was determined by the Board based on his proximity to the Reservoir and the area rivers and streams.[26] Specifically, Lenge had attempted to introduce information about all waterbodies hydrologically connected to the Reservoir in the area of the proposed Interconnect Project that were part of the existing snowmaking water withdrawal and delivery system for Killington Resort. The way the Water Resources Board defined the key term "Associated Waterbodies," however, artificially constrained the kind of information Lenge could submit from an ecosystem perspective by narrowing the scope of the review to a limited number of waterbodies, and kept the analysis limited to Reservoir-specific impacts, which in turn prevented a watershed analysis.

---

24 Vermont Water Res. Bd., Findings of Fact, Conclusions of Law and Order, Docket Nos. MLP-97-09 and WQC-97-10, at 54–55 (Aug. 14, 1998).

25 *Id.*

26 *Id.* at 6–9.

As part of the review of the section 401 Water Quality Certification analysis, the Water Resources Board also reviewed the ANR's Rules for Water Withdrawals for Snowmaking and determined that the project complied with the rules. These rules, notably, are geared toward requiring the applicant to complete feasibility analyses regarding the need to use water from one source versus another. The rules incorporate the February Median Flow provision, and in this regard they recognize the ecological connections between winter stream flows and aquatic biota. The snowmaking rules, however, are based on the assumption that withdrawals for snowmaking are a foregone conclusion and that the only question to be answered is which waterbody best serves that purpose. According to these rules, it is the policy of the State to "help to provide for and enhance the viability of Vermont's ski industry, which uses certain of the state's waters for snowmaking."[27] Therefore, a review under these rules does not necessarily lend an ecosystem perspective to the analysis.

The Woodward Reservoir Act 250 Proceeding

While Lenge battled the issues on appeal from the ANR's decisions to the Water Resources Board, he was also involved in the Act 250 hearings for ASC's Woodward Reservoir project. In the case of Act 250, however, nine other individuals who sought and were granted party status as adjoining property owners joined him. On November 24, 1997, the District Commission granted ASC's Act 250 permit and incorporated into the permit the conditions from the 401 Water Quality Certification.[28] Lenge appealed the issuance of the permit for Woodward Reservoir to the Environmental Board.

During the course of the Act 250 appeal, ASC and Farm and Wilderness, the co-applicants and parties to the Agreement, raised a number of objections to Lenge's testimony. The District Commission had granted Lenge standing under criterion 1(F), which concerns the effects of a proposed development project on shorelines.[29] ASC asserted on appeal that Lenge's testimony should be stricken because it focused on criterion 1(G) (wetlands), a criterion for which Lenge was not granted standing.[30] ASC also used the opportunity to criticize Lenge's expertise or specialized knowledge.[31] Farm and Wilderness separately objected to Lenge's

27 State of Vermont, Agency of Natural Resources, Water Withdrawals for Snowmaking §16.02(2), *available at* http://www.anr.state.vt.us/dec/rules/pdf/chap16.pdf (last visited June 14, 2007).

28 Woodward Reservoir Act 250 Permit Decision, *supra* note 18, at 13.

29 *Id.*

30 *In re* Killington, Ltd., Permit Application, No. 1R0813-5, Objections of Killington, Ltd. to Prefiled Testimony (June 18, 1998). Lenge's proffered exhibits were also criticized as irrelevant to the Act 250 proceeding. *Id.* at 23.

31 *Id.*

testimony on the same grounds.[32] As a result of unified and strong objections and skillful use of the rules by opponents, Lenge and the other parties seeking to participate were effectively prevented from introducing an ecosystem perspective to the proceedings. For example, Lenge sought to introduce testimony about the effect of the drawdowns on a floating peat mat that was part of the adjacent wetland. His testimony attempted to draw connections between the shoreline project, the water level in the Reservoir, and the macroinvertebrate life.[33] However, ASC and Farm and Wilderness objected to this testimony about the wetland and the Board sustained those objections. ASC and Farm and Wilderness argued that criterion 1(G) (wetlands) was not the subject of the appeal; therefore, Lenge did not have standing to introduce information under criterion 1(G) about the peat mat. Because the Board agreed with this argument, none of this information was admitted.

Despite Lenge's attempts to show interrelationships among waterbodies that would be affected by water withdrawals for snowmaking, and to interject a broader ecosystem perspective into the various permit proceedings, his efforts were unsuccessful. On August 14, 1998, the Water Resources Board upheld the ANR's issuance of the encroachment permit and the 401 Water Quality Certification. On August 25, 1998, the Environmental Board upheld the District Commission's decision on the Act 250 permit and issued an amended Act 250 Permit to ASC and Farm and Wilderness.[34] The Environmental Board recognized, however, the link between criterion 1(F) (shorelines) and criterion 1(C) (water conservation) when it acknowledged that the faster the Reservoir is replenished with water, the faster the local habitat and its inhabitants will benefit.[35]

By 1999, ASC had acquired all of the necessary permits to withdraw water from Woodward Reservoir.[36] In 2000, Killington Resort increased snowmaking capacity by 30 percent, when it completed the six-mile, four million dollar pipeline from the Reservoir to the ski area.[37]

In the context of the Woodward Reservoir project, it appears that the other proceedings outside of Act 250 did not take an ecosystems perspective, due in large measure to the operation of the Agreement, the operative standards in those proceedings, and the rules regarding participation in appeals. We conclude, however, that this need not be the case in other situations. It is possible

---

32 *In re* Killington, Ltd., Permit Application, No. 1R0813-5, Farm and Wilderness Foundation's Objections to Pre-Filed Testimony and Exhibits (June 18, 1998).

33 *Id.*

34 *In re* Killington, Ltd. and Farm and Wilderness, Amended Land Use Permit, No. 1RO813-5-EB (Aug. 25, 1998).

35 *Id.*

36 See the discussion in Chapter 15, footnote 22 and the accompanying text regarding necessary permits.

37 Laurie Lynn Fischer, *There's No Business Like Snow Business*, RUTLAND HERALD, Jan. 8, 2001, *available at* http://rutlandherald.nybr.com/Archive/Articles/Article/18107 (last visited Mar. 16, 2002).

that the analysis undertaken in other proceedings outside of the Act 250 process can help to create an ecological foundation for Act 250 decisions.

Optimistically, some information presented by individuals at the outset of certain proceedings, like the section 404 and the section 401 proceedings, may contribute to an ecosystem perspective. This is due in part to the fact that there are no restrictions on who can be involved in public hearings on permits and certifications and who can provide comments on draft documents—in other words, no standing rules. For instance, in the context of the Section 401 Water Quality Certification by the ANR, draft certifications are published for public inspection and the public has 30 days to provide comments to the ANR.[38] In this context, members of the public can provide comments and information to the ANR without meeting any particular standing or party status requirements. Similarly, to the extent members of the public or conservation-minded groups have a desire to explain to the ANR how a proposed activity will impact the ecosystem, the public process provides that opportunity.

In the case of a Water Quality Certification, the ANR is required only to find that the proposed activity will not violate applicable provisions of the Clean Water Act, as administered by the ANR, including the Vermont Water Quality Standards. The information provided by the public, therefore, could be expansive in scope and describe cumulative impacts on climatology, wildlife, and vegetation, but the ANR has the authority to deny certifications, only on the grounds that a provision of the Clean Water Act is violated.

This conclusion may be different in the context of other permitting decisions. For instance, before issuing an encroachment permit, the ANR must review the proposed project's effect on the public good. Because the public good analysis is multi-factored and less rigid than the Water Quality Certification analysis, there is a greater opportunity to inject the process with an ecosystem perspective. Unlike the public process in the Water Quality Certification context, however, notice of the application for an encroachment permit is sent with a request for comments only to adjoining landowners, local, regional and state offices, and other interested people or groups. Any person requesting a copy may receive one, but a group must know that the application is pending and ask for a copy so that it can provide comments in a timely manner. Staying abreast of development and the issuance of draft permits, therefore, is key, and in some cases essential to keep the door open for comments that might offer an ecosystem perspective.

We conclude that the need for approvals outside of the Act 250 process has the potential to interject an ecosystem perspective into the Act 250 process, because the decision-makers are not required to assess applications under the same criteria as the District Commission. Whether involvement in non-Act 250 proceedings leads to an ecosystem perspective, however, depends on the standards used by the reviewing agency and whether the procedural rules allow for

---

38 *See* ANR Permit Handbook, *available at* http://www.anr.state.vt.us/dec/permit_hb/sheet27.pdf (last visited June 16, 2007).

participation. In the end, while the different standards in other proceedings may present an opportunity for an ecosystem analysis, in practice they do not usually take an ecosystem perspective. Similarly, participation in public processes at an appellate level often involves an entirely different set of rules regarding standing and evidentiary submissions that may defeat any attempt to infuse these processes with a broader perspective. In the case of the Woodward Reservoir, parties who had been excluded from the negotiations that led to the Agreement and who attempted to participate in other proceedings found themselves stymied by rules that prevented the meaningful introduction of ecosystem-based information when it came to appeal decisions.

There appears to be an opportunity to influence the discussions and thoughts of permitting agencies early on in the process and to advocate for an ecosystem perspective. It is at this point in the process, the outset, where rules governing appeals or other participation are at a minimum and parties are free to actively participate. While it is important to craft an ecosystem perspective that addresses the permitting criteria, it is at this point when decision-makers are the most open to an ecosystem perspective and stakeholders can educate the parties about the ecological interrelationships. By interjecting the ecosystem perspective at this stage, the information and the perspective has the best chance of making its way into final decisions and ultimately into Act 250 permits.

The Resort Village and Master Plan Review Under Act 250

In September 1998, Killington applied to the District Commission for master plan permit review of Phase One of its proposed Resort Village.[39] Phase One of the project envisioned

> the construction of 520 hotel rooms, 700 hotel suites, 160 townhouses, 20 duplexes or single family homes, 180,000 square feet of retail/commercial space, 50,000 feet of public assembly/indoor sports space, 96.5 acres of new trails and other on-mountain improvements at Killington Resort (warming huts, restaurants, etc.), 22.3 acres of new trails and other on- and off-mountain improvements at Pico, and three new parking lots at Killington Resort.[40]

At the time Killington made its application, it proposed to construct Phase One before the end of 2003. Phases Two and Three of the Resort Village contemplated expanding Killington Resort in the same manner over 20 years.

---

39 *In re* Killington, Ltd., Resort Village Master Plan Application, No. 1R0835, Findings of Fact, Conclusion of Law and Order, at 1 (Vt. Dist. Envtl. Comm'n #1, Apr. 11, 1999) [hereinafter Resort Village Act 250 Permit Decision].

40 *Id.*

One of the benefits of master plan review is that it identifies for the applicant the potential opponents and supporters of a project, and what, specifically, they oppose or support. Killington asked the District Commission to make affirmative findings under Act 250 that certain aspects of the project conformed to Act 250's requirements. When such findings are made and not reversed on appeal, the applicant need not submit additional evidence to the District Commission when it later seeks an Act 250 permit to construct a discrete element of the approved master plan. This benefit inures to the applicant during the five-year term of those findings so long as the construction of the discrete element conforms to the information presented during the Act 250 master plan review.

The District Commission granted the Vermont Natural Resources Council (VNRC), the Green Mountain Club, and the Appalachian Trail Conference permission to participate as parties in the proceeding. The Green Mountain Club and the Appalachian Trail Conference's standing was limited to criteria 8 (scenic beauty, historic sites, and natural areas) and 9(K) (public investments). The VNRC was granted status under nearly every criterion.

At the outset of the proceeding, before any discussion of criteria, the VNRC objected to the District Commission's phased review of the Resort Village. The District Commission overruled this objection on the grounds that it had no legal authority to require the applicant to plan past five years. The District Commission expressed its view that long-term planning was rightfully the province of the local and regional bodies, and that even their plans were likely to change within five years. The District Commission "note[d] that there are positive benefits of master planning for the community-at-large, but question[ed] whether Act 250 is the appropriate forum to make final, wide-ranging planning decisions which may impact a community far into the future."[41]

Because the District Commission must review the Resort Village plan for its conformity with Act 250, Killington presented evidence relating to each of the ten criteria. On April 21, 1999, the District Commission issued affirmative findings under criteria 1(D) (floodways), 9(B) (primary agricultural soils), 9(D) (earth resources) and (E) (same) and 9(L) (rural growth areas).[42] It was, arguably,

41 *Id.* at 3

42 The Vermont Natural Resources Council appealed the Commission's decision, alleging that the Commission "erred in its findings concerning [Act 250 criteria] 1(A), 1(B), 6, 7, 8, 9(A), 9(H) and 9(L)…." *In re* Killington, Ltd. 1999 WL 1027239 (Vt. Envtl. Bd. 1999). The VNRC did not dispute the affirmative findings the Commission made. Instead, the VNRC argued that it should be able to appeal findings the Commission made that were *not* binding, and that were *not* being incorporated into the partial permit. *Id.* at *6. On appeal, the Board upheld the District Commission's exercise of jurisdiction over Phase One of the Resort Village, after considering the object and purpose of the master permit process. *Id.* The Board also found that because the Commission had essentially "made findings of fact sufficient to support a conclusion that [Phase One] complies with criterion 9(H), …this criterion is ripe for appeal." The Board conducted a *de novo* hearing on whether Phase One met criteria 9(H) and (L). *In re* Killington, Ltd., 2000 WL 1099082 at *2 (Vt. Envtl. Bd.

fairly easy for the District Commission to make affirmative findings under these particular criteria, because the information presented by Killington showed that the proposed plans would not impact the resources protected by those criteria. For instance, criterion 1(D), relating to floodways, requires the applicant to show that the project will not "restrict or divert the flow of flood waters or significantly increase peak discharges."[43] The analysis under criterion 1(D) in this proceeding simply asked the question: are any floodways present in the Phase One development area? Because the District Commission's answer was no, based on information provided by Killington, the District Commission found that criterion 1(D) had been met.

An argument could be made, however, that because Phase One involved increasing the acreage devoted to trails, and the associated tree clearing could increase stream flow, it may in turn ultimately adversely affect the ability of floodways to handle flood waters entering the various streams in the watershed during storm events or snowmelt. Similarly, because Phase One also involved increasing the amount of impervious surfaces (for example new units, new parking lots, new commercial space), which could also increase stream flow and erosion, it may in turn also ultimately adversely affect the ability of floodways to handle floodwaters.

Importantly, the VNRC had requested and received permission to participate as a party under criterion 1(D). In fact, the VNRC noted in its petition for party status the effect Phase One could have on peak runoff, flood flows, and "floodway integrity."[44] It does not appear from the Findings of Fact, however, that the VNRC ever introduced evidence into the record to address this issue or make the argument. As a result, Killington's testimony went unchallenged and it satisfied its burden of proof.

Turning next to one of the many criteria for which the District Commission did not make an affirmative finding (criterion 1 relating to air pollution), the Resort Village project illustrates how Act 250 attempts to consider cumulative and speculative effects of long term, phased projects. In the case of criterion 1, several facts played a prominent role in the District Commission's finding that while the applicant had met its burden of proof regarding air pollution from mobile sources (such as the additional cars driving to and parking in the new parking lots proposed under the Resort Village), it had not done so with respect to dust and other pollution from fireplaces to be installed in the proposed, new residential units.

Killington obtained an air permit from the ANR that covered all of the "indirect source air pollution" caused by parking areas. It introduced the permit as evidence of Phase One of the Resort Village's satisfaction of criterion 1, which established

---

2000). Because these two criteria do not directly address the ecosystem issue, we will not go into detail on the Board's findings on appeal.

43 Resort Village Act 250 Permit Decision, *supra* note 39, at 25.

44 Petition of Vermont Natural Resources Council, Dist. Envtl. Comm'n Docket No. 1R0835, at 9.

a rebuttable presumption that criterion 1 was satisfied.[45] No other party offered evidence that rebutted the presumption. However, because ASC failed to address a neighboring condominium association's separate concerns about the increase in pollution from the fireplaces, which were not covered by the air pollution permit, the District Commission found that subsequent applications would need to address this issue, among others.

Killington's Resort Village master permit expired in 2004. In July of 2004, Killington applied for a minor permit amendment and asked the District Commission to renew the findings, made five years earlier in 1999, for an additional five year period (to 2009). Recall from the discussion above that the life span of the findings made in 1999 was one of the VNRC's concerns. The District Commission granted the permit amendment to extend the validity of its 1999 findings without a hearing, because no party requested one and the District Commission did not deem one necessary in the absence of any objection.[46] This example illustrates that fact that findings made five years ago may be renewed with little consideration by the District Commission as to whether circumstances have changed or the progress under other permits or new permits necessitates some sort of cumulative impacts analysis.

Another aspect of the Resort Village master permit application process is that the Act 250 Master Permit Guidance Policy actually encourages piecemeal review of phased projects, resulting in an embedded policy against considering cumulative impacts.[47] This is not to say that a District Commission cannot or will not examine cumulative impacts at later stages. The Environmental Board, in the Resort Village and Parker's Gore East appeals, indicated that cumulative impacts would be considered. However, this is entirely subject to the discretion of the members of the Board or District Commission.

Like other Act 250 master plan development permits granted throughout Vermont,[48] Killington's permit represents the state's general acceptance of Killington's long-term development goals.[49] In granting the permit, the state gave

45 See the discussion in Chapter 16 on the role of rebuttable presumptions in Act 250.

46 *In re* Killington, Ltd., Resort Village Master Plan Application, No. 1R0835, Permit Amendment (Aug. 23, 2004).

47 Vermont Environmental Board, Master Permit Guidance Document (May 19, 1999), *available at* www.nrb.state.vt.us/lup/publications/maguide7.doc (last visited Mar. 18, 2008).

48 Marcy Harding, former chair of the Environmental Board, mentioned two other examples in an interview with the *Rutland Herald*: Maple Tree Place, a retail complex in Williston, Vermont, and the Town of Stowe sewer line, a quadrupling of the town sewer plant with extensions of sewer lines up the Mountain Road in Stowe. Bruce Edwards, *Act 250: A View from the Top*, Rutland Herald, July 3, 2000 *available at* http://rutlandherald.nybor.com/Archive/Articles/Article/9551 (last visited on May 14, 2002).

49 Isham interview with Tim Clapp, Director of Planning & Development, Killington, Ltd. (Mar. 15, 2002).

guidance to Killington and the other stakeholders with respect to the ten Act 250 criteria including impact on wildlife habitat, primary agricultural soils, traffic, aesthetics, and headwaters.[50]

While Act 250 review of the master plan is not the only opportunity the applicant has to present information to the District Commission, it is clear that citizen involvement at this phase is critical if there is any hope to encourage an ecosystem analysis of the cumulative impacts of phased developments. As noted above, the VNRC had an opportunity to introduce this type of information, but did not do so with respect to criterion 1(D). Because the District Commission ultimately did not make affirmative findings under criterion 1(D), the parties to future applications to build discrete elements of the Resort Village will not be saddled with findings based on incomplete information. However, it represents a missed opportunity to affect the process and the thinking of both the applicant and the District Commission. The failure to intercede in the master permit extension application presents another missed opportunity to bring to the District Commission's attention changed circumstances that might militate against renewing five year old findings.

The Act 250 review of the Resort Village project under Act 250's master plan review differs from the Act 250 proceedings discussed earlier in this chapter because the resulting permit did not authorize ASC to construct any improvements or begin development. Rather, the benefit to an applicant of submitting a master plan for review is to obtain findings from the District Commission on the project as proposed, before going forward with more time consuming and costly implementation measures. These findings can provide guidance to the applicant when it later proceeds with future, separate applications to construct the improvements. Ideally, the master plan review process identifies areas that will need additional attention from the applicant before the applicant files individual project permit applications. The same rules of engagement apply in these proceedings, so earlier criticism of the rules and their impact on the ability of stakeholders to introduce ecosystem-oriented information remains. The fact that this type of review is done on a larger scale, with all aspects of a future project considered together rather than piecemeal, may encourage more of an ecosystem perspective than other types of review.

The Power of the Tenth Criterion: Local Planning

An important thread runs throughout all of these projects—criterion 10—the requirement that projects conform to adopted local or regional plans or capital programs. While a representative of a local or regional planning board or commission may opine as to the conformity of a proposed project with the applicable plan, the decision is ultimately up to the District Commission or the Board to make a final consistency determination. Again, because Act 250 is a

50 *See* Edwards, *supra* note 48.

permitting statute and contains no prospective planning component, local and regional plans provide a potential opportunity to incorporate ecosystem principles into planning and thereby affect permitting decisions.

Local and regional plans are powerful tools. Land use plans serve as guides to organize community growth.[51] Land use plans operate in conjunction with zoning codes or ordinances and may include maps and other illustrations. Land use plans often describe and visually represent areas that have been targeted for growth, or areas in the community that will be preserved as open space.

We saw the relevance of a local plan at work, to some extent, in the early Parker's Gore East Act 250 proceedings discussed in Chapter 16, where the Town of Mendon's land use plan, through Act 250's criterion 10, protected high-elevation land from virtually all development. While it is not clear whether the rationale for that protection was truly ecosystem based, the power of the tool is apparent. As a result of the plan's protection of high-elevation land, Killington's early expansion efforts in Parker's Gore East failed. In contrast, the other three projects discussed in this case study provide examples of local and regional plans that instead encourage mountain resort development and do not take an ecosystem approach and, therefore, do not provide a mechanism to introduce those concepts into permitting decisions.

In the Interconnect and Woodward Reservoir proceedings, the District Commission found that the projects conformed to the applicable local and regional plans.[52] In each case, those findings were made based on the evidence provided by the applicant in its application, as opposed to any information provided by representatives of the local or regional planning bodies. The local and regional planning bodies were statutory parties, but they submitted no information and did not impact the proceedings.

In connection with its Resort Village application, ASC did not request affirmative findings under criterion 10. The District Commission noted that review under this criterion would occur when ASC made individual project applications.[53] At that point in time, ASC undoubtedly expected that the Town of Killington planning board would have revised the local plan to incorporate the new acreage that ASC acquired in the land swap with the State of Vermont under the Agreement, because that land had never been included in the local plan. The town did not disappoint its economic engine and essentially incorporated the provisions of the Resort Village into the town plan in 1999.

The District Commission also noted that the Rutland Regional Plan identified the area in which the proposed development would occur as a "Resort/Recreation Center," and that the regional planning commission had "determined that the proposed [Killington Resort Village] plan is in conformance with the Future Land

51 *See generally* Am. Jur. Zoning § 17.

52 Interconnect Permit Decision, *supra* note 1, at 62; Woodward Reservoir Act 250 Permit Decision, *supra* note 18, at 22.

53 Resort Village Act 250 Permit Decision, *supra* note 39, at 81

Use Goals [of the regional plan]."[54] In addition, the regional plan encouraged locating new resort and recreation development in the same region, or in similar areas designated in town plans. The regional planning commission also encouraged the development of sewage treatment facilities in these areas to be done in a manner that would "allow for clustered or concentrated development."[55]

Two questions remain: whether the local and regional plans foster or promote an ecosystem perspective and, if they do, did that ecosystem perspective shape or in any way impact the mountain resort development at Killington Resort. One example that we noted in the previous paragraph is the provision in the Rutland Regional Plan encouraging infrastructure improvements to be developed in a way that promotes clustered development. While one could make the argument that an ecosystem perspective infused the Rutland Regional Plan and led the regional planning commission to promote clustered development, there is no evidence of that in the plan itself. Clearly, promoting clustered development may reduce sprawl and impervious surfaces, which in turn reduces storm water runoff, which in turn benefits water quality. Although there is no way to know whether the clustered development goal in the Rutland Regional Plan is the result of an ecosystem perspective, and more likely than not it is a function of economics, it will impact future development and may potentially lead to a positive ecosystem result in future projects.

While it has a few elements of environmental sensitivity, the Killington Town Plan does not appear to take an ecosystem perspective to planning. Economics are at the heart of nearly every planning recommendation made in the Killington Town Plan. The Killington Planning Commission notes in the introduction to the current plan, adopted October 18, 1999, that the plan is in essence a response to, or ratification of, the Killington Resort Village.[56] Both the economic development and land use objectives for development center on maintaining and enhancing the viability of the ski industry and the resources vital to that industry (water for snowmaking, area for trails), as well as encouraging the growth of the area as a four-season resort community (golfing, hiking, fishing, hunting, mountain biking to name a few) so that Killington is not entirely dependent on winter ski business.[57] Even the scenic and historic objectives are geared toward making the area aesthetically pleasing for visitors so they will come and enjoy the area all year round.[58] The plan mentions fragile areas like peaks and wetlands, and discusses, for example, their susceptibility to erosion and value as habitat. When it comes to recognizing the interrelationships between the fragile areas and the effects of development, however, the plan does not appear to prohibit development in those areas to protect the resources. Additionally, the Killington Zoning Regulations

54 *Id.* at 289.

55 *Id.* at 288.

56 Town of Killington, Killington Town Plan 5 (Oct. 1998).

57 *Id.* at 10-11.

58 *Id.* at 12.

incorporate by reference Killington's Resort Village and require development in that area to be in conformance with the Killington Resort Village.[59]

It appeared that Killington Resort's most recent owners were moving ahead at the beginning of 2008. In January 2008, SP Land Co., the entity that controls real estate development at Killington Resort and operates the ski area with Powdr, appeared before the Killington Planning Commission at an informational meeting. At the meeting, Killington officials discussed the status of Phase One of the Killington Resort Village and indicated that Phase One would itself be built in phases. Killington indicated that it would seek extensions of its existing permits from the Town of Killington for a 400-acre Planned Unit Development (PUD) and a 408-acre PUD to ensure that Killington could pursue Act 250 approvals for discrete elements of the Resort Village without being concerned about the expiration of existing local development approvals.[60]

At the same time, the Town of Killington Planning Commission put out a request for proposals to the land use consulting communities, seeking assistance with the upcoming review of Killington's Planned Unit Development application. The proposal specifically mentions the desire for analysis of the economic impact of the Resort Village on the existing commercial base and on public services and facilities.[61]

Only one month later, arguably in response to what was a perceived "lack of support for extending the PUD application," Killington notified the Town of Killington Planning Commission in February 2008 that it would not request an extension of its expiring PUD permits.[62] Killington stated that it would "put [its] plans on hold indefinitely and [] abandon the effort to pursue an extension of the currently effectively PUDs." One of the reasons cited is the fact that recent Resort Village plans submitted by Killington to the Planning Commission reflect changes to the plans originally submitted by Killington when it received approval for the PUDs.[63] As a result, the Planning Commission suggested a new PUD application would be necessary.[64] According to the Town Manager, this suggestion

59 Town of Killington Zoning Regulations 69.

60 Town of Killington Planning Commission, Meeting Minutes of January 9, 2008, *available at* http://www.killingtontown.com/vertical/Sites/%7BE4345A2E-9636-47A3-9B74-2E6220745729%7D/uploads/%7BC739C465-209A-49F6-9682-80EE12E59167%7D.PDF (last visited Jan. 28, 2008). A planned unit development is a permitting tool designed to facilitate the creation of districts in which there is a planned mix of uses. This planning tool is often uses where large tracts of land can be developed by a single entity. American Law of Zoning § 11:12.

61 Town of Killington, Request for Proposal—Killington Village Master Plan Review (undated) (on file with author).

62 Bruce Edwards, *SP Land Shelves Ski Village Plans*, Rutland Herald, Feb. 16, 2008, *available at* http://www.rutlandherald.com/apps/pbcs.dll/article?AID=/20080216/NEWS04/802160375/1002/NEWS01 (last visited Apr. 2, 2008).

63 *Id.*

64 *Id.*

stemmed from public concern about the new owner forging ahead with concrete development plans that appear to deviate from the concept plan set forth in the PUDs.[65] Without any changes to the Killington Town Plan, however, it is unlikely that the Killington Resort Village, whatever its configuration, will be deemed inconsistent with the plan for purposes of Act 250.

If advocates for an ecosystem perspective are able to involve themselves at the local and regional levels and introduce an ecosystem perspective into the plans, then there is a possibility that this perspective will find its way into subsequent Act 250 proceedings through criterion 10. And even if the ecosystem is not expressly addressed when reviewing proposed projects for compliance with the criterion 10, the work and effort that went into the planning process may foster an ecosystem perspective by encouraging the developer to consider broader issues when complying with local plans.

65 *Id.*

Chapter 18
Conclusion

Killington's three approved development proposals are inextricably linked—more residential and commercial capacity at the mountain base to attract more people; more trails with the Interconnect to fuel demand at the mountain base; and more snowmaking capacity to serve the additional trails. All of these activities take place in the context of a larger landscape.

Act 250 does not take an ecosystem perspective, but it does an admirable job of protecting individual media, for example air and water, via the narrower interests of adjacent property owners and environmental groups. The absence of a state-level planning component in Act 250, a component that was proposed in the initial legislation but never adopted, appears to be a fundamental flaw that prevents Act 250 from taking a broader perspective. This flaw is compounded by the piecemeal review of projects under Act 250 and sometimes hostile rules regarding participation.

The piecemeal review stems from the fact that Act 250 provides for an application-by-application analysis of the impacts a proposed project will have in a particular area. One problem with this approach is that there is no specific requirement that decision-makers review the proposed project with an eye toward the impacts that previously approved projects have had or may still have on the area. Additionally, there also appears to be little consideration of the cumulative impacts of *multiple applications* pending simultaneously in Act 250.

As demonstrated by the discussion in Chapter 17, for example, there is no comprehensive analysis of the three Killington Resort applications that looks at the comprehensive effect on the ecosystem. While the three proceedings relied on some of the same information, testimony and exhibits, there is little discussion in the findings to suggest that the decision-makers referred back to earlier findings or to other related, pending applications to guide findings in new applications. The Parker's Gore East example, discussed in Chapter 16 of this case study, provides a bright spot on this point, because in that case, the District Commission and the Environmental Board clearly looked past the individual applications before it and considered the collective impacts of both the logging project and the Madden Pond project.

The fact that certain amendments to permits can be made administratively and with greatly reduced levels of oversight and public participation may lead to additional impacts on the ecosystem without an analysis of the cumulative effects. The amendment by the District Commission extending the Resort Master Plan approval for an additional five years as noted in Chapter 17 for Killington provides an example of this phenomenon.

Further, Act 250 does not currently have any mandate to consider the broader ecological impacts of any one application. This is due primarily to the separateness of the ten Act 250 criteria and the procedural rules that require parties to prove standing with respect to each individual criterion and allow parties to provide information only as it relates to that criterion. Advocates in the Parker's Gore East appeal to the Board effectively brought to the attention of the Board the various interrelationships and interdependencies that extended past a simple analysis of wetlands, for instance, and delved into bear feeding activities. This did not occur in the Interconnect, Woodward Reservoir or Resort Village proceedings. Notably, both ASC and Farm and Wilderness worked to affirmatively block Nicholas Lenge from introducing a watershed perspective into the Woodward Reservoir proceedings.

Several of the Act 250's criteria suggest that the Vermont Legislature saw value in using the analysis performed under a media-specific criteria to inform the analysis of whether the proposed project would cause unacceptable secondary impacts. Specifically, criteria 9(H) (scattered development) and 9(K) (public investments) provide support for the proposition that the legislature recognized potential harms from proposed development may manifest themselves away from the actual project site. Both of these criteria require the District Commission to make findings as to how the proposed project will affect other geographic areas or public investments. In making findings under criteria 9(H) and 9(K), District Commissions may look to how other criteria are being satisfied. For instance, in the District Commission's findings relating to the Woodward Reservoir application relating to criterion 9(K), the District Commission incorporated by reference the findings made under criterion 1(E) (stream condition) and 1(F) (access and erosion control) to find that the project would not endanger an adjacent public investment, namely the Reservoir itself. This represents an instance in which the manner in which Act 250 is being interpreted or applied, as opposed to the actual language of the Act, dictates how inclusive of interrelated ecosystem components the analysis can be.

The robustness of local land use planning may also create an ecological backstop that can guard against ecologically negative cumulative impacts of development projects. As noted in the Chapter 16, one of the requirements within Act 250 is that the proposed project be consistent with local and regional land use plans. There is reason to believe, therefore, that an ecosystem analysis might stem not from the Act 250 permitting process itself, but from local land use planning and the way it is ultimately incorporated into Act 250 through criterion 10. This approach restores the focus to planning, which is, by its very nature, prospective in nature. In contrast, Act 250 is a permitting scheme with specific criteria by which applications can be examined and adjudicated.[1] In the absence of changes to the language of Act 250, individual municipalities can engage in long-range planning that incorporates an ecosystem perspective to guide future land use decisions

1 See Chapter 16 discussing the history of the passage of Act 250.

and development. This in turn would infuse the Act 250 process because of the consistency requirement under criterion 10.

As this case study illustrates, Act 250 is not just about criteria and impacts, but also about people and how they operate within the legal system. Because of the Killington Resort's magnitude, and its owner's goal of making its investment as profitable as possible, "Killington has attracted attention from a range of stakeholders [and agencies]."[2] Not all of these stakeholders can and will ever agree on the effect of the resort's development activity on the local ecosystem. On the one hand, there are the Killington Resort workers who may be inclined to elevate salary concerns over those of the local ecosystem, as well as those businesses that depend on the seasonal and year-round activities offered by the resort. On the other hand, there are the recreationists who enjoy the seasonal and year-round activities but also have a deep appreciation for the landscape that surrounds Killington Resort. In a practical sense, however, most of the aforementioned stakeholders lack the resources to actively engage in Act 250 proceedings themselves. Most of the Act 250 proceedings, therefore, depend on the expertise offered by state agencies, nongovernmental organizations (NGOs), and local interest groups.

State agencies, such as the Agency of Natural Resources, have a staff and resources to assess the impacts of proposed development projects on local ecosystems,[3] but their review is done to ensure compliance with existing regulations. These regulations tend to be straightforward, addressing the effects of proposed development projects on individual environmental media, as required by Act 250, as opposed to the larger ecosystem. Even if ecosystem concerns are warranted, agency staff has no constituency to answer to, unlike NGOs that exist based on the support that they receive from members.

NGOs, such as the Green Mountain Club, Vermont Natural Resources Council, and Conservation Law Foundation, have been instrumental in bringing their resources to Act 250 proceedings,[4] making them very familiar with the process. In fact, these groups have played important roles in the development of Killington Resort.[5] Many battles would not have been fought and won on behalf of the

---

2 *See generally*, Savage et al., *The Changing Composition and Influence of Land-Based Groups: Evidence from Two Counties in Vermont*, Middlebury College Working Paper Series 0306, Middlebury College, Department of Economics (2003), *available at* http://www.middlebury.edu/services/econ/repec/mdl/ancoec/0306.pdf (last visited Jan. 5, 2008).

3 These agencies are staffed by full-time scientists with expertise and knowledge on a range of matters.

4 *In re* Killington, Ltd., et al., No. 1R0813-2, Findings of Fact, Conclusion of Law and Order, at 2 (Vt. Dist. Envtl. Comm'n #1, Nov. 24, 1997).

5 The Green Mountain Club was an active participant in the Interconnect project between Killington and Pico Mountains, with its particular focus on the "preservation and upkeep of Vermont hiking trails." *See* Jonathan Isham and Jeff Polubinski, *Killington Mountain Resort: A Case Study of "Green" Expansion in Vermont,* 26 Vt L. Rev. 565, 578 (Spring 2002) (citing the Green Mountain Club, http://www.greenmountainclub.

environment and the ecosystem without their involvement in the Act 250 process. Their involvement, however, should not overshadow the important work of local interest groups.

Local groups are likely to have insight into a proposed development's project effect on a locally cherished ecosystem. The involvement of Nancy Bell in the Parker's Gore East proceeding discussed in Chapter 16 of this case study provides an example of the power and expertise true grassroots groups can have. While they may lack the technical resources of state agencies and NGOs, they are often able to provide anecdotal evidence concerning a local ecosystem that may be of great value to Act 250 decision-makers. Local groups may also be less familiar with the procedural workings of Act 250, particularly because their concerns are generally focused on discrete issues that may only involve one-time matters. To adequately address their concerns without divorcing them from Act 250 proceedings, they might consider joining in the activities of statewide NGOs. Such involvement, however, must be guarded so as not to subsume the interests of one group for the other.

While a group protective of local ecosystems may either be acting alone or in concert with each other in Act 250 proceedings, decision-makers will independently scrutinize their participation and testimony so as to comply with the law. With no guiding Act 250 language concerning the effects of proposed development projects on local ecosystems, and limited efforts by decision-makers to help evolve the Act into a ecosystem-oriented law, the efforts of regional NGOs and local groups to address the effects of proposed development projects on local ecosystems may have little legal relevancy. Legal relevancy must be found in the Act 250 criteria. Unless one can show a clear connection between any of the Act 250 criteria and the ecosystem, little will be accomplished in protecting the ecosystem from the adverse effects of proposed development projects. There is promise, however, that such a connection among the Act 250 criteria can be made, particularly since federal laws have begun to embrace an ecosystem perspective.[6]

The lack of a mandated ecosystem analysis, coupled with certain procedural aspects of Act 250, hinders a full ecosystem perspective. Specifically, we have shown, through the discussion of Killington Resort's expansion plans in the 1980 and 1990s, that the piecemeal aspects of Act 250 undermined its comprehensive

---

org/headqt.htm). The Vermont Natural Resources Council has frequently and actively opposed development activity at Killington Resort. *Id.* (citing Vt. Natural Res. Council, About VNRC, http://www.vnrc.org/aboutvnrc.htm). The Conservation Law Foundation was actively involved with the Killington's Resort Village Master Plan process in the form of advice. *Id.* at 579 (citing Conservation Law Foundation, About CLF, http://www.clf.org/aboutclf/home.htm).

6 For a discussion about how an ecosystem analysis has been applied in specific instances, please refer generally to the discussion of the Endangered Species Act and the National Forest Management Act, in Robert F. Gruenig, *Killington Mountain and Act 250: An Eco-Legal Perspective*, 26 Vt. L. Rev. 552–53. Please also see Roger Fleming's discussion in Part II about Loon Mountain.

appearance. Act 250 does not guarantee a consideration of the cumulative and interrelated impacts of development on the ecosystem. Act 250 is impeded from taking this approach because of the following characteristics: (1) disjointed consideration of the merits, given decisions along a (somewhat) linear path; (2) piecemeal submission of evidence, given the standing rules; and (3) separate consideration of individual activities, which does not necessarily take into account the cumulative effects of multiple applications or activities that do not trigger Act 250 review.

Furthermore, one also should acknowledge that some of Act 250's fundamental original features have been stripped away, since these four projects were originally vetted: ecosystem protection under Act 250 is now more difficult. As discussed in Chapter 16, since February 1, 2005, appeals from District Commission decisions no longer go to the Environmental Board. Act 115 of the Vermont Legislature abolished the Environmental Board, and in its place vested the Environmental Court with jurisdiction over appeals from District Commissions.[7] And critically, with respect to party status, the rules no longer allow parties to participate in an appeal of a District Commission decision if they were not a party to the District Commission proceeding. Had the recent changes to Act 250 been in effect at the time that Killington was beginning its expansion plans in the mid 1980s, it is likely that there would have been a different result. Under the new rules, for example, Nancy Bell and the Friends of Parker's Gore would have been unable to participate in the appeal of the Parker's Gore East projects because they did not participate in the initial proceeding at the District Commission level. And with respect to the Board's review of issues beyond those contained in S-K-I's notice of appeal, the new rules no longer allow the Environmental Court to consider issues that were not noticed in the appeal. Therefore, the Environmental Court may not have been able to consider the impact on the wetland and then examine how the wetland provides necessary wildlife habitat to black bears in the area because those issues were not raised in the notice of appeal.

As noted in our introduction to Act 250, there is nothing explicit in the language of Act 250 that requires decision-makers to assess impacts on the ecosystem, as opposed to one element of the ecosystem. Neither the word "ecosystem," nor any of its derivatives can be found within Act 250's language. The absence of such language, however, should not deter decision-makers from interpreting such a need, particularly based on the intent of the Vermont legislature to protect the state's landscape, which is part of a larger ecosystem.

While decision-makers have attempted to assess impacts of proposed development projects on local ecosystems in finding compliance under individual Act 250 criterion, in some cases they have gone further by finding certain criteria are inextricably linked. By linking different criteria together, one can make the

7 See the discussion in Chapter 15 at note 12 regarding the abolishment of the Environmental Board and the creation of the Natural Resources Board and the Environmental Court.

argument that decision-makers are assessing the impacts of proposed development projects on local ecosystems, particularly since each criterion by itself has a narrower focus and linking these criteria broadens the ecological impact assessment of the projects. Linking of criteria, however, was not commonly practiced in connection with the various Killington applications and therefore, Act 250 proceedings are piecemeal efforts for addressing the impacts of proposed development projects on local ecosystems.

We conclude this chapter with a perhaps wistful suggestion as to how the Act 250 process can be improved so that it better protects ecosystems, or at a minimum incorporates an ecosystem perspective. Given Act 250's structure around ten criteria related to the impact of development on the environment, we would propose criterion 11: ecosystem protection. Such a criterion, with detailed subcriteria like those of criterion 1, could explicitly link different media—such as water use and wildlife habitat—and therefore give parties with current or potential standing the authority to present evidence on ecological interrelationships. Indeed, given the comprehensive nature of Act 250's current set of ten criteria, we speculate that criterion 11 would be in keeping with the original intention of this Act back when it was crafted in 1970—to reflect the ecological stewardship valued by so many Vermonters. It might be possible to achieve a similar result by amending Act 250 to allow the District Commission and stakeholders the ability to use evidence introduced under any one criterion to build a case under any other criterion.

We admit that, at first glance, it seems unlikely that the political pressure for such a change in Act 250 will materialize soon. Indeed, as noted above, the most recent major change in Act 250 reflects the sometimes-competing value that Vermonters' also hold: to keep their economy moving forward. But we hold out hope that the political winds could change, particularly as diverse coalitions in this state reflect on the likely shocks to the state's economy associated with global climate change. In December 2005, Governor Jim Douglas signed on to the seven-state Regional Greenhouse Gas Initiative (RGGI) and also appointed a six-person commission on Climate Change, "representing a broad variety of interests," to develop a Climate Change Action Plan to reduce Vermont's greenhouse gas emissions. One of the commission members is Parker Riehle, the Vice President of the Vermont Ski Areas Association.[8]

So just as Governor Deane Davis and other political and civic leaders helped to shepherd in the original Act 250 in the face of Vermonters' urgency about excessive and unchecked development as the age of environmentalism began, we speculate that a new "Ecosystems" criterion could emerge from Vermonters' sense of urgency about our latest ecological challenges. Such a criterion could reduce the piecemeal aspect of this still innovative law, thereby better protecting ecosystems in the Green Mountains.

8 Press Release, Governor Douglas Leads On Climate Change—VSAA's Riehle Appointed To Commission" December 20, 2005, *available at* http://www.skivermont.com/nerve/press_releases.php?tid=2755 (last visited Feb. 9, 2006).

PART V
Mont Tremblant, Quebec

Canadian Law and the Ecological Footprint of a Four-Season Resort

Jane Matthews Glenn[1]

> "There's nothing that can be done now—the train has left the station. You either hop on or you get out of the way."
>
> Mont Tremblant resident, 2004[2]

1 The author wishes to thank Anne Drost for her encouragement and insightful comments and Carole Chan and Alexandre Gagnon for their assistance with the research for this case study. Comprehensive research was completed in November 2005, and has been selectively up-dated since then.

2 Quoted in Unnati Gandhi, *Changing a Mountain's Face: Project draws mixed reviews*, The [Montreal] Gazette, Aug. 11, 2004, at A3.

Editor's Note: Citations herein generally conform to The Bluebook: A Uniform System of Citation (Columbia Law Review Ass'n et al. eds., 17th ed. 2000). In order to make the citations more useful for Commonwealth readers, abbreviations and certain other conventions have been adopted from the Canadian Guide to Uniform Legal Citation (McGill Law Journal) eds., 6th ed. 2006. English rather than French hyphen conventions have been used throughout, including in proper names.

Chapter 19

An Introduction to Mont Tremblant and the Issues

Mont Tremblant is the largest and most popular ski resort in eastern Canada. It is located about 90 miles north of Montreal, Canada, on the slopes of one of Quebec's highest mountains (altitude 3,176 feet), tucked into the southwest corner of Mont Tremblant Park. The Park, which covers approximately 585 square miles, was first created in 1895 as Trembling Mountain Park,[1] and was so named because the Amerindians (Algonquins, who called it *manitonga soutana*, meaning "mountain of the spirits") thought that the trembling that climbers sometimes felt beneath their feet signified that man had disturbed the spirits.

The ski resort was first established in 1938, with the opening of Mont Tremblant Lodge by Philadelphia millionaire Joseph Bondurant Ryan, and is said to be the second oldest ski resort in North America.[2] By the late 1980s, however, Mont Tremblant was struggling for survival, as were many ski resorts in North America and elsewhere. A Canadian real estate development company, Intrawest Development Corporation, headquartered in Vancouver, British Columbia, took over the then almost bankrupt station in 1991.

Mont Tremblant's expansion under Intrawest has been spectacular. The recreational facilities now consist of 94 trails covering some 625 acres of skiable area serviced by 14 lifts (eight of them high speed) on the mountain, as well as golf courses, tennis courts and other facilities at its base.

This case study examines how and to what extent the law protects the ecosystem of Mont Tremblant and the resort area at its base in the face of considerable tourism and development pressures. It focuses on three different areas: the skiable domain on the mountain itself, the base camps—including the golf courses—on the lower reaches of the mountain, and an immediately adjacent protected land trust area,

---

1 Act to Establish Trembling Mountain Park [Parc de la Montagne Tremblante], S.Q. 1895, 58 Vict., c. 23. *See* C. Pierre Deschênes, *Tremblant, Mont*, The Canadian Encyclopedia 2192 (2nd ed., Vol. IV, 1988). The mountain's name was changed to Mont Tremblant in 1961.

2 Gray Rocks Inn, located just a couple of miles away, dates from 1906 (see map in Chapter 21, Figure 21.2). Ville de Mont Tremblant, Règlement de Plan d'urbanisme: Proposition préliminaire 11, http://www.villedemont-tremblant.qc.ca/jahia/Jahia/pid/695 (last visited July 31, 2007) [hereinafter "Règlement de Plan d'urbanisme: Proposition préliminaire"].

Domaine Saint Bernard, skirting the foot of the mountain. The three areas transect the mountain from top to bottom.

Each of the three areas is governed by its own set of rules. In examining them, this case study will attempt to respond to two questions. Firstly, do the various sets of rules form what might be described as a "legal ecosystem" in which the rules—federal, provincial and local rules; ownership and management-based legal regimes; and public and private law—peaceably co-exist in their own, often overlapping, habitats? In other words, do they constitute an "integrated network" for the management of land and the ecosystems it supports, which the government has called for on several occasions over the past decade? As Quebec's Ministry of the Environment has stated:

> What is now needed is a unified viewpoint, or a more harmonized intervention framework for enhancing our protected areas. The time has come to update the concept of an "integrated network" according to which each stakeholder, while remaining independent, will allow for the reaching of common objectives to protect a representative sampling of Quebec's biodiversity, the sharing of common data bases, and the development of actions focused on a more complementary intervention of actions and the sharing of responsibilities.[3]

Secondly, if the rules do form such a legal ecosystem, does this legal ecosystem adequately protect the physical ecosystem of Mont Tremblant?

Two preliminary issues condition the responses to these questions. One is the economic and social issues raised by Intrawest's operations and the second is the Canadian constitutional and administrative context. These are discussed in the present chapter.

Economic and Social Issues

Intrawest is the largest owner and operator of "village-centered destination leisure resorts" in North America. It combines recreational operations and base camp

---

3 Environnement Québec, Protected Areas in Quebec: A Pledge for the Future. Government Guidelines with a View to Adopting a Quebec Strategy, http://www.menv.gouv.qc.ca/biodiversite/aires_protegees/orientation-en/index.htm (last visited Feb. 3, 2002); *see also* Gouvernement du Québec, Les orientations du Gouvernement en matière d'aménagement du territoire 1994, at 41, http://www.mamm.gouv.qc.ca/pdf_mamm/amenag/oramenag.pdf, (last visited May 15, 2002):

Based on consultation and agreement, this approach [integrated land management] is aimed at both the satisfaction of human needs and the maintenance of the characteristics of ecosystems by taking account of the long-term objectives concerning the production and use of each resource, is such a way that an action in favor of one resource does not compromise objectives relating to other resources. *Id.* (author's translation).

(village) development at 12 mountain resorts, four in Canada—including Whistler/Blackcomb (its first acquisition, bought in 1986, and planned site of the 2010 Winter Olympics) and Tremblant—and eight in the United States; it has village developments at a further five mountain locations, three in the United States and two in France.[4]

This expansion can be largely attributed to Intrawest's "success formula," which it describes in vivid, even exuberant, terms on its website as follows:

> Each gear of Intrawest's revenue clock produces increased guest visits, increased revenue per visit and higher real estate values at every turn. The design's elegance is that the gears work in sync, causing a compounding effect. …
>
> 1. We start with a resort and enhance the experience.
> 2. Then build an animated village so people stay longer.
> 3. All this attracts more visitors who come more often, spend more money and bring their friends.
> 4. More real estate is built and attractions are added, drawing yet more people.
> 5. More people, more often, leads to the expansion of year-round facilities, maximizing use of shops, hotels, convention facilities and restaurants.
> 6. As occupancy and room rates climb, so does demand for resort real estate, creating a surge in real estate sales.
> 7. All this results in a total resort experience which brings year-round destination visitors, generating financial critical mass which …
> 8. Leads to more resorts. …[5]

In short, this means "[m]ore people spending more time generating revenue 24 hours a day, 7 days a week, 365 days a year".[6]

Intrawest's success formula thus involves the upgrading and expansion of on-mountain recreational facilities and the construction and development of animated village accommodations at the base. It has applied this two-pronged approach at Mont Tremblant. It rapidly expanded the on-mountain winter facilities, so that the skiable area now covers more than 625 acres on three separate slopes, the number of trails has more than doubled, and the lift capacity has increased significantly; summer facility development has proceeded apace, with golf course development

4 Crédit Suisse First Boston Corporation, Equity Research: Intrawest Corporation (Mar. 26, 2001) 1; *see also* http://intrawest.com/ and Intrawest Corporation Quick Facts (to 2005), http://media.intrawest.com/snowshoe/media_docs/QuickFacts2005.pdf (last visited July 31, 2007). Intrawest is also active in a number of warm weather resorts.

5 Intrawest, Our Success Formula, http://www.intrawest.com/about/overview/successformula.html (last visited Apr. 2, 2004).

6 Intrawest, Our Success Formula in Action—Tremblant, http://www.intrawest.com/about/overview/success_tremblant.html (last visited Apr. 2, 2004).

having pride of place. At the same time, the first base camp, Base Sud, was built at the foot of Versant Sud on the shore of Lac Tremblant. It contains just under 2,000 lodging units and some 145,000 square feet of commercial space.[7] It is now being followed by construction of two new high-density base camps, at Versant Soleil and Camp Nord, which will about treble these amounts, and a further 455 acres are to be added to the skiable domain.[8] The readers of *SKI Magazine* regularly rate Mont Tremblant as the "Number 1 Resort in the East",[9] with comments stressing the attractiveness and convenience of the pedestrian village as much as, if not more than, the quality of the skiing itself. Mont Tremblant is no longer just a ski resort: it is one of the most popular four-season resort destinations in eastern North America.

A central element of Intrawest's formula is "warm-bed" accommodation. Purchasers of the townhouse and condominium units in the pedestrian villages are required to place their units in a rental pool for a designated number of weeks each year. This ensures that the unit is occupied when it is not being used by the owner, thereby increasing the volume of "destination visitors" at the resort throughout the year, particularly in off-peak periods.[10] More destination visitors increase both Intrawest's recreational revenues (lift tickets, green fees and so on) and its nonrecreational revenues, as destination visitors are "less price-sensitive"[11] than single-day visitors. They are generally more affluent, with more disposable income to spend on leisure activities, and tend to spend more of it on peripheral (i.e., non-lift or non-green fee) recreational and nonrecreational items than do single-day visitors.[12] Intrawest captures this extra spending through vertical integration, as it owns or manages 80 percent of the available lodging units and commercial facilities (boutiques, restaurants, bars and so on) at Tremblant.[13] The introduction of "all inclusive" vacation packages will increase Intrawest's capture rate.[14] The following table indicates the relative importance of the various sources of Intrawest's resort revenues.

---

7 *See* Daniel Malo, *The Economics of Mont Tremblant: Remaining Questions and Preliminary Answers*, 26 Vt. L. Rev. 629, 633 (2002).

8 Infrastructure Canada & Fisheries and Oceans Canada, Environmental Assessment Screening Report, Mont Tremblant: Development of Versant Soleil and Camp Nord, Mont Tremblant (Phases 3 and 4) item 5.3 (Aug. 2004), http://www.infrastructure.gc.ca/pn/csif/mont-tremblant/report_e.shtml (last visited Dec. 7, 2004).

9 Crédit Suisse First Boston Corporation, *supra* note 4, at 16; SKI Magazine Readers Rank the Top 10 Resorts in the East for 2006–07, *available at* http://www.skinet.com/skinet/photos/article/0,26964,1539448,00.html (last visited July 31, 2007).

10 Credit Suisse First Boston Corporation, *supra* note 4, at 22.

11 *Id.* at 9.

12 *Id.* at 9, 11.

13 *Id.* at 14.

14 André Courey, *Tremblant Addresses Tourism's New Challenges*, Tremblant Express, July 2004, *available at* http://www.tremblantexpress.com/ (last visited July 13, 2004) ("Once at the resort, no further cash payments need be made; the vacation experience is hassle-free for the parents.").

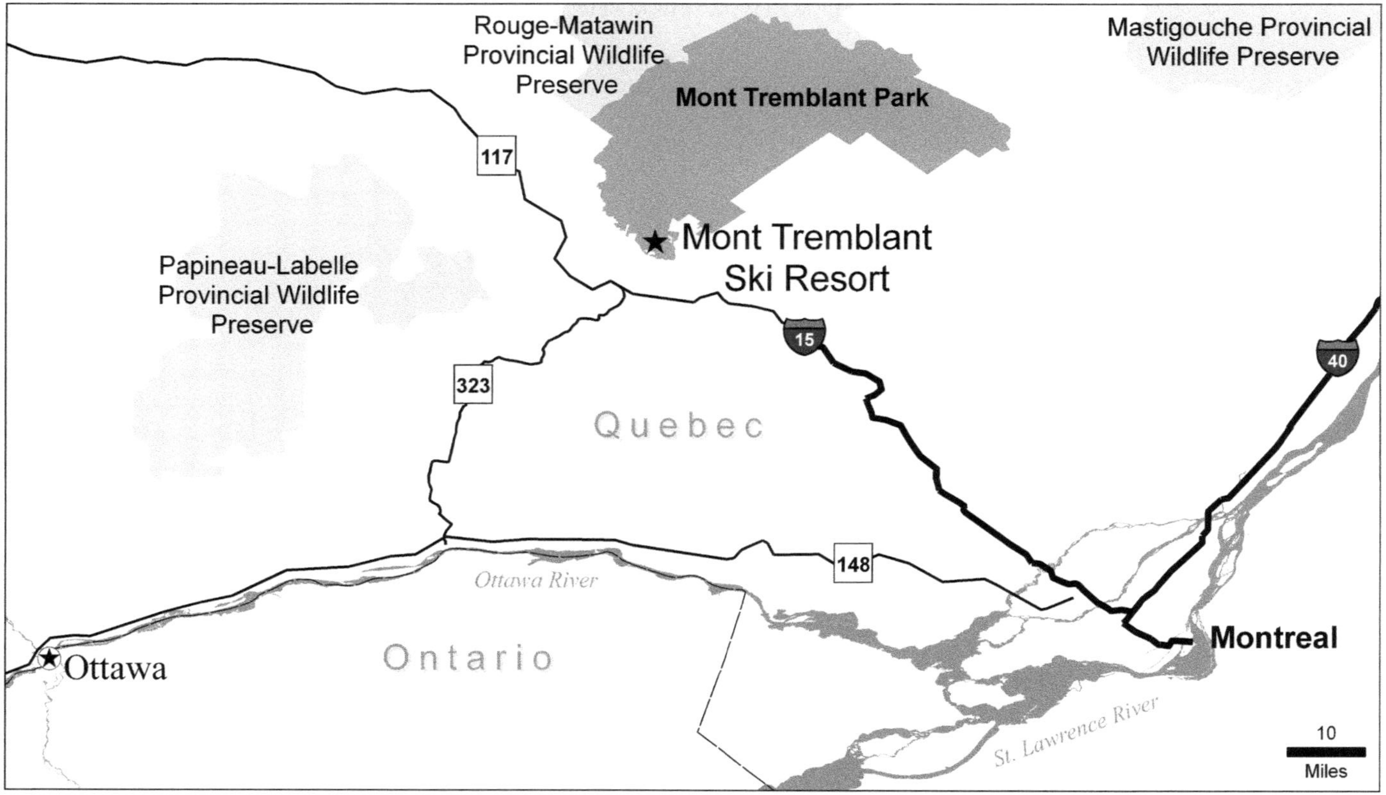

Figure 19.1 The Setting of Mont Tremblant Park

Data Sources: DMTI Spatial Inc.; ESRI; ©Department of Natural Resources Canada, all rights reserved.

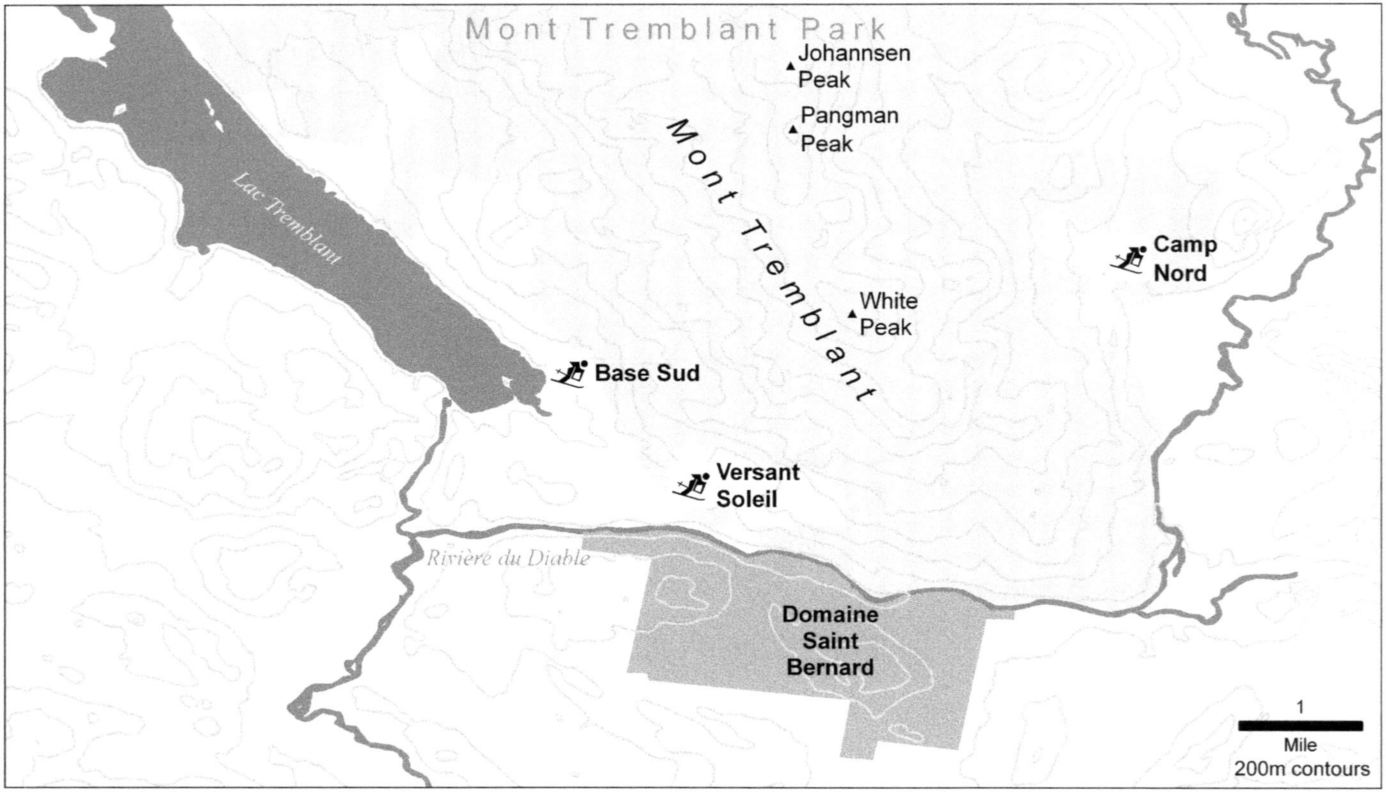

Figure 19.2 Mont Tremblant and its Base Camps

Data Sources: DMTI Spatial Inc.; ESRI; ©Department of Natural Resources Canada, all rights reserved.

Table 19.1 Intrawest Resort Revenues by Segment, 1999–2002

Revenue source	1999A		2000A		2001E		2002E		% variation
	$US M	%	$US M	%	$US M	%	$US M	%	1999–2002
Mountain operations	159.7	41.1	177.1	39.2	190.6	38.1	200.1	36.9	+25.3%
Retail & rental shops	62.6	16.1	72.8	16.1	84.0	16.8	92.4	17.0	+47.5%
Food & beverage	56.3	14.5	60.1	13.3	68.3	13.6	75.1	13.9	+33.5%
Lodging & property mgmt	39.4	10.2	53.5	11.8	62.8	12.6	72.3	13.3	+83.4%
Ski school	22.8	5.9	25.8	5.7	29.9	6.0	32.9	6.1	+44.1%
Golf	21.8	5.6	30.9	6.8	35.3	7.1	38.8	7.2	+77.8%
Other	25.8	6.6	31.9	7.1	29.2	5.8	30.6	5.6	+18.6%
Total	**388.4**	**100**	**452.1**	**100**	**500.1**	**100**	**542.2**		**+39.6%**

(A=Actual; E=Estimated)

Source: Crédit Suisse First Boston Corporation Equity Research: Intrawest Corporation (Mar. 26, 2001) 3

It shows that although revenues from all sources of activity are increasing, the increase is greatest in the areas of lodging and property management, golf, and retail shops (including equipment rental). More generally, it shows a declining importance of mountain operations compared to off-mountain activities. (See Table 19.1).

This change in revenue emphasis reflects another key element in Intrawest's success formula, which is to extend the season—to keep the "warm-beds" warmer longer, not just during the ski season but throughout the year. Golf is the obvious summer drawing card, and there are now seven golf courses in the Tremblant area, six of which are located in the Town of Mont Tremblant and two of which are owned by Intrawest. Other warm weather activities include hiking, biking and various water sports on Lac Tremblant and elsewhere. A concrete luge run on the mountain is a new summer attraction. Convention centers are planned for the two new base camps. Ongoing summer events range from street "animation" in the pedestrian village—street performers, group animation troupes, face-painting, parades, arts and crafts workshops, and so on—through to more sedate features such as small concerts, musical happy hours, and evening lectures ("nature under the stars") on topics related to the flora and fauna of Mont Tremblant Park. Special events are sprinkled throughout the warm weather season. These include *Les 6 Heures du Circuit Mont Tremblant* car race[15] and the Canada-Quebec Cup mountain bike competition in May; a women's tennis competition, a celebrity golf tournament

15 Anne Desjardins, *Wheels on the Track: Circuit Mont Tremblant Roars Again*, Nuvo, Autumn 2004, at 112, 114 . The course has "some enormous elevation changes along with 15 corners which makes it all the more exciting for the driver and for the spectator as well". *Id.* at 114. Enthusiasts love it ("the roar of high performance engines still echoes in the Laurentian Mountains": *id.*). Some local residents are less enthusiastic.

and a triathlon in June; shooting stars seen from the summit in August; and a second charitable golf tournament and the "Grand Prix of Colours" in September ("...a race against the clock to the top of the tallest peak in the Laurentians. A breathtaking activity, a spectacular panorama!"[16]).

> Intrawest has found that an effective way to increase returns is to encourage visitation at historically low periods by creating an experience with corporate sponsorship ... targeted at a specific demographic segment, to create demand that would otherwise not be there. This marketing technique is particularly effective with singles and couples without children, as they have the greatest flexibility as to travel times and the most disposable income.[17]

These activities are financed in large measure by a "royalty" added to all charges (1 percent for accommodation and 2 percent for goods and services), the purpose of which is "to allow the Tremblant Resort Association, a non-profit organization, to ensure that guests enjoy a unique and truly memorable experience by offering top-notch entertainment, events and shows, the majority being free, as well as world-class services and facilities."[18] They all increase the size and weight of the human footprint on the mountain ecology.

Intrawest's presence at Mont-Tremblant has been a considerable boost to the area's economy.[19] The company spent approximately $1 billion Can. in the first phases, improving the recreational facilities and constructing the first base camp, and is projecting to spend another $500 million Can. on each of the two new base camps and related improvements. Employment increased by almost 70 percent in the

16 Mont Tremblant Resort, Mount Tremblant Sports and Cultural Events in Winter and Summer, http://www.tremblant.ca/events/evenements.asp?SelectEvent=ete2004 (last visited June 29, 2004).

17 Crédit Suisse First Boston Corporation, *supra* note 4, at 33. Some of the Tremblant events are charitable ("Fondation Tremblant", set up by Tremblant Resort to aid underprivileged children in the Mont Tremblant region, is a frequent beneficiary), as for example the golf tournaments, the triathlon and a mid-December ski event (Grand Prix 24h de Tremblant, organized by Jacques Villeneuve and other Formula One drivers and modeled on a similar event in Villars, Switzerland). *See* http://www.24heures.tremblant.ca/ (last visited June 29, 2004). Prizes are return visits to Mont Tremblant.

18 Royalty, http://tremblant.com/whattoexpect/local_customs/intex-f.htm (last visited Apr. 6, 2004). *See* Act respecting the Association de Villégiature de la Station Mont Tremblant, S.Q. 1993, c. 106.

19 Most of the following information is drawn from CLD [Centre local de développement] Laurentides, Cahier d'information socio-économique: Portrait de la zone Mont Tremblant (Feb. 2002), based on Statistics Canada data from 1998 (business and employment) and 2001 (population), http://www.cldlaurentides.org/indexf.htm (last visited June 9, 2004). *See generally* Les Conseillers ADEC Inc., Les impacts socio-économiques de développements majeurs dans le secteur Mont Tremblant: Rapport sommaire (Oct. 2003), http://www.cldlaurentides.org/indexf.htm (last visited June 9, 2004).

Mont Tremblant area from 1991 to 1998, one of the most impressive jobs creation rates in North America for the period; over half of these jobs are in the tourism sector, which grew by almost 160 percent in the period under consideration, with Intrawest alone employing over 2,800 people.[20] The number of businesses rose by about a third, with almost a quarter of the new businesses being in the tourism sector. The population grew by some 15 percent, ten times more than the province as a whole. Land prices soared, and local revenues (property taxes, land transfer duties, construction permits) increased apace. The level of investment in local infrastructure (local roads, parks, trails, a heritage site, and other local improvements) rose, and a public transportation system was put in place to assist local residents and workers commuting from other areas. A new airport was built.[21]

The federal and provincial governments recognize the importance of Intrawest's development for the economy of the region, and have supported it generously. The former (Parti Québécois) provincial government, for example, granted Intrawest a subsidy of $79 million Can. to begin the first phases of the development in the early 1990s, and promised a further $75 million Can. to help start the next phases of construction.[22] The present (Liberal) provincial government and the federal government each promised $47.5 million Can. in funding for Versant Soleil and Camp Nord, to be used mainly for roads, sewers and other infrastructure.[23] The promise of federal funding triggered a federal environmental review.[24]

But the picture is not entirely rosy. More recent statistics, from 2001, put the Town of Mont Tremblant's unemployment rate at 9.8 percent, higher than the regional (9.6 percent) and provincial (8.2 percent) rates for the same period.[25] Much of the employment generated consists of seasonal, relatively unskilled, minimum-wage jobs.[26] Rising real estate prices and property taxes mean a dearth of affordable housing, and subsidized housing now has to be provided.[27] The school

---

20 Intrawest Resort Real Estate, Tremblant's Success is a True Fairy Tale, One We Never Tire of Telling, http://www.livetremblant.com/vision/index.html (last visited May 27, 2004).

21 André Courey, *Airport Puts Tremblant in League with Vail and Aspen*, TREMBLANT EXPRESS, May 2003, *available at* http://www.tremblantexpress.com/ (last visited May 28, 2004); André Courey, *Airport Gets Green Light*, TREMBLANT EXPRESS, Sept. 2004, *available at* http://www.tremblantexpress.com/ (last visited Sept. 21, 2004).

22 André Courey, *Tremblant-Québec Subsidy Talks Continue for Versant Soleil*, TREMBLANT EXPRESS, Feb. 2004, *available at* http://www.tremblantexpress.com/ (last visited May 28, 2004).

23 Kristin Goff, *Investors Cool to Mont Tremblant Plan*, THE [MONTREAL] GAZETTE, Aug. 12, 2004, at B1, B2.

24 *Growth's Effect on Watershed Studied*, THE [MONTREAL] GAZETTE, Dec. 11, 2004, at B2. See the discussion *infra* in the text in Chapter 20 at note 38 and Chapter 21 at note 99.

25 Règlement de Plan d'urbanisme: Proposition préliminaire, *supra* note 2, at 16.

26 Les Conseillers ADEC Inc., *supra* note 19, at 25. Most of the construction work is done by workers from outside the region, for construction firms also from outside. *Id.* at 17.

27 A $10.2 M. Can. project is being subsidized by the municipality ($1.2 M.) and the provincial government (through the Société d'habitation du Québec) ($5 M.). André

drop-out rate is one of the highest in the province, and the availability of low-level jobs undoubtedly exacerbates this situation.[28] Local residents are concerned about the effect of such a major development on their own identity, including their access to the recreational amenities of their area. Infrastructure provision also is costly.[29]

And many people are concerned about the effect of the development on the region's ecosystem. Various nongovernmental environmental umbrella organizations, such as the *Conseil régional de l'environnement des Laurentides* (CRELA) [Laurentian Regional Environmental Council], have called for an independent evaluation of the cumulative effect of development, not just Intrawest's project but in the Mont Tremblant area.

> What is required is a "comprehensive environmental and social" assessment of the region, said the ... [CRELA] president. Currently, there are known to be "125 other projects in the area, some of which involve 200 to 400 housing units", Ruelland said. There are now six golf courses, plus ski hills that, when they are making artificial snow, consume the same amount of water as all the other businesses and residents, he said. "All of that has an impact. We have to analyze what the hydrological network can handle and what it can't."[30]

These calls have generally gone unheeded although, as we shall see, the environmental screening under the federal Canadian Environmental Assessment Act,[31] triggered by a demand for federal funding for the developments at Versant Soleil and Camp Nord, goes some way to remedy this.

Courey, *City to Borrow 1.5 Million for Affordable Housing*, TREMBLANT EXPRESS, Aug. 2003, and André Courey, *Affordable Housing on the Way*, TREMBLANT EXPRESS, Apr. 2004, *available at* http://www.tremblantexpress.com/ (last visited May 28, 2004).

28 Louis-Gilles Francoeur, Plan de développement de 1,2 milliard à Mont Tremblant: Les projets d'Intrawest inquiètent citoyens et villégiateurs, LE DEVOIR [DE MONTRÉAL], Jan. 13, 2003, available at http://www.geocities.com/ericsquire/articles/misc/dev030113.htm (last visited Feb. 4, 2004).

29 About $20 M. Can. was spent on road access improvement between 1993 and 2002, and about $100 M. Can. more will be needed to service the proposed two new pedestrian villages: Les Conseillers ADEC Inc., *supra* note 19, at 27. Much of this will be financed by the federal and provincial governments, as noted above, but the Act respecting the Agence de Développement Station Mont Tremblant, S.Q. 1997, c. 100, provides for the setting up of a joint municipal/Station Mont Tremblant body, the "Station Mont Tremblant Development Agency", to provide for infrastructure provision and financing in the base camp areas. The Agency has authority to borrow up to $12.1 M. Can.

30 Lynn Moore, *Public to Have Say on Tremblant*, THE [MONTREAL] GAZETTE, Aug. 21, 2004, at B1; *see also* Francoeur, *supra* note 28.

31 Canadian Environmental Assessment Act, S.C. 1992, c. 37. See the discussion *infra* in the text in Chapter 20 at note 38 and Chapter 21 at note 99.

In sum, Intrawest's economic model underlines that a successful ski resort is no longer simply a place where people come to ski during the winter months, leaving the ecosystem time to recover during the rest of the year. A four-season resort, especially one focused on generating revenue "24 hours a day, 7 days a week, 365 days a year"[32]—with the myriad of activities this entails—leaves no time for recovery. The human footprint on the mountain ecology is not just larger and heavier; it is more unrelenting.

Constitutional and Administrative Considerations

The Canadian constitution, adopted at the time of Confederation in 1867,[33] does not specifically mention the environment. Constitutional jurisdiction must thus be teased out of the existing division of powers sections, notably sections 91 (matters of federal jurisdiction) and 92 (provincial jurisdiction).[34] As Mr. Justice La Forest put it in the Supreme Court of Canada, "It must be recognized that the environment is not an independent matter of legislation under the Constitution Act, 1867 and that it is a constitutionally abstruse matter which does not comfortably fit within the existing division of powers without considerable overlap and uncertainty."[35] While the result is sometimes a patchwork quilt, jurisdiction over the Mont Tremblant ecosystem is predominantly provincial.

Jurisdiction over the skiable domain, which is located inside the boundary of Mont Tremblant Park, falls under provincial jurisdiction by virtue of the constitutional authority of the provinces over "the Management and Sale of the Public Lands belonging to the Province and of the Timber and Wood thereon."[36] Privately owned lands outside the Park, which include the base camps and Domaine Saint Bernard, also fall under provincial jurisdiction, this time under the authority of the provinces in relation to "Property and Civil Rights in the Province"[37] as well as "Matters of a merely local or private Nature in the Province."[38] Quebec, like the other provinces, has delegated the bulk of its regulatory authority to local governments under its constitutional authority over "Municipal Institutions in the Province."[39] Jurisdiction over infrastructure equally falls under provincial and, by

32 *Supra* note 6.

33 Constitution Act, 1867 (U.K.), 30 & 31 Vict., c. 3, *reprinted in* R.S.C. 1985, App. II, No. 5.

34 *See generally* Peter W. Hogg, Constitutional Law of Canada 735 (4th ed. 1997); Jamie Benidickson, Environmental Law 21–24 (1997).

35 Friends of the Oldham River Society v. Canada (Minister of Transport), [1992] 1 S.C.R. 3 at 71.

36 Constitution Act, 1867 (U.K.), 30 & 31 Vict., c. 3, s. 92(5); *see also* ss. 92A(1)(b) & 109.

37 *Id.* at s. 92(13).

38 *Id.* at s. 92(16).

39 *Id.* at s. 92(8).

extension, municipal authority over "Local Works and Undertakings."[40] Private law, for example, contracts and torts, is similarly a matter of provincial jurisdiction under the above-mentioned head of "Property and Civil Rights in the Province." Unlike the other Canadian provinces, where the common law prevails, the private law of Quebec is the civil law. This is the main source of law governing Domaine Saint Bernard.

More generally, jurisdiction over the basic components of the ecosystem—air, water, flora and fauna—is similarly provincial, although the federal government does have some role to play. For example, control over navigable waters, including Lac Tremblant at the base of the mountain, is a matter of federal jurisdiction by virtue of its authority over "Navigation and Shipping."[41] Other sources of federal authority include its jurisdiction over "Inland Fisheries"[42] and the general (although restrictively interpreted) residual authority "to make Laws for the Peace, Order and good Government of Canada".[43]

Most of the province's legislation comes under the responsibility of, or provides a role for, the ministers responsible for environment, natural resources, wildlife and parks, with their various roles depending on how ministerial responsibilities are distributed from time-to-time. Since 2006, responsibility for both parks and the environment has come under the aegis of the same minister—the Minister of Sustainable Development, Environment and Parks—rather than been divided between the Minister of the Environment and the Minister of Natural Resources, Wildlife and Parks as was the case in the past. Responsibility of a single minister facilitates a coordinated ecosystem approach in these key areas. Responsibility for wildlife remains under a separate minister, the Minister of Natural Resources and Wildlife,[44] although the 2006 legislative package instructs the two ministers to sign a formal memorandum of agreement to work together "[i]n keeping with the principles of sustainable development and integrated management".[45]

---

40 *Id.* at s. 92(10).

41 *Id.* at s. 91(10). Municipal regulations attempting to restrict navigation or the use of boats on lakes and rivers have thus been challenged in Quebec courts and held to be unconstitutional. *See* Québec (Procureure Générale) v. Larochelle, Que. C.A., Dec. 22, 2003, *available at* http://www.jugements.qc.ca. Quebec has adopted two regulations under the Environment Quality Act, R.S.Q. c. Q-2, dealing with the protection of the waters of particular lakes from discharge from pleasure boats: O.C. 896-92, G.O.Q. 1992.II.2978 (Lac Memphrémagog) and O.C. 203-95, G.O.Q. 1995.II.463 (Lac Mégantic). However, a similar regulation has not been adopted for Lac Tremblant.

42 Constitution Act, 1867 (U.K.), 30 & 31 Vict., c. 3, s. 91(12).

43 *Id.* at s. 91, preamble. *See* Hogg, *supra* note 34, at 443–45.

44 *See* Act respecting the Ministère du Développement Durable, de l'Environnement et des Parcs, R.S.Q., c. M-300.001, and Act respecting the Ministère des Ressources Naturelles et de la Faune, R.S.Q., c. M-25.2. For current Quebec legislation and regulations, see http://www.publicationsduquebec.gouv.qc.ca/home.php# (last visited July 30, 2007).

45 Act respecting the Ministère des Ressources Naturelles et de la Faune, R.S.Q., c. M-25.2, s. 11.1, para. 2.

A key function of the Minister of Sustainable Development, Environment and Parks is to assume responsibility for "coordinating government action in the area of sustainable development and for promoting compliance with the principles of sustainable development, especially their environmental aspects, within the Administration and among the public", by means of the development and implementation of government policies concerning, *inter alia*, "the protection of ecosystems and biodiversity."[46] The Minister is also responsible for the administration of the Environment Quality Act, the main objective of which is to control the introduction of contaminants into the environment;[47] the environment is defined as "the water, atmosphere and soil or a combination of any of them or, generally, the ambient milieu *with which living species have dynamic relations*."[48] The Environment Quality Act also guarantees everyone an enforceable right "to a healthy environment and its protection, and to the protection of the living species inhabiting it" but only "to the extent provided for by this Act and the regulations, orders, approvals and authorizations" issued under it, which gives the right somewhat of a "now you see it, now you don't" air.[49] The Minister may draw upon the *Bureau d'audiences publiques sur l'environnement* (BAPE) [Office of Public Hearings on the Environment] in fulfilling his or her responsibilities (see textbox in the following pages). As for the Minister of Natural Resources and Wildlife, his or her mission is to ensure, "in a manner consistent with sustainable development and the integrated management of resources," the conservation of both natural resources, including wildlife and wildlife habitats, and public lands (excluding parks).[50]

46 Act respecting the Ministère du Développement Durable, de l'Environnement et des Parcs, R.S.Q., c. M-300.001, ss. 10 and 11. Other matters for ministerial attention include the prevention, abatement or elimination of water, air and soil contamination; the establishment and management of aquatic reserves, biodiversity reserves, ecological reserves and man-made landscapes; the protection of threatened or vulnerable plant species; and the development and carrying out of activities related to the observation and knowledge of nature.

47 R.S.Q., c. Q-2. Much of the Act is taken up with such specific matters such as air pollution (s. 47), industrial pollution (s. 31.11), decontamination and restoration of contaminated sites (s. 31.42), quality of water and management of water including sewage treatment plants (s. 32), solid waste management including hazardous materials (s. 53.1), and protection from radiation.

48 *Id.* at s. 1, para. 1(4) (emphasis added).

49 *Id.* at s. 19.1. In a similar vein, the recently adopted Sustainable Development Act, R.S.Q., c. D-8.1.1 (adopted as S.Q. 2006, c. 3), amends the Charter of Human Rights and Freedoms to include the following: "Every person has a right to live in a healthful environment in which biodiversity is preserved, to the extent and according to the standards provided by law." S. 18, adding a new s. 46.1.

50 Act respecting the Ministère des Ressources Naturelles et de la Faune, R.S.Q., c. M-25.2, s. 11.1.

Bureau d'Audiences Publiques sur l'Environnement (BAPE)
[Office of Public Hearings on the Environment]
The BAPE is an independent, quasi-judicial body whose function is to provide for public input into decisions to be taken by the provincial government (and other bodies under its jurisdiction) which could affect the quality of the environment. It was added to the Environment Quality Act in 1978 along with provisions for environmental impact assessments, and much of its activity relates to EIAs under the Act. However, the Minister responsible (the Minister of Sustainable Development, Environment and Parks) may submit other questions to the BAPE, and this could include changes to park boundaries.

The BAPE's goal is to have informed citizen participation and transparent decision-making. All documents, including environmental impact studies, are published on its website. In a typical case, the BAPE facilitates public participation by opening consultation centres in the region concerned, making the relevant documents available, holding information sessions, registering public questions and comments, and reporting on them to the Minister. The BAPE might then be asked by the Minister either to mediate or to hold a public hearing. A public hearing consists of two phases. The first is an information-gathering phase, and involves presentations to the BAPE panel by both opponents and proponents of the project, followed by questions from the public; there is no time limit on this phase and often a question period continues over several days. The second phase centres on obtaining the opinion of the public, through written briefs and oral presentations to the panel. The *Bureau* also conducts its own inquiries and can request additional information from the promoter or government agencies involved. It then analyses the information and submits its report to the Minister.

The BAPE is thus an important vehicle for public consultation. However, it is only an advisory body and its report is only a recommendation. The Minister or relevant government agency has the final say.

Sources: Environment Quality Act, R.S.Q., c. Q-2, s. 6.1 & following; BAPE, Rapports, publications et conferences, *at* http://www.bape.gouv.qc.ca/sections/rapports/ (last visited Jan. 12, 2008); "The BAPE: A participative democracy tool", *available at* http://www.bape.gouv.qc.ca (last visited Oct. 11, 2007).

In other words, the rather fastidious constitutional disaggregation of jurisdiction over the components of a mountain ecosystem between federal and provincial (and, by extension, municipal) governments, coupled with the spread of administrative responsibility for the various components of the ecosystem amongst the different ministries at each level, hampers the ability of the public sector to protect the ecosystem as an integrated whole. It falls short of the ideal framework to foster a legal ecosystem.

Conclusions

Intrawest is an experienced ski resort developer with a coherent, integrated economic approach, one which necessarily extends, intensifies, and prolongs the human footprint on the mountain ecology. It is to be controlled in this by a legal system in which the constitutional and administrative authority governing its activities is disaggregated over a wide range of government agencies, none of which specializes in ski hill development and mountain ecosystem protection and all of which must respond to pressures for economic development as well as for environmental protection.

The next two chapters explore in detail how this disaggregation of authority affects the government's ability to evaluate and regulate development impacts from an ecosystem perspective. By focusing on specific governmental decisions that were pivotal to the recent growth of the resort at Mont Tremblant, the reader can see the extent to which the law does or does not create a coherent legal ecosystem in very specific factual contexts. Chapter 20 explores the actions required to authorize Intrawest's expansion of ski trails and other human activities on the skiable domain, and Chapter 21 evaluates how the law and its administrators addressed Intrawest's proposals for expanding the villages and golf courses at the base of the mountain. Although some of the applicable rules contain elements that suggest an integrated ecosystem perspective, they fail to require and implement a full ecosystems analysis consistently and successfully. In addition, significant procedural features, most notably the limited rights of public disclosure and participation, discourage the public from reinforcing the ecosystem perspective or evaluating the extent to which the government has adequately protected the ecosystem. Chapter 21 also introduces the alternative of achieving ecosystem protection through private, nongovernmental action. Chapter 22 provides a summary of the gaps in the legal ecosystem and suggestions about how they might be filled.

Chapter 20
Intrawest's Development of the Skiable Domain

The skiable domain consists of just over 625 acres on the slopes of Mont Tremblant. The mountain is located in Mont Tremblant Park, as we have seen, and this conditions the legal regime applicable to the skiable domain. The general orientation of the Park is east-west, and it represents an area of transition between the privately owned lands of the inhabited south and the publicly owned lands of the (relatively) uninhabited north, and between the different geographic regions of the Laurentian highlands to the south and the Canadian shield to the north. The Park is more open, with more lakes, in the north, and more mountainous in the south. It is located at the headwaters of three different hydrological systems, which adds to its overall ecological importance.

The World Wildlife Fund places the Park in a wider eco-region of "eastern forest-boreal transition,"[1] which it accords an overall conservation status of "fragile." This is mainly because much of the area has been highly fragmented by forestry and, increasingly, tourism activities (including skiing facilities), leading to substantial habitat loss. Only about 10 percent of this wider eco-region remains intact, with Mont Tremblant Park being one of the larger areas.[2] This, together with the differences in latitude and altitude within the Park, and its diverse physical features, make it important for biodiversity. The mountain itself plays an important role in this regard.

Because Mont Tremblant Park is a provincial park and hence publicly owned land, the provincial government exercises both regulatory authority and ownership rights in controlling the activities in the Park. Its ownership rights over the skiable domain are those of landlord, with Intrawest (operating as Station Mont Tremblant)

---

1 Comprising most of the southern Canadian Shield north and west of the Saint Lawrence Lowlands as well as a "disjunct" section, the Adirondack Mountains in upper New York State. World Wildlife Fund, Terrestrial Ecoregions: Eastern Forest-boreal Transition, http://www.worldwildlife.org/wildworld/profiles/terrestrial/na/na0406_full.html (last visited Mar. 6, 2004).

2 *Id.* There are two other protected areas in the general vicinity of Mont Tremblant. One is the 4,572-acre Jackrabbit Ecological Reserve (named after well-known Quebec cross-country skiing pioneer Hermann "Jackrabbit" Johannsen), designated in 1992 under the then Ecological Reserves Act, R.S.Q., c. R-26.1, to preserve a representative Laurentian ecosystem in its natural state. The second is the 538 square mile Rouge-Matawin Wildlife Sanctuary, which was created in 1981 under the Act respecting the Conservation and Development of Wildlife, R.S.Q., c. C-61.1, s. 111, and abuts Mont Tremblant Park to the north.

as its tenant. When Station Mont Tremblant took over the ski resort in 1991, one of its assets was a fifty-year lease (ending in 2033) to the mountain slopes. The government, as lessor, consented to the assignment of the lease and also agreed to an extension of its term, so that the present lease will end in 2051; the annual rent of $5,000 Can. is subject to increase every five years to reflect inflation.[3]

There are two main issues relating to the skiable domain. First is a land exchange between Station Mont Tremblant and the government in 2000 and a resulting rezoning, and a second relates to the activities taking place on this domain.

Land Exchange and Park Rezoning

The area leased to Station Mont Tremblant in 1991 included some of the more ecologically sensitive areas of the Park. However, in 1995, to mark the centenary of Mont Tremblant Park and to reflect the increasing emphasis on conservation in the wake of the Rio Summit, the then Minister of the Environment proposed to change the classification of Mont Tremblant Park from a "recreation park" to a "conservation park"[4]—that is, "a park primarily intended to ensure the conservation and permanent protection of territory representative of the natural regions of Quebec, or of natural sites presenting exceptional features, while rendering them accessible to the public for the purposes of education and cross-country recreation".[5] A reclassification required an increase in the area dedicated to conservation and a corresponding decrease in the intensive recreation area under Intrawest's control. This meant that the lease had to be renegotiated, and Intrawest agreed to a rezoning of the leased area in return for a land exchange whereby Intrawest would receive title to land previously held within the park in exchange for land it had owned outside the park

Section 4 of the Parks Act requires that a public hearing be held before the boundaries of a park can be changed. At the Mont Tremblant hearing, there was general agreement about the substance of the proposed changes but not about the procedure followed. For example, the *Conseil régional de l'environnement des Laurentides* (CRELA) [Laurentian Regional Environmental Council] objected to

---

3 Transfert et refonte du bail [Assignment and Revision of Lease] between the government (or more precisely "Sa Majesté du chef du Québec") and Station Mont Tremblant, Aug. 31, 1991, Clauses 5 and 6.

4 Québec, Société de la faune et des parcs du Québec, Plan directeur: Parc du Mont Tremblant vii–viii (Dec. 2000), *available at* http://www.fapaq.gouv.qc.ca/fr/consultation/mont_tremblant/plandir_Tremblant.pdf (last visited Aug. 30, 2004); *see also* Quèbec, Ministère de l'Environnement et de la Faune, Le parc du Mont Tremblant: a conservation park (1998).

5 Parks Act, R.S.Q., c. P-9, s. 1(c). "Cross-country recreation" [*récréation extensive*] is defined as "a type of recreation characterized by the use of little frequented territory and the use of relatively simple equipment." *Id.* at s. 1(e).

the lack of available information (such as studies evaluating the overall long-term impacts of the proposal, particularly the economic and environmental impacts as well as the impact on flora and fauna). It also contested the possible partiality of a hearing run by a government department—rather than by the independent *Bureau d'audiences publiques sur l'environnement* (BAPE) [Office of Public Hearings on the Environment] as is usually the case for environmental issues—, and the limited scope of the hearing. (See textbox in the preceding chapter.) It argued as well that the new park zoning seemed to have been chosen for administrative rather than ecological reasons, and suggested that it should be determined by biologists and other specialists.[6] Finally, CRELA feared that the intensive development proposed by Intrawest would adversely affect the ecological balance of the Park, citing in this regard the federal government's concern about increased commercial development in and around Banff National Park, which it described as being in a state of "ecological crisis."[7]

Banff National Park

Banff National Park, located in the Rocky Mountains in Alberta, is Canada's first national park, established in 1885. It spans 2,564 square miles of valleys, mountains, glaciers, forests, meadows and rivers, and boasts several major ski areas, including Norquay, Skiing Louise and Sunshine. It is one of four adjoining federal parks and three provincial parks which together play a core role in ecosystem protection. This is recognized by their designation as the UNESCO Rocky Mountain World Heritage Site.

Banff National Park is nevertheless "a mountain ecosystem under stress." Millions of visitors to the Park, development pressures in and around the town of Banff and the Trans-Canada Highway traversing the Park all contribute to the stress. In 1994, the government appointed an independent task force to review the status of the Park. Its 1996 report, "Banff-Bow Valley: At the Crossroads", is a "blue-print for managing Canada's National Parks." It led to some 95 percent of the Park being zoned as wilderness, and a Park Management Plan incorporating many of its more than 500 recommendations was adopted in April 1997 and revised in May 2004.

New legislation governing Canada's national parks was also adopted in response. The 2000 Canada National Parks Act now puts ecological integrity of park land at the

6 CRELA, Mémoire sur le changement de classification du parc du Mont Tremblant (Oct. 24, 1998), http://www.crelaurentides.org/PDF/tremblant.pdf (last visited Aug. 30, 2004) [hereinafter CRELA, Mémoire sur le changement de classification]; *see also* Union québécoise pour la conservation de la nature (UQCN), Avis sur le changement de vocation du Parc du Mont Tremblant (Sept. 4, 1998), http://ecoroute.uqcn.qc.ca/group/uqcn/org/doc/mem/m_tremblant.htm (last visited Aug. 30, 2004); Pierre Dupuy, Les audiences publiques: Le territoire sous bail, Les enjeux environnementaux de l'éntente de principe (Sept. 1998).

7 Citing Banff-Bow Valley Task Force, Banff-Bow Valley: At the Crossroads (a report submitted to the Minister of Canadian Heritage) (Oct. 1996), *available at available at* http://www.nationaltrail.ca/BOW%20VALLEY%20ALBERTA.pdf (last visited Apr. 22, 2008).

heart of the planning process: "Maintenance or restoration of ecological integrity, through the protection of natural resources and natural processes, shall be the first priority of the Minister when considering all aspects of the management of parks." The revised Management Plan's strategic goal for summer and winter use of the three ski areas is to implement a strategy which will "support the long-term viability of the ski-hills, while keeping the impact on ecological integrity to a minimum". The Plan thus calls for capacity limits for the ski areas and establishing a boundary to the Sunshine Ski area to restrict expansion.

The ski areas may propose improvements or expansions through the development of long-range plans. Such work may not include tree cutting and must conform to the principle of "no net negative environmental impact." Norquay, Skiing Louise and Sunshine Ski areas have approved long-range development plans. Under a Development Review and Approval Process, any proposed development must be consistent with the long-range plans and is subject to public review.

Sources: Banff-Bow Valley Task Force, Banff-Bow Valley at the Crossroads (a report submitted to the Minister of Canadian Heritage) (October 1996), *available at* http://www.nationaltrail.ca/BOW%20VALLEY%20ALBERTA.pdf (last visited Apr. 22, 2008); Speaker Abstracts, The National Mountain Conference, Stewardship and Human Powered Recreation for the New Century, September 14-16, 2000, Golden, Colorado, http://www.mountainforums.org/resources/library/nmconooa.htm (last visited April 26, 2005); Parks Canada, Banff National Park Management Plan (Apr. 1997, am. 2004), *available at* http://www.pc.gc.ca/pn-np/ab/banff/docs/plan1/plan1a_E.asp (last visited Apr. 22, 2008); and Canada National Parks Act, S.C. 2000, c. 32, replacing National Parks Act, R.S.C. 1985, c. N-14.

As one possible remedial measure to prevent similar stress to Mont Tremblant Park, CRELA suggested the creation of buffer zones between the Park's commercialized and conservation zones. However, the present Park director favors an interrelationship between the two, such as increased trail linkages between the resort and the Park proper to make the longest cross-country ski network in North America, "park discovery packages" (in Indian war canoes) with naturalists for resort visitors, and an outdoor theatre in easy proximity to the resort. Environmentalists are increasingly concerned about the extent to which "the human footprint can be allowed in the park without too much encroachment on fauna and flora".[8]

Under the land exchange, lands along the Rivière du Diable at the base of the mountain and part of the ski area on Mont Tremblant, both owned by Intrawest, were

8 André Courey, *Mont Tremblant Park New Approach*, Tremblant Express, June 2003, *available at* http://www.tremblantexpress.com (last visited May 28, 2004)*; see also* André Courey, *Tremblant Addresses Tourism's New Challenges*, Tremblant Express, July 2004 (last visited July 13, 2004) ("Today's vacationers are also looking for a learning experience of the kind that eco-tourism proffers. ... This summer, for the first time, the resort is offering excursions into Mont Tremblant Park.").

included within the Park boundaries, and an equivalent 395 acres were excluded from the Park and granted to Intrawest for the development of the two new base camps (*Falaise de l'avalanche*, renamed Versant Soleil, and Camp Nord) at the bottom of the slopes.[9] Under the Park rezoning, parts of the leased lands which had previously been available for development by the Station as either an "intensive recreation zone" or a "service zone" were rezoned as either a "preservation zone" or a "natural environment zone."[10] (See Figure 20.1). The rezoning enabled the government to accomplish the following ecological objectives: to safeguard the natural characteristics of the highest point in the Park, Johannsen Peak, and the forest cover on its most visible flank; to protect the habitat of the Bicknell's thrush (above 2,460 feet); to safeguard a representative transect of vegetation from Johannsen Peak down both the east and west flanks of the mountain; to preserve a representative sample of the Park's southern forest types (e.g., red oak, American linden, white ash and many herbaceous plants); and to maximize the long-term protection of the white-tailed deer yard (or winter habitat).[11] These changes improved the development potential of the resort while protecting ecologically sensitive areas within the Park. They are reflected in the master plan of the Park, which was approved in January 2001 by the board of directors of the *Société de la faune et des parcs du Québec* [Quebec Wildlife and Parks Board], the agency then responsible for park policy.[12]

9 *See* (untitled) Revision of Lease between the Société de la faune et des parcs du Québec and Station Mont Tremblant, Jan. 28, 2000. Note that the part of the ski area formerly belonging outright to Station Mont Tremblant and now included in the Park boundaries was added to the area leased to Station Mont Tremblant.

10 Comparative maps showing the boundaries and zoning of Mont Tremblant Park can be found in Regulation respecting the Parc du Mont Tremblant, R.R.Q., c. P-9, r. 5 (pre-exchange) and Parks Regulation, Schedule 6, O.C. 838-2000, G.O.Q.2000.II.3356 at 3567 (post-exchange); *see also* Regulation to amend Parks Regulation, Schedule 6, O.C. 157-2002, G.O.Q.2002.II.1489 at 1490.

11 Dupuy, *supra* note 6, at 18–20. The leased lands include 6.6 sq. miles of the 53.8 sq. mile yard, all of which were subject to development under the original lease; the rezoning left as developable only 1.9 sq. miles, with the remainder left either in the preservation zone (3.3 sq. miles), or the natural environment zone (1.4 sq. miles). *Id.* at 20. Intrawest was named as a "Phénix de l'environnement 2000" finalist in the biodiversity and conservation category for its participation in the land exchange. Mont Tremblant Resort, Station Mont Tremblant Environmental Prizes, http:www.tremblant.ca/about/environnement_prix.asp (last visited Mar. 17, 2005). However, the new development at Versant Soleil will result in a significant reduction of the extent of the protected area. See the discussion in Chapter 21 *infra* at note 74.

12 Press Release, Société de la faune et des parcs, Le Conseil d'administration de la faune et des parcs du Québec donne son accord, http://www.fapaq.gouv.qc.ca/fr/c_press/2001_nat/ c010130.htm (last visited Jan. 19, 2004). A new ten-year "strategic plan" for the Park was reported as under preparation in 2003. André Courey, *Mont Tremblant Park New Approach*, Tremblant Express, June 2003, *available at* http://www.tremblantexpress.com (last visited May 28, 2004).

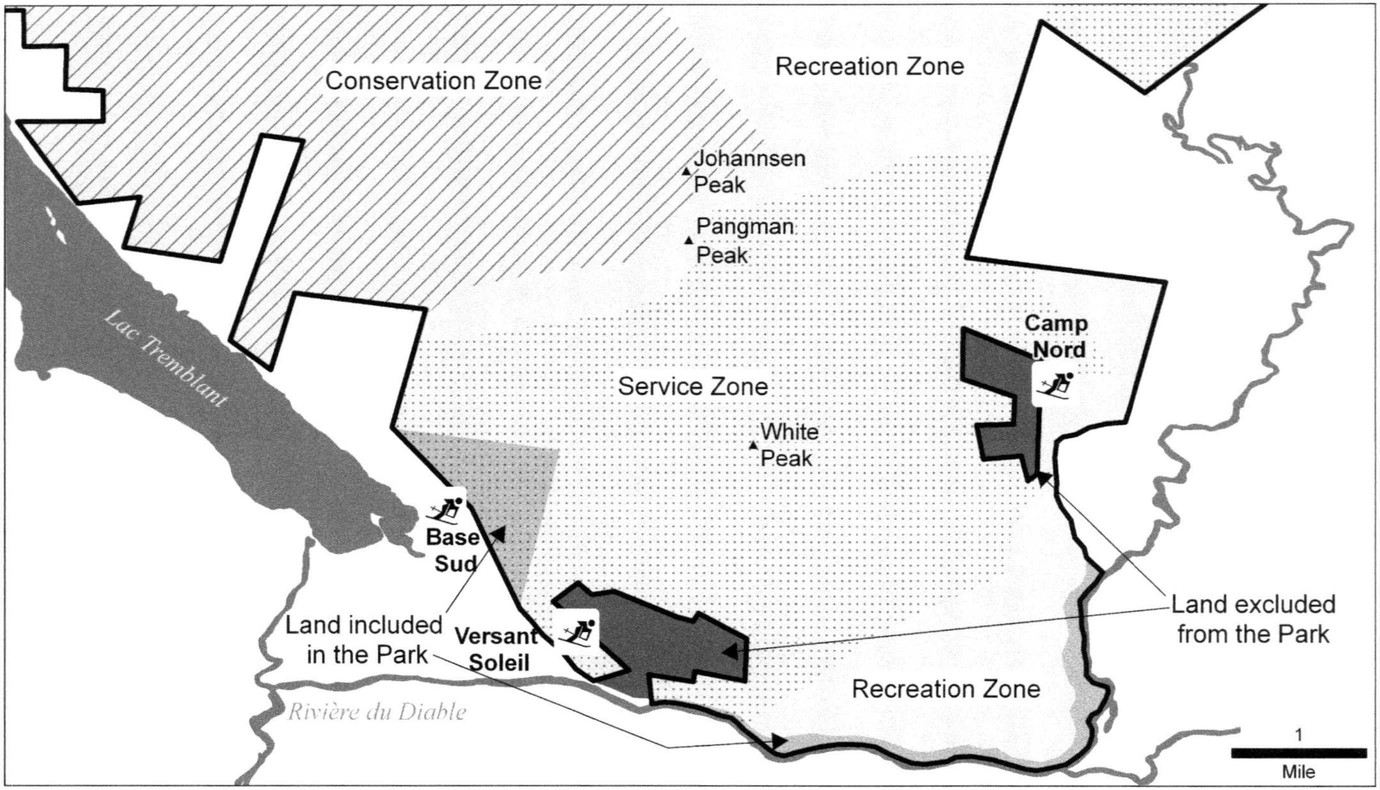

Figure 20.1 The Land Exchange

Data Sources: Société de la faune et des parcs du Québec; DMTI Spatial Inc.; ESRI; ©Department of Natural Resources Canada, all rights reserved.

Rather than simply change the classification of Mont Tremblant Park from "recreation" to "conservation" as intended in 1995, the government amended the Parks Act in 2001[13] to eliminate the basic distinction between recreation and conservation parks, as the de Belleval Committee had recommended in 1996.[14] All provincial parks are now classified as "national parks" whose primary purpose is

> to ensure the conservation and permanent protection of areas representative of the natural regions of Québec and of natural sites with outstanding features, in particular because of their biological diversity, while providing the public with access to those areas or sites for educational or cross-country recreation purposes.[15]

The operation of the ski resort at Mont Tremblant would appear to be at odds with this purpose. This was recognized by the *Société* in 2002:

> Certain activities practiced in Québec parks have led, at the time of their introduction, to a major transformation of the natural environment; such is the case with golf and downhill skiing and to a lesser extent, cross-country skiing skating style and inline skating. These activities belong to the category *activities exceptionally authorized* in the parks of Quebec. Their offer is supported only in parks where they are presently offered. Elsewhere, the development of these activities is forbidden. In parks where these activities are promoted, we try to limit the possible impacts that they may have on the natural environment.[16]

These three things—the change in classification for Mont Tremblant Park, the land exchange and the rezoning—are positive contributions to the protection of the Mont Tremblant ecosystem. They provide enhanced protection for ecologically significant habitat for the Bicknell's thrush and representative vegetation. However, it is not clear that the new park boundaries were delineated based on an ecosystems analysis, rather than administrative concerns or the desire to accommodate growth of the resort-related activities. The law allowed the government, as landlord and regulator, to negotiate change, but it did not mandate either an ecosystems analysis

---

13 An Act to amend the Parks Act, S.Q. 2001, c. 63.

14 Comité de Belleval, Rapport du Comité conseil sur la relance des parcs québécois (Nov. 1996) at 34, quoted in CRELA, Mémoire sur le changement de classification, *supra* note 6, at 8; *see also* Environnement Québec, Communiqués de presse: Relance des parcs québécois: Dépôt du rapport au Comité conseil (Dec. 19, 1996), http://www.menv.gouv.qc.ca/communiques/1996/c961219.htm (last visited Aug. 30, 2004).

15 Parks Act, R.S.Q., c. P-9, s. 1(c).

16 Société de la faune et des parcs du Québec (Sépaq), Parks policy: Activities and Services—Summary, 2, http://www.fapaq.gouv.qc.ca/en/parc_que/parc_que.htm (last visited Aug. 31, 2004). For a copy of the full report, LES PARCS NATIONAUX DU QUÉBEC: LES ACTIVITES ET LES SERVICES : LA POLITIQUE SUR LES PARCS, 4th ed. (2002), see http://www.fapaq.gouv.qc.ca/fr/parc_que/politique_parcs.pdf (last visited Aug. 31, 2004).

Figure 20.2 Mont Tremblant's Ski Slopes

Data Sources: DMTI Spatial Inc.; ESRI; ©Department of Natural Resources Canada, all rights reserved.

or a specific ecological net result. In addition, the extent to which this protection will prove effective in the face of ongoing development pressures remains to be seen.

Mountain Activities

The mountain recreational facilities at Mont Tremblant presently consist of 94 trails totaling 47.6 miles serviced by 14 lifts located at three different sites (Base Sud, Versant Soleil and Camp Nord) around the mountain, for a total skiable area of 625.5 acres, including 479.5 acres (over three-quarters of the total) of fabricated snow.[17] (See Figure 20.2). Several trails are lighted for night skiing.[18] Half of the trails are in the "expert" category, and thus relatively steep (with some reaching 42 degrees of inclination). Glade skiing makes up 31 acres of the total, with most being concentrated at Versant Soleil (60 percent of its skiable area) and a recently opened expert-level area at Camp Nord. There are also three snowboarding "parks" totaling some 40 acres, including one 18-acre park which includes a 150-yard long, 10-yard high "half-pipe."[19] A concrete luge track—almost a mile long and just over four yards wide, the first of its kind in North America—has recently been built on one of the ski trails for summer use.[20] Finally, a 1,000-seat restaurant at the summit services the three ski sites.

What role does the law play to ensure that these facilities are built and used in way that is respectful of the mountain ecosystem? We look at trail development, snowmaking and non-ski mountain activities in an attempt to answer this question.

Trail Development

Trail development at Mont Tremblant is conditioned by a variety of legislative provisions, contractual terms and codes of conduct.

Legislation New ski trail development in the Park is subject to a number of laws and regulations, the most obvious of which is the Parks Act. Under this Act, all works of "maintenance, development or construction in a park"[21] must be authorized

17 *See generally* Mont Tremblant Resort, The Mountain at Mt Tremblant, http://www.tremblant.ca/mountain/statistiques.asp (last visited May 31, 2004).

18 These lighted runs are now open more often than formerly. André Courey, *New on the Mountain*, Tremblant Express, Nov. 2003, *available at* http://www.tremblantexpress.com (last visited May 28, 2004).

19 *See* Snow Park, http://www.tremblant.ca/activities/winter/activities/index-e.htm (last visited July 30, 2007).

20 André Courey, *The Luge: Another Activity at Tremblant*, Tremblant Express, June 2003, *available at* http://www.tremblantexpress.com (last visited May 28, 2004).

21 R.S.Q., c. P-9, ss. 6 & 8.

by the Minister of Sustainable Development, Environment and Parks, who can authorize only those works which respect the conservation purpose of parks[22] and thus "serve to maintain or improve the quality of the park"[23] and are "compatible with continued conservation of the natural environment or preservation of the recreational potential of the park".[24] The Minister's decisions under the Parks Act must also respect the requirements of the Environmental Quality Act, where applicable, and the fact that the same minister is presently responsible for both Acts[25] promotes an integrated approach under the two statutes.

The Environment Quality Act is thus another important statute, of which section 22 is the principal section. This section requires a certificate of authorization from the Minister to "erect or alter a structure . . . [or] carry on an activity" either because of the anticipated consequences (if it seems likely that it "will result in an emission, deposit, issuance or discharge of contaminants into the environment or *a change in the quality of the environment*"[26]) or because of the locale (when it takes place "in a constant or intermittent watercourse, a lake, pond, marsh, swamp or bog"[27]). More precise screening criteria are provided in the Regulation respecting the Application of the Environment Quality Act[28] which lists those projects which are generally exempt from the need for section 22 authorization (basically, projects undertaken in conformity with other acts or regulations, such as those governing the management of forests in the public domain) and—more importantly in the present context—those which are exempt from scrutiny based on anticipated consequences[29] or from scrutiny based on their hydrological locale.[30] These lists, although helpful, are fastidiously drafted: the second and third lists identify 14 and 3 exempted projects, respectively; and some of the listed exemptions contain their own specific exceptions which are then subject to section 22. The most specific reference to trail development is found in section 3 of the Regulation, which screens out sports and recreational activities in hydrological or wetland areas "*except* construction or development work required for such activities";[31] this exception therefore screens them in as requiring authorization

22 *Supra* the text at note 15.

23 R.S.Q., c. P-9, s. 6.

24 *Id.* at s. 8.2 as am. by S.Q. 2004, c. 11, s. 56.

25 See the text in Chapter 19 *supra* at note 47 and following.

26 R.S.Q., c. Q-2, s. 22, para. 1 (emphasis added).

27 *Id.* at s. 22, para. 2.

28 Regulation respecting the Application of the Environment Quality Act, c. Q-2, r. 1.001 (O.C. 1529-93, G.O.Q.1993.II.5996 as am. by O.C.333-2003, G.O.Q.2003.II.1273).

29 *Id.* at s. 2.

30 *Id.* at s. 3. On screening generally, see Joe Weston, *EIA, Decision-making Theory and Screening and Scoping in UK Practice* 43 J. Envtl. Plan. & Mgmt 185–203 (2000).

31 Regulation respecting the Application of the Environment Quality Act, s. 3, para. 1(1) (emphasis added); *see also* Environnement Québec, Demande de certificat d'autorisation: Milieux du loisir et de la villegiature, http://www.menv.gouv.qc.ca/ministere/certif/fiche6.htm (last visited Sept. 2, 2004).

under the "locale" criterion set out in section 22 itself. In non-hydrological and wetland areas, sports and recreation related construction or development work is screened in as requiring authorization under section 22's "consequence" provision (i.e. "change in the quality of the environment"). As the government has applied section 22, the development of ski trails of more than a kilometer (.62 miles) in length needs section 22 approval.[32] Other relevant listed projects, drafted in the same exemption/exclusion style, relate to forest and wildlife management, work involving pesticide use, and construction of forest roads.

Moreover, a section 22 authorization does not necessarily mean that a full environmental impact assessment (EIA) will be held. EIAs are governed by Division IV.1 of the Act, which was added to the legislation in 1978 to provide for a process of impact assessment and review, with public consultation and a possible public hearing before the *Bureau d'audiences publiques sur l'environnement* (BAPE).[33] (See textbox in the preceding chapter.) But the statute requires an environmental impact assessment only "in the cases provided for by regulation of the Government,"[34] which considerably reduces the reach and effect of EIAs in Quebec. The Regulation respecting Environmental Impact Assessment and Review[35] lists some 37 projects subject to review, which have limited, if any, relevance to trail development at Mont Tremblant. The most possible include dredging and filling operations in watercourses ultimately draining into the Saint Lawrence River, modifying the course of a river, and roadworks on forest roads over 2 kilometers long.

The rather tortuous drafting of the Quebec Act's screening provisions thus invites the disaggregation of larger projects into smaller discrete ones: trails in hydrological and wetland areas or outside them, longer and shorter trails, trails

32 Entente cadre entre la Ville de Mont Tremblant et Station Mont Tremblant Société en Commandite sur l'aménagement du complexe touristique Versant Soleil [hereinafter Entente cadre 2003], Annexe G: Évaluation environnementale et plan d'orientation du programme de contrôle et de suivi environnemental des projets de construction, d'entretien et de gestion du site du Versant Soleil de la Station Mont Tremblant sur le territoire de la Ville de Mont Tremblant [hereinafter Annexe G], 8, 16.

33 Environment Quality Act, s. 31.3, requires the Minister to make the environmental impact statement public and to have the proponent's undertake the "public information and consultation" process provided by regulation (*see* Regulation respecting Environmental Impact Assessment and Review R.R.Q. 1981, c. Q-2, r. 9, ss. 6-16); s. 31.3 of the Act also authorizes "[a]ny person, group or a municipality" to apply to the Minister for a public hearing, which the Minister must accept unless he considers the application to be "frivolous." *See* Rules of Procedure relating to the Conduct of Public Hearings, R.R.Q. 1981, c. Q-2.

34 R.S.Q. c. Q-2, s. 31.1. Note that the Act's basic presumption against public consultation (unless required by regulation) is more restrictive than the usual legislative model's basic presumption in favor of public consultation (unless exempted by regulation).

35 Regulation respecting Environmental Impact Assessment and Review, s. 2.

subject to an EIA and trails not subject, and so on. The assessment of each project might be holistic—and the Regulation respecting Environmental Impact Assessment and Review calls for an evaluation of the "positive, negative and residual impacts of the project on the environment, including indirect, cumulative, latent and irreversible effects" on "the aspects of the environment which could be affected by the project, such as fauna, flora, human communities, the cultural, archeological and historical heritage of the area, agricultural resources and the use made of resources of the area".[36] As a result, the government could take an ecosystems perspective for each discrete portion. However, the limited scope of the discrete project to be evaluated militates against a comprehensive, holistic assessment of the cumulative ecosystem impacts of the larger project of which it is part.

The Minister does have the power under the Act to submit more comprehensive questions to the BAPE for inquiry and analysis; he or she may submit "any question relating to the quality of the environment" and may require it to hold a public hearing.[37] This could have included a request for a comprehensive study of the cumulative effects of the entire four-season development proposed by Intrawest (and perhaps even by others) at Mont Tremblant—on all mountain slopes and for all base camps, winter and summer. However, this was not done. No comprehensive study was requested by the Minister and no public hearing was held, despite calls for one.

The Saga Of Mont Orford, Quebec

Contrary to the relative ease with which Intrawest obtained government approval for expansion at Mont Tremblant through a land exchange and other concessions, a similar project at the Mont Orford ski area was hotly contested and ultimately blocked.

Mont Orford is a Quebec national park, like Mont Tremblant, and is located in the Eastern Townships close to the border between Quebec and Vermont. The developer and operator of the ski hill, Mont Orford Inc., wanted the land located at the base of the ski hill to build 1,400 condominium units and a golf course. This would entail a change in the park boundaries as private ownership and commercial activities of the nature proposed are prohibited there. As we saw for Mont Tremblant, a public hearing is a prerequisite for a change in park boundaries, and the Minister responsible for the environment submitted the question to the *Bureau d'audiences publiques sur l'environnement* (BAPE) [Office of Public Hearings on the Environment] for hearing, rather than simply have a meeting run by a government department as had been done for Mont Tremblant.

The 2005 BAPE report recommended against government approval of the project, as it found it would have adverse impacts in terms of both biodiversity and ecological integrity. The BAPE also called for further studies to be conducted, including a study of the quantity of water that could be taken without modifying the aquatic ecosystem, and for an examination of the legality of the exchange under the Parks Act.

36 *Id.* at s. 3, para. 1 (b) and (c).

37 Environment Quality Act, R.S.Q., c. Q-2, s. 6.3.

However, the BAPE's reports are advisory only; the developer pressured the government, threatening to lay off all employees until the project was approved; and the government eventually decided to authorize the project. The opaquely named "Act to Ensure the Enlargement of Parc National du Mont Orford, the Preservation of the Biodiversity of Adjacent Lands, and the Maintenance of Recreational Tourism Activities" was adopted in June 2006, after an acrimonious debate in the National Assembly culminating in the government's imposition of closure. Special legislation was necessary to counter objections that a sale of land was illegal under the Parks Act. The 2006 Act changed the boundaries of the Park to exclude the lands in question; it provided for their sale by public tender, with the proceeds to be used to buy other (but less attractive or environmentally important) park land on the northern boundary; and it set out the land use controls and regulations that apply to the land, including the residential and commercial portions, specifically overriding the provisions of any by-laws adopted under the Act respecting Land Use Planning and Development—thereby preventing the municipalities from blocking the development, as had occurred at Mont Pinacle (see textbox in Chapter 21).

Opponents of the project argued strenuously that adopting the special legislation put at risk all protected lands, publicly and privately owned alike. For example, the *Fiducie foncière Mont Pinacle* sent a strongly worded letter to Quebec's Premier, underlining the chilling effect this would have on private donations of land. The government proposed a modified project, which would entail the sale of land at the base of the mountain but not the mountain itself. This proposal was acceptable to local mayors but not to an influential citizens' group, SOS Orford. A class action was brought against the government in December 2006 on behalf of all those who had donated either money or land for the creation or consolidation of Parc Mont Orford. The fate of Mont Orford was an important issue in a provincial election held the following spring, and when the government was returned with only a minority of members in the legislature, it decided not to go through with the project. In June 2007 it amended the special legislation to preclude the sale of lands excluded from the Park. It also bought out the remainder of Mont Orford Inc.'s 70-year lease to the ski hill and turned it over to a government agency (the *Société des établissements de plein air du Québec*) to run until May 2009, at which time local residents must have agreed on a plan to operate it or it will be closed. But the mountain ecosystem remains vulnerable, as the lands are still outside the Park's boundaries and outside the land use control jurisdiction of the local municipality.

Sources: Parks Act, R.S.Q., c. P-9; BAPE, Les répercutions d'un échange de terrains sur la biodiversité et l'intégrité écologique du parc national de Mont Orford : Rapport d'enquête et d'audience publique, Rapport 209, mars 2005, *available at* http://www.bape.gouv.qc.ca/sections/rapports/publications/bape209.pdf (last visited, Jan. 12, 2008); Act to Ensure the Enlargement of Parc National du Mont Orford, the Preservation of the Biodiversity of Adjacent Lands, and the Maintenance of Recreational Tourism Activities, S.Q. 2006, c. 14, as am. by S.Q. 2007, c. 9; Saint-Pierre and Gravel v. Procurer Général du Québec, *available at* http://www.sosorford.org/IGM/pdf/Requete_autorisation_06_12_13.pdf (last visited Sept. 4, 2007).

The federal Canadian Environmental Assessment Act[38] applies to the developments at Versant Soleil and Camp Nord as a result of application for federal funding for two sites. It is more cumulative in approach than the Quebec legislation in that it provides, for example, that closely related projects may be evaluated as a single project.[39] The Mont Tremblant assessment therefore looked at Intrawest's Versant Soleil and Camp Nord development as a whole, both on the mountain and in the base camps. The Screening Report recognizes that the development of the skiable domain will result in a range of adverse environmental effects, many of which cannot be completely attenuated (e.g., effects relating to hydraulics and hydrology; surface waters; aquatic, riparian and terrestrial vegetation; and herpetic, aquatic and avian fauna and their habitat), although it does not regard their residual effects as either individually or cumulatively significant.[40] Nevertheless, the Screening Report set out a number of mitigation measures to be taken,[41] some ten of which relate to watercourse crossings (19 new ones were planned for the skiable domain), eight to the aquatic milieu in general (e.g., creating buffer zones along water courses, replanting banks with native shrubs and plants, protecting identified wetlands), seven to terrestrial fauna and flora (including limiting forest clearing to the strict minimum,[42] conserving active deer travel corridors, and working outside birds' nesting and breeding periods[43]) and 24 measures relating to the skiable area and multifunctional trails (including using a variety of erosion reduction measures, limiting the use of heavy machinery, protecting watercourses by sediment ponds and other filtering devices, replanting with indigenous plants, etc.).

Other laws and regulations that might affect trail development focus on specific elements of the ecosystem: watercourses, fauna and flora. The Protection Policy for Lakeshores, Riverbanks, Littoral Zones and Floodplains, adopted under section 2.1 of Quebec's Environment Quality Act, provides for the protection of banks, shores and floodplains as being "critical to the survival of the ecological

---

38 S.C. 1992, c. 37.

39 *Id.* at s. 15(2)*; see also* Chapter 21 *infra*, the text following note 99.

40 Infrastructure Canada & Fisheries and Oceans Canada, Environmental Assessment Screening Report, Mont Tremblant: Development of Versant Soleil and Camp Nord, Mont Tremblant (Phases 3 and 4) para. 7.0 (August 2004), http://www.infrastructure.gc.ca/pn/csif/mont-tremblant/report_e.shtml (last visited Dec. 7, 2004) [hereinafter Environmental Assessment Screening Report].

41 *Id.* at para. 8.0.

42 Although safety concerns could militate against this. For example, three skiers died in just over a month after hitting trees on Quebec slopes in the 2005 ski season, and coroners' inquests were called to investigate at least two of them. *Skier Killed When He Hits Tree*, THE [MONTREAL] GAZETTE, Mar. 5, 2005, at A9.

43 Environmental Assessment Screening Report, *supra* note 40, para. 8.0. Clearing in the Bicknell's thrush habitat is authorized as long as it is done outside their breeding period; a Bicknell's thrush habitat is defined as "dominant or co-dominant balsam fir habitats … above 800 m [2625 ft] altitude".

and biological components of watercourses and bodies of water."[44] It requires the authorization of the Minister responsible for the environment for most construction and other activities carried out in protected areas. This would include the cutting and filling necessary to construct ski trails where this affects mountain streams.

Legislation relating to the protection of flora and fauna includes the Act respecting the Conservation and Development of Wildlife. This Act provides for the designation of "wildlife habitats," in which "[n]o person may . . . carry on an activity that may alter any biological, physical or chemical component peculiar to the habitat of the animal or fish concerned," unless the activity is exempted by regulation, carried out according to regulation, or "authorized by the Minister or the Government under this Act."[45] The leased lands in the Park are governed by the Regulation respecting Wildlife Habitats, which applies to habitats located on public lands.[46] Protected habitats under the Regulation include a "water fowl gathering area," a "habitat of a threatened or vulnerable wildlife species," a "fish habitat," a "muskrat habitat," a "heronry" and a "white-tailed deer yard." Mont Tremblant is at the northern limit of the distribution area of white-tailed deer.[47] The Regulation defines a deer yard as "a wooded area measuring at least 250 hectares [617.8 acres] where white-tailed deer gather during the period when snow cover exceeds ... 50 centimetres [16.7 in.]....",[48] and this would include some of the lands leased by Station Mont Tremblant.[49] The Regulation sets out standards

44 Preamble, Protection Policy for Lakeshores, Riverbanks, Littoral Zones and Floodplains, c. Q-2, r. 17.3 (O.C. 468-2005, G.O.Q.2005.II.1441), *available at* http://www2.publicationsduquebec.gouv.qc.ca/home.php# (last visited July 31, 2007). This Policy, which was first adopted in 1987 and revised in 1991, 1996 and 2005, is discussed in more detail in relation to golf course construction. See the text in Chapter 21 *infra* at note 96.

45 R.S.Q., c. C-61.1, s. 128.6.

46 Regulation respecting Wildlife Habitat, r. 0.1.5 (O.C. 905-93, G.O.Q. 1993. II.3536), s. 1. The Act respecting the Conservation and Development of Wildlife provides that wildlife "preserves" may be established on privately owned land with the consent of the owner (s. 122) and wildlife "habitats" may be designated with or without consent (ss. 128.1ff), although the Minister "may grant financial assistance" to an owner if the designation is "harmful to his interests" (s. 128.17). And the Act respecting Nature Reserves on Private Land, S.C. 2001, c. 14 (since incorporated into the National Heritage Conservation Act, R.S.Q., c. C-61.01, at s. 54), provides for the protection of privately owned areas having "significant biological, ecological, wildlife, floristic, geological, geomorphic or landscape features"; *see also* Environnement Québec, Protected Areas: Private Land, http://www.menv.gouv.qc.ca/biodiversite/prive/terres-priv-en.htm (last visited Aug. 31, 2004).

47 Ville de Mont Tremblant, *Le Versant Soleil ... Des Réponses à vos Questions*, INFO MONT TREMBLANT, Autumn 2002, at 4, 6, *available at* http://www.villedemont-tremblant.qc.ca/jahia/Jahia/pid/53 (last visited Mar. 16, 2005). Tremblant's deer population has increased over the last decade, as winters have been moderate, but this could change.

48 Regulation respecting Wildlife Habitat, s. 1(2).

49 The protected habitats must also be demarcated on a map prepared by the Minister; some 700 habitats have been mapped to date (Environnement Québec, Répertoire des aires protégées et des aires de conservation gérées au Québec,"Deuxième partie" (1999), http://www.

in regard to various activities in the designated wildlife habitats, including the development of recreational sites. For example, the Regulation permits "laying out of trails for hiking, riding, cycling or cross-country skiing" in a white-tailed deer yard only under certain conditions, including that the activity take place "only between May 1 and December 1" and that "the sum of the areas used for such activities ... not represent more than 2% of the total wooded area of the .... yard or more than 2% of the total area of all the shelter stands located within the yard."[50] Versant Soleil is located in a white-tailed deer yard, and these dispositions do not permit alpine skiing (nor does the seasonal proviso accommodate the otherwise permitted cross-country skiing). However, the Act provides that the Minister "may authorize the carrying on of an activity that alters a wildlife habitat:"[51]

> Before issuing an authorization, the Minister shall take into account, in particular but not exclusively, the physical features of the area, the nature of the proposed activity, *the economic and social consequences of the proposed activities*, the impact of the activity on the conservation of the wildlife and its habitat and the possibility of substituting another habitat.[52]

The ski station would thus presumably have (or have had) no difficulty obtaining an authorization, should one be necessary.

In a similar vein, the Act respecting Threatened or Vulnerable Species[53] provides for the protection of threatened or vulnerable plant and animal species through a process of listing and habitat designation, with the protected species and habitats then being governed by the provisions of the Act respecting the Conservation and Development of Wildlife. This Act has limited effect on the recreational development at Mont Tremblant, mainly because none of the wildlife species listed as threatened or vulnerable and only one of the plant species (wild leeks) are found in the area.[54] Moreover, the Act provides that the government may,

---

menv.gouv.qc.ca/biodiversite/aires_protegees/repertoire/partie2.htm, at 2 (last visited Feb. 5, 2002)), and we assume that these include relevant habitats in the Mont Tremblant area.

50 Regulation respecting Wildlife Habitat, s. 27 (2) & (3). A "shelter stand" is defined as "a softwood stand or a softwood-dominant mixed stand 7 meters [7.7 yds] high or more, that has a canopy of 60% or more and is located in a white-tailed deer yard." *Id.* at s. 2.

51 R.S.Q., c. C-61.1, s. 128.7.

52 *Id.* (emphasis added).

53 R.S.Q., c. E-12.01. The federal government also has jurisdiction in relation to wildlife habitat in general (*see* Environment Canada, Habitat Conservation: Laws and Policies, http://www.cws-scf.ec.gc.ca/habitat/laws_e.cfm (last visited Sept. 2, 2004)) and endangered species in particular (*see* Government of Canada, Species at Risk Act Public Registry, http://www.sararegistry.gc.ca/default_e.cfm (last visited Sept. 2, 2004)).

54 *See* Regulation respecting Threatened or Vulnerable [wildlife] Species and their Habitats, r. 0.2.3 (O.C. 950-2001, G.O.Q.2001.II.4851, as am. by O.C. 902-2003, G.O.Q.2003.II.2787); and Regulation respecting Threatened or Vulnerable Plant Species and their Habitats, r. 0.4 (O.C. 757-2005, G.O.Q.2005.II.3611, replacing O.C. 489-98

on the advice of the Minister responsible for the environment and after a public hearing, authorize a particular activity "if it considers that the consequences of not carrying on or of abandoning the activity would be more harmful *to the public* than the alteration of the habitat of the plant species concerned."[55] Once again, this provides the possibility for an exemption favoring Station Mont Tremblant, should one be necessary. Finally, the Act also stipulates that the government may adopt a regulation of general application, identifying activities which do not require authorization even though they "may alter the ecosystem, biological diversity and physical or chemical components of the habitat of a threatened or vulnerable plant species."[56] No such regulation has been adopted to date.

In sum, Quebec's regulations appear on their face to consider and constrain the ecological impact of ski trail development, but they may in fact have limited effect. The regulations under the Environment Quality Act are sensitive to the ecosystem functions of wetlands, water bodies, and littoral zones, but the disaggregated way the Act is drafted encourages a restricted and fragmented ecological analysis, with limited public input. The legislation governing wildlife addresses the potential conflict between trail development and habitat protection, such as deer yards, but the protection it provides can be overridden to accommodate countervailing economic and social priorities. Given the limits on public disclosure and hearings, little is publicly available about the extent to which the various provincial laws have affected Intrawest's construction of new trails. The federal Canadian Environmental Assessment Act, on the other hand, takes a broader ecological perspective, looking at the cumulative effects of the resort development as a whole, not just some or even all of the trails, and provides for some measure of public input. The federal review, triggered by the investment of federal funds, thus provides a more comprehensive, publicly available ecological assessment and protection than does provincial law.

Contract Law The 1991 lease of the skiable domain between Station Mont Tremblant and the government[57] is another source of law governing trail development. Clause 7 of the lease authorizes Station Mont Tremblant, as lessee, to use the area only for the development and operation of a "centre for ski and [other] sports and leisure activities," including downhill and cross-country skiing, recreational tourism, walking and hiking, bicycling and other similar activities; it provides that the lessee may, at its own expense, open ski trails and install and operate ski lifts, artificial snowmaking and other necessary equipment; and it requires that

---

as am.). The latter Regulation prohibits the harvesting of wild leeks in parks, ecological reserves and wildlife preserves (although a limited quantity of leeks may be harvested for personal consumption elsewhere). *Id.* at s. 4.

55 R.S.Q., c. E-12.01, s. 19 (emphasis added).

56 *Id.* at s. 39.

57 Transfert et refonte du bail [Assignment and Revision of Lease] between the government and Station Mont Tremblant, Aug. 31, 1991.

all of this be done in conformity with a development master plan, revised every five years, for the leased area. The plan must include "a study of matters related to the maintenance of the recreational potential of the park" and a land use map, as well as set out all development projects.[58] It is to be prepared by the lessee and submitted to the Minister responsible for the Park for approval;[59] the Minister then has 60 days in which to grant or refuse approval, in default of which the plan is deemed to be approved.[60] Station Mont Tremblant is not to undertake any project (including "the modification of any natural milieu (watercourses, tree cutting, etc.)") without the prior authorization of the Minister, although this authorization may be given through approval (or deemed approval) of the development master plan and related documents.[61] The lease provides that the lessee must carry out its activities in conformity with the master plan and "following generally accepted practices",[62] but it does not contain any other clauses addressing ecosystem issues in a more explicit manner. Intrawest's first ten-year plan was approved in 1992,[63] but it is not available to the public; nor is any information available about a second ten-year plan. Consequently, it is difficult to assess whether the master planning process reflects an ecosystems analysis.

However, more specifically ecological control is provided in development agreements subsequently entered into between the Municipality of Mont Tremblant and Station Mont Tremblant in the context of the construction of the base camps. A first development agreement, dated December 23, 1992,[64] related to the construction of the first pedestrian village, Base Sud. Under this agreement, Station Mont Tremblant contracted to invest about $30.5 million Can. in the ski facilities in return for the right to build a designated number of housing units (with housing construction being linked to progress in developing the ski station). Both activities (ski facility development as well as base camp construction) were to be done in conformity with an "environmental control, monitoring and evaluation program" annexed to the agreement. The environmental requirements of this program related to a wide range of issues, including erosion control on slopes and banks, conservation of wooded edges of waterways, road construction, water quality control, protection of the deer yard, fish habitat preservation, forest conservation and wetland preservation. The environmental protection measures to be taken at each stage of the project were to be decided in advance and set out in the various applications for building and other permits. Compliance with the program was to be monitored by a qualified professional chosen by Station

58 Clause 8.3.

59 Clauses 7 and 8.

60 Clause 29.

61 Clause 9.2.

62 Clause 7.3 ["suivant les règles de l'art"].

63 Dupuy, *supra* note 6, at 16 n. 14.

64 Protocole d'entente entre Municipalité de Mont Tremblant et Station Mont Tremblant société en commandite.

Mont Tremblant during construction and for two years following completion. In the event that the Municipality and the Station did not agree with the evaluator's reports, they could commence arbitration proceedings. It is difficult to assess the effectiveness of this regime, as the document includes a confidentiality provision under which the Municipality undertook not to make public any of the information it receives under the agreement.

An "environmental control and monitoring program" is annexed to a framework agreement, dated April 8, 2003,[65] between Station Mont Tremblant and the municipality[66] relating to Versant Soleil. However, this program has only limited application to mountain developments on the leased land and will thus be discussed in the next chapter on base camp development.

Voluntary Codes of Conduct Station Mont Tremblant has followed its own "Trail Development Guide" ["Guide d'aménagement des pistes"] since 1994 in order to limit adverse environmental impacts as much as possible.[67] Trail design favors a slope's natural topography in order to limit the amount of cutting and filling, and avoids ecologically sensitive areas such as wetlands and watercourses as much as possible. Construction (tree-cutting and terracing) techniques limit run-off and sedimentation which affect fish habitats and the general health of ponds and lakes; the cut trees and roots are used in the fill, which facilitates site regeneration and avoids overuse of heavy machinery (thereby limiting soil compaction which exacerbates run-off and erosion); trail replanting follows immediately.

Station Mont Tremblant also adheres to the National Ski Areas Association's "Sustainable Slopes" environmental charter, adopted in 2000. This sets out guidelines relating to wildlife habitat protection and forest and vegetation management as well as to other matters such as water and energy conservation, water quality protection and solid waste reduction. Station Mont Tremblant is conducting a comprehensive audit of its environmental practices as part of its adherence to the charter,[68] with a biologist as one of the members the team.[69]

Intrawest's attention to environmental matters in trail design is recognized by the ski industry. Whistler/Blackcomb has received Mountain Sports Media's "Silver Eagle Award" five times in the last decade, and the "Golden Eagle Award

65 Entente cadre 2003, Annexe G, *supra* note 32.

66 That is, the recently merged Town of Mont Tremblant. See the discussion in Chapter 21 *infra* at note 3.

67 Tremblant: Deux nouvelles pistes dans le respect de l'environnement, http://www.carnetduski.com/actualit%C3%A9s/decembres03/Tremblant_NllesPistes.htm (last visited Sept. 2, 2004).

68 André Courey, *Tremblant Conducts Environmental Audit*, Tremblant Express, Jan. 2003, *available at* http://www.tremblantexpress.com/ (last visited May 28, 2004); *see also* Station Mont Tremblant, Tremblant's Environmental Values, http://www.tremblant.ca/about/environment.asp (last visited Mar. 6, 2004).

69 *Id.* ("Tremblant is one of very few ski resorts in North America to have a full-time biologist.")

for Overall Environmental Excellence" in 2003;[70] Station Mont Tremblant was a finalist for a Silver Eagle Award in 2000, for trail development at Versant Soleil:

> Tremblant Resort designed its narrow, winding trails in such a way as to leave an untouched strip of vegetation beside its mountain streams, which in turn prevents warm-up and sediment contamination. This innovative trail layout was made possible by judicious planning, the use of a helicopter to haul materials, the minimal use of equipment, as well as by immediate replanting.[71]

Mont Tremblant thus receives good marks for its trail development. One cannot help wondering, however, about the extent to which the cumulative effect of the trails adversely affects surrounding flora and fauna. For example, the trails converge like spokes on a wheel at the summit restaurant, so that the contiguous natural areas remaining in this fragile area are proportionally less.[72] Local bears probably object to a new trail, "La Griffe" (named for bear-claw markings on the trees), through their mountain territory.[73] Lighted trails and night-skiing also affect habitat environment. Glade skiing leaves an enlarged footprint on the mountain. Eighteen-acre snowboard parks are large gaps to cross. And the four-yard wide concrete luge trail must be equally daunting to local fauna in summer. As indicated above, however, the federal and provincial regulations play a relatively small role in moderating the ecological impacts of these activities, and it is difficult to know the extent to which the contractual arrangements address their effects.

Snowmaking

Snowmaking is an increasingly important aspect of a successful ski resort operation, and this is particularly so in northeast North America with its lower mountain ranges. Warmer winters are taking their toll, and the average snowfall in the Northeast has dropped by about a third during the last decade.[74] Snowmaking helps insulate a resort against unpredictable snowfall levels in any given year, and extends the ski season every year, which increases a resort's profitability. As we have seen, just over three-quarters of the total skiable area of Mont Tremblant (479.5

---

70 SKI Magazine Announces 2003 Golden Eagle Award Winner http://www.skimag.com/skimag/travel/article/0,12795,594177,00.html (last visited Sept. 2, 2004).

71 Mont Tremblant Resort, Station Mont Tremblant Environmental Prizes, http://www.tremblant.ca/about/environmental/prizes-e.htm (last visited Mar. 17, 2005).

72 *See* Mont Tremblant Resort, Hiking Trail Map, http://www.tremblant.ca/activities/pdf/carte_des_sentiers.pdf (last visited Sept. 2, 2004).

73 André Courey, *New on the Mountain*, Tremblant Express, Nov. 2003, *available at* http://www.tremblantexpress.com/ (last visited May 28, 2004) ("Don't worry about the bears. They sleep all winter!").

74 Crédit Suisse First Boston Corporation, Equity Research: Intrawest Corporation (March 26, 2001) 10.

of 625.5 acres) are provided with artificial snow. Station Mont Tremblant began using more efficient equipment in 2002–2003, which increased its snowmaking capacity by 30 percent.[75]

The use of artificial snowmaking equipment for the Base Sud trails is specifically authorized by clause 7 of the 1991 lease between Station Mont Tremblant and the government, discussed above. It provides that the water for snowmaking and base camp consumption is to be drawn from Lac Tremblant, at the southeastern foot of the mountain near the first base camp.[76] Other possible sources of water in the area are Rivière du Diable, running along the base of the mountain into Lac Tremblant, and groundwater. These are to be tapped for the new development at Camp Nord.[77] The overall amounts needed now raise concerns about the capacity of these sources to meet the new demands. Snowmaking is not regulated under the Environment Quality Act.[78]

Thus, the ecological impacts of snowmaking, both in terms of its demand on water supplies and its impact on slopes, are not subject to regulation. If the government considered them, it would have been in the context of the initial lease negotiations, where the government was acting as landlord, but the record does not indicate whether any environmental assessment was made then about water capacity.

Non-Ski Mountain Activities

As we have seen, mountain resorts are no longer single-purpose ski resorts. To be economically viable today, they have to position themselves as four-season resorts offering a panoply of on-mountain and off-mountain activities. Of particular concern for a mountain ecology is the use of off-road vehicles, both motorized (snowmobiles and all-terrain vehicles) and non-motorized (mountain bikes).

A mountain resort's vehicular traffic is a source of ecosystem disturbance. Access roads to the resort must be constructed or widened; roads must be kept passable (cleared and salted or sanded) in the winter; adequate parking at the mountain base must be provided; service roads for the mountain facilities must be built; and non-ski recreational activities must be provided.

75 Mont Tremblant Resort, Trail Maps: South Slope, http://www.tremblant.ca/mountain/pdf/cartedespistes_sud.pdf (last visited Sept. 2, 2004).

76 The water thus reaches the leased land through an aqueduct crossing some of Station Mont Tremblant's own land, and the lease (clause 11) therefore provides for a perpetual servitude [easement] over the Station's lands in favor of the leased lands to accommodate the aqueduct.

77 See the discussion in Chapter 21 *infra* following note 8.

78 R.S.Q., c. Q-2. The only explicit mention of snow under the Act is the Regulation respecting Snow Elimination Sites, O.C. 1063-97, G.O.Q. 1997.II.4522, which limits the places where cleared snow may be deposited, particularly with a view to restricting the former practice of discharging it into a body of water or a watercourse. This addresses issues of water quality, rather than quantity.

Off-road motorized vehicles are of particular concern in this regard. A mountain resort's facilities (particularly its service roads and cleared trails) are attractive for snowmobiles in the winter and all-terrain vehicles (ATVs) in the summer, and their uncontrolled use could be particularly deleterious to a mountain's ecosystem. In Quebec, the Act respecting Off-highway Vehicles[79] permits the use of snowmobiles, ATVs and other off-road vehicles on publicly owned lands "subject to the conditions, restrictions and prohibitions imposed" under several statutes, including the Parks Act.[80] On land leased under these statutes, such as Mont Tremblant, operation of an off-road vehicle must be authorized by the tenant (i.e., Station Mont Tremblant).[81] Quebec's park policy puts motorized sports in the class of "forbidden activities" as they are "not compatible with the [conservation] mission of Quebec's parks."[82] However, the government continues to permit the circulation of snowmobiles in some parks, including Mont Tremblant Park, a decision which is contested by environmental groups.[83] Station Mont Tremblant now provides snowmobiles for recreational use by visitors over "[t]housands of kilometres of forested trails and snow covered fields",[84] although in the past their

79 R.S.Q., c. V-1.2 (adopted by S.Q. 1996, c. 60). It applies to snowmobiles, motocross vehicles (that is, "a motorized all-terrain vehicle equipped with handlebars and at least two wheels, that is designed to be straddled and whose mass does not exceed 600 kilograms": *id.* at s. 1) and other motorized off-road vehicles designated by regulation. The Regulation respecting Motor Vehicle Traffic in Certain Fragile Environments, O.C. 1143-97, G.O.Q. 1997.II.4595, adopted under the Environment Quality Act, R.S.Q., c. Q-2, is of limited effect. For one thing, a mountain per se is not a fragile environment under the Act, which is defined to include marshes, swamps and peat bogs (as well as dunes, offshore bars and beaches). S. 1. As well, snowmobiles are exempted from most of its provisions. Ss. 3 & 4.

80 Act respecting Off-highway Vehicles, R.S.Q., c. V-1.2, s. 8.

81 *Id.*

82 Société de la faune et des parcs, The National Parks of Quebec: Nature—The road to discovery: Activities and Services, http://www.fapaq.gouv.qc.ca/en/parc_que/parc_act_ser_Ang.pdf (last visited Dec. 7, 2004). Down-hill skiing and other activities "requiring major modifications to a large surface of the natural environment" are also prohibited, but are "exceptionally authorized" in parks where they were offered when the new policy was adopted in 2001.

83 Conseil régional de l'environnement des Laurentides (CRELA), Le CRELA demande l'imposition d'une tarification d'accès aux motoneiges qui circule dans le Parc du Mont Tremblant (Press Release Mar. 14, 2001), http://uqcn.qc.ca/aires_protegees/motoneiges/tarification.html (last visited July 13, 2004) ("The absence of a precise timeframe for the exclusion of snowmobiles leads us to believe that the authorities are ready to tolerate this ecological aberration for a long time more so as not to offend [*froisser*] the snowmobile lobby") (author's translation).

84 Mont Tremblant Resort, Winter Activities—Snowmobiling, http://tremblant.com/whattoseedo/winter_activities/snowmobiling/index-e.htm (last visited Aug. 31, 2004).

use was limited to employees for work[85] and for ferrying privileged clients to the top of the mountain.[86]

Snowmobile Noise and Pollution Lawsuits
Snowmobile use has become a controversial issue in Quebec. In 2004, a group of affected residents in the Mont Tremblant area succeeded at trial in a class action for noise and pollution resulting from snowmobile use. The action was brought by residents along the P'tit Train du Nord Linear Park (the present right-of-way of a former, immensely popular and affectionately remembered ski train to the Laurentian ski areas) against the Quebec government and the regional municipality which manages the park trail. (See map in Chapter 21, Figure 21.2.) The favorable trial decision has been described as "historic."

In the face of dire warnings about the decision's effect on the tourist industry, the Quebec government immediately responded with a moratorium on similar lawsuits. This 2004 moratorium was made to apply retroactively from December 2001; it was initially slated to expire in May 2006 but has been extended to May 2011. The controversy surrounding the issue is illustrated both by the retroactivity of the legislation and by the fact the legislation was adopted during the Christmas rush to end of the session; it was given all three readings on Dec. 16, 2004, and was assented to the following day.

Sources: Coalition pour la protection de l'environnement du Parc linéaire "Petit Train du Nord" et al. v. Municipalité Régionale de Comté des Laurentides et al., Que. Sup. Ct, Nov. 30, 2004, available at http://www.jugements.qc.ca: Bruno Bisson, Les Motoneiges Bannies du Parc Linéaire des Laurentides: Décision historique de la Cour supérieure, La Presse [de Montréal], Dec. 2, 2004, at A1; André Duchesne, L'industrie Touristique des Laurentides Catastrophée: L'interdiction des motoneiges dans le parc du Petit Train du Nord la priverait de retombées de 100 millions, La Presse [de Montréal], Dec. 3, 2004, at A1; and Act respecting Off-highway Vehicles, s. 87.1 (added by S.Q. 2004, c. 27, and am. by S.Q. 2006, c. 12).

The rules applicable to ATVs are similar to those applying to snowmobiles. An off-highway vehicle club may establish trails on private land with permission of the owner; and on public land, it may do so "according to law," with the express authorization "of the Minister or the body having authority over the land or responsible for the management or administration of the land.[87] We have no evidence about the use of ATVs in Mont Tremblant Park itself, but Station Mont Tremblant now offers ATV tours as one of its featured activities: "Ride dirt roads

85 André Courey, *Club Produit Motoneige: Snowmobile Industry Getting Organized*, Tremblant Express, Feb, 2003, *available at* http://www.tremblantexpress.com/ (last visited May 28, 2004).

86 CRELA, Mémoire sur le changement de classification, *supra* note 6, at 14.

87 Act respecting Off-highway Vehicles, R.S.Q., c. V-1.2, s. 15.

and backcountry trails on an all-terrain vehicle. Bump over rocks and through dried-up river beds, then *ride up a mountain top and enjoy the views*."[88]

The use of off-road non-motorized vehicles, principally mountain bikes, is also a concern as they can be used far off the beaten track, thereby extending the potential for and range of ecosystem disturbance. Careening pell-mell down steep, wooded slopes seems particularly attractive to mountain bikers. Unlike motorized off-road vehicles, non-motorized vehicles are not the subject of any special rules and regulations. In particular, neither the Act respecting Off-highway Vehicles[89] nor the Regulation respecting Motor Vehicle Traffic in Certain Fragile Environments[90] applies to mountain bikes. Quebec's park policy classes "outings on an all-terrain bike" among "generally permitted secondary activities." It notes that "[r]epeated passing of all-terrain bikes causes soil erosion", but states that "strict conditions for practice of this sport will limit these impacts to an acceptable level so as to maintain the integrity of the heritage".[91] Although such potential impacts are recognized, "strict conditions" have not been implemented. In fact, mountain biking is a feature of Station Mont Tremblant's summer activities. It sponsors guided mountain biking tours, which now include "an initiation to single track mountain biking on the forested trails of Mt.-Tremblant"[92] for the more adventurous, as well as tours along the linear park "P'tit Train du Nord" and on Domaine Saint Bernard's cross-country trails at the base of the mountain for the more sedate. New mountain bike trails are planned as part of the expansion of the skiable area of Versant Soleil and Camp Nord.[93] Moreover, one of Station Mont Tremblant's summer drawing cards is the "Canada-Quebec Cup", an annual three-day mountain bike competition attracting some 1,000 participants, including top international riders. The highlight is Sunday's downhill event down the face of the mountain—"a 2.4 km [1.5 mi.] run featuring a staggering 319 m. [1,047 ft] unlevel"[94] starting at the top of one of the major ski trails about half way up the

---

88 Mont Tremblant Resort, Summer Activities—ATV Tours, http://tremblant.com/whattoseedo/summer_activities/atvtours/index-e.htm (last visited Aug. 31, 2004) (emphasis added).

89 R.S.Q., c. V-1.2.

90 O.C. 1143-97, G.O.Q. 1997.II.4595, adopted under the Environment Quality Act, R.S.Q., c. Q-2.

91 Société de la faune et des parcs, The National Parks of Quebec: Nature—The Road to Discovery: Activities and Services, http://www.fapaq.gouv.qc.ca/en/parc_que/parc_act_ser_Ang.pdf (last visited Dec. 7, 2004).

92 Mont Tremblant Resort, Summer Activities – Guided Bike Tours, http://tremblant.com/whattoseedo/summer_activities/biketours/index-e.htm (last visited Aug. 31, 2004); see also Guided Mountain Biking, http://www.tremblant.ca/activities/velo.asp (last visited June 29, 2004).

93 Environmental Assessment Screening Report, *supra* note 40, para. 5.3.

94 Mont Tremblant Resort, Events – Canada and Quebec Cup of Mountain Biking, http://www.tremblant.ca/activities/velo.asp (last visited June 29, 2004); *see also* Christophe Cullis, *Canada-Quebec Cup: Not Your Ordinary Bike Ride*, TREMBLANT EXPRESS, June 2003,

mountain. As well, the local cycling club is to publish a map and guide of the area's mountain biking trails, with the trails running the gamut from easy to very difficult ("more than rugged enough to offer an interesting ride").[95] All of this emphasis on mountain biking is sure to attract riders to the mountain slopes, with obvious adverse effect on the mountain ecosystem.

Conclusions

Overall, therefore, recreational activities have a mixed effect on the mountain ecosystem. The ski trails are constructed in as ecologically sensitive manner as possible, and this is probably due as much to the internal codes of conduct to which Intrawest adheres as to any externally imposed legislative and contractual controls. However, the cumulative effect of the number of ski trails and snowboard parks is more open to question. The impact of non-ski activities on the mountain ecosystem is equally worrisome, as snowmobiles, ATVs and mountain bikes are not subject to any meaningful regulation, and their use is not just tolerated but encouraged. Finally, the possible effect of snowmaking on the mountain aquifer is a matter of increasing concern, particularly when this is coupled with the increased demands resulting from new ski area and base camp development. The snowmaking provisions in the 1992 lease were negotiated with only the first phase at Base Sud in mind.

This review of the various on-mountain activities and the law that governs them—or does not govern them—illustrates the intricate array of public laws, public-private contractual arrangements, and voluntary codes. It shows that the government has not taken a comprehensive approach to the on-mountain ecosystem. It has chosen a piecemeal alternative, with some activities or ecological assets subject to regulation or negotiation, and others not. Moreover, the regulations or negotiated terms tend not to evaluate the cumulative, comprehensive ecological impact of discrete activities, although the absence of publicly available information hinders the ability to evaluate fully the extent to which ecological considerations are taken into account. The strengths and weaknesses of this approach will be discussed at more length in Chapter 22, following the next chapter, which moves off the mountain to the base camps and golf courses and brings other legal regimes into play.

---

available at http://www.tremblantexpress.com/ (last visited May 28, 2004); Aimée Belec, *Canada-Quebec Mountain Biking Cup: Registration Increases for Mountain Biking Event*, TREMBLANT EXPRESS, May 2004 (last visited June 29, 2004) ("downhill racers will speed down a steep, windy path to the finish").

95 André Courey, *Maps and Guides for Cycling Available Soon*, TREMBLANT EXPRESS, June 2004, available at http://www.tremblantexpress.com/ (last visited June 29, 2004); see also 3-D trail map at http://pages.infinit.net/endo99/tremb.html (last visited Sept. 19, 2005).

Chapter 21
Base Camps, Golf Courses and Land Protection at the Mountain's Base

The ski station itself is not the only, or even the major, drawing card at Mont Tremblant. Most people come for the entire complement of activities offered in and around the base camps, and golf is an increasingly important three-season activity. The base camps (existing and proposed) and golf courses are located at the foot of Mont Tremblant just outside the boundaries of the Park. They therefore come under the jurisdiction of the local municipalities rather than the Parks authorities.

Canadian municipalities play a strong role in land use control for traditional reasons. Although municipalities have no independent constitutional protection and are simply "creatures of the province" under provincial constitutional authority over "Municipal Institutions in the Province,"[1] provinces have traditionally delegated their regulatory authority over privately owned land and their responsibility for all but the most important infrastructure (major highways, for example) to local municipalities.

Quebec's municipal structure is two-tiered: local and regional. Station Mont Tremblant's lands are located in the Town of Mont Tremblant, which is part of the *Municipalité régionale de comté des Laurentides* [Laurentides Regional County Municipality]. Until recently, the Town of Mont Tremblant was four separate municipalities—the Parish of Saint Jovite (established 1881), the Municipality of Lac Tremblant Nord (established 1915), the Town of Saint Jovite (established 1917) and the Municipality of Mont Tremblant (established 1940)[2]—with Intrawest's first base camp development being located in the former Municipality of Mont Tremblant. In 1999, the four municipalities were merged into a new Town of Mont Tremblant,[3] a forced merger which the former Municipality contested unsuccessfully before the Superior Court.[4] The council of the former Municipality, considered "pro-environment" in approach, contested the merger in the belief that

1 Constitution Act, 1867 (U.K.), 30 & 31 Vict., c. 3, s. 92(8). *See, e.g.* Public School Boards' Association of Alberta v. Alberta (Attorney General), [2000] 2 S.C.R. 409 at 428; Pacific National Investments Ltd. v. Victoria (City), [2000] 2 S.C.R. 919 at 941.

2 Town of Mont Tremblant, Règlements, http://www.villedemont-tremblant.qc.ca/Jahia/pid/18 (last visited Sept. 21, 2004).

3 Act respecting the Amalgamation of Municipalité de Mont Tremblant, Ville de Saint Jovite, Municipalité de Lac Tremblant Nord and Paroisse de Saint Jovite, S.Q. 1999, c. 88; *see also* Décret 1294-2000, G.O.Q. 2000.II.6971 (in French only).

4 Municipalité de Mont Tremblant v. Paroisse de Saint Jovite, [2000] R.J.Q. 2299.

the council of the merged municipality, with a majority of its members coming from the other former municipal areas, would be "pro-development."

Forced mergers, not only in Mont Tremblant but throughout the province, became an issue in the provincial election of 2002, and the new government provided for possible "demerger" of the merged municipalities, albeit under a somewhat complicated procedure.[5] In the end, the residents of the former Municipality of Mont Tremblant—more likely to be wary of the proposed Versant Soleil development—were not successful in their bid to demerge.[6]

Station Mont Tremblant's present and proposed base camps and golf courses are located in the merged Town of Mont Tremblant, at the base of Mont Tremblant. Their development obviously affects the mountain ecosystem, and this section of the chapter examines how and to what extent the law attenuates their impact. The chapter ends by looking at the role of a land trust in protecting ecologically significant land at the mountain's base.

Base Camp Development

Intrawest has completed the development of one base camp, Base Sud; two more, Versant Soleil and Camp Nord, are either under construction or planned for the near future. These are usually referred to as "pedestrian villages" but this is somewhat of a misnomer as not all residential development is located in the compact central core. Base Sud, for example, has dispersed residential development around a golf course and in a forested area on the mountain flank near the pedestrian core.[7]

5 Act respecting the Consultation of Citizens with respect to the Territorial Reorganization of Certain Municipalities, S.Q. 2003, c. 14. At least 10% of qualified voters had to sign a register requesting that a referendum be held; and in the referendum, the number of votes in favor of demerger had not only to exceed the number of votes cast against (simple majority) but also to be greater than 35% of all those entitled to vote (weighted absolute majority).

6 The large number of nonresident owners (73%) in the former municipality, many in Intrawest's pedestrian village, undoubtedly made success difficult, if not impossible. Although 21% of persons on the electoral list in the former municipality petitioned for a referendum (well over the 10% threshold), and demerger won 71% of the votes cast in the referendum, this represented only 31% of the full electoral list (just short of the required 35%). The absentee owners would have been unlikely to vote. *See* André Courey, *Referendums at Mont Tremblant and Lac Tremblant Nord*, Tremblant Express, June 2004, *available at* http://www.tremblantexpress.com/ (last visited June 29, 2004). *See also* Municality of Mont Tremblant, Mémoire de Ville de Mont Tremblant présenté à la Commission de l'aménagement du territoire à l'égard de projet de loi numéro 9, Loi concernant la consultation des citoyens sur la reorganisation territoriale de certaines Municipalités (Aug. 21, 2003), = http://www.villedemont-tremblant.qc.ca/jahia/Jahia/pid/91 (last visited Aug. 31, 2004) (advocating weighted voting).

7 *See, e.g.*, Intrawest, Real Estate at Mont Tremblant, http://www.livetremblant.com/residences/index.html (last visited March 17, 2005).

Construction is underway at the second site, Versant Soleil, which is to be developed around an artificial lake.[8] It will include a central core of some 1,360 accommodation units and about 97,000 square feet of commercial space, with an additional 650 housing units on the periphery. It is to focus on corporate and convention business, and feature a 95,000 square-foot convention center, a spa, an arena and an aquatic center. Some 2,750 parking spaces (1,200 underground) are also planned. Drinking water will be provided by the existing municipal system, which draws its water from Lac Tremblant, and wastewater will be directed to the municipality's existing aeration ponds located nearby.

Construction of Camp Nord is scheduled to start when Versant Soleil is substantially completed. Its central core is to include about 1,000 accommodation units and a further 97,000 square feet of commercial space; an additional 500 accommodation units are to be built on both sides of the central area. Camp Nord is described as a "rustic, family-oriented development", with a youth camp and equestrian, curling and aquatic centers. It will also include two small artificial ponds as well as a smaller conference center and 1,000 outdoor parking spaces. Drinking water is to come from groundwater sources, with the Rivière du Diable as a possible supplementary or alternative source. Some 233,000 cubic feet per day will be required during the snowmaking season (November to February) and about 25,000 cubic feet per day for the rest of the year. Wastewater is to be directed to new aeration ponds and eventually discharged into the Rivière du Diable below the water intake.

To what extent does the law play a role in controlling the construction of the base camps, and mitigating their effect on the mountain ecosystems? The two sources of control are the rules relating to land use planning and to environmental assessment.

Land Use Planning

Land use planning in Quebec is governed by the Act respecting Land Use Planning and Development.[9] This Act sets out the legal framework for the developments at the base of Mont Tremblant, outside the boundaries of the Park. It reflects Quebec's two-tiered municipal structure, and provides for the adoption of regional plans ("development plans") at the regional level, to be followed up by more detailed plans ("planning programs")[10] and implementing by-laws at the local level.

---

8 The information about Versant Soleil and Camp Nord is taken mainly from Infrastructure Canada & Fisheries and Oceans Canada, Environmental Assessment Screening Report, Mont Tremblant: Development of Versant Soleil and Camp Nord, Mont Tremblant (Phases 3 and 4) item 5.0 (August 2004), *available at* http://www.infrastructure.gc.ca/pn/csif/mont-tremblant/report_e.shtml (last visited Dec. 7, 2004) [hereinafter Environmental Assessment Screening Report].

9 R.S.Q., c. A-19.1.

10 *See generally* Jacques L'Heureux, *Nature et effets d'un schéma d'aménagement et d'un plan d'urbanisme*, 31 Revue de droit Université de Sherbrooke 2 (2000–2001).

Regional Plans The regional plan is the most important integrative planning tool, as it coordinates the land use policies of the provincial, regional and local governments ("vertical integration") in the region. The regional planning process also facilitates "horizontal integration", that is the coordination of the policies of various sectorial (or "line") ministries—such as Transport, the Environment, Municipal Affairs, Natural Resources, etc.—at the provincial level through the requirement that regional plans must be consistent with the government's aims and projects as articulated by the government as a whole, not just by the separate ministries;[11] a regional plan also coordinates the policies of the various local municipalities in the region.[12]

The statutory content of regional plans emphasizes their integrative role. Integration is implicit in the usual sort of requirement that the plan articulate policies relating to land development, land use, transportation and other infrastructure, etc. It is more explicit in other, more overtly ecological, provisions. A regional plan must identify the "zones where land occupation is subject to special restrictions … for reasons of environmental protection regarding riverbanks and lakeshores, littoral zones and floodplains," as well as those parts of the territory that are "of historical, cultural, aesthetic or ecological interest in the regional county municipality."[13] Optional components include the identification of priority zones for development and land uses and approximate density of occupation for such zones, and the determination of guidelines to promote the sustainable development of private forests.[14] A plan must also include a "complementary document" setting out minimum requirements that municipalities must include in their zoning and

11 Two policy documents informed the recent round of regional plan revisions: Gouvernement du Québec, Les orientations du Gouvernement en matière d'aménagement du territoire 1994, http://www.mamm.gouv.qc.ca/pdf_mamm/amenag/oramenag.pdf (last visited May 15, 2002); Gouvernement du Québec, Les orientations du Gouvernement en matière d'aménagement du territoire [Document complémentaire] (1995) http://www.mamm.gouv.qc.ca/pdf_mamm/amen/orcomp.pdf (last visited Dec. 4, 2001).

The Sustainable Development Act, R. S.Q., c. D-8.1.1, further promotes horizontal integration of government activities through the articulation of five-year "sustainable development strategies", adopted by the government and tabled in the legislature with a view to fostering "an integrated approach and the coherence of the various interventions undertaken" in the area of sustainable development not only by the various provincial government departments but also by "the local and regional authorities concerned". S. 11. Sustainable development requires that the relevant authorities take account of such principles as "protection of cultural heritage" (including landscapes), "biodiversity preservation", "respect for ecosystem support capacity" and "subsidiarity". S. 6.

12 Horizontal and vertical integration are explored more fully in Anne Drost & Jane Matthews Glenn, *Mont Tremblant Resort: An Integrated Approach to Ecosystem Protection,* 26 Vt. L. Rev. 593–628 (2002).

13 The obligatory content of regional plans is set out in s. 5 of the Act respecting Land Use Planning and Development, R.S.Q., c. A-19.1.

14 *Id.* at s. 6.

subdivision by-laws concerning the regulation or prohibition of the incompatible use or subdivision of environmentally sensitive land.[15]

The Laurentides Regional County Municipality regional plan, revised in July 1999 and in force in June 2000,[16] articulates the need to balance tourist development and ecological protection with increasing specificity throughout the document. Two of the development orientations, set out in broad-brush terms, capture the ecosystem balancing act facing an area such as Mont Tremblant: the plan calls for continued efforts to protect and promote the environment, including wildlife habitats and watercourses and wetlands, while at the same time recognizing the need to offer "a more diversified and integrated recreo-touristic product" (one which recognizes the importance of the drawing power of "the existing major infrastructure," i.e., Station Mont Tremblant).

The heart of the regional plan is the chapter identifying the main land use designations for the territory and the general principles governing each. Issues of protecting watercourses, wetlands, and wildlife habitats, particularly the white-tailed deer yard, as well as limiting the visual impact of residential development on the existing landscape, run like a thread through this chapter. It also sets out more specific objectives concerning the resort area adjacent to Station Mont Tremblant, including the protection of sensitive natural areas. For example, the plan states:

> The zone adjacent to Station Mont Tremblant contains several important sensitive natural areas which must be the subject of particular attention when planning the road network and residential development.
>
> It is in the sector of Domaine Saint Bernard and the corridor of Rivière du Diable that one finds the most strategic zones of wildlife habitat and those subject to natural constraints, in the sense that they are increasingly subject to strong development pressures generated by Station Mont Tremblant.
>
> In the context of an integrated approach to planning, municipalities must provide themselves with local plans and implementing by-laws which clearly set out objectives, criteria and norms which support the concepts of development in which the protection of white-tailed deer yards (including their displacement corridors), blue spaces (lakes, watercourses, wetlands and flood plains) and landscapes must be closely linked to the development of large recreational networks and green spaces.
>
> More specifically, municipalities must include in their plans and by-laws objectives, means and/or criteria designed to do the following:

---

15 *Id.* at s. 5, para. 2. The complementary document may, however, provide for exemptions in certain cases. *Id.* at s. 6, para. 3 (1.1).

16 Municipalité Régionale de Comté Laurentides, Schéma d'aménagement révisé: Version définitive, July 1999 (Regional County Municipality, adopted by Bylaw 154-99) [hereinafter Schéma d'aménagement].

a. preservation of the spaces that are essential to white-tailed deer, consisting of areas of shelter, feeding and feeding-shelter as well as the main displacement corridor along the Rivière du Diable by the Domaine Saint Bernard as well as to the west of Tremblant Village; the complementary document [to the regional plan] sets out certain rules relating particularly to cutting of trees, subdivision of land, residential development, river frontages and spaces essential to the survival of this habitat;
b. integral protection of flood plains, areas prone to landslides and wetlands;
c. special rules relating to the cutting of trees in white-tailed deer yards;
d. integral protection of a heronry and its immediate environs situated near Lac Gautier Road, in the municipality of Saint Jovite Paroisse.[17]

Other relevant chapters focus on recreational networks and environmental issues. The recreational network chapter discusses the development of hiking, bicycling, snowmobile and all terrain vehicle trails and their linkages to a cross-Quebec network of trails. It recognizes the tension between the increasing economic importance of the recreational use of ATVs and the adverse environmental impact of their use in ecologically sensitive areas, such as wildlife habitats and wetlands, and recommends the development of a regional network of appropriately located ATV trails.

The chapter on environmental issues goes into detail about the conservation of wildlife habitats and the forest milieu, threatened and vulnerable species, protected watercourses and lakes, floodplains, wetlands, and landslide areas. Potentially threatened or vulnerable species (flora and fauna) are identified, and the measures to be taken by local municipalities to protect them are set out in the "complementary document," which is included as a separate chapter in the plan. The complementary document outlines the rules and regulations that must be adopted by the local municipalities in relation to constructions or activities on foreshores, the banks of lakes and rivers, floodplains, wetlands, potential landslide zones, heronries, white-tailed deer yards, residential development in tourist areas, and so on.

In sum, the Laurentides region's plan recognizes that tourist development cannot be at the expense of the ecological milieu in which it takes place, and identifies ample measures to protect local flora and fauna and their habitat. These measures are to be then taken up and implemented at the local level by virtue of a requirement that local municipalities bring their own land use planning and control documents into line with the revised regional plan within two years of it coming into force, and keep amendments in line subsequently.[18] Local documents include both a local plan

17 *Id.* at 3-50 (author's translation).

18 Act respecting Land Use Planning and Development, R.S.Q., c. A-19.1, s. 3, ss. 59, 59.5 (revised plan; *see also* s. 33 (initial plan) & s. 58 (amended plan)), and ss. 137.3–137.8. *See, e.g.*, MRC des Laurentides, "Rés. 2004.10.3354: Avis de non-conformité au schéma d'aménagement révisé relatif au règlement 87-02-140 modifiant la réglementation d'urbanisme numéro 87-02 de l'ancienne municipalité de Mont Tremblant", Procès-verbal

and by-laws implementing the plan. The discussion which follows looks at these local-level documents, and shows how they were used to control the development of the original base camp at Base Sud and the new one at Versant Soleil.

Local Plans Generally speaking, a local plan sets out more detailed land use planning and development policies for its territory within the general parameters provided in the regional plan. Quebec's Act respecting Land Use Planning and Development is much less specific about the content for a local plan, or "planning program," than for a regional plan, and simply requires that it include the "general aims of land development policy", the "general policies on land uses and occupation densities" and the "planned layout and the type of the principal thoroughfares and transport systems".[19] The Act also provides that a local plan may include more specific components, including a "special planning program" for part of the municipal territory (such as a base camp).[20] A special planning program includes such matters as the detailed land use and land occupation density, the proposed zoning, subdivision and building rules, the provision of public services and infrastructure (including the sequence of their provision) and "the special land redevelopment, restoration and demolition provisions".[21] As we will see, a special planning program served as the principal vehicle for implementing an agreement between Station Mont Tremblant and the municipality governing base camp development at Versant Soleil.[22]

The transitional measures accompanying the municipal mergers provide that existing regulations, including land use plans and implementing by-laws, of the constituent municipalities remain in force until replaced.[23] The local plan of the

[Minutes] du Conseil du 21 octobre 2004, agenda item 9, http://www.mrclaurentides.qc.ca/fr/services/administration/pdf/pvcm/pvcm%202004-10-21.pdf (last visited Sept. 4, 2007) (zoning amendments to facilitate a private sector development at the base of Mont Tremblant did not protect deer habitat as required by the regional plan).

The Laurentides Regional County Municipality is also preparing a nonstatutory "strategy for sustainable development" for the area, which will focus on the effect of Mont Tremblant's economic growth on the area's natural environment. One of the issues is "whether the MRC's ideas on sustainable development will be more or less demanding in matters of real estate development." André Courey, *Sustainable Development as Seen by MRC*, Tremblant Express, Mar. 2005, *available at* http://www.tremblantexpress.com/ (last visited March 15, 2005). *See also* Minutes of March 9, 2006, agenda item 11, http://www.mrclaurentides.qc.ca/fr/services/administration/pdf/pvcm/pvcm%202006-03-09.pdf (last visited Sept. 4, 2007).

19 Act respecting Land Use Planning and Development, R.S.Q., c. A-19.1, s. 83.

20 *Id.* at ss. 84, 85. A regional municipality may require a local municipality to include one or more of these otherwise optional components. S. 86.

21 *Id.* at s. 85, para. 2 (8).

22 See the discussion *infra* in the text at note 71.

23 Act respecting Municipal Territorial Organisation, R.S.Q., c. O-9; Act respecting the Amalgamation of Municipalité de Mont Tremblant, Ville de Saint Jovite, Municipalité de Lac Tremblant Nord and Paroisse de Saint Jovite, S.Q. 1999, c. 88, s. 4.

former Municipality of Mont Tremblant was adopted in 1989 (thus prior even to Intrawest's acquisition of the ski station) and conformed to the Laurentides Regional County Municipality's plan in force at that time.[24] It should have been modified by 2001 to bring it into conformity with the 1999 revised regional plan, but the uncertainty surrounding the merger/demerger process and the pressure of other demands on the planning staff's time had delayed this. During the course of 2003, the merged Town adopted a strategic action plan to serve as "a frame of reference in daily decision-making" (in which "[e]conomic development is high on the list of priorities but the environment is said to be the city's wealth and main attraction"),[25] an "environmental master plan" (calling for "an ecosystemic approach in environmental management recognizing that each part of an ecosystem affects the others and impacts on any one of them to have a cumulative effect on the whole"[26]) and a parks and green spaces plan.[27] These are nonstatutory plans and hence without legal force and effect. However, they have been "integrated into the process of deliberation"[28] for the adoption of the revised planning program (local plan) required by the Act respecting Land Use Planning and Development.

The Town commenced the process of adopting a statutory local plan with the preparation of a "preliminary planning proposal" of its planning program in

---

24 Ville de Mont Tremblant, Règlement de Plan d'urbanisme: Proposition préliminaire 3, *available at* http://www.villedemont-tremblant.qc.ca/jahia/Jahia/pid/695 (last visited July 31, 2007). The plans of the other constituent municipalities are more recent, dating from 1995 (Municipality of Lac Tremblant Nord), 1996 (Parish of Saint Jovite) and 1997 (Town of Saint Jovite).

25 André Courey, *Council Adopts Master Development Plan*, Tremblant Express, Feb. 2003, *available at* http://www.tremblantexpress.com (last visited May 28, 2004) ("Among these [specific programs] is the conclusion of a protocol with Intrawest for the construction of Versant Soleil...."); *see* Ville de Mont Tremblant, Plan stratégique de développement, http://www.villedemont-tremblant.qc.ca/jahia/Jahia/pid/413 (last visited July 31, 2007).

26 André Courey, *Environment Master Plan Adopted*, Tremblant Express, Oct. 2003, and *Development: The Environment and Quality of Life*, Tremblant Express, June 2004 ("...a necessarily holistic approach—looking at ecosystems as a whole and their interconnection as part of a closely-linked chain..."), *available at* http://www.tremblantexpress.com (last visited May 28, 2004). *See* Del Degan, Massé et Associés, Plan directeur en environnement Ville de Mont Tremblant, 2 vols. (July 2003), *available at* http://www.villedemont-tremblant.qc.ca/jahia/Jahia/pid/535 (last visited July 31, 2007).

The Town also created a new environmental department, headed by a biologist. Serge Léonard, *Le directeur de l'environnement assume une tâche essentielle*, Tremblant Express, May 2004, *available at* http://www.tremblantexpress.com (last visited June 29, 2004).

27 André Courey, *Parks and Trails Plan Adopted*, Tremblant Express, Jan. 2004, *available at* http://www.tremblantexpress.com (last visited May 28, 2004).

28 Town of Mont Tremblant, Summary of the Preliminary Proposal for the Planning Programme (Dec. 2003) 1, http://www.villedemont-tremblant.qc.ca/ jahia/Jahia/pid/55 (last visited Sept. 23, 2004) [hereinafter Summary of Preliminary Proposal].

2003.[29] Although this step is optional under the Act, some mandatory rules apply to it should this step be taken. A key procedural element is the holding of a public meeting to "explain the preliminary proposal and hear every person and body wishing to be heard".[30] The extent of public consultation by the Town is not clear: the preliminary proposal itself suggests that public consultation is optional;[31] notices spoke of a meeting for the "unveiling"[32] of the proposal, at which the public would presumably hear council but not the reverse;[33] but interested persons were invited to submit written comments by a given date.[34]

The discussion of the Station Mont Tremblant resort area in the preliminary planning proposal is surprisingly succinct, being slightly more than two pages in total.[35] The overall objective is to ensure a coherent development of the Station, "linked to the presence of Mont Tremblant and to the natural, social and economic milieu of the Town."[36] The preliminary proposal supports the two new developments at Versant Soleil and Camp Nord set out in the Station's own master plan, and recommends that the Town sign a development agreement with Station Mont Tremblant relating to Camp Nord (in addition to the one already signed for Versant Soleil) (see Figure 21.1); and it recognizes that care must be taken to

---

29 Ville de Mont Tremblant, "Résolution 2003-909: Adoption de la proposition préliminaire—Plan d'urbanisme—Ville de Mont Tremblant", Procès verbal de la séance [Minutes of meeting] du 10 novembre 2003, agenda item 4.1, http://www.villedemont-tremblant,qc.ca (last visited Sept. 21, 2004). *See* Règlement de Plan d'urbanisme: Proposition préliminaire, *supra* note 24.

A preliminary proposal is in the nature of a tentative first draft, intended to sound out opinion on various options ("The preliminary planning proposal shall be presented as a series of alternatives, with an indication of the estimated cost of each": Act respecting Land Use Planning and Development, R.S.Q., c. A-19.1, s. 88). It is followed by the adoption of a final draft, and then ultimately by the adoption of the plan itself.

30 Act respecting Land Use Planning and Development, R.S.Q., c. A-19.1, ss. 90 ("The municipality *shall* hold a public meeting ..." (emphasis added)) & 93.

31 Règlement de Plan d'urbanisme: Proposition préliminaire, *supra* note 24, at 2.

32 Ville de Mont Tremblant, Refonte de la réglementation d'urbanisme (March 2004), http://www.villedemont-tremblant.qc.ca/jahia/Jahia/pid/54 (last visited July 31, 2007) ["*dévoilement*"].

33 "Next December 1st is thus an important appointment for all citizens of Mont Tremblant who want to know the major orientations of the Town in regard to development and land use planning." Ville de Mont Tremblant, Le 1er décembre prochain à Mont Tremblant: Présentation de la proposition préliminaire du plan d'urbanisme de la Ville de Mont Tremblant, Communiqués, Nov. 12, 2003, http://www.villedemont-tremblant.gc.ca/ (last visited April 1, 2005) (author□s translation, emphasis added).

34 Ville de Mont Tremblant, Refonte de la réglementation d'urbanisme (March 2004), http://www.villedemont-tremblant.qc.ca/ jahia/Jahia/pid/54 (last visited July 31, 2007).

35 Règlement de Plan d'urbanisme: Proposition préliminaire, *supra* note 24, at 28, 57–58, 93–94,179–180.

36 *Id.* at 179.

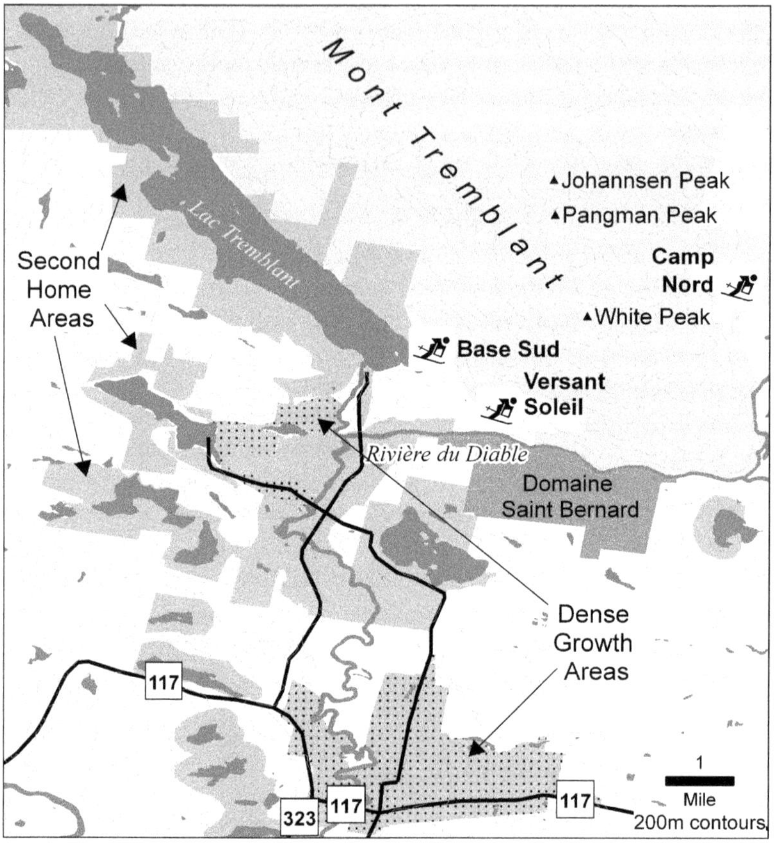

Figure 21.1 Municipality of Mont Tremblant's Existing Development

Data Sources: Ville de Mont Tremblant, Règlement de Plan d'urbanisme: Proposition préliminaire; DMTI Spatial Inc.; ESRI; ©Department of Natural Resources Canada, all rights reserved.

ensure that the Station's activities do not adversely affect the other areas of the municipality.[37]

The preliminary proposal's discussion relating to the environment is more detailed. The proposal recognizes that environmental matters are often governed by specific provincial or federal laws and regulations, but stresses that a pillar of the Town's development is to protect and enhance "the authenticity of the environment as a resource".[38] It identifies the need to balance the pace of development with

37 *Id.* at 57–58, 180.

38 *Id.* at 26–27 ["de protéger et de mettre en valeur l'authenticité de la ressource 'environnement'"].

the environment's ability to support it as the main environmental issue facing the town, and recognizes the interrelated nature of the environment:

> Indeed, the [municipal] territory includes several wetland zones to preserve, as well as essential white-tailed deer habitats and first-rate fish habitats and spawning grounds. Fauna development is tied to the integrity and conservation of these sites since certain actions such as draining, filling, and destroying vegetation can have disastrous effects on these ecosystems. These ecologically important areas thus require the protection of densely forested zones.[39]

The preliminary proposal therefore recommends that the Town take a number of steps to protect the environment, including: integrating environmental concerns (particularly as set out in the Town's environmental master plan) into the Town's regulatory framework; subjecting new projects to a biological assessment; adopting a potable water use policy and regulatory provisions to protect both the water quality in lakes and rivers and the supply for human consumption; prohibiting or limiting development in environmentally sensitive areas; adopting regulations and other measures to minimize nuisances (emanating from Circuit Mont Tremblant, snowmobile noise, night lighting, etc.); adopting more stringent regulations relating to pesticide and fertilizer use; and so on.[40] Two particularly interesting environmental recommendations are that the Town's environmental department "study the *cumulative* effects of present and proposed developments on the fundamental environmental values of Mont Tremblant"[41] and that "the [environmental] impacts linked to the development of Station Mont Tremblant" be controlled by regulation and cooperation with the Station.[42]

More generally still, "environment" and "landscape" (or more precisely—and somewhat more commercially—the "landscape resource") are identified as being at the centre of the preliminary planning proposal's drafting philosophy.[43] The proposal sets out a "frame of reference"—which includes "landscape units"

---

39 *Id.* at 40 (author's translation). Other environmental matters mentioned in the preliminary proposal include the importance of watershed planning, the provision of potable water and the treatment of water, sewerage (including by septic tank) and used snow. Flood, erosion and landslide zones, outdoor lighting, automobile racing, snowmobile, motorboat and other traffic and pesticide and other chemical uses are also identified as affecting both the environment and the quality of life. *Id.* at 40–42.

40 *Id.* at 158–162.

41 *Id.* at 162 (emphasis added).

42 *Id.*

43 Règlement de Plan d'urbanisme: Proposition préliminaire, *supra* note 24, at 2; Summary of Preliminary Proposal, *supra* note 28, at 1. This approach reflects a growing interest in the planning profession to integrate landscape protection into the planning process. *See, e.g.*, Conseil du paysage québécois, Guide du paysage : Un outil pour l'application d'une Charte de paysage (Oct. 2002), *available at* http://www.paysage.qc.ca/Application-charte.pdf (last visited March 10, 2005); Charte des paysages naturels et bâtis

(identified by their vulnerability in the face of development), "signature corridors" (access routes to the principal tourist destinations) and the Mont Tremblant "label" (the totality of unique and spectacular landscapes that draw tourists)[44] — to serve as a backdrop to all planning decisions. The impact of development on Mont Tremblant's landscape is to be assessed in terms of "visual absorption capacity, panoramic views, symbolic or identity landscapes, wetlands, lakes and mountain peaks, and human creations (roads, urban and tourist milieu), etc."[45]

Under the Act respecting Land Use Planning and Development, the municipality must take the preliminary planning proposal and the results of public consultation on it into account when drafting the final plan.[46] Another public meeting must be held prior to adoption of the plan,[47] and the regional municipality must assess the conformity of the local plan with the provisions of its own regional plan.[48] If this assessment is affirmative, the local municipality must then implement the plan.[49]

The 2003 preliminary proposal was approved as a draft by council in December 2003. However, the press of other business caused the planning process to be put aside during the next two years, and the draft was then "completely revised" in 2006 and 2007 in light of the over 100 submissions received since 2003 from the public (citizens and promoters) and other considerations. The revised draft places more emphasis on sustainable development, and integrates a "watershed management" planning approach.[50] The provisions relating to Station Mont Tremblant reflect the

---

des Laurentides, *available at* http://www.mcreq.org/bulletin/04.11.04B.html (last visited March 10, 2005).

44 Règlement de Plan d'urbanisme: Proposition préliminaire, *supra* note 24, at 25–26; Summary of Preliminary Proposal, *supra* note 28, at 2. The English summary refers to the Mont Tremblant "trademark", rather than "label", but "trademark" does not capture the flavor of the French text, "*griffe*", a word usually used in the context of designer clothes and similar luxury goods.

Other framework elements include transportation and infrastructure (especially roads), tourism (with mention of the Park, but not Mont Tremblant itself), and various tourist-related elements such as nautical activities, plane and helicopter transportation (but not skiing), parks and green spaces (Mont Tremblant Park, Domaine Saint Bernard, *P'tit Train du Nord* Linear Park and a multifunctional trail network) and the environment.

45 Règlement de Plan d'urbanisme: Proposition préliminaire, *supra* note 24, at 141 (author's translation).

46 R.S.Q., c. A-19.1, s. 94.

47 *Id.* at ss. 95–96. This meeting must be held "even where the preliminary proposal had been submitted to consultation". Id. at s. 95, para. 1.

48 *Id.* at s. 36. A local municipality may appeal a decision of non-conformity to the Quebec Municipal Commission. Id. at ss. 37–44.

49 *Id.* at ss. 102, 110.4. The regional council must also confirm the conformity of the implementing by-laws with the regional plan (*id.* at ss. 137.1–137.3, 137.8) with a possibility of appeal to the Quebec Municipal Commission. *Id.* at ss. 137.4–137.6.

50 Info Mont Tremblant (Dec. 2006) Vol. 5:4, at 4, and (Mar. 2007) Vol. 6:1, at 9, *available at* http://www.villedemont-tremblant.qc.ca/jahia/Jahia/pid/626 (last visited Aug. 1, 2007); Ville de Mont Tremblant, Projet de Règlement (2008)-100: Plan d'urbanisme,

terms of the 2003 framework agreement between the Station and the municipality, set out below. The process of public consultation (a public meeting in February 2008 and follow-up written submissions) on the revised proposal is now complete, but council has not yet adopted a final revised plan.[51]

In other words, the new municipality has been actively engaged in the planning process since the merger, and has adopted several policy documents setting out frameworks for future development. Two of them, the strategic action plan and the environmental master plan, are nonstatutory documents, without constraining effect; the former is more development-oriented in nature, whereas the latter advocates an integrative ecosystem approach to decision making. Adoption of a revised statutory plan as required under the Act respecting Land Use Planning and Development is ongoing. The 2003 preliminary planning proposal, approved as a first step in the procedure, adopted an environmental discourse; and this is also the case with the more recent proposal. But what is striking about these various local planning documents is their commercial flavor, coloring even the environmental discourse: the environment does not come through as something to be protected in and of itself, but rather as an asset of commercial value to the tourist industry.

In the meantime, the 1989 local plan remains in effect until it is replaced by a revised statutory plan, and the implementing by-laws relate to this plan (as punctually amended)-and not to the proposed revision of it. The by-laws discussed below give a flavor of the types of tools available to a Quebec municipality to implement a plan, and how these tools have been used in relation to the original base camp developments at Base Sud and the new development at Versant Soleil.

Local Implementing By-Laws Implementing by-laws include not only the traditional regulatory by-laws (zoning, subdivision and building by-laws) but also those relating to the more discretionary tools that have been added to the Quebec planning legislation over the last 15 years, notably comprehensive development program by-laws, site planning and architectural integration program by-laws, and municipal works agreement by-laws.[52]

Regulatory By-Laws A local municipality is authorized under the statute to include provisions which address environmental issues in its regulatory by-laws. For example, zoning by-laws may "regulate or restrict, by zone, the excavation of

---

available at http://www.villedemont-tremblant.qc.ca/servicesMunicipaux.php?section=245 (last visited Oct. 27, 2008).

51 *Id.*

52 The difference between regulatory and discretionary tools is that the former set out in the by-laws themselves what property owners can and cannot do with their property ("rights in advance") whereas the latter set out what sort of thing the approval authority must take into consideration when deciding whether or not to approve a development application ("parameters of discretion"), and this usually involves negotiation between applicant and municipality. *See generally* Philip Girard, *Discretionary versus Regulatory Controls: A Canadian perspective*, in C. Toppin-Allahar & B.A. Chow, eds., Taking up the Challenge of Designing Indigenous Planning Laws 51–55 (1994)

the ground, the removal of humus, the planting and felling of trees and all works of clearing and filling [and] compel any owner to put grass, shrubs or trees on his landsite;" they may also "regulate or restrict the planting or felling of trees to ensure protection of forest cover and promote sustainable development of private forests."[53] Both zoning and subdivision by-laws may:

> regulate or prohibit all or certain land uses, structures or works [or subdivision operations], taking into account the topography of the landsite, the proximity of a stream or lake, the danger of flood, rockfall, landslide or other disaster, or any other factor specific to the nature of a place which may be taken into consideration for reasons of public safety or of environmental protection regarding riverbanks and lakeshores, littoral zones or floodplains; …[54]

Subdivision by-laws may also "prescribe the minimum area and minimum dimensions of the lots at the time of a cadastral operation, taking into account the nature of the land, the proximity of public works, or the presence or, as the case may be, the absence of septic installations, waterworks or a sanitary sewer system".[55] Moreover, a municipality may make the granting of a building permit conditional upon the existence of waterworks and sewer services, or alternatively, that "the drinking water supply and waste water treatment planned for the structure to be erected on the land comply with the Environment Quality Act . . . and the regulations thereunder or with the municipal by-laws dealing with the same object."[56] The issuance of a building permit may also be made conditional upon an undertaking by the owner to donate land or pay a sum of money to the municipality "for the establishment or enlargement of a park or playground or for the preservation of a natural area."[57]

The pre-merger Municipality of Mont Tremblant made ample use of these and other similar regulatory provisions in its implementing by-laws.[58] For example, it restricted "conservation" zones to public, semi-public and private recreational and leisure activities and constructions of a light nature, such as cross-country ski trails, hiking trails and bicycle paths.[59] Other provisions dealt with the use of land on floodplains, constructions and improvements on riverbanks and lakeshores

53 Act respecting Land Use Planning and Development, s.113, para. 2(12) & (12.1).

54 *Id.* at s. 113, para. 2(16), s. 115, para. 2(4). Note that the Watercourses Act, R.S.Q., c. R-13, s. 8, stipulates that "[i]n no case may a local municipality issue a building permit to build in a flood plain recognized by government regulation" until the municipality has adopted the relevant by-law under section 113, para. 1(16).

55 Act respecting Land Use Planning and Development, R.S.Q., c. A-19.1, s. 115, para. 2(3).

56 *Id.* at s. 116, para. (2) and (3).

57 *Id.* at s. 117.2.

58 Municipalité de Mont Tremblant, Réglementation d'urbanisme, By-law 87-02 (1987, as amended Mar. 2001) [hereinafter Réglementation d'urbanisme].

59 *Id.* at s. 4.2.7.

for recreational and other purposes, subdivision and construction in white-tailed deer yards (lots to be unfenced, and at least 10,000 square meters in area) and in fish spawning grounds and marshlands (no subdivision of land or construction of buildings allowed; no improvements to respect the land's natural state and appearance and no interference with its natural drainage pattern).[60]

The merged municipality has also made use of these provisions. In 2004, for example, it adopted two by-laws tightening the rules governing construction on mountain flanks and summits in the tourist area. One is designed to ensure that buildings are integrated into the natural surroundings and their visual impact lessened:

> It also seeks to prevent soil erosion and excessive deforestation in areas where the ground gradient is greater than 15%. The other regulation protects the mountain landscape by increasing the proportion of natural area that must be left intact on a building lot and imposing greater restraints on deforestation on mountains. Basically, 65% of a lot in an area designated as residential must be left intact and 70% of a lot in an area designated as "resort" must be left untouched. On larger lots, deforestation is limited to a maximum of 850 square meters per residence although there are exceptions made to the rule.[61]

These various measures, pre- and post-merger, remain in force until modified by the municipality. Quebec residents have traditionally benefited from a particularly vigorous form of public input in the case of amendments to zoning, subdivision and building by-laws, in that they are provided not only with the usual opportunity to make their views known in a public meeting[62] but also with the chance to veto an amendment in a subsequent referendum.[63] However, an important exception relates to "concordance by-laws", that is zoning and other by-law amendments that are necessary to bring the by-laws into conformity with revised regional and local plans,[64] and this exception was invoked to restrict the possibility of veto in the case of Versant Soleil, as explained below.[65]

Discretionary Tools The newer discretionary land use control tools, added to the Act respecting Land Use Planning and Development in the mid 1980s, allow for site-specific solutions to ecological and other problems through negotiation with the owner. This flexibility makes them more useful for addressing ecological

60 *Id.* at s. 4.5.2.

61 André Courey, *Construction Rules Tightened*, TREMBLANT EXPRESS, July 2004, *available at* http://www.tremblantexpress.com (last visited July 13, 2004) (discussing By-laws 2004-479 and 2004-480).

62 Act respecting Land Use Planning and Development, R.S.Q., c. A-19.1, ss. 123–127.

63 *Id.* at ss. 123, 128–133.

64 *Id.* at s. 123, para. 3.

65 See *infra* the discussion at note 87.

issues than the regulatory tools, which simply set out general minimum standards throughout a zone. Two discretionary tools warrant particular mention: one is "comprehensive development programs"[66] and the other, "site planning and architectural integration programs."[67]

Comprehensive development programs allow a municipality to delay development in a given area until it has had the opportunity to review a developer's plans for all the land it holds in the area, rather than being limited to considering discrete applications on a piecemeal basis. This is a two-stage process. The first is to establish a freeze on development of the lands in question, which is done through a municipal by-law identifying the area in which a comprehensive development program is required and setting out the general parameters of an acceptable development (e.g., land uses, occupation densities, nature conservation and so on). The second stage is to lift the freeze once the developer has submitted an acceptable development proposal covering all lands he owns in the area. Approval of the proposal involves negotiation between the municipality and developer about its details and about the conditions (such as forest cover, infrastructure provision, etc.) attached to approval. The agreement is reflected in the requisite change in zoning to permit the project. The public is consulted in regard to both the initial comprehensive development program by-law and the subsequent amending by-laws to give effect to a program.

Mont Pinacle, Quebec

Comprehensive development programs were recently put to the test in a hotly contested proposal to develop a ski, golf and condominium recreational complex on the privately owned summit of Mont Pinacle, in Quebec's Eastern Townships. This development was initially favored by the regional and local municipal authorities—the 1987 and 1990 regional plans of the area permitted it, and the local municipality supported the withdrawal of some 2,000 acres from the agricultural land preservation regime to allow the development to go ahead.

However, local opposition became increasingly strong, and when the developer applied in 1993 for a change in zoning and the issuance of building permits for a residential development on the south face of the summit, a newly elected conservation-oriented Council responded with the adoption of a comprehensive development program by-law, freezing development until it had a chance to consider the developer's plans for the entire summit. The developer realized that the overall project would not be approved by the conservation-minded Council, and sued in tort for economic loss.

The Supreme Court of Canada unanimously approved the Council's actions. The Court held that the municipality was entitled to evaluate the cumulative effect of a projected downhill ski run on the north face as well as a residential development on

66 *Id.* at ss. 145.9–145.14.

67 *Id.* at s. 145.15 (added in 1989). *See generally* Marc-André LeChasseur, *Les règlements à caractère discrétionnaire en vertu de la Loi sur l'aménagement et l'urbanisme*, 31 Revue de droit Université de Sherbrooke 199 (2000–2001).

the south face rather than being limited to considering discrete applications (in this case, for the residential development) in a piecemeal fashion, citing Mr. Justice Mailhot in the Court of Appeal: "Preserving the natural environment of Mount Pinacle called for more than merely checking the aesthetics of the architecture. The municipal council had to get a comprehensive picture of the project before approving it and allowing the appropriate zoning change."

Most of the summit is now owned by a Montreal company active in heritage preservation and key areas of the north slope are controlled by the *Fiducie Foncière Mont Pinacle* [Mount Pinnacle Land Trust], a non-profit company set up in 1991.

Sources: Act respecting Land Use Planning and Development, R.S.Q., c. A-19.1, s. 145.9 and following; Enterprises Sibeca Inc. v. Frelighsburg (Municipality), [2004] 3 S.C.R. 304; and Fiducie Foncière Mont Pinacle, *at* http://www.montpinacle.ca (last visited Aug. 23, 2007).

Site planning and architectural integration programs are designed to ensure the appropriate integration of a development into the surrounding milieu. The general procedure is similar to that outlined above for comprehensive development programs: adoption of an initial by-law setting out the requirements governing the submission and assessment of a program, and subsequent approval of the program by resolution, with or without conditions.[68] The public must be consulted on the initial by-law but not necessarily on the subsequent program.[69]

The former Municipality of Mont Tremblant availed itself of these discretionary tools to control all aspects of the base camp development of Base Sud. Under the development agreement negotiated for Base Sud in 1992, the by-law criteria relating to ecological aspects of base camp and other residential developments included: natural treatment of the interface between the main parking area and the adjacent wetland, and protection of the wetland itself; protection of the environment, particularly as it concerns water quality; conservation of the wooded areas along waterways; respect for natural drainage patterns; maintenance of vegetation cover on slopes; and protection of the deer yard. For example, a development proposal for some zones in the white-tailed deer yard would not be approved unless it: (1) preserved one or more wooded corridors at least 32 yards wide to permit the movement of the herd from one feeding area to another; (2) prohibited the construction of fences to facilitate their free movement; (3) left at least 15 percent of the zone in its natural state; and (4) favored the clustering of buildings rather than their dispersal.[70] Intrawest and other developers then

68 Act respecting Land Use Planning and Development, R.S.Q., c. A-19.1, ss. 145.16, 145.19, 145.20.

69 *Id.* at ss. 123, para. 1(3) and 145.18.

70 Réglementation d'urbanisme, *supra* note 58, at s. 4.5.2.9.3. These by-laws provisions implemented the changes agreed to in the 1992 development agreement (Protocole d'entente entre Municipalité de Mont Tremblant et Station Mont Tremblant

submitted voluminous development programs, or plans, in conformity with the by-law criteria. The Municipality approved these programs by resolution, the developers signed development agreements, or contracts, binding themselves to implement the programs, and the Municipality adopted the necessary by-laws attendant on its approval.

As for the more recent base camp at Versant Soleil, the key instrument governing its development is a negotiated "special planning program"[71] contained in Annex E to the 2003 framework agreement between the merged Town of Mont Tremblant and Station Mont Tremblant.[72] Under this agreement, Station Mont Tremblant undertakes to realize "diligently" the project set out in its own master plan for the site, and the municipality contracts to employ "its best efforts" to ensure the adoption and approval of land use by-laws prepared by Station Mont Tremblant in consultation with the municipality and annexed to the agreement.

Annex E to the framework agreement sets out the amendments to be made to the 1989 local plan. Some of the general provisions affecting the natural environment include the elimination of a designated park and green space area along the main road by Rivière du Diable leading to Versant Soleil,[73] a change in the boundaries of the protected white-tailed deer yard so as to exclude the base camp site,[74] an extension of the "visual basin" up to the mountain summit so as to include both the residential area and the entire flank of Versant Soleil within it[75] and—more positively—the protection of a salmon spawning ground at the mouth of a small stream flowing out of the Versant Soleil site.

But the heart of Annex E is a 48-page proposed "special planning program" dealing specifically with the base camp development.[76] The program adopts an environmental discourse, with watercourse issues having pride of place. The development objectives include: "to concentrate development so as to minimize its impact on the surrounding natural environment;" "to plan interventions in the

---

société en commandite [hereinafter Protocole 1992]). See the discussion in Chapter 20 *supra* at note 64.

71 See *supra* the text at note 20 and following text.

72 Entente cadre entre la Ville de Mont Tremblant et Station Mont Tremblant Société en Commandite sur l'aménagement du complexe touristique Versant Soleil [hereinafter Entente cadre 2003].-

73 Annexe E, s. 4.1.

74 *Id.* at s. 4.2. The site is now identified as being one where the deer are unlikely to winter over because of the dearth of evergreens to provide the necessary shelter; however, the program recognizes that deer are nevertheless present in the area and contains the objective of planning the development "in such a way as to permit the white-tailed deer to continue to traverse the property". Ss. 3.2.5 and 4.3 of the special planning program (author's translation). See the discussion *supra*, the text at notes 20–22.

75 *Id.* at s. 4.6. This relates to the regional plan objective of limiting the visual impact of residential development on the natural landscape. See the discussion *supra*, the text following note 16.

76 *Id.* at s. 12.

natural milieu in such a way as to recreate a sustainable environmental equilibrium through ... environmental improvements to the lake and streams which will have been the object of an environmental impact assessment;" "to construct works in sensitive natural environments with a view to the creation of ecosystems;" and "to respect the support capacity of the milieu in terms of the provision of potable water from Lac Tremblant and the transmission of treated sewerage into Rivière du Diable."[77] A central environmental objective in the special planning program is "to create from a badly drained area an interesting and aesthetic tourist milieu, one which is balanced from an environmental point of view."[78] The proposed residential area—a ten-hectare plateau, or bowl, nestled in the mountain about 100 meters from its foot—is crossed by three drainage systems which form a wetland (or "badly drained area") in the bowl before ultimately flowing into Rivière du Diable. Frogs and salamander thrive in this milieu, and beaver are active. The plan is to transform this area into a 2.5-hectare retaining pond, or lake, integrated into the built environment. Part of the banks will be urbanized, but for the rest:

> the objective is to make it a window on nature, representative of a natural Laurentian lake ... [with] indigenous plants, typical of our lakes, planted along the shore... The lake will not be stocked with fish, to protect the spawning ground downstream from it. However, with its diversified bank plantings, its floating and emerging swamp areas, its wooded banks and perhaps some tiny islands, the lake will certainly become a living environment for numerous species of amphibians, reptiles, aquatic birds and small mammals.[79]

As would be expected, the proposed amendments to the local plan were picked up in the amendments to the implementing by-laws, set out in Annex F, with the bulk of this Annex being devoted to Versant Soleil.[80] Annex F includes proposed amendments to the existing regulatory framework (zoning, subdivision control, and signage by-laws, etc.) and the existing site plan and architectural integration by-law so as to bring them into conformity with the amended plan.[81]

---

77 S. 4.3 of the special planning program (author's translation).

78 *Id.*

79 *Id.* at s. 5.1.1 b) (author's translation). Annexe H of the Entente cadre 2003, which sets out development principles for streams and bodies of water, focuses almost exclusively on the artificial lake. One wishes that the same care and attention would be devoted to the preservation of the ecosystem of the truly natural Laurentian lake, Lac Tremblant, on the shores of which Base Sud is situated.

80 Annexe F to Entente cadre 2003, *supra* note 72, particularly s. 12 (Chapitre 6: Dispositions spéciales applicables au Versant Soleil).

81 The agreement also includes dispositions relating to such matters as water withdrawal from Lac Tremblant, solid waste management, parks and trail networks, local access to recreational facilities, and so on. The local access provision (Entente cadre 2003 supra note 72, s. 5.8.5) can hardly be called generous, as it provides for a 60% discounts on lift tickets every Tuesday throughout the season (except for a two-week period from

What procedure has been followed for the adoption and implementation of this framework agreement? The agreement package was the product of negotiation between Station Mont Tremblant and the merged municipality. The latter was aided by a "Station Mont Tremblant Technical Committee", which it had set up in July 2001 and consisted of council members, members of a planning advisory committee established under the Act respecting Land Use Planning and Development, municipal employees and outside experts.[82] The municipal council reviewed the final draft of the agreement at a closed meeting on March 17, 2003, at which representatives of Station Mont Tremblant (but apparently not opponents of the project) were present to explain the project and answer questions.[83] A public meeting was held four days later, also attended by the Station's representatives, to explain the project and answer questions;[84] and Council authorized signature of the agreement at its meeting of March 24.[85] At this same meeting, Council also adopted a by-law amending the local plan and another amending the implementing by-laws to accommodate Versant Soleil.[86] There is no indication in the minutes of a discussion of these changes, and they were but two of some 60 items on the agenda (including a public meeting on four unrelated draft by-laws and two question

Christmas to New Years) and every Wednesday from April 1 to the end of the season, as well as one free lift ticket on an "Open Door" day on a designated Sunday in early June. Most local people will be working or in school on Tuesdays; and lift tickets prices at Mont Tremblant are presently about double other Laurentian destinations. The [Montreal] Gazette, Nov. 20, 2004, at W7.

82 The mandate of the Committee was "to analyse the applications of Station Mont Tremblant for the project and all related elements, to work in collaboration with Station Mont Tremblant, to draft a regulatory framework, to define the content of any agreements between Station Mont Tremblant and the Town of Mont Tremblant, and to advise the Council about them". Preamble to Annexe E to the Entente cadre 2003, supra note 72 (author's translation).

83 André Courey, *Versant Soleil Rising Soon*, Tremblant Express, Mar./Apr. 2003, http://www.tremblantexpress.com/ (last visited May 28, 2004).

84 *Id.* Pharand reports that about 250 persons attended the meeting. "Despite the significant level of attendance by residents …, the attendees were only provided opportunities to ask questions of clarification regarding the development. Participants were not able to contribute to the development of the protocol content … City representatives suggested that since the council was 'given an opportunity to give Intrawest feedback and since [they] represented the community, residents were able to provide indirect feedback.'" Carolyn Pharand, Stakeholder Involvement in Corporate Social and Environmental Strategies in Mont Tremblant, Supervised Research Project, Master of Resource Management, Simon Fraser University, 56-57 (2005), available at http://ir.lib.sfu.ca/retrieve/2178/etd1825.pdf (last visited Aug. 2, 2007).

85 Ville de Mont Tremblant, Procès-verbal de la séance [Minutes of the meeting] du 24 mars 2003, agenda item 5.3, available at http://www.villedemont-tremblant.qc.ca (last visited Sept 16, 2005).

86 *Id.*, agenda items 4.4 and 4.5 (By-laws 2003-200 and 2003-2001 respectively). It also adopted several other, less encompassing, by-laws relating to Versant Soleil.

periods) for the two-and-one-half hour meeting. This way of proceeding (plan amendment and implementing by-laws) meant that the amended implementing by-laws were classified as "concordance by-laws" and thus not subject to the referendum procedure with its attendant risk of veto by local residents.[87]

Thus, discretionary tools provided the main means for mediating the environmental, social, and economic priorities of the area. The development of Intrawest's camps at Mont Trembant was clearly negotiation-based, and the outcomes of the negotiations were reflected principally in the two development agreements for the two base camps. The 1992 agreement for Base Sud, negotiated by the pre-merger municipality, provided for comprehensive development programs and site planning and architectural integration programs as the key discretionary tools to implement the agreement; utilization of these tools led to further, more detailed negotiation. The 2003 agreement for Versant Soleil, negotiated by the post-merger municipality, featured the special planning program as the key implementing vehicle. Its subsequent inclusion in the local plan meant that all implementing by-laws, regulatory and discretionary alike, also had to be amended to reflect the terms of the special planning program; utilization of the discretionary tools also involved further, more detailed negotiations, as with Base Sud, but these negotiations were conditioned by the terms of the special planning program, as their outcomes had to accord with it. In the end, therefore, the extent to which discretionary tools in fact mediate environmental, social, and economic priorities depends on the negotiating position of the parties to the agreement, and Mont Tremblant's case, Intrawest's economic priorities necessarily weighed heavily in the results.

These land use planning rules apply to golf courses in the same way they apply to base camps, but before considering golf course development in detail, the following section looks at the explicit environmental rules that apply to base camp development.

Environmental Assessment

Land use planning law is not the only source of rules applicable to Intrawest's base camp development. Environmental law also plays a role, both as set out in the negotiated agreements between Station Mont Tremblant and the municipality and under legislation.

The contractual provisions are found in the "environmental control and monitoring programs" included as annexes to both the 1992 and 2003 agreements between the Station and the municipality. As we have seen, the environmental monitoring program annexed to the 1992 development agreement, relating to Base Sud, encompassed ski facility development and base camp construction alike.[88] The 2003 Versant Soleil monitoring program, however, is more carefully circumscribed in scope. For one thing, it applies only to developments within

87 See the discussion *supra*, text at note 64.

88 See the discussion in Chapter 20 *supra* at note 64.

the Town of Mont Tremblant (i.e. the base camp) and not to developments on the leased lands in the Park (i.e. the ski area) except to the extent that the Park developments affect the Town portion of the site; and for another, it applies only to those developments (wherever located) that are not subject to an environmental assessment by the provincial or federal governments. This latter exception means, for example, that the diversion of streams and the development of the artificial lake at the base camp are outside the scope of the program, as are potable water supply and waste water treatment facilities.[89] In fact, the Versant Soleil program really applies only to the proposed residential and commercial development in the base camp, and its ecosystems reach is thus limited. However, the framework agreement itself provides for the establishment of a joint technical committee to "study and examine *all aspects* of the natural environment related to the realization of the project,"[90] with the natural environment being understood for this purpose to mean "the water, air, land or any combination thereof or, generally, the ambient milieu with which living species interrelate dynamically."[91] This suggests a more holistic appreciation of the ecosystem, but the public record does not indicate whether the committee has been established or the study completed.

As for legislation, the most important statute is Quebec's Environment Quality Act,[92] which applies to base camp development in much the same way as it applies to trail development.[93] Particularly important for Versant Soleil is the need for section 22 ministerial approval for any construction or other activities "in a constant or intermittent watercourse, a lake, pond, marsh, swamp or bog."[94] This includes the matters identified in the 2003 framework agreement's environmental control and monitoring program as being outside its scope (stream diversion, artificial lake construction, water supply, wastewater treatment). However, ministerial authorization does not imply a comprehensive environmental impact assessment, complete with public hearing, as we have seen. Rather, individual authorizations are given for each discrete aspect of the project. The whole is disaggregated into its several parts.[95]

Base camp development also brings into play the provincial government's Protection Policy for Lakeshores, Riverbanks, Littoral Zones and Floodplains,

---

89 Entente cadre 2003, *supra* note 72, Annexe G: Évaluation environnementale et plan d'orientation du programme de contrôle et de suivi environnemental des projets de construction, d'entretien et de gestion du site du Versant Soleil de la Station Mont Tremblant sur le territoire de la Ville de Mont Tremblant, para. 2.3.1.

90 Entente cadre 2003, *supra* note 72, at s. 5.1.2 (emphasis added).

91 *Id.* at s. 5.1.4.

92 R.S.Q., c. Q-2.

93 See the discussion in Chapter 20 *supra* at note 26 and the following text.

94 Environment Quality Act, R.S.Q., c. Q-2, s. 22, para. 2. This paragraph was added to the Act in 1988 and entered into force in 1993. Environnement Québec, Demande de certificat d'autorisation: Milieux du loisir et de la villegiature, http://www.menv.gouv.qc.ca/ministere/certif/fiche6.htm (last visited Sept. 2, 2004) (emphasis added).

95 See the discussion in Chapter 20 *supra* at note 33 and following text.

adopted under section 2.1 of the Environment Quality Act.[96] The various provisions in the Policy are framed as guidelines rather than as provincial regulations so that they will be integrated into local and municipal planning documents and thus implemented in a more decentralized manner. Accordingly, the Laurentides Regional County Municipality's regional plan stipulates that projects that do not require ministerial approval under the Act must nevertheless, for example, "ensure the natural flow of water" and "protect the typical plants of wetland areas, threatened or vulnerable species and the wildlife, and guarantee that they will not incur damage."[97] These provisions are then to be reflected at the local level in the local plan and implementing by-laws, under the principle of vertical integration, and the Act respecting Land Use Planning and Development stipulates that if the Minister responsible for the environment concludes that a municipal zoning, subdivision or building by-law "fails to conform with the policy of the Government contemplated in section 2.1 of the Environment Quality Act" or "considering the distinctive features of the locality, fails to provide adequate protection for lakeshores, riverbanks, littoral zones and floodplains", he or she may request the municipality to amend the by-law and, if the municipality fails to do so, may amend it himself.[98]

As for the federal Canadian Environmental Assessment Act,[99] it applies to the Versant Soleil and Camp Nord developments, as we have seen, mainly as a result of Station Mont Tremblant's application for federal government infrastructure financing. This was not the case for the Base Sud development, and the federal procedure differs from Quebec's in two important respects—scope and public input—making it a stronger ecological instrument. Firstly, the scope of the assessment is more comprehensive or holistic, and includes an evaluation of "the *cumulative effects* that the carrying out of the project, combined with the existence of other projects or activities, is likely to cause to the environment."[100] "Environmental effects" are defined widely under the Act to include "changes caused by the project to the biophysical environment and the direct effects of these changes on human health, socio-economic conditions, natural and cultural heritage (historical, archaeological, paleontological and architectural)."[101] The anticipated

---

96 Preamble, Protection Policy for Lakeshores, Riverbanks, Littoral Zones and Floodplains, c. Q-2, r. 17.3 (O.C. 468-2005, G.O.Q.2005.II.1441), *available at* http://www2.publicationsduquebec.gouv.qc.ca/home.php# (last visited July 31, 2007) [hereinafter Protection Policy].

97 Schéma d'aménagement, *supra* note 16, "Document complémentaire," ch. 10, art. 32 (author's translation).

98 Act respecting Land Use Planning and Development, R.S.Q., c. A-19.1, ss. 165.2 and 165.4.

99 Canadian Environmental Assessment Act, S.C. 1992, c. 37. See the discussion in Chapter 20 *supra* at note 38 and following text.

100 Environmental Assessment Screening Report, *supra* note 8, para. 4.2 (emphasis added).

101 *Id.* at para. 4.2, paraphrasing Canadian Environmental Assessment Act, S.C. 1992, c. 37, s. 2 (1).

environmental effects of the Versant Soleil development were identified in the Screening Report as including (but not being limited to) the following:

> hydrology and the drainage system, hydrogeology (groundwater), surface waters, soil quality, terrestrial, riparian and aquatic vegetation and wetlands, fish and fish habitat, herpetofauna, terrestrial and semi-aquatic fauna, avian fauna, navigation, land use planning and land use, ambient sound, air quality, landscape, heritage and archaeological potential.[102]

The evaluation was conducted under the aegis of Infrastructure Canada and Fisheries and Oceans Canada, with input from other federal and provincial authorities.[103] The overall conclusion of the assessment was that the development projects "are not likely to cause significant adverse environmental effects."[104] More precisely, it concluded that the developments in the three locations (the two new base camps and the skiable domain) will have possible adverse environmental effects under most headings,[105] that complete attenuation of the adverse environmental effects will rarely be possible,[106] but that the residual effects will not be significant under any heading. The report includes a long list of mitigation measures to be taken relating to the application of pesticides and fertilizers in proximity to watercourses, the prevention of watercourse sedimentation, the protection of wildlife habitats, the restriction of construction activity during sensitive breeding and spawning periods, the restriction of forest clearing, the use of indigenous plant species for

---

102 *Id.* at para. 4.1.

103 Fisheries and Oceans Canada was involved because the "destruction, harmful alteration or disruption of fish habitat" require its authorization under s. 35 (2) of the Fisheries Act, R.S.C. 1985, c. F-14. Natural Resources Canada advised on hydrology and forestry; Environment Canada was consulted on wetlands and avian fauna; Public Works and Government Services Canada provided input concerning hydrology and water quality; and Transport Canada was consulted in the context of its jurisdiction over navigable waters. Several provincial bodies were also consulted: the Quebec environment ministry on matters within its jurisdiction (identified as wastewater management, watercourse crossings, hydrology, etc.); and the Société de la faune et des parcs du Québec concerning wildlife protection (white-tailed deer, ichthyologic fauna, avifauna, etc.) in particular, as well as activities on the leased lands in general. *Id.* at para. 2.0.

104 *Id.* at para. 10.0.

105 The only exceptions for the two base camp developments were "archaeology" and "heritage" under human environment; and for the skiable domain, "hydrology" (physical environment); and "land use planning and land use", "ambient noise", "air quality" and "archaeology" and heritage" (human environment). *Id.* at para. 7.0.

106 It would be possible only in regard to "soil quality" (physical environment) and "wetland" and "ichthyofauna/habitat" (aquatic biological environment) in the three locations; attenuation would also be possible for "land use planning and land use" and "ambient noise" (human environment) in regard to the two base camps; neither was identified as a problem in the skiable domain. *Id.*

revegetation, and so on.[107] It also provides for several compensation projects to be undertaken relating to fish habitat (management of 880 yards of an identified stream to support breeding and feeding needs of particular fish) and wetlands (management of filter marshes to compensate for the loss of wetlands).[108] The developments are to be monitored during and after construction, and Infrastructure Canada and Fisheries and Oceans Canada representatives are to be allowed to make such site visits as they deem necessary.[109]

A second difference between the federal and provincial environmental control procedures concerns public input. As we have seen, this is the exception rather than the rule under the Quebec legislation, as it is required only for those projects subject to an environmental impact assessment. Under the federal legislation, public consultation is a requirement for all assessments, although a public hearing is required only when a project is referred by the Minister to a review panel for more detailed consideration either because the initial screening indicates significant adverse environmental effects or because public concern warrants it.[110] The Mont Tremblant development was not referred to a review panel, so no public hearing was held. The Screening Report was simply made available in August 2004 for public comments "to ensure that all pertinent components of the environmental assessment have been considered".[111] As a leading environmentalist observed:

> It's not a lot, but it's better than doing nothing … which is what the provincial government is doing. … While Quebec recently launched public environmental hearings for a highway bypass for two villages just north of Mont Tremblant, it refused to do so for Intrawest's project, a venture that will create new villages, new ski slopes and bring thousands more into a region that has already experienced rapid development.[112]

Eight responses were received by the late September deadline: five from property-owner associations, environmental, outdoor, and other groups; two from individuals; and one from the Laurentides Regional County Municipality.[113] The concerns focused on the capacity of Rivière du Diable to meet further demands, pollution issues, the cumulative effect of development projects, and the need for public hearings.[114]

---

107 *Id.* at para. 8.0.

108 *Id.*

109 *Id.* at para. 9.0.

110 Canadian Environmental Assessment Act, S.C. 1992, c. 37, ss. 28(1) and 34(b).

111 Environmental Assessment Screening Report, *supra* note 8, para. 10.0.

112 Jacques Ruelland, President of the Comité regional environnemental des Laurentides (CRELA), as quoted in Lynn Moore, *Public to Have Say on Tremblant*, The [Montreal] Gazette, Aug. 21, 2004, at B1.

113 *Growth's Effect on Watershed Studied*, The [Montreal] Gazette, Dec. 11, 2004, at B2.

114 *Id.*; Pharand, *supra* note 84, at 58–59.

Water is thus a central environmental issue. The water supply in the Mont Tremblant area is said to be excellent,[115] with Lac Tremblant and Rivière du Diable said to provide enough water to meet demands for snowmaking and golf course watering as well as for human consumption.[116] But concerns remain. In 2004, the Municipality of Mont Tremblant introduced measures to limit water consumption,[117] and asked its Consultative Committee on the Environment to draft a town water policy for managing and preserving water resources.[118] It had the *Comité régional environnemental des Laurentides* (CRELA) [Laurentian Regional Environmental Council] co-ordinate the setting up of an independent Diable River catchment area management committee composed of all the major players (Mont Tremblant Park, the municipality, ecological organizations and—presumably—Station Mont Tremblant), to focus on protecting the quality of the water in Rivière du Diable.[119] And it hired one of Quebec's leading engineering firms to undertake a new study of the proposed use of Rivière du Diable as Camp Nord's main water source, even though several previous studies had concluded that it would not jeopardize the water supply of communities downstream. One of the concerns is that extraction from Rivière du Diable when water levels are low (late fall, for example) could "jeopardize the river's ecological stability" as well as affect the quantity and quality available for communities downstream.[120] The ecological equilibrium of Lac Tremblant is equally of concern, and Quebec's Ministry of the Environment has enacted regulations designed to maintain a minimal level of

115 André Courey, Mont Tremblant*'s Water Gets Good Marks*, TREMBLANT EXPRESS, Apr. 2004, *available at* http://www.tremblantexpress.com (last visited May 28, 2004) ("The quality of fresh water in the region is not lacking and the quality is among the best to be found anywhere").

116 *Id.* Little is known about the state of the groundwater, although it is an increasingly important source of potable water. *Id.*

117 By-law 2004-63, adopted Feb. 9, 2004, http://www.villedemont-tremblant.qc.ca/jahia/webdav/site/tremblant/shared/Fichiers/Proces_verbaux/2004-02-09%20pvo.pdf (last visited Sept. 16, 2005); André Courey, *City Watches Over Water Consumption*, TREMBLANT EXPRESS, Mar. 2004), *available at* http://www.tremblantexpress.com (last visited May 28, 2004).

118 André Courey, *Municipal Affairs: Water Resources Protection*, TREMBLANT EXPRESS, May 2004, *available at* http://www.tremblantexpress.com (last visited May 28, 2004).

119 *Id.*; Mise sur Pied d'un Comité de Gestion de Bassin Versant de la Rivière du Diable, INFO MONT TREMBLANT (Nov. 2004) 4, *available at* http://www.villedemont-tremblant.qc.ca/jahia/webdav/site/tremblant/shared/Fichiers/Bulletins/Info%20Mont-Tremblant_volume_3_no_3_novembre_2004.pdf (last visited Aug. 8, 2007). This committee, AGIR pour la Diable (Alliance pour un Gestion Intégrée et Responsable du basin versant de la rivière du Diable), is in the process of drafting a master plan for the river. *See* Plan directeur de l'eau, http://www.agirpourladiable.org/portail/index.html (last visited Aug. 8, 2007).

120 André Courey, *Camp Nord Water Supply Assessed Again*, TREMBLANT EXPRESS, Apr. 2004, *available at* http://www.tremblantexpress.com (last visited May 28, 2004).

water in the lake, as well as an "ecologically minimum outflow" from Rivière du Diable and another river (Rivière Cachée), "measured so as to take account of the surrounding hydrological network".[121]

In sum, the base camp development at Base Sud was subjected to a more comprehensive environmental assessment under contract law, as the environmental control and monitoring program in the 1992 agreement applied to the entire development, mountain and base camp alike, whereas the 2003 agreement for Versant Soleil limited the reach of the equivalent program much more severely. On the other hand, the development at Versant Soleil was subjected to a more comprehensive and public legislative assessment under the federal environmental protection statute, whereas Base Sud was governed solely by the Quebec legislation, without public input.

Because golf courses are an integral element of the base camp experience and fall under the same land use planning regime, let us look at this topic before drawing some general conclusions about the two.

Golf Course Development

As we have seen, golf course development is integral to the economic viability of a four-season resort, and the Mont Tremblant area boasts seven courses, six of which are located in the Town of Mont Tremblant. (See Figure 21.2). Two of the six are owned by Intrawest (or more precisely, Station Mont Tremblant): Le Diable, an "Arizona style" 7,056-yard championship course, with glens, imposing bunkers and long, narrow, "impeccably green" fairways; and Le Géant, a 6,836-yard course constructed on multi-level plateaus "sculpted right into the mountainside", with two artificial lakes and 52 bunkers.[122] Golf course development causes problems of habitat fragmentation, gaps and edges similar to ski trail development. An additional concern is their possible adverse affect on water quality and quantity. All six golf courses in the Town of Mont Tremblant are built along or near the Rivière du Diable. Golf course development raises issues relating to construction and operation.

Golf Course Construction

Golf courses can be constructed only in areas designated for this use in municipal plans and their implementing by-laws, as discussed above. They are also governed by Quebec's Environment Quality Act, which identifies golf course

121 Ville de Mont Tremblant, Le Versant Soleil … Des Réponses à vos Questions, INFO MONT TREMBLANT (Automne 2002) 4 at 5, *available at* http://www.villedemont-tremblant.qc.ca/jahia/Jahia/pid/53 (last visited March 16, 2005).

122 Mont Tremblant Resort, A Paradise of Green: Superb Scenery, Exceptional Courses, http://www.tremblant.ca/golf/index-e.htm (last visited March 16, 2005).

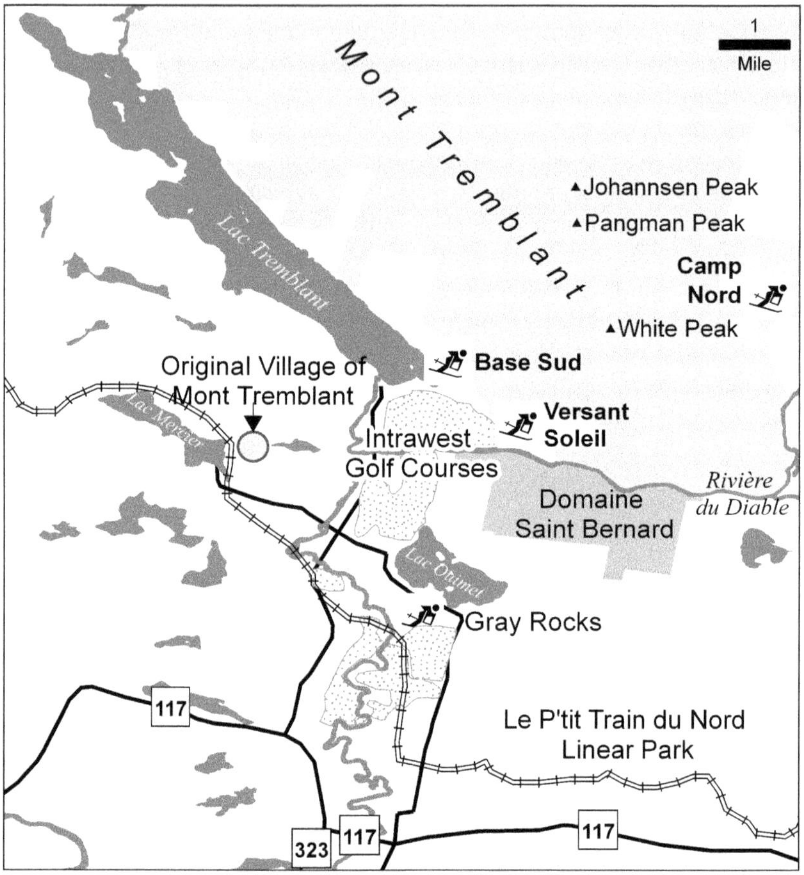

Figure 21.2 Golf Courses and Domaine St. Bernard

Data Sources: DMTI Spatial Inc.; ESRI; ©Department of Natural Resources Canada, all rights reserved.

construction, like trail development, as an activity likely to result in "a change in the quality of the environment," one that usually takes place in an area of "constant or intermittent watercourse, a lake, pond, marsh, swamp or bog."[123] For this reason, construction of a new golf course or enlargement of an existing one requires a certificate of authorization from the Quebec Minister of the Sustainable Development, Environment and Parks under section 22 of the Act. The application for a certificate must be accompanied by preliminary studies of the environmental impact of the project, particularly with regard to the construction phase, the space occupied by the golf course, the use of fertilizers and pesticides, and drainage and

123 Environment Quality Act, R.S.Q., c. Q-2, s. 22, paras. 1 & 2.

water withdrawal for irrigation.[124] As we have seen, section 22 does not provide for a public hearing prior to the granting of a certificate of authorization.

The provincial government's Protection Policy for Lakeshores, Riverbanks, Littoral Zones and Floodplains,[125] adopted under section 2.1 of the Environment Quality Act, also plays a role in regard to golf course construction. Floodplain protection is of particular concern because golf course construction involves cutting and filling to shape the course. Under the Policy as it existed prior to a 2005 amendment, golf course construction was not permitted as of right in flood-prone areas, although an exemption was possible for "the development of a parcel of land for recreational purposes . . . which requires cutting and filling in flood-prone areas (such as . . . *golf courses*, hiking trails, cycling paths, etc.)."[126] At least one golf course in the Mont Tremblant area was granted such an exception by the Minister responsible for the environment and was constructed in a designated floodplain area. The revised Policy is stricter, and specifically excludes any possibility of an exemption for golf courses, whether or not they require cutting and filling to construct. A list of structures, undertakings, and works that "may be permitted" in a flood-prone area includes "an open-air undertaking, *other than a golf course*, intended for recreation purposes and that does not require filling or removal of fill;" and a list of structures, undertakings and works eligible for an exemption includes "development of land for recreational purposes ... that requires filling or the removal of fill, involving such undertakings as roads, footpaths and bicycle paths; ... *golf courses are not eligible for an exemption.*"[127]

No new golf courses are planned for construction by Station Mont Tremblant as part of the Versant Soleil or Camp Nord developments. However, an agreement of August 24, 2001, relating to the construction of a golf course owned by another corporation[128] contains a number of clauses dealing with environmental matters, such as prevention of erosion and sedimentation of water courses, creation of buffer zones along the Rivière du Diable and around wetlands, noninterference with floodplain capacity and spring runoff channels, limits on the quantity of water used for irrigation, restrictions on pesticide use around existing and future wells for drinking water, control of the storage and use of chemicals, and ongoing monitoring of the quality of surface and underground water.[129] This goes further

---

124 Québec, Ministère de l'Environnement, Fiche technique no. 16: Golf.

125 Protection Policy, *supra* note 96.

126 The former Politique de Protection des Rives, du Littoral et des Plaines Inondables, Décret 103-96, G.O.Q. 1996.II.1263 & 1483 [available in French only], Annex 1, Item 13, and Annex 2, Item 15 (emphasis added). A "flood-prone area" [*zone de grand courant*] is defined in the Politique de Protection as being an area susceptible of recurring flooding within twenty-year periods.

127 Protection Policy, *supra* note 96, at ss. 4.2.1 (g) and 4.2.2 (k) (emphasis added).

128 Project de Golf Le Manitou: Protocole d'entente entre Ville de Mont Tremblant et Golf Manitou Inc. 10, Annexes [hereinafter Protocole 2001].

129 *Id.* at Annex A.

than the provisions relating to golf courses in the earlier, more general 1992 agreement[130] between the municipality and Station Mont Tremblant governing the development at Base Sud. As with the 1992 agreement, compliance under the 2001 agreement was determined by an evaluator's report and possible arbitration.[131]

Golf Course Operation

The major concerns regarding golf course operation are the application of chemicals—herbicides, pesticides and fertilizers—and the use of water to maintain the verdant green conditions to which golfers have become accustomed and are regarded as the hallmark of a first-class course.[132] Golf course watering is part-and-parcel of the general concerns about water supply in the Mont Tremblant area, as discussed above. The focus here is on pesticide and other chemical use. Rules about their use are often negotiated on a case-by-case basis at the time of construction, as noted above; they can also be set out in more generally applicable instruments.

The distribution and use of pesticides is controlled mainly by the provincial Pesticide Act.[133] The Pesticide Management Code, adopted under the Act in 2003, prohibits any nonagricultural pesticide application within three meters (3.28 yards) of a watercourse or body of water.[134] Golf courses fall under this general prohibition. They also fall under a more specific provision of the Code providing for the submission of triennial golf course "pesticide reduction plans" to the Minister responsible for the environment, starting in April 2006. These plans must be signed by a member of the Ordre des agronomes du Québec [Quebec Order of Agronomists], and must identify: the total quantity of pesticides (fungicides, insecticides, herbicides, rodenticides and other pesticides) applied annually in each of the three preceding years, and the area treated by each class of pesticide; the pesticide reduction objectives for the next three years, in percentage or quantity, for each class of pesticide; measures to be taken to attain pesticide reduction; measures taken to prevent migration of pesticides outside premises; and an evaluation of the results obtained under the reduction plan during the preceding three years.[135] The goals of the Minister are therefore to reduce the overall amount of pesticides used,

130 Protocole 1992, *supra* note 70.

131 Protocole 2001, *supra* note 128, at art. 2 and Annex E.

132 A government guide acknowledges that golf course superintendents often feel pressure to maintain courses to tournament standards, so that mowing heights are kept very low and the resulting stress on plants fosters pest development and a concomitant reliance, or overreliance, on pesticides. Environnement Québec, Section 73 of the Pesticides Management Code: Pesticide Reduction Plan for Golf Courses, http://www.menv.gouv.qc.ca/pesticides/permis-en/code-gestion-en/guide-golf/index.htm (last visited March 16, 2004).

133 Pesticides Act, R.S.Q., c. P-9.3.

134 Pesticide Management Code, O.C. 331-2003, 2003 G.O.Q. II.1255, s. 29.

135 *Id.* at s. 73.

particularly toxic and persistent ones; to reduce health and environmental risks associated with pesticide use; and to foster better cultivation practices, integrated pest management and environmentally sound management. Effective integrated pest management requires an understanding of a golf course ecosystem.

Regulation of pesticide use is not just a provincial matter. It may also take place at the municipal level, as the Supreme Court of Canada has recognized in holding that a municipality may prohibit pesticide use on lawns within a municipality under its general power to adopt by-laws "to secure peace, order, good government, health and general welfare in the territory of the municipality."[136] The Town of Mont Tremblant's response to this has been both regulatory and contractual. In May 2004, it adopted a new by-law on pesticides and fertilizers,[137] which severely restricts the use of pesticides and prohibits the use of chemical fertilizers within the municipality. In June 2004, it signed an agreement with the six golf courses within its territory providing for the management and storage of pesticides on golf courses, as well as for emergency measures to be taken should this be necessary; it also provides for regular assessment of the water quality in the Rivière du Diable and other watercourses downstream from it, a matter of ongoing concern as all six of the area's golf courses border this river.[138] This agreement is a first of its kind in Quebec, and was negotiated with the participation of Quebec's Ministry of the Environment.[139]

There are thus encouraging examples of an ecosystems approach being taken in regard to base camp and golf course development at Mont Tremblant. Environmental issues received a good deal of attention in the regional plan; and planning documents at the local level—notably the "environmental master plan," but also the "preliminary proposal"—are more overtly ecosystemic, or integrative, in their discourse and approach. These environmental concerns then flow into the regulatory and discretionary implementing by-laws adopted by both the pre-merger and post-merger councils, which contain measures relating to the white-tailed deer yard, wetlands, forest coverage, and so on. Provincial and federal environmental assessment legislation and contractual environmental monitoring agreements reinforce this approach. Although the limited scope of most of the projects evaluated militates against the adoption of a truly holistic approach, there are encouraging

---

136 Cities and Towns Act, R.S.Q., c. C-19, s. 410, para. 1(1); 114957 Canada Ltée v. Town of Hudson, [2001] 2 S.C.R. 241. The Hudson by-law exempted the use of pesticides on golf courses for a period of five years from 1991, the date the by-law came into force.

137 Ville de Mont Tremblant, Règlement sur les Pesticides et Fertilisants, By-law 2004-67, http://www.villedemont-tremblant.qc.ca/ (last visited April 1, 2005)*; see also* Ville de Mont Tremblant, Nouveau règlement sur les pesticides et fertilisants, http://www.villedemont-tremblant.qc.caécgi-binécommuniques.cgi (last visited May 28, 2004).

138 Ville de Mont Tremblant, Une première au Québec: La signature d'un protocole d'entente entre la Ville de Mont Tremblant et les six golfs de son territoire pour la protection de l'environnement, http:www.villedemont-tremblant.qc.ca/jahiad/Jahia/pid/227 (last visited July 13, 2004); André Courey, *Town Signs Agreement with Golf Courses*, TREMBLANT EXPRESS, July 2004, *available at* http:www.tremblantexpress.com (last visited July 12, 2004).

139 *Id.*

signs of focus on dynamic interrelationships and cumulative effects. Concerns about water runs like a thread through all of these documents, with issues such as maintaining an ecological balance as well as simply ensuring an adequate supply of potable water coming to the fore. Golf courses are increasingly subject to control.

But the development pressures are enormous, and the discourse sometimes changes to accommodate new developments. For example, trees can be cut in the Bicknell thrush's habitat, but not during breeding season; parts of the white-tailed deer yard protected by the land exchange are subsequently included in the Versant Soleil base camp site; and wetlands become an artificial pond.

And the applicable legal rules can also change to accommodate new development, and this is particularly true of the land use planning rules. In principle, the various instruments are to nest together in a hierarchical way: the regional plan articulates a vision for the future growth of the region, in broad-brush terms, which the local plans of the constituent municipalities then reflect in more detailed terms; these plans then condition the content of the various implementing by-laws. However, the process does not often work out so neatly, as it is impossible to foresee the future with complete accuracy. Changed economic conditions, new councils with different policies, new owners with different ideas often require an adjustment to the plans and by-laws to accommodate developments not allowed under the existing rules, and these adjustments usually result from negotiations between municipality and developer. Pushed to the limit, this suggests that the process is not one in which the legal instruments control the form and nature of development, but rather the reverse—one in which development proposals shape the content of plans and their implementing by-laws—but this would be overstating the case: there is always some negotiation with most developments, and in the end, it is a matter of degree—as the Versant Soleil development illustrates.

Versant Soleil is not the only development to benefit in this way from extensive changes to the local plans and implementing by-laws.[140] Zoning changes and variances at Mont Tremblant have been said to "flow like water, overriding rules about frontage on lakes and distances between buildings and building densities", and the fear is that "willy-nilly zoning" is undermining not only the environment but also Mont Tremblant's attraction as an international tourist destination.[141] As one newspaper editorial put it:

> The prospect of a billion-dollar project carries with it the potential of overdevelopment, environmental and otherwise. The town of Tremblant cannot expect to keep all its quaintness, and the highest peak in the province will seem

140 "While Intrawest grabs the headlines—and some media and government scrutiny—other developers quietly obtain zoning changes and derogations [i.e. variances]". Lynn Moore, *'The Old Orchard Syndrome': Welcome to Tremblant, where many feel development projects will damage not only the environment, but the area's appeal to tourists*, The [Montreal] Gazette, Dec. 11, 2004, at B1.

141 *Id.* at B1, B3.

> even more populated when ski runs are cut onto the north face of the mountain and a convention centre is built on the south. Still, this is Quebec's oldest provincial park, and no wilderness area.[142]

This possibility of change in the public law rules is the reason why the council of the pre-merger municipality turned to the private law tool of a land trust to protect Domaine Saint Bernard.

Domaine Saint Bernard

The third protected area of importance in the Mont Tremblant area is Domaine Saint Bernard, an area of some 1,485 acres situated immediately across the Rivière du Diable from Versant Soleil. The majority of the site is forest-covered, and it contains two 1,300-foot mountains, Mont Bellevue and Mont Saint Bernard, as well as Lac Raynaud, numerous streams and a peat bog. Wildlife is abundant, notably white-tailed deer and herons. Once the site of a small hotel or health resort, Onontio Inn, the Domaine was purchased in 1951 by a religious community, *Les Frères de l'Instruction Chrétienne* [Brothers of Christian Education], as a retreat for its members. The property was later also used for cross-country skiing and hiking, with its network of trails attracting people from far and wide. Some 120,000 trees of varying species were planted on the site over the years.[143]

The Brothers decided to sell the property in the late 1990s. Because of the enormous development potential of the site and its strategic location at the foot of the mountain, several offers were made for high-income residential development. The pre-merger Municipality of Mont Tremblant was concerned about the possible loss to the community of such an important natural area, and decided to purchase the property itself "with the principal objective of maintaining the local and regional network of green trails in a truly natural setting that is economically accessible to all."[144] This decision was enthusiastically endorsed by the community, 98 percent of whom voted in favor of it in a referendum and accepted an eight to 10 percent increase in property taxes to help finance the eventual purchase.[145]

---

142 Editorial, *Mining Tourist Gold from Mont Tremblant*, THE [MONTREAL] GAZETTE, Aug. 12, 2004, at A18. The mayor's position is more pragmatic and he is quoted as saying, "I don't think any one can tell [where overdevelopment begins], and experts will differ, but I think the market will usually take care of that. You'll know that when there are [new] condos and nobody is buying them." *Id.*

143 Information on the domaine is taken from Le Domaine Saint Bernard: Patrimoine naturel et historique. Un lieu pour la collectivité 7 Annexes (2000).

144 Letter from André Sigouin, Mayor of Mont Tremblant, to the Conseil des monuments et sites du Québec (author's translation) (May 10, 2000); *see also The Choice We Face: Turn the Domaine Over to Developers, or Preserve a Garden Open to the Entire Local and Regional Population*, NEWS BULLETIN (Municipality of Mont Tremblant), July 1999, at 2.

145 *Id.*

The municipality decided not to simply create a municipal park of the newly acquired lands, although this was the most usual and straightforward option open to it, because this would not guarantee the preservation of the land in perpetuity. The council was aware that the then imminent forced municipal merger would modify the composition of the municipal council, and that the new council could then decide to replace the park designation with one permitting commercial or residential development on the site. To prevent this from happening, and to preserve one of the last large undeveloped areas remaining at the foot of Mont Tremblant, the pre-merger municipal council decided to place the newly acquired Domaine Saint Bernard in a perpetual trust.

The concept of a land trust, which is a popular land conservation tool in the United States, presents great potential for the protection and preservation of natural areas in Quebec.[146] Like other protected areas, land or green trusts may contribute to a community's health and welfare, prevent pollution of surface and ground waters, maintain wildlife habitats and ecosystems, preserve the natural heritage and provide recreational areas for the population. The concept of a land trust is relatively new in Quebec, and has been recognized in the Civil Code of Quebec only since 1994, with the inclusion of dispositions relating to a social trust. Article 1270 of the Code provides: "A social trust is a trust constituted for a purpose of general interest, such as a cultural, educative, philanthropic, religious or scientific purpose. It does not have the making of profit or the operation of an enterprise as its main object."[147] A social trust is thus distinguished from a private trust in that its object is to benefit the general public. Both "private [and] social trusts may be perpetual."[148]

The trust deed was signed on November 20, 2000, and registered on title.[149] It provides that the settlor, the Municipality of Mont Tremblant, transfers the property to be held in perpetuity for social purposes. The beneficiaries are identified widely, as being "collectively or individually, both at the present time and in the future, without limitation as to time, the citizens of the Municipality of Mont Tremblant as well as any physical or legal person using the Domaine Saint Bernard in accordance with the purposes for which the trust is created."[150] The trust purposes are more specifically defined to include the following:

---

146 Quebec's protected areas strategy includes utilizing land trusts to preserve natural lands. Environnement Québec, *Aires protégées au Québec: Contexte, constats et enjeux pour l'avenir*, http://www.menv.gouv.qc.ca/biodiversite/aires_protegees/contexte/partie2.htm (last visited May 15, 2002).

147 Art. 1270 Civil Code of Quebec (C.C.Q.).

148 Art. 1273 C.C.Q. *See generally* Remi Moreau, La Protection du Milieu Naturel par les Fiducies Foncières (1995). On the trust in Quebec law, *see* Madeleine Cantin Cumyn, L'Administration du Bien d'Autrui (2000).

149 Acte de fiducie d'utilité sociale créant la fiducie du Domaine Saint Bernard (Nov. 20, 2000) [hereinafter Trust Deed].

150 *Id.* at clause 2(i) (author's translation).

> ecological protection: to preserve the Domain in its natural state, as a true wildlife and flora sanctuary, in perpetuity for present and future generations, and to respect the natural evolution of this ecosystem;
>
> social: to permit the beneficiaries (constituting the citizens of the municipality and other users of the site) access to the site for a moderate fee;
>
> recreation and sports: to permit the beneficiaries to carry on non-motorized outdoor activities, while respecting the ecological conservationist character of the site.[151]

The trust is administered by ten named trustees, under the general supervision of the municipality. The trustees must administer the property in accordance with the trust's purposes; they may not alienate the property; they must permit the beneficiaries to use the property in accordance with its purposes and with any regulations adopted by them; and they must hold an annual meeting to advise the beneficiaries of the trustees' activities and decisions. The legislation merging the four municipalities formally recognizes the creation of the Domaine Saint Bernard land trust, and provides that the agreed property tax increase may be levied against all property owners of the enlarged municipality.[152]

There are signs of post-merger strain about the future of Domaine Saint Bernard. In June 2003, four of the original ten trustees stepped down and had to be replaced. Under the trust deed, trustees are named for life, and some councilors argued that this was not conducive to good park management and should be changed.[153] A motion to change the terms of the trust so as to reduce the trustees' term of office to two years was defeated by a bare majority of councilors.[154] However, the only manner in which the trust may be modified or dissolved is upon application by an interested person to court. The court may only order such termination if the trust ceases to meet the intent of the settlor or becomes impossible or too onerous to continue. Any modifications must be consistent with the initial intent of the settlor.[155] Given the intent of the former Municipality of Mont Tremblant to preserve Domaine Saint Bernard in perpetuity, it will be difficult to amend the trust or terminate it.

---

151 *Id.* at clause 1 (author's translation). Other purposes relate to culture and heritage preservation, science and education.

152 Act respecting the Amalgamation of the Municipalité de Mont Tremblant, Ville de Saint Jovite, Municiaplité de Lac Tremblant Nord and Paroisse de Saint Jovite, S.Q.1999, c.88, ss. 6–9.

153 Under clause 14 of the Trust Deed, trustees may resign their position in writing, and may be replaced by the settlor.

154 André Courey, *Domaine Saint Bernard: Can it be kept out of politics?*, TREMBLANT EXPRESS, June 2003, available at http:www.tremblantexpress.com (last visited May 28, 2004).

155 Art. 1294 C.C.Q.

Domaine Saint Bernard provides the greatest ecosystem protection at the present time, as the entire area is impressed with a trust to preserve it, in perpetuity, "in its natural state, as a true wildlife and flora sanctuary" and to respect "the natural evolution of this ecosystem"; limited recreational use is permitted, but only if it respects "the ecological conservationist character of the site". Increased residential and tourist development at Mont Tremblant will increase the recreational use,[156] but the trust is the strongest way possible to protect the Domaine from conversion to another use.

Conclusions

This chapter has examined the rules and regulations applying to privately owned land at the base of Mont Tremblant, outside park boundaries. In the end, three points stand out. The first is that the rules consist of a mixture of land use and environmental rules. The land use rules operate mainly at the municipal level within a provincial legislative framework. The regional and proposed local plans for the Mont Tremblant area have a strong environmental content, with protection of watercourses, wetlands and wildlife habitats having pride of place; water quality and quantity are an emerging concern. However, the land use tools are multifunctional in the sense that they must have regard to all aspects of a community's development and must thus balance ecological protection with possibly competing economic and social concerns, a balance particularly difficult to strike in an ecologically sensitive resort area such as Mont Tremblant. This highlights the importance of the role played by explicitly environmental tools, with are unifunctional in focus. The environmental rules operate mainly at the provincial level, although there is some filtering down of the provincial rules to the local level through their integration into local planning documents, with the Protection Policy for Lakeshores, Riverbanks, Littorals Zones and Floodplains being a good example of this. Environmental rules can operate also at the federal level, and the applicability of the Canadian Environmental Assessment Act to the Versant Soleil development provided important ecosystem protection.

The second main point is the limited amount of public input in both sets of rules—land use and environmental—and at all levels of government—municipal, provincial and federal. At the municipal level, the format of public hearings for both the preliminary planning proposal and the Versant Soleil framework agreement and its attendant plan and by-law amendments discouraged rather than encouraged a full and open interchange of ideas; and the centrality of the special planning program under the Versant Soleil agreement avoided the need for a referendum on

156 Station Mont Tremblant's cross-country ski webpage highlights the access to Domaine Saint Bernard, and a pedestrian bridge now spans Rivière du Diable, connecting the two areas. *See* Mont Tremblant Resort, Cross Country Skiing, http://www.tremblant.ca/activities/winter/activities/cross_country/index-e.htm (last visited Aug. 8, 2007).

the amending by-laws. At the provincial level, environmental approvals were given without public input or hearings. And even at the federal level, the public input was by way of written comments rather than oral presentations at a public hearing.

The third main point is the interplay between public law tools (laws, regulations and policy statements) and private law tools (contract and trust). Some of the contracts deal specifically with environmental concerns, as for example, the monitoring programs included in the two development agreements for Base Sud and Versant Soleil; the several golf course construction and operation agreements are other examples. Negotiation and contract played a key role in shaping the land use rules for Versant Soleil in particular, and this reinforces the issue of limited public input, as the public are neither privy to the negotiations nor party to the contracts. Whether or not the contract provides effective environmental protection depends on the interests and bargaining power of the parties, and Station Mont Tremblant's ongoing economic success is important not only to Intrawest but also to the municipality. Recourse to trust law protects Domaine Saint Bernard from the reach of contract law and regulatory change.

Chapter 22
Legal Diversity and Legal Ecosystems

This case study has examined how and to what extent the law protects the ecosystem of Mont Tremblant and the resort area at its base in the face of considerable tourism and development pressures. It focused on three different areas which transect the mountain from top to bottom: the skiable domain on the mountain itself, the base camps on the lower reaches of the mountain, and a protected trust area at the foot. Each of these areas is governed by its own set of basic rules—the Parks Act for the skiable domain, the Land Use Planning and Development Act for the base camps, and the Civil Code of Quebec for the trust area—although some sets of rules apply to all three areas. This is notably the case for Quebec's Environment Quality Act (and the federal Canadian Environmental Assessment Act when triggered) as well as legislation protecting flora and fauna such as Quebec's Act respecting the Conservation and Development of Wildlife. In short, Mont Tremblant's legal diversity matches its ecological diversity.

Does this legal diversity form a "legal ecosystem" in which the various sets of rules—federal, provincial and municipal regulations; ownership-based and management-based legal regimes; and public and private law—coexist in their own, often overlapping, habitats? The answer is more "yes" than "no."

The most obvious examples of a legal ecosystem are what might be described as legislative "nesting", which favors a more coherent, holistic approach to what would otherwise be treated as separate issues. For example, the Act respecting Threatened or Vulnerable Species protects them through a process of listing and habitat designation, with the protected species and habitats then being governed by the provisions of the Act respecting the Conservation and Development of Wildlife. As well, the Environment Quality Act provides for the adoption of guidelines for the protection of banks, shores, and floodplains, which are found in the Protection Policy for Lakeshores, Riverbanks, Littoral Zones and Floodplains; these guidelines are then implemented in both centralized and decentralized ways, through the need for Ministerial authorization under the Environment Quality Act for most developments in protected areas, on the one hand, and through integration in regional and municipal plans adopted under the Act respecting Land Use Planning and Development, on the other; the Minister responsible for the environment may require the amendment of municipal land use by-laws that do not follow the Policy. Further, the Act respecting Land Use Planning and Development authorizes a municipality to make the issuance of a building permit conditional on the existence of water and sewer services that comply with the Environment Quality Act, another example of legislative nesting.

Administrative nesting similarly illustrates a legal ecosystem, and the requirement that the Minister of Sustainable Development, Environment and Parks and the Minster of Natural Resources and Wildlife sign a formal memorandum of agreement is an example of this; and uniting ministerial responsibility in one person is an even clearer example.

Policy nesting is a further example of a legal ecosystem, and this is particularly promoted through regional plans adopted under the Act respecting Land Use Planning and Development. Regional plans both facilitate the horizontal coordination of ministerial policy at the provincial level and the integration of provincial, regional, and local land use policies in the region.

However, this nesting, or integration, is not complete. The most notable exception is the divide between the rules governing provincially owned land (Mont Tremblant Park) and those governing privately owned, municipally regulated land (the base camps in the Town of Mont Tremblant). While some legislation—the Environment Quality Act and the Act respecting the Conservation and Development of Wildlife, for example—bridges this divide to some extent, there is little if any interrelationship between the two basic statutes, the Parks Act and the Act respecting Land Use Planning and Development. This is unlike the town of Banff in Alberta, which is located within Park boundaries and is thus subject to the Canada National Parks Act. Moreover, nesting of the private law rules (the lease) governing the leased land and the public law rules (the Parks Act) otherwise governing the Park is limited. The leased land is, in a sense, a private law enclave in an public law area. Domaine Saint Bernard is a similar legal enclave, with the terms of the private law trust deed forming a sort of buffer, or filter, to the application of the public law rules adopted under the Act respecting Land Use Planning and Development. The principal difference between the two civil law enclaves is that the objective of the lease is development and that of the trust deed is conservation.

Does this legal ecosystem adequately protect the physical ecosystem of Mont Tremblant? Here the answer is more "no" than "yes."

Clearly, much has been done. At the provincial level, the Park rezoning to preserve ecologically sensitive areas of the mountain, the guidelines to protect riverbanks and wetlands and its pesticide management provisions to control water quality are but three examples. At the municipal level, many of the actions of both the pre- and post-merger councils have had a clear ecological focus: putting Domaine Saint Bernard out of developers' reach, stressing ecological protection in land use planning documents and agreements, controlling and monitoring water quality, and so on. And Intrawest adheres to its own or other voluntary codes of conduct to limit adverse environmental impacts in trail design and development.

But the legal ecosystem, like the physical ecosystem, has "gaps" and "edges", of which Intrawest and other developers can take advantage, as they are entitled to do. We have already mentioned the sharpness of the legal "edge" between the rules applicable inside and outside the Park, and between those applicable in the leased land in the Park and those applicable elsewhere in the Park. There are three significant legal "gaps."

A first gap is the discretionary element of some of the rules, which are then vulnerable to the economic clout of Intrawest and other developers. One example is the possibility of an exemption from general rules, such as ministerial permission to carry out otherwise unauthorized activities in wildlife habitats protected under the Act respecting the Conservation and Development of Wildlife or in floodplains protected under the Protection Policy for Lakeshores, Riverbanks, Littoral Zones and Floodplains. A second example is the retroactive moratorium imposed by statute on snowmobile nuisance actions. A third is the municipal-private sector contract negotiations that are part of the process of application of the discretionary land use control tools. Economic clout, and the bargaining power that goes with it, clearly plays an important role.

A second gap is the discrete, or piecemeal, nature of much of the assessment process. One example is in regard to land use planning. The procedure usually favors a comprehensive approach to development assessment because it moves from general to specific, from broad-brush to fine-grain, with provincial land use policy objectives, including the strategy adopted under the Sustainable Development Act, informing the content of regional plans which in turn condition and constrain local municipal plans and implementing by-laws. This means that specific projects are assessed in light of more general, more comprehensive considerations. However, because planning is not prescient, the legislation provides that plans can be amended to accommodate specific projects. When this happens, the assessment process privileges the fine-grain, and more comprehensive, holistic considerations can easily get lost in the process.

The assessment procedure under Quebec's Environment Quality Act is also discrete, or piecemeal, in approach. Although the evaluation of projects is done in a comprehensive way, the projects subject to evaluation are limited in scope. This results from the way in which the Act's screening provisions are drafted. The distinctions between projects for which authorization is or is not required, those which do or do not require an environmental impact assessment, and those for which a hearing by the *Bureau d'audiences publiques sur l'environnement* (BAPE) [Office of Public Hearings on the Environment] are or are not required invites the disaggregation of larger projects into more discrete ones. This militates against scrutiny of the cumulative environmental impacts of the overall whole. For example, the land exchange and rezoning assessment did not evaluate the overall impact of the base camp developments at Versant Soleil and Camp Nord. Nor is the "environmental control and monitoring program" included in Versant Soleil development agreement between the Town and Station Mont Tremblant comprehensive in scope; it takes full advantage of the possibility to disaggregate and limits its application to those developments in the Town that are not subject to an environmental assessment by the provincial or federal governments. On the other hand, a comprehensive approach is possible. The evaluation of Versant Soleil under the Canadian Environmental Assessment Act included mountain and base camp developments. And a more holistic approach was taken to the Mont Orford development than to Mont Tremblant's as a result of the decision of Quebec's environment minister to use his jurisdiction to submit "any question" relating to the quality of the environment to the BAPE for assessment and public hearing.

A third gap is the limited provision for public input in the evaluation processes. Although public hearings are an integral part of the regulatory procedure under the Act respecting Land Use Planning and Development (although the time allotted by the municipality for the Versant Soleil hearings could be criticized), the public is excluded from the negotiation process for any development agreement that forms part of the discretionary tools provided under the Act. And both the Quebec Environment Quality Act and the Canadian Environmental Assessment Act are even more circumspect in regard to public input. Under the Quebec Act, public consultation is required only for projects that are subject to environmental impact assessment and review under Division IV.1 of the Act, and not for those for which a simple section 22 authorization is required; and even under Division IV.1, public consultation does not necessarily entail a public hearing before BAPE, although anyone can request a hearing which must be accepted unless the request is deemed frivolous. Public consultation through the submission of written comments is part of all environmental assessments under the federal Act, but a public hearing is required only if a project is referred by the Minister to a review panel.

Two things in particular stand out about public input in regard to Mont Tremblant. One is the minimalist approach to public input at each stage of the process. Each time a choice is available between a wide public consultation and a narrow one, the authority in question has chosen the latter: a hearing led by a government department rather than one led by the BAPE for the land exchange; simple ministerial authorization (without consultation) rather than fuller environmental impact assessments (with public consultation and possible public hearing) under Quebec's Environment Quality Act for both the mountain and base camp developments; public consultation rather than public hearing for the Versant Soleil and Camp Nord developments under the Canadian Environmental Assessment Act; and a public meeting rather than a referendum for the Versant Soleil development under Quebec's Act respecting Land Use Planning and Development.

The second thing that stands out is the limited extent to which the public ultimately availed itself of the limited consultation possibilities that were made available to it. Participation at the land exchange hearing was keen. We have no evidence about the Versant Soleil public meeting, but the land use changes were then adopted by Council without discussion and only eight public comments were submitted to the federal environmental review process. By that time, however, opposition was probably felt to be fruitless. The negative ecological and social impacts of development at Mont Tremblant are extensive and irreversible; the train has, in fact, left the station, and people who have not hopped on have simply got out of the way.

Does the identification of these gaps in the legal ecosystem suggest ways in which the legislation might be changed to provide better protection of the physical ecosystem? The first gap we identified was the discretionary element of some of the rules and the economic leverage that discretion gives. However, discretion is part of any development process (even the firmest rules can be changed) and it is better to have points of discretion being identified explicitly, overtly, in the legislation rather than occurring implicitly, covertly, in practice. The main issue with discretion is to ensure, as much as possible, equality of bargaining power between those who seek and those who grant exceptions. The principle of "subsidiarity", as set out in the proposed Sustainable Development Act, requires that powers and responsibilities be delegated "to the appropriate level of authority" and that decision-making centers be "as close as possible to the citizen and communities concerned".[1] This means that land-related decisions should be taken at the municipal level whenever possible; but unequal economic clout might militate against this on occasion, and any decision-making process must be carefully reviewed to ensure that the appropriate checks and balances are in place. In the case of Mont Tremblant, the provincial government was as much in favor of the Intrawest development for economic reasons as was the merged municipality, and the federal government had to place its assessment in the wider context of ongoing federal-provincial relations. It is difficult to see how the legislation could be changed to eliminate such economic and political pressure.

However, the other two gaps in the legal ecosystem are amenable to legislative reform. A first recommendation is therefore that Quebec's Environment Quality Act be amended to require more integrated, comprehensive assessments of projects as a whole, rather than permitting, even encouraging, piecemeal assessments of their component parts. The Canadian Environmental Assessment Act is one example of how this might be accomplished, but this is only one example. There are many others.

A second recommendation is that both the provincial and the federal environmental statutes be amended to require more extensive public consultation, particularly in the form of public hearings. In our view, public consultation through a simple submission of written views is significantly different from one through a public hearing. The former is an individual act which takes place in isolation, with little or no possibility of learning of the views of other people or of being sure that the points being made are understood; the latter is a collective act which takes place in a group, where all hear each other's views, all can express an opinion about them and all can be questioned by the hearing authority if need be. Internet postings will never replace face-to-face contact.

These recommendations are too late to change the course of development at Mont Tremblant. But Mont Tremblant is not the only mountain in Quebec. Mont Orford Inc. tried very hard to replicate Intrawest's real estate development success, and this could become the model for mountain development throughout the province.

---

1 Sustainable Development Act, R.S.Q., c D-8.1.1, s. 6(7).

PART VI
A Vision for the Mountains

Chapter 23
The Challenges of Joining Ecology with the Law: A Vision for the Mountains

Janet E. Milne and Ross A. Virginia

In some respects, mountain resorts—in the abstract—appear to provide a relatively easy framework for evaluating whether the law applies an ecosystem perspective as it regulates uses on the mountains. The mountains lie largely "upstream" from many societal sources of ecological interferences. They often do not experience the ecological consequences of activities well beyond their bases, with the significant exceptions of airborne pollution and impaired habitat of species that range beyond the mountains. The human activities at the mountain resorts are also relatively discrete, the number of players is quite small, and the land is often held in large tracts. Thus, not having to disentangle as many ecological and human factors, one in theory can focus more easily on the ecosystem impacts of mountain resorts than some other types of human development or uses elsewhere on the landscape.

As the chapters of this book illustrate, however, even this seemingly simple situation illustrates the complexities of fully evaluating the impacts of human activities on an ecosystem and integrating an ecosystem perspective with the law. By taking a somewhat anecdotal view of specific mountain resorts at a certain point in time, the chapters portray gritty illustrations of the difficulties and successes in trying to bridge the boundaries among the scientific disciplines and the boundaries between law and science. This chapter provides some concluding thoughts about the analyses in this book and some suggestions for ways to maximize opportunities to elevate the status of the ecosystem within the law as people govern the creation and growth of mountain resorts in the future.

The Ecosystem Challenge: Redux

Perhaps a starting point is to underscore the magnitude of the challenge of building an ecosystem perspective into the law. The ecosystem—that "dynamic complex of plant, animal, and microorganism communities and the nonliving environment interacting as a functional unit"[1]—is inherently intricate, and scientific understanding of the mountain ecosystem is still unfolding. The scientific

1 Convention on Biological Diversity, art. 2, 31 I.L.M. 818 (entered into force Dec. 29, 1993).

task alone is somewhat daunting, particularly given that each mountain ecosystem will have its own special characteristics that affect the interactions between the ecosystem and humans, so each in the ideal world warrants its own detailed study.

How can or will the relatively linear world of the law deal with the scientific complexity and uncertainty of this kaleidoscope, ever changing as new understanding emerges and as the ecosystem evolves and responds to external forces? The law must create some degree of certainty in its rules that will guide behavior. It must define when those rules apply and what standard of behavior it will require. The blunt reality is that lawmakers and regulators must choose a limited number of words, written into law in black and white until changed by subsequent legislative or administrative act. This relatively definitive concreteness stands in sharp contrast to the gloriously complex, partially understood, and evolving ecosystem we would like it to consider.

As seen in the preceding chapters, the law focuses on specific, triggering human activities and, through a decision-making process, will yield a decision of no, yes, or yes if done in a certain way. If it uses an ecosystem perspective, it must look at the consequences of those human activities for the ecosystem, which in turn requires an analysis of the functional relationships and processes affected by that action. The analysis quickly turns from being a sharply focused to a multifaceted, interactive inquiry that features uncertainty.

The case studies in this book have considered the extent to which the law currently requires or allows this challenging ecosystem perspective. They identify a number of obstacles and some evidence of hope. The remainder of this chapter does not attempt to summarize the case studies. It focuses instead on some observations about the past and future that flow from the preceding chapters, highlighting three key characters that play dominant roles in these plots—the science, the law, and the people.[2]

The Science: Uncertainty and a Possible Model

The complexity of the mountain ecosystem invites one to seek an overarching conceptual model that encompasses the full range of both natural and anthropogenic activities that take place. Equally important, to protect the mountain environments while permitting appropriate and sustainable development requires both a more specific description and assessment of the current environmental functioning of these mountains, that is more science, and science that is updated to meet the challenges of understanding mountains in a rapidly changing climate. Given knowledge of the natural processes unique or most important to mountain

2 The views or characterizations of the case studies in this chapter are solely ours. We are grateful to the extraordinary analysis of the authors in other chapters, but we do not want to saddle them with our interpretations or opinions, with which they may or may not agree.

systems, one can begin to understand the impacts of mountain resorts on that functioning, and also the extent to which the present environmental law regimes might properly regulate mountain development and management. Ultimately, we hope to have demonstrated how some legal regimes can accommodate ecosystem-based regulation of mountain development or how existing regimes can provide the basis for recommendations for changes in law and regulation.

Our scientific knowledge of mountains lags behind that of many other ecosystem types. The reasons are many. Mountain access is often difficult and extremes in climate add to the challenges and costs of conducting research in mountain environments. The significant economic resources (most notably trees) are most often located at lower elevations where research is concentrated, and higher-elevation forests and alpine zones favored by skiers remain less studied. A simple scan of the expertise of ecological researchers on any large university faculty will demonstrate how few scientists specialize on mountain ecosystems. As a consequence, those seeking to develop law or regulate mountain resorts, or specific activities within mountain regions, will usually face a paucity of detailed site-specific information.

This lack of site-specific data creates significant challenges to science and to the law. First, the development of mountain models that could be used in an ecosystem legal regime may require the extensive use of information derived from ecosystems other than mountains to fill in gaps in our knowledge of mountain functioning. This could have the effect of lower confidence in the applicability of the model to address mountain development issues, especially when conflicting stakeholders are each interpreting the science and the model predictions. In addition, our limited scientific capacity for mountain research places pressure on identifying and selecting the key ecological features of mountains for study if one wants to take an ecosystem perspective in considering whether to permit resort-related activities. The recurrent emphasis in this book on the importance of understanding the ecological significance of tree removal (from the scale of individual trees to stands) is an obvious example of opportunities to match scientific effort to meet the information needs around issues arising from resort development. Additional areas of research discussed in this volume with high potential to support better mountain law are biogeochemical cycling (nutrient losses and stream water quality), biodiversity maintenance and invasive species, and habitat fragmentation.

The Hubbard Brook Ecosystem Model: A Way Forward?

We suggest that one path forward for northeastern North America is to adapt the Hubbard Brook Forest Ecosystem Model to better incorporate the special features of mountain resorts.[3] The Hubbard Brook project began in 1963 in the White Mountains of New Hampshire to understand the process of forest succession

---

3 *See generally* GENE E. LIKENS ET AL., BIOGEOCHEMISTRY OF A FORESTED ECOSYSTEM (1977).

following harvest with a focus on the ecosystem functions of production and nutrient cycling. Baseline studies showed that the mature intact deciduous forest lost less than 0.1 percent of the nitrogen contained in living forest biomass and dead organic matter in the soil and litter in stream flow (a "closed" nutrient cycle defined by its minimal nutrient export in streams). When one entire Hubbard Brook watershed was then clear-cut of trees, a 40 percent increase in stream flow occurred because water use by trees had been almost eliminated by the forest harvest. Biological controls over stream flow are important to know in predicting consequences of water extraction by resorts for snowmaking. With increased stream flow the "closed" nutrient cycle of the Hubbard Brook forest became "open" (more nutrients were lost). The concentration of nitrogen as nitrate in the stream increased about 60 times above the background levels measured in the forested watershed. Concentrations of elements that are important to the biology of the ecosystem leaked into the streams and were exported from the ecosystem. Odum's ideas on ecosystem function suggested that nutrient losses would decline as the clear-cut forest regenerated and biodiversity was reestablished.[4] This pattern was observed as the Hubbard Brook forest was allowed to recover (undergo succession); nutrient losses to streams declined to near baseline levels. The Hubbard Brook experiment shows land mangers how the processes of forest removal and regrowth affect the retention of soil nutrients and influence the quality of stream waters.

Ecosystem scale experiments, such as Hubbard Brook, provide the framework for working conceptual models of ecosystem function and their responses to human activities. In many cases these conceptual models have led to the development of predictive computer simulation models that allow testing of "what if" scenarios to aid basic understanding and management. The Hubbard Brook Forest Watershed Model relates the output of nutrients in stream water to a set of interacting compartments representing atmospheric inputs (acid rain), soil nutrient reserves, biological biomass and diversity, and biotic interactions regulating nutrient levels available for biota. This model has evolved in its sophistication and ability to handle more ecological variables in simulating the biogeochemical responses of forests to both human and natural disturbances.

In 2004, the conceptual framework of the Hubbard Brook model was modified and expanded in three important ways (Figure 23.1).[5] The conceptual framework was altered through the addition of three interacting components: state factors, stochastic factors (natural and anthropogenic), and ecosystem functions and services. The Hubbard Brook researchers proposed that the "new model will help ensure a comprehensive approach to forest ecosystem analysis and will facilitate interactions of research with policy and management at many locations."[6]

---

4 Eugene P. Odum, *The Strategy of Ecosystem Development*, 164 Science 262 (1969).

5 Peter M. Groffman, Charles T. Driscoll, et. al., *Nor Gloom of Night: A New Conceptual Model for the Hubbard Brook Ecosystem Study*, 54 BioScience 139 (2004).

6 *Id.* at 139.

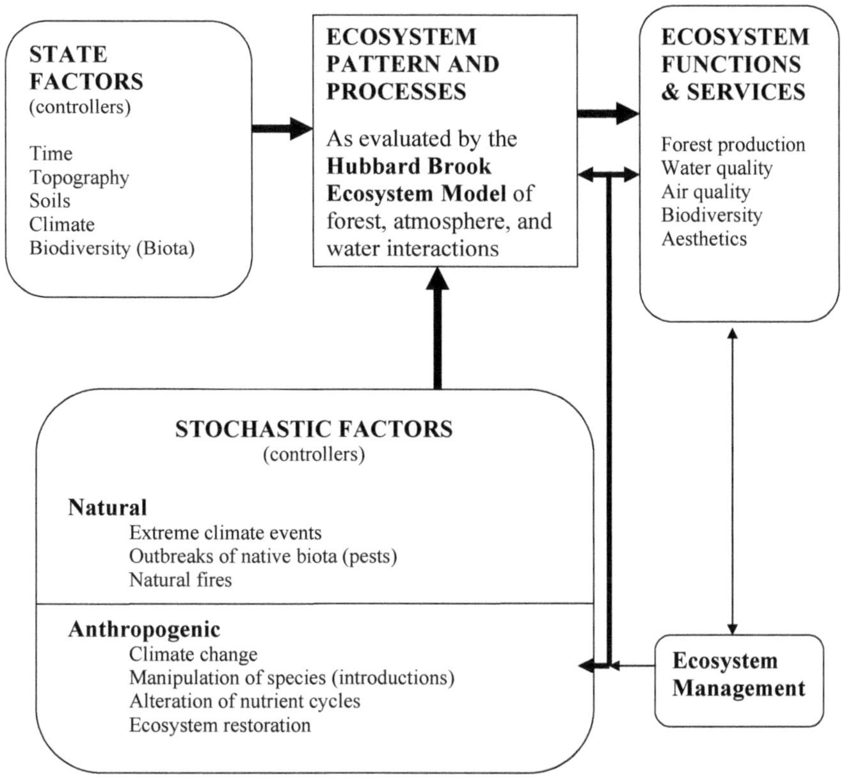

Figure 23.1 A Conceptual Model for Possible Application to Mountain Ecosystems

Note: The model depicted is a slightly revised version of the new Hubbard Brook Ecosystem Study Model as presented by Groffman et al, *Nor Gloom of Night: A New Conceptual Model for the Hubbard Brook Ecosystem Study*, 54 BioScience 139 (2004).

The model identifies "controllers" that drive the pattern and processes of the ecosystem (the functioning of the ecosystem). Controllers fall into two groups. "State factors" predict the condition of the ecosystem at any given time using traditional ecosystem metrics for time, topography, parent material, climate, and biota. Inclusion of these factors allows the model to be parameterized for the specific conditions (soils, topography, etc.) found at each resort. "Stochastic factors" are variable interventions, both natural and anthropogenic, that impinge on the ecosystem and its myriad of processes. For our purposes, a selected number of these ecosystem processes lead to ecosystem functions and services (including forest production, water quality, biodiversity maintenance, and aesthetics) that we value and hope to maintain through sound management practices. People can alter the basic relationships between process and functions and services at the local scale of the mountain through management practices. In contrast, anthropogenic factors such as climate change that operate at regional to global scales, although important to the ecosystem, must remain largely outside the immediate legal regime for the mountain.

The new emphasis of the model on understanding the factors that control the provision of ecosystem services makes this approach more useful in the realms of management, economics, and the law. The model, although general and broadly conceptual, identifies the critical interactions that must be quantified to achieve the level of modeling necessary to satisfy the requirements of an ecosystem-based legal regime.

There are many opportunities to adjust the new Hubbard Brook model to focus on resort development issues. The value of such a model comes when it is used to direct the kinds of research questions that are asked such that they have relevance to needs of the law. For example, information on snowmaking and water extraction from streams could be linked to the Hubbard Brook hydrology submodel, which would provide output to the ecosystem functions and services compartment of the new Hubbard Brook model. This could provide resorts with information on snow depth and quality and trail coverage and how these essentials might be altered by climate change and other stochastic factors. This model framework provides space for the interactions between human factors that directly or indirectly alter mountains (acid rain, stream water removal, forest clearing for trails and lodges, paved surfaces and runoff, increased fire risk, introductions of invasive species, etc.) and the features of the mountain ecosystem controlling production, nutrient cycling, and biodiversity.

Providing ways for the social sciences (law and economics) to link with biological process models is an area of intense research, with limited success in most cases. The Hubbard Brook model and the conceptual model in Figure 23.1 clearly outline the difficult challenge in achieving a balanced integration of science, social science, and law to manage mountain ecosystems. As discussed earlier, we lack empirical data concerning the response of mountains to specific development plans and regulatory regimes. These outcomes are inferred from our knowledge of basic ecosystem functioning. The unique characteristics of individual mountains and the past land use histories also complicate this task. Nonetheless, the chapters in this book suggest areas where we can begin to make these linkages and prioritize research.

The Law: Observations about the Legal Mechanisms, Triggers, and Standards

As demonstrated in the discussion above, the science of mountain ecosystems is evolving, and to a large extent, the players in the four case studies in this book did not have the benefit of sophisticated, scientific ecosystem analyses. Moreover, as the case studies in this book illustrate repeatedly, they often were making decisions under legal regimes not explicitly designed to require an ecosystem-based analysis. Ideally one would understand the science and then decide whether or how to build a legal regime around that understanding, but in fact the science of (mountain) ecosystems and the law's appreciation for that perspective often are evolving on parallel tracks, a premise of this book series. Hence, the case studies have evaluated the extent to which, often without explicit mandate, an ecosystem perspective can nonetheless enter the legal analysis and the situations where the law hinders it from doing so.

In the case studies, the law uses various legal mechanisms, which focus on different triggering actions and apply different standards:

- *Ownership and conveyance rules for governmentally owned land* govern the ability of government (through direct transfer of the title to land, lease, or permit) to allow a private operator to use government lands for the development of a resort. Those rules set the framework for the government, as the landowner, as it decides whether or how to allow the private uses on its land, and they vary significantly from one resort to another.
  - A feature present at Loon, Killington, and Mont Tremblant.
- *Zoning*, a planning mechanism, can create geographic zones that identify specific types of permissible uses or limits on uses.
  - In all four case studies, private lands are subject to municipal zoning.
  - The Quebec government used its power to zone its park lands.
  - New York's constitution designated the public land areas in the Adirondack Park as forever wild, a form of zoning writ large.
- *Negotiated development agreements* can allow local government, through its land use planning powers, to amend zoning ordinances to allow for uses under negotiated terms.
  - As at Mont Tremblant.
- *Periodic planning requirements* can also install a planning perspective in a different way, calling on the resort owner or operator to engage in ongoing planning by submitting periodic plans for the operation of the resort.
  - Such as the unit management plans for the Whiteface Mountain Ski Center.
  - Master plans for Mont Tremblant (required by the lease of provincial lands).
  - The national forest management plan that identified land for resort expansion at Loon.
- *Environmental impact assessments* can evaluate the environmental consequences of proposed actions, potentially effective mechanisms for current science, empirical research and modeling to enter into decision making.
  - Federal environmental impact statements were used at Loon.
  - State environmental impact statements at Whiteface.
  - Provincial and federal environmental impact assessments at Mont Tremblant.

- *Permit review processes* also can mandate consideration of a variety of environmentally oriented and other criteria and, in effect, operate as an assessment of the environmental consequences.
  - As seen at Killington.
- *Media-specific or activity-specific regulations* can also come into play, as evidenced by the panoply of environmental laws governing issues such as endangered or threatened species, shoreline protection, snow removal, the use of fertilizer and pesticides, and snowmobiling. Whether they represent an ecosystem perspective will depend on the extent to which they accurately target the important interactions among multiple components of the ecosystem.
  - For example, at Mont Tremblant.
- *Private conservation law* can also significantly affect the future use of the land.
  - Notably the land trust to protect Domaine Saint Bernard near the base of Mont Tremblant.
  - The conservation easement on land near Killington.
  - New York's program to acquire conservation easements on private lands within the boundaries of the Adirondack Park.

The discussion below focuses on the ecosystem-oriented potential of these various legal mechanisms, structured around the activities that occur at mountain resorts rather than the types of law at play. The activities generate the ecological consequences and the law often uses specific activities as its trigger points, so they provide the organizational anchor—the decision to create the resort, access to government land, on-mountain activities, and secondary growth.

The Law and the Original Creation of the Resort

In all of the case studies, the decision to create the mountain resort occurred before the time under analysis—and before society had started to think extensively in terms of ecosystems. The case studies focus on subsequent points of expansion, but the mere fact of the resorts' existence almost inevitably influences and constrains the discussions about whether to allow them to expand and the conditions under which they will operate. The public has grown accustomed to using them; the local economy is dependent upon them; and the owners have invested significant capital into them. For example, the Loon Resort's existence was the premise in the argument for permit renewal and expansion, even though that premise apparently was not based on an ecosystem analysis. As a result, the analytical table for evaluating expansions may have a potential tilt in favor of development, even though the original decision was not ecosystem-based. Proposals for new resorts today might undergo a different level of ecological scrutiny, building ecological factors into the foundational analysis and establishing an ecological baseline against which future impacts can be measured if the resort is approved. Tied to this process, resorts could be compelled to meet standards of sustainability and certification around energy, materials, and operations.

The Law and Access to Government Land for Expansion

The case studies illustrate how government, as landowner, can influence the shape of a mountain resort within or near its boundaries. It can decide whether to allow the expanded use on its land and under what terms, subject to any legal limitations on its powers, and it can determine the relative merits of the ecological and economic factors and public and private factors. As the understanding of mountain ecosystems increases in the future, it can use that knowledge to better inform its decisions and to design conditions on leases or land exchanges that can minimize impacts on the ecosystem. Its ownership of land gives it a powerful card that it can play as it negotiates terms—if it chooses to do so. The relatively unconstrained discretion to exchange public and private land seen in the Killington and Mont Tremblant situations[7] might give a government committed to an ecosystem perspective more leverage than the government constrained, as in the Loon case, by federal policies contemplating private uses.[8] By the same token, however, a government less interested in mountain ecosystems would have more authority to discount the ecosystem perspective. Herein lies an important space for NGOs such as environmental organizations and special use groups to exert influence or to directly participate in agreements. Whiteface presents a very different situation, where the voters, by constitutional amendment, chose to designate the public

7 The land transactions at Killington and Mont Tremblant were essentially standardless from an ecosystem perspective. At Killington, the criteria of Act 250 may have influenced the shape of the land exchange, because the prospect of litigating expansion proposals under Act 250 provided some impetus for Killington Resort to enter into an agreement, with the land exchange as one element. Nonetheless, the decision by the government administrators and legislators to execute the exchange was governed by strategic and political considerations, not legal or ecological standards that might consider issues such as habitat fragmentation or habitat quality for selected species such as Bicknell's thrush. Similarly at Mont Tremblant, the decision to extend the lease when Intrawest took over the resort in 1991, and the land exchange that gave Intrawest land for two new base camps, fell within the provincial government's discretionary powers, which were not bounded by an explicit substantive mandate to consider ecological consequences (although the land exchange did arise from the provincial government's interest in rezoning the park from "recreation" to "conservation").

8 At Loon, the federal law governing the Forest Service both explicitly anticipated the possibility of private uses of national forest lands and required an environmental impact assessment of proposed uses. While environmental and, arguably, ecosystem factors can be part of the decision-making process governing the use of national forest land for mountain resorts, they will not necessarily prevail because the legislative and regulatory regimes do not clearly establish the relative priorities of ecosystem protection and economic considerations.

land in the Adirondack Park as forever wild with exacting specifications for the maximum resort development, strictly limiting the government officials' discretion by creating a de facto precautionary principle. In short, the legal ground rules affecting a government's range of choices as a landowner are very important.

If the government considers allowing resorts to use its land and wants to base its decision on an ecosystem perspective, it must decide the relevant geographic scale for the ecosystem analysis. The immediate mountain setting is obviously the starting point, but the expansion decision also should look at the adjacent ecosystems on up to the scale of the region, not only to put the proposed on-mountain activities into a broader ecological setting, but also to bring the secondary growth from the expansion into the ecological analysis. The environmental impact analysis for the expansion onto additional federal lands at Loon, for example, required the identification of different scales and an analysis at each scale, a useful step in the right direction. The issue of scale is relevant to many of the activities discussed below, but it is particularly important to the decision about whether the resort will get the land it needs, because that decision is the predicate for the activities that follow.

Finally, as noted in all the case studies in various ways, economic considerations are very real and powerful as government balances the range of societal goals affecting how it will use public land, sometimes creating pressure to expand resorts and in other instances creating demand for constrained growth. We must note that the case studies in this book admittedly have not been able to undertake significant analysis of the economic benefits and costs of mountain resorts, tending to focus more on the ecological side of the equation.[9] An important companion book would be one that considers more fully the economic ecosystem that arises out of these mountains and their resorts and the extent to which the law considers that ecosystem.

The Law and On-mountain Activities—Trails, Lifts, Snowmaking, Base Lodges, and Four-Season Use of the Slopes

Each of the case studies focused on proposals to expand the basic facilities on the mountain to improve the skiing and boarding experience. The major construction activities on the slopes—the cutting of new trails, construction of new lifts and lodges, and installation of snowmaking facilities—triggered legal review. At Loon,

9 For one example of a study that incorporates significant economic considerations, including the amenity value of mountain settings, see Timonty P. Duane, Shaping the Sierra (1999). The economic impacts of amenity migration are also examined in Laurence A.G. Moss, Ed., The Amenity Migrants (2006), which contains two chapters with particular relevance to the mountain resorts in this book—a chapter on Whistler, British Columbia, home of an Intrawest resort, which examines the impacts of amenity migration on affordable housing in particular, and a chapter on the Adirondacks, which looks at trends in tourism, second homes, employment opportunities, and affordable housing.

the request to expand onto more federal land required the government to review the environmental impact of the activities that will be conducted on the land. At Whiteface, the expansion activities could not go forward without approval through the periodic unit management planning process and accompanying environmental impact assessment. At Killington, the commercial use of acreage in excess of the statutory minimum of ten acres and above 2,500 feet triggered review under Act 250. And at Mont Tremblant, the patchwork of legal regimes (regulations, lease terms, and development agreements) for the public and private land on the mountain addressed trail work and facilities' construction. The nature of the review may be different under each (as discussed further below), but the law generally gained oversight of the major construction activities. Perhaps the most notable deviation from the norm is that snowmaking facilities at Mont Tremblant were not subject to regulatory review, although they were addressed in the terms of Intrawest's lease.

Four general observations seem to emerge from the analyses of the legal review of the expansion proposals. First, at a very basic level, if the goal is to instill an ecosystem analysis into the review of major on-mountain facility expansions, the law should contain explicit mandates to consider impacts from a more fully attenuated ecosystem perspective. Quebec has taken some steps in this direction with explicit direction for its Minister of Sustainable Development, Environment and Parks to consider developing policies to protect "the ecosystem."[10] However, the authors predominantly found that injecting an ecosystem perspective often requires trying to harness old law with a relatively poor grounding in ecosystem science in creative ways that will allow the introduction of new, broader, scientific views.

Second, although the legal regimes tend to address the major activities, snowmaking stands out as an example of an activity where future proceedings might look more closely at ecological consequences. Regulatory attention to date seems to have focused largely on the question of whether water withdrawals will harm aquatic species, leading to the use of measures such as the median February flow. This result is positive, but not necessarily driven by a full ecosystem analysis. The litigation at Loon introduced questions about the ecological effect of water transfers from one body to another, and as Chapter 4 suggests, transfers of water from one source to the slopes, in the form of manmade snow, can have other complex ecological consequences that we are only starting to understand. Human accelerated climate change may require even more snowmaking capacity if resorts are to be sustainable.[11] As knowledge grows, this major activity might be subject to more rigorous, ecosystem-based analysis.

Third, a number of ecological consequences of the major facility expansions often arise from the details of the ways in which the plans are executed and the resort is operated thereafter—the seemingly minor questions of where and when trees are cut, how slopes are maintained, whether fill might bring in invasive

10 See Chapter 19 *infra* at note 46 (quoting Act respecting the Ministère des Ressources du Développement Durable, de l'Environnement et des Parcs, R.S.Q., c. M-300.001).

11 Daniel Scott et al., *Climate Change and Quebec's Ski Industry*, 17 Global Environmental Change 181 (2007).

species, whether to allow non-skiing uses that do not require new facilities, such as mountain biking. Although the construction and expansion of major, winter facilities tend to occupy the regulatory spotlight, it is important to find legal mechanisms that consider the ecological impact of these directly and indirectly associated management or operational activities that might otherwise slide under the regulatory radar.

The case studies suggest approaches for addressing these details. In some instances, government may simply choose to require a certain substantive result, just as Quebec allows bans on pesticides, the Banff National Park's Management Plan prohibits tree cutting, and best management practices apply to storm water in the Whiteface case study. Whether such bans or regulations reflect an ecosystem perspective will depend on whether their rationale rests on a sound, ecosystem-based analysis. Ongoing planning regimes also may be useful for applying an ecosystem perspective to these seemingly minor but ecologically significant activities. The periodic unit management plans at Whiteface have the potential to address a wide range of management activities, not just in the initial construction stage, but also as the Olympic Regional Development Agency continues its management of the approved facilities over the years, providing an opportunity to adapt over time to new understandings of ecological consequences. Conditions attached to permits or agreements also can address the ecological impacts of these initial and ongoing activities. At Killington, the government required that the resort owner prepare a study of the impact of the Interconnect trail system on upland watersheds, and it retained the right to impose conditions to protect water quality. At Mont Tremblant, the Municipality of Mont Tremblant's development agreement with Intrawest required Intrawest to monitor the environmental effects of its expansion activities. These types of ongoing study and monitoring obligations hold the potential to build the base of knowledge about ecosystem impacts and offer opportunities to reevaluate management techniques, provided they are stated in ways that require as broad an ecosystem analysis as possible and both the government and the resort operator take the conditions seriously. Whether they yield actual change will depend on the voluntary will of the resort operator or reevaluation obligations under a legal regime.

Finally, this question of major and minor activities relates to the broader challenge of analytical integration versus segregation. In evaluating expansions of the on-slope activities, does one look at the full range of activities and impacts and their interactions or just target some? In an ecosystem-based legal analysis of on-slope activities, the ideal goal would be to consider the full extent of the human activities, both in terms of the immediate activity proposed for the mountainside and the secondary activities that will flow from it, such as how building the new trails and lifts will involve not only the ultimate change in the trail pattern, but construction activities along the way, increased usage which increases demands for residential and retail support facilities on and off the mountain, the opening of new areas for non-winter use, and so on. This broad view would capture the full width of the human footprint on the ecosystem. In evaluating the ecological impacts of all these activities, one then would consider how deeply their ecological consequences flow through the web of interrelationships in the ecosystem—the ecological depth of the human footprint. And finally, there is the question of the consequences of these impacts over the course of time not just at the moment in which they first occur— the length of time that the human footprint will last.[12]

If the law seeks to achieve this fully attenuated width-depth-length analysis, either it needs to have the freedom to look very broadly or it needs to focus on key ecological impacts that can represent by proxy the other attenuated impacts. The approach of looking broadly involves both the question of which activities are brought into the review and how far out the law follows their ecological consequences. The more the law brings the range of human activities into view by looking at the full width of the footprint, and the more it studies the ecological depth and length of the footprint, the better the chances for instilling an ecosystem perspective.

The case studies yield mixed results on this score. The review process under Vermont's Act 250 would apply to all commercial activities conducted above a certain altitude or involving a specified acreage. This broad triggering mechanism can create the flexibility to bring into consideration the more minor activities, or at least those known at the time of application, but it may take initiative to ensure that the activities are identified as fully as possible, major and minor, primary and secondary. As seen in the Killington case study, however, separate proceedings focused on different aspects of the expansion, undercutting the ability to analyze the full footprint in a consolidated fashion. In addition, while each of Act 250's criteria focuses on a specific aspect of the ecosystem, the criterion-by-criterion analysis creates a barrier to looking at the true depth and intricacy of the ecological footprint unless the consequential ecosystem effects can be drawn into each criterion's analysis. This points to the need for conceptual and analytical models that encompass the critical features of both the ecosystem and the resort which determine the sustainability of each. Quebec's environmental impact assessment at Mont Tremblant appears comprehensive, allowing evaluation of "direct, cumulative, latent and irreversible effects"[13] but the review looks at only elements of the expansion project, not its entirety. The planning and environmental impact assessment regimes at Loon and Whiteface offer interesting opportunities for a

---

12 A width-depth-length analysis in a very different legal setting appears in Justice Stephens' dissent in First Lutheran Church v. Los Angeles County, 482 U.S. 304, 330 (1987), and echoes in his majority opinion in Tahoe-Sierra Preservation Council, Inc. v. Tahoe Regional Planning Agency, 535 U.S. 302, 318 (2002). Those cases involved the question of when a regulation effects a taking compensable under the Fifth Amendment of the United States constitution, which under Justice Stephens' analysis will turn in part of the width, depth, and length of the regulatory intrusion into the landowners' property interests. Although the analytical setting is different, the concept is useful to our ecosystem discussions.

13 See Chapter 20 *infra* at note 36 (quoting the Regulation respecting Environmental Impact Assessment and Review, s. 3).

broader approach, but they could be strengthened by more explicit requirements to apply an ecosystem analysis.

Laws that take a piecemeal approach, by focusing on specific segments of the ecosystem, are not likely to achieve the broader analysis unless that specific segment has been identified as a proxy based on a broader ecosystem analysis. We have seen little evidence in the case studies that the law to date has effectively identified proxies for the impacts of on-mountain resort development, a result that is not surprising given that science has not yet identified clear proxies for the range of ecosystem impacts desired by the law. As scientific understanding of the mountain ecosystem and the ecological impacts of resort activities grows, the law may be in a position to sharpen its focus on certain proxies. This sharpening may not necessarily require legislative changes. For example, if hypothetically the health of the salamander population were identified as a worthy surrogate for the health of the mountain ecosystem when considering trail development, regulators could focus on whether the trails would impair salamander habitat as they assess the impact on wildlife habitat under Vermont Act 250 or conduct environmental impact assessments under the legal regimes at play in the other resorts.

The Law and Secondary Growth

In considering new residential growth, golf courses, and other types of secondary growth, a threshold question is whether off-mountain associated growth should be analyzed under its own legal regimes, or whether it should be analyzed as part of the legal regime that governs the on-mountain activities. If one takes the approach of looking at the width, depth, and length of the ecological footprint of resort activities, then the associated growth is part of the width of the on-mountain activities' footprint, and its ecological impacts should be considered when the on-mountain activities are under review. This broader view would allow decision-makers to maximize the opportunities to look at the full footprint before allowing new development.[14] The federal regime operating in national forests potentially could take this broader view, allowing the environmental impact assessment of the expansion of the slopes onto federal lands to consider the impacts of the anticipated real estate development just outside the boundaries of the federal lands. By contrast, the Act 250 proceedings at Killington separated the environmental analysis of the resort village from the analysis of the expansion of trails and snowmaking facilities for the Interconnect.

Part of the challenge in evaluating and planning for associated growth is the fragmentation of governmental authority among different branches and layers

14 A corollary question is whether the resort operator should be held responsible for secondary development where it is not the owner or entrepreneur, such as golf courses, condominiums, or hotels built by third parties. On the fiscal side of the picture, Act 250 has been interpreted to allocate the fiscal impacts of secondary growth (including third parties' activities) to the applicant. *See In re* Wal*Mart Stores, Inc., 207 A.2d 397, 402 (Vt. 1997).

of government. Government officials making decisions about the on-mountain activities may operate under different regimes than those responsible for off-mountain activities. For example, the extent of the off-mountain growth will depend in part on the local zoning, and that local land use regime is not always fully integrated with the planning or permitting process for the on-mountain activities, nor does it necessarily consider impacts on and interests of surrounding communities. Who is responsible for which types of growth, and whose priorities should govern?

Each of the case studies offers a different technique for at least partially addressing this challenge. At Loon, the federal environmental impact statement should consider the effects of secondary growth. The federal government has no influence over the local zoning governing the private land at the mountain's base, but it can at least consider how the expansion of the on-mountain resort will influence growth patterns and environmental consequences on the private land. While possibly generating a more ecosystem-oriented analysis, this approach potentially puts more power in the hands of the federal government. At Killington, Act 250 considers the extent to which the proposed activity is consistent with the municipal and regional plans, a bottom-up approach to integration that places some control in the hands of the community. At Mont Tremblant, the provincial government uses the opposite, top-down technique, requiring municipalities to conform their plans and ordinances to provincial and regional goals.[15] At Whiteface, the Adirondack Park regime allows the state to step in directly and apply intensity guidelines to private land, with more constrained authority left in the hands of the municipalities.

The extent to which each of these techniques can achieve an ecosystem perspective varies. The federal environmental impact assessment could over time introduce a more comprehensive, ecosystem-based analysis; municipalities in Vermont could choose to base their town plans on ecosystem principles; the environmental master plan in the municipality of Mont Tremblant already calls for "an ecosystemic approach in environmental management;"[16] and over the course of time, the Adirondack Park's zoning regime might be refined or more explicitly framed in ecosystem terms.

The allocation of power will directly affect the question of who decides the relative merits of economic development, ecosystem protection, and quality of life when or if those values compete. Often the local governments may be more susceptible, understandably so, to the pressure for jobs and new tax revenues, as demonstrated in the Killington and Mont Tremblant case studies, but they are also confronted with the challenges of affordable housing, as seen at Whiteface

15 The development agreement involving Base Sud illustrates how the community may negotiate terms that covers both on- and off-slope growth, because some of the on-slope activities were on private land subject to the municipality's jurisdiction.

16 See Chapter 21 *infra* at note 26 (quoting André Courey, *Development: The Environment and Quality of Life*, Tremblant Express, June 4, 2004).

and Mont Tremblant. To the extent that the legal regimes rest more authority in their hands, they will be more responsible for striking the balance. They may also be keenly aware of the economic value of the ecosystem and its ecological services or at least its aesthetic attributes, such as Lake Placid's marketing of its relatively unspoiled setting and the municipality of Mont Tremblant's desire to protect its ambiance. Although Vermont's Act 250 defers to municipal plans to some extent, it also sometimes puts decisions about economic consequences in the hands of the administrators and judges implementing the law. Under the criterion governing the impact on wildlife habitat, the government will not grant a permit if an opponent shows that the activity will imperil necessary wildlife habitat and that the economic or recreational benefit to the public does not outweigh the public loss from imperiling the habitat, a form of cost-benefit analysis.[17]

Finally, the associated growth issues are inextricably linked to the question of what type of resort-based development is sound from an ecosystem perspective—compact, traditional villages that are pedestrian friendly (sometimes called "smart growth") or more dispersed growth that is more dependent on vehicles ("sprawl"). The ecosystem implications of each involve the extent of habitat fragmentation, air pollution from transportation, runoff from impervious surfaces, and more, and those in turn depend on the amount and location of development.

Intuitively, it would seem that the traditional villages surrounded by relatively undeveloped land are likely to minimize ecosystem impacts, and the case studies illustrate the different ways that the law can achieve this result, even though the present law may not be based on an ecosystem analysis. At Whiteface, the Adirondack Park's precautionary principle locks development out of substantial areas of land and its zoning regime directs growth toward traditional town centers, which reduces habitat fragmentation and its effects on species and biodiversity. The New York open space plan, implemented by the acquisition of conservation easements, further limits growth potential in outlying areas. At Mont Tremblant, Intrawest's business plan is built in part on the economic attributes of the pedestrian village, and the creation of the trust at Domaine Saint Bernard removed land from the development market. As ecosystem analysis of the impacts of the below-mountain growth improves, it can better inform the decisions about where growth should occur and how to design it in ways that can reduce its ecological footprint.

In sum, from an ecosystem perspective, it is important to try to integrate the decision making about on-mountain growth and off-mountain growth as much as possible, whether by building an analysis of cumulative impacts into the review of on-mountain activities or by using integrated planning or permitting mechanisms that cross the artificial boundaries that sometimes divide the on-mountain legal regimes from the off-mountain regimes. There is no one silver bullet, but policymakers need to keep the target of integration clearly in their sights.

17 Vt. Stat. Ann. tit. x, § 6086(a)(8)(A) (criterion 8A).

The People

The state of understanding about the mountain ecosystem has depended in large part of the sometimes fortuitous interest of scientists in researching seemingly narrow topics that can have broader effects. For example, the scientists studying the Bicknell's thrush did not do so because they foresaw the need for that information at Whiteface or Killington, but because they happened to be pursuing their independent professional interests. Yet that knowledge helped stimulate of the analysis at Whiteface, and the Tree Island Pod proposal in turn helped make possible more research and analysis. The ecosystem perspective depends upon having scientific knowledge available, and that depends on capturing the interest of people who can then find a way to help intellectually assemble and understand the pieces of the puzzle of the mountain ecosystem.

The government officials and resort managers also, obviously, play a significant part in decision making, but decisions again can reflect the particular interests of the individuals. At Whiteface, the mix of individuals interested in Bicknell's thrush helped put a more ecologically-oriented perspective on the table. Perhaps the presence of a biologist on Intrawest's team at Mont Tremblant can reinforce an ecosystem perspective. Institutional structures for personnel may also become significant over time, such as Quebec's consolidation of a range of environmental responsibilities in the hands of one minister, who then might be able to more easily see relationships among issues. In addition, industry standards, such as Sustainable Slopes, offer a potential vehicle for the resort industry to engage in ecologically-oriented self-regulation.

Evident throughout the case studies are the key roles played by people who, just because they cared, chose to voluntarily involve themselves in the legal processes for guiding mountain development—Roland Dubois at Loon, Nancy Bell and Nicholas Lenge at Killington, the residents of the municipality of Mont Tremblant who almost unanimously committed themselves to purchasing Domaine Saint Bernard, even at the cost of up to a 10 percent increase in their property taxes, and numerous nongovernmental organizations. One cannot conclude that these participants always employed a full ecosystem analysis, but they exemplify the significance of voluntary commitments which, as the science evolves, can increasingly provide that perspective.

Yet legal barriers may limit the rights of these voluntary participants. The rules governing standing to participate in the Killington Act 250 proceedings restrained Nicholas Lenge from participating as fully as he wanted. And very significantly, at Mont Tremblant, public access to information is sometimes limited. For example, a confidentiality agreement prevents the public from obtaining the results of the environmental monitoring and evaluation that Intrawest must perform under the development agreement with the municipality. These barriers to information can preclude interested individuals from understanding the facts and formulating their views, and as also noted in the Mont Tremblant case study, they may prevent the public from presenting their views at hearings. Akin to a fourth estate, these voluntary public participants can contribute significantly to the injection of an ecosystem perspective, but they need access and opportunity, and the issue of public participation echoes through these case studies like a constant, quiet drumbeat.

The opportunities for voluntary involvement can be direct—participation in hearings, filing of lawsuits—but these direct actions can also yield negotiations, as happened at Killington and Loon. While the law can create leverage for negotiations, the negotiations are not formally constrained by procedures or standards of law, opening the potential for ecosystem-based rationales even when not required by letter of the law.

It is perhaps also useful to think about "people" in the broadest sense—the attitudes of the general population that govern the priorities government sets, the standards it adopts, the appeal of the private sector's products and image, and choices about how lives are lived on and around the mountains. The public understanding of ecosystems is still in its infancy, but as that understanding grows, people may more fully appreciate the extent to which one action has numerous and potentially far-flung consequences. Perhaps the current discussions about climate change and the services provided by healthy ecosystems are serving not only to educate people about the ecological impact of greenhouse gas emissions, but also to educate them about the basic notion of the "marvelously complex interrelationships of life forms"[18] that lies at the core of the ecosystem perspective. If that notion becomes part of the national frame of mind, resort operators, policymakers, the public, and people who voluntarily choose to participate may start viewing issues more broadly and think more about the width, depth, and length of our ecological footprint.

Going Forward by Harnessing Existing Law: Carpe Diem

As we reach the end of this book, we see two basic routes ahead for people interested in trying to increase the extent to which the law considers the ecosystem at mountain resorts. The first is to take maximum advantage of opportunities under existing law, and the second is to look for ways to create new or different legal regimes that can provide greater assurance that decision-makers will take an ecosystem perspective. Both require a better understanding of the ecosystem, calling for the types of research identified earlier in this chapter.

A limited number of relatively simple guiding rules seem to emerge from the case studies about how best to take advantage of existing law even where it does not explicitly require an ecosystem-based analysis. The specific opportunities will vary with the legal regime, but the following may be common to many situations.

---

18 Ernest Callenback, Ecology: A Pocket Guide 1 (1998).

Interpret Existing Environmental Legal Standards as Broadly as Possible For analytical purposes, the editors of this book have drawn a distinction between a traditional environmental perspective, which tends to focus on the individual components of the ecosystem, and a broader, ecosystem perspective, which looks more holistically. Yet as our scientific and public understanding of ecosystems increases, that distinction may become artificial. It will be more difficult and illogical—even in looking at just one component—to ignore its relationship with other components. Consequently, when legal regimes call for an analysis of the impacts of human activities on individual components of the ecosystem, that analysis may increasingly be susceptible to a broader interpretation that recognizes cross-component interrelationships. It would seem that this broader interpretation could easily be applied to traditional environmental impact assessment and planning regimes that contain environmentally-oriented mandates or goals.

Interpret the Relevant Activity as Broadly as Possible Taking an ecosystem perspective involves not only looking at the cascade of ecological effects of a proposed activity across the multiple components of the ecosystem; it can also involve an examination of how one particular proposed activity puts in motion other human activities, which can create their own ecological impacts. To the extent that the analysis can bring in the multiple dimensions of the human activities, it will more thoroughly comprehend the ecological consequences that will arise from the initial, focal activity. Decision-makers and interested participants can look for opportunities to apply broader definitions of the activities under review, which take into account these consequential activities. Again, environmental impact assessment and planning regimes may offer this flexibility for those seeking to use it.

Take Advantage of Opportunities to Participate and Influence To the extent that legal regimes have the flexibility to allow the introduction of an ecosystem perspective, success will depend on the willingness of participants—government administrators or decision-makers, resort operators, abutters, interested citizens, nongovernmental organizations, scientists, and others—to look for opportunities within the legal regimes and to invest in the scientific inquiries that can credibly elucidate the ecological interrelationships. The procedures of the law will yield decisions, but the people who participate in that process can significantly influence the nature of those decisions.

Use Updating Procedures to Build Ecosystem-Based Language into Existing Legal Regimes Some legal regimes call for periodic updates, such as updated management plans or master plans or periodic reviews of zoning. As understanding of the mountain ecosystem grows, periodic updates can reflect that increased understanding. In the case of an existing mountain resort, those updates may be able to influence ongoing management practices or decisions about continued secondary growth, particularly if there are incentives or requirements for adapting over time.

Remember the Potential Power of Conditions Conditions attached to permits or leases may help refine a blunt, yes-or-no decision into a decision that allows an activity to occur if it complies with specified requirements designed to minimize ecological impacts. This possibility may be particularly significant for addressing the construction and ongoing management techniques. In addition, conditions may anticipate periodic planning, which can allow for a reevaluation of the ecological impact of practices, or they may require further scientific study. Given the inevitably evolving state of understanding of the mountain ecosystem, yet the need to decide whether to allow a proposed resort activity at a given point in time, these ongoing reviews may help bridge the gap between the known and the unknown and between certainty and flexibility.

Negotiate Based on an Ecosystem Analysis Even if a legal regime does not demand an ecosystem perspective, it may create an impetus for negotiations, and parties to those negotiations have opportunities to base their horse trading (or perhaps bear trading) on ecosystem-oriented outcomes. The de facto rules of a negotiation may be broader than those of the black letter of the law.

Look for Opportunities to Enhance Research on Mountain Ecosystems It is very important for mountain constituents to find opportunities to advance the state of knowledge about the mountain ecosystem. The law may help force this understanding, by requiring investments in environmental impact assessments or ongoing monitoring studies, and participants should look for opportunities to use the law's leverage to generate new research. New knowledge will also flow independently from the academic, government and nongovernmental sectors, where people may choose to focus on mountain ecosystems. Advancing research will require not only interest, but funding, and it could be enhanced by discussion of research priorities and increased interdisciplinary and transdisciplinary efforts (as discussed more below).[19] Better understandings can help provide the sound basis for discussions about how to work within existing laws, as well as how to design more ecosystem-oriented laws in the future. Mountain constituencies should insist that the ecosystem science is presented for the public in a clear and understandable format and that the credentials and professional interests of the scientists are freely available.

Live with Uncertainty Finally, the task of trying to comprehend the mountain ecosystems and the impact of resorts on those ecosystems can be paralytically daunting and defeating, perhaps a reason why it is easier and more comfortable to focus on the components of the ecosystem rather than its whole. Consequently, part of the task is to remember and accept what we do not yet know, while working with what we do know.

---

19 *See* Martin F. Price, ed., Mountain Area Research and Management 2–5 (2007).

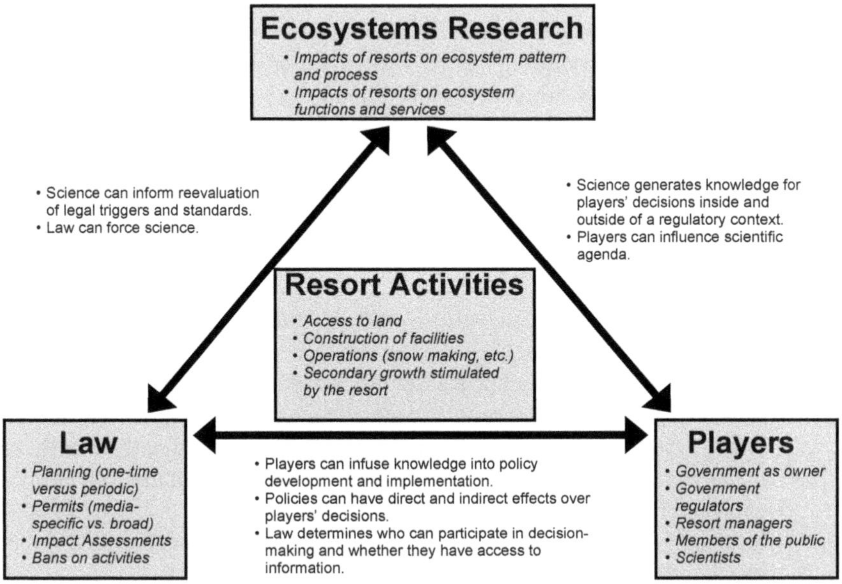

Figure 23.2 A Conceptual Diagram of a Mountain System to Include the Interactions Between Science and Research, the Stakeholders, and the Resultant Law that Comes to Bear on the Development and Operations of Mountain Resorts

Going Forward by Creating New Frameworks for the Integration of Ecosystems and Law

The alternative route is to try to aggressively create new regimes explicitly incorporating an ecosystem-based approach. Because it would be a new regime, interdisciplinary research—and not just research about ecosystem science—would play a critical role, particularly at the start. Figure 23.2 depicts one configuration of the structure and complexity of a coupled human-mountain system. It highlights the key interactions that coalesce to create the legal regime regulating resort activities.

The Research Agenda

The application of ecology to inform law and policy has the opportunity to take new shape through the emergence of sustainability science and its focus on environment and development.[20] Although sustainability science is often seen as

20 Robert W. Kates et al., *Environment and Development: Sustainability Science*. 292 SCIENCE 641–642 (2001)

focused on large scale global problems, it recognizes the essential need to approach problems from an understanding of the ecological and social characteristics of specific places and the stakeholders involved in managing for sustainability. At the heart of sustainability science is the framing of a research agenda to provide more effective communication between science and human institutions. We propose that the law should be included in this partnership. Selected organizing questions that define sustainability science and can inform the discussion of the research agenda for mountain resorts are:[21]

- How can the dynamic interactions between nature and society (including lags and feedback) be better incorporated into emerging models and conceptualizations that integrate development and sustainability?
- What determines the vulnerability or resilience of the ecosystem (the nature-society system) in particular kinds of places (for example, the Northeast) and for particular types of ecosystems (mountains) and human livelihoods (resort operation)?
- Can scientifically meaningful "limits" or "boundaries" be defined that would provide effective warning of conditions beyond which the nature-society systems incur a significantly increased risk of serious degradation?
- What systems of incentive structures (markets, rules, norms, and scientific information) can most effectively improve social capacity to guide interactions between nature and society toward more sustainable trajectories?
- How can today's operational systems for monitoring and reporting on environmental and social conditions be integrated or extended to provide more useful guidance for efforts to navigate a transition toward sustainability?
- How can today's relatively independent activities of research planning, monitoring, assessment, and decision support be better integrated into systems for adaptive management and societal learning?

As evident from this list, the research agenda must be grounded in science. Models, such as the Hubbard Brook model, could significantly increase understanding of the impacts of resort development on the mountain ecosystem. It can help identify the dynamic interactions, vulnerabilities or resilience of the ecosystem, and the limits and boundaries described in the first three questions above. That increased understanding is essential to infusing an ecosystem perspective into decision making at mountain resorts.

As suggested by the questions above, however, scientific research needs to be integrated with other disciplines to examine the relationship between the ecosystem and livelihoods and economic enterprises to determine their interactions, vulnerabilities and limits. We would interpret our "ecosystem science" compartment in Figure 23.2

21 *Id.*

broadly to include the full array of research bearing on the relationship between the mountain ecosystem and society. Moreover, as indicated by the last three questions above, research and debate must examine ways to improve incentive structures, operational systems, and ongoing management. This book perhaps represents a small, interdisciplinary venture into some of these research questions for mountain resorts, but much more is needed in order to develop a better understanding of the mountain ecosystem and the relationship to that ecosystem and society.

The Action Agenda

The research described above can vastly increase our understanding of the nature-society relationship at mountain resorts and elsewhere. However, we think that the chapters in this book generate some tentative conclusions about the types of legal considerations that may be key at mountain resorts if decision-makers are to take an ecosystem perspective. They suggest a possible agenda for action, with the sustainability-science issues running as themes through it. This agenda may change over time with the deeper understandings that can flow from the research described above, but we did not want to close this book without some concrete suggestions for how a new, integrated set of legal mechanisms might encourage a more ecosystem-oriented approach to mountain resorts.[22]

Agenda Item 1: Thorough Ecosystem Evaluation at the Resort's Inception Advocates of ecosystem-based approaches often endorse the concept of adaptive management, which can offer flexibility to reevaluate with changes in the ecosystem and the state of knowledge,[23] and the last sustainability-science question above calls for the integration of research into adaptive management. The challenge for mountain resorts, however, is that the foundational decisions about whether to allow the resort in the first instance or to allow significant expansions are not easily be revisited, once made. With authorizations in hand, the resort owners or operators will invest significant capital in building—or expanding—the mountainside facility, and they or other enterprises will invest in developing the associated residential and retail complexes. The growth will influence the economic profile of the region and decisions about public infrastructure. These activities would not occur without a significant degree of relatively long-term certainty. The decision creates a "dynamic interaction" between nature and society.

---

22 Given the focus of this book on the natural ecosystem, agenda items may focus more on this side of the equation than the economic side. This emphasis, however, is not meant to diminish the significance of, and need for, a more comprehensive analysis that explicitly addresses the economic issues, which are part of the sustainability-science approach.

23 *See, e.g.*, Decision V/6 of the Conference of the Parties to the Convention on Biological Diversity, Ecosystem Approach, ¶ A.4 (2000); *The Report of the Ecological Society of American Committee on Scientific Basis for Ecosystem Management*, 6 Ecological Applications, No. 3, 665, 683 (1996).

Consequently, it is very important to inject the ecosystem perspective into those fundamental decisions about the existence and scale of the resort at the start. The decision-making process at that point in time should look as extensively as possible at the fully attenuated effects of the proposed expansion and its associated growth on the local and regional ecosystem. If the government owns land where the resort might operate, it can build a thorough assessment into its review of a proposed lease, permit or land exchange, either by virtue of its freedom as a landowner or by virtue of legislation requiring it to do so. If the government is acting in its capacity as regulator, it could enact regulations requiring activities of a certain magnitude or location to undergo heightened, ecosystem-based scrutiny through a permitting or planning process using environmental impact assessment. Whether in its capacity as landowner or regulator, government would need to ensure that the criteria for the analysis of the impacts require the fullest possible attenuation across the components of the ecosystem and that the studies are based on the best available scientific information. Independent permits for specific activities, such as the alteration of wetlands, might provide relevant evidence, but they would not be conclusive or might even be procedurally integrated into the same comprehensive review to avoid conflicting results.

Implementation of this review would also require decisions about who should pay for this analysis—the government or the entity proposing the resort? Because the resorts in most cases are operated by the private sector, it seems only fair to allocate that burden in large part to the private players who will ultimately reap the financial benefit, in part from public goods. Although the resort will produce public benefits, such as jobs, the private sector is converting the value of the mountain resource into cash flow and it should bear at least the cost of assessing its impact on that resource—a potential restructuring of "incentive structures" noted in the sustainability questions above. The government would need to have the authority to deny activities for failure to produce credible analyses, and interested parties, broadly defined, should have the ability to intervene in the proceedings, access records, and submit evidence, aspects of the decision-support question also noted above.

Implementation would also require a definition of the ultimate standard for determining whether to authorize the resort—what is the permissible degree of ecological impact and when should economic benefits trump ecological impact? Government as landowner may have some freedom to exercise discretion, but government as regulator will have to adopt a standard of some sort. These are highly qualitative, societal judgments that should lie in the hands of relevant legislative or executive bodies, which can make politically accountable decisions that reflect their constituencies' priorities. There is no one right answer, underscoring the significance better understanding and defining of the ecosystem-society relationship over time.

Even so, it may be difficult to reach agreement and find words that can meaningfully express an ecosystem-oriented standard. All activities will have an impact on the ecosystem, so how does one define by legal standard the impacts that are undue? The refinement of understanding of the "vulnerabilities and resiliences" and "limits and boundaries" can help inform these definitions of the ecosystem-society relationship over time. It would seem either that standards would have to be based on broad goals or targets, such as "no impact that will significantly impair the long-term sustainability of the ecosystem (with an accompanying definition of "the ecosystem"), or perhaps more likely they would have to focus on components (pattern and processes, ecosystem functions and services, as in the new Hubbard Brook model) of the ecosystem that can serve as proxies for the health of the ecosystem. The latter approach will require the types of research advances in understanding of the mountain ecosystem described above. As a complementary policy, government can also set aside for conservation those ecologically significant mountain areas that should not be open to development, whether by designating governmentally owned land as wilderness or by acquiring ownership or conservation easements of privately owned mountain land. A change in the "incentive system," this preemptive planning component implicitly recognizes the remaining areas as potentially more susceptible to development. In addition, if state or provincial governments integrate their planning with regional and local planning, they can increase the chances of agreeing upon and harmonizing the potentially divergent priorities at different levels.

Agenda Item 2: Loudly Explicit Assumption of Risk for the Resort Operator and the Regional Economy and the Power of Renegotiation As the case studies illustrate, government may own part of the land where the resort will operate, granting long-term leases or permits to use. Technically speaking, government has the option of not renewing the arrangements when they expire, but practically, the private and public economic interests seem to create a momentum for continuation. To incorporate an ecosystem perspective, one should take seriously the possibility of nonrenewal at the expiration of the term. By that time, the ecosystem may have changed in significant ways or science may more fully understand the impacts of the resort on the ecosystem. While not rising to the level of adaptive management, a rigorous, objective, ecological assessment at the end of the term can at least offer the opportunity to revisit the fundamental question of the existence of the resort, considering the relative health of the ecosystem with and without the continued resort on government land and what is then known about the ecosystem-society relationship. Such an assessment is also essential when expansions are proposed, which significantly affect the dynamic interactions between nature and society, increasing expectations and the economic difficulty of nonrenewal. In reality, however, it has often proven difficult for government to resist the gravitational pull of renewal and expansion. Consequently, high standards and a thorough evaluation under Agenda Item 1 are especially critical. In addition, if renewal or expansion seems almost inevitable, government nonetheless should maximize opportunities to impose conditions that will recognize new understandings about ecological vulnerabilities and limits.

Agenda Item 3: Ongoing Ecosystem-Based Planning Requirements for the Mountainside Activities The concept of adaptive management can more easily enter the picture once the mountain resort is functioning, as resort operators make decisions about how to use and manage their slopes. Those smaller scale but sometimes ecologically significant decisions are easier to revisit those involving substantial, one-time capital investments. Whether through conditions attached to leases or conditions attached to regulatory permits, government could require the submission and approval of periodic management plan and associated environmental impact analyses and monitoring. These issues links directly to the sustainability-science question about how operational systems for monitoring can better move toward sustainability and allow for adaptation over time.

Agenda Item 4: Ecologically-Based Regulation for Secondary Growth The periodic reviews suggested in Agenda 3 would have limited application to the secondary growth, which often is beyond the control of the resort operator and involves numerous actors. Although the ecological impact of that projected growth would have been considered under Agenda 1 above, its ecological impacts on an ongoing basis will largely be controlled by local planning and media-specific regulations (such as pesticide regulations). Hence, applying an ecosystem perspective to secondary growth will require the development of local and state regulations that reflect a heightened understanding of the ecological impacts of secondary growth. Those regulations may vary significantly, depending on relevant ecosystem and its potential vulnerabilities, again a matter of developing a greater scientific base of knowledge about the ecological-societal impacts of growth. Very likely, it will also be a matter of reevaluating the current incentive structures (rules) that can disaggregate decision making among different bodies—a politically difficult but significant inquiry.

Agenda Item 5: Price Signals Finally, one can look for ways to shape and educate views of the mountain ecosystem by using price signals as one form of incentive structure. Mountain resorts are popular because people want not only exercise but also beauty and fresh air, yet the aesthetics of nature, the view from the top of the mountain, and the crisp air—valuable, marketable assets—come largely free of charge for the resort operator. Perhaps the government's leases for the land should reflect that value, or visitors to the mountain resort should pay an ecological tax or charge in recognition of the contributions of the ecosystem, or resort operators should pay for water extracted for snowmaking. These types of price signals may help build understanding that the ecosystem is providing valuable services; they may influence resort operators' decisions; and they may also be able to provide revenue for investing in science, protecting the ecosystem, and educating society about the marvelous complexities of the ecosystem.

> "In passing over these heights of land, through their thin atmosphere, the follies of the plain are refined and purified."[24]
>
> Henry David Thoreau on mountains

Thoreau saw the mountains as a special and pure environment rising above the problems created by people at its base. Unfortunately, today these problems have reached all parts of the mountain and these fragile ecosystems will require an effective ecosystem legal regime if they are to have a sustainable ecological and economic future. In the short term, our mountain agenda does not rely on path breaking—new legal instruments. Rather, based on this book's journey through the science and law of mountains, it tries to synthesize relatively traditional but enhanced techniques in a way that can more effectively allow decision-makers to focus on the mountain ecosystem using a holistic framework to connect people and ecosystems through the law. Much of this agenda might apply to non-mountain settings as well. In the longer term, if we are truly to apply an ecosystem perspective, we cannot artificially set mountains apart from the rest of the landscape or mountain resorts apart from other uses. Like the extraordinary interrelatedness that animates the concept of the ecosystem, all parts are connected and future legal regimes must be designed to respond to a broad range of ever changing issues. We hope the perspectives from these mountains may provide some inspiration for positive change in the relationships between law and ecology.

24 Henry David Thoreau, Excursions 182 (Houghton Mifflin Company 1893).

Index

Note: *italic* page numbers denote references to Figures/Tables.

accommodation 234, 334, 375
acid rain 16, 90, 218n17, 265–6
Act 250 (Vermont) (1970) 271, 273–4, 275, 278, 279–99, 323–8
  burden of proof 286–7
  habitat protection 108–9
  Interconnect project 301–5
  land exchange 427n7
  local planning 317–21, 324–5
  Parker's Gore East expansion 288–94
  party status 285–6, 302, 305, 315, 327
  public participation 299, 308, 435
  rebuttable presumption 287
  Resort Village 314–17
  secondary growth 432, 433
  ten criteria 282–4, 324, 326, 328, 431
  triggering events 281–2, 431
  wildlife 108–9, 432, 434
  Woodward Reservoir 306–7, 310–13
Act respecting Land Use Planning and Development 375, 379–81, 384–5, 387–8, 392, 395, 411–12, 414
Act respecting Nature Reserves on Private Land 361n46
Act respecting Off-highway Vehicles 368, 370
Act respecting the Conservation and Development of Wildlife 347n2, 361–2, 411, 412, 413
Act respecting Threatened or Vulnerable Species 362–3, 411
Adams, Sherman 136–7, 138, 144, 145, 201
adaptive management 15, 441, 443
Adirondack Mountain Club 230
Adirondack Mountains 1, 6, 27
Adirondack Park 10, 211–13, 234, 265–8, 427–8
  Adirondack Atlas 254, 255
  conservation easements 266, 426
  ecological consequences of development 262–3
  ecology of 31
  intensity guidelines 256, 257n15, *259*, 260–1, 433
  Land Use and Development Plan 224, 226, 255–6, 257–8, 260, 262–3, 266–7
  legal regime 220–6, 266, 267–8
  Open Space Plan 241, 434
  State Land Master Plan 223, 225, 226, 235–40, 241, 243
  wetlands 261–2
  zoning 425, 433, 434
Adirondack Park Agency 213, 221, 235–7, 240, 242–3, 250–1
  intensity guidelines 256, *259*, 260, 261
  local land use programs 225, 256, 257–8
  Open Space Plan 241
  regional assessment 263
  storm water runoff 249
Adirondack Park Agency Act (1971) 221, 242n51, 265
  intensity guidelines 256, 257n15
  Land Use and Development Plan 224, 255
  purpose of 258–60
  State Land Master Plan 223, 235–7, 238
  wetlands 261–2
Administrative Procedure Act (APA) 193n13, 194n15, 197, 206n7
Agence de Développement Station Mont Tremblant 340n29
Agenda 21 (Rio Earth Summit) 19
air pollution 90, 106, 218, 265, 315–16
algae 88, 89, 180
Alliance pour un Gestion Intégrée et Responsable du basin versant de la rivière du Diable (AGIR) 398n119

all-terrain vehicles (ATVs) 367, 368, 369–70, 378
alpine communities 57–9, 63
Alps 3, 82, 114
American Skiing Company (ASC) 10, 11, 275, 276, 324
    Interconnect project 301–5
    Memorandum of Agreement 294–6
    Resort Village 316, 317, 318
    Woodward Reservoir 306–7, 310–11
amphibians 114, 115
Appalachian Mountain Club 3, 136
Appalachian Mountains 27, 29–30, 132
Appalachian Trail Club 296
Appalachian Trail Conference 302, 314
appurtenances 232–3
aquatic salamanders 106–8, *107*, 126
Arlberg 3
aspen 41, 45, 47–8, 48n35
Associated Waterbodies 309
Ausable River 31, 215, 218, 248, *249*
Austria 3, 4

balsam fir 43–4, 100, 105, 106, 123, 360n43
Bamforth Ridge 44n17
Banff National Park 349–50, 412, 430
Banta, John S. 209–68
Barten, Paul K. 95
Base Sud 334, *336*, *354*, 374, 433n15
    agreement with municipality 364–5, 393, 402
    discretionary tools 389–90, 393
    environmental assessment 395, 399
    environmental control and monitoring program 393, 409
    lifts 355
    snowmaking 367, 371
base-facilities
    environmental assessment 393–9
    forest fragmentation 55
    hydrological impact of 56
    Intrawest 332–3
    Loon Resort 160, 161, 167, 184
    Mont Tremblant 331, 334, *336*, 364–5, 373, 374–99
    Whiteface Mountain 218
    see also secondary growth
bears 119, 123, 126
    Act 250 habitat protection 108–9
    habitat fragmentation *116*, 117
    Killington Resort 288–91, 292–3, 295, 302, 327
    Mont Tremblant 366
    seeps 56
bedrock 70–1
beech 28, 41, 49, 54
    black bears 108, 290, 292–3
    Northern Hardwood Forests 43
    Parker's Gore East 288, 292–3
    shade tolerance 45
Bell, Nancy 294, 296, 326, 327, 435
Bellayre 232
Bicknell's thrush 100, *101*, 104–6, 126
    Act 250 habitat protection 108–9
    edge effects 114
    gap-crossing ability 115
    Interconnect project 303
    Mont Tremblant 351, 353, 360n43, 404
    vegetation management 122, 123
    Whiteface Mountain 218, 239, 243, 244–7, 250, 251, 435
Big Tupper 229n11
biking 35, 219, 367, 370–1
biodiversity 24, 32–3, 36, 117–18
    2008 Planning Rule 206n7
    Adirondack Park 434
    definition of 37
    disturbance patches 41
    Forest Management Plans 149
    habitat fragmentation 53, 54, 55
    Hubbard Brook model 422, 424
    Loon Resort 175, 177
    Mont Tremblant 347
    national parks 353
    NFMA 173–4, 202
    old-age forests 51–2, 53
    patch communities 55, 63
    research 421
biogeochemical cycling 37, 421
biogeochemistry 74
biomass 67n16
birch 27, 28, 41, 44, 49
    Northern Hardwood Forests 43
    seed germination 47–8, 48n35
    shade tolerance 45

birds 16–17
  Bicknell's thrush 100, *101*, 104–6, 126
    Act 250 habitat protection 108–9
    edge effects 114
    gap-crossing ability 115
    Interconnect project 303
    Mont Tremblant 351, 353, 360n43, 404
    vegetation management 122, 123
    Whiteface Mountain 218, 239, 243, 244–7, 250, 251, 435
  Killington Mountain 30, 303, 304
  Mont Tremblant 32
  ovenbirds 115
  seed dispersal 48
  songbirds 118–19, 123
  synanthropic species 119
  Whiteface Mountain 31
  see also wildlife
blackbears 123, 126
  Act 250 habitat protection 108–9
  habitat fragmentation *116*, 117
  Killington Resort 288–91, 292–3, 295, 302, 327
Black Forest, Germany 87–8
Blue Line 221
Boehlert, Sherwood 266
Booth Creek Ski Holdings, Inc. 8, 139, 142, 143, 164n28
Bosch, J.M. 77
Boyle Brook 141, 179
Boyne USA, Inc. 9n36, 143
"bridge documents" 196
Brown, A.E. 77–8
Buchanan, Stu 250, 251
buckthorns 60–1
buffer zones 122, 123, 350, 360, 401
burden of proof 286–7, 315
Bureau d'audiences publiques sur l'environnement (BAPE) 343, 344, 349, 357, 358–9, 413, 414
Bush, George W. 148n24, 205–6
by-laws 375, 377, 379, 385–93, 395, 403, 404

Callenback, Ernest 13–14
Camp Nord 334, *336*, *354*, 375
  environmental assessment 360, 395, 413
  federal funding 340, 360, 395
  glade skiing 355
  land exchange and rezoning 351
  lifts 355
  local planning 381
  mountain biking 370
  public consultation 414
  snowmaking 367
  water source 398
Canada
  Environmental Assessment Act 340, 360, 363, 395–6, 408, 411, 413–14, 415
  National Parks Act 349–50, 353, 355–6, 358–9, 411, 412
  ski resorts 4, 5
  see also Quebec
Canadian Shield 32
carabid beetle 117
carbon emissions 16
Cascade Range 81
Centex Destination Properties 142, 143
Centre local de développement (CLD) 338n19
charity events 338n17
Chase, James E. 80, 84, 88, 95
chestnut 28
chloride *94*, 95
Civil Code of Quebec (C.C.Q.) 406, 411
Clean Air Act (1970) 14
Clean Water Act (CWA) (1972)
  Adirondack Park 223–4
  Loon Resort 179, 191–7, 199–200, 202n2
  storm water runoff 249
  Water Quality Certification 312
  Woodward Reservoir project 307–8
climate 26, 57–9
climate change 16, 125, 424, 436
  Bicknell's thrush 106
  snowmaking 429
  Vermont commission on 328
climax communities 41
clustered development 319
CNL Income Properties, Inc. 8n36, 143
codes of conduct 365–6, 371, 412
communities 42
community ecology 24
competition 44–6, 47, *62*

comprehensive development programs 388, 393
conditions 438, 444
coniferous trees 40, 43–4
Conseil régional de l'environnement des Laurentides (CRELA) 340, 348–50, 368n83, 398
conservation
  Adirondack Park 266
  Endangered Species Act 197–8
  government policy 443
  Mont Tremblant 348
  private law 426
  species-based approach 126
  Weeks Act 135
Conservation Law Foundation 286n28, 296, 302, 325
constitutional provisions
  Canadian Constitution 341
  New York State Constitution 10, 211, 213, 221, 225, 226
    Article XIV 223, 227–34, 251
    local land use 256n8
    zoning 212, 425
contract law 363–5, 399, 409
Coolidge State Forest 288, 290, 295, *297*
Council on Environmental Quality (CEQ) 194n19
courts 196–7
Cowles, Henry 24
cranefly orchid 52–3
Crawford Notch 49–50, 51
cumulative impacts 120–1, 126, 434
  Cumulative Watershed Effects 87
  Environment Quality Act 358
  Killington Resort 291, 315, 316, 317, 323, 327
  Mont Pinacle 388–9
  Mont Tremblant 340, 366, 371, 383, 395, 413, 431
Cumulative Watershed Effects (CWE) 87
Czechoslovakia 4

Dartmouth College Outing Club 3, 136
Davis, Deane 279, 328
Davos 3
Dean, Howard 296
deciduous trees 40, 44, 422
decomposition 58
deer
  as keystone species 118–19
  Mont Tremblant 351, 361–2, 377–8, 383, 387, 389–90, 404
deforestation
  hydrological impact of 97
  Loon Resort 173–8
  Mont Tremblant 387, 396
  see also logging; tree cutting
Department of Environmental Conservation (DEC) 213, 221–3, 240, 242, 250–1
  Open Space Plan 241
  State Land Master Plan 237, 238
  storm water runoff 249
discretionary tools 385n52, 387–93, 413, 415
dissolved substances 73, 74
District Environmental Commission (Vermont) 280, 281, 285, 287–8, 290–4, 328
  appeals 327
  Interconnect project 302–4
  local planning 317, 318
  Parker's Gore East 323
  Resort Village 313, 314–15, 316, 317
  Woodward Reservoir 310, 311, 324
disturbance 30, 46–51, 99
  alpine communities 59
  hydrology 66
  resort development *62*
  species response to 103–10
  weather 100
disturbance patches 41, 42, 48, 49–50
  see also habitat fragmentation; patch communities
Domaine Saint Bernard 370, 377, 378
  golf courses *400*
  land trust 405–8, 409, 412, 426, 434
  provincial jurisdiction 341, 342
  residents 435
dominant species 42
Douglas, Jim 328
draft environmental impact statement (DEIS) 152, 170–1
dredging permits 307–8
Dubois, Roland 139, 193–7, 435

eastern hemlock 45–6
Eastern Wilderness Act (1975) 204n3
ecological community 37
Ecological Reserves Act 347n2
ecological succession *see* succession
ecology 13–14, 23–5
Adirondack Park 238–40, 262–3, 265, 267
Canada National Parks Act 349–50
definition of 36
Domaine Saint Bernard 407, 408
Killington Mountain 29–30
Mont Tremblant 32, 340, 341
resort development impact on 33–5, 39–40, 41, 61–3, 429–32, 440
variation in 26
Whiteface Mountain 31–2, 218, 250–1
see also ecosystem perspective
economic value 123–5, 428
Adirondack Park 265
Killington Resort 277–8, 319, 328
Loon Resort 155, 185–6
Mont Tremblant 333–41
Whiteface Mountain 220
ecosystem ecology 36–7
ecosystem functioning 37, 422, *423*, 423–4
ecosystem management 15–16
ecosystem perspective 1–2, 13–18, 19, 23–38, 201, 205
Act 250 (Vermont) 271, 284, 312–13, 324, 326, 327–8
Adirondack Park 213, 238–40
Canadian Environmental Assessment Act 363
complex interrelationships 436
cumulative impacts 317
definition of scope 169
existing law 436–8
federal law 187–8, 191–200, 205–7
Interconnect project 302, 303, 304
legal regimes 419–20, 421, 424–34
local planning 318, 319, 321, 324–5
Loon Resort 161, 164–5, 172, 178, 183, 186–7, 202–3
master plan review process 317
Mont Tremblant 345, 353–5, 380, 403–4
national forests 207–8
new legal frameworks 439–45
New York State Constitution 234
provincial jurisdiction 342
Quebec Environment Quality Act 358
side agreements 296–8
traditional environmental perspective distinction 437
Whiteface Mountain 227, 252
Woodward Reservoir project 311, 312, 313
ecosystem services 36, 38, 61, 436
economic value 124
Hubbard Brook model 422, *423*, 423–4
price signals 444
ecosystems
Act 250 (Vermont) 284
definitions of 14, 16, 24, 37, 419
Hubbard Brook model 421–4, 440, 443
landscape ecology 40
loss of components and function 174–5
NEPA 152
provincial jurisdiction 342
see also mountain ecosystems
edge effects 50, 110, 173
buffering 122
spatial analysis *111*, 111–12, *112*
species risk analysis 114–15
elevation 42, 69, 100
emergent properties 37
employment 338–9
encroachment permits 307, 308, 311, 312
endangered species 55, 63, 181
Act 250 (Vermont) *283*, 284
definition of 198n36
Killington Resort 303
see also threatened species
Endangered Species Act (ESA) (1973) 191, 197–200, 202n2, 206n7
energy consumption 6
Environment Quality Act (Quebec) 342n41, 343, 344, 411, 412, 413
amendment to 415
base camp development 394–5
building permits 386
golf courses 399–400, 401
off-road vehicles 368n79
public participation 414
snowmaking 367
trail development 356–8, 360–1, 363

Environmental Assessment Act (Canadian) (1992) 340, 360, 363, 395–6, 408, 411, 413–14, 415
Environmental Board (Vermont) 280–1, 291–4, 316, 327
  adjoining landowners 285n26
  habitat protection 108
  Parker's Gore East 323, 324
  party status 286n29
  public participation 286n28
  Resort Village 314n42
  snowmaking 84n140
Environmental Conservation Law 237
environmental groups 277, 279, 294, 298, 301–2, 325–6
environmental impact assessment (EIA) *13*, 425, 442
  Adirondack Park 225, 261, 265
  BAPE 344
  Environment Quality Act 357, 358
  federal law 427n8
  Mont Tremblant 393–9, 413, 431
  periodic planning 444
  secondary growth 432
  traditional 437
  Whiteface Mountain 242, 252
environmental impact statement (EIS) 12, 425
  2008 Planning Rule 206n7
  Environment Quality Act 357n33
  Lake Placid 257
  Loon Resort 155, 159, 162, 165, 166–71, 185, 187, 194–5
  NEPA 151–3, 159–60, 162, 166, 202
  public participation 170–1
  scope 166–7
  secondary growth impacts 185, 186
  Whiteface Mountain 219n19, 223, 242, 244, 245, 252, 267
environmental lapse rate 26n8
Environmental Protection Agency (EPA) 5, 125, 192, 263
epiphytes 52–3, 63
erosion *see* soil erosion
evaporation 67–8
evapotranspiration 68, 69, 78, 81, 85
evergreens 43–4
Fallon, Kathleen S. 95
Farm and Wilderness Foundation, Inc. 294–5, 301, 306, 307, 310–11, 324
February Median Flow (FMF) 83, 307, 310, 429
federal law 12, 186–9, 191–200, 201, 202n2, 205–7, 427
fertilizers 86, 88–9
  golf courses 400, 402
  Mont Tremblant 383, 396, 402, 403
Final Environmental Impact Statement (FEIS) 130n10, 152, 197
  public participation 170
  secondary growth impacts 184–5, 186
  tree cutting 173, 174–7
  water resources 181, 183, 192, 194–5
fir 27–8, 43–4, 123
  Bicknell's thrush 100, 105, 106, 360n43
  old-age forests 52
  Parker's Gore East 288
fire 46
fish
  Clean Water Act 191
  Loon Mountain 29, 182
  Mont Tremblant 32, 383, 387, 396n103, 397
  sedimentation impact on 86–7, 180–1
  streamflow requirements 83
  water quality 75, 89
  water withdrawals 180
  Whiteface Mountain 31
  see also wildlife
Fleming, Roger 127–208
floodplains 401
floods 66, 72–3, 82, 315
Forest Management Plans 148–50
  environmental impact statements 152, 153
  Management Indicator Species 174
  White Mountain 153–6, 158, 160, 163, 164, 165–6, 203
Forest Service Organic Administration Act (1897) 145–6, 201
Forest Service Recreation Agenda 157
forests 26, 43–55, 129–30
  Adirondack Park 239
  alpine communities 57–9

competition 44–6, 47
disturbance and recovery 46–51
edge effects 50, 110–12, *111*, *112*, 114–15, 122, 173
fragmentation 34, 41, 53–5, 62, 109–10, 113–17, 173
Green Mountains 30
Hubbard Brook model 421–4
hydrological impact of 74, 79, 89, 97
Loon Mountain 130–1
matrix concept 41, 42
Mont Tremblant 32, 351, 360
old-age 51–3, 54, 63
Parker's Gore East 288
patch communities 55–7
precipitation 79
resort development 36
stream temperatures 89
White Mountains National Forest 132, 136
Whiteface Mountain 31
see also deforestation; trees; vegetation
"forever wild" principles 212, 213, 223, 228–9, 234, 265
exceptions to 229–30, 239
New York State Constitution 221, 226
Foster, Jeffrey 49–50
four-seasons activities 4, 5
Killington Resort 319
Loon Resort 144, 202
Mont Tremblant 11, 334, 337–8, 341, 367
species response to disturbances 104
water extraction 81–2
Whiteface Mountain 216, 219
fragility 33, 59, 99, 347
fragmentation *see* habitat fragmentation
France 3, 4
Freshwater Wetlands Act (New York State) 261–2
Friends of Parker's Gore 296, 302, 327
frost action 26
fugitive species 48

Germany 3, 87–8
Gifford Woods 52
glacial tills 44
glaciation 26, 27, 28, 32
glade skiing 50, 62, 123
Mont Tremblant 355, 366
Whiteface Mountain 232
Gleason, Henry 24
Glenn, Jane Matthews 329–415
golf courses
Mont Tremblant 333–4, 337, 373, 399–404
water pollution 88–9
water use 81–2
Gore Mountain Ski Center 217, 229n11, 231–2, 237, 242n51
Gosz, James R. 90
government investment 339, 340n29
Green Mountain Club 296, 302, 314, 325
Green Mountains 1, 6, 29–30, 274, 288
greenhouse gases 16, 328, 436
groundwater 70, 90

habitat diversity 45
habitat fragmentation 34, 53–5, 62, 99, 102–3, 109–10, 125–6
Adirondack Park 434
black bears 288, 293
cumulative effects of development 120–1
forest matrix 41
golf courses 399
invisibility 125
management recommendations 122–3
Mont Tremblant Park 347
natural 100, 104–5
population decline 115, *116*
research 421
spatial analysis 110–13, 126
species risk analysis 113–17
trail width 303
tree cutting 173
see also disturbance patches
habitat loss 99, 104–8, 121, 125–6
habitat modification 99, 102, 110, 118, 121, 125–6
Haeckel, Ernst 24
Hagen, Kimberly 99–126
Hannah, Sel 136, 137
Helvey, J.D. 78
hemlock 28, 43, 45–6, 49, 52, 54
herbicides 402

herbivory *62*
Hewlett, J.D. 77, 78
high mountains 26
High Peaks wilderness area 31
honeysuckles 60–1
Hornbeck, J.W. 77, 79, 80
Houseal, Brian 250
Hubbard Brook Experimental Forest 74, 77, 79
Hubbard Brook Forest Ecosystem Model 421–4, 440, 443
hydrology *see* water

ice encasement 51
indicator species 123, 298
  Loon Resort 175n76, 176–7, 181, 182, 183, 204
  NFMA 149, 154, 174, 187, 202
  water quality 75
insects 119
integrated land management 332, 342, 376
Interconnect project (Killington) 273, 277, 295, 296, 301–5, 318, 323, 430
interdisciplinary approach 149, 151, 439
Intrawest Development Corporation 11, 331, 344–5, 409, 415
  barriers to information 435
  base camps 374, 393
  codes of conduct 365–6, 371, 412
  contract law 363–5
  development of skiable domain 347–71
  discretionary tools 389–90, 413
  economic and social issues 332–41
  golf courses 399
  land exchange and rezoning 348–55, 427n7
  revenues *337*
  see also Station Mont Tremblant
invasive species 60–1, *62*, 63
"iron seeps" 90
Isham, Jonathan 269–328
Italy 4

Jackrabbit Ecological Reserve 347n2
Japan 4
Japanese knotweed 60
Johannsen Peak 351
Jones, J.A. 77

keystone species 42, 118, 123, 298
Killington Mountain, ecology of 29–30
Killington Resort 3, 6, 10–11, 269–328, 429
  conclusions 323–8
  conservation easement 426
  economic value 277–8
  forest fragmentation 54
  Gifford Woods 52
  Interconnect project 273, 277, 295, 296, 301–5, 318, 323, 430
  land exchange 427
  legal features 12, *13*
  local planning 317–21
  location *7*, *272*, *289*, *297*
  Memorandum of Agreement 294–8
  operational features *9*
  opposition to expansion 298–9, 305
  ownership 12, 425
  permit review process 426
  Planned Unit Development 320–1
  Resort Village 273, 277, 287, 305, 313–17, 318, 320–1
  scientists 435
  secondary growth 432, 433
  snowmaking 84n140
  Town Plan 319, 321
  water usage 6n29
  Woodward Reservoir 273, 276–7, 294–5, 305, 306–13, 318, 324
  see also Parker's Gore East
King, R.M. 78
knotweed 60
krummholz 30, 31, 58
K-selected species 103

Lac Tremblant 342, 367, 375, 391, 398–9
Lake Placid 6, 10, 211, 212, 215–16, 253, 265
  constitutional amendment 229
  Land Use and Development Plan 255, 266–7
  local land use programs 256, 257
  revenues from tourism 220
  skiing competitions 244
  tourism marketing 251, 434
  Winter Olympic Games 230
Lake Tahoe 87

land exchanges
government constraints 427
Killington Resort *13*, 295–6, 302–3, 304, 305, 318, 427n7
Mont Orford 358
Mont Tremblant *13*, 348, 350–1, *352*, 427n7
land trusts 406–8, 409, 412, 426, 434
Land Use and Development Law *see* Act 250
Land Use and Development Plan (LUDP) 224, 226, 255–6, 257–8, 260, 262–3, 266–7
land use classifications 235–7, *236*, 239, 258–60
landscape 37, 207
landscape ecology 37, 40, 41, 208
landslides 46, 48, 85
Laurel Highlands 90
Laurentian Mountains 1, 6, 27, 32
Laurentides Regional Council Municipality 377–8, 379n18, 380, 395
law 12–13
access to government land 427–8
Adirondack Park 211–12, 213
Canada 345
conceptual framework *439*
conservation 426
contract law 363–5, 399, 409
creation of resorts 426–7
Domaine Saint Bernard land trust 405–8, 409, 412
ecosystem perspective 14–15, 18–19, 419–20, 424–34, 436–45
federal 12, 186–9, 191–200, 201, 202n2, 205–7, 427
habitat protection 108–9
interested parties 18–19
"legal ecosystem" concept 332, 344, 345, 411–15
Loon Resort 131, 144, 145–58, 186–9, 201
new legal frameworks 439–45
on-mountain activities 428–32
patch communities 57
Quebec 341–3, 363
secondary growth impacts 432–4
snowmaking 84n140
taking advantage of existing law 436–8
Total Maximum Daily Load 97
Whiteface Mountain 220–6, 227–52
see also legislation; planning law
leaching 34, *62*
leaf area index (LAI) 58n77
"legal ecosystem" concept 332, 344, 345, 411–15
legislation
Act 250 (Vermont) (1970) 271, 273–4, 275, 278, 279–99, 323–8
burden of proof 286–7
habitat protection 108–9
Interconnect project 301–5
land exchange 427n7
local planning 317–21, 324–5
Parker's Gore East expansion 288–94
party status 285–6, 302, 305, 315, 327
public participation 299, 308, 435
rebuttable presumption 287
Resort Village 314–17
secondary growth 432, 433
ten criteria 282–4, 324, 326, 328, 431
triggering events 281–2, 431
wildlife 108–9, 432, 434
Woodward Reservoir 306–7, 310–13
Act respecting Land Use Planning and Development 375, 379–81, 384–5, 387–8, 392, 395, 411–12, 414
Act respecting Nature Reserves on Private Land 361n46
Act respecting Off-highway Vehicles 368, 370
Act respecting the Conservation and Development of Wildlife 347n2, 361–2, 411, 412, 413
Act respecting Threatened or Vulnerable Species 362–3, 411
Adirondack Park Agency Act (1971) 221, 242n51, 265
intensity guidelines 256, 257n15
Land Use and Development Plan 224, 255
purpose of 258–60

State Land Master Plan 223, 235–7, 238
wetlands 261–2
Administrative Procedure Act 193n13, 194n15, 197, 206n7
Civil Code of Quebec 406, 411
Clean Air Act (1970) 14
Clean Water Act (1972)
Adirondack Park 223–4
Loon Resort 179, 191–7, 199–200, 202n2
storm water runoff 249
Water Quality Certification 312
Woodward Reservoir project 307–8
Eastern Wilderness Act (1975) 204n3
Ecological Reserves Act 347n2
Endangered Species Act (1973) 191, 197–200, 202n2, 206n7
Environment Quality Act (Quebec) 342n41, 343, 344, 411, 412, 413
amendment to 415
base camp development 394–5
building permits 386
golf courses 399–400, 401
off-road vehicles 368n79
public participation 414
snowmaking 367
trail development 356–8, 360–1, 363
environmental assessment 397, 398, 399
Environmental Assessment Act (Canadian) (1992) 340, 360, 363, 395–6, 408, 411, 413–14, 415
Environmental Conservation Law 237
Forest Service Organic Administration Act (1897) 145–6, 201
Freshwater Wetlands Act (New York State) 261–2
Mont Orford 359
Multiple Use Sustainable Yield Act (1960) 145, 146, 147, 201, 204, 208
National Environmental Policy Act (1969) 150–3
2005/2008 Planning Rules 206n7
amendments to 205–7
Clean Water Act 196, 197
EIS regulations 162, 193, 194–5
forest management plan amendments 160n5
Loon Resort 156, 159, 166, 168–9, 173, 187–8, 202–5
procedural requirements 151, 164n26, 172, 173, 187–8, 199
public participation 149, 169, 171, 188
scope 166, 168n43
secondary growth impacts 184
substantive provisions 188n133
Whiteface Mountain 225
National Forest Management Act (1976) 129, 147, 148–50, 159, 187–8, 202–5
amendments to 205–7
Forest Management Plan 154, 156
pre-NFMA planning 146
public participation 169
substantive requirements 164n26, 171–2, 173, 174, 199
tree cutting 173–4, 178
water resources 179, 183
National Forest Ski Area Permit Act (1986) 145n4, 156–7, 204
National Parks Act (Canada) (2000) 349–50, 353, 355–6, 358–9, 411, 412
"nesting" 411–12
Occupancy Act (1915) 145
Pesticide Act 402
Regulation respecting Motor Vehicle Traffic in Certain Fragile Environments 368n79, 370
Regulation respecting Wildlife Habitats 361–2
Resource Conservation and Recovery Act (1976) 14
snowmobiles 369
State Environmental Quality Review Act 223, 225, 226, 242, 250, 252, 261
Sustainable Development Act 376n11, 413, 415
Water Pollution Control Act Amendments (1972) 14
Watercourses Act 386n54

Weeks Act (1911) 135, 146, 201
Wild, Scenic and Recreational Rivers Act (New York State) (1975) 215n7, 218, 248
Wilderness Act (1964) 130n11, 204–5, 207, 239
see also constitutional procedures; law
LeMense, Julia 269–328
Lenge, Nicholas 308, 309, 310–11, 324, 435
Leopold, Aldo 120
lichens 52–3, 56
lifts 3
Killington Resort 301
Loon Resort 141, 143
Mont Tremblant 333, 355, 391n81
light 34, 45–6, 47
Lincoln 130–1, 132–5, 136, 138, 144, 184–6, 196, 201
litigation
2005/2008 Planning Rules 206n7
Endangered Species Act 199n45
Loon Resort 192–7
Little Whiteface Peak 213, 218, 234
local access provisions 391n81
local planning
Act 250 (Vermont) 317–21, 324–5
Adirondack Park 225, 256, 257–8
Mont Tremblant 375, 377, 378–85, 395, 403–4, 408, 411–12, 413
secondary growth 444
see also planning law
logging
forest fragmentation 53, 54, 293
invasive species 61
Killington Resort 291
Loon Mountain 201
soil erosion 56
see also timber trade
Loon Mountain, ecology of 28–9
Loon Mountain Project (LMP) 174–6, 182
Loon Mountain Recreation Corporation (LMRC) 8, 130, 136–8, 202
definition of purpose and need 162–3, 187
legal challenge to water proposals 192, 193, 196
permits 145, 152, 203
public participation 171
South Mountain Expansion 138–44, 154–6, 158, 160
South Peak Resort 143, 167–8, 184
Loon Mountain Ski Resort 6, 8–10, 127–208, 426, 428–9, 431–2
birth and growth 135–8
conclusions 201–8
definition of purpose and need 162–6, 172, 187, 203–4
definition of scope 166–9, 172, 187
early permits 145–7, 202
Endangered Species Act 199
environmental impact statements 425
federal law 186–9, 191–200, 202n2, 427
Forest Management Plans 158, 425
framing of expansion proposal analysis 161–6, 171–2, 187, 204
legal features 12, *13*
location *7*, 132, *133*
operational features *9*
opposition to expansion 163n22, 193–7
ownership 12, 425
public participation 169–71
scales of analysis 174–5, 177, 185, 428
secondary growth 184–6, 433
tree cutting analysis 173–8
visitor numbers 164, 165n29
water demand and storage 6n29, 179–83, 192–7
Loon Pond 29, 138, 141, 177n92, 179, 182–3, 193–7
low mountains 26
luge tracks 337, 355, 366
lumbering 32
see also timber trade
Lunn, Arnold 3

macroinvertebrates 66, 75, 86, 180–1
Madden Brook 288, 290, 292, *297*
Management Indicator Species (MIS)
aquatic 181, 183
Loon Resort 175n76, 176
NFMA 149, 174, 202
maple 28, 41, 43, 288
mass wasting 26
matrix concept 41, 42

McFarland, Kent P. 99–126
Memorandum of Agreement (MOA) 273, 294–8
 Interconnect project 302–3, 305
 Woodward Reservoir 306–7
mercury 90, 106
metapopulations 109–10
middle mountains 26
Milne, Janet E. 1–19, 419–45
Minister of Natural Resources and Wildlife (Quebec) 342, 343, 412
Minister of Sustainable Development, Environment and Parks (Quebec) 342–3, 355–6, 400, 412, 429
Mont Orford 358–9, 414, 415
Mont Pinacle 388–9
Mont Tremblant 6, 11, 329–415, 429
 base camps *336*, 373, 374–99
 constitutional and administrative considerations 341–4
 ecology of 32
 economic and social issues 332–41
 environmental impact assessment 425, 430, 431
 golf course development 399–404
 land exchange and rezoning 348–55, 427
 land use planning 375–93, 404, 408, 411, 412, 413, 425
 "legal ecosystem" concept 411–15
 legal features 12, *13*
 local government 433–4
 location *7*, *335*
 non-ski activities 367–71
 operational features *9*
 ownership 12, 425
 public access to information 435
 secondary growth 433
 ski slopes *354*
 snowmaking 366–7, 371
 Town of 373–4, 380–3, 390, 393–4, 399, 403, 413
 trail development 355–66
 see also Domaine Saint Bernard
Mont Tremblant Park 331, 341, 347, 412
 base camp developments 394
 off-road vehicles 368
 reclassification 348–53
Montreal 8
mosses 56
Mount Equinox 61
Mount Mansfield 59, 60, 80n108
 Bicknell's thrush *101*, 105–6, 114, 245
 fracture flow 71
 habitat fragmentation 109
 hydrology 91–6
 precipitation 69
 spatial analysis of wildlife habitats 112
Mount Van Hoevenberg 216–17, 244
mountain biking 35, 219, 367, 370–1
mountain ecosystems 19, 23, 25–7, 419–20, 445
 fragility 33
 models 35–6
 price signals 444
 resort development impact on 33–5
 scientific understanding 432
Moynihan, Daniel 266
Multiple Use Sustainable Yield Act (MUSYA) (1960) 145, 146, 147, 201, 204, 208
multiple-use objectives 146, 147, 188, 201, 202, 204, 205, 207

National Environmental Policy Act (NEPA) (1969) 150–3
 2005/2008 Planning Rules 206n7
 amendments to 205–7
 Clean Water Act 196, 197
 EIS regulations 162, 193, 194–5
 forest management plan amendments 160n5
 Loon Resort 156, 159, 166, 168–9, 173, 187–8, 202–5
 procedural requirements 151, 164n26, 172, 173, 187–8, 199
 public participation 149, 169, 171, 188
 scope 166, 168n43
 secondary growth impacts 184
 substantive provisions 188n133
 Whiteface Mountain 225
National Forest Management Act (NFMA) (1976) 129, 147, 148–50, 159, 187–8, 202–5
 amendments to 205–7
 Forest Management Plan 154, 156

pre-NFMA planning 146
public participation 169
substantive requirements 164n26, 171–2, 173, 174, 199
tree cutting 173–4, 178
water resources 179, 183
National Forest Service (NFS) 130, 137, 159–89, 201–8
definition of purpose and need 162–6, 172, 187, 203–4
definition of scope 166–9, 187
early permits 145–7, 202
evolution of South Mountain expansion proposal 138–42, 154–6
federal law 186–9
framing of expansion proposal analysis 161–6, 187, 204
NEPA 152, 153
NFMA 148–50
public participation 169–71
purchase of land by 135, 146
revision of planning regulations 148n24, 206n7
scales of analysis 174–5, 177, 185, 204
secondary growth 184–6
ski industry relationship 156–8, 204
tree cutting analysis 173–8
water demand and storage 179–83, 192–7
White Mountain Forest Management Plan 153–6
National Forest Ski Area Permit Act (1986) 145n4, 156–7, 204
national forests 129–30, 145–6, 147, 207–8, 432
National Park Service 302
national parks 349–50, 353, 355–6
National Parks Act (Canada) (2000) 349–50, 353, 355–6, 358–9, 411, 412
National Pollutant Discharge Elimination System (NPDES) 191n5
National Ski Areas Association (NSAA) 97, 243, 251, 365
New Hampshire 6, 8, 132, 186, 201
Hubbard Brook Experimental Forest 74, 77, 79, 80
ski resorts 164n28
Tuckerman's Ravine 81
New York State 211, 212, 216
conservation easements 426
Open Space Plan 241, 434
rivers 215n7, 221
New York State Constitution 10, 211, 213, 221, 225, 226
Article XIV 223, 227–34, 251
local land use 256n8
zoning 212, 425
nitrogen 43n14, 85n155, 88, 422
nongovernmental organizations (NGOs) 325–6, 427
Nordic skiing 144, 157
North Elba 32, 215, 225, 253, 257
Northern Hardwood Forests 43
Norway 2
nutrient cycling 32–3, 36, *62*, 421, 422, 424

oak 41, 48n35
Occupancy Act (1915) 145
Odum, Eugene 24–5, 422
off-road vehicles 367–71, 378
Olympic Games
1924 3
1932 3, 211, 228, 267
1980 211, 216, 218, 230, 231, 241, 253, 267
2010 11
facilities 216–17
Olympic Regional Development Authority (ORDA) 216–17, 219, 227, 267
Bicknell's thrush 245, 247
creation of 231
planning 240, 241–3, 248, 252, 430
revenues 220
snowmaking 248
State Land Master Plan 238
storm water runoff 249, 250
Sustainable Slopes principles 251
Whiteface Mountain highway 237n38
Open Space Plan 241, 434
orchids 52–3
Organic Administration Act (1897) 145–6, 201
orographic lifting 72n52
orthophotography 110–11
outcrop communities 56, 57

out-of-bounds skiing 50, 55, 62, 123
ovenbirds 115
oxygen 75, 89, 90

Parker Young Company 134, 135, 146
Parker's Gore East 271–3, 276, 288–94, 305, 324
  cumulative impacts 316, 323
  local planning 318
  Memorandum of Agreement 295, 296
  negotiations 298
  public participation 327
particulate matter 73, 74
patch communities 34, 41, 42, 55–7, 63, 177
  see also disturbance patches
Pemigewasset River 29, 134, 138, 141, 179, 193–5, 196
percolation thresholds 120, 121, 126
periodic planning 12, 425, 438, 444
permits 66, 426, 442
  Act 250 (Vermont) 273, 280–8, 306
  Adirondack Park 224, 225–6, 242, 257–8, 261, 263
  air pollution 315–16
  amendments to 323
  by-laws 386
  conditions 438, 444
  expiration 208
  habitat protection 108–9
  Killington Resort 276n23, 294, 296, 301n2, 302–3, 307–10, 311–12, 315–17
  Loon Resort 136–7, 145–7, 152–3, 186, 203
  master plan review process 313–17
  nonrenewal 443
  NPDES 191n5
  Ski Area Permit Act 145n4, 156–7, 204
  see also special use permits
Pesticide Act 402
pesticides 86, 87, 88–9
  Environment Quality Act 357
  golf courses 400, 402–3
  Mont Tremblant 383, 396, 401, 402–3, 412
  Quebec ban on 430
  special use permits 147
phosphorus 88, 97
photosynthesis 57–8, 67, 68
Pico 10, 11, 273, 275, 296, 301
pine 28, 49
Planned Unit Development (PUD) 320–1
planning law
  Act 250 (Vermont) 317–21, 324–5
  Adirondack Park 211–12, 221–3, 224–5, 240, 263, 267
  Canada National Parks Act 349–50
  discretionary tools 385n52, 387–93
  ecological approach 207n8
  ecosystem-based 443–4
  Killington Resort 12, 273–4, 314
  Loon Resort 146, 186, 203
  master plan review process 313–17
  Mont Tremblant 12, 375–93, 395, 403–4, 408, 411–12, 413
  NFMA 148, 149, 154, 188
  periodic planning 12, 425, 438, 444
  preemptive planning 443
  regulatory by-laws 385–7
  revision of Forest Service regulations 148n24, 206n7
  Vermont 279–80
  White Mountain Forest Management Plan 153n65, 154
  Whiteface Mountain 12, 219n19, 241–3, 248, 252, 430
plant communities 39–63
  alpine 57–9, 63
  competition 44–6
  disturbance and recovery 46–51
  fragmentation 53–5
  invasive species 60–1, 63
  patch communities 55–7, 63
  see also forests; trees
pollination 57
pollution 14, 16
  Act 250 (Vermont) 282–3, *283*
  air 90, 106, 218, 265, 315–16
  Environment Quality Act 343, 356
  snowmobiles 369
  special use permits 147
  Total Maximum Daily Load 97
  water 73, 86–7, 88–90, 191–2, 193–4, 195, 196
pools 65–6
population viability analysis (PVA) 121–2

populations
  decline due to habitat fragmentation 115, *116*
  edge effects 111–12
  species response to disturbances 103
  viability analysis 121–2
Powdr Resorts 10–11
precautionary principle 212, 232, 234, 252, 265, 434
precipitation 26–7, 71
  annual cycle *68*, 68–9
  cloudwater interception 81
  evapotranspiration 68
  Mount Mansfield 91
  resort development 76, 79
  see also snow
price signals 444
private sector 12, 207–8, 442
  Adirondack Park 211, 220, 221–3, *222*, 224–5, 226
  Loon Resort 157, 164n26, 204
  Whiteface Mountain 216
productivity 32–3, 37, 58
protected habitats 361–2
Protection Policy for Lakeshores, Riverbanks, Littoral Zones and Floodplains 360–1, 394–5, 401, 408, 411, 413
public good 308, 309, 312
public ownership 12, 425
  access to government land 427–8
  Adirondack Park 211, 221–3, *222*, 224–5, 226, 234
  Mont Tremblant 347–8
  New York State Constitution 227–8
  Whiteface Mountain Ski Center 10, 216
public participation 149–50, 152
  Act 250 (Vermont) 299, 308, 327, 435
  BAPE 344
  by-laws 387, 392–3
  comprehensive development programs 388
  Environment Quality Act 357
  Killington Resort 294, 435
  limited 345, 435–6
  Loon Resort expansion 169–71, 203
  Mont Tremblant 381, 384, 392–3, 397, 408–9, 414, 415, 435–6
  NEPA 188
  Water Quality Certification 312
  White Mountain Forest Management Plan 154, 156
  Woodward Reservoir project 308, 313

Quebec 11, 341–3, 363, 435
  ecosystem perspective 429
  environmental impact assessment 431
  land use planning 375
  Ministry of the Environment 332, 398–9, 403
  municipal structure 373
  pesticides 430
  protected areas 406
  zoning 425
  see also Environment Quality Act; Mont Tremblant

railroads 134–5
rain *see* precipitation
real estate 4
  Loon Resort 137–8, 142, 143
  Mont Tremblant 339
  see also residential development
rebuttable presumption 287
Record of Decision (ROD) 174, 177, 182–3, 185
recovery 59
red spruce 43–4
red-backed salamander 117
Regional Greenhouse Gas Initiative (RGGI) 328
regional planning
  Adirondack Park 263
  Killington Resort 318–19
  Mont Tremblant 375, 376–9, 380, 384, 403–4, 408, 411–12, 413
  see also planning law
Regulation respecting Motor Vehicle Traffic in Certain Fragile Environments 368n79, 370
Regulation respecting Wildlife Habitats 361–2
Reiners, William 49–50
research 17, 98, 438, 439–41
  conceptual framework *439*
  hydrology 96–7

lack of site-specific information 421, 424
Mount Mansfield 95–6
reservoirs 83–4
residential development
Domaine Saint Bernard 405
Killington Resort 323
Lake Placid 254–5
Loon Resort 142, 143–4, 167–8, 184–5
Mont Tremblant 334, 364, 374–5, 377
"undue adverse impact" 256–7
Whiteface Mountain 215, 216
see also real estate
resilience 33, 37, 59, 99
resistance 33, 37
resort development
cumulative effects 120–1, 126, 316, 317, 323, 327
disturbance 50
ecosystem evaluation 441–2
federal law 186–9, 208
habitat fragmentation 54–5, 102–3
Hubbard Brook model 424
hydrological impact of 56, 57, 63, 66, 75–82, 85–90
impact on ecology 33–5, 39–40, 41, 61–3, 429–32, 440
Mont Orford 358–9
patch communities 57, 63
secondary growth 119, 184–6, 432–4
wildlife 119
see also Killington Resort; Loon Mountain Ski Resort; Mont Tremblant; Whiteface Mountain Ski Center
Resort Village (Killington) 273, 277, 287, 305, 313–17, 318, 320–1
Resource Conservation and Recovery Act (1976) 14
RESTORE 139, 193–7
revenues 5
Lake Placid 220
Loon Resort 155
Mont Tremblant *337*, 341
Vermont 124
see also economic value
Riehle, Parker 328
Ries, Johannes B. 87–8
riffles 65n4, 66, 89
Rimmer, Christopher C. 99–126
Rio Earth Summit (1992) 19, 348
rivers
Loon Mountain 29
New York State 215n7, 221
patch communities 56
Whiteface Mountain 31
see also streams; water
road development
barriers to dispersal 63
Environment Quality Act 357
hydrological impact of 78, 79–80, 89
invasive species 60, 61
Mont Tremblant 384n44
patch communities 57
vehicular traffic 367
rocks 70–1
Rocky Mountains 5, 82, 98, 349–50
Rouge-Matawin Wildlife Sanctuary 347n2
r-selected species 103, 118
runoff
annual cycle *68*
Mont Tremblant 365
Mount Mansfield 91, 92, 95
resort development impact on 34, 76, 79, 80, 85–6
storm water 66, 72–3, *94*, 95, 249–50, 430
Total Maximum Daily Load 97
Rutland Regional Plan 318–19
Ryan, Joseph Bondurant 331

salamanders 106–8, *107*, 123, 126, 432
habitat fragmentation *116*, 117
sedimentation impact on 180–1
seeps 56
saturation 70
scenery 125, 177
Schneider, Hannes 3
science 420–1, 424–5, *439*
secondary growth 119, 184–6, 324, 432–4, 444
sediment 66, 74, 75, 85–8
Loon Resort 182
Mont Tremblant 365, 396, 401
Mount Mansfield *94*, 95
snowmaking 180
Total Maximum Daily Load 97

seed banks 48–9
seed dispersal 47, 48, 49, 53, 57, *62*, 63
seed germination 47–8, 49
seed predation *62*
seeps 56, 57, 90
sewage 89–90, 196, 220, 391
shade tolerance 34, 45–6, 47
Shanley, James B. 65–98
Sherburne Corporation 274, 275
shrubs 28, 48, 56, 58
  see also vegetation
site planning and architectural integration programs 389, 391, 393
S-K-I, Ltd. 275, 276, 288, 290–1, 292–3, 296, 327
Ski Area Permit Act (1986) 145n4, 156–7, 204
ski lifts 3
  Killington Resort 301
  Loon Resort 141, 143
  Mont Tremblant 333, 355, 391n81
skiing 2–6, 125
  alpine communities 59
  Forest Service/ski industry relationship 156–8, 204
  Loon Resort 135–6, 137, 144, 164–5
  out-of-bounds 50, 55, 62, 123
  Quebec national parks 353
  revenues from 155
  Whiteface Mountain 211, 212, 217–18, 229
  see also trails
Smith, Preston Leete 274, 275
snow 34, 69, 71, 81
  air pollution 90
  compaction 80, 84
  snowmelt 71–2, 80, 84, 92, 181
snowboarding 4, 144, 355, 366
snowmaking 5–6, *13*, 15, 82–5
  ANR Rules 310
  climate change impact on 429
  Hubbard Brook model 424
  hydrological impact of 80
  impact on ecosystem 34
  Killington Resort 276–7, 288, 290, 301n2, 306–7, 310–11, 323
  Loon Resort 138–9, 141, 160–1, 179–81, 184, 192–3
  Mont Tremblant 340, 366–7, 371, 429
  Mount Mansfield 95
  patch communities 57
  Whiteface Mountain 218, 248–9
snowmobiles 234, 367, 368–9
snowshoeing 130, 136, 144
Société de la faune et des parcs du Québec 351, 353
soil erosion 34, 59, 85, 87, 88
  Act 250 (Vermont) *283*
  alpine communities 63
  Mont Tremblant 360, 365, 387
  mountain biking 370
  outcrop communities 56
  steep slopes 97
  tree cutting analysis 176
  water pollution 73
soils *25*, 27
  alpine communities 58–9
  forest communities 44
  Loon Mountain 28
  moisture content 70
  patch communities 55
  resort development *62*
  seed germination 48
  shallow 102
  tree cutting impact on 176
  Whiteface Mountain 31
songbirds 118–19, 123
South Peak Resort (Loon Mountain) 142, 143–4, 167–9, 171, 184–5, 204
SP Land Co. 10, 320
Spangler, Carl 294
special use permits (SUPs) 145, 147, 148, 152
  Loon Resort 159–60, 161, 163, 165–6, 174, 202
  NEPA 162
  Ski Area Permit Act 156–7
specialization 104, 108
species diversity 32–3
species extinction 56–7, 124
spruce 27–8, 43–4, 54
  management recommendations 122
  old-age forests 52
  Parker's Gore East 288
  Whiteface Mountain 218–19
squashberry 303
St. Anton 3

St. Lawrence River 211, 357
St. Moritz 3
stakeholders 288, 294, 325, *439*
State Environmental Quality Review (SEQR) Act 223, 225, 226, 242, 250, 252, 261
Station Mont Tremblant 347–8, 351, 363, 392
  contract law 363, 364
  economic success 409
  environmental assessment 413
  golf courses 399, 401
  local planning 381–5
  mountain biking 370
  off-road vehicles 368–70
  regional planning 377
  snowmaking 367
  "special planning program" 390
  voluntary codes of conduct 365–6
  see also Intrawest Development Corporation
storm water runoff
  Mount Mansfield *94*, 95
  peak flows 66, 72–3
  Whiteface Mountain 249–50, 430
storms 46
Stowe Mountain Resort 60, 80n108, 89, *96*
  Bicknell's thrush 245
  hydrology 91
  percolation threshold 121
  spatial analysis of wildlife habitats 110–12
Stratton Mountain
  Bicknell's thrush *101*, 105, 106, 114, 245
  percolation threshold 121
  spatial analysis of wildlife habitats 110–13
streamflow 67, 70
  annual cycle *68*, 68–9
  annual peak flow 72–3
  Hubbard Brook model 422
  Killington Resort 315
  Loon Resort 182, 183, 196
  Mount Mansfield 91–6
  resort development impact on 76–8
  snow impact on 71–2
  snowmaking 83, 180
  Total Maximum Daily Load 97
  water quality 74
  Whiteface Mountain 248
  see also water
streams *25*, 27, 65–6, 97–8
  Act 250 (Vermont) 283–4
  ANR Rules 310
  aquatic salamanders 106–8
  definition of 65n1
  downstream environments 82
  fracture flow 71
  Hubbard Brook model 422, 424
  Interconnect project 303–5
  Mount Mansfield 91–6
  resort development impact on 75–82, 85–90
  restoration 122–3
  snowmaking 82–5
  water extraction 81–2, 83, 85
  water movement 69–70
  water quality 73–5, 76, 86, 89–90, 97
  Woodward Reservoir project 306–7
  see also rivers; water
stress 33
Strimbeck, G. Richard 39–63
Strong, Allan M. 99–126
Stuart, G. 79, 80
subdivision by-laws 386
subsidiarity 415
succession
  definition of 38
  disturbance 49
  Hubbard Brook model 421–2
  resort development *62*
  secondary 41, 47, *62*
summer activities 4, 5, 81–2
  see also four-seasons activities
Summit House 30
Sun Valley, Idaho 3–4
supplemental environmental impact statement (SEIS) 152n58, 193, 195n24
sustainability 185, 188, 205, 427, 444
sustainability science 23, 439–40, 441
sustainable development 266, 342–3, 376, 384, 386, 420
Sustainable Development Act 376n11, 413, 415
Sustainable Slopes initiative 125, 251, 365, 435
Sweden 4

Switzerland 3, 4
synanthropic species 119
systems approach 24–5

Tansley, Arthur 24
temperature 57–9, 97
  environmental lapse rate 26n8
  streams 75
  water quality 89
Thomas, Lowell 230
Thoreau, Henry David 445
threatened species 55, 63, 198n36, 362–3, 378, 411
  see also endangered species
thrushes *see* Bicknell's thrush
timber management 154
timber trade 134, 135, 136, 201, 291
  see also logging
Titus, John H. 88
Total Maximum Daily Load (TMDL) 97
tourism
  Banff National Park 349
  Killington Resort 274–5
  Lake Placid 220, 253, 267
  Mont Tremblant 331, 332–9, 341, 347, 377, 378, 384n44
  wildlife 124
  Wilmington 253–4
  see also visitor numbers
Town of Mont Tremblant 373–4, 380–3, 390, 393–4, 399, 403, 413
trails *13*, 15, 34, 62
  barriers to seed dispersal 53, 63
  gap-crossing ability of species 115, 117
  habitat fragmentation 54–5, 102, 120, 126
  hydrological impact of 79, 80
  invasive species 61, 63
  Killington Resort 276, 296, 301, 303, 323
  Loon Resort 141, 143, 160, 173–8
  management recommendations 122–3
  Mont Tremblant 333, 355–66, 371
  patch communities 57
  soil movement 88
  species response to disturbances 104, 105
  Whiteface Mountain 218, 219–20, 227, 229–31, 232, *233*, 245–7
trampling 59, *62*, 63, 85n155
transpiration 67–8
tree cutting 421
  Loon Resort 173–8
  Mont Tremblant 365, 404
  New York State Constitution 228–9
  see also deforestation; logging
"Tree Island Pod" 220, 227, 232, *233*, 243, 244–8, 250, 435
trees *25*, 27–8, 40–2
  alpine communities 57–9
  aspen 41, 45, 47–8, 48n35
  beech 28, 41, 49, 54
    black bears 108, 290, 292–3
    Northern Hardwood Forests 43
    Parker's Gore East 288, 292–3
    shade tolerance 45
  birch 27, 28, 41, 44, 49
    Northern Hardwood Forests 43
    seed germination 47–8, 48n35
    shade tolerance 45
  competition 44–6
  Domaine Saint Bernard 405
  evaporation 68
  fir 27–8, 43–4, 123
    Bicknell's thrush 100, 105, 106, 360n43
    old-age forests 52
    Parker's Gore East 288
  Green Mountains 30
  hemlock 28, 43, 45–6, 49, 52, 54
  Loon Mountain 28
  management recommendations 122, 123
  maple 28, 41, 43, 288
  Mont Tremblant 32
  oak 41, 48n35
  pine 28, 49
  spruce 27–8, 43–4, 54
    management recommendations 122
    old-age forests 52
    Parker's Gore East 288
    Whiteface Mountain 218–19
  Vermont community classification system 43–4
  Whiteface Mountain 31
  see also forests; plant communities; vegetation
Tremblant Resort Association 338
Troendle, C.A. 78
trust law 406–8, 409, 412, 426

Tsuyuzaki, Shiro 88
Tuckerman's Ravine 81
tundra 26, 27, 30
Tupper Lake 229n11

uncertainty 420, 438
"undue adverse impact" 256–7, 258, 261, 263
United States, ski resorts 4–5
updating procedures 437–8

valleys 55, 82
values 123–4, 125
vegetation 39–63
  Green Mountains 30
  invasive species 60–1, 63
  Loon Mountain 28
  management recommendations 122
  Mont Tremblant 32, 351, 353, 360, 366, 383, 389, 396–7
  resort development impact 33–5
  transpiration 67–8
  tree cutting impact on 176
  Whiteface Mountain 31
  see also forests; plant communities; trees
Vermont 10–11, 271, 328
  District Environmental Commission 280, 281, 285, 287–8, 290–4, 328
    appeals 327
    Interconnect project 302–4
    local planning 317, 318
    Parker's Gore East 323
    Resort Village 313, 314–15, 316, 317
    Woodward Reservoir 310, 311, 324
  Environmental Board 280–1, 291–4, 316, 327
    adjoining landowners 285n26
    habitat protection 108
    Parker's Gore East 323, 324
    party status 286n29
    public participation 286n28
    Resort Village 314n42
    snowmaking 84n140
  environmental groups 279
  Memorandum of Agreement 295
  minimum streamflow 83
  stream quality 75
  tourism revenues 124
  town plans 433
  Water Quality Standards 307–8, 312
  see also Act 250
Vermont Agency of Natural Resources (ANR) 288, 292, 295–6, 325
  air pollution 315
  Interconnect project 301, 302–5
  Rules for Water Withdrawal 310
  Woodward Reservoir project 306–8, 310, 311–12
Vermont Center for Ecostudies (VCE) 105–6
Vermont community classification system 43–4
Vermont Institute of Natural Science (VINS) 105–6, 245, 247, 251
Vermont Monitoring Cooperative (VMC) 95, 96
Vermont Natural Resources Council (VNRC) 285n27, 302, 314, 315, 316, 325
Vermont Ski Areas Association (VSAA) 328
Versant Soleil 334, *336*, *354*, 375
  agreement with municipality 379, 392, 393
  by-laws 387, 404
  environmental assessment 360, 393–4, 395, 396, 399, 413–14
  environmental control and monitoring program 365, 393–4, 409, 413
  federal funding 340, 360, 395
  glade skiing 355
  land exchange and rezoning 351
  lifts 355
  local planning 381, 408
  mountain biking 370
  public consultation 414
  "special planning program" 390–1, 393, 408–9
  trail development 366
  white-tailed deer 362, 404
views 39, 384, 444
villages 55, 56, 434
  see also base-facilities
Virginia, Ross A. 23–38, 419–45
visitor numbers 4–5
  Killington Resort 275–6
  Loon Resort 164, 165n29
  Mont Tremblant 334
  Whiteface Mountain Ski Center 219
voluntary codes of conduct 365–6, 371, 412

water 5–6, 27, 57, 63, 65–98
Act 250 (Vermont) *283*, 283–4
Adirondack Park 261
ecosystem perspective 15
Killington Resort 276–7, 288, 294–5, 306–12
Loon Resort 29, 138, 141, 179–83, 192–7, 429
Mont Tremblant 340, 360–1, 367, 375, 383, 389, 390–1, 394–9, 401, 404
Mount Mansfield 91–6
pollution 73, 86–7, 88–90, 191–2, 193–4, 195, 196
quality 73–5, 76, 86, 89–90, 97
Clean Water Act 191–2, 196
golf courses 399
Hubbard Brook model 422
Killington Resort 307–10, 312
Mont Tremblant 383, 389, 398, 399, 401, 403, 412
resort development impact on 34, 75–82, 85–90
rights 84
seeps 56
snowmaking 82–5
storage 83–4, 141, 179–80, 182–3, 193, 194–5, 196
storm water runoff 66, 72–3, *94*, 95, 249–50, 430
Whiteface Mountain 234, 249–50
see also rivers; streams; watersheds; wetlands
Water Pollution Control Act Amendments (1972) 14
Watercourses Act 386n54
watersheds 66, 76
Cumulative Watershed Effects 87
Hubbard Brook model 422
Killington Resort 304–5
Mont Tremblant 384
Mount Mansfield 91–5, *92*
weather disturbances 100
Weeks Act (1911) 135, 146, 201
Wemple, Beverley 65–98
wetlands
Adirondack Park 261–2, 263
black bears 290, 327
Environment Quality Act 356–7
invasive species 61
Killington Mountain 30, 292–3, 294
Mont Tremblant 365, 377–8, 383, 389, 391, 395, 397, 401, 404, 412
patch communities 56, 57
Whiteface Mountain 31
Woodward Reservoir project 311
White, Carleton S. 90
White Mountains 1, 6, 8–10
disturbance patches 49–50
ecology 28
Forest Management Plan 153–6, 158, 160, 163, 164, 165–6, 203
National Forest 132, 136, 148
old-age forests 52
timber harvesting 135
Whiteface Mountain, ecology of 31–2
Whiteface Mountain Ski Center 6, 10, 209–68, 429, 431–2
alpine zone 59
Bicknell's thrush 244–7
constitutional limitations 227–35, 251, 427–8
environmental impact statements 425
growth of resort communities 253–5
intensity guidelines 433
legal regime 12, *13*, 220–6, 227–52
local government 433–4
location *7*, *214*
operational features *9*
ownership 12
private lands around 253–63, 266–7
roads 80n108
scientists 435
snowmaking 248–9
State Land Master Plan 223, 225, 226, 235–40, 241, 243, 251–2
storm water runoff 249–50, 430
Unit Management Plan 219–20, 223, 227, 232–3, 237, 240–52, 267, 425, 430
visitor numbers 219
white-tailed deer
as keystone species 118–19
Mont Tremblant 351, 361–2, 377–8, 383, 387, 389–90, 404
Wild, Scenic and Recreational Rivers Act (New York State) (1975) 215n7, 218, 248

Wilderness Act (1964) 130n11, 204–5, 207, 239
wilderness areas 31, 205n4
  Adirondack Park 235, 238, 239, 267
  Banff National Park 349
  Lake Placid 253
wildflower species 53
wildlife *25*, 27, 99–126
  2008 Planning Rule 206n7
  Act 250 (Vermont) 108–9, *283*, 284, 291, 292–3, 432, 434
  Adirondack Park 241
  aquatic 180, 181–2, 191
  bears 119, 123, 126
    Act 250 habitat protection 108–9
    habitat fragmentation *116*, 117
    Killington Resort 288–91, 292–3, 295, 302, 327
    Mont Tremblant 366
    seeps 56
  cumulative effects of development 120–1, 126
  disruption of ecological processes 117–20
  Domaine Saint Bernard 408
  economic value 123–5
  Endangered Species Act 197–200
  Forest Management Plans 149, 154
  Killington Mountain 30
  Loon Mountain 29, 176, 177, 179
  Mont Tremblant 32, 360, 377, 378, 383, 396, 413
  NFMA 173–4
  patch communities 57
  population viability analysis 121–2
  predator-prey interactions 55
  Quebec legislation 361–2, 363
  Quebec Minister of Natural Resources and Wildlife 342, 343
  response to disturbances 103–10
  salamanders 106–8, *107*, 123, 126, 432
    habitat fragmentation *116*, 117
    sedimentation impact on 180–1
    seeps 56
  sedimentation impact on 86–7
  societal values 123, 125
  spatial analysis 110–13, 126
  species risk analysis 113–17
  tree cutting impact on 173, 176
  vegetation changes 34–5
  Whiteface Mountain 31
  white-tailed deer 118–19, 351, 361–2, 377–8, 383, 387, 389–90, 404
  see also birds; fish
Wildlife Conservation Society 240, 244, 245, 251, 254
Wilmington 10, 211, 212, 215, 253–4, 265
  Land Use and Development Plan 255, 266–7
  local land use programs 225, 256
  water services 220, 234
wind 46, 50, 58, 81
Winter Olympic Games
  1924 3
  1932 3, 211, 228, 267
  1980 211, 216, 218, 230, 231, 241, 253, 267
  2010 11
  facilities 216–17
wood sorrel 45n23
Woodward Reservoir 273, 276–7, 294–5, 305, 306–13, 318, 324
World Wildlife Fund 347

Zdarsky, Mathias 3
zoning 425
  Adirondack Park 223, 224, 226, 255–6, 263, 434
  by-laws 385–6
  Killington Resort 319–20
  Loon Resort 147, 167n40
  Mont Pinacle 388–9
  Mont Tremblant 348–55, 404, 412
  regional planning in Quebec 376–7
  secondary growth 433
  Whiteface Mountain 212, 216

For Product Safety Concerns and Information please contact our EU
representative GPSR@taylorandfrancis.com
Taylor & Francis Verlag GmbH, Kaufingerstraße 24, 80331 München, Germany

www.ingramcontent.com/pod-product-compliance
Ingram Content Group UK Ltd.
Pitfield, Milton Keynes, MK11 3LW, UK
UKHW020024200926
475702UK00014B/2050
* 9 7 8 1 1 3 8 2 7 7 4 6 5 *